STRATEGIC PLANNING for HUMAN RESOURCES

First Edition

Julie Bulmash
George Brown College

Nita Chhinzer
University of Guelph

Elizabeth Speers
George Brown College

McGraw-Hill
Ryerson
Connect. Learn. Succeed.

The McGraw·Hill Companies

McGraw-Hill
Ryerson
Connect. Learn. Succeed.

Strategic Planning for Human Resources
First Edition

Statistics Canada information is used with the permission of Statistics Canada. Users are forbidden to copy this material and/or redisseminate the data, in an original or modified form, for commercial purposes, without the expressed permission of Statistics Canada. Information on the availability of the wide range of data from Statistics Canada can be obtained from Statistics Canada's Regional Offices, its World Wide Web site at http://www.statcan.ca and its toll-free access number 1-800-263-1136.

ISBN-13: 978-0-07-095177-8
ISBN-10: 0-07-095177-2

1 2 3 4 5 6 7 8 9 10 CCI 10

Printed and bound in the United States of America

Care has been taken to trace ownership of copyright material contained in this text; however, the publisher will welcome any information that enables it to rectify any reference or credit for subsequent editions.

Vice-President and Editor-in-Chief: *Joanna Cotton*
Senior Sponsoring Editor: *Kim Brewster*
Marketing Manager: *Cathie Lefebvre*
Developmental Editor: *Lori McLellan*
Senior Editorial Associate: *Christine Lomas*
Supervising Editor: *Cathy Biribauer*
Copy Editor: *Carrie McGregor*
Production Coordinator: *Sheryl MacAdam*
Inside Design: *Katherine Strain*
Composition: *Laserwords Private Limited*
Cover Design: *Katherine Strain*
Cover Photo: © *Marshall Sokoloff/Corbis*
Printer: *Courier Companies Inc.*

Library and Archives Canada Cataloguing in Publication Data

Bulmash, Julie
    Strategic planning for human resources / Julie Bulmash, Nita Chhinzer, Elizabeth Speers. — 1st ed.
    Includes index.

ISBN 978-0-07-095177-8

    1. Manpower planning—Textbooks.   2. Strategic planning—Textbooks.
I. Chhinzer, Nita
II. Speers, Elizabeth, 1947- III. Title.
HF5549.5.M3B84 2010   658.3'01   C2009-905810-3

DEDICATION

Julie Bulmash would like to dedicate this book to her husband, Hank, and her children, Lorin, Eric, and Benjamin for their unwavering support and encouragement.

Nita Chhinzer would like to dedicate this book to her supportive husband and her inspiring children.

Elizabeth Speers would like to dedicate this book to her family for their support and encouragement.

ABOUT THE AUTHORS

Julie Bulmash

Julie Bulmash is a professor at George Brown College in Toronto where she coordinates the human resources program and teaches courses in organizational behaviour, human resource management, compensation, management of change, and organizational effectiveness.

Julie began her career in social services as a psycho-educational consultant for a large Toronto hospital. In the early 1990s, Julie entered the private sector and held progressively senior human resources management positions, garnering over 15 years of experience in the chemical, software development, and telecommunication industries.

Julie began her academic career several years ago. She has taught at Humber College, Ryerson University, the University of Toronto, and George Brown College, where she is currently a professor in the School of Business. In addition, she is the co-author of *Managing Organizational Behaviour in Canada*, now in its second edition, and she has contributed to other human resource publications.

Julie has extensive experience in the design, development, and delivery of human resource strategies intended to assist organizations in achieving their objectives. She has developed compensation and benefit systems, redesigned performance management programs, implemented human resource information systems, and has worked to ensure the effective management of change in both profit and not-for-profit sectors.

Julie obtained her undergraduate degree with honours in psychology at Concordia University in Montreal. She did graduate work in assessment and counselling at the University of Toronto, and took her MBA from Heriot-Watt University in Edinburgh, Scotland.

With her extensive business background and her practical focus, Julie provides her students with the opportunity to integrate academic theory with an understanding of real-life business experiences. Her students are challenged to compare what they have learned in the classroom with the best practices of organizations within a collaborative learning environment.

Julie is an enthusiastic and creative educator with a passion for teaching. At George Brown, she won the prestigious award for Excellence in Teaching and Learning, which recognizes an instructor's ability to motivate and inspire through quality teaching methods.

Julie is active in the social service community. Currently she is on the Board of Directors of the Family Service Association Toronto (FSA), was past president of the Canadian Mental Health Association (CMHA) for York Region in Ontario, and served on the Ontario Board of the CMHA.

Nita N. Chhinzer

Nita N. Chhinzer is an Assistant Professor of Human Resources at the Department of Business at the University of Guelph. She also has teaching experience at undergraduate and graduate levels at McMaster University and Ryerson University. Her research is concentrated on strategic human resource management with a strong focus on downsizing practices, procedures, and ethics.

Dr. Chhinzer's program of research includes securing a stronger understanding of downsizing activity in the Canadian context with an aim to effect public policy and legislation regarding layoffs. Her contributions to conferences, publications, and consulting cover a broad range of HR topics, including human capital metrics, recruitment, compensation, labour relations, knowledge management, and training. She is also a member of the Research Advisory Board of the Canadian Tourism Human Resources Council and an active member of the Administrative Sciences Association of Canada (Human Resources Division). Dr. Chhinzer was a visiting professor in the area of human resource management and downsizing at the Graduate School of Business, University of Paris 1: Sorbonne-Pantheon.

Elizabeth Speers

Elizabeth Speers is Academic Director at the Centre for Business at George Brown College in Toronto, where she manages both the School of Business and the School of Financial Services. Elizabeth began her career as a medical researcher at Queen's University. She has experience teaching in high schools, colleges, and universities—Durham College, Seneca College, the University of Alberta, and Ryerson University. Elizabeth's work experience includes supervisory roles at Ontario Hydro in Nuclear Services and Energy Services and management and director roles at Canadian Tire in Supply Chain and Human Resources.

Elizabeth has extensive experience in the design, development, and delivery of human resources strategies, including change management, succession planning, leadership development, and executive coaching. Her contribution to conferences, publications, and consulting cover the areas of mentoring, coaching, succession planning, organizational development, and consulting. Elizabeth obtained her undergraduate degree with honours in chemistry and biology from York University in Toronto. She also holds a Masters of Science in Microbiology from the University of Alberta, a Bachelors of Education with specialist certificate in Chemistry and Biology, a Masters of Education in Administration, and a Doctorate of Education in Developing Human Resources from the University of Toronto.

Brief Contents

Preface   xv

PART 1
Introduction   1

Chapter 1
Introduction to Human Resource Planning   1

PART 2
Forecasting Demand and Supply   25

Chapter 2
Forecasting Demand and Supply   25

Chapter 3
Labour Shortage   52

Chapter 4
Labour Surplus   77

PART 3
Optimizing Existing Human Resources   107

Chapter 5
Career Development   107

Chapter 6
Succession Management: Planning for the Future   133

Chapter 7
Human Resource Planning and Technology   158

PART 4
Key Considerations and the HR Decision   181

Chapter 8
International Human Resources: Planning for Resources in a Global Economy   181

Chapter 9
Mergers and Acquisitions   204

Chapter 10
Specific Applications in Human Resource Measurement Systems   227

Chapter 11
Future Developments in the Field of Human Resource Planning   259

Appendix   283
Glossary   296
Endnotes   303
Name Index   331
Subject Index   334
Photo Credits   344

TABLE OF CONTENTS

Preface   xv

PART 1:
Introduction   1

Chapter 1
Introduction to Human Resource Planning   1
Profile: The 2010 Vancouver Olympics   2
What is Human Resource Planning?   3
The Evolution of Human Resource Planning   3
 The 1970s—The Beginning of Strategic Human
  Resource Management   4
 The 1980s Resource-Based View—The Value of a
  Firm's Internal Human Resources   5
 The 1990s—HRP and a Focus on the
  Customer   6
 Current Challenges—HRP Becomes a Decision Tool
  Focused on *Results*   7
Why is Human Resource Planning Important?   7
 The "Readi" Paradigm   8
  Results   8
  Enables   8
  Aligns   9
  Directs   9
  Instills   9
Key Human Resource Planning Characteristics   9
 Informal or Formal   10
 Short-Term or Long-Term   10
 Static or Dynamic   10
HRP in the News   11
 Tied to Business Strategy or Stand-Alone   11
 The Strategic Management Processes—Corporate,
  Business, and Functional   12
  Corporate Strategy   12

 Business Strategy   13
 Functional Strategies   14
 Integrated Across HR Processes or Operating as an
  Independent Activity   14
  Recruitment and Selection   15
  Training and Career Development   15
HRP and the Small Business   15
Five Stages of Planning Sophistication   16
HRP in the News   17
 The Human Resource Planning Process   18
  1. *Forecast Labour Demand and Labour
   Supply*   18
  2. *Establish Human Resource Objectives*   19
  3. *Design and Implement Human Resource
   Programs to Achieve Objectives*   19
  4. *Evaluate the Effectiveness of the Programs*   19
Framework and Organization of the Textbook   20
Chapter Summary   20
Key Terms   21
Review Questions   21
Discussion Questions   21
Web Exercise   22
Case Incident   22
Required Professional Capabilities Referenced in this
 Chapter   23

PART 2:
Forecasting Demand and Supply   25

Chapter 2
Forecasting Demand and Supply   25
Profile: The Great Pyramid of Giza   26
Why is Human Resource Planning
 Important?   26

Information Required to Successfully Forecast Human Resources Demand and Supply   27
  The Human Resources Planning Team   27
  Determining the Appropriate Planning Horizon   27
    Immediate versus Long-Term Workforce Considerations When Determining the Appropriate Planning Horizon   28
  Evaluating the Current Human Resources Situation   28
    Defining the Internal Labour Force   28
  HR Inventory   29
  Defining the External Labour Force   30
The Human Resource Planning Process   31
Step 1: Forecast Labour Demand and Supply   31
  Forecasting HR Supply   31
    Forecasting External HR Supply   31
HRP in the News   33
    Forecasting Internal HR Supply   35
  Forecasting HR Demand   39
    Quantitative Techniques for Forecasting HR Demand   40
HRP and Ethics   41
    Qualitative Techniques for Forecasting HR Demand   43
HRP and the Small Business   45
Step 2: Establish Human Resource Objectives   46
Step 3: Design and Implement HR Programs   46
Step 4: Evaluate the Effectiveness of the Programs   47
Chapter Summary   47
Key Terms   48
Review Questions   48
Discussion Questions   48
Web Exercise   49
Case Incident   49
Required Professional Capabilities Referenced in this Chapter   51

Chapter 3
Labour Shortage   52

Profile: The Canadian Province that Just Keeps Growing!   53
What is a Labour Shortage?   53
Managing Labour Shortages—Alternative Staffing Strategies   56

Staffing Option #1—Hire Employees   56
  Part-Time or Full-Time Workers?   56
  Recruit Internally or Externally?   57
Staffing Option #2—Contract Out the Work   58
  Different Types of Contractual Relationships   58
  Outsourcing   59
HRP in the News   60
  Crowdsourcing—A Novel Way to Source Talent   61
The Contingent Workforce—Leveraging the Mix of Staffing Options   61
  The Contingent Workforce—Some Trends   62
  Managing the Contingent Relationship   63
    Administrative Considerations   63
    Legal Considerations   64
    Operational Considerations   64
    Compensational Considerations   64
  Staffing Option #3—Develop Employees Internally   64
  Staffing Option #4—Leverage Work Arrangements   65
    Work Arrangement—Overtime   65
HRP and Ethics   66
    Work Arrangement—Flexible Hours, Schedules, or Location   67
    Work Arrangement—Flexible Retirements   67
HRP and Strategic Partners   68
    Work Arrangement: Float and Transfer   68
Key Factors that Determine the Best Available Staffing Option   69
  Urgency and Importance   69
  Speed   69
  Quality of Service   70
  Financial Constraints   70
  Managerial Preferences   70
  Revocability   71
    HR Role in Managing the Work Arrangements   71
The Ultimate Labour Shortage—What If There Is a Pandemic?   71
Chapter Summary   72
Key Terms   73
Review Questions   73
Discussion Questions   74
Web Exercise   74
Experiential Exercise   74

Case Incident   75
Required Professional Capabilities Referenced in
  this Chapter   76

Chapter 4
Labour Surplus   77
Profile: Canada's Automotive Sector   78
What Is a Labour Surplus?   78
Managing a Labour Surplus   79
  Labour Reduction Methods   79
Immediate Headcount Reduction Strategies   80
HRP in the News   80
  Layoffs   81
  Incentives for Voluntary Separations   82
    Notice Periods and Timing of the Terminations
      (Layoffs and Separations)   83
    Severance Pay   84
HRP and the Small Business   85
  Leave Without Pay   86
Attrition Strategies   86
  Hiring Freeze   86
  Early Retirement   87
Work-Term Change Strategies   88
  Job-Sharing   88
  Reduction in Hours   89
  Wage or Benefit Concessions   89
HRP and Strategic Partners   90
  Retraining/Moving Employees   90
Mixed Methods of Downsizing   90
The Challenges of Downsizing and Methods to
  Overcome Them   91
  Equity Theory   92
  Organizational Justice   93
    Procedural Justice   93
    Distributive Justice   93
    Interactional Justice   94
  Downsizing Agents   94
    Human Resources Management   94
    Department or Line Managers and
      Supervisors   94
HRP and Ethics   95
  Communication with Employees During a Labour
    Surplus   96
  Outplacement Services to Downsized
    Employees   97
Union Impact During a Time of Labour Surplus   99
Chapter Summary   100
Key Terms   101

Review Questions   101
Discussion Questions   101
Web Exercise   102
Case Incident   102
Appendix: Jurisdictional Effects of Legislation on
  Layoffs   104
  Ontario Jurisdiction Employees   104
  Federal Jurisdiction Employees   104
Required Professional Capabilities Referenced in this
  Chapter   106

PART 3:
Optimizing Existing Human Resources   107

Chapter 5
Career Development   107
Profile: Talent Management in the 21st Century   108
Career Development and Human Resource
  Planning   108
  Why Would an Organization Support Career
    Development?   110
  Who is Responsible for Career Development?   110
HRP and Ethics   110
Human Capital   111
  Buy Versus Develop   111
  Talent Crunch   111
  Potential Value of an Employee   112
  Career   112
  Career Path   113
  Career Goals and Career Planning   113
Career Management and the Balance between
  Organizational and Individual Need   114
  Organizational Career Development
    Planning   116
Career Models   117
  Career Ladder   117
  Sonnenfeld's Career System Typology
    Model   118
  Competency-Based Career Model at
    Microsoft   119
  Goals of Microsoft's Career Model   121
The Career Model of the 21st Century   122
  Mentoring   122
  Networking   123
  Coaching   123
Role of Human Resources in Facilitating Career
  Development   124

Talent Management   124
    The Role of Leaders in Talent Management   125
    Competency-Based Approach to Talent
        Management   125
Supply-Chain Model of Talent Development   126
    Talent-Based Approach to Talent
        Development   126
Talent Development—A Burning Priority   127
Chapter Summary   128
Key Terms   129
Review Questions   130
Discussion Questions   130
Web Exercise   130
Experiential Exercise   130
Case Incident   131
Required Professional Capabilities Referenced in this
    Chapter   132

Chapter 6
Succession Management: Planning for the
Future   133
Profile: The Kellogg's Conundrum—A Leader in the
    Wings   134
What is Succession Management?   134
Why is Managing Succession Important?   135
    Ensures Organizational Sustainability   136
    Attracts and Retains Key Talent   136
    Leverages Workforce Diversity—A Diverse Talent
        Tool   137
Key Elements that Characterize Effective Succession
    Management   138
    The Succession Planning Process   139
        Step 1: Determine the Need for the
            Program   140
        Step 2: Decide on the Type of Program
            Required   140
        Step 3: Review Existing Work Requirements to
            Determine Critical Positions   141
        Step 4: Review Individual Performance to
            Determine the Availability of Leadership Talent
            and Bench Strength   141
        Step 5: Determine Future Work Requirements
            and Assess Individual Performance
            Potential   142
        Step 6: Implement Development
            Programs   143
        Step 7: Evaluate the Process   144
    Succession Policies/Guidelines   145

HRP and the Small Business   145
    Business Environment   146
    Links to Other Business and HR–Related
        Functions   147
    Evaluation, Feedback, and Measurement   147
        Customer Satisfaction   148
        Effective Placements   148
        Process Progress   148
        Organizational Results   148
        Administration   148
Constraints Facing Succession Planning   149
    Lack of Management Commitment   149
    Unclear Selection Criteria, Rater Errors, and
        Questionable Data   149
    Insufficient Attention to Development   150
    Timing of Developmental Assignments   150
    Lack of HR Credibility   150
Trends in Succession Management   150
HRP in the News   151
    A Difficult Choice—Hire an External Candidate or
        Fill the Role Internally?   151
HRP in the News   152
Chapter Summary   153
Key Terms   153
Review Questions   154
Discussion Questions   154
Web Exercise   154
Case Incident   155
Required Professional Capabilities Referenced in this
    Chapter   157

Chapter 7
Human Resource Planning and Technology   158
Profile: Ryerson University   159
Introduction—Technology and Human
    Resources   160
Human Resource Planning and Technology   160
    Evolution of Data Management in Human
        Resources   160
What is a HRMS?   161
    The Stakeholders   161
    Overall Impact of Information Technology on
        Functional Activities   162
Why is a HRMS Important to Human Resource
    Planning?   162
    Why Invest in a HRMS?   162
        Specific Applications of a HRMS   163
    Outsourcing   164

Global Needs   164
Human Resources Efficiencies   165
Components to Consider in the Design of a
    HRMS   165
    Development of a HRMS   165
    Relational Databases   165
    Web-Based Technology   166
Critical Components of a HRMS   167
What is a HRMS Used For?   167
IT Solutions for Different Needs   168
Enterprise Resource Planning Systems   168
How Does an Organization Determine Their HRMS
    Requirements?   169
HRP and Strategic Partners   170
    Investigation of Needs   170
    Marketplace Investigation   171
        Request for Proposal   171
    Evaluation of Products   172
    Implementation   172
        The Implementation Process   172
The Future of Human Resources Technology   172
Measuring the Performance of a HR Information
    System   173
Confidentiality Versus Security   173
    Confidentiality Issues   173
    Security Issues   174
The Impact of a HRMS on Human Resources
    Professionals and Line Managers   175
        Challenges of MSS Rollout and
            Implementation   175
The Impact of a HRMS in Organizations   175
Chapter Summary   176
Key Terms   177
Review Questions   178
Discussion Questions   178
Web Exercise   178
Case Incident   178
Required Professional Capabilities Referenced in this
    Chapter   180

PART 4:
Key Considerations and the HR Decision   181

Chapter 8
International Human Resources: Planning for
Resources in a Global Economy   181

Profile: Honda—A Global Company with Significant
    Resource Opportunities   182
Introduction—Human Resource Planning in a
    Multinational Enterprise   182
    Four Stages of Corporate Evolution: Resource
        Planning Implications   183
        Domestic Firms and HRP Implications   184
        International Firms and HRP Implications   184
        Multinational Firms and HRP
            Implications   185
        Global Firms and HRP Implications   185
HRP in the News   186
Human Resource Planning—External and Internal
    Factors that Influence Planning Decisions   187
External Contextual Factors   187
    Country Culture   187
    Labour Economy   188
    Labour Legislation—Employment   189
        Leave Entitlements/Vacation   189
    Termination Provisions/Severance Cost   190
        Human Rights and Anti-Discrimination   190
    Labour Legislation—Labour Relations   190
    Immigration Policies   191
Internal Contextual Factors   192
    How Corporate Social Responsibility Influences the
        Global HR Plan   192
HRP and Ethics   193
    Managerial Preference—Staffing
        Alternatives   193
        Ethnocentrism   194
        Polycentrism   194
        Geocentrism   194
        Regiocentrism   194
    The Staffing Mix—Advantages and Disadvantages
        of PCNs, TCNs, and HCNs   194
        Host Country National—Local Presence   194
        Parent Country National—Integrating Global
            Standards   194
        Third Country National—Integrating Global
            Standards   195
Current Trends in Staffing the International
    Organization—"The Assignment"   196
The Expatriate—Costs and Benefits   196
Key Elements of a Successful Expatriate
    Experience   197
    Policies—HRM, Travel, and Relocation   197
        Administrative Processing   198
        Candidate Selection Criteria   198
        Repatriation   199
        HR Planning Implications   199

Chapter Summary   199
Key Terms   200
Review Questions   201
Discussion Questions   201
Web Exercise   201
Case Incident   202
Required Professional Capabilities Referenced in this
   Chapter   203

Chapter 9
Mergers and Acquisitions   204
Profile: The Urge to Merge   205
Mergers and Acquisitions   205
A Canadian Overview of Mergers   206
Why Merge?   207
Strategic Benefits of Merging   208
Financial Advantages   209
   Managerial Needs   209
How Do Mergers Occur?   210
   Friendly Mergers   210
   Hostile Mergers   210
   Waves of Change   211
Merger and Acquisition Process   211
   Pre-Deal Stage   211
   Due Diligence Stage   212
   Integration Planning Stage   212
   Implementation Stage   212
How Can Human Resources Professionals Add Value
   to a Merger?   213
Major Obstacles to Successful Mergers and
   Acquisitions   213
   Human Resources Due Diligence   215
HRP in the News   215
Impact of Mergers and Acquisitions on
   Employees   216
   Loss of Key Talent   216
   Turnover—Especially of Key Managers   216
   Context of Work During Mergers   217
   Communication Challenges   217
   Clash of Corporate Cultures   217
Mergers and Human Resource Planning   218
   Human Resources as Part of the Merger Team   219
   Other Areas to Consider as Part of Human
      Resource Planning   219
      Redundancies   219
      Organizational Structure   219
      Staffing Decisions   220
      Communication   220

      Compensation   220
      Labour Relations   220
      Performance Appraisal   221
      Training and Development   221
Organizational Skills Required to Support a Successful
   Merger   221
Management Capabilities   221
   The Skill of Communication   221
Human Resource Capabilities   222
Gaps in Human Resources Skills   222
Chapter Summary   223
Key Terms   224
Review Questions   224
Discussion Questions   224
Web Exercise   224
Case Incident   225
Required Professional Capabilities Referenced in this
   Chapter   226

Chapter 10
Specific Applications in Human Resource
Measurement Systems   227
Profile: Sysco Corporation   228
The Balanced Scorecard Approach   228
   The HR Scorecard Approach   229
Alignment of HR Measures with Organizational
   Strategy   231
HRP and the Small Business   232
   What Defines Meaningful HR Metrics?   233
Preparing for HR Measurement   234
HRP and Ethics   234
Alternative Approaches to Segmenting HR
   Metrics   235
Measures Using the Life-Cycle Approach   235
   Return on Investment   235
   Economic Value Added   236
   Productivity   237
   Stage 1 of the HR Life Cycle: Attract and
      Acquire   237
      Attract and Acquire: Cost Metrics   238
   HRP and Strategic Partners   238
      Attract and Acquire: Quality Metrics   239
      Attract and Acquire: Quantity Metrics   241
      Attract and Acquire: Time Metrics   242
   Stage 2 of the Life Cycle: Develop   242
      Develop: Cost Metrics   243
      Develop: Internal Mobility Metrics   244
      Develop: Time and Efficiency Metrics   245

Stage 3 of the Life Cycle: Utilize   246
   Utilize: Performance Metrics   246
   Utilize: Lost-Productivity Metrics   247
   Utilize: Span-of-Control Metrics   248
   Utilize: Overtime Metrics   250
Stage 4 of the Life Cycle: Separate   250
   Separate: Turnover Metrics   250
   Separate: Vacancy Metrics   253
Strategic versus Operational Metrics   254
Target Audience   254
Chapter Summary   255
Key Terms   256
Review Questions   256
Discussion Questions   256
Web Exercise   256
Case Incident   257
Required Professional Capabilities Referenced in this
   Chapter   258

CHAPTER 11
**Future Developments in the Field of Human
Resource Planning   259**
Profile: Recommendations for Canada's Future
   Economic and Labour Prosperity   260
Labour Force Changes   261
   Labour Shortage and Talent Mismatch   261
   The Aging Workforce   262
   Diversity Management   263
      Immigrants   264
      Visible Minorities   265
      Women   266
      Persons with Disability   267
   Impact of Labour Force Trends on Human Resource
      Planning   267
HRP and the Small Business   269

Alternative Work Arrangements   269
   Flextime   270
   Compressed Workweek   270
   Annualized or Banked Hours   270
   Reduced Hours or Part-Time Work   271
   Telecommuting   271
   Impact of Alternative Work Arrangements on
      Human Resource Planning   272
Outsourcing   273
   Labour Market Trends Impacting
      Outsourcing   273
   The Outsourcing of HR   274
      Pre-Employment Background Screening   274
      Recruitment   274
HRP and Ethics   275
   Performance Management   275
   Compensation   276
   Benefits   276
   Training   276
   Impact of Outsourcing on Human Resource
      Planning   276
HRP and Strategic Partners   277
   Outsourcing Challenges   277
Chapter Summary   278
Key Terms   278
Review Questions   279
Discussion Questions   279
Web Exercise   279
Case Incident   280
Required Professional Capabilities Referenced in this
   Chapter   282

Appendix   283
Glossary   296
Endnotes   303
Name Index   331
Subject Index   334
Photo Credits   344

PREFACE

Strategic Planning for Human Resources provides students with comprehensive, up-to-date, and integrative information about the needs, methods, uses, risks, and future trends in human resource planning. There are three distinct features of this book that offer a significant link to the business-relevant approach to human resource planning (theoretical and operational):

1. With a focus on the Canadian landscape, this text includes a review of relevant political, economical, legal, demographic, and social factors and their impact on human resource planning. To complement this, many of the examples, methods, and processes discussed are applicable globally. This focus allows students and teachers to concentrate on developing an understanding of unique Canadian human resource planning challenges and opportunities while developing transferrable knowledge about global issues.

2. The framework of this book centres on an accessibility approach. Learning objectives are introduced at the beginning of each chapter; they outline the goals for study and are reinforced throughout the chapters. Each chapter discusses a concept or theory, which is then illustrated with examples, case studies, company reviews, exercises, and web-based cases. This experiential style of the pedagogy reinforces learning for students.

3. The career orientation of this book is notable. Identification of national human resource certification requirements (Required Professional Capabilities) assists students in connecting the text and course as whole to their future career plans. In addition, the spotlight on strategic partners, ethics, small business, current technology, and new human resource directions aims to fulfill human resource's mandate to be a business partner.

■ ORGANIZATION OF THE TEXTBOOK

- **Chapter 1: Introduction to Human Resource Planning** introduces the topic of human resource planning and explains the key steps in the HRP process, including its relationship to overall business activities.
- **Chapter 2: Forecasting Demand and Supply** details the four main steps of the human resource planning process, including qualitative and quantitative forecasting methods.
- **Chapter 3: Labour Shortage** explores the topic of labour shortage and identifies alternative staffing strategies. It examines the factors that can influence the choice of strategies and the types of initiatives that organizations take when faced with a prolonged shortage situation.
- **Chapter 4: Labour Surplus** highlights the management of labour surplus, including methods for reducing headcount, communication strategies, and the risks associated with downsizing.
- **Chapter 5: Career Development** describes the relationship between human resource planning and career development of employees so as to meet organizational needs as well as employee needs.

- **Chapter 6: Succession Management: Planning for the Future** describes the succession planning process and why it is an important activity. It explores the relationship between succession planning and other HR functions such as career planning, workforce planning, and talent management.
- **Chapter 7: Human Resource Planning and Technology** focuses on the role of technology in human resource planning and how technology can facilitate the human resource planning process. The role of the human resources professional and line staff in the use of technology is described.
- **Chapter 8: International Human Resources: Planning for Resources in a Global Economy** introduces the topic of global human resource planning within multinational corporations. It discusses the types of global staffing assignments and the key contextual factors that influence a global human resource plan.
- **Chapter 9: Mergers and Acquisitions** focuses on the role of human resource planning in the business practice of mergers and acquisitions. The skills required by the organization for a successful merger, especially those of human resources professionals, are discussed.
- **Chapter 10: Specific Applications in Human Resource Measurement Systems** focuses on developing methods to measure, benchmark, and communicate the value of human resource planning to multiple stakeholders.
- **Chapter 11: Future Developments in the Field of Human Resource Planning** provides a forward-looking view of human resource planning, identifying existing trends and the potential impact of these trends on human resources professionals and organizations at large.
- **Appendix: Building Strategic Partnerships** examines what it means to be a strategic partner and how it impacts the human resource planning process.

Learning Objectives are highlighted at the beginning of each chapter, and the chapter's **Summary,** relating to these learning outcomes, is included at the end of each chapter.

LEARNING OBJECTIVES

- Define human resource planning (HRP) and how it has evolved as a key human resource activity
- Explain why HRP is important
- Describe the five key HRP characteristics
- Determine the link between HRP and business strategy
- Describe the relationship between HRP and human resource management
- Identify the various levels of HRP sophistication in organizations
- Discuss the key steps of the HRP process

CHAPTER SUMMARY

- Human resource planning (HRP) is a process used to determine future human resource requirements by anticipating future business demands, analyzing the impacts of these demands on the organization, and making decisions on how to effectively acquire and utilize firms' human resources. Its goal is to ensure that the right people are available at the right place at the right time.
- HRP is an important HR activity. It ensures that the organization is ready—ready to focus on results that contribute to organizational productivity, ready to help the organization adequately forecast its resource requirements, ready to align its activities to corporate and business strategy, and ready to ensure that employee skills and abilities in the organization are valued.
- There are five key HRP characteristics that describe the multifaceted nature of HRP. These attributes are: formal or informal, short-term or long-term, static or dynamic, aligned to business strategy or stand-alone, integrated across HRM processes or operating as an independent activity.
- Organizations are unique in term of how they plan, with each organization operating at a different level of sophistication. At the extreme end are those organizations that view

Each chapter begins with an **Opening Profile** that highlights the key concepts in the chapter. The students are engaged by the conversational tone and can relate to the companies that are referenced.

■ **PROFILE**

Canada's Automotive Sector[1]

According to the Canadian Auto Workers union (CAW), in 2007 the Canadian auto industry directly employed 150,000 people. There are also 340,000 jobs related to the auto industry in Canada, including jobs in parts supply, materials, and services. Traditionally referred to as the "Big Three," GM, Ford, and Chrysler were the major Canadian employers in the auto industry.

The Canadian automobile sector experienced a number of structural and macroeconomic challenges that forced the industry into decline in 2008 and 2009. Canadian automakers lost $2.7 billion in 2008 and were estimated to lose an additional $2.1 billion in 2009. The industry is not projected to see profits until 2012.

Following many rounds of layoffs in the Canadian auto sector, in April 2009 the Canadian government agreed to provide up to $700 million (CDN) in funding for the industry, to help auto parts suppliers, provide consumer protection by backstopping auto warranties, and help struggling companies. Additional funding for GM, Chrysler, and Ford was contingent on demonstration of a feasible restructuring plan.

Each chapter includes several boxed features (**HRP in the News, HRP and the Small Business, Ethics and HRP,** and **HRP and Strategic Partners**), which highlight comprehensive, real-world examples of the material in the chapter.

HRP AND THE SMALL BUSINESS

BioWare—Creator of the "Knights of the Republic"

The gaming industry is thriving in Canada. The global market is $30 billion in sales, with Canada accounting for 3 percent of the sales, or over $1 billion. One such company whose products are in demand is Bioware Corp. Based in Edmonton, Alberta and founded in the 90s by two physicians, this company has grown significantly over the past twelve years. They recently opened a studio in Austin, Texas and now employ over 340 employees in Austin and Edmonton. They recently merged with Pandemic Studios to create one of the strongest independent game companies in the industry. Its sales have grown exponentially.[67]

Bioware is well-known in the industry, collaborating with such high-profile artists as George Lucas on their game "Knights of the Republic." They have won over one hundred awards and have been listed as one of Canada's top 100 employers. Their latest game is called "Jade Empire" and is an action-martial arts game. Currently they have three new games in development and they are on a recruitment drive, sourcing candidates throughout North America. Numerous job openings are available in such roles as animation, marketing, design, technology, and artists to name a few.[68]

Getting the right people in the right place when they need them is a major priority for this firm!

Exhibits are interspersed throughout the text to illustrate concepts and provide a visual framework for students.

EXHIBIT	**1.2**	The READI Paradigm—Why Planning Is Important
R		**R**esults—contributes to organization profitability and productivity
E		**E**nables the organization to project its resource needs
A		**A**ligns to business strategy
D		**D**irects the activities of the HR function
I		**I**nstills pride in employees that their organization values its human capital

Definitions of **Key Terms** highlighted in each chapter are provided in the margins, and a list of these terms with page references is provided at the end of each chapter.

> **human resource planning (HRP)**
>
> A process used to determine future human resource requirements by anticipating future business demands, analyzing the impacts of these demands on the organization, and making decisions on how to effectively acquire and utilize firms' human resources

Review and **Discussion Questions** appear at the end of each chapter. In response to instructor suggestions, these real-life exercises require the application of learned concepts and techniques.

REVIEW QUESTIONS

1. Describe the HRP process.
2. Discuss the evolution of HRP.
3. Differentiate between HRP and SHRP.
4. What are the five key characteristics that can be used to describe HRP?
5. Discuss the link between HRP and business strategy.
6. Discuss the link between HRP and HRM.
7. How would you describe the different levels of HRP sophistication?

DISCUSSION QUESTIONS

1. As an employee in an organization, what reasons would you give to convince your organization to develop its employees internally?
2. Using the "Readi" paradigm discussed in this chapter, explain why HRP is an important HR activity.
3. If HR is going to add value, it must demonstrate that it is a strategic partner. How does the function of HRP enable HR to achieve these goals?
4. What challenges do you think organizations are facing today that might influence the way they plan their human resources?
5. Consider different sized organizations and the types of planning activities that would be applicable. How sophisticated do you think the planning function should be for a small organization of fewer than 50 employees? What about an organization with over 1,500 employees? What type of planning activities do you think would be appropriate?

A **Web Exercise** at the end of each chapter will familiarize the student with a wealth of compensation-related material available on the Internet. Also included at the end of each chapter is a **Case Incident** requiring application of the chapter material.

WEB EXERCISE

Visit the following websites and answer the questions listed below:

    Statistics Canada: www.statcan.gc.ca/start-debut-eng.html (Access the current labour market survey and click on the detailed summary)

    Job Futures www.jobfutures.ca/en/home.shtml (Click on "I want to know more about the world of work")

    Human Resources and Skills Development: www.hrsdc.gc.ca/eng/workplaceskills/labour_market_information/index.shtml (Look under Labour Market Information and Labour Market Bulletins)

Questions

1. What are the hottest jobs in each province right now?
2. Where are the greatest skill shortages in your province?
3. What industries have had the most growth over the past several years?
4. What are the projections with respect to job growth?
5. Do certain industries have greater opportunities than others?

CASE INCIDENT

What Does the Weather Have to Do with Human Resource Planning?

The fall-out from global warming will be felt for more than 1,000 years. There is significant evidence that the world is heating up! The arctic ice cap is melting much faster than expected and is now about thirty years ahead of what was originally predicted.[79] Significant increases in heat waves, rainstorms, and severe hurricanes and typhoons, and a warming of the earth's core are predicted. The climate has been projected to change significantly over the next several decades—ocean currents will slow by as much as 25 percent, global temperatures will be 1.7 to 4 degrees higher, and sea levels are expected to rise. If this trend continues, global warming can lead to a complete elimination of the Greenland ice sheet and a rise of about seven metres in sea levels.

    The warming of the climate system is going to continue. In fact, 11 out of the last 12 years rank among the warmest since the 1950s.[80] What does this mean for specific industries? Consider the sporting goods industry or those manufacturing firms who make boots, winter apparel, or snow equipment. Or the travel industries who specialize in ski vacations. What challenges do you think these firms will face?

Questions

1. What industries do you think would be most affected by this change in weather?
2. What are some specific jobs that would be in demand?
3. What are some specific jobs that might be compromised? When may there be an oversupply if these trends continue?
4. What initiatives are being planned to help combat global warming? Vist the Environment Canada website at www.ec.gc.ca.

■ REQUIRED PROFESSIONAL CAPABILITIES (RPCs)

As of March 2003, provincial human resources associations throughout Canada have successfully agreed on a framework for achieving the designation of Certified Human Resources Professional (CHRP). This national accreditation process was launched by the Canadian Council of Human Resources Associations (CCHRA); see **www.cchra-ccarh.ca/parc/en/section_3/ss_3/333e.asp** for entry-level RPCs and **www.cchra-ccarh.ca/parc/en/section_3/ss_3/33X3e.asp** for experienced-professional RPCs.

The national CHRP certification program has raised the bar for human resources practitioners across the country who must now meet an even more demanding set of professional performance standards and acquire knowledge and skills covering a wide range of required professional capabilities (RPCs). Specifically, in the area of human resource planning (which includes staffing, succession planning, talent management, and career development), the accredited CHRP must possess the following capabilities to effectively plan for its human resources:

- Contributes to the development of the organization's vision, goals, and strategies with a focus on human capabilities
- Translates the organization's business plan into issues, priorities, and human resource strategies and objectives
- Develops and implements an HR plan that supports the organization's strategic objectives
- Assesses the effectiveness of people and talent management plans

Look to the end of each chapter to see the set of the specific RPCs required for human resource planning. You will see these referenced throughout the chapter with the icon shown here in the margin. Whenever you see this icon in the margin beside chapter content, simply look to the end of the chapter to link to the required human resource planning competency. Please note that for the sake of brevity and simplicity, we have included only the human resource planning competencies upon which students will be responsible for in the CHRP exams, and not cross-referenced to other functional areas.

■ INSTRUCTOR AND STUDENT SUPPORT

Integrated Learning System

Great care was used in the creation of the supplemental materials to accompany *Strategic Planning for Human Resources,* First Edition. Whether you are a seasoned faculty member or a newly minted instructor, you will find the support materials to be comprehensive and practical.

Instructor and Student Online Learning Centres (www.mcgrawhill.ca/olc/bulmash)

This online learning centre is a text website that follows the text material chapter-by-chapter. Students will find custom quizzes for chapter content and a searchable glossary.

Instructors will find downloadable supplements, including the Instructor's Manual, Computerized Test Bank, and Powerpoint Presentations.

*i*Learning Sales Specialist

Your Integrated Learning Sales Specialist is a McGraw-Hill Ryerson representative who has the experience, product knowledge, training, and support to help you assess and integrate any of our products, technology, and services into your course for optimum teaching and learning performance. Whether it's how to use our test bank software, helping your students improve their grades, or how to put your entire course online, your *i*Learning Sales Specialist is there to help. Contact your local *i*Learning Sales Specialist today to learn how to maximize all McGraw-Hill Ryerson resources!

*i*Services Program

McGraw-Hill Ryerson offers a unique *i*Services package designed for Canadian faculty. Our mission is to equip providers of higher education with superior tools and resources required for excellence in teaching. For additional information, visit **www.mcgrawhill.ca/highereducation/iservices.**

WebCT/BlackBoard

This text is available in two of the most popular course-delivery platforms—WebCT and BlackBoard—for more user-friendly and enhanced features. Contact your local McGraw-Hill *i*Learning Sales Specialist for more information.

ACKNOWLEDGEMENTS

In preparation of this book, we have benefitted greatly from the helpful critiques and suggestions of numerous professors across the country. Their assistance was invaluable and we extend our many thanks to the following reviewers:

Eddy Ng, *Trent University*

Gerald Hunt, *Ryerson University*

Carol Ann Samhaber, *Algonquin College*

Julie Aitken Schermer, *University of Western Ontario*

Lynn Buckerfield, *George Brown College*

Anna Bortolon, *Conestoga College*

Deborah Zinni, *Brock University*

Cheryl Dowell, *Algonquin College*

Holly Seebach, *Niagara College of Applied Arts and Technology*

Greg Irving, *Wilfrid Laurier University*

Nelson Lacroix, *Niagara College of Applied Arts and Technology*

Sujay Vardhmane, *George Brown College*

Don Miskiman, *Vancouver Island University*

Alan Saks, *University of Toronto*

Sue Deegan, *Georgian College*

Julie Bulmash would like to extend a special note of thanks to Lisa Whitt and Cheryl Tsang, students in the postgraduate human resources program at George Brown College, for their research assistance and support.

Many thanks are also due to the following McGraw-Hill Ryerson staff who worked hard to make this book a reality: Kim Brewster, Senior Sponsoring Editor; Lori McLellan, Developmental Editor; Cathy Biribauer, Supervising Editor; Sheryl MacAdam, Production Coordinator; and Carrie McGregor, Copy Editor.

INTRODUCTION TO HUMAN RESOURCE PLANNING

LEARNING OBJECTIVES

- Define human resource planning (HRP) and how it has evolved as a key human resource activity
- Explain why HRP is important
- Describe the five key HRP characteristics
- Determine the link between HRP and business strategy
- Describe the relationship between HRP and human resource management
- Identify the various levels of HRP sophistication in organizations
- Discuss the key steps of the HRP process

■ **PROFILE**

The 2010 Vancouver Olympics

The 2010 Vancouver Olympic games will be an event celebrated around the globe, when athletes from around the world come together to celebrate. There will be over eighty countries participating in the Olympic winter games, 5,000 Olympic athletes and officials, seventeen days of events, and 10,000 media representatives. Three billion people worldwide are expected to watch the games and 1.8 million tickets are available for those lucky individuals who will be present at this historic event![1]

Imagine the manpower required to get a monumental event such as the Olympics up and running. Consider the types of *human resources* British Columbia will need in order to ensure that the games are a success.

In 2005, venue construction began on all 2010 competition and non-competition sites, with an expected start date of 2007 to start construction on the Vancouver Olympic Village and the Whistler Olympic and Paralympic Village. The completion date for the games venue for athletic training was 2007/2008.

John Furlong, the CEO of the Olympic Committee, indicated in his speech to the Vancouver Board of Trade on November 18, 2005, that there was approximately $70 to 75 billion worth of construction projects anticipated over the next three years.[2] Consider what types of skills would be required to ensure that these construction projects will be met on time and on budget. Project management, heating, plumbing and electrical, general contracting, engineering, welders, and technologists would be some of the many required skills.

In addition to the actual building of the Olympic Village, the Olympic organization itself has resource requirements. This organization is comprised of a body of individuals who are responsible for delivering the games. Initially, this committee had 150 to 200 employees and projections indicated that the committee was expected to grow to 1,200 full-time and 3,000 part-time individuals plus approximately 25,000 volunteers by 2010. With a significant influx of people both delivering services and those individuals lucky enough to attend the games, the economic impact is significant.

As far back as 2005, John Furlong expressed great concerns over the availability of labour, cost of labour, and having a place to house the workers who had been hired to work on these projects. He indicated that the economic impacts were $2.1 to 3.3 billion in 2005 and that the city and its surrounding communities would need increased accommodation, transportation, restaurants, bars, retail stores, and security.[3] With this increase comes the need for resources—human resources.

Fast forward to today and the year 2010. Canada is in a recession and many companies are struggling to manage labour costs. Many people have lost their jobs and there is an oversupply of resources in the marketplace. The unemployment rate across Canada has risen and Western Canada is feeling the effects. What has changed is the availability of labour, but not the need for specific skill sets and not the need to ensure that these skills sets are available when needed.

It was expected that the village would be completed by 2007, however there were significant delays due to budgetary reasons. A recent review of the employment website showed only 33 open positions[4] and due to the number of résumés, the volunteer opportunities are diminishing and we are seeing more unpaid jobs. However, the need for some key skills still remains. For example, a recent article highlighted the need for fire services during the games. Planning for the safety and security of the games is a major issue. The British Columbia Ambulance Service plans on staffing 125 to 150 paid paramedics a day. They will add 60 new ambulances to its fleet and staffing will draw on a pool of 2,100 part-time paramedics that British Columbia Ambulance Service employs across the province.

Mind boggling, isn't it, when you think of what resources are needed in order for these games to be enjoyed by all?

Looking for some work experience? Vancouver can be a very pleasant place to be in the winter!

■ WHAT IS HUMAN RESOURCE PLANNING?

**human resource
planning (HRP)**

A process used to
determine future human
resource requirements
by anticipating future
business demands,
analyzing the impacts of
these demands on the
organization, and mak-
ing decisions on how
to effectively acquire
and utilize firms' human
resources

Human resource planning (HRP) is a process used to determine future human resource requirements by anticipating future business demands, analyzing the impacts of these demands on the organization, and making decisions on how to effectively acquire and utilize firms' human resources.[5] It helps identify what human resources are needed to ensure that the organization can respond to change and provides resource plans to help the organization respond effectively.[6] It is a dynamic process and implies movement from an existing state to a future state.[7] The major objective of human resource planning is to ensure that the organization has the *right people with the right skills at the right time* in order for the organization to fulfill its organizational and individual objectives.[8] The desired outcomes of planning focus on business competitiveness through effectively allocating "people" resources and prioritizing human resource initiatives.[9]

Human resource planning has evolved throughout the decades. It is highly valued and widely used by some organizations, but not effectively used by others. A recent survey conducted by the IPMA-HR (International Public Management Association for Human Resources) found that only 37 percent indicated that their organizations had workforce planning activities in place.[10]

Just think about our opening Olympics example. The chairman of the committee is a critical position. This role sets the vision and mission for the organization, establishes organizational goals, and ensures that key performance objectives are achieved. This leadership is critical, and sourcing individuals with specific skill sets to lead the Olympic organization is challenging. Consider the number of people in Canada or in the U.S. who would possess this type of experience and skill set and the length of time it would take to find such an individual. Planning for this takes time and significant resource planning.

These concerns over resource planning and the repercussions of not finding the right people with the rights skills at the right time is what this textbook is all about.

This text is divided into four parts. Part One (Chapter 1) presents an overview of human resource planning. Part Two (Chapters 2, 3, and 4) focuses on the various models used to forecast demand and supply and the staffing options that can be considered. Part Three (Chapters 5, 6, and 7) explores the various human resource–related programs that enable an organization to leverage its existing workforce skills and experience and the technological tools to facilitate these activities. Part Four (Chapters 8, 9, 10, and 11) highlights specific challenges that organizations face today, such as mergers and acquisitions, globalization, and managing diversity within a multinational enterprise, as well as examining the human resource planning challenges facing organizations in the future.

So let's begin. This chapter will introduce the concept of HRP. We will examine its historical roots and explore how it has evolved as a key strategic HR activity. Next we will discuss some of the characteristics that describe planning activities, concluding with the major HRP process steps.

■ THE EVOLUTION OF HUMAN RESOURCE PLANNING

As demonstrated in Exhibit 1.1, HRP has evolved significantly over the past four decades, from a process that was considered merely an add-on to the human resource function, to one where it is now a major decision-making tool enabling organizations to optimally leverage their human resources to ensure organizational continuity.[11] In the 1970s, HRP was referred to as personnel, workforce, or manpower planning. It was defined as a process.

In the 1980s and 1990s, terms such as human resource planning, strategic human resource planning, human resource strategy, and human capital planning began to be used to

EXHIBIT | **1.1** | The Evolution of HRP

Date	HRP Application	Who is Responsible for Planning
1970 ⟶	Minimum HR involvement Activities centred around staffing patterns with the planner projecting future staffing, taking into account data mainly from attrition and internal movement	Line Manager
1980 ⟶	Resource-based view (RBV)—emphasized the value that people bring to an organization. Recognition that capabilities of an organization can come from its "intellectual capital"	HR involvement begins—there is a recognition that HR processes can be a valuable tool in planning
1990 ⟶	Customer focused—practical relevant applications	HR–strategic—demonstrating its understanding of the business and internal customer requirements
2000 ⟶	Decision tool—results-based	HR—full partnership with the business

describe the planning process. Today, human resource planning and human capital planning are widely accepted as descriptors of the process. This text will use the term *human resource planning*.

The 1970s—The Beginning of Strategic Human Resource Management

Prior to the 1970s, the economy had been relatively stable—corporations experienced minimal change and there were very few competitors to be concerned about. Organizations did engage in planning, but they carried out this activity in a rudimentary fashion, practising it on a very basic level. The line manager was primarily responsible for planning which centred on past staffing patterns with the planner projecting future staffing, taking into account some basic data such as attrition and internal movements.[12] The past was an important factor for determining future planning. This process was thought of as linear. **Manpower planning,** a process by which management determines how the organization should move from its current to its desired human resources position, was used to describe human resource planning.[13] Planning was relatively short-term and manpower planners thought more about quantity of resources versus the quality of resources.[14]

    Then, in the 1970s, the economic environment began to change—the energy crisis, uncertainty regarding company profits, increased government regulations, advances in affirmative action, advances in women's rights, concerns over reverse discrimination, increased space exploration, and the arrival of the microprocessor all impacted organizations. The term manpower planning began to be replaced with human resource, which helped broaden the scope, and emphasized

manpower planning

A process by which management determines how the organization should move from its current to its desired human resources position

that employees were an important resource to a company. The Human Resource Planning Society started in 1977 to aid in broadening the knowledge in the field.[15]

Numerous researchers wrote about the challenges these changes posed and stressed that if organizations were going to survive, they had to be adept at anticipating these changes. It meant understanding what challenges organizations were facing, anticipating these changes, forecasting resource requirements, and helping the organization identify its human resource requirements. The focus shifted and suddenly the organization's future business activities became an important input into ensuring an effective human resource plan.[16]

One prolific researcher was James W. Walker. In the late 1970s he wrote about the importance of creating a link between human resource planning and the business strategic plan. He stressed that a relationship existed between the planning function and the business and individual objectives. He suggested that a comprehensive approach to planning would enable management to attract and retain, and develop and utilize talent to meet the challenges of the future.[17] This link implied that HRP could become an integral part of an organization's business planning activities.

Early on, Walker identified three key fundamental elements of HRP: forecasting, programming, and evaluation. Forecasting focuses on identifying the type of talent an organization needs, as executed by a thorough examination of the business and individual development plans. Programming means establishing HR–related objectives and determining the HR functions that are impacted. Evaluation stresses the impact that these elements have on business and individual objectives, and the importance of using quantitative measures such as cost and auditing of the HR practices to analyze the gaps in service delivery.[18] These three elements formed the basis for the planning process today and are discussed in greater depth throughout this text.

Suddenly, this activity was recognized as one that could add value to an organization, but only if HR demonstrated an understanding of an organization's business needs and linked its activities accordingly. This revelation was considered a significant event in the evolution of HRP as no one prior to this point had so clearly articulated this link. Some researchers even heralded this finding as the *conception* of **strategic human resource management (SHRM)**.[19] SHRM is the linking of HRM with the strategic goals and objectives of the organization to improve organizational performance.

Several researchers began writing about this strategic connection and the literature offered several examples of how several large and well-known companies engaged in these planning activities. One such company was Eastman Kodak. Kodak had experimented with different approaches to human resource planning, viewing planning from a three-dimensional focus on "diversity, decentralization, and dynamism."[20]

A new definition of human resource planning emerged, describing HRP as a formal process of linking business strategy with human resource practices.[21] HRP started to be referred to as SHRP. "Strategic" meant helping the organization anticipate and manage rapid change, enabling managers to make informed decisions regarding the acquisition and the effective utilization of its human resources so that an organization could achieve its objectives. There was a growing realization that firms' human resources provided a "pipeline of talent" and, if developed, nurtured, and groomed, could help organizations meet their labour challenges.[22]

> **strategic human resource management (SHRM)**
>
> The linking of HRM with the strategic goals and objectives of the organization to improve organizational performance

The 1980s Resource-Based View—The Value of a Firm's Internal Human Resources

The 1980s brought new challenges to organizations, such as the me generation, hostile takeovers, leverage buyouts, rising unemployment, significant advancements in science and technology, cable TV, and MTV. Japan was gaining strength economically and it started to play a major role in investments. In order to compete with Japan, companies became aware that total quality management (TQM) practices were necessary. By involving employees and increasing quality in production, TQM became a fundamental aspect of doing business. Corporations had to undergo radical changes in order to adapt to these new processes.

Companies began to downsize, reduce overheads, and in order to compete, companies became more lean and mean. There was a philosophical shift in thinking whereby researchers began to focus on organizations' *internal* human resources and explore the value that these resources could bring to help maintain a competitive advantage. This was referred to as a **resource-based view (RBV)** and it emphasized an organization's resources, including financial and physical. It highlighted the importance of the skills and competencies possessed by a firm's human resources. This view emphasized the value that these resources bring to the organization. It referred to these assets as "intangible assets" and suggested that the capabilities that an organization possesses must be considered not only from the organizational perspective, but from the employee perspective as well.[23]

These capabilities were defined as the collective skills, abilities, and expertise of an organization—stable over time and more difficult for competitors to copy.[24] Terms such as knowledge management, human capital, and learning organizations were used to describe this *value*. Seminal books such as *In Search of Excellence* and *Iacocca: An Autobiography* referred to the critical importance of these *human assets,* describing how organizations could differentiate themselves and become "distinctive" by leveraging their internal human resource capabilities.[25]

At this point, we began to see human resource planning utilizing and engaging several other HR processes to leverage its internal capabilities and resources. We see a greater focus on succession planning, training, and career development and how these processes could support and facilitate overall HRP objectives.[26]

This integration was another major milestone in the development of HRP. HR systems that were once considered a *collection* of functional areas (computers, training, and staffing) now were being viewed as *enablers* to help plan ahead and support the development of an organization's human capital. The realization that these processes could be integrated with the HR plan was an important realization.[27]

For example, in the 1980s, Eastman Kodak found itself in a highly competitive environment with the Japanese who were making significant gains in penetrating the market with advanced camera technology. In 1985, the company decided to restructure and establish new management processes. They decentralized, diversified, and became more dynamic in terms of establishing matrix organizations and pushing decision-making down to the lowest levels. The human resource team at Kodak worked at integrating management themes with planning processes at the business and corporate levels and building competencies internally to ensure the organization was able to make this change. They called this "planning in 3D." The three D's stood for diverse, decentralized, and dynamic.[28]

The 1990s—HRP and a Focus on the Customer

In the 1990s, the challenges facing organizations continued. This was the electronic age, with the Internet discovered in 1992. Globalization was in full force. The economy was booming and merger activity escalated. Companies began to expand their markets globally. This led to companies learning to develop effective cross-cultural communication techniques. There was an increased emphasis on quality, costs, and productivity. Flexible management practices and companies were indicating that planning was even more important as global companies such as Kodak set up global or regional areas for "research, engineering, manufacturing and distribution." Foreign competition was significant and companies such as British Petroleum rose to the challenge. This company gained an advantage by "forging 90 distinct business entities around the world."[29]

Human resource planning responded by becoming more flexible. The focus was on practical and relevant solutions, more pragmatic solutions to translate issues into action, and recognizing that with the fast pace of change, a shorter-term focus with respect to planning had to be considered. There continued to be an even greater focus on capabilities and how human resources could

---

resource-based view (RBV)

An organization's resources, such as financial and physical; it highlights the importance of the skills and competencies possessed by a firm's human resources

leverage its "human advantage."[30] Tony Grundy spoke of this human advantage as contributing to human resources by adding value and managing cost.[31]

A major thrust was demonstrating how human resource planning added value for its customers, how it contributed toward managing costs, and how it was optimizing its resource capabilities and knowledge to accelerate operational and management processes and help organizations manage change. Flexibility coupled with a customer focus and bottom-line impact now took precedence over other concerns.

Current Challenges—HRP Becomes a Decision Tool Focused on *Results*

Today, organizations continue to face significant challenges—globalization, significant labour shortages, changes in the way we work, a greater focus on work–life balance, a fluctuating economy, and significant environmental concerns. Many organizations are finding that their domestic markets are saturated and they need to operate in foreign markets. Managing internationally has become the norm and the challenges of managing human resources globally are fast becoming a critical skill required by human resources professionals.

environmental scanning

A process of systematic surveillance and interpretation designed to identify events, elements, and conditions of the environment that have potential relevance and impact for an organization

Worldwide labour shortages are a major concern and organizations must be prepared to meet the ever-increasing challenge of finding the right people at the right time by seeking alternative staffing sources and focusing on ways to effectively evaluate resources and capabilities to determine strengths, opportunities, and weaknesses. One method that can be used is **environmental scanning.** This is a process of systematic surveillance and interpretation designed to identify events, elements, and conditions of the environment that have potential relevance and impact for an organization.[32] Organizations must be aware of the type of people that they need and the demand that exists in their industry. This is discussed in more detail in Chapter 2.

The focus of human resource planning is on the demonstration of results and providing managers with decision-making tools so that they can meet their resource requirements and capitalize on their "human advantage."[33]

In order for human resource planning to be a valuable process, its value must be "transparent" to all its stakeholders. Regrettably, at this point in time, HRP is still not valued as a core activity. The results of a recent IPMA-HR survey that measured the extent to which public agencies used a workforce plan indicated that HRP is still considered a new concept for many organizations. Of those surveyed, 21.6 percent indicated they had a plan, 18.6 percent indicated that they were in the process of developing a plan, 26.8 percent indicated that they were planning on developing a plan, and 30.9 percent indicated no immediate plans to develop a plan.[34]

The next section will further our understanding as to why planning is an important HR activity.

■ WHY IS HUMAN RESOURCE PLANNING IMPORTANT?

In summary, we can view human resource planning as an enabler, mobilizing organizational resources so that the organization is *ready*—ready to ensure that the *right people are in the right place at the right time* and that the customers' needs are met.

Interested in retail, love chic fashion and love travel? Ever heard of Zara? Zara is the premier fashion brand for Industria de Diseno Textil (known as Inditex) and a highly profitable apparel retailer in Europe. Zara sells chic, high-fashion clothing at a low price. It operates in sixty countries and has more than 850 stores that carry women's, men's, and children's apparel. This Spanish fashion chain is fast becoming a major presence, with stores opening across the globe.[35] Inditex has grown exponentially since 2000. Sales and profits have tripled and the number of stores has doubled. Zara is the largest of their brands and accounts for over 66 percent of its total revenues. Inditex's goal is one of growth.[36] Very recently Inditex signed an agreement with Tata Group to form a join venture to develop Zara stores in India. They plan to open up stores in New Delhi, Mumbai, and other major cities in India.[37]

What type of skills do you think Zara will need in order to staff and provide administrative support for these stores? Perhaps marketing, accounting, sales staff, facilities, and IT skills? At what level will they require senior roles such as directors and managers? Or will the bulk of the staff needed be more junior? How many jobs do you think this expansion will generate? Where do you think the bulk of these jobs will be?

This expansion will take a lot of planning. Of course, it is not just human resource planning. Planning will include finding facilities, getting the facilities up and running, and ensuring financing is available. From a resource perspective, this growth strategy will bring new human resource demands in the form of staffing.

A major objective of planning is to ensure that the organization is ready. Ready to compete, ready to deploy its strategy, and ready with the right number of people and skills to meet its objectives. The next section will discuss the importance of planning and explore the reasons why organizations cannot afford to ignore this activity.

The "READI" Paradigm

Planning is important as it enables an organization to be *"readi,"—ready* to meet its business challenges through the effective mobilization of its talent resources and by mobilizing the applicable HR function to help it achieve its goals. An easy way to remember why it is important is to use the "READI" paradigm, as outlined in Exhibit 1.2.

Results   HRP focuses on results. It contributes to the organization's productivity and profitability objectives and people and operational measures.[38]

According to a study conducted by the Hackett group, high-performing organizations who plan effectively achieve 67 percent less voluntary staff turnover and require 46 percent fewer new recruits than companies who do not. In terms of cost, these organizations spend 13 percent less than their peers and operate with 15 percent fewer staff.[39]

Enables   HRP enables an organization to project its resource requirements. The organization forecasts the types of skills required, the number of positions that must be filled, when to fill these positions, and leverages its internal resources capabilities to help make this happen.[40] For example, Cognos, a Canadian business software company, has projected significant financial growth over the next three years. This growth is a result of the fact that more companies are buying software and Cognos will need resources to help build products. Such resources include individuals with specialized software skills and individuals who will help them expand sales. Cognos has predicated that this growth will require an additional workforce of 5,000 staff.[41]

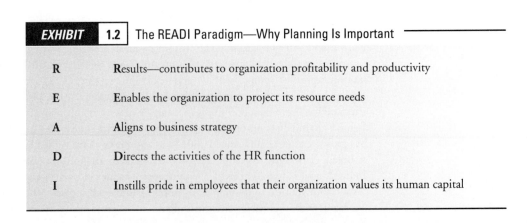

EXHIBIT	1.2	The READI Paradigm—Why Planning Is Important
R		Results—contributes to organization profitability and productivity
E		Enables the organization to project its resource needs
A		Aligns to business strategy
D		Directs the activities of the HR function
I		Instills pride in employees that their organization values its human capital

Aligns   HRP is a proactive process that aligns the activities of human resource management with the overall strategic direction of the organization, linking its actions to the overall strategic plan. HRP enables the human resource function to be proactive and provides human resources with an opportunity to demonstrate that it understands the business challenges and that it can provide the targeted services that are valued by the organization.[42] For example, Microsoft recently launched a new project called "Agility," recognizing that in order to compete effectively against Google and other competitors, it needed to build new capabilities. Skilled talent professionals from across the organization worked with the business to identify and develop the necessary skills and behaviours that its workforce required. Talent management was no longer considered solely the domain of the HR department. The focus became organization-wide, and a key activity for HR was to ensure that employees understood the link between strategy, organizational capabilities, and these talent initiatives.[43]

Directs   HRP directs the human resource activities of the organization, driving the need to establish HR–related objectives and to work with managers in the organization to ensure that human capital needs are met.[44] For example, IBM was concerned about having the skills required to meet their customers' needs in addition to being able to deploy resources in a timely fashion. They decide to create a resource capacity index called "hot skills." The purpose of this index was to provide an inventory of skills so that IBM could match the current skills of its employees to projected demands in a timely fashion. They decided to catalogue all skill sets as human inventory. The key business driver was to ensure that they were able to deploy their resources whenever it was required by a customer.[45]

Instills   It instills a sense of pride in employees when their organization values its human capital and leverages its resource capabilities to help maintain a competitive advantage in the marketplace. For example, Dofasco Inc., one of North America's most progressive and profitable steel makers, believes in its employees. Its slogan is, "Our Product is Steel, Our Strength is People." Dofasco has been ranked as one of the fifty best companies to work for in Canada. They invest in their employees by providing significant training and development opportunities. Their employees are proud to work at Dofasco because of its commitment to people.[46]

In summary, we can say that human resource planning ensures the organization is *ready*, so that it is able to obtain the right people with the right skills in the right place at the right time.

Next, we will discuss several key attributes that can be used to describe an HRP plan.

■ KEY HUMAN RESOURCE PLANNING CHARACTERISTICS

HR planning is multifaceted in nature in that is there are different characteristics that we can use to describe any HR plan. Thinking about these attributes in an organized manner brings clarity to our understanding of HRP. Exhibit 1.3 outlines these different attributes.[47]

For example, we can describe the HR activities of a large organization as being formal, long-term, dynamic, tied to the business strategy, and integrated across HR processes. To illustrate, let's

---

EXHIBIT   1.3 | HRP Characteristics ————————————————————

1. Informal or formal
2. Short-term or long-term
3. Static or dynamic
4. Tied to business plan or stand-alone
5. Integrated across HR processes or operating as an independent activity

consider the challenges faced by the three big automakers over the past several years. The auto industry is a multibillion-dollar industry that over the past decade has faced significant challenges. Work has been moved offshore, labour costs have been rising, customer requirements have been changing, and environmental issues have become a issue, all leading to an overall downturn in the industry. Massive job cuts, restructurings, and plant closings have been reported by General Motors, Chrysler, and Ford. In late 2005, GM announced a restructuring plan that included 30,000 layoffs and a dozen plant closings in Canada and the U.S. This plan was to be completed by the year 2008. Upon completion, GM expected to cut more than 25 percent of its U.S. and Canadian workforce and will make 30 percent fewer cars than it did in 2002.[48]

This plan was formalized and structured. It was linked to the business plan which focused on cutting costs, restructuring, and reducing operating margins. It was integrated across other human resource management functions, impacting recruitment, retention, and employee relations. The resource plan involved discussions with respect to what skills GM would require in the future and what skills it no longer needed, what positions were critical to retain, and where the work would be located. Some individuals were earmarked to receive severance packages and others were offered positions at other sites. A clear well-thought-out termination process was shared with the unions and communicated to employees. The plan that called for plant closings required that HR in Canada notify the Ministry of Labour for approval.

Unfortunately, due to today's economic climate, these plans were not effective. Today, the current recession has significantly impacted the auto industry and automakers have had to accelerate their planning activities and aggressively restructure their organizations at a more rapid rate. Sadly, as of February 2009, GM announced that it was going to cut an additional 47,000 jobs and close five more plants in the U.S. by 2012. And Chrysler announced that it was going to eliminate an additional 3,000 jobs.[49]

Informal or Formal

This HRP characteristic refers to the degree to which planning procedures are rigorous or laissez-faire, whether they are standardized and documented, whether the planner engages in a clearly defined methodology, and whether these activities are evaluated. Some questions to consider are: Does the organization use specific models to plan? Have the planners created formal schedules to follow? Is there a willingness to consider the impact of planning on HRM functions? Are there clearly defined steps?[50]

Short-Term or Long-Term

This HRP characteristic defines the time horizon, the length of time over which the objectives and the plan for ensuring that these objectives will be met will occur. The time horizon can be short, intermediate and/or long-term. Short-term refers to one year in length, an intermediate plan focuses on a two- to three-year time frame, and long-term refers to plans that span three to five years in length. A short-term focus typically corresponds to organizations' annual budgeting cycle, whereas intermediate and long-term plans typically correlate to an organization's strategic planning activities.[51]

Static or Dynamic

This HRP characteristic refers to the degree to which the human resource planning is flexible and malleable. Can the plan be changed when the organization experiences a major resource challenge or is the plan fixed and static? Is the plan amenable to major challenges facing the organization?[52]

Consider the impact of the SARS crisis when suddenly the number of people travelling around the world came to a halt. Some people were quarantined, others did not come to work,

Intel and Human Resource Planning: Alignment to Business Strategy

Intel is a company that has a robust planning process that is both aligned to the business strategy and integrated across human resource functions. Paul Otellini, the new CEO of Intel and the first non-engineer to lead the company, embarked on a business strategy to change the way Intel does business. The company decided to revise its business strategy and extend its product offerings. The old model was primarily focused on providing memory chips for PCs. The new strategy focused on creating all types of chips and software, bringing them together in what they call "platforms" for consumer electronics, communications, and health care industries. Intel's plan was to launch more products than it had in the past. The shift is due to the fact that the PC market is shrinking. The effects can be seen in decreasing revenue growth and profit margins.

What is the link between a new business strategy and human resource management? How does this change impact human resource planning? Otellini has decided to reorganize the company by putting its 98,000 employees in new jobs. In addition, he added 20,000 new employees. The resource planning for the 20,000 new jobs involved identifying the types of skills needed and then using the recruiting function to source these individuals, determine when they needed them, and where their skills were needed. Otellini also focused on the type of skills needed to ensure optimum deployment of the business strategy. He brought in employees with marketing skills, sociologists, ethnographers, and doctors, and shifted the focus to marketing, creating a new culture. Intel also embarked on training its existing staff and helped them integrate in the new culture—one that emphasized teamwork, focused on the customer, communicated what Intel could do for customers, and created a more global mindset.[53] New leader, new culture, new business strategy, and new challenges for HRP!

and stress levels increased significantly. The travel and tourism industry was severely impacted. Companies allowed people to work from home, they cross-trained others to ensure backup, they outsourced work in order to meet their revenue targets, and they increased their employee assistance program (EAP) support.

Tied to Business Strategy or Stand-Alone

This HRP characteristic refers to the link between human resource planning and the organization's business strategy. Is the plan aligned to the business strategy or is it a stand-alone process? Total alignment results in a two-way dialogue between human resources and the business. It is one where human resources provide information to help management optimize their resource requirements and this information in turn is fed into and integrated with the business plans. Once integrated with other business processes, human resources respond accordingly. This two-way dialogue enables human resources to be proactive.

A stand-alone process is one whereby human resources are *told* what information is relevant and what resources are important. It is based on the premise that HR does not understand the business strategy, nor do they incorporate these details into their resource plan. When HR is *being told,* they receive the information downstream (from business forecasts as opposed to from the strategic plan) and as a result they are put in a position of *reacting to* the information rather than being proactive.[54]

EXHIBIT **1.4** The Link Between Human Resource Planning and Business Strategy

```
                    ┌─────────────────────┐
                    │ Corporate Strategy  │
                    └─────────────────────┘
                              │
                              ▼
                    ┌─────────────────────┐
                    │ Business Unit Strategy │
                    └─────────────────────┘
                              │
                              ▼
                    ┌─────────────────────┐
                    │  Functional Strategy │
                    └─────────────────────┘
                     ╱        │         ╲
              ┌───────────┐ ┌──────────┐ ┌──────────────────────────────────┐
              │ Marketing │ │ Finance  │ │ Human Resources                  │
              └───────────┘ └──────────┘ │ HR Strategy                      │
                                          │ HR Goals                         │
                                          │ HR Initiatives—HR Programs and Services │
                                          └──────────────────────────────────┘
```

strategy

An organization's plan of action, a pattern of decisions that determines objectives and purposes, and produces principles, policies, and plans for achieving these goals

In order to clarify this relationship and ascertain the degree of alignment, we need an understanding of the strategic management process and the relationship that can potentially exist between corporate, business, and functional strategies. Exhibit 1.4 illustrates the corporate and business strategies that are commonly referred to by strategic planners and shows the relationship of human resource planning to each of these strategies.

The Strategic Management Processes—Corporate, Business, and Functional

corporate strategy

The selection of business areas in which organizations will compete

Almost all organizations engage on some level in a strategic management process, developing a strategic plan that is unique to its circumstances. These circumstances are determined by a plethora of internal and external factors. A **strategy** is an organization's plan of action, a pattern of decisions that determines objectives and purposes, and produces principles, policies, and plans for achieving these goals. Effective strategies help the organization marshal and allocate its resources in a unique way that is based on its internal competencies and shortcomings, while taking into account environmental changes and anticipated competitor moves.[55]

business strategy

A strategy that identifies how businesses compete in the areas they have selected

Strategies exist at three different levels in an organization. They are corporate, business unit, or functional strategies. **Corporate strategy** refers to the selection of business areas in which organizations will compete. A **business strategy** identifies how businesses compete in the areas they have selected. **Functional strategies** implement these business strategies by making decisions and taking actions that support this process. HR is a function and, as such, is responsible for creating a functional strategy.[56]

functional strategy

Strategies implemented by making decisions and taking actions that support this process

Corporate Strategy   There are three general approaches to corporate strategies: concentration, vertical integration, and diversification. Concentration refers to the focus of an organization on a single or small group of products or services in a single market. Vertical integration occurs when a company decides to expand its business into areas that are in the same industry. They are then involved in different stages of the industry supply chain.

Diversification refers to activities that will enable an organization to achieve greater market share, acquire new skills and knowledge, and enter into new geographic regions. Diversification enables organizations to achieve some economy of scale. There are several approaches that organizations use to diversify—internal ventures, mergers and acquisitions, or joint ventures. A merger occurs when two organizations combine into one, whereas an acquisition involves one organization buying another from its owners.[57] Mergers and acquisitions require significant HR planning. Questions such as what skills are needed, who the organization will retain, what positions are critical, and where the resources should be located, are all important HR–related questions that are raised when organizations engage in this form of activity. Chapter 9 will discuss this in more detail.

Business Strategy   A business strategy identifies how businesses compete in the areas they have selected. It answers the questions about the appropriateness of the business objectives.

In 1980, Michael Porter, an economist at Harvard, identified three generic business strategies in his seminal book, *Competitive Strategy.* His focus was on determining an appropriate competitive strategy based on examining the influences of customers, suppliers, and competitors on industry competition. He determined that organizations could achieve a competitive advantage by offering products or services that were different than their competitors, the same but at a lower cost, and or a combination of the two. He referred to these strategies as cost leadership, differentiation, and focus.

cost leadership

A strategy that focuses the organization on becoming the lowest cost provider of goods or services

Cost Leadership   **Cost leadership** is a strategy that focuses the organization on becoming the lowest cost provider of goods or services. These organizations typically compete by lowering prices when needed, but do not compromise profitability. They attempt to achieve this through economies of scale, technological advances, ensuring that they continuously improve, learning through experience, and ensuring process efficiencies. Dell would be an example of a company that employs a cost leadership strategy.

differentiation

An emphasis on the creation of value through being unique

Differentiation   **Differentiation** emphasizes the creation of value through being unique. Organizations provide superior quality and services, superior supplier relationships, and product innovations. In this instance, customers have to be willing to pay more for the specialness of the product versus what the firm spent to create it. Apple would be an example of a company that uses the strategy of differentiation.

focused differentiation

A strategy that is a combination of cost leadership and differentiation; it focuses on a segment of the market, providing a product or service to this segment

Focused Differentiation   **Focused differentiation** is a strategy that is a combination of cost leadership and differentiation. It focuses on a segment of the market, providing a product or service to this segment. For companies engaging in this strategy, understanding the needs of this target market are critical to success. At this point, Nortel could be considered an example of such a company.

Two other prolific researchers on the subject of business strategy are Raymond Miles from Berkeley and Charles Snow from Pennsylvania State. They took a slightly different approach from Porter. They examined corporate growth strategies, focusing on the timing of growth moves as it related to their competitors, and they proposed that there were certain "types" of organizations.[58] They referred to these business strategies as defenders, prospectors, and analyzers.[59]

defenders

Organizations that operate in stable markets and simple markets; they compete on cost and their strategy is to protect their market share by cost controls and operational efficiencies

Defenders   **Defenders** are organizations that operate in stable markets and simple markets. They compete on cost and their strategy is to protect their market share by cost controls and operational efficiencies. Typically these types operate in stable environments. These organizations engage in standardized processes to minimize cost and have centralized structures in order to manage the flow of information.

Prospectors   **Prospectors** operate in unstable, dynamic, and complex environments. They compete on innovation and creativity. They differentiate themselves from their competitors by developing strategies that focus on market growth with respect to product and/or service innovation. They have organic/decentralized structures and flexible processes.

Analyzers   **Analyzers** are firms that can operate in both a stable and unstable environment. They combine the strengths of the defender and prospector into one system and can operate in product areas that are low-cost or innovative. These types of organizations operate in mixed environments. Focused operation or nichemanship can be used to describe this type of organization.

Functional Strategies   Functional strategies contain details of how functional areas such as marketing, operations, and human resources should work together to achieve business level strategy.[60]

Each function identifies programs and activities that support and align to the plan. These strategies result in a plan of action. HR is a function and as such it is responsible for creating a "functional" strategy, receiving direction from the business strategy. This strategy "helps focus, mobilize, and direct all HR activities on issues that most directly affect the business and involves multiple programs, typically involving multiple functions."[61]

The human resource planning process provides information, guidance, and direction to human resources so that it can develop a "targeted" strategy, one that is aligned to the business. The degree to which human resource planning is aligned to the business strategy and fully integrated with other human resource activities is largely dependant on an organization's level of sophistication with respect to its HR practices.

Integrated Across HR Processes or Operating as an Independent Activity

This HRP characteristic focuses on the degree to which resource planning is integrated with other human resource management processes. Early on in the research conducted by Miles and Snow, a link was found between business strategy and human resource management. They determined that when organizations adopt a specific business strategy, there is a common set of "traits" that are exhibited, if human resource activities are aligned. These traits refer to the type of environment the organizations operate within; the design of their processes; their communication, coordination, and control mechanisms; and the design of their jobs.[62]

Organizations that chose to follow a defender strategy, where the focus was on managing efficiencies and being effective in order to manage costs, would create standards and insist on procedural uniformity. Job designs would be rigid, rules and procedures would be explicit, communication would be vertical, and control mechanisms would be tight. Training programs would be focused on skill building, recruiting would be limited to entry-level positions, and selection mechanisms would be focused on low cost. Here, human resource planning would be long-term, formalized forecasting and planning of labour.[63] An example would be McDonald's mechanized processes and clearly defined jobs.

Organizations who chose a prospector strategy, where innovation and creativity were important, typically would exhibit decentralized organizational structures. Their processes were not as formalized, communication was horizontal, there were few rules and procedures, job design was broad, there was sophisticated recruiting at all levels, and numerous selection mechanisms were used. Human resource planning is typically short-range and must be flexible.[64]

An example of a prospector company would be Google, an organization that has experienced significant growth and is very specific about its recruitment and selection practices. It has been noted that an individual applying for a position with Google may have up to fifteen interviews, as well as undergoing extensive testing that focuses on a candidate's creativity and innovation.

Recent literature has further confirmed the importance of the link between business strategy and human resource planning, and the importance of integrating planning with other HR functions. As Jackson and Schuler so elegantly expressed, "HR planning will be the thread that ties together all other HR resources activities and integrates these with the rest of the organization."[65]

Growing the firm's intangible assets through significant investments in HR functions such as staffing, training, and compensation are considered necessary to ensure optimum utilization of the firm's internal resources.

Recruitment and Selection   Let's consider the recruitment and selection process. Planning determines the number of people needed, the skills required, and when they are needed. Recruitment identifies and attracts an adequate number of candidates. These individuals can be internal or external. The recruitment function gets its direction from planning to narrow the pool to the appropriate candidates and then utilizes various selection tools to choose the best fit.

Training and Career Development   Planning determines what skills are required and when these skills and competencies are needed. Training provides employees with the skills or competencies to do their jobs and development prepares employees for future positions. Career paths are developed and development and succession plans are created to ensure optimum utilization of human capital. Organizations that are in growth mode and who are unique in terms of their products or services, typically have multiple career paths, significant development opportunities, broad applications, a lot of participation organizations, and find ways to improve staff utilization.[66]

These are just a few illustrations as to how human resource planning deploys and integrates across human resource management processes and functions. This relationship will be discussed in more detail in the subsequent chapters.

HRP AND THE SMALL BUSINESS

BioWare—Creator of the "Knights of the Republic"

The gaming industry is thriving in Canada. The global market is $30 billion in sales, with Canada accounting for 3 percent of the sales, or over $1 billion. One such company whose products are in demand is Bioware Corp. Based in Edmonton, Alberta and founded in the 90s by two physicians, this company has grown significantly over the past twelve years. They recently opened a studio in Austin, Texas and now employ over 340 employees in Austin and Edmonton. They recently merged with Pandemic Studios to create one of the strongest independent game companies in the industry. Its sales have grown exponentially.[67]

Bioware is well-known in the industry, collaborating with such high-profile artists as George Lucas on their game "Knights of the Republic." They have won over one hundred awards and have been listed as one of Canada's top 100 employers. Their latest game is called "Jade Empire" and is an action-martial arts game. Currently they have three new games in development and they are on a recruitment drive, sourcing candidates throughout North America. Numerous job openings are available in such roles as animation, marketing, design, technology, and artists to name a few.[68]

Getting the right people in the right place when they need them is a major priority for this firm!

■ FIVE STAGES OF PLANNING SOPHISTICATION

Every organization is unique and they are very different in terms of how they plan. Some organizations create robust plans—ones that are structured, tied to the business plan, integrated with HR functions, and dynamic in nature—whereas other organizations plan informally. Researchers have attempted to ascertain what, if any, are the differentiating factors that can lead us to understand these differences. Daniel Quinn Mills, a professor at Harvard and MIT, observed that organizations evolve through various stages and that each organization can be different in terms of its level of planning sophistication.

Noting that different industries had different planning horizons based on their unique circumstances, he categorized organizations with respect to the degree and scope of their planning activities and the level of acceptance of the human resource planning process within these organizations.[69] He examined the number of people-planning elements used in the company, the degree to which resource plans were integrated into the business plan, and the commitment made to planning itself. Dr. Mills identified five stages of planning sophistication, as shown in Exhibit 1.5.

Stage one companies do not engage in any form of planning, whether it be business- or human resource–related. Recruitment and training are considered an afterthought. An example would be a family-owned or small organization where the leadership style is paternalistic in nature.

Stage two companies do engage in some long-term business planning, but minimal human resource planning. Resource planning is solely focused on headcount forecasts. The planning is static in nature and receives minimal weight in terms of importance within the organization.

We can describe stage three companies as engaging in moderate planning activities, creating longer-term forecasts, and projecting their needs three to five years ahead. However, these organizations still do not integrate their people planning efforts into the long-term business plan.

EXHIBIT   1.5   Five Stages of Planning Sophistication

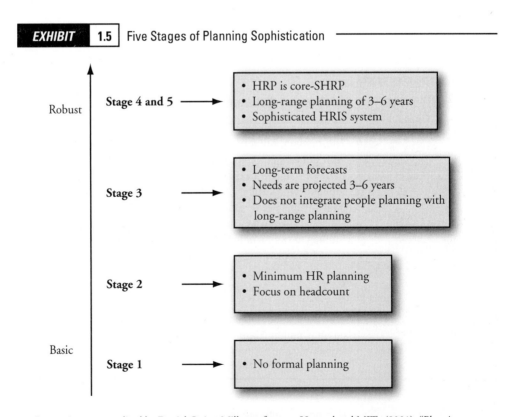

Robust

Stage 4 and 5 ──────▶
- HRP is core-SHRP
- Long-range planning of 3–6 years
- Sophisticated HRIS system

Stage 3 ──────▶
- Long-term forecasts
- Needs are projected 3–6 years
- Does not integrate people planning with long-range planning

Stage 2 ──────▶
- Minimum HR planning
- Focus on headcount

Basic

Stage 1 ──────▶
- No formal planning

Source: As conceptualized by Daniel Quinn Mills, professor at Harvard and MIT, (2001), "Planning with People in Mind," *Harvard Business Review,* 97–105.

Stage four and five companies are considered advanced in terms of their planning sophistication. Here, human resource planning becomes a core process. At this stage we begin to see organizations valuing their human resources and embracing the value that these assets can deliver. Managers are enthusiastic about planning and there is a growing recognition that anticipating resource requirements for the future is imperative to ensure organizational sustainability.

Stage four and five organizations engage in long-range human resource planning and their resource requirements span three to six years. Over 80 percent of the organizations studied incorporated at least one human resource component into their long-range plan. We could describe these types of organizations as engaging in SHRP.

Stage five organizations are considered role-model organizations that engage in best practice resource planning principles. At this stage, human resource planning is considered a key

HRP IN THE NEWS

Corning Inc.—A Sophisticated Human Resource Planning Process

Corning Inc., a world leader in specialty glass and ceramics, is a company who has a 150-year-old history of success with process and material innovation. For many years, Corning maintained a diverse portfolio of business. However, the collapse of the telecom bubble severely impacted Corning's profitability, and the company decided to re-evaluate its business goals and processes. It shed half its workforce and shrank from over 40,000 to 20,000 employees, embarking on a strategy to redefine its business processes. The mix of skills and talent which once specialized in optical and electronic areas now shifted back to material and process specialties.

To respond to this change, the HR department embarked on some key activities, engaging in human capital planning (HCP) to help the organization achieve its goals. HR established four key transformational goals. The first was business linkage, which aligned the planning activities to the business planning processes. The second and third goals were global and scalable, highlighting the need for HR to build capabilities when and where needed on a real-time basis, and deploying these capabilities wherever required. HR reviewed its employees' existing skill sets, engaged managers in dialogue about their staff, and considered the appropriate investments needed for its staff. HR refused to outsource work and looked towards "building functional capability and the service excellence that ensure[s] that each business ha[s] the right number, quality, and type of talent needed to execute the strategy." To get information on its employees, it leveraged its HRIS system—a very sophisticated system called "People Soft." HR broadened its perspective and approach to an international perspective, developing expertise in international HR practices and arming its existing workforce with the appropriate skills. The fourth transformational goal was "top quartile cost," meaning that HR engaged and delivered these activities on budget. They used sophisticated evaluation tools and benchmarked their progress by using qualitative and quantitative measures.

We can say that Corning operated at a sophisticated level and demonstrated a robust human resource planning process that delivered significant value to the organization. For more information about Corning, go to www.corning.com.[70]

Source: Brush, M.C. & Ruse, D. H. (2005). "Driving strategic success through human capital planning: How Corning links business and HR strategy to improve the value and impact of its HR function" [electronic version]. HR. *Human Resource Planning*, 28 (1), 49–60.

priority. The plan can be described as long range with the time frame being three to six years. The planning is formal, flexible, dynamic, and adjusts to change as circumstances dictate. The human resource components are fully integrated with the business plan. Recruitment and training are anticipated and succession planning is considered a critical activity to ensure sustainability. Stage five organizations utilize robust evaluation tools, illustrating how human resource planning activities contribute to the bottom line.

We can conclude that stage four and five companies engage in a greater degree of SHRP planning as their HR processes are aligned, their activities integrated, and their processes and systems are more sophisticated. Corning Inc. is a company that utilizes sophisticated planning practices.

Next, we turn our attention to the actual human resource planning process and explore the key steps involved.

The Human Resource Planning Process

Human resource planning is a process. The definition of a process is a specific ordering of activities across time and space with a beginning and an end, and with clearly identified outputs and inputs. It provides a structure for action and identifies how work is to be done.[71] HRP adds value by helping managers focus on the issues that are most important. This helps the organization become competitive and enhance decisions about human capital.[72] The human resource planning process itself is not strategic or unique. As shown in Exhibit 1.6, it is merely a set of four generic steps.[73]

What *is* unique is how organizations choose to engage in the planning process, the degree of sophistication with respect to these practices, how urgent and important the resource needs are, and the overall importance that senior management places on resolving resource challenges.

The steps of human resource planning are as follows:

1. Forecast Labour Demand and Labour Supply This activity answers the question about what type of talent is required to meet organizational objectives. Planners must review the corporate and business strategies and understand the type of organization, its environment, the industry challenges, and resident skills sets. What type of business strategy has been chosen by the organization? Is the organization facing a merger? Does the organization operate locally or globally? This phase identifies and prioritizes talent gaps, estimating the number of people and type of skills required over the term of the critical business cycle. It answers the question of *how many*

EXHIBIT 1.6 The Human Resource Planning Process ———————————

human resources are needed, *when* this talent is needed, and *where* it is needed. It forecasts this demand by looking at many factors, such as business strategy, technological advances, and sales forecasts. This is followed by an assessment of the internal supply of resources through examining the capabilities and skills of its employees and the external supply of labour in the marketplace. How this is done is largely dependant on the level of the organization's sophistication, the view management has regarding human resource planning, and whether or not talent management is a priority. Chapters 2, 9, and 10 will discuss this in more detail.

2. Establish Human Resource Objectives   This step identifies what the planners expect to accomplish as a result of their actions. It directs the planning process, identifies what the planner will do in order to achieve their goals, and sets a baseline to determine whether the organization has achieved its goals. For example, if the organization's strategy is to grow revenue by 20 percent, the HR objective would be to add a certain number of "headcount" with a certain set of skills by a predetermined date. However, if the organization's objective is to reduce labour costs by 20 percent, then the objective might be to reduce the workforce in each department by five percent by a certain date, carefully taking into account the preservation of individuals with critical skills sets and significant ongoing potential. Chapter 2 and Appendix A will discuss this in more detail.

3. Design and Implement Human Resource Programs to Achieve Objectives   In this step, the planners decide what type of human resource programs will be developed in order to achieve their objectives. These programs attempt to balance demand and supply. For example, if the organization is projecting a labour shortage, it may choose to outsource or use overtime. Or in a surplus, it may decide to job-share versus downsize. Considerations will be given to whether there is time to develop employees internally or whether an outside source is required. This will be discussed in greater detail throughout the book.

people equity

An approach used by an organization to measure and manage human capital using three elements—alignment, capabilities, and engagement

4. Evaluate the Effectiveness of the Programs   Measurement provides a tangible link, a "bridge" between investments in human resource programs and organizational sustainability.[74] A major goal of human resource measurement is to enhance decisions about human capital and connect human resources to strategy.[75] W. Schiemann used the term **people equity** to explain how organizations measure and manage their human capital to maximize its value. The concept of people equity comprises three main elements and looks at how a firm optimizes its return on investment. He referred to these three elements as alignment, capabilities, and engagement (ACE). Alignment refers to the degree of alignment between strategy and people's activities. Capabilities are the talent resources to execute the strategy. Engagement is the degree of commitment that people have to the organization.[76]

To measure human capital effectively, the planner is responsible for evaluating its processes and continuously improving the technical and strategic aspects of this process. This improvement must be evident from year to year. To ensure continuous improvement, all processes must be measured, a baseline developed, and initiatives put in place. It is imperative that the human resources professional use key business metrics and develop a thorough understanding of how human resource planning can contribute to the bottom line.[77] Evaluation is dependant on the criteria the organization uses to discern whether the human resource planning function is effective. Typically, processes are measured in terms of the time and cost associated with their deployment. They can be assessed with respect to their usefulness, consistency, variability, and robustness.[78]

There are a variety of mechanisms or tools that can be used to demonstrate this value. The ability to do this in a compressive way largely depends on the level of technological sophistication—the systems that are available and the robust nature of the tools chosen. Chapters 7, 10, and 11 will discuss this process step in more detail.

EXHIBIT | **1.7** | Roadmap: Framework and Organization of the Textbook

HR PROCESS STEPS	FORECAST LABOUR DEMAND AND LABOUR SUPPLY	ESTABLISH HR OBJECTIVES	DESIGN AND IMPLEMENT HR PROGRAMS TO ACHIEVE OBJECTIVENESS	PROGRAM EVALUATION AND CONTROL
	→	→	→	
HR ACTIONS	Review corporate/business strategy and determine talent requirements	Estimate number of people required and forecast internal and external supply	Identify and prioritize talent gaps and take action to close gaps Consider data sources	Evaluate, monitor, and continuously improve
CHAPTER REFERENCE	1, 2, 8, 9	1, 2	3, 4, 5, 6, 7, 8, 9	7, 10, 11

■ FRAMEWORK AND ORGANIZATION OF THE TEXTBOOK

Throughout the textbook, we will explore the human resource planning process and examine each of these process steps in much greater detail. In Exhibit 1.7, we have created a roadmap to guide you throughout the text. This roadmap explains how the text is organized and highlights the link between the human resource process steps, human resource actions, and chapter references.

CHAPTER SUMMARY

- Human resource planning (HRP) is a process used to determine future human resource requirements by anticipating future business demands, analyzing the impacts of these demands on the organization, and making decisions on how to effectively acquire and utilize firms' human resources. Its goal is to ensure that the right people are available at the right place at the right time.
- HRP is an important HR activity. It ensures that the organization is ready—ready to focus on results that contribute to organizational productivity, ready to help the organization adequately forecast its resource requirements, ready to align its activities to corporate and business strategy, and ready to ensure that employee skills and abilities in the organization are valued.
- There are five key HRP characteristics that describe the multifaceted nature of HRP. These attributes are: formal or informal, short-term or long-term, static or dynamic, aligned to business strategy or stand-alone, integrated across HRM processes or operating as an independent activity.
- Organizations are unique in term of how they plan, with each organization operating at a different level of sophistication. At the extreme end are those organizations that view

planning as merely an add-on and react to challenges rather than being proactive and integrating its planning activities as part of the business planning cycle. Daniel Quinn Mills identified five stages of sophistication.

- The HR planning process is a four-step process. Step one is to forecast labor demand and supply. Step 2 is to establish organizational objectives. Step 3 is to design and implement HR programs to achieve these objectives. Step 4 is to evaluate the program and continuously improve. However, because all organizations are different—they operate in very different environments, with different management philosophies and different levels of sophistication—these steps are interpreted in many different ways.

KEY TERMS

- analyzers 14
- business strategy 12
- corporate strategy 12
- cost leadership 13
- defenders 13
- differentiation 13
- environmental scanning 7

- focused differentiation 13
- functional strategy 12
- human resource planning (HRP) 3
- manpower planning 4
- people equity 19
- prospectors 14

- resource-based view (RBV) 16
- strategic human resource management (SHRM) 5
- strategy 12

REVIEW QUESTIONS

1. Describe the HRP process.
2. Discuss the evolution of HRP.
3. Differentiate between HRP and SHRP.
4. What are the five key characteristics that can be used to describe HRP?
5. Discuss the link between HRP and business strategy.
6. Discuss the link between HRP and HRM.
7. How would you describe the different levels of HRP sophistication?

DISCUSSION QUESTIONS

1. As an employee in an organization, what reasons would you give to convince your organization to develop its employees internally?
2. Using the "Readi" paradigm discussed in this chapter, explain why HRP is an important HR activity.
3. If HR is going to add value, it must demonstrate that it is a strategic partner. How does the function of HRP enable HR to achieve these goals?
4. What challenges do you think organizations are facing today that might influence the way they plan their human resources?
5. Consider different sized organizations and the types of planning activities that would be applicable. How sophisticated do you think the planning function should be for a small organization of fewer than 50 employees? What about an organization with over 1,500 employees? What type of planning activities do you think would be appropriate?

WEB EXERCISE

Visit the following websites and answer the questions listed below:

Statistics Canada: www.statcan.gc.ca/start-debut-eng.html (Access the current labour market survey and click on the detailed summary)

Job Futures www.jobfutures.ca/en/home.shtml (Click on "I want to know more about the world of work")

Human Resources and Skills Development: www.hrsdc.gc.ca/eng/workplaceskills/labour_market_information/index.shtml (Look under Labour Market Information and Labour Market Bulletins)

Questions

1. What are the hottest jobs in each province right now?
2. Where are the greatest skill shortages in your province?
3. What industries have had the most growth over the past several years?
4. What are the projections with respect to job growth?
5. Do certain industries have greater opportunities than others?

CASE INCIDENT

What Does the Weather Have to Do with Human Resource Planning?

The fall-out from global warming will be felt for more than 1,000 years. There is significant evidence that the world is heating up! The arctic ice cap is melting much faster than expected and is now about thirty years ahead of what was originally predicted.[79] Significant increases in heat waves, rainstorms, and severe hurricanes and typhoons, and a warming of the earth's core are predicted. The climate has been projected to change significantly over the next several decades—ocean currents will slow by as much as 25 percent, global temperatures will be 1.7 to 4 degrees higher, and sea levels are expected to rise. If this trend continues, global warming can lead to a complete elimination of the Greenland ice sheet and a rise of about seven metres in sea levels.

The warming of the climate system is going to continue. In fact, 11 out of the last 12 years rank among the warmest since the 1950s.[80] What does this mean for specific industries? Consider the sporting goods industry or those manufacturing firms who make boots, winter apparel, or snow equipment. Or the travel industries who specialize in ski vacations. What challenges do you think these firms will face?

Questions

1. What industries do you think would be most affected by this change in weather?
2. What are some specific jobs that would be in demand?
3. What are some specific jobs that might be compromised? When may there be an oversupply if these trends continue?
4. What initiatives are being planned to help combat global warming? Vist the Environment Canada website at www.ec.gc.ca.

■ REQUIRED PROFESSIONAL CAPABILITIES REFERENCED IN THIS CHAPTER

1. Contributes to the development of the organization's visions, goals, and strategies with a focus on human capabilities.
2. Translates the organization's business plan into issues, priorities, and human resources strategies and objectives.
6. Develops and implements a human resources plan that supports the organization's strategic objectives.
7. Audits existing HR programs to ensure they are aligned with business objectives.
8. Provides the information necessary for organizations to effectively manage its people practices.
9. Evaluates the effectiveness of HR strategies, applying various measurement and assessment programs.
10. Applies business fundamentals of production, operations management, accounting and finance, information technology, marketing, and strategic planning to people management issues.
65. Forecasts HR supply and demand conditions.

FORECASTING DEMAND AND SUPPLY

LEARNING OBJECTIVES

- Understand and select information required to forecast HRP
- Identify members of the HR planning team
- Understand the four steps in the HRP process
- Apply techniques to forecast HR demand and supply
- Describe various methods for assessing labour planning (quantitative and qualitative)
- Discuss key challenges in forecasting HR demand and supply

■ PROFILE

The Great Pyramid of Giza

The Great Pyramid of Giza has fascinated the world for centuries and is revered as one of the greatest mysteries of time. When it was first built it was 145 metres tall, making it the tallest structure on the earth for over 4,300 years. Egyptologists argue that even with all of the human and computer advancements achieved to date, it would be near impossible to replicate the production of these pyramids. The HR planning scale of the project would be among the biggest challenges to face.

Archaeologists have their own methods for determining how many workers (mostly slaves) were employed at Giza, but a majority agree that the Great Pyramid was built by approximately 4,000 primary labourers—quarry workers, haulers, and masons. These primary labourers would have been supported by 16,000 to 20,000 secondary workers—ramp builders, tool-makers, mortar mixers, and those providing back-up services such as supplying food, clothing, and fuel. These estimates suggest a total of 20,000 to 25,000 employees who laboured for 22 years to build the pyramids.

Although the concept of HRP as it is currently known did not exist at this time, determining how many employees, at what time, in which location, and with which specific skill sets was in fact a function of HRP. Multiple factors affected the HR planning forecasts, including the number of blocks delivered and installed per day via mud ramps, the number of trips to the quarry per day, the length of the workday and workweek, the amount of food distributed, and the amount of housing needed.

One theory suggests that the workers may have been subdivided into a permanent workforce of approximately 5,000 salaried employees who lived together with their families and dependents in a well-established pyramid village. In addition, there were up to 20,000 temporary workers who arrived to work three- or four-month shifts. These temporary workers lived in a less sophisticated camp established alongside the pyramid village.

Another theory suggests that the employees were split into one of three groups for the production of the pyramids. One group went to Giza to work on the pyramids, the second worked in the fields to farm the food required for the workers, and the third would rest. These groups of employees would rotate every four months to ensure that within a one-year span the full cycle would be completed.

What unique challenges are presented in the HR planning for the pyramids? What factors influenced the supply of labour for the building of the pyramids and how could these be prevented or responded to?

This chapter will provide a clear awareness of the human resource planning process, specifically focusing on the forecasting of labour supply and labour demand. Both qualitative and quantitative methods of forecasting will be outlined.

■ WHY IS HUMAN RESOURCE PLANNING IMPORTANT?

As discussed in Chapter 1, a key goal of HRP is to get the right number of people with the right skills, experience, and competencies in the right jobs at the right time and at the right cost. This ensures that the business production requirements are met in an efficient and effective manner. Having too many employees is problematic due to the risk of high labour expenses, downsizing, or layoffs. Having too few employees is also problematic due to high overtime costs, the risk of unmet production requirements, and the challenge of finding the instant human resources needed to get the job done. According to the Government of Canada, human resource planning links people management to the organization's mission, vision, goals and objectives, as well as its strategic plan and budgetary resources. A critical component of an

forecasting

The interaction between the decision maker's perceptual and cognitive processes and the objective characteristics of their environment

effective HR plan is the method of forecasting. **Forecasting** refers to the interaction between the decision maker's perceptual and cognitive processes and the objective characteristics of their environment.

The opening case in this chapter identifies the HRP issues associated with the building of the Great Pyramid of Giza in 2620 BC, where tens of thousands of workers were employed for almost 22 years. Since then, the nature of organizations has changed, but HRP issues remain imperative in the establishment and maintenance of a successful organization. In recent times of hyper-competition and knowledge-based economies, more complex models of HR planning are needed to account for more dynamic business models. Additionally, as labour expenses become a large portion of the costs of operation, planning the appropriate "mix" of human resources becomes a priority for the organization.

Securing management and staff commitment to the HRP process is fundamental to the development of a successful workforce plan. Before launching the HRP process, it is important to build commitment and awareness in the process at multiple levels in the organization.

■ INFORMATION REQUIRED TO SUCCESSFULLY FORECAST HUMAN RESOURCES DEMAND AND SUPPLY

There are three important elements to consider in order to successfully forecast labour demand and supply: identifying stakeholders who will be involved, determining the appropriate planning horizon, and defining the internal and external labour force.

The Human Resources Planning Team

groupthink

The tendency for group members to avoid introducing novel ideas that are outside of the group's normal mode of thinking for fear that they will disrupt the group consensus process

The HRP team should include all relevant stakeholders across multiple functional areas and organizational levels. Explicitly developing a team for the HRP process helps ensure success of the strategies within the plan and holds those who are not meeting the goals accountable. Also, the diversity in the team will reduce **groupthink,** the tendency for group members to avoid introducing novel ideas that are outside of the group's normal mode of thinking for fear that they will disrupt the group consensus process. Listed in Exhibit 2.1 are suggestions for whom to include.

For example, senior leaders must understand the value of the HR plan to the organization in order to build their commitment to the execution of the plan. It is critical not only to align the HR plan to the organization's strategic plan, but to also communicate how the plan will affect future operations, financial goals, and market position of the company. Doing so will build the confidence of the leaders and convince them that the change is required.

Determining the Appropriate Planning Horizon

appropriate planning horizon

A judgement about how far into the future predictions can be made, taking into consideration acceptable levels of operational, organizational, and environmental uncertainties

Similar to the development of an organizational strategy, a human resources strategy must have a horizon or timeline. The **appropriate planning horizon** is a judgement about how far into the future predictions can be made, taking into consideration acceptable levels of operational, organizational, and environmental uncertainties. This is highly subjective as it is based on the decision maker's cognitive processes and perceptions of the organization's position in the market.

As discussed in Chapter 1, the typical planning horizon is two-tiered. The first horizon, usually a year in duration, identifies more immediate workforce concerns that can be addressed quickly, such as known employee exits, replacements, promotions, etc. The second horizon is usually longer, approximately 3 to 6 years, allowing for enough lead time to actively recruit, select, train, and transfer staff as needed. Regardless of how sophisticated the planning techniques, the further into the future HR plans are, the higher the level of uncertainty. Planning is not a static

| **EXHIBIT 2.1** | Strategic Partners in HR Planning |

Strategic Partners	Rationale
Senior Leaders or Business Executives	Leaders are accountable for recognizing the need for workforce planning, demonstrating commitment, and making it happen.
Line or Department Managers	Department managers are responsible for using the HR plan as a process for aligning the right people actions, such as recruitment and selection, with strategic goals and objectives.
HR Professionals	HR professionals provide support, workforce data, and HR strategic goals. They should work closely with department managers to implement the process.
IT Professionals	IT professionals aid in data collection, especially when the process is automated.
Strategic Planners	Strategic planners ensure linkages between the organizational strategic plans and the HR plans.
Finance or Accounting Budget Analysts	Budget analysts ensure linkages between the organizational financial limits or goals and the HR plans.

activity; HR plans are frequently updated and should be reviewed annually to ensure they are still appropriate for the organization.

Immediate versus Long-Term Workforce Considerations When Determining the Appropriate Planning Horizon   Here are some examples of immediate workforce concerns:

- Replacing personnel known to be retiring
- Promoting employees within departments when positions become available
- Filling vacancies due to turnover

Here are some examples of long-term workforce concerns:

- Succession planning for key management positions
- Developing employee skill sets to launch new products or processes
- Working with colleges or universities to increase the number of graduates with a specific desirable educational background
- Responding to future government or union policy changes

Evaluating the Current Human Resources Situation

internal labour force

Those who perform the work or provide services within the company under the control or supervision of the organization's management team

Defining the Internal Labour Force   When assessing the current HR situation, it is important to define who is included in the **internal labour force.** A fatal flaw in the HR planning process is conducting a human resources audit on a limited or non-representative sample of employees. When determining which persons should be considered employees, a good measure is those who perform the work or provide services within the company under the control or supervision of the organization's management team. This includes contingent employees.

R**P**C® 73

R**P**C® 16

contingent workforce

The class of individual workers who are not regular, full-time employees of a company

The **contingent workforce,** while having no precise definition, essentially encompasses the class of individual workers who are not regular, full-time employees of a company.[1] This includes part-time, temporary, seasonal, contractual, and intern employees. These employees are hired by staffing organizations, through independent contracts, or by the company itself. Currently, almost one-third of Canadian workers are defined as part of a contingent workforce.[2] Organizations typically rely on a contingent workforce to address short-term labour needs or when they are in need of a specific expertise. Chapter 3 will discuss this in more detail.

HR Inventory

 72

Identifying current workforce dynamics is a critical step in the development of an HR plan. A **skills inventory** is a computerized or manual system designed to take stock of information about current employees' experience, education, compensation history, and/or unique abilities. A skills inventory can be useful in revealing what skills are immediately available in an organization by providing a snapshot view of the existing talent in an organization.

skills inventory

A computerized or manual system designed to take stock of information about current employees' experience, education, compensation history, and/or unique abilities

As an alternative or complement to the skills inventory, a **human resource audit** is a systematic examination and analysis of an organizational workforce in an effort to create an understanding of the current staffing situation. The HR audit compares the past with the present labour specifications to identify trends and patterns in multiple aspects, including turnover, training, absence, and diversity. An HR audit can identify key information about HR operations, including how well they work, and where improvement may be needed. It is an extremely useful tool in HR planning.

The information provided in an audit or skills inventory (as shown in Exhibit 2.2) can be useful in identifying a number of workforce trends. For example, is turnover increasing or decreasing? Is the organization becoming more or less diverse? What factors influence the turnover

human resource audit

A systematic examination and analysis of an organizational workforce in an effort to create an understanding of the current staffing situation

EXHIBIT 2.2 Information Commonly Included in an HR Audit or Skills Inventory

The following information should be included in current staffing plans:

- Budget information
- Classification information
- Compensation and benefits information
- Demographic data
- Diversity issues
- Employee experience (internal and external)
- Health and safety issues
- Identification of unionization and bargaining units
- Job analysis information (e.g., employee knowledge, skills, and abilities)
- Labour market analyses
- Performance data and evaluations
- Recruiting sources
- Redeployment plans
- Retention data
- Retirement plans
- Selection and staffing information
- Succession planning information
- Technology use
- Training and development information
- Turnover data
- Work–life balance issues

rate? Are these short-term or long-term factors? What types of positions have been filled recently within the company and which ones have recently been vacated? Developing an awareness of these factors can help predict change in an organization's human resources.

Some organizations conduct active HR audits or skills inventories as part of specific legislation requirements (e.g., occupational health and safety, pay equity, employment equity), as part of a human resources information system (HRIS), or as part of another HR activity (e.g., merger, acquisition, downsizing, etc.). If no HR audit or skills inventories exist, creating one can be very labour-intensive and time-consuming. Sources of information for an HR audit or skills inventory are the same as the sources for collecting job analysis information.

Defining the External Labour Force

external labour force

Potential sources of human resources outside of an organization that can affect the future supply of employees

The **external labour force** refers to potential sources of human resources outside of an organization that can affect the future supply of employees. Evaluation of the external labour force relies on labour market estimates based on regional and global economic, environmental, and demographic changes. Economic and environment factors include interest rates, unionization, economic growth, unemployment rates, and political climate. Demographic factors include population-based information such as retirement rates, birth/mortality rates, educational attainment, primary language, labour shifts (location), etc. Chapter 11 provides a detailed discussion of the major external labour force changes that are affecting HR planning.

Since the external labour force provides designated group members from which the employer can reasonably be expected to recruit, any changes to that population must be considered when conducting an HR planning exercise to help develop an understanding of projected HR supply. Human Resources and Social Development Canada (HRSDC) recommends that the external labour force representation (availability) include the most accurate estimates by using information on the Canadian workforce in specific occupational groupings and analysing that information based on qualifications, eligibility, and geography.

Qualifications for inclusion in the external workforce analysis can include the use of census data (e.g., education levels, industry of employment) to align with the desired skill level and skill type required by the organization. In addition, organizations use eligibility and geography as criteria for determining whom to include in the external workforce. Eligibility can include professional designations (e.g., Chartered Management Accountants) or licenses required by the organization. Geography refers to the area from which the organization can be reasonably expected to recruit. Generally, more critical positions, such as CEOs or executive management positions, involved a wider geographic search than less critical positions in an organization.

In the 2006 Canadian Census, the fastest growth industry in terms of employment was the mining and oil and gas extraction industry. In this industry, employment increased nearly four times the national average. Alberta accounted for 70 percent of the employment growth in this industry. An Alberta organization in this industry can interpret this data to indicate heavy competition for labour in the external workforce and due to the employment growth in this industry, low future HR supply of labour. Comparably, the decline of manufacturing jobs in Ontario in recent years indicates a high supply of potential labour in the external workforce for organizations in this industry.

There are also general trends in the external labour force that can affect future HR supply. For example, a mix of low birth rates, the baby-boom generation, and increasing average life expectancy in Canada increased the average age of members of the labour force from 37.1 years old in 1991 to 41.2 years old in 2006. At the same time, the Canadian labour force grew by 9.5 percent (from 15.6 million to 16.9 million), with immigrants accounting for 70 percent of the labour force growth.[3] Thus, the Canadian labour force is growing significantly while becoming older and more diverse.

An awareness of external labour force pressures, changes, and trends can aid an organization in understanding its potential to recruit labour in the future, and thus is a critical component of forecasting future HR supply.

THE HUMAN RESOURCE PLANNING PROCESS

strategic plan

A macro-level set of directives that identify how the organization will achieve its mission and move toward its vision

An organization's **strategic plan** leads the overall HR strategic plan. The strategic plan is a macro-level set of directives that identifies how the organization will achieve its mission and move toward its vision. Workforce planning offers a means of systematically aligning organizational and program priorities with the budgetary and human resources needed to accomplish them. By beginning the planning process with identified strategic objectives, managers and their organizations can develop workforce plans that will help them accomplish those objectives. At the same time, these plans provide a sound basis for justifying budget and staffing requests, since there is a clear connection between objectives, the budget, and the human resources needed to accomplish them.

The strategic plan for human resources should follow organizational goals, including the types of projects and activities that the organization aims to execute. For example, if the organization aims to grow its market and expand sales by 25 percent, HR planning should align itself to grow the organization. Likewise, if the strategic plan is for maximizing efficiencies and lowering overhead costs, the HR plan should have the same goals.

As we learned in Chapter 1, the HR planning process involves four steps. Forecasting labour demand and supply is the first step and can be accomplished using multiple methods. The second step is the establishment of human resource objectives as ascertained by comparing demand and supply forecasts and assessing workforce imbalances. The third step is the design and implementation of HR programs to achieve objectives. The fourth and final step is the evaluation of the effectiveness of the programs, which feeds back into the first step. The result is a cyclical HR planning process.

STEP 1: FORECAST LABOUR DEMAND AND SUPPLY

Decisions made about projections of future labour supply and demand are affected by the decision maker's environment (organizational characteristics) and their own beliefs or perceptions relating to the environmental uncertainty. Labour forecasting is key to an organization's ability to achieve its operational, production, and strategic goals.

Forecasting HR Supply

The purpose of identifying future HR supply requirements is to determine the number of employees in each job and their knowledge, skills, abilities, and other characteristics (KSAOs). In addition, forecasting HR supply is essential in determining the characteristics of hiring sources within the predetermined planning horizon in order to establish whether future HR supply is sufficient to match future HR demands. To forecast HR supply, an organization needs to evaluate both their internal and external labour force. This step is dependent on an accurate assessment of the current workforce situation.

Forecasting HR supply involves an understanding of internal and external potential human resource supplies. Due to the availability of data and the multiple methods that can be used, internal supply is usually easier to establish than external supply. However, it is still important to try to determine external supply as accurately as possible.

Forecasting External HR Supply   There are multiple levels at which external HR supply can be predicted, including global, national, provincial, regional, and local. Information that will help develop an understanding of external HR supply includes:

- Supply and demand of jobs or skills
- Educational attainment levels within a region
- Compensation patterns based on experience, education, or occupation
- Immigration and emigration patterns within an area
- Forecasts of economic growth or decline
- Competition for talent
- Industry or occupational expected growth levels

- Public policy, government, and legal changes
- Trends in labour force participation (including entry and exit)
- Technological development patterns

National information is available through a number of departments in the Government of Canada, including Statistics Canada, the Ministry of Labour, and the Human Resources and Social Development Canada (HRSDC) department.

Information may also be available at specific levels. For example, predictions of enrolment and graduation levels in specific majors from academic institutions can identify the number of new entrants in the external labour force who possess a specific skill set. The Canadian Occupational Projection System (COPS) has developed a Job Futures databank with supply and demand information for 265 occupational groups and 155 fields of study. In addition, industry specific information can be secured from industry associations and subsets. For example, the Canadian construction industry can access updated labour market supply information from the Construction Sector Council website (www.csc-ca.org). Similarly, labour market information on the tourism labour sector in Canada can be explored with the help of the Canadian Tourism Human Resource Council (www.cthrc.ca).

This type of information can be very useful in developing an understanding of future HR supply. Exhibit 2.3 presents an example from a Job Futures article in 2007.[4] Organizations in the

EXHIBIT   2.3   Projected Job Growth by Occupational Grouping (2007–2012)

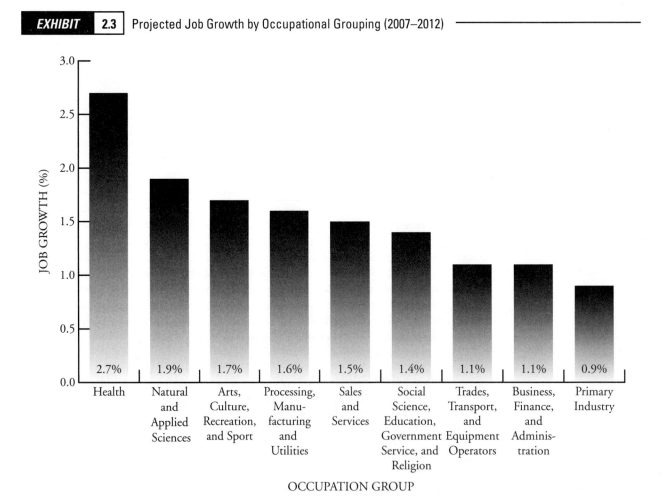

Source: Policy Research and Coordination Directorate, HRSDC.

HRP IN THE NEWS

Doctor Shortage at a Crisis Stage in Canada[5]

The History

- Based on a 1991 federal and provincial government report aimed at reducing growing health care expenses, recommendations were made to cut medical school admissions by 10 percent and impose limits on the recruitment of foreign-educated doctors. At the time, there was no doctor surplus or imbalance, and these recommendations were adopted. Due to a lack of HR planning, there was no awareness of the impact that these changes, along with economic and demographic changes, would have in creating a severe labour shortage of qualified doctors in Canada.
- Since 1993, provincial governments have decreased enrolment in medical schools and associated postgraduate training programs. There were 1,825 medical school graduates in Canada in 1985, which dwindled down to 1,599 graduates in 2007, representing a 12.4 percent decline in medical school graduation rates. In contrast, the Canadian population in 1985 was 25.8 million, compared with 33.1 million in 2007, representing a 30 percent growth in population.

The Existing Situation

- Among industrialized nations identified as OECD (Organization for Economic Co-operation and Development) countries, the Canadian doctor-patient ratio is among the lowest ranked (24 out of 28). In 2008, there were 2.2 doctors for every 1,000 patients. To meet the OECD *average,* the Canadian Medical Association (CMA) suggests a need to hire 26,000 new doctors immediately.
- Almost five million Canadians in 2008 have no family doctor, and 25 percent of the population is unable to schedule an appointment to see a doctor within a day. Among those without a regular physician, 64 percent opt for walk-in clinics, 12 percent visit the hospital emergency room, and 10 percent visit community health centres. Those who are wait-listed for family doctors may experience undiagnosed or chronic health issues, thus adding pressure to an already extended health care system in Canada. It is estimated that the wait-lists for family doctors is responsible for $14 billion in lost economic activity at the national level. The scarcity of labour is so pronounced that in areas such as Belleville and Bancroft, Ontario, new recruits are offered $250,000 bonuses.
- The past and current physician population is male-dominated (in 2007, 67 percent of physicians were males), but at the same time, 52 percent of doctors under the age of 35 are female. The age factor impacts work commitment with doctors aged 55–65 years averaging 54 hours per week, and those under 35 years averaging 47.3 hours per week.
- Presently, 47 percent of general practitioners in Canada are female. Despite training and skill set, female doctors are still given a bigger proportion of childcare, eldercare, and housekeeping responsibilities. In an average week, male doctors dedicate 79 hours to tasks and professional duties outside of their work requirements, while females average 103 hours per week on the same tasks. Directly related to this, female doctors work an average of 48 hours per week, while male doctors average 56 hours per week. It is not surprising that burnout is a severe issue among physicians in Canada. Almost 46 percent of the physician population is near burnout, and Canadian doctors are twice as likely to commit suicide as the general population.

Continued

Doctor Shortage at a Crisis Stage in Canada

- Not only are the working hours different between genders, productivity rates differ as well. A female physician will average 12 minutes per patient, while male physicians average 10 minutes per patient. Patients do appreciate the greater time investment, and the results are evident in the higher patient satisfaction scores for physicians who spend more time with each patient. However, lower productivity in female doctors (in this measure, patients per hour) increases demand factors for doctors.
- The majority of current medical students in Canada are female, including 70 percent of Laval University's medical student population and 66 percent of the University of Montreal's medical cohort. From an HR planning perspective, there is a leakage problem with the training programs offered in Canada. Although there are 2,400 medical school admissions annually in Canada, in 2007, the number of graduates from these programs was only 1,599. In addition, 1 in 9 doctors who graduated from Canada have now migrated to the United States. The imbalance becomes even more prevalent because for every 19 doctors who emigrate from Canada to the United States, only 1 doctor from the United States immigrates into Canada.
- Each year, 1,500 Canadians enrol in medical schools outside of Canada, demonstrating the severity of the supply and demand imbalance in Canada. Education fees are significantly higher for international students, resulting in heavy debt loads (upwards of $500,000 per graduate) for foreign-trained medical graduates. Canadians educated abroad are still considered International Medical Graduates (IMG's) and therefore compete with non-Canadians for the limited number of IMG categorized residency positions. As a result, 50 to 75 percent of foreign trained Canadians do not return to Canada.
- In 2004/2005, the average gross pay for a family doctor was $202,219, for specialists it was $269,606, and for surgeons was $347,720 per year. A challenge for family doctors is the fact that that overhead costs are estimated at $80,000, significantly reducing the gross earning of this group.
- Recently, Brian Day, the President of the Canadian Medical Association, stated, "Until more openings exist in Canadian schools, repatriation of Canadian students is a cost-effective way of addressing the shortage." However, Canadians with foreign training express discontent with this proposal since they were initially displaced and forced to pay higher international education fees, while those with Canadian medical training had their education subsidized through government funding.

Challenges to Balancing Supply and Demand in the Future

- By 2015, without adequate integration and availability of foreign trained doctors, the number of physicians per capita in Canada will continue to decline.
- By 2015, women will make up 40 percent of the total physician workforce in Canada.
- The Canadian population is estimated to continue to increase by 2 to 3 percent per year.
- By 2056, 1 in 4 Canadians will be over the age of 65 (currently 13 percent of the population is over 65).

Continued

HRP IN THE NEWS   **Doctor Shortage at a Crisis Stage in Canada**

Based on the historical, current, and projected information provided above, how would you address the following questions?

1. Using your expertise in HR planning, what factors should have been included in projecting HR demand and supply that may have been overlooked?
2. Based on the current situation, what additional HR planning challenges do you foresee in the future? How might you address the challenges presented in the article, as well as any other challenges you foresee?
3. If you were part of an HR planning team in the health care industry, what actions would you recommend to help balance supply and demand for doctors in Canada?

actuarial losses

Life events that affect all populations (i.e., death, disability, and retirement)

turnover

Termination of an individual's employment with an organization

total turnover

Total number of employees leaving an organization divided by the total number of employees in an organization, regardless of whether the turnover was voluntary or involuntary

voluntary turnover

Employee-initiated turnover, mainly in the form of quits or resignations

involuntary turnover

Employer-initiated turnover, mainly in the form of dismissals or layoffs

health industry can predict high competition for talent. Thus, they may make changes to internal efforts such as training and educational support, as well as to external efforts, including university relationships and recruitments techniques, in an effort to help combat a potentially low level of forecasted HR supply over the next six years.

Forecasting Internal HR Supply   By reviewing the data in the HR audits, projections can be made for future HR supply. The internal labour force may be affected by temporary absences such as leaves of absence (e.g., educational leave, maternity/paternity leave), permanent absences (e.g., death, disability, retirement), or turnover (e.g., resignations, dismissals, layoffs). Death, disability, and retirement are considered **actuarial losses** in that these are life events that affect all populations. These can be predicted with some degree of accuracy by using mortality rates, understanding occupational health and safety risks, or reviewing demographic information about the population.

Turnover refers to the termination of an individual's employment with an organization.[6] The standard definition of **total turnover** is the total number of employees leaving an organization divided by the total number of employees in an organization, regardless of whether the turnover was voluntary or involuntary. Turnover can be classified into two sub groups—voluntary and involuntary. **Voluntary turnover** is defined as employee-initiated turnover, mainly in the form of quits or resignations. In this instance, the decision to terminate employment with the firm is made by the employee, without management enticement. **Involuntary turnover** is defined as employer-initiated turnover, mainly in the form of dismissals or layoffs. The employee has little or no personal say in this turnover decision.[7]

It is possible to estimate labour supply changes for the specified planning horizon by estimating labour movement, absences, and turnover. There are a variety of methods to forecast future HR supply. They include trend analysis, skills/competency inventories, replacement charts, succession planning, staffing tables, and Markov analysis. In the following section, these methods will be explained with some examples.

Trend Analysis   **Trend analysis** is considered one of the simplest methods of forecasting future HR supply. It assumes that past trends and ratios in employee movement are stable and indicative of future trends and ratios in employee movement. The information collected in the HR audit is used to identify labour patterns—hiring patterns, retirement patterns, productivity patterns, and turnover patterns. By examining the trends of the past, the HR department can predict the effect of the same activity on the future of the organization, because it is assumed that these patterns will

69

trend analysis

A method of forecasting that assumes past trends and ratios in employee movement are stable and indicative of future trends and ratios in employee movement

competency

A set of behaviours that encompass skills, knowledge, abilities, and personal attributes, that taken together, are critical to successful work accomplishment

competency model

A future-oriented model that first reviews competencies that are aligned with an organization's mission, vision, and strategy, and then aims to identify an ideal workforce in terms of these competencies

replacement chart

A chart used to estimate vacancies in higher level jobs and identify how potential HR supply can fill these vacancies via internal movements from lower levels jobs

remain stable. In more complex models, trend analysis is not used alone, rather is treated as a necessary step in understanding the current workforce profile and the assumptions that can be made.

For example, an organization reviewing historical data may realize that every year, approximately five percent of their staff retire, six percent resign, and three percent are dismissed. Using a simple trend analysis, future HR supply forecasts can be established by assuming an average reduction in internal HR supply of 14 percent per year.

Skills/Competency Models Building on the skills inventory, the skills/competency models focus on matching the right skills or competencies needed for each job with the skills available within the organization. Unlike other models that predict headcount (e.g., trend analysis or Markov models), the skills/competency models focus on identifying the skills/competency supply within the organization, and helping focus future recruitment, selection, retention, and training activity in core areas of key skills/competencies needed for the organization to succeed.

Recently, organizations have been moving away from a focus on skills to a focus on competencies. A **competency** is a set of behaviours that encompass skills, knowledge, abilities, and personal attributes, that taken together, are critical to successful work accomplishment. These are usually determined by studying top performers' activity within their job context, which identifies the attributes that separate top performers from other employees within the organization.

The **competency model** is a future-oriented model that first reviews competencies that are aligned with an organization's mission, vision, and strategy, and then aims to identify an ideal workforce in terms of those competencies. However, a competency model cannot be applied without the previous information obtained in the HR audit. Thus, the reliability and validity of the information collected earlier in the process is important in determining the accuracy of a competency model.

Replacement Charts A **replacement chart** is used to estimate vacancies in higher level jobs and identify how potential HR supply can fill these vacancies via internal movements from lower levels jobs. A comprehensive replacement chart will include information regarding possible replacements for vertical or horizontal movement. Generally, a replacement chart includes information about employees' performance, readiness to fill the position, and education. Exhibit 2.4 shows a detailed example of a replacement chart. In some cases, a replacement chart will include information about an employee's age, tenure, gender, and visible minority status in addition to required experiences, education, or skills needed for the position. The demographic information provided is an effort to manage firm diversity, but HR and management teams must be careful when conducting a replacement plan not to allow such information to result in any potential illegal discrimination.

In Canada, the aging workforce presents a unique challenge to replacement planning. According to the 2007 HRSDC Job Futures report, over 45 percent of all retirements in Canada from 2007 to 2012 will be in the areas of sales and service, business, finance, and administration. Over the same time periods, there will be over two million jobs that need replacing due to the aging of the workforce and the accompanying retirement of employees.[8] Replacement planning to prepare for these departures—through recruitment, orientation, training, and skills development of the replacements—will be critical to ensure an organization's ability to meet their goals.

Succession Planning While replacement charts provide identification of potential replacements for vacancies within an organization, succession planning focuses on identifying, developing, and tracking future leaders for executive positions or positions that are critical to the success of the organization. Succession planning is a longer-term process of grooming a successor (selected from a pool of candidates on the basis of perceived competency) for management or critical positions. An organization can use the skills inventory, HR audit, or a succession summary to help identify potential successors and skill gaps that can be addressed through succession planning.[9]

EXHIBIT 2.4 | Sample Replacement Chart

PRESIDENT/CEO
Possible Replacements
L. Moffat	E/2/M
J. Bennett	S/2/P
R. Ellis	E/3/M
M. Manoy	S/1/M

VICE PRESIDENT HUMAN RESOURCES
L. Moffat

Possible Replacements
K. Nagra	S/1/B
J. Lee*	S/2/M
T. Cox	E/1/M

VICE PRESIDENT SALES & MARKETING
T. Bennett

Possible Replacements
M. Sanghera*	E/3/B
T. Mitchell	N/1/P
F. Hewer	S/2/M

VICE PRESIDENT FINANCE
R. Ellis

Possible Replacements
L. Anderson	S/2/M
M. Harding	N/1/P
R. Allen	S/2/M

VICE PRESIDENT OPERATIONS/DISTRIBUTION
M. Manoy

Possible Replacements
S. Mayer*	E/3/B
L. Bonett	E/2/M
N. Fernandez	N/2/C

* Identifies minority membership   **Key**

Present Performance	E=Excellent
	S=Satisfactory
	N=Needs Improvement
Promotional Potential	1=Ready Now
	2=Training Required
	3=Questionable
Education	P=Doctorate level
	M=Masters level or Professional certificate
	B=Bachelors level
	C=College or less

---

staffing table

A clear graphical view of all organizational jobs and the current number of employees at each job

 64

Markov analysis

Analysis that helps predict internal employee movement from one year to another by identifying percentages of employees who remain in their jobs, get promoted or demoted, transfer, and exit out of the organization

Staffing Tables   To assess internal HR supply, a **staffing table** provides a clear graphical view of all organizational jobs and the current number of employees at each job. It presents a simple visual understanding of an organization's staffing level within each department and the organization as a whole, in an effort to help understand the combination of employees that make up an organization's internal workforce. This information is useful in evaluating staffing levels by department, branch, or project; the types of staff at each level; and the combination of staff in all categories.

Developed using information collected in the assessment of the existing labour force in the HR inventory, an organization can predict future HR supply by assuming a constant mix of employees in the organization, based on the staff table, or they can make adjustments based on projected growth or decline at each staffing level within the organization. Since staffing tables are relatively simple, they are frequently used as a precursor to more complex methods of forecasting future HR supply, such as a Markov analysis.

Markov Analysis   A **Markov analysis** extends beyond the staffing table to help predict internal employee movement from one year to another by identifying percentages of employees who remain in their jobs, get promoted or demoted, transfer, and exit out of the organization. By tracking and predicting employment movement within an organization, the Markov analysis allows for the development of a transition matrix to forecast internal labour supply.

The Markov analysis extends beyond a simple exit and retention understanding to provide valuable information on employee movement within the firm, clearly identifying projected labour supply for the following year. This represents both a stock approach (quantities in a point of time) and a flow approach (comparing quantities that change over a period of time). Exhibit 2.5 provides a sample of a Markov analysis. In this example, the stock approach is represented in the number of employees for each job in 2009, and the flow approach is represented in the predicted movements from 2009 to 2010. Through merging a stock-and-flow approach, the analysis allows for forecasting future supply of labour for each job within the organization for a period of time.

The Markov analysis example in Exhibit 2.5 includes estimates of employee movement within each level for a hypothetical manufacturing firm. As can be seen in this example, 67 percent of the employees in a general labourer position will continue in this position next year. One in ten general labourers (10 percent) will be eligible for a promotion next year, and should be promoted accordingly. The remaining 23 percent of general labourers will be exiting the firm. It is clear that some employees should be eligible for a promotion next year, while others should actually be demoted based on their performance and skill set. As well, the exit predictions highlight

EXHIBIT **2.5**	A Markov Analysis for a Hypothetical Manufacturing Firm

2009 ＼ 2010	PLANT MANAGER	DEPARTMENT SUPERVISOR	FOREMAN	MACHINE OPERATOR	GENERAL LABOUR	EXITS
PLANT MANAGER n=3	87% / 3	7% / 0				6% / 0
DEPARTMENT SUPERVISOR n=15	7% / 1	76% / 11	12% / 2			5% / 1
FOREMAN n=60		3% / 2	75% / 45	9% / 5		13% / 8
MACHINE OPERATOR n=102			15% / 15	48% / 49	12% / 12	25% / 26
GENERAL LABOUR n=306				10% / 31	67% / 205	23% / 70
PROJECTED SUPPLY 2010	4	13	62	85	217	105

Percentages represent estimated transactions for next year
Actual numbers represent projections for next year of actual employee count

that both the machine operator and general labour levels suffer from high turnover via exits, which identifies an area for HR to explore and explain.

The Markov analysis identifies a need for 31 machine operators next year in order to accommodate for losses at that level. In this case, 31 general labourers will be eligible for a promotion next year. The organization can fill these positions with internal candidates or external candidates. If the organization does not promote an internal candidate who is available, it may experience employee demotivation, distrust in management, or turnover. However, if the company fills all of the positions with internal candidates, they may forfeit new perspectives and ideas that could be brought to the machine operator level.

In the case where there are not enough openings in the higher levels to accommodate those who eligible for a promotion, the organization must determine the best course of action to ensure productivity, job satisfaction, and performance management of all the employees involved.

The downward flow of an employee in an organization is known as a demotion. Situations are also highlighted where an employee's performance and skill set are below the level that they currently work at, leading to some expectation of a demotion next year. This is a challenge for the organization. The organization may choose to invest in training to ensure that these employees are capable of performing at their assigned levels next year, or they could demote the employees according to skill level. Few organizations would choose the latter option.

The Markov analysis also identifies areas of high turnover, specifically at general labourer and machine operator levels. It may be of interest to the organization to assess the causes of turnover at these levels and identify whether the turnover can be minimized.

While this provides a very clear approach to forecasting HR supply, there are two key challenges to using a Markov analysis. First, the organization must be large enough to provide information on different jobs and occupations. Second, organizations that are experiencing periods of change or very high turnover might find that this model does not accurately predict future supply. However, with reasonably stable skill sets and fair scenarios about the economy, historical time series analyses of labour supply can be used to predict the numbers for each cell in the diagram, allowing for accurate and clear predictions of future labour movement and supply.

Forecasting HR Demand

demand analysis

Analysis that identifies the future workforce requirements needed to maintain the organization's mission and goals

Demand analysis identifies the future workforce requirements needed to maintain the organization's mission and goals. The end result of a demand analysis is the identification of the required number of employees in an organization and the necessary functions that the employee must perform to meet organizational objectives. In HR planning, labour demand is determined separately from supply estimates because it facilitates a re-examination of embedded assumptions about the labour force. As well, different variables affect demand analysis. Due to the high number of factors that influence demand, demand is often more difficult to predict than supply. Factors that need to be considered when forecasting demand include the following:

- Environmental scanning, including economic, legislative, and competitive pressures
- The organization's future strategic goals and plans
- Expected demand for products or services, including expected sales (across the organization or at the business unit level)
- Estimated productivity measures of workforce (can be stable, increase, or decrease)
- Organizational design or job design, including technological advancements and administrative changes
- Projected budgets or financial resource availability
- New products/processes/ventures that the organization will be launching in the future

Due to the high number of environment- and organization-specific variables that influence demand analysis, there is no single correct way to estimate future HR demand. Instead, a number of quantitative and qualitative methods, as shown in Exhibit 2.6, are available to

®
65

EXHIBIT 2.6	Summary of Methods Used to Forecast HR Demand
Quantitative Techniques	**Qualitative Techniques**
• Trend analysis	• Delphi method
• Ratio analysis	• Nominal group technique
• Regression analysis	• Scenario analysis

aid HR professionals in this step. Ultimately, the decision of which method to use will be dependant on the size of the organization, the resources available, and the expertise of the HR planning team. Quantitative techniques for determining HR requirements include trend analysis, ratio analysis, and regression analysis. Qualitative approaches to forecasting HR demand require managers to use their experiences to make expert judgements about future forecasts. This can occur in the form of a Delphi method, a nominal group technique, or a scenario analysis.

Quantitative Techniques for Forecasting HR Demand

Trend Analysis   Similar to trend analysis used to forecast internal HR supply, past trends and ratios can also be used to forecast HR demand. For this purpose, **trend analysis** predicts the demand for labour based on projections of past relationship patterns over a number of years between an operational index (e.g., revenue per employee, productivity per employee) and the demand for labour (number of employees). As one of the simpler methods of forecasting HR demand, trend analysis assumes that an organization's past employment needs are indicative of future needs when linked with an operational index.

There are a number of steps required to successfully complete a trend analysis. First, it is critical to select the right business or operational index. A hotel chain may select the number of rooms a housekeeper can clean in a set time frame to predict the number of housekeepers needed. A service provider may select the number of customers each customer service representative can effectively deal with to estimate the number of customer service representatives needed. A large business may select sales volume per sales employee to predict the number of employees needed.

Next, the organization tracks the business index and the size of the workforce over time. Typically, five years of historical data is sufficient in a trend analysis, but this can vary based on organization history and industry. With this information, the planning team can calculate the average ratio of the business or operational index and the workforce size in the past. This information is used to forecast HR demand.

As a simple example, a hotel determines that each housekeeper can clean 20 rooms a day (an operational index). The hotel has 1,000 rooms and is projected to be at 100 percent capacity in the summer season, but 80 percent capacity in the fall season. In this example, the hotel would use trend analysis to determine that it will need 50 housekeepers for the summer season and 40 in the fall season (rooms occupied daily/index of 20 rooms per housekeeper per day).

ratio analysis

Analysis that determines future HR demand based on ratios between assumed casual factors and the number of employees needed

Ratio Analysis   **Ratio analysis** determines future HR demand based on ratios between assumed casual factors and the number of employees needed. Ratio analysis appears very similar to trend analysis, but the primary difference is that there is no requirement for significant historical data collection. This allows organizations that do not have easy access to multiple years' worth of data to use current ratios to help estimate future demand. In addition, while trend analysis links one business or operational index over time, ratio analysis allows for multiple causal factors to

HRP AND ETHICS

Quantitative and Qualitative Forecasting

There are ethical issues with both quantitative forecasting techniques and qualitative forecasting techniques. An optimistic perspective is that no technique can be completely void of ethical issues and therefore an organization must select the most appropriate technique given their strategic alignment as well as resource and time limitations. A pessimistic perspective is that all of the many alternatives offer results with ethical implications and therefore HR planning as an activity has embedded ethical dilemmas.

For quantitative techniques, the ethical challenges include the limitations associated with viewing human resources based on measures or quantities. When conducting quantitative methods, mathematical equations can help determine how many more or how many fewer human resources are needed in an organization, without ever considering the human element of the employee–organization relationship. For example, when forecasting a labour surplus, an organization can determine that there are 15 percent more employees in a department than needed, leading to an effort to lay off 15 percent of the employees in the department. In this simple example, it is evident that when using quantitative techniques, what does not factor into the decision is the human element, the expectations of the employer to provide a stable work environment, and an awareness of the human relationships that have existed within the teams.

In contrast, the qualitative techniques associated with HR planning can be viewed as open to higher levels of personal bias or subjectivity. For example, with the Delphi technique, a manager can purposely over-predict the productivity of a department or the projected growth rate of the HR needs to secure additional resources or employees, or conversely they can deflate these values if they are interested in reducing headcount. In qualitative techniques, there is a risk that the expert's personal agenda is influencing the results. Through the use of accountability measures, these risks can be reduced or mitigated.

be used to predict demand. Ratio analysis is also useful in benchmarking organizational efforts with industry or competitive standards to help identify areas of strength or weakness in an organization.

Extending on the example from the Markov analysis (see Exhibit 2.5), a ratio analysis can be used to determine HR requirements for the following year (see Exhibit 2.7). In this example, the organization's estimated rate of sales growth rate is 25 percent from 2009 to 2010. Assuming the same employee distribution from 2009, HR requirements at each level can be predicted, as shown in Exhibit 2.7. (Note: Growth rate can be calculated by using 2009 actual employee count at each level multiplied by 1.25 to represent a 25 percent projected growth.)

The next example, in Exhibit 2.8, provides a more complicated prediction of HR demand, but still relies on ratio analysis. In 2009, the organization needed 486 employees to meet the requirements for $9.72 million in sales. The result is a revenue-to-employee ratio of $200,000:1. In 2010, the organization predicts sales of $11 million. Therefore, using ratio analysis, the organization estimates a requirement of 550 employees. In addition, another level of ratio analysis can be used to determine where employees will be needed, in an effort to predict HR demand.

EXHIBIT	2.7	Ratio Analysis on a Hypothetical Manufacturing Firm (25 Percent Growth)

Level	2009 Actual Employee Count	Est. 25% Growth Requirements for 2010
Plant manager	3	4
Department supervisor	15	19
Foreman	60	75
Machine operator	105	128
General labourer	306	383
Total	486	609

EXHIBIT	2.8	Ratio Analysis on a Hypothetical Manufacturing Firm, 550 Employees

Level	2009 Actual Employee Count	% of Workforce (2009)	Demand for 550 Employees in 2010
Plant manager	3	0.6	3
Department supervisor	15	3.1	17[1]
Foreman	60	12.3	68
Machine operator	105	20.9	115
General labourer	306	62.9	346
Total	486	99.8*	549

*due to rounding, values do not add up to 100%

Note: In 2009, 3.1% of the internal labour force was supervisors. Using an organizational forecast of 550 employees in 2010, the organization would need 17 supervisors (3.1% of 550)

Specifically, in this example, the ratio of employees at each level within the organization (percentage of workforce) can help predict demand. Assuming the ratio of employees within each level of the workforce is fixed, estimates about how many employees are needed at each level can be secured.

Regression Analysis **Regression analysis** is a more complicated method of estimating HR demand, but allows for adjustment of seasonal fluctuation, long-term trends, and random movement when forecasting. This method provides statistical projections using mathematical formulas to determine the correlation between multiple measureable output factors (independent variables) and an organization's employment level (dependent variable). A regression analysis is useful in predicting the strength and direction of a linear relationship between two variables, but in situations of a non-linear relationship, estimates would not be valid.

When there is one independent variable, there is one regression. When there are multiple independent variables, there are multiple regressions. A correlation depicts a value between -1 and 1. The closer the value is to 0, the less predictive of the relationship between the two variables. The closer the value is to either -1 or 1, the more predictive the relationship between two variables. The positive or negative sign in front of the correlation number indicates the nature or direction of the relationship.

regression analysis

A method of estimating HR demand that provides statistical projections using mathematical formulas to determine the correlation between multiple measureable output factors (independent variables) and an organization's employment level (dependent variable)

For example, if the correlation between sales and the number of employees is 0.897, then an organization can interpret that an increase in sales is accompanied by an increase in the number of employees. In contrast, a correlation between investment in technology and the number of employees of −0.713 suggests that an increase in technology investments in the company would decrease the number of employees in the organization. Similarly, a correlation level of 0.012 between productivity and the number of employees represents no significant relationship between the two variables.

To effectively conduct a regression analysis, the planning team must have access to a large sample size of data (individual or group level data); have or be able to acquire the statistical skill set required to run the regression (most often completed using regression software); and be educated on the interpretation and use of this data. As a result, regression analysis is most often used in large organizations. This approach is also purely statistical, assuming that the past is the best predictor of the future. Any changes that alter this assumption while forecasting HR demand (e.g., new product lines, new ventures, technology, etc.) should be adjusted for accordingly.

Qualitative Techniques for Forecasting HR Demand

Delphi method

A method of forecasting HR demand that involves a panel of experts using their judgements to make estimates of short-term future demands

Delphi Method   The origins of the **Delphi method** can be traced back to the late 1940s when the RAND Corporation used a famed "think tank" to estimate how future events effected HR projections for an organization.[10] This process involves a panel of experts using their judgements to make estimates of short-term future demands. Experts use a variety of factors to make their judgements, including economical, demographical, technological, legal, and social conditions outside of the organization, as well as production, sales, turnover, experiences, and education levels of the workforce within the organization.

This method involves a number of steps. During the process, experts are not permitted to engage in direct face-to-face contact or communication. This is in an effort to prevent groupthink, influence of others, or confrontation of experts, which can influence the results. First, experts must be identified to participate in this task. Second, each expert is asked to submit HR demand forecasts, including specification of sources of information and assumptions used to estimate demand. Next, each submission is gathered by the HR planning group, which then summarizes the results. The aggregated results are sent back to the experts, who are given an opportunity to adjust their forecasts based on the information provided in the summaries. These steps are repeated until the expert opinions converge, something that may occur after three to five rounds.[11] Each feedback loop provides an opportunity for experts to understand their position relative to others and the reactions of others to the summaries provided.

One of the criticisms of the Delphi method is that it is subjective in nature, and thus may be difficult for those who prefer quantitative approaches to fully commit to. In addition, the organization should be explicit with experts not to discuss their estimates with others, something that can happen when experts have strong working relationships or work in close proximity to others.

nominal group technique (NGT)

A method of forecasting HR demand that involves multiple experts (usually line and department managers) meeting face to face to discuss independently formulated positions of an organizational issue, with the ultimate aim of securing an accurate assessment of a given situation

Nominal Group Technique   The **nominal group technique (NGT)** was first developed by Delbecq and VandeVen as an alternative to simple, individual brainstorming of ideas.[12] This process involves multiple experts (usually line and department managers) meeting face to face to discuss independently formulated positions of an organizational issue, with the ultimate aim of securing an accurate assessment of a given situation. NGT can be used to help forecast HR demand for an organization or can be used to solve other organizational issues (e.g., decisions about launching new products or processes, managing change, establishing sales targets, etc.).

This technique differs from the Delphi technique in that it encourages face-to-face meetings and discussions about an issue as a critical step in the decision-making process. There are four main steps in this process:

1. **Step 1:** Generally five or six experts are solicited to participate in the NGT. Each expert is asked the same specific question (e.g., What are your predictions for future HR demand in this branch/unit/department/organization for the next X number of years? What are the causes of any expected changes in demand?). Independently, each expert writes down their solutions to the issue or question.

2. **Step 2:** Experts then meet face to face (usually around a table) and are asked to individually present their solutions. These solutions are often recorded on flipcharts or blackboards to allow for comparisons in later steps. During this process, each member is encouraged to freely present their results, and interruption or discussion from other group members on the results is discouraged at this point. This allows for each member to present their ideas completely, without judgement or influence.

3. **Step 3:** After all experts have presented their results, clarification questions are solicited. A facilitator should encourage questions on clarification of information so as to encourage group dialogue and discourage self-protectiveness about estimates.

4. **Step 4:** Each expert is asked to secretly rank estimates. Voting is anonymous and calculated using equal participation from team members. The facilitator then uses the estimate from step 1 that draws the highest ranking as the estimate used to forecast HR demands.

In a case where there are two or more close high ranking estimates of future HR demand, steps 3 and 4 can be repeated, with only these estimates presented, to allow for further discussion and to build confidence in the results.

scenario analysis

A method that provides multiple estimates of future HR demand, contingent on a unique set of assumptions and circumstances for each scenario

Scenario Analysis   Due to the high number of factors that can affect predictions of HR demand, some organizations prefer to conduct a scenario analysis rather than determining a single demand scenario (as in the previous methods discussed in this step). **Scenario analysis** provides multiple estimates of future HR demand, contingent on a unique set of assumptions and circumstances for each scenario. This method involves recognizing uncertainties about the future. For example, forecasts are contingent upon the overall economic outlook of the firm's output. An organization could create three different estimates accordingly, one for a constant economic situation (e.g., zero growth), a second for some anticipated economic growth (e.g., five percent growth), and a third for the possibility of economic decline (e.g., five percent reduction).

Expert brainstorming activities help to develop agreement on long-range factors and the impact of changes on the HR forecasts. These can include internal changes (e.g., adoption of new technology, productivity or workforce changes) or external changes (economic position, legal requirements, competitive changes) that cannot be predicted with confidence to have a single effect. The possible result of these changes will create a forecast for each possible scenario that the organization can expect. The group will assess potential uncertainty and estimate realistic potential future scenarios. Generally, there will be three estimates secured, one at the level of continuance with the status quo, one best-case or optimistic scenario, and one worst-case or pessimistic scenario. As a result, the organization secures a range of forecasted HR demand and must continuously monitor influencing factors to narrow that range as time progresses.

While this method is the least effective in determining a single estimate of future HR needs, this option provides some clarity as to future estimates for dynamic organizations, organizations that are experiencing high change, or in cases where the past is not the best predictor of the future.

HRP AND THE SMALL BUSINESS

Human Resource Planning Challenges Unique to Small Businesses

Regardless of how large or small the organization is, all organizations require HR planning to secure the right resources in the right positions at the right time. However, there are unique challenges that small businesses face in terms of the HR planning process.

For small businesses that may be in an initial start-up stage or may be experiencing high growth, there is the option of conducting an HR plan for a horizon that is measured in unique units. For example, if a small business expects 50 percent revenue growth per quarter, then the horizon for HR planning would be a predetermined number of quarters, rather than annual estimates. Similarly, if a small business anticipates growth or decline using six-month periods, then the unit for the HR planning horizon can be each half year.

Small businesses can also track the current workforce using manual measures or off-the-shelf computer software. For smaller organizations, the investment in a proprietary HR auditor skills inventory tool may not be advisable.

Rather than investing in primary research to forecast external HR supply, many small businesses can benefit from reviewing existing secondary data as previously highlighted. However, rather than utilizing national or international data, small businesses might find that regional or local government offices provide data that is more transferrable for their needs.

One of the biggest challenges that small businesses face in terms of forecasting HR supply is effectively and proactively managing succession planning. In publicly managed firms, the successor is selected from a pool of qualified applicants by the board of directors. In a small business, little attention is paid to succession planning since it is assumed to be a rare event (once per generation) and the pool of potential successors is very small (often the first-born male).[13] In family-owned small businesses, tacit, procedural, and social capital is passed on from one generation to another.[14] Due to high levels of loyalty and trust among family members, the succession plan for these businesses is assumed, rather than planned for. As a result, owners take a reactive approach to succession planning in small businesses. Roughly 3 in every 10 small businesses survive when the second generation becomes the successor.[15]

The succession plan in small and medium enterprises should be a formal and communicated process whereby the potential successor is trained and integrated into the work efforts with the owner-operator. In order to build commitment from the remaining employees, it should be explicitly discussed why this successor was selected and what unique abilities they possess. Education levels of potential successors should also match the expected education level of the position they will be filling. The training efforts and communications should develop the core competencies and skill sets of the successor, which will also aid in building confidence of the succession plan with the remaining workforce.

Forecasting HR demand is usually completed using qualitative methods in small businesses, rather than quantitative methods, due to the expertise of management in the organization, the lack of historical data in the organization, and the dynamic nature of the businesses. Many small businesses would benefit from combining either an NGT or Delphi technique with a scenario analysis to predict a range of potential needs for the future.

■ STEP 2: ESTABLISH HUMAN RESOURCE OBJECTIVES

gap analysis

Analysis that identifies the differences between the forecasted HR supply and the forecasted HR demand, focusing on balancing the number and characteristics of employees needed and available to ensure that supply equals demand

Organizational objectives help determine what organization action is required to align HR demand with HR supply. Organizational objectives direct the planning process by identifying the desired activity to achieve organizational goals.

A **gap analysis** identifies the differences between the forecasted HR supply and the forecasted HR demand, focusing on balancing the number and characteristics of employees needed and available to ensure that supply equals demand. Ideally, the estimated demand and supply could balance out (identifying no gap in HR forecasts), but this is a rare situation. Most likely, either HR supply exceeds demand, identifying a projected labour surplus, or HR demand exceeds supply, identifying a labour shortage.

Using the hypothetical manufacturing firm previously discussed in the chapter, an example of a gap analysis can be examined. Forecasted HR supply was determined using a Markov analysis in Exhibit 2.5. Forecasted HR demand was determined using a ratio analysis in Exhibit 2.7. Using these forecasts, predicted gaps in the labour force are identified in Exhibit 2.9. In total, a labour shortage of 195 employees is predicted, but this analysis also identifies which levels have a surplus and which have a shortage and by what degree.

solutions analysis

Analysis that creates a strategic plan to address labour surpluses or shortages, including creating an awareness of changes that continually occur in the workforce (e.g., retirements, turnover, etc.)

Gaps and surpluses are alleviated through solutions analysis. **Solutions analysis** involves creating a strategic plan to address the labour surplus or shortage, including creating an awareness of changes that continually occur in the workforce (e.g., retirements, turnover, etc.). The solutions analysis should clearly identify what actions are required to mitigate the gaps and what the most effective options are for addressing these gaps.

Due to the volume and complexities associated with managing a labour surplus and labour shortage, these issues are dealt with in greater detail in later chapters. Chapter 3 includes an extensive review of strategies, challenges, and alternatives to address labour shortages, while Chapter 4 focuses on solutions for labour surpluses.

■ STEP 3: DESIGN AND IMPLEMENT HR PROGRAMS

As discussed throughout this text, a comprehensive HR planning team can aid in the successful implementation of the HR plan. The design and implementation of a plan to correct workforce imbalances can include the need to increase productivity or the size of the workforce in a labour shortage situation or the need to change work-terms or decrease the size of the workforce in a labour surplus situation.

Chapters 3 and 4 provide not only a detailed discussion of the multiple options available to correct a workforce imbalance, but also a discussion of the resources, costs, appropriateness, and advantages

| **EXHIBIT 2.9** | Gap Analysis on a Hypothetical Manufacturing Firm, 550 Employees |

Level	2010 Projected Supply	2010 Projected Demand	Gap in Demand for 550 Employees in 2010
Plant manager	4	3	−1
Department supervisor	16	17	1
Foreman	32	68	36
Machine operator	85	115	30
General labourer	217	346	129
Total	354	549	195

Note: The gap is calculated by subtracting projected demand from projected supply. A negative value indicates a labour shortage and a positive value indicates a labour surplus.

and disadvantages of these options. Regardless of what methods are used to correct the workforce imbalance, the implementation of the plan must adhere to applicable legislation and regulations.

■ STEP 4: EVALUATE THE EFFECTIVENESS OF THE PROGRAMS

Evaluating the effectiveness of the programs implemented as part of the HR plan is both the final step and a step that loops back to the first step in the HR planning process. Thus, planning is not linear, but cyclical in that evaluation of the results of one planning cycle establishes input for the next planning cycle. Chapter 10 identifies the importance of knowing what to measure and why, as well as developing an understanding of how systems are used to measure HR metrics (e.g., productivity, turnover, quality, etc.).

In conclusion, the forecasting of human resource supply and demand can project a labour surplus or shortage. The next two chapters will discuss methods to deal with a labour shortage (Chapter 3) and a labour surplus (Chapter 4).

CHAPTER SUMMARY

- HR planning is a critical component of organizational planning that ensures that the right resources are available at the right time to achieve organizational goals, vision, and strategy. HR plans affect many elements of HR, including recruitment, selection, training, development, organizational structure, and compensation.
- There are four steps in the HR planning process. Before embarking on the HR planning process, an organization must determine the appropriate planning horizon. This includes creating an awareness of both immediate and long-term staffing concerns. As well, planners should assess and accurately understand the current staffing situation in the organization. An HR audit is useful for collecting information in a meaningful way, but depends on the level of clarity regarding who is considered to be in the workforce.
- Forecasting HR supply is a component of the first step. There are a number of different triggers for changes in the internal labour force, including actuary losses, voluntary turnover, and involuntary turnover. As well, the supply of human resources available outside of the organization is also in flux. Thus, this step requires the effective mapping of the effects of internal and external labour forces changes to the organization. Tools such as trend analysis, skills/competency models, replacement charts, succession planning, staffing tables, and Markov analysis can be used in this step.
- Also part of the first step, an HR demand analysis predicts the number of required employees (quantity and quality) within the predetermined time horizon. This forecast can use quantitative techniques (trend analysis, ration analysis, regression analysis) or qualitative techniques (Delphi method, nominal group technique, scenario analysis) to increase the accuracy of the HR demand forecast.
- In the second step, evaluation of organizational objectives will drive gap analysis and solutions analysis. The organizational objectives help determine which program is the most appropriate for responding to imbalances in required HR demand and projected HR supply within the organization. In this step, the projected supply is compared to the projected demand to determine if the organization will experience a labour equilibrium, shortage, or surplus in the future.
- The third step is implementation of the HR plan.
- The fourth and final step is the evaluation of the plan's effectiveness, which then loops back to the initial HR planning step. This creates cyclicality in the HR plan. Potential HR metrics that can be used in this step are outlined in Chapter 10.

KEY TERMS

- actuarial losses   35
- appropriate planning horizon   27
- competency   36
- competency model   36
- contingent workforce   29
- Delphi method   43
- demand analysis   39
- external labour force   30
- forecasting   27
- gap analysis   46
- groupthink   27
- human resource audit   29
- internal labour force   28
- involuntary turnover   35
- Markov analysis   37
- nominal group technique (NGT)   43
- ratio analysis   40
- regression analysis   42
- replacement chart   36
- scenario analysis   44
- skills inventory   29
- solutions analysis   46
- staffing table   37
- strategic plan   31
- total turnover   35
- trend analysis   36
- turnover   35
- voluntary turnover   35

REVIEW QUESTIONS

1. Identify the four steps in the HR planning process and discuss the importance of the cyclicality of the process.
2. Who should be included in the HR planning committee and why?
3. What are the various options available for forecasting HR supply?
4. Identify when the use of each option would be feasible.
5. Outline the quantitative and qualitative methods for forecasting HR demand. What are some of the challenges in determining demand and how can these be overcome using the techniques outlined?
6. What are the differences and similarities between the each pair: Delphi technique and nominal group technique; trend analysis and ratio analysis; succession planning and replacement planning?

DISCUSSION QUESTIONS

1. Your organization is launching a brand-new product line, investing a significant amount of resources into technology and eliminating a business line that they feel is not profitable. Given the highly dynamic nature of the business, what method would you recommend to forecast HR supply and demand? Provide a rationale for your selection.
2. A colleague of yours does not support the HR planning activities that the organization is currently engaged in. She suggests that planning is a fruitless exercise for an organization since the results may be outdated by the time the process is complete. Using your expertise in HR planning, either support or refute this argument. Include a discussion of the inherent assumptions in your position and the position of your co-worker.
3. Assume your organization has asked you to help facilitate a nominal group technique. Who would you include in the process and why? What materials might you need for this process? What obstacles or challenges should you be careful to avoid?
4. Your organization has conducted a Markov analysis. Next year, you predict that 42 employees at level 1 will be eligible for a promotion into level 2 jobs. Level 2 is predicted

to have 30 vacancies. Would you hire from within the organization, hire from outside the organization, or use a combination of both for the expected vacancies in level 2 next year? Why? How will you deal with the employees who are predicted to be promoted but are not? How will you keep them motivated?

WEB EXERCISE

Conducting a Nominal Group Technique to Estimate University Professor Forecasts

Assume you are working for a large comprehensive university in Canada. Working in teams of six, use the information below to establish estimates of demand for university professors within Canada. Assign one person to the role of facilitator to help manage the process. In step 1 of the NGT, complete the following:

1. Identify factors that contribute to the demand of university professors in Canada. You can use websites such as www.statscan.com, www.caut.ca, www.aucc.ca, your university or college website, and other websites for information to guide your discussion.
2. Estimate a projected growth or decline rate (percentage) of university professors for 2010 and 2015 using this information and other information you may have available.
3. Determine factors that could impact the accuracy of your HR demand estimates.

CASE INCIDENT

Predicting Supply and Demand for a Call Centre

A call centre out of Halifax, Nova Scotia is currently in the process of conducting an HR planning exercise. They have estimated employee flow throughout the organization and have mapped this information onto the following Markov matrix:

	A	B	C	D	Exits
A. Shift manager (n = 6)	0.70	0.05	0.00	0.00	0.25
B. Department supervisor (n = 18)	0.13	0.82	0.03	0.00	0.02
C. Team leader (n = 105)	0.05	0.10	0.62	0.05	0.08
D. Customer service representatives (n = 590)	0.00	0.00	0.22	0.54	0.24

1. Outline employee movement projections and the supply estimates for each level for next year.
2. What trends in the predicted workforce movement should be highlighted as potentially problematic?

In addition, the HR department suggests that three percent of the workforce this year will be retiring next year. These departures are expected to be experienced proportionately at all levels in the organization. These are not included in the exit estimations. After you have completed your Markov analysis, factor in these exits in your supply estimates based on this year's HR supply to help get a more accurate prediction of next year's estimates.

This year, the call centre had 5,200,000 clients. Due to a new project, the call centre expects an additional 1,500,000 clients next year. They do not anticipate any changes in the distribution of the workforce. What HR demand estimates would you calculate for the organization?

Comparing the forecasted HR supply and demand, conduct a gap analysis. What levels have a labour surplus and what levels have a labour shortage? How many employees would the company need to meet demands for next year?

CASE INCIDENT

Forecasting HR Supply Using a Ratio Analysis

As an HR manager in a national bank, you have access to historical data about branch activity and employment across Canada from 2001 to 2009. These two variables develop a productivity ratio in terms of how many customers each teller is able to serve per year. You are asked to make a quick and rough estimate of teller projections for the bank using this information, and are expected to apply a ratio analysis.

The bank is expecting a five percent annual growth rate in their number of customers from 2009 to 2012. This is due to an aggressive marketing technique and the launch of a high-interest banking incentive for customers who leave their existing bank to join yours. As well, because of plans to launch a training and orientation program targeted at all employees, the bank also expects an annual increase in productivity over the next two years.

Using this information and the chart with data provided below, predict the organization's 2010 and 2011 forecasts for HR demand.

Year	Number of Customers	Number of Tellers	Productivity (customers served per teller)
01	650,000	580	1,120.69
02	690,000	610	1,131.15
03	640,000	575	1,130.04
04	585,000	550	1,063.64
05	550,000	515	1,067.96
06	605,000	560	1,080.36
07	625,000	570	1,096.49
08	659,000	590	1,116.95
09	680,000	605	1,123.97
10*			
11*			

*Helpful information: Productivity was calculated by dividing the number of customers by the number of tellers per year. Average productivity can be calculated using previous data to help predict future expected productivity. Expected number of customers can be calculated using growth estimates above.

■ REQUIRED PROFESSIONAL CAPABILITIES REFERENCED IN THIS CHAPTER

11. Gathers, analyzes, and reports relevant business and industry information (including global trends) to influence development of strategic business HR plans.
16. Provides the organization with timely and accurate HR information.
64. Researches, analyzes, and reports on potential people issues affecting the organization.
65. Forecasts HR supply and demand conditions.
67. Develops people plans that support the organization's strategic directions.
69. Maintains an inventory of people talent for the use of the organization.
70. Develops systems and processes that link the career plans and skill sets of employees with the requirements of the organization.
72. Identifies the organization's staffing needs.
73. Identifies the potential source of internal and external qualified candidates.

LABOUR SHORTAGE

LEARNING OBJECTIVES

- Discuss the Canadian labour shortage problem and how it compares to other countries across the globe
- Describe the alternative staffing strategies that can be considered to help manage a shortage of labour
- Identify the various ways organizations can source services from an independent vendor
- Describe what is meant by the term "contingent workforce" and discuss the challenges that organizations face managing these relationships
- Describe the various types of flexible work arrangements and the impact of employment legislation
- Identify the factors that can influence the type of alternative staffing strategy chosen
- Discuss the initiatives that organizations are taking to prepare for the possibility of a prolonged major labour shortage, such as a pandemic

■ PROFILE

The Canadian Province that Just Keeps Growing!

Imagine living in a province where the jobs are abundant, the compensation is significantly higher than anywhere else in Canada, and the opportunities for career development are plentiful. Imagine a province where the population has increased so significantly over the past few years that its rate of growth is almost three times the national average. In fact, in 2006, over 58 percent of the population came from interprovincial migration.[1]

Alberta is that province. Alberta has an enormous wealth of natural resources. It is oil-rich and it has been a leader in economic growth in Canada over the past decade. Its total income (GDP) rose 43 percent between 2002 and 2005.[2] The number of projects that have been approved or are under construction has increased from $47 billion in 1998 to approximately $137 billion worth of new projects as of July 2006.[3] Its unemployment rate has steadily declined over the past decade, obtaining virtually zero unemployment prior to the 2009 global recession. As of February 2009, Alberta's unemployment rate of 4.4 percent continues to impress, being significantly lower than the national average of 7.2 percent.[4]

Today, Alberta continues to experience a significant demand for labour. A recent survey showed that 56 percent of Alberta's employers indicated that they were having significant difficulties hiring skilled and semi-skilled workers.[5] However, due to the current recessionary environment, the search for talent has been alleviated to some degree. Nonetheless, significant shortages still exist in some industries requiring specific skill sets, notably in the oil and gas industries.[6]

Alberta has experienced a significant challenge with respect to the attraction and retention of talent over the past several years. The types of initiatives that Alberta has undertaken to address these concerns have been impressive and include launching innovative immigration programs, developing long-term workforce planning strategies for many of its industries, creating labour market partnerships, and offering candidates attractive compensation and innovative reward packages, such as signing bonuses, higher pay, and enhanced relocation packages. These are just of few examples of innovative planning practices.[7]

Labour shortage is a problem experienced across the globe. Falling birth rates, the pending retirement of the baby-boom generation, and significant concern for quality of work–life balance are major reasons why this is a worldwide problem. In Canada, the baby-boom generation comprises one third of Canada's population and many of the boomers will soon leave their jobs, resulting in a sharp drop of talent exiting the workforce. The first wave of retirements has already begun, with the first wave impacting Canada in 2001. It has been projected that by 2055, Canada will experience a potential shortfall of twelve million workers. Canada's unemployment rate has reached a thirty-year low. In the U.S., the problem is identical. Experts have forecasted that by the year 2010, more than 25 percent of the working population will reach retirement age, resulting in a potential shortage of ten million workers, a number that will increase to thirty-five million by 2030.[8] Europe is also experiencing similar problems. Evidence of worker shortages is obvious in unemployment rates, where Europe is currently experiencing a fourteen-year low.[9]

This chapter will explore several staffing options that organizations may consider when faced with a talent shortage as well as current staffing trends and how to objectively determine the best available option(s).

RPC ® 36

labour shortage

A shortage that occurs when there is not enough qualified talent to fill the demand for labour

■ WHAT IS A LABOUR SHORTAGE?

A **labour shortage** occurs when there is not enough qualified talent to fill the demand for labour. Organizations experience a shortage when they cannot fill their open positions. A skill shortage refers to specific skills that the organization requires. It occurs when the demand for workers with specific skills exceeds the available supply of workers with these specialized skills.[10]

There are a number of variables that influence the nature, timing, and extent of a labour shortage, including economic conditions, productivity gains, immigration policies, and workforce participation.[11]

Shortages can be experienced in various ways. They can be global in scope, nationwide, or limited to a particular province or region. They can occur in a specific occupation, indicating an imbalance in the number of people entering into an occupation. In addition, shortages can be skill-based, whereby a particular occupation has a skill set that is in demand and there is not enough talent to fill the need. A recent survey by the SHRM found that 62 percent of HR professionals reported difficulties hiring workers with the skills critical for the 21st century.[12]

Shortages can be seasonal, cyclical, or structural. Structural factors refer to demographics such as aging populations, fluctuations in consumer tastes and technology, and various *institutional* changes such as settlements of labour agreements and government legislation.

Below are some examples to illustrate the challenges facing specific industries and occupational groups, and some of the initiatives taken to help alleviate these concerns.

1. Nurse and Physician Shortage—Global   Highlighted in Chapter 2, Canada has experienced a significant physician shortage. This shortage encompasses the nursing profession as well and is a global issue as the quality of health care across the globe has been negatively affected. The World Health Organization (WHO) Report of 2006 estimated a global shortage of 2.3 million physicians, nurses, and midwives in order to meet the workforce levels needed to strengthen health systems. They identified 57 counties where there was a significant shortage.[13] The report found vast differences in health care occurred within countries and even within individual cities. The WHO organization has made significant recommendations including that primary health care, including integrated services at the community level, can help save lives.[14]

In Canada, doctors and nurses are in short supply. In fact, the shortage of physicians is critical. In British Columbia, more than 100,000 people do not have a family doctor and in Ontario, more than one million people do not have a doctor. Specialists are needed all across Canada. For example, in Ontario and Alberta, there is a shortage of anesthesiologists and a shortage of specialists has been reported all across Saskatchewan.[15]

Canada has found several ways to ameliorate the problem. They rely on internationally trained doctors,[16] increase the intake of Canadian students into medical schools in Canada, and in The Pas, Manitoba, the doctors have found job sharing to be one solution to the shortage.[17] The Ontario Nurses' Association is trying to make the public aware of the nursing crisis and has started a campaign called "Not Enough Nurses."[18] The education system has responded by increasing the number of nursing programs offered, expanding the number of specialties, and changing the way in which nurses are trained.

2. Shipping Industry—Canada and Worldwide   It is forecasted that by 2015, a worldwide shortage of ship officers will reach 27,000 as fewer people enter the industry. A career at sea is not one that many people aspire to, and as a result, this industry is experiencing a talent shortage. Finding ways to attract people to merchant marine careers is very difficult. In 2003, there were 5,341 officers from Eastern Canada working in the marine industry across the world; 1,300 of the 5,341 were from Newfoundland and Labrador. Programs such as the Marine Institute in St. John's, Newfoundland offer courses and distance learning programs focusing on nautical science. And the industry itself has developed robust career paths for individuals who want to pursue a career in this industry.[19]

3. Applied Science Technologists and Technicians—British Columbia   The Applied Science Technologists & Technicians of British Columbia (ASTTBC) has indicated that they expect a 70 percent shortage of supervisors, managers, and contractors in trades and technologies in 2010. In order to combat this shortage, the industry is targeting schools and government to help recruit the needed talent. They are establishing standards of excellence and asking that members register with the ASTTBC so they can uphold these standards of excellence and ensure ongoing education regarding best practices.[20]

4. Aerospace—British Columbia   The aerospace industry in B.C. is also facing a skills shortage. Viking Air Ltd., a Victoria-based firm, reported difficulty finding skilled workers. The company, who recently bought the intellectual property rights to the "Twin Otter," is expanding its workforce. They are finding it extremely difficult to find skilled workers such as aeronautical engineers. Reports from other aerospace firms in B.C. who are also experiencing this problem indicate that this shortage is going to be a major challenge over the next several years. To manage this, Viking Air plans to enter into a partnership with the Southern Alberta Institute of Technology to train students for its current projects. The company also plans to continually train its employees so that they are able to keep on top of the industry.[21]

5. IT Specialists—Canada   A study that was carried out by the Information Technology Association of America (ITTA) found that more than 346,000 IT jobs are not being filled because of a lack of skilled workers. Three out of ten vacancies relating to computers are taking six months or longer to fill. This data highlights a skills shortage. In addition to specific skills required, this industry is expected to experience an overall labour shortage. *The Financial Post* reported that Canada's technology companies will face a labour shortage due to a significant drop in university enrolments in IT programs, negative perceptions of the technology sector, and the fact that 31,000 of the 600,000 Canadians employed in the IT sector will retire in the near term.[22] Statistics Canada has confirmed these findings. An independent study commissioned by Statistics Canada and conducted by the Software Human Resource Council confirmed that the high tech industry has been severely compromised due to a labour shortage. As a result, it found that the industry has been operating at 75 to 80 percent capacity.[23]

6. Environmental Occupations—Canada and the U.S.   It is no surprise that with a renewed interest in environmental issues globally, individuals with these skills are in great demand. Business is booming in the environmental section, employment in this field is steadily increasing, and the demand for human resources with these specific skills sets is at an all-time high.

Recently, *The National Post* featured an article highlighting the shortage of environmental workers in Canada. A report produced by Grant Trump, president of Calgary's Environmental Careers Organization (ECO Canada), indicated that 3.2 percent of the working-age population are environmental employees. Of these employees, 54 percent of senior environmental managers are over forty-five years of age, whereas the national average is 44 percent. Most disconcerting was that out of the ten universities polled, eight indicated that enrolments are declining in environmental fields.[24]

7. Intelligence and Security—Global   Al-Qaeda, the events of 9/11, and counter-terrorism factions are major issues that concern many people across the globe. Worldwide interest in the intelligence and security industry has been renewed. Demand is so high for these skills that there are significant signs of a looming shortage. Canadian universities are experiencing a significant surge in enrolments for programs related to security and intelligence and are unable to hire the staff needed to head these departments. This popular ever-growing field is in dire need of funding and research or academic specialists in this field will seek their education outside of Canada.[25]

8. Labour Skills in Demand Across the Globe—Mexico, Japan, U.S., Canada, Europe, China   *Business Week* recently reported that different countries are experiencing different types of skill shortages. For example, in Mexico, 82 percent of companies say that the skills most in demand are factory workers, labourers, and accountants. Japan reports that 61 percent of companies are finding it difficult to fill jobs such as sales representatives and secretaries. The U.S. indicates that 41 percent of companies are struggling to fill positions such as sales representatives and teachers. In Canada, 36 percent of companies indicated a shortage of plumbers, electricians, welders, and sales representatives. Europe reports that 31 percent of companies experience difficulty finding plumbers, electricians, and engineers. Finally, 19 percent of companies in China report shortages in laboratory workers, labourers, and factory workers,[26] and a recent McKinsey report identified that "insufficient executive talent was the biggest barrier to China's global ambitions."[27]

These examples illustrate just how prevalent the labour shortage problem is and the challenges that they entail. Next, we will discuss what organizations can do to manage these challenges and the various staffing alternatives that are available.

■ MANAGING LABOUR SHORTAGES—ALTERNATIVE STAFFING STRATEGIES

Organizations that engage in effective HR planning utilize a variety of staffing strategies to ensure that they have the right people with the right skills at the right place and at the right time. There are several staffing options available and there are numerous criteria to consider to make the best possible decision. We will begin by discussing the four main options. These options are: hiring employees, contracting out the work to another firm, developing existing employees internally and leveraging existing work arrangements to optimize the way work is accomplished. See Exhibit 3.1.

Staffing Option #1—Hire Employees

One way to address a labour shortage is simply to hire an employee to fill an open position. However, there are several decisions that managers must make with respect to hiring. Managers must decide if they need someone full-time or part-time, if the employment relationship will be ongoing or for a specific period of time, and if they should hire someone externally or fill the position from the firm's internal talent pool.

Part-Time or Full-Time Workers?   Largely dependant on labour budgets and a manager's view as to how to effectively run their department, decisions are made about hiring an employee to work full- or part-time and whether the individual will be hired on a temporary or permanent basis. Some common terms used to describe these types of employment relationships are permanent full-time (PFT), permanent part-time (PPT), temporary full-time (TFT), and temporary part-time (TPT). In Canada, a **full-time employee** works 37.5 to 40 hours in a workweek.

full-time employee
An employee who works 37.5 to 40 hours in a workweek

EXHIBIT 3.1	Alternative Staffing Strategies		
Hire Employees	**Source Service Providers**	**Develops Employees Internally**	**Work Arrangements**
PFT	Independent contractor	Replacement charts	Overtime
PPT	Third party	Succession planning	Flexible schedules
TFT	Outsource	Career development	Flexible time and location
TPT	Crowdsource	Float and transfer	Flex Policies

Part-time workers are employed persons whose normal hours of work are less than those of a comparable full-time worker. They typically work approximately 20 to 25 hours per week. Temporary workers are sometimes called "contract" workers. Typically, employees who are PFT or PPT are eligible for company benefits whereas employees who are TFT or TPT may not. Another type of temporary worker can be a casual or seasonal employee.

It is important to note that *employees* of an organization are all paid via the company payroll system. The organization deducts and remits taxes to the government on the employee's behalf, as indicated by Revenue Canada, and their employment agreements are subject to the *Canada Labour Code* or applicable provincial legislation.

Recruit Internally or Externally?   In addition to determining the applicable employment relationship, organizations must decide whether to recruit internally or externally.

Internal recruitment is typically facilitated by the company's job posting process and has some advantages, including a more accurate assessment of the person's abilities, a demonstration that the organization is supportive of employee development, and less orientation costs as the employee is already familiar with company practices. However, external recruitment may be desired if the company wants new blood, if they do not have the skills internally, or if the position requires the application of a particular set of skills in a timely fashion when there is no time to train existing employees.

Effective organizations think not only about whether to fill roles internally or externally, but they also look for novel ways to accelerate the available supply of candidates. They devise strategies that enable them to tap the hidden job market by actively pursuing a variety of alternative programs. Some examples include accessing the immigrant population, determining which jobs can be performed by people with disabilities and sourcing applicable candidates, and partnering up with universities and colleges to create a co-op/internship program.

Companies who choose to hire people with disabilities illustrate that they embrace diversity and recognize the need for employment for all members of the community. Workers with disabilities can be employed in many facets of business and this should be considered a viable option with the impending labour shortage. In British Columbia, Stephen Peters, manager of the Pan Pacific Hotel, has been hiring workers with disabilities since 2003. He points out that with the labour shortage, hiring people with disabilities is a great solution since there is a large pool of talent among people with disabilities.[28]

Many firms are now implementing a co-operative student or internship program. These programs not only fill the labour gap and provide the employer with skills, but they provide the student with much needed work experience and the ability to apply their education in a business-related environment.[29]

Hiring immigrants is another approach to filling the gap. For example, one firm who hires immigrants is Friesens Corp., a commercial printer located in Altona, Manitoba. They have a significant need for trained press operators and due to the specialized nature of these skills they have had to bring people in from Germany and Uruguay to fill their gaps. The problem for Friesen is the wait for these immigrants. Due to immigration policies, the wait has been up to three years. However, recently the province of Manitoba embarked on a program to accelerate this process. They have targeted immigration policies and created a system that expedites the number and type of immigrants who are granted permanent visas into Canada. The province has created a system that identifies key employability factors, such as skill shortages specific to their region, and has developed their own selection criteria for accepting immigrants into their province. They have created a nomination system, choosing from a "backlogged pool" of permanent visa applications overseen by Ottawa. Those immigrants have the skills needed to fill their shortages. Manitoba then expedites the immigrant's visa application process, accelerating wait times. As a result, the wait time for Friesen is now one year.[30]

Staffing Option #2—Contract Out the Work

contractor

Someone who provides goods or services to another entity under the terms of a specific contract

consultants

Professionals who provide expert advice and counsel in a particular area

The next alternative that organizations may consider to manage a labour shortage is sourcing services from an independent vendor by entering into a service agreement with a contractor. A **contractor** is someone who provides goods or services to another entity under the terms of a specific contract.

Contractors are not employees of an organization. They are governed under contract law, not employment legislation. The contractor typically invoices the organization and the organization pays for these services via the accounting function. The contractor's "contract" ends when the services that they have agreed to provide are complete and the services have been delivered. On occasion, organizations will choose to engage a "consultant." **Consultants** are professionals who provide expert advice and counsel in a particular area.

Contractors determine their own work hours, typically have their own offices, and can work on multiple contracts at the same time. They can hire other persons to perform the work, they are not eligible for benefits, and they supply all their own equipment and supplies. Revenue Canada has provided a number of tests to determine whether someone is a contractor. Revenue Canada policies are very strict and assess companies' practices to ensure that the relationship is at arm's length. The tests are related to control, ownership of tools, chance of profit, risk of loss, and payment. Exhibit 3.2 explains five tests to determine if a person is a contractor or an employee.

Different Types of Contractual Relationships   There are several different types of relationships that organizations can choose to engage in when purchasing the services of a contractor. An independent contractor can be a sole owner of a business or one of multiple owners. Contractors can provide the services themselves or they can contract out the work. The contractor can perform the work on company property or from an alternative location. There are several reasons

EXHIBIT	**3.2**	Five Key Tests to Determine Contractor/Employee Status

Control	• Is the person under the direction and control of another with respect to the time the person works, where the person works, and the way in which the work is done?
	• The greater employer's control, the more likely the person is an employee. The contractor determines the result. As an employee, the employer has the right to determine the way the task is carried out.
Ownership of Tools	• Does the person use the tools, space, supplies, and/or equipment owned by someone else? If so, this may be an indication the person is an employee.
	• The contractor should supply their own tools.
Profit	• Does the person make a profit? If the person profits, then they could be a contractor. If the person's income is always the difference between the cost of providing the service and the price charged for the service, then they are deemed an independent contractor.
	• An employee has no risk of loss.
Risk of Loss	• If the person risks losing money and/or if the cost of doing the job is more than the price charged, then they can be considered contractor status.
Payment	• If the person receives payments at regular intervals, regardless of customer satisfaction, then they may be an employee.

why companies may choose to purchase services from a third party. They may simply require additional expertise, or perhaps there is a significant volume of work and the organization requires additional resources to ensure that the work is accomplished. Or, the work itself may be considered non-core and the organization does not have the time or the skill sets internally.

Here are some examples that illustrate a firm's typical contractual relationships:

a) A company hires a recruiting firm to screen all its résumés, interview its candidates, and provide a short list of candidates. In this case, the recruiting firm bills the organization for the service and the recruiting firm pays whoever did the work.

b) A company hires a temporary help agency to supply them with workers to do a specific job. The workers will be paid by a temporary help agency and the temporary help agency will invoice the organization for its services.

c) An organization requires an interim executive due to the unexpected departure of one of their key employees. The organization contracts with a third-party vendor, such as a career transition firm, who can supply the organization with an interim executive. This executive is someone with senior-level skills and experience who can step into the job for a period of time. The career transition firm would be paid to source the candidate and the candidate would be paid to deliver the services.[31]

Exhibit 3.3 highlights the different types of contractor relationships.

Outsourcing

The subcontracting of activities that are not regarded as part of a company's core business, in an effort to reduce costs

Outsourcing   The term **outsourcing** has been used extensively in the past decade. Outsourcing refers to the subcontracting of activities (production processes or services) that are not regarded as part of a company's core business, in an effort to reduce costs by transferring portions of work to outside suppliers, rather than completing the work internally. The organization purchases services from an outside vendor rather than using internal resources. Outsourcing or contracting out work is typically associated with work that is non-core to an organization, and where the outsourcing firm has special skills, technology, and expertise to manage this work. Outsourcing is a business decision made by executives, not human resource planners. Outsourcing is considered

EXHIBIT 3.3	Different Types of Contractor Relationships	
Type	**Description**	**Example**
Third party	Organization purchases services from an outside vendor	Temporary help agencies who supply seasonal and temporary help
	Vendor can be an independent contractor or a firm with specific expertise who employs the employees with specific expertise	Recruitment firms who help the organization manage its recruitment volumes or who source candidates
		Outsource firms such as Ceridian and ADP. They may have service agreements with an organization to manage their payroll and benefit administration—perhaps the entire function
Crowdsourcing	A function once performed by employees is outsourced to an undefined and generally large network in the form of an "open call"	The company iStockphoto requires some additional inventory so an open call is sent via the web to anyone who would like to submit their work

by a company as way of saving money, improving quality, or freeing up company resources for other activities so that the organization can focus on those activities that it does best. A subset of the term, offshoring, involves transferring jobs to another country by either hiring local subcontractors or building a facility in an area where labour is inexpensive.[32]

Several types of outsourcing relationships can exist. There are joint ventures and equity partnerships, external co-sourcing, vendor co-sourcing, and employee swapping. Joint ventures and equity partnerships are used when the focus is on long-term goals. External co-sourcing involves pooling the operations of many different companies, something that can prove difficult. Vendor co-sourcing occurs when the company controls the processes, but not the rest of the operations, usually encompassing the best of both companies. Employee swapping uses former employees. These employees are "swapped" to another company, but still contribute to their former company. For example, at Semco and Rhino Foods, employees who left the company became satellite workers, working externally to provide the company with supplies.[33]

To effectively managing these outsourcing relationships, the organization must engage in a series of steps. Step one is to evaluate the vendor organization. This evaluation should take into consideration the company's needs, ensuring that there is a good fit. The organization must then negotiate the contract and determine who internally will manage the vendor. The organizational structure and skills need to be taken into consideration. Next, the organization will transition the work to the vendor of choice and manage the vendor's ongoing performance.[34]

A recent trend has been for firms to outsource some of their HR–related functions. In an effort to manage costs and focus on its core competencies, Bank of Montreal decided to outsource its HR processing functions to alleviate its administrative burden and utilize the technologies of the outsourcing firm. The agreement between BMO and Exult was valued at $75 million per year

---

HRP IN THE NEWS   **The IBM Transformation**

The computer industry has shifted and IBM has taken on the challenge. Once a company who sold and serviced technology, IBM is now embracing the future and the future looks bright! IBM is moving to a business consulting and outsourcing business model, projecting that within ten years this model could build a revenue stream of over $50 billion. Its business strategy has changed forever as necessitated by the weak projected growth of a meagre 6 percent for the $1.2 trillion computer industry. The computer industry has become commoditized and there are some very formidable market competitors such as Dell and Hewlett-Packard.

From an HRP perspective, IBM has decided to optimize its existing talent base. It has dug deep into its talent pool to leverage its existing knowledge and skills. These individuals possess vast experience in areas such as research and development (R&D), software programming, and networking skills. IBM is focusing on this talent pool and for the past few years has directed the attention of its workforce to its new strategy, emphasizing what is important to business growth. It is actively engaging employees in these talent-management activities and since 2002 the number of employees focused on the business rather than technology has increased from 3,500 in 2002 to more than 50,000 today.[35]

What types of skills and competencies do you think IBM needs to achieve its objectives? What type of training and developments would be most applicable? What specific human resource plans do you think need to be considered?

and affected about 250 positions both in Canada and in the U.S.[36] Human resources often play a significant role when HR is outsourced. They must focus on service delivery and ensure that the transition is seamless. Ultimately, HR has direct responsibility for service quality and results and they must manage the vendor to ensure that the service is value-added and business objectives are met.[37]

crowdsourcing

Act of taking on a a function once performed by employees and outsourcing it to an undefined (and generally large) network of people in the form of an open call

Crowdsourcing—A Novel Way to Source Talent   **Crowdsourcing** is a relatively new term that describes a novel way for companies to meet their resource requirements. It is the act of taking on a function once performed by employees and outsourcing it to an undefined (and generally large) network of people in the form of an open call. The term was coined in June 2006 by *Wired* magazine writer Jeff Howe and editor Mark Robinson.[38]

In this model, the organization has a need for human resources. It then communicates this need to the public via the Internet. It is an "open call" to interested parties who decide, based on their own interests and their own time, if they want to help the organization by providing a service or filling a need. The work is done outside the traditional company walls. If the organization feels that the contribution is valuable, the organization will pay the contributor for their efforts in some way.

In outsourcing, the organization typically sends out a formal request for proposal (RFP) and they review potential vendors before deciding on the best one. Typically, lower-paid professionals do the work itself. In crowdsourcing, the problem is communicated through the net and it is virtually *out there* for those individuals who are interested to respond.

Several companies have used this option with great success. Procter and Gamble, Cambridge House, and iStock photo are a few examples. Calgary-based firm, iStockphoto, sells stock photography online at a minimal cost. They can do this because it sources its content from the *crowd* and pays them royalties depending on how popular their images are. From time to time, Procter and Gamble has R&D problems that its 9,000 scientists and researchers have trouble solving. They now post these problems on a website called "InnoCentive," offering large cash rewards to more than 90,000 *solvers* who make up this network of backyard scientists. Cambridge House, based in Calgary, is another example of a company that uses crowdsourcing to manage labour requirements. Entrepreneurs can throw out ideas for a software product and then peers evaluate the idea. If accepted, the entrepreneur will get the appropriate people to work on the product and then pay royalty points to everyone involved. Points can then be traded in for cash, based on how successful the product is.[39]

The main advantage of crowdsourcing is that innovative ideas can be explored at relatively little cost. Furthermore, it also helps reduce costs and makes use of the *crowd* to communicate its requirements.

■ THE CONTINGENT WORKFORCE—LEVERAGING THE MIX OF STAFFING OPTIONS

Over the past decade, the trend has been for firms to consider a combination of staffing options to optimally manage labour costs and effectively leverage their intellectual capital in a variety of different ways. A significant approach has been for firms to utilize part-time workers, seasonal workers, self-employed workers, and temporary help to manage their labour demand fluctuations in the most cost-effective manner. The term **contingent workforce** has become a popular word to describe this type of approach to managing labour demand. This section will discuss these trends and the advantages of using a contingent workforce. In addition, we will consider some of the issues that managers must take into account when engaging the contingent workforce.

contingent workforce

The class of individual workers who are not regular, full-time employees of a company

Audrey Freedman coined the term "contingency workforce" in 1985 to describe a management technique of employing workers only when there was an immediate or direct need for their services. Hence, the word *contingent* is used. It has been used to describe various forms of employment and contractual relationships. Since then, the term has been used in many different contexts and now is defined as individuals performing a job who do not have an explicit or implicit contract for long-term employment.[40] This means that the employees who are permanent full-time are not considered *contingent.*

Contingency can be applied in such employment practices as part-time work, temporary help service employment, self employment, contracting out work, and seasonal and casual worker situations. However, researchers have found that the word itself can be misleading as it has been loosely used to refer to many different types of relationships. And, "referring to workers as 'contingent' causes many workers to be misclassified and many analysts to be confused about what actually is being described or studied."[41] To simplify, we will define contingent work as all temporary and contract employment.[42]

Attracting and maintaining a good temporary pool of employees who are willing to work intermittently is a challenge for many organizations today. However, the benefits of doing so are enormous. As discussed earlier, there is a general belief that using contingent workers is an effective way to handle shortage problems for a period of time and can help an organization sustain its competitive advantage. Contingent workers can be used to handle business activity fluctuations and provide their knowledge and skills on a short-term basis. They provide the organization with the flexibility needed to handle the ebbs and flows of work. These workers can help when an organization has extended operating and production schedules and are useful for organizations that want to ensure work life–balance for its existing employees. They can fill in for a maternity or extended leave of absence, lend their expertise in areas where the organization does not have any expertise, or simply fill a gap. A major benefit of hiring contingent workers is that these workers bring knowledge and skills into the workplace, and organizations increase workforce diversity because they typically get a wide variety of employees from all backgrounds. In terms of costs, because these workers are not permanent employees, the organization can avoid any long-term commitment (e.g., severance costs).[43] The costs associated with engaging contingent workers are variable, not fixed.

The Contingent Workforce—Some Trends

Just how prevalent is the use of the contingent worker? The following data illustrates the widespread use of the various contingency-staffing options:

- Typically, conventional employees make up about 60 percent of the workforce, with the remaining 40 percent engaged in some type of alternative staffing arrangement.[44]
- A recent survey found that among 136 respondents, 58.8 percent use contract workers on a freelance basis, 19.1 percent use seasonal workers, 75 percent use temporary workers, 64.7 percent use part-time workers, and 13.2 percent use some other type of additional support worker to help manage additional work requirements.[45]
- Over the last ten years, employment in companies providing employment-related services—placement agencies, temporary help services, and leasing services—has increased significantly. In 2000, an additional 17,000 people worked in employment services. This increased to 85,000 by the end of 2000, doubling the number from 1994.[46] This suggests that many organizations have decided to outsource or hire temporary employees to fill a shortage.
- In 2000, there was an increase of 319,000 jobs. Some 263,000 jobs were full-time, while 56,000 were part-time.[47]
- The number of people working fewer than thirty hours a week has increased significantly over the last three decades. In 2005, one in five Canadians worked part-time as their main job, compared to one in eight in 1976.[48]
- Growth in part-time employment is occurring around the globe. The Netherlands, the U.K., Japan, and Australia had higher part-time employment rates in 2002 than Canada.[49]

EXHIBIT **3.4** Contingent Workforce Considerations

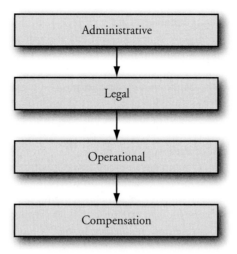

- Part-time work has increased in youths. More than two in five 15- to 24-year-olds worked part-time in 2005 compared to one in five in 1976. Youth work in retail, food services, recreation, and culture. Of the Canadians youths who started jobs in 2006, 25 percent were temporary.
- Part-time work is also common for women aged 25–54.[50]

Managing the Contingent Relationship

Managing the contingent workforce can be extremely challenging. The very nature of the word *contingency* denotes a sense of transience and unpredictability and describes a workforce that is on the periphery of organizational life. If you have ever worked part-time, seasonally, or as a contractor, you might be aware of the feelings associated with being a part-time worker, your commitment to the organization, and the level of connection you felt to the organization.

Several elements must be considered in order to ensure that this option is managed effectively. These considerations, outlined in Exhibit 3.4, are administrative, legal, operational, and compensation.

Administrative Considerations   When addressing administrative considerations, the first decision is to determine the applicable employment relationship. Will the person provide services or will they be an *employee* of the corporation? From that point, managers must ensure that the payment delivery, the relevant employment status codes, and the security clearance authorization are all recorded accurately with the relevant documentation and that there is a system in place to track the resource. In terms of pay, the employee will be set up on the company payroll with the applicable deductions, whereas the contractor will be set up in the accounting system as a vendor providing services. The vendor will be required to invoice the organization and funds will need to be allocated to the applicable labour budget. Depending on the employment relationship, the codes that will be entered into the HRIS system will be different so as to accurately reflect the employee or contractor status, hours worked, etc. Security clearances are often different based on the status. For example, an employee will always be given access to its web-based intranet resources, whereas the contractor will maintain an arm's length relationship.

Another important administrative activity relates to the tracking of these individuals. Information such as when their agreements are ending and what notice the company must provide if they want to terminate the contract early is important for managers to know so that they can plan their workforce needs accordingly.[51]

Legal Considerations   As previously discussed, Revenue Canada has very strict rules regarding *contractors*. It is important that the managers who engage these individuals review the guidelines and establish upfront the parameters in which the contractor will be expected to operate. A major challenge is ensuring that supervisors and managers avoid treating these contractors as full-time employees, thereby creating an employment relationship that does not exist. Refer back to Exhibit 3.2: Five Key Tests to Determine Contractor/Employee Status.

Organizations that use temporary agencies need to assess and scrutinize the agencies' practices. Does the agency treat its workers respectfully and engage only workers who are legally entitled to work in Canada? Does the agency take advantage of or exploit its workers? Recently, the Ontario government has addressed the problem of temporary agencies' practices. They have introduced legislation to protect part-time workers who are employed by part-time agencies. The legislation sets out some basic rights, such as ensuring that workers receive holiday pay and not charging fees to part-time workers. The law requires agencies to ensure that their practices are fair, equitable, and nondiscriminatory.[52]

Operational Considerations   Managers need to decide how best to engage the contingent worker. The challenge is to get the maximum value from this form of labour. There are many different points of view as to how to best utilize contingent workers' skills. Some researchers have advocated that contingent workers should only be used for non-core aspects of the business, because there is a general belief that exposing these workers to business knowledge may be a risk, as it could end up in the public domain. Others believe that it does not matter. They believe that engaging or employing these workers in core activities will enable an organization to incorporate best practice methods into their processes and as a result their employees will benefit from this increase in knowledge.[53] Whichever viewpoint organizations subscribe to, managers must ensure that they understand the company philosophy and adhere to these practices.

Most importantly, managers must ensure that they manage the performance of the contingent workforce just as they would their permanent staff. Performance expectations should be clear and performance tracked, reviewed, and recorded. Managers need to provide feedback to the employee or contractor as to whether they are meeting the requirements.

Compensation Considerations   Making decisions regarding how much to pay a part-time employee or a contractor can be an issue. This issue must be resolved and agreed to prior to the employee/contractor starting work. Typically, contractors are compensated with a higher rate of pay. This is because they do not get benefits, they may have other costs such as having to pay workers' compensation premiums, and they do not have on-going work. However, issues can then arise with respect to the wage differentials between the various groups. In this case HR has to be prepared to objectively defend these decisions.[54]

Staffing Option #3—Develop Employees Internally

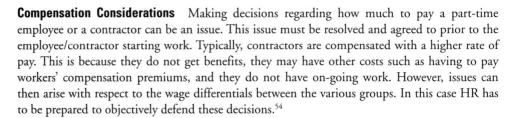

When faced with a labour shortage, organizations can choose to optimize their internal supply by focusing on their existing employees. This option considers the strength of an organization's internal workforce with respect to the skills and knowledge employees possess and the future skills and knowledge employees will need in order for the organization to meet its labour requirements. Organizations use various mechanisms, such as promotions, replacement charts, and succession and career plans to ascertain employees' interests, the types of training and development required, and when employees will be ready to fill a future labour requirement. Organizations utilize their internal HR–related processes to facilitate these activities, optimizing their human resources' talent pool. Chapter 2 (Forecasting Demand and Supply), Chapter 5

(Career Development), and Chapter 6 (Succession Management) discuss these options in much greater depth.

Staffing Option #4—Leverage Work Arrangements

A mother who can only work daycare hours, a person who has to care for a sick parent and must work from home, or an parent who has to drop children off at school are all examples of employees who benefit from a flexible work environment. Research has indicated that companies who demonstrate significant flexibility and utilize a variety of work arrangements are not only better able to attract a supply of labour, but also score higher in terms of employee satisfaction.

This final staffing option focuses on the various types of *work arrangements*. A work arrangement refers to a firm's use of work hours, schedules, and location to ensure that the goals of the organization and the needs of employees are optimally met. We will be discussing four types of arrangements: overtime; flexible hours, location, and schedule; flexible retirements; and float and transfer. See Exhibit 3.5.

These types of arrangements are all based on *choices*. The organization can make the choice to offer these options to the employees and the employees make a choice about whether to accept. In this reciprocal relationship, both the employer and the employee typically benefit as a result. For example, if the employee agrees to overtime, then they will receive money or time in lieu, and the organization will be able to manage its staffing shortage.

Work Arrangement—Overtime   Have you ever been asked to work overtime for an extended period of time? Working overtime can be a blessing for some, but disliked by others. We all have different reactions to these types of organization requests. Some of us enjoy having the extra money and do not mind being at work and away from home pressures while others feel cheated about not having a *life* and may feel that the organization is taking advantage of them.

Overtime provides many advantages such as enabling an organization to deal with busy times, bottlenecks, and employee absences. It can provide additional income to employees and can avoid disruption to jobs where the workload might be difficult to share. However, there can be many disadvantages. It can increase salary expenses or contribute to inefficiency due to increased hours of work, fatigue, and exhaustion. It can impact employees by creating more stress and can contribute to increased health and safety issues. A Statistics Canada study revealed that 51 percent of employees in unstable positions were more stressed than 38 percent of employees who worked standard schedules.[55] In addition, employees might feel that they are entitled to overtime, which could lead to resentment if the organization decides on an alternative course of action.[56]

It is important for organizations to understand the legislation as it relates to overtime provisions. Legislation on hours of work and overtime varies depending on the province. There

EXHIBIT   3.5   Types of Work Arrangements

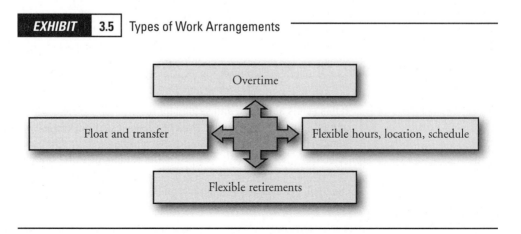

are two basic concepts—the standard workweek and the maximum workweek. Some provinces indicate that overtime should be paid after the standard work has been exceeded, whereas others provide a legal maximum number of hours per day or per week. For example, in Ontario, the standard workday is eight hours and the standard workweek is forty-four hours. The maximum number of hours is eight per day, or if the employer has established a workday longer than eight hours, it is forty-eight hours per week. When these standards are exceeded, overtime is paid. In Ontario, the Employment Standards Act allows employers and employees to enter into averaging agreements that allow them to average hours of work over one to four weeks when

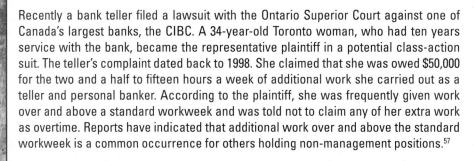

HRP AND ETHICS   The Overtime Lawsuit and the Bank Teller

Recently a bank teller filed a lawsuit with the Ontario Superior Court against one of Canada's largest banks, the CIBC. A 34-year-old Toronto woman, who had ten years service with the bank, became the representative plaintiff in a potential class-action suit. The teller's complaint dated back to 1998. She claimed that she was owed $50,000 for the two and a half to fifteen hours a week of additional work she carried out as a teller and personal banker. According to the plaintiff, she was frequently given work over and above a standard workweek and was told not to claim any of her extra work as overtime. Reports have indicated that additional work over and above the standard workweek is a common occurrence for others holding non-management positions.[57]

The plaintiffs are seeking $600 million in retroactive pay, $500 million in compensation, and $100 million in punitive damages. It is expected that the suit will cover approximately 10,000 current and former non-management, non-unionized employees. Tellers make about $30,700 a year.[58]

These lawsuits are common in the U.S., but this is the largest one in Canadian history to date. Banks operate under federal legislation, which has clearly defined requirements with respect to hours of work and overtime. The bank has indicated that its policies are progressive, clearly defined, and exceed legislative requirements. The bank has urged all employees who feel they have issues to come forward. Overtime is prevalent in Canada. In a recent Statistic Canada report, more than 1.6 million Canadians put in unpaid overtime work in the month of April 2007.[59] A recent survey conducted by COMPAS Inc. surveyed 129 CEOs and leaders from various sized firms. The majority surveyed (39 percent) indicated that the best way to compensate would be time off in lieu. More than 25 percent indicated the legislative requirement as it related to overtime (typically time and a half) was a better alternative. And a much smaller portion indicated that perks and incentives or bonuses would be appropriate ways to compensate for overtime. However, an overwhelming 44 percent said they felt that overtime was a moderate factor in burnout.[60]

If this suit is accepted and settled for the plaintiff(s), the costs could have a significant impact on the bank. Do you think the bank exploited the teller? Do you think that the banks should pay overtime or is there another way to compensate these employees? Should the banks decide to use a different mix of staff? Should they contract out the work to avoid the burden of overtime pay? What about work–life balance? Should the bank place greater emphasis on this? Could this suit have been avoided? Consider the impacts on HRP if this lawsuit is successful.

calculating the entitlement to overtime.[61] There are exceptions for various employee groups that may be exempted from hours of work and overtime pay provision, including students, domestics, and construction workers. In addition, these provisions can be exceeded in the case of emergencies.[62]

Every week in Canada, 20 percent of workers put in nine hours of overtime.[63] Is this good or bad? Is there an alternative way that organizations can manage an increase in work?

Work Arrangement—Flexible Hours, Schedules, or Location   Have you ever thought that the work that you do could be done partially from your home? Do you ever wonder why you must go into the office? Is it possible for you to deliver the work from a remote facility? Or perhaps you have to go into work because you require some data that is only accessible at work. Organizations are currently exploring how to accommodate today's workforce. With the change in demographics, growth in wireless technology, and the value placed by employees on work–life balance, there are numerous opportunities for organizations to explore how work is done, where it is done, and when it should be done. There has been a significant trend in terms of how organizations are leveraging flexible work arrangements to manage their manpower shortage. According to a recent survey conducted by Hewitt, 84 percent of Canadian companies offer some flextime to their employees. This is expected to increase to 90 percent by 2009. In addition, an increase from 60 to 71 percent is expected for part-time workers working from home and an increase from 34 to 41 percent is expected for full-time employment.[64] Flexible work arrangements can expand business flexibility, save costs, increase employee engagement, and demonstrate a concern for people and recognition as to the diverse nature of their needs. A study by Watson Wyatt showed that a collegial flexible workplace has a nine percent impact on market value.

There are three basic flexible options to consider: flexible time, reduced time, and flexible place.[65] Flextime includes flex hours, schedules, and compressed workweeks. **Flex hours** mean variable start and stop times. **Flex schedules** refer to any type of variation in traditional work schedules. **Compressed workweeks** refer to a reduction in the number of days per week in which full-time work is performed, but not in the number of weekly hours.[66] Reduced time includes part-time and seasonal work, job sharing, reduced hours, and any assignments that are not full-time in nature. Flexible location refers to *where* work is done. It can include telecommuting, mobile work, and other types of offsite work.[67]

Providing employees with the ability to choose their work location is another opportunity for organizations to demonstrate flexibility. **Telecommuting** refers to a situation where an employee conducts at least some of his/her regular work hours from home instead of going into the office setting. For telework to be successful, the organization must have top-notch telecom and IT support for home offices. Clear policies must be in place regarding how often the employees are expected to attend meetings in the office. Also, there must be structured performance management guidelines to ensure that the quality of work is maintained, performance goals are established, and telecommuters are held to the same standard as others who do the same work. In addition, organizations must ensure that when these individuals do come into the office a workspace is available for them and they are welcomed as part of the team.[68]

This option can be attractive to many types of workers, such as the retired, disabled, and part-time workforce.

Work Arrangement—Flexible Retirements   Another way for firms to manage shortages is to target those employees who are close to retirement with a view to extending their contributions. The challenge has been balancing the needs of these employees with the needs of the organization. Organizations for quite some time have attempted to slow this process down by offering employees a phased approach to retirement whereby the individual's hours and responsibilities are reduced ahead of full retirement. However, this approach only works well if the organization isn't facing a significant labour shortage where the need for the employee skills and knowledge would be required on an ongoing basis.[69]

flex hours

Variable start and stop times

flex schedules

Any type of variation in traditional work schedules

compressed workweek

A reduction in the number of days per week in which full-time work is performed, but not in the number of weekly hours

telecommuting

A situation where an employee conducts at least some of his/her regular work hours from home instead of going into the office setting

HRP AND STRATEGIC PARTNERS

Best Buy

Consider how Best Buy Company Inc. is leveraging flexible work arrangements. Best Buy is a specialty retailer of consumer electronics, home-office products, entertainment software, and appliances, operating primarily in Canada, the U.S., and China. They have recently implemented a new program called ROWE, Results Only Work Environment. This means that the age-old face-time culture at Best Buy has been abandoned for a results culture. Employees can create their own schedules, there are no mandatory meetings, and there are no impression management concerns. People can work where they want, when they want, and how they want as long as they produce. It was hoped that by creating more freedom in terms of decision-making employees' morale and level of service would increase. It is working; productivity is up 35 percent in departments that have switched to ROWE. Employees are more engaged, satisfied, and there is an increase in retention.[70]

flexible retirement

A novel approach to optimizing the talent of recent retirees, thus extending their contributions and continuing their engagement in organizational activities

A relatively new approach to managing retirement is **flexible retirement.** This term has been used to describe a novel approach to optimizing the talent of recent retirees by extending their contributions and continuing their engagement in organizational activities. Called "retiree-return" programs, these programs provide retirees with the opportunity to work after they have retired and provide them with significant flexibility in terms of how they work, what they work on, when they work, and where they work. These programs are flexible in the sense that they take into account the retirees' needs and tailor the work accordingly. These programs typically begin prior to retirement and continue after the employee has officially retired. One can say that these retirees take on an *active* retiree status, whereby they continue their involvement in the organizations long after they have officially retired.

The benefits are substantial as the organization will be able to retain its intellectual capital long after they have left the organization. The firm will be able to retain its talent to fill unexpected gaps, institutional knowledge and transfer of this knowledge will not be lost, and the organization will be able to control its labour costs since retirees do not receive any additional benefits. It is projected that phased retirement programs will double over the next several years from 26 to 55 percent.[71] In a recent William Mercer study, 23 percent of the surveyed companies had some form of the program to provide mature workers with flexibility.

In addition to the programs that organizations are offering, the Ontario government has recently passed legislation that prohibits mandatory retirement. This legislation came into effect on December 12, 2006. It provides older people with a choice as to when they want to retire and how long they want to work. They no longer have to retire at age sixty-five.[72] This change enables organizations to have access to a greater supply of resources and to engage these resources to help them manage swings in demand, and it enables the employee to continue to work for as long as they wish to.

Work Arrangement—Float and Transfer　Ever wonder what it would be like to do someone else's job? Ever wish you could trade places with someone for a bit of time so that you can get away from your boss or the monotony of the work you do or the people you work with, but you're concerned it may not be the right move? Another flexible arrangement that organizations use to manage shifts in work is through a policy that enables its full-time resources to be transferred when needed, or if the need is for a very short time, they *float* the worker. Organizations rely on their training programs to ensure that their employees are cross-trained and that they can secure these resources when they need them. Another term that we can use to describe this arrangement is job rotation. For example, Capital One used this arrangement when they had significant demand in their payment processing area. Employees who normally worked in other areas were deployed to work in the payment processing area.[73]

Next, we will turn our attention to how organizations choose the best possible staffing options and the criteria they can use to help make an effective decision.

KEY FACTORS THAT DETERMINE THE BEST AVAILABLE STAFFING OPTION

Now that we have identified the four main options for filling labour shortages, let us turn our attention to how an organization determines the best option. Seven key criteria, as shown in Exhibit 3.6, should be considered: urgency, importance, speed, quality of service, financial constraints, managerial preference, and revocability (ease with which the relationship can be terminated).

Urgency and Importance

Urgency and importance are determined by organizational requirements and refer to the salience of the need and how quickly the organization requires the skill. In order to determine urgency and importance, organizations must ascertain whether it will be able to meet its customer requirements, its ability to deliver its services at an acceptable level, and just how critical the time frame is. Consider a person who does the payroll of a company division. An important skill, don't you agree? Now imagine that this person is suddenly called away and the person who is supposed to be on backup has to take her maternity leave earlier than expected. The customers, also the internal employees of the organization, expect their paycheques at a certain time and they expect them to be processed accurately. Clearly, the delivery of this service is important, a certain level of service is expected, and the timeframe in which this service is delivered is not negotiable. Finding someone to do this work in a timely fashion is urgent and important and if this does not happen, the organization will not be able to meet its customer and legislative requirements. However, it is important to note that what may be urgent and important to one manager may not be urgent and important to others. In order to ascertain the degree of importance, it is advised that the HR planners engage in meaningful discussions with managers to understand specific circumstances and build a plan that can adequately address concerns.

Speed

Speed relates to how long it takes to fill the shortage. It refers to the external environment that the organization operates in. It relates to the supply of labour in the marketplace and whether there is an abundance of resources or just a few and whether there are some skills that are *hot,* meaning

---

EXHIBIT 3.6 Criteria to Consider When Choosing a Staffing Option

- Urgency
- Importance
- Speed
- Quality of service
- Financial constraints
- Managerial preferences
- Revocability

in very high demand, and others that are not. When choosing an option, the company must consider how long it will take to find the right resource within the time frame determined by the customer. For example, in the early nineties there was a shortage of SAP developers. Organizations had to source these individuals from across the nation. Germany was one key source of talent, but the hiring process was a lengthy one. It took a significant amount of time to find these candidates, secure work permits, and relocate them from their home county. If their customers required immediate services, these organizations had to either contract out the work or hire a third party to help them deliver the service. Contracting out the work may have required that organizations initiate the request for proposal (RFP) process, which in itself could be a lengthy process. On the other hand, some organizations decided that they would train their existing employees if time permitted. Lots of options exist, but it all depends on when these resources are needed.

Quality of Service

Another consideration when choosing a staffing option is how much expertise and sophistication the organization requires. Can the organization hire a junior person, such as a co-op student, or do they need someone who is very experienced? Do they require someone who has worked or provided services only to large multi-national corporations or do they need resources that focus on a specialized niche or market segment? These factors must be considered when organizations make choices about how to manage their shortages.

Financial Constraints

Ever heard a manager say they cannot hire someone because of their budgets? Ever been told that a position that you held was not going to be renewed because of the budget? The choices that managers make will usually be influenced by how much they have to spend. Managers are also trying to find ways to minimize costs and maximize benefits, ensuring optimum quality of work and service delivery with minimal cost.

Managers consider several budgetary options and are always cognizant of where resource dollars will be allocated, when the dollars will be available, and how many dollars will be allocated. Do managers have funds to support a full-time person? For example, full-time employees get benefits and in Ontario, when managers terminate these employees, they have to pay notice and severance. Temporary employees and contractors do not get benefits and a typical termination clause in a contractual agreement is two weeks' notice. With benefits costs ranging from 15 to 40 percent, managers may decide that they can employ two temporary employees instead of one full-time employee. This would save on benefits, hiring, severance costs, and lead times would be shorter. Also, the cost to recruit full-time employees can be very expensive. The average cost per hire in Canada (CPH) is $7,123, and the average time to fill is thirty-seven days. And these numbers increase when looking for knowledge workers.[74] Another option that managers typically consider is the use of overtime, choosing to balance their resource needs by offering overtime to existing employees for a certain period of time. If they do this, managers must consider not only the cost of overtime, but also the legal and humanistic repercussions.

Managerial Preferences

In addition to budgetary concerns, managers have certain preferences. Sometimes a manager prefers to have a permanent employee work overtime rather than hire a part-time or temporary person to fill the void. In addition, some managers are more concerned with work–life balance. Managers might be concerned about burnout, excess stress, and poor quality of work. These managers would prefer to engage the services of a contractor rather than burden an existing employee with a large number of overtime hours. Another preference relates to the manager's concern over control. The more a manager needs to control the work activities of his or her work unit, the more that manager will choose an option where they will be able to directly manage the service provided. These managers will typically hire temporary employees who can work on site as opposed to outsourcing the work.

Revocability

This factor refers to the ease with which an agreement can be terminated. For example, when an organization hires a temporary employee or contractor, the agreement terminates on the last day of the contract. If the organization chooses to end the contract early, as previously stated, a clause is built into the agreement that can be executed with the party providing two weeks' notice. This is not the case with a permanent full-time or part-time employee where employment law provisions prevail.[75] In Ontario, for example, notice in lieu of pay or pay in lieu of notice must be given. In organizations with an Ontario payroll of $2.5 million or more, compensation based on years of service must be given to any employee who has been with the organization for five years or more.[76]

Organizations have several different options to consider when faced with a shortage of manpower. In order to determine the one that is right for them, they must weigh the various criteria, determine the degree to which each of the criteria is relevant to their situation, and choose an option that will meet its manpower needs.

Before we leave this topic, we will briefly discuss HR's role in helping manage these work arrangements.

HR Role in Managing the Work Arrangements
HR typically creates policies and procedures that govern the administration of these work arrangements and sets out the parameters under which each option can be considered. In addition, HR communicates these policies to employees, helps employees manage flexibility, and works with managers to track employee use. Also, they seek feedback from the manager to determine if these arrangements are meeting the manager's needs. HR evaluates these policies and procedures and makes the necessary changes based on feedback and any relevant legislative requirements so as to continuously improve the effective utilization of each option.

■ THE ULTIMATE LABOUR SHORTAGE—WHAT IF THERE IS A PANDEMIC?

On a final note, any discussion of labour shortages must address the "what-if" scenario. A major worldwide concern today is how organizations will manage if a pandemic strikes. It is called continuity planning and there is an overwhelming view that it is not a matter of *if*, but *when* the pandemic will strike.

It is expected that a third of the population will become ill with the pandemic, with a mortality rate of one percent for the whole population. The pandemic is expected to last several months and will come in waves of illness epidemics. These waves are expected to last from six to eight weeks.[77]

The effects from this disaster will pose a major threat to businesses' operations across the globe. Statistics suggest that businesses should plan for up to 50 percent of staff absences during the peak and these absences may last for two weeks or longer. Some employees will be stricken directly, while others will take care of sick family members. It is expected that movement and quarantine restrictions will disrupt organizations' supply chains and, as a result, they will most likely not be able to get inventory. From a macro perspective, the impact of the pandemic is expected to cost up to five percent of the GDP. In Canada, that number translates to up to $60 billion.[78]

The demand for certain business services and goods will fluctuate significantly depending on the type of good or service offered by the firm. Industries such as retail, tourism, and restaurants will be devastated, while industries such as health care will experience major demand. One report suggested a decline in demand of 17 to 67 percent in transportation and warehousing, 20 to 80 percent in arts and entertainment, and a 3 to 10 percent decline in manufacturing. On the other hand, health care could experience a 4 to15 percent increase in demand.[79]

What should organizations do? Companies, first and foremost, cannot afford to ignore this threat. They must create a pandemic preparedness plan. This plan must be designed to protect employees' health, reduce the adverse impact on business, and help the organization manage during this crisis so that it can effectively carry on its operations. It must ensure adequate control of the business operations and it must help its employees cope with this catastrophe. It is perfectly reasonable to assume that employees will have many concerns and questions and many employees will be very stressed and worried. Employees will have queries about the company's sick policies and loss of wages if the company's operations decline. As well, they will be concerned about working with others for fear that someone may be infected. They will need emotional support and information so that they can understand what the company is doing to help them.

The plan must address a number of areas, not just the labour issues. However, we will specifically focus on how an organization should manage these prolonged labour shortages. It must look at the impact of these absences. Initially, the firm must identify its essential operations and the people who are currently carrying out these activities, as well as those individuals who have the skills to carry out the essential operations. Backup employees should be in place and additional employees trained so they can provide these essential services. In addition, organizations can consider deploying others from different divisions or bringing back recent retirees. HR must review the company policies and make provisions to its sick leave policies to accommodate these longer-term absences. They must consider leveraging different types of flexible work arrangements, such as allowing employees to work from home, and have in place a robust technology support system to ensure connectivity. In addition, HR should review both their return-to-work and travel policies to curb the spread of illness.[80]

These are just some of the initiatives that organizations can take. Alcan is an example of an organization that is implementing a robust pandemic plan. In addition, several organizations are providing firms with some direction as to the crucial elements that must be in a plan. Some of these organizations are the Canadian Manufacturers and Exporters, Ontario Chamber of Commerce and Public Safety, and Emergency Preparedness Canada.[81]

CHAPTER SUMMARY

- The Canadian labour shortage problem, which is also a global issue, encompasses falling birth rates, pending retirements of the baby-boom generation, and quality of work–life balance.
- In order to manage a shortage of labour there are alternative staffing strategies that should be considered including: hiring more employees, contracting out work to another firm, developing existing employees, or leveraging existing work arrangements to optimize the way work is accomplished.
- Organizations can choose to source services from an independent vendor to help with their labour shortages. One option is to enter into a service agreement with a contractor. Another option is to outsource services to a third party. Crowdsourcing is a novel way to source services.

- The trend today is to consider a mix of staffing options, obtaining optimal flexibility by utilizing the contingent workforce. A contingent workforce is one where the workers do not have a contract for long-term employment.
- There are four elements that managers should consider in order to effectively manage the contingent worker relationship. These are administration, legal, operational, and compensation.
- There are various types of flexible work arrangements: overtime; flexible hours, schedules, and locations; flexible retirement options; and providing employees with the opportunity to transfer across the organization.
- Several factors can influence the type of staffing strategy chosen: urgency and importance, speed, quality of service, financial constraints, managerial preferences, and revocability.
- Organizations are taking initiatives in order to prepare for the possibility of a prolonged major labour shortage such as a pandemic. Companies are creating detailed plans that outline the impact on their businesses, the control of the business operations, and how to address employees' concerns.

KEY TERMS

- compressed workweek   67
- consultants   58
- contingent workforce   61
- contractor   58
- crowdsourcing   61
- flex hours   67
- flex schedules   67
- flexible retirement   68
- full-time employee   56
- labour shortage   53
- outsourcing   59
- part-time worker   57
- telecommuting   67

REVIEW QUESTIONS

1. What is meant by the term "labour shortage"?
2. What are some ways to describe a labour shortage?
3. What are the four main staffing strategies that an organization can use to manage its labour shortages?
4. What does the term "contingent workforce" mean?
5. The chapter discusses several different types of flexible work arrangements. What are they?
6. What are some of the reasons why an organization may decide to engage a contingent worker?
7. What criteria should managers consider when choosing a staffing option?

DISCUSSION QUESTIONS

1. Think about the labour shortage problem facing a company that you have worked for. How would you describe their challenges? What critical skills do you think this firm has in the future? How do you think they should address this problem?
2. Do you think any type of work would lend itself to flexible hours and schedules? Think about various industries like retail, telecommunication, and manufacturing. Which industries would have the greatest need for flexibility?
3. Outsourcing work has become very prevalent in the past decade. Do you think that an organization should outsource its HR activities? If so, which activities do you think would be most appropriate?
4. If you were the human resources manager of a mid-sized call center in Canada, what flexible policies and practices would you recommend the company institute and why? Would your answer be any different if the firm had fewer employees?

WEB EXERCISE

1. Visit the Statistics Canada website www.statcan.gc.ca/start-debut-eng.html (click on the Labour Force Survey) and/or visit www.jobfutures.ca/en/home.shtml (click on I want to know more about the world of work, then on Work Prospects). Identify the industries and occupations that are most affected by labour shortages. Compare and contrast these differences in various provinces. Are there any patterns or trends?
2. Visit the website for Human Resources and Social Development (www.sdc.gc.ca/en/ home.shtml) and review the section that addresses workplace innovation. What are some of the changes taking place in the workplace?
3. Go the website of any international newspaper such as www.theglobeandmail.com, www. nationalpost.com or www.nytimes.com and identify some recent initiatives that organizations are taking to manage their specific labour shortages. Describe these initiatives and comment on whether you think they will be effective. How is the current recession affecting these organizations?

EXPERIENTIAL EXERCISE

Determine Whether This Person Is a Contractor or an Employee

An IT company hired a worker to code a specific algorithm. The company had the worker sign a written agreement saying the person declared himself an independent contractor. The company supplied the work and asked that the person come into the office on several occasions to discuss the implications of his work with senior IT managers. During these visits, the individual was expected to work onsite using his own computer. However, on two occasions, the individual forgot to bring his laptop and had to use the company property. The individual invoiced the company, charged GST, and the company paid the person via their accounts payable system. Using the tests set out by Revenue Canada, is this person an employee or a contractor? How can the organization effectively manage this person's performance? What policies and practices do you think the organization should have in place to manage this effectively?

CASE INCIDENT

Zebra Ltd.

Zebra Ltd. is a mid-size IT organization with revenues of over $1 million. They currently employ 250 employees and are located in Canada and the U.S. Zebra is well known in the industry for providing software that helps organizations address their Internet/intranet security needs and is well respected for its strong focus on R & D activities.

Recently Zebra had a major breakthrough, inventing a new and innovative software program that will ensure better encryption of data across the web. The industry is truly impressed with this innovation. Blogs are heralding the technical genius and several articles about this company have appeared in national newspapers and IT–related publications. The CEO, Brent Talver, is very pleased with the attention as it has resulted in a significant demand for its products and services over the past several months. In fact, the vice president of sales is projecting an increase of 50 percent in new orders within the next 12 to 15 months.

Talver is wondering how the organization is going to manage the volume of work. He is thinking about the kinds of labour resources he will need, when these resources will be needed, and where. Notably he is concerned about cost and availability of some critical skill sets, especially in light of the current economic recession. His senior employees have all spoken to him about the need for more resources. The VP of sales says she needs more sales representatives, the engineering department is asking for more software engineers, HR is overwhelmed by the sudden need to hire, and new employees are complaining that they are not being signed up on the company benefit plans in a timely fashion.

Talver has asked you for advice as to what should he do to manage this volume of work.

Questions

1. What staffing options does he have available? Determine what the advantages may be for each option.
2. What specific skills would he need? How would he go about finding out this information?
3. Where should he go to find these skills? Can some skill sets be sourced locally or will the organization need to look nationally?
4. Assuming the organization is going to hire contract employees, what advice would you give the managers with respect to managing this group?

■ REQUIRED PROFESSIONAL CAPABILITIES REFERENCED IN THIS CHAPTER

5. Keeps current with emerging HR trends.
7. Audits existing HR programs to ensure they are aligned with business objectives.
8. Provides the information necessary for organization to effectively manage its people practices.
9. Evaluates the effectiveness of HR strategies, applying various measurement and assessment programs.
10. Applies business fundamentals of production, operations management, accounting and finance, information technology, marketing, and strategic planning to people management issues.
23. Develops budgets, monitors expenditures and performance of outside HR contractors and other specialists.
36. Stays current with professional knowledge.
66. Identifies the data required to support HR planning.
68. Assesses the effectiveness of people and talent management plans.
69. Maintains an inventory of people talent for the use of the organization.
70. Develops systems and processes that link the career plans and skill sets of employees with the requirements of the organization.

Labour Surplus

LEARNING OBJECTIVES

- Identify and evaluate the available methods for managing a labour surplus
- Differentiate between immediate workforce reduction strategies, attrition strategies, and work-term change strategies, including examples of each.
- Evaluate the impact of downsizing strategies on organizations and their employees
- Recognize the challenges of downsizing, and consider the methods and tools to overcome these challenges
- Understand the role of the downsizing agent, the union, and communication in effectively managing a labour surplus

■ PROFILE

Canada's Automotive Sector[1]

According to the Canadian Auto Workers union (CAW), in 2007 the Canadian auto industry directly employed 150,000 people. There are also 340,000 jobs related to the auto industry in Canada, including jobs in parts supply, materials, and services. Traditionally referred to as the "Big Three," GM, Ford, and Chrysler were the major Canadian employers in the auto industry.

The Canadian automobile sector experienced a number of structural and macroeconomic challenges that forced the industry into decline in 2008 and 2009. Canadian automakers lost $2.7 billion in 2008 and were estimated to lose an additional $2.1 billion in 2009. The industry is not projected to see profits until 2012.

Following many rounds of layoffs in the Canadian auto sector, in April 2009 the Canadian government agreed to provide up to $700 million (CDN) in funding for the industry, to help auto parts suppliers, provide consumer protection by backstopping auto warranties, and help struggling companies. Additional funding for GM, Chrysler, and Ford was contingent on demonstration of a feasible restructuring plan.

In 2009, as a precondition to government aid, the ailing Canadian auto manufacturers (Chrysler, GM, and Ford) were forced to make labour costs more competitive with nonunionized auto manufacturers in Canada (e.g., Toyota and Honda). Estimates of the hourly labour costs at the Big Three in Canada ranged from $75 to $80, whereas the wage rate for nonunionized automakers in Canada ranged from $45 to $55 per hour.

Chryslers aim was to reduce labour costs by $19 an hour. They did this by reducing break times, eliminating a cost-of-living increase, and cancelling the $600 Christmas bonus per employee. In March 2009, GM and the CAW union representing GM workers agreed to wage and benefit concessions equalling roughly $7 per hour per employee.

Another round of negotiations at GM in May 2009 resulted in concessions of an additional $15 to $16 in benefits per hour per employee. These concessions came in the form of wage freezes, increased employee health benefit costs, pension freezes, elimination of cost-of-living increases, and a reduction in paid time off. Ford concessions included a 3-year wage freeze, elimination of 40 hours of vacation pay per year, a reduction in long-term medical care, increased employee co-pays on prescription drugs, a reduction in pension entitlements, and elimination of cost-of-living adjustments.

The HR planning process provides an awareness of whether or not forecasted HR supply matches forecasted HR demand in an organization. When supply exceeds demand, a labour surplus exists. This chapter examines a number of alternative techniques to manage a labour surplus, as well as outlines relevant legal, psychological, ethical, and practical issues that can impact the success or failure of the labour surplus management initiative.

■ WHAT IS A LABOUR SURPLUS?

labour surplus

A condition when labour supply exceeds demand of labour in an organization or business unit

A **labour surplus** occurs when labour supply exceeds demand of labour in an organization or business unit. A labour surplus can be characterized using both quantity and quality dimensions. Quality refers to the skills and work-related characteristics that an employee brings to the organization. Quantity refers to the number and placement of employees throughout the organization.[2]

An organization can absorb an employment disequilibrium for some time, but they risk inflated labour costs, employee loafing, employee motivation problems, perceptions of equity among productive versus non-productive employees, and possible declining profit margins. Thus, organizations with a labour surplus usually take action to align the quantity and quality of their workforce supply with the projected workforce demand in an effort to secure continuous success of the organization.

■ MANAGING A LABOUR SURPLUS

downsizing

An intentional organizational action that affects work process, which involves workforce reduction in an effort to improve efficiency and effectiveness of the organization

In an era of globalization, hyper-competition, and rapid technological changes, workforce planning is a critical component of an organization's success. In order to ensure an optimal workforce, organizations must regularly adjust their workforce to the changing business conditions. In situations of a labour surplus, **downsizing** has emerged as a widely used workforce adjustment tool. Rather than being considered a final attempt to save a failing company (as it was in considered in the late 1970s), downsizing has become an accepted and familiar way to manage an organization. In a survey of 1,149 large Canadian companies, over 50 percent of organizations reported efforts to permanently reduce their workforce.[3]

Although downsizing has become an acceptable and frequent organizational activity, there are a limited number of supported best practices to guide management in downsizing. The scarcity of research on workforce reduction is surprising given that a firm's decision of which employees to keep has a large impact on future organizational performance.[4] Also, downsizing is considered by some researchers as the "most pervasive yet understudied phenomenon in the business world."[5]

For a clear definition of organizational downsizing, Kim Cameron identifies four main facets of the downsizing phenomena:[6]

1. Downsizing is an *intentional action*. Downsizing only occurs based on internal decisions and actions in an organization. Executives within the organization intentionally engage in downsizing activities to achieve a desired goal.
2. Downsizing usually involves a *reduction in the workforce*. Downsizing is frequently defined as an organization's deliberate intention of mass headcount reductions.[7] As a result, a number of terms are used synonymously with the term "downsizing" in academic and mass media literature. See Exhibit 4.1 for a list of such terms.
3. Downsizing focuses on *improving efficiency or effectiveness* of the organization. This can be a proactive or reactive reaction to internal and external pressures, but the primary purpose of downsizing is a targeted organizational improvement (e.g., cost containment, increase competitiveness).
4. Downsizing *affects work processes*. In situations where downsizing is not accompanied by a reduction in the amount of overall expected work, the same amount of work is expected from a smaller number of employees. This affects what work gets done and how. Alternatively, downsizing can include elimination of work, or restructuring, which can result in some form of organizational redesign.

Labour Force Reduction Methods

An organization can engage in many activities to actively reduce the size of their workforce. As outlined in Exhibit 4.2, temporary layoffs, permanent layoffs, incentives for voluntary separation, and leaves without pay all represent forms of immediate workforce reductions. Hiring freezes and

EXHIBIT	**4.1**	Synonyms Commonly Used for Downsizing

building-down	compressing	consolidation	contracting out
cut-backs	declining	de-hiring	de-layering
de-massing	de-recruiting	downscaling	downshifting
job cuts	job separation	layoff	leaning-up
optimization	rationalizing	reallocating	reassigning
redirecting	reduction-in-force	redundancies	re-engineering
rebalancing	rebuilding	redeploying	redesigning
reorganizing	resizing	restructuring	retrenching
revitalizing	rightsizing	slimming	streamlining

EXHIBIT 4.2	Methods for Managing a Labour Surplus
Immediate Headcount Reduction Strategies	• Layoffs (permanent or temporary) • Incentives for voluntary separation • Leaves without pay
Attrition Strategies	• Hiring freeze • Early retirement
Work-Term Change Strategies	• Job-sharing • Reduction in hours • Wage or benefit concessions • Retraining and/or moving employee

early retirement packages represent forms of attrition, which take longer, but do not cause an immediate disruption of the workforce. An organization can also reduce full-time employment by changing the nature of the work. Such strategies include job sharing, reduction in hours, wage concessions, and employee retraining.

In Canada, layoffs are the most widely used strategy for labour reduction. Early retirement and voluntary resignations account for about one-quarter of workforce reduction strategies, while attrition techniques are used in about one-third of labour surplus cases. The remaining organizations deploy layoffs as their primary method of responding to a labour surplus.[8] Layoffs are the norm in a variety of industries, such as automobile, forestry, financial, telecom, and pharmaceutical.[9] Given the proliferation of layoffs in Canada, this chapter begins with a detailed discussion of layoffs.

IMMEDIATE HEADCOUNT REDUCTION STRATEGIES

Immediate headcount reduction strategies focus on severing the employment relationship for non-natural reasons (e.g., attrition). These strategies result in an immediate reduction in the size

HRP IN THE NEWS[8]   **Manufacturing Sector Decline[10]**

The Canadian manufacturing industry has experienced long-term and short-term decline. In the long term, the manufacturing sectors' total share of employment in Canada fell from 19.1 percent in 1976 to 11.7 percent in 2007. Gains in productivity, foreign competition, and a move towards service activity in Canada have all contributed to the long-term decline in manufacturing in Canada.

In the short term, Canadian manufacturers are being challenged by the high dollar, falling U.S. demand, inroads by lower-cost Asian competitors, and high energy prices. Statistics Canada reports that job losses in the manufacturing sector from 2002 to 2007 exceeded 344,000. Ontario and Quebec were hit the hardest. Ontario lost about 1 in 8 manufacturing jobs, while Quebec lost 1 in 5 manufacturing jobs from 2002 to 2007.

Some argue that the decline in manufacturing in Canada is a part of a structural reorientation of Canada to become more service-oriented, similar to the shift from manufacturing to services in other industrialized nations. Others suggest that an increase in domestic demand, the improved profitability of the sector, and the eventual recovery of the U.S. economy will sustain Canada's manufacturing industry.

immediate headcount reduction strategies

Strategies for addressing labour surpluses that focus on severing the employment relationship for non-natural reasons

of the workforce. As well, through providing an organization with the ability to select which employees separate, management maintains some strategic control over who leaves and stays, helping align the quality and quantity of the workforce with long-term organizational objectives.

While allowing for control and timely reaction to a labour surplus, immediate workforce reductions may demoralize the workforce. Although widely used, due to poor planning and execution, these strategies have not proven to be effective. This has resulted in an increase in wrongful dismissal lawsuits. In addition, in Canada many employees qualify for legislated minimum notice periods and severance packages if they become unemployed due to an organization's decision to downsize. Thus, these strategies have the highest short-term expense of the alternatives available. Options for immediate reductions in headcount include layoffs, incentives for voluntary separations, and leaves without pay. Following a discussion of each of these three alternatives below, a review of applicable legislation (as of 2009) is presented.

Layoffs

layoff

A permanent or temporary separation of employees from employment for business or economic reasons

A **layoff** is defined as a permanent or temporary separation of employees from employment for business or economic reasons. This assumes that there is no cause or fault on the employee's behalf (e.g., quit, resignation, or dismissal). Instead, the separation is the result of an intentional organizational activity to reduce workforce size. The separation can be either permanent or temporary, based on organizational needs and strategic direction. **Temporary layoffs** are defined in slightly different terms in different Canadian jurisdictions, but a common interpretation refers to a layoff where employees experience a temporary interruption of the employment relationship, due to a lack of work, and with the potential for recall. **Permanent layoffs** are also called terminations in that the organization has no intent to re-establish a working relationship with the employee and there are no recall rights. In a layoff situation, the organization unilaterally selects the quantity and combination of employees to lay off, forcing the employee into unemployment involuntarily.

temporary layoff

Layoff where employees experience a temporary interruption of the employment relationship due to a lack of work and have the potential for recall

There is some discussion in downsizing research about the distinction between a layoff and competing workforce reduction strategies (e.g., early retirements, attrition).[11] Specifically, layoffs provide the option of managing a labour surplus with some strategic control. Management determines the depth of the labour reduction and targets specific employees based on criteria aligned with the organizational strategy. In addition, layoffs are a relatively quick solution, allowing an organization to modify its internal labour force based on skills and competencies, thus increasing workplace responsiveness to environmental changes. Instead of a longer-term solution, layoffs can encourage a drastic change in the business strategy, product line, or processes due to the short execution time of a layoff. In addition, layoffs may be perceived as a more cost-effective solution to changing a labour force skill set. Rather than investing in training an existing workforce, layoffs give an organization the option of replacing individuals with non-aligned skills with new employees immediately able to apply the desired skills.

permanent layoff

Layoffs where the organization has no intent to re-establish a working relationship with the employee and there are no recall rights; also called terminations

Many argue that layoffs are the primary tool used in Canada to respond to a labour surplus. In fact, the average annual layoff rate (temporary and permanent layoffs combined) in Canada ranges from 13.20 to 17.30 percent a year.[12] Put another way, even in years of strong economic growth, more than one in every eight employees experiences a layoff. For approximately one in every six workers in Canada, layoffs are not a rare event; they are part of a continuation or long string of layoffs. These individuals experience five or more layoffs within ten years.[13] For one in every three persons who experience a layoff, the layoff is a rare event, with "rare" defined as a layoff once or twice in a ten-year span. Even in the case of rare-event layoffs, an individual would expect four to eight layoffs in a 40-year career span in Canada. Even the booming petroleum industry in Canada had a 6.6 percent average annual permanent layoff rate from 2007 to 2008.[14] These statistics highlight the proliferation of layoffs in Canada.

Layoffs present considerable challenges. Employees who survive layoffs may suffer negative psychological and work-related attitudes leading to mistrust in management, lack of perceived control or involvement in the workplace, high stress levels, and reduced productivity. The negative impact of the layoff on remaining employees may hinder the organization's ability to recover and achieve desired targets. These negative aspects can be partially mitigated by managing the layoff process in a manner that is perceived as both fair and equal. The negative aspects of layoffs often lead to something commonly referred to as "survivor syndrome," a condition discussed in greater detail later in this chapter.

A survey of HR vice presidents in 1,400 companies revealed that only 36 percent of companies have a layoff policy in place. Of the organizations with a policy in place, only 64.1 percent included detailed decision rules. Furthermore, 94 percent of organizations plan and implement layoffs in less than two months.[15] This means that the vast majority of organizations execute layoffs with no policy in place and under severe time constraints. This lack of control can result in a remaining workforce that is not aligned with organizational goals and strategies. Thus, layoffs are often seen as a quick fix to a labour surplus, but one that is not well developed or executed.

Although using layoffs as a tool to manage labour surplus poses a number of challenges, they have become the strategy of choice among employers who want to quickly adapt their workforce for future HR demand. The critical challenge becomes the effective management of layoffs. Some companies such as Merge Technologies opt for a phased approach to layoffs, focusing on maintaining the morale and loyalty of employees during the change process (see Exhibit 4.3). A later section of this chapter includes many examples and guidelines on the effective execution of layoffs, as well as competing workforce reduction strategies.

Incentives for Voluntary Separations

incentives for voluntary separations

An organization's attempt to entice employees to self-select employment termination during a time downsizing in exchange for a monetary benefit (e.g., cash bonuses, retraining expenses, outplacement service); also called buyouts

Incentives for voluntary separations are also referred to as buyouts. They occur when the organization attempts to entice employees to self-select employment termination at a time of downsizing in exchange for a monetary benefit (e.g., cash bonuses, retraining expenses, outplacement services).

Organizations generally view voluntary separations as a more humane, efficient, and timely method for managing a labour surplus than involuntary layoffs. As well, the risk of an employee filing a wrongful dismissal lawsuits can be managed when employees are involved in the decision-making process during a downsizing.[17] Companies such as IBM, Air Canada, Associated Press, Nortel Networks, HP, GM, CBC, Bell South, United Airlines, Ford, and Berkeley University actively and aggressively use voluntary separation to correct workforce imbalances.

One of the challenges involved with providing incentives for voluntary separation is the risk that more than the required number of employees may participate in the plan. For example, when DuPont used voluntary separations as its downsizing strategy, it lost twice as many employees as it

---

EXHIBIT   **4.3**   A Phased Approach to Layoffs ──────────────────

When Merge Technologies Inc. announced a reduction of 28 percent of its workforce in 2006, they took a phased approach to the layoffs. Concurrent with the loss of 150 jobs in Canada, the organization planned to offshore and increase resources to its software development and support centre in India. Due to the timing and structure of the reductions, the company anticipated it would incur retention costs and stay bonuses of $1 to $2 million, as well as an additional $3 to $5 million cost in severance. That translated to an average stay bonus or retention bonus of $6,778–$13,333 per remaining employee and an average severance of $20,000–$33,333 per employee. In an effort to help to transition work from the Canadian locations to the India location, some of the staff reductions occurred immediately, while others occurred six months after the announcement. Those who remained with the organization during the transition focused on ensuring continuity and customer satisfaction until the move to the offshore location was complete.[16]

originally targeted. This can lead to a labour shortage post-downsizing. As well, the organization loses control over the types of individuals applying for the program, which can erode company-specific skills or result in the elimination of the best performers. Employees with highly transferrable skills are probably the most likely to respond to an incentive for voluntary separation, because they can "grab the money, go for a long holiday, and get another job the next day."[18]

Another challenge with encouraging voluntary separation is that the organization loses control of who exits and who remains with the company. For example, senior employees may be less likely to volunteer for separation as they may not want to jeopardize retirement plans, may have highly firm-specific skills, and therefore less transferrable skills, and may not feel that they are as mobile in the open labour market. High tenure with a company also suggests that the individual employee may have more invested with the company, such as a house near work, work friendships that extend to personal life, an attachment to the job, or vested pensions. Voluntary separations may change the composition of the workforce and the result may not be aligned with the original strategic goals of the workforce reduction.

These challenges can be overcome by providing clarity as to the number, priority, eligibility, and strategic reason for the separations. Organizations should also devise an action plan that takes into account a situation where more employees volunteer for a separation than is required. Such strategies can include retention plans or alternative forms of work-term changes.

Notice Periods and Timing of the Terminations (Layoffs and Separations)

In Canada, a person whose employment has been severed for non-disciplinary reasons is entitled to notice or pay in lieu of notice for all terminations. This includes layoffs, as well as voluntary separations at the time of a downsizing, as defined above. A few exceptions exist, such as if the employee:

1. Has not completed three consecutive months of continuous employment
2. Has terminated their own employment (e.g., quit, resigned)
3. Has been dismissed for just cause
4. Is on a layoff that does not qualify as termination of employment (e.g., contractual workers, seasonal workers, etc.)

Traditionally, the judicial system reactively determined a reasonable-notice period, based on individual employee factors—the nature of the work; skill or responsibility level; age, tenure, and training level; and an assessment of how long it would take the employee to find another suitable job. However, the incorporation of federal and provincial employment legislation resulted in a more proactive approach to the management of layoffs and terminations. As highlighted in Exhibit 4.4 and Exhibit 4.5, each jurisdiction in Canada has established minimum guidelines on statutory notice periods for layoffs and terminations (excluding the four exemptions above) as of 2009.

Exhibit 4.4 reviews mass terminations based on layoff size and the minimum notice period legislated. For example, in Quebec, a mass layoff of 10–99 employees would require that employees receive a minimum of eight weeks' notice. If the mass layoff in Quebec was for 100–299 employees, the minimum notice period increases to 12 weeks' notice. As well, to be considered a mass layoff, an organization must conduct all of the layoffs within a maximum period of time, ranging from four weeks to two months.

Although there is no standardization regarding mass layoff regulations across Canada, there are some similarities within most jurisdictions. In most jurisdictions, the larger the number of layoffs the longer the required notice period. A number of jurisdictions offer the employer the right to pay an employee in lieu of providing notice of the layoff, including British Columbia, Manitoba, New Brunswick, Newfoundland, Nova Scotia, and Ontario. British Columbia and Alberta specify that a layoff is considered a mass layoff if 50 or more employees are laid off in *a single location,* while other jurisdictions do not specify any location constraints.

When an employer lays off less than the minimum required for mass layoff, the employer must adhere to individual layoff notice periods, as highlighted in Exhibit 4.5. In these cases, minimum notice periods are directly determined by individual employee tenure (years of experience

EXHIBIT 4.4 Mass Layoffs—Minimum Notice Requirements According to Jurisdiction and Layoff Size

Jurisdiction	Maximum Time to Conduct Layoffs	Conditions for Event to Be Considered a Mass Layoff	Layoff Size 10–24	25–49	50–99	100	100–199	200–299	300	301–499	500+
Quebec	2 months	Layoffs must be due to technology or economy	8 weeks	8 weeks	8 weeks	8 weeks	12 weeks	12 weeks	12 weeks	16 weeks	16 weeks
Nova Scotia [1]	4 weeks		8 weeks	8 weeks	8 weeks	8 weeks	12 weeks	12 weeks	12 weeks	16 weeks	16 weeks
Prince Edward Island	4 weeks		8 weeks	8 weeks	8 weeks	8 weeks	8 weeks	8 weeks	8 weeks	8 weeks	8 weeks
Sakatchewan	4 weeks		4 weeks	4 weeks	4 weeks	8 weeks	12 weeks	12 weeks	12 weeks	12 weeks	12 weeks
New Brunswick [1]	4 weeks	Layoffs must affect at least 25% of employer's workforce	6 weeks	6 weeks	6 weeks	6 weeks	6 weeks	6 weeks	6 weeks	6 weeks	6 weeks
Northwest Territories	4 weeks				4 weeks	8 weeks	12 weeks	12 weeks	16 weeks	16 weeks	16 weeks
Nunavet	4 weeks				4 weeks	8 weeks	12 weeks	12 weeks	16 weeks	16 weeks	16 weeks
Yukon	4 weeks				4 weeks	8 weeks					
Federal	4 weeks	Applies only to industrial establishments			16 weeks	16 weeks	16 weeks	16 weeks	16 weeks	16 weeks	16 weeks
Manitoba [1]	4 weeks					10 weeks	10 weeks	14 weeks	14 weeks	18 weeks	18 weeks
Newfoundland [1]	4 weeks	Pay in lieu of notice must include expected overtime			8 weeks	8 weeks	8 weeks	12 weeks	12 weeks	12 weeks	16 weeks
British Columbia [1]	2 months	Can offer combination of notice and pay in lieu of notice			8 weeks	8 weeks	8 weeks	12 weeks	12 weeks	12 weeks	16 weeks
Ontario [1]	4 weeks	See Ontario Employment Standards Act			8 weeks	8 weeks	8 weeks	12 weeks	12 weeks	12 weeks	16 weeks
Alberta	4 weeks	Minimum layoff size per single location			4 weeks	4 weeks	4 weeks	4 weeks	4 weeks	4 weeks	4 weeks

Note: (1) Employers can offer employees pay in lieu of notice

---

with the company). While these are considered minimum notice periods, employees may be offered more than the minimum notice or pay in lieu of the minimum notice.

In a study of 3,359 workers who experienced a permanent layoff in Canada, it was found that regardless of the length of the notice period, workers who lost their jobs in a permanent layoff and were given advanced notice find employment sooner than workers who are not given notice. One possible explanation for this is that the employee may be more accepting of the employment relationship termination and therefore dedicate more time to job searching, rather than waiting for a recall or feeling that the layoff is a temporary one.[19]

Severance Pay   **Severance pay** is additional compensation provided to employees whose employment relationship with an organization is severed due to an organizational decision to reduce workforce size. Since employees become unemployed through no fault of their own (i.e., they were not let go for performance-related issues, they did not actively quit their job), a severance package is intended to compensate employees for loss of seniority and work-related benefits. It is provided in addition to the minimum notice period outlined above. Employees whose employment is terminated

severance pay

Additional compensation provided to employees whose employment relationship with an organization is severed due to an organizational decision to reduce workforce size

EXHIBIT 4.5   Individual Layoffs—Minimum Notice Requirements According to Jurisdiction and Employee Tenure

Jurisdiction	Layoff Size												
	> 3 mos	3–6 mos	6 mos–1 yrs	1–2 yrs	2–3 yrs	3–4 yrs	4–5 yrs	5–6 yrs	6–7 yrs	7–8 yrs	8–10 yrs	10–15 yrs	15 yrs +
Quebec		1 week	1 week	2 weeks	2 weeks	2 weeks	2 weeks	4 weeks	4 weeks	4 weeks	4 weeks	8 weeks	8 weeks
Nova Scotia	1 week	1 week	1 week	2 weeks	2 weeks	2 weeks	2 weeks	4 weeks	4 weeks	4 weeks	4 weeks	8 weeks	8 weeks
Prince Edward Island			2 weeks	2 weeks	2 weeks	2 weeks	2 weeks	4 weeks	4 weeks	4 weeks	4 weeks	6 weeks	8 weeks
Sakatchewan		1 week	1 week	2 weeks	2 weeks	4 weeks	4 weeks	6 weeks	6 weeks	6 weeks	6 weeks	8 weeks	8 weeks
New Brunswick			2 weeks	2 weeks	2 weeks	2 weeks	2 weeks	4 weeks	4 weeks	4 weeks	4 weeks	4 weeks	4 weeks
Northwest Territories	2 weeks	2 weeks	2 weeks	2 weeks	2 weeks	3 weeks	4 weeks	5 weeks	6 weeks	7 weeks	8 weeks	8 weeks	8 weeks
Nunavet	2 week	2 week	2 week	2 week	2 week	3 weeks	4 weeks	5 weeks	6 weeks	7 weeks	8 weeks	8 weeks	8 weeks
Yukon		1 week	2 weeks	2 weeks	2 weeks	3 weeks	4 weeks	5 weeks	6 weeks	7 weeks	8 weeks	8 weeks	8 weeks
Federal	2 weeks	2 weeks	2 weeks	2 weeks	2 weeks	2 weeks	2 weeks	2 weeks	2 weeks	2 weeks	2 weeks	2 weeks	2 weeks
Manitoba [1]	1 week	1 week	1 week	2 weeks	2 weeks	4 weeks	4 weeks	6 weeks	6 weeks	6 weeks	6 weeks	8 weeks	8 weeks
Newfoundland		1 week	1 week	1 week	2 weeks	2 weeks	2 weeks	3 weeks	3 weeks	3 weeks	4 weeks	4 weeks	6 weeks
British Columbia		1 week	1 week	2 weeks	2 weeks	3 weeks	4 weeks	5 weeks	6 weeks	7 weeks	8 weeks	8 weeks	8 weeks
Ontario		1 week	1 week	2 weeks	2 weeks	3 weeks	4 weeks	5 weeks	6 weeks	7 weeks	8 weeks	8 weeks	8 weeks
Alberta		1 week	1 week	1 week	2 weeks	2 weeks	4 weeks	4 weeks	4 weeks	5 weeks	5 weeks	6 weeks	8 weeks

Note: (1) Eligibility for notice begins after the 30th day of employment

---

HRP AND THE SMALL BUSINESS

Downsizing in a Small Business

Small businesses face unique challenges when in a labour surplus situation. First, the organization may not be able to use the sophisticated tools outlined in Chapter 2 to predict if a labour surplus or shortage will occur and as such they are usually unprepared for any imbalances in the workforce. A smaller firm may not have the financial resources to keep talent on board without a corresponding HR need, so they may have to execute workforce reduction quickly.

In addition, smaller organizations may not have an HR department to help guide the downsizing process, so using a HR consultant or a third-party firm specializing in downsizing may be beneficial. For example, a small business must still ensure that the termination process includes minimum notice periods and any applicable severance pay as per the minimums outlined in their jurisdiction. Through the aid of third-party experts in the field, the small business can mitigate any potential wrongful dismissal lawsuits and ensure that a labour surplus is handled in a manner that minimizes survivor syndrome.

Often, small businesses make an effort to manage labour surpluses in a way that involves the employees, usually in the form of voluntary separation incentives or unpaid leaves. Through employee participation in the decision-making process, many small-business owners can overcome the negative psychological effects of letting someone go.

due to downsizing must receive their severance pay within a week of their last employment date. With prior approval from the Ministry of Labour, organizations can develop an instalment-based severance program (up to a maximum of three years' duration) for downsized employees.

In Canada, only employees who fall under federal or Ontario jurisdictions have legislated severance packages for downsized employees. Similar to the notice period, these requirements are considered minimums and many severance packages exceed the legislated requirements. See the Appendix at the end of this chapter for the application of these regulations.

Leave Without Pay

leave without pay

A situation where an employee agrees to a temporary leave of absence without compensation while retaining seniority and, in some cases, benefits

A short-term labour surplus can be managed through a voluntary **leave without pay.** In this situation, an employee agrees to a temporary leave of absence without compensation while retaining seniority and, in some cases, benefits. Examples include leaves for educational purposes, leaves to pursue personal interests, or extended vacations. Before the leave commences, it must be authorized by the relevant authority in the organization, and the terms and length of the leave must be explicitly defined. Employees should be made aware of potential conflicts of interest with regard to their pursuits while on leave as well as any activities while on leave that would jeopardize their relationship with the organization or the organizational image. The implications of continuity of employment following the end of the leave period must also be outlined.

■ ATTRITION STRATEGIES

attrition

The natural and continuous departure of employees in an organization through methods that affect the population at large, such as quits, retirements, disabilities, and deaths

In an organizational context, **attrition** refers to the natural and continuous departure of employees in an organization through methods that affect the population at large, such as quits, retirements, disabilities, and deaths. This strategy does not involve the severance of employment by the organization, but rather relies on natural reasons for employees to exit the firm. In these cases, it is not an organization's decision to severe the employment relationship; it is an individual employee's decision. A recent Ipsos Reid poll revealed that in Canada one in every three employees plan to leave their job within the next two years.[20]

Attrition strategies can be useful in predicting and controlling compensation expenses, since voluntary or natural departures do not require legislated minimum notice period, or any severance compensation from the firm. These strategies are also useful in keeping morale high, since there is no immediate workforce reduction beyond a level that the organization normally experiences. Negative aspects of attrition strategies include the length of time it takes to correct the workforce imbalance as well as a loss of management's ability to control who leaves. Additional attrition-based strategies to manage a labour surplus include hiring freezes and incentives for early retirement.

Hiring Freeze

hiring freeze

A form of attrition where openings created from natural attrition (e.g., quits, resignations, retirements, etc.) are not filled with new employees

A **hiring freeze** is a form of attrition where no new employees are added to the organization. The organization experiences a steady and predictable form of workforce reduction in the form of natural turnover in the organization (e.g., quits, resignations, retirements, etc.). The openings that are created from this natural attrition are not filled with new employees, and thus the workforce size steadily declines. Most organizations rely on historic data to predict future attrition rates, and estimate the time required to achieve the desired headcount reductions accordingly.

Organizations can use a hiring freeze as their primary means of reducing headcount. While this strategy results in a much slower reduction in the number of employees in an organization, employees are not being forced out of a job. Thus, the negative aspects associated with immediate workforce reduction can be minimized when employing this strategy.

However, an organization may find it becomes stagnant and resistant to change if no new talent, ideas, or perspectives are brought into the organization. As well, if an organization has a skills mismatch between the existing labour force and the desired labour force of the future, a hiring freeze may not assist in aligning the talent of the organization with its desired strategy.

Many times, during a labour surplus, an organization will immediately institute a hiring freeze. If an organization does not implement a hiring freeze at a time of layoff, employees experiencing a downsizing may find it unfair that the organization is hiring to replace positions where attrition has occurred, while actively trying to reduce headcount in the organization elsewhere. This can demoralize employees.

Early Retirement

early retirements

A situation that allows employees with either long service or older age, or a combination of the two, to retire before their eligible retirement date

Early retirements are a special form of attrition that can be actively controlled. These programs are designed to allow employees with either long service or older age, or a combination of the two, to retire before their eligible retirement date. In some companies the eligible retirement date is when age and service exceed a predetermined number, while in other companies retirement eligibility is tied to age alone. When employees retire early, they draw benefits longer, so early retirement packages are usually accompanied by a proportionate reduction in retirement pay or benefits.

From the 1960s to 2005, the average retirement age in Canada fell by 6 percent, from 66 to 62 years of age. For more than 50 percent of male workers and about 30 percent of female workers, entry into retirement is triggered by downsizing activity in Canada, suggesting that early retirement is a tool used actively by organizations to reduce headcount.[21]

In Canada, labour laws do not specify the retirement age for employees, except in certain occupations such as military personnel, pilots, judges, and firefighters. By 2009, all jurisdictions in Canada will have eliminated a mandatory retirement age. However, age 65 is still the benchmark used for calculating and evaluating pensions. It is critical to note that the elimination of mandatory retirement means that an employee cannot be forced by a company to take retirement based on their age factor alone. However, in cases where an employee chooses to participate in retirement activities, they can do so. The pension amount and eligibility for government assistance relating to retirement will be dependant on an individual's age, and should be clearly understood by the employee.

In Alberta, Manitoba, Newfoundland and Labrador, Ontario, P.E.I., Yukon Territory, British Columbia, Saskatchewan, Northwest Territories, and Nunavut, mandatory retirement is considered discriminatory under the Charter of Human Rights and Freedoms. However, there are two exceptions in which mandatory retirement is not considered discrimination:

1. There is a bona fide occupation requirement (BFOR) for employees to be within a certain age. The Supreme Court of Canada rulings have developed and revised the standards that are to be applied in establishing a defence under the BFOR exception.
2. An employee's employment is terminated because he or she has reached the normal age of retirement for an employee working in positions similar to the position the employee holds.

Under these exceptions, an employer can raise a complete defence for a policy of mandatory retirement, not only at age 65, but also at lower ages.

If early retirement is used as a method to manage a labour surplus, an organization must avoid making employees feel forced to take the retirement packages as part of the downsizing activity. If an employee feels that they have been coerced or pressured into taking the early retirement option, they can file a labour complaint based on age discrimination, which is considered to be a human rights issue.

An alternative to early retirement is phased-in retirement. In this circumstance, older employees reduce their work hours in increments to eventually phase into retirement completely when they have reached eligibility. For example, if an employee is four years away from retirement, they can choose to reduce work activities by 30 percent for the first and second year, then another 30 percent in the third and fourth year. By the time they are ready to retire, they will be on a reduced workload of 40 percent, so the transition to retirement may be smoother. This reduces the size of the full-time workforce in the organization, but does not sever the employment relationship immediately.[22]

■ WORK-TERM CHANGE STRATEGIES

work-term change strategies

Strategies aimed at minimizing or removing the need for mass headcount reductions in a time of labour surplus through changing the terms of employment for multiple employees

Work-term change strategies aim to minimize or remove the need for mass headcount reductions in a time of labour surplus through changing the terms of employment for multiple employees. Assuming a shared responsibility model, some or all employees in the organization agree to reduce their hours and spreadout available work to avoid ending the employment relationship of individual employees. Examples of work-term change strategies include job sharing, reduction in hours, wage or benefit concessions, and retraining and moving employees.

An important concept in these strategies is the issue of full-time equivalents (FTE). The HR planning process can establish current and future full-time employee requirements. However, part-time workers and employees in non-traditional work arrangements must be converted to FTEs to ensure that the downsizing activity is effective in reducing the workforce.

To calculate FTE, the organization must first determine what constitutes a full-time work load. In the majority of the cases, this is calculated using hours worked per week, but alternatives can include production outputs, calls serviced, or various other workplace outputs. Second, the number of hours worked by an employee (or other measure used) is divided by the full-time work load to determine the percent of a FTE that the employee contributes.

constructive dismissal

Occurs when the employer unilaterally makes changes to the employment terms and conditions thereby altering work terms and the employee resigns within a reasonable time after these changes occur

A risk with work-term changes as a response to a labour surplus is the threat of perceived **constructive dismissal.** In some Canadian provinces, an employee is considered constructively dismissed if the employer makes changes to the employment terms and conditions (e.g., reduction in salary, work locations, hours of work, authority or position) and the employee resigns within a reasonable time after these changes occur. Therefore, work-term changes must be voluntary.

Job-Sharing

job-sharing

A work-term change strategy where the duties, compensation, and/or benefits of one position are split among two or more employees

Job-sharing is also known as job-splitting, since the duties, compensation, and/or benefits of one position are split among two or more employees. This is generally perceived as an alternative to layoffs, in that employees maintain their employment, but with reduced workloads. For example, if an organization currently employs 12 full-time administrative assistants, but only forecasts a need for 6 FTEs in the future, they can either sever the employment relationship for 6 employees or use job-sharing to ensure that all 12 employees stay with the organization under an altered work arrangement.

In this case, if the organization assumes that 36 hours is a full-time work load, they can reduce hours for each administrative assistant by 50 percent (6/12) to ensure that there are still 6 FTEs without forcing any employee out of the organization. In this case, each administrative assistant would work 18 hours as part of the job-sharing plan.

Job-sharing is complicated in an administrative sense. The organization is required to track information on two employees who combined complete the work of one full-time employee (e.g., training two employees on a new technology rather than one, managing benefits for two employees rather than one). Employees who share one full-time job equally may share benefits, work stations, and responsibilities. It may be difficult to measure performance if the job is interdependent. Thus, job-sharing is best suited for independent work, given that communication may be difficult between both parties sharing a job. Also, job-sharing may be beneficial for employees who prefer part-time hours to balance non-work commitments (e.g., school, training, family, etc.).

Job-sharing should be a voluntary reduction in hours. If work hours are reduced by 50 percent it is technically considered a layoff in some Canadian provinces. Therefore, compensation in terms of notice period and severance increases the expense of this option. As well, depending on the jurisdiction, employees who experience job-sharing may be entitled to employment insurance assistance from the government to compensate for the wage reductions associated with job-sharing.

Reduction in Hours

reduction in hours

A situation where work hours for full-time employees are reduced to less than full-time.

A **reduction in hours** involves work hours for full-time employees being reduced to less than full-time in an effort to prevent the elimination of employees from a workforce. A reduction in work hours does not involve sharing work, rather it reduces each employee's contribution to the workforce.

In Canada, a part-time employee is one who works fewer than 30 hours per week. Moving from full-time to part-time employment results in cost savings for the organization because often part-time employees have limited or reduced benefits, such as health care and pensions.

A benefit of this alternative is that the organization can determine the required reduction in hours based on HR demand. For example, if an organization has a supply of 200 production employees, but only demand for 150, the organization is free to use various options to secure an overall 25 percent reduction in hours for each employee. Assuming that production occurs eight hours a day from Monday to Friday, where a full-time workload is 40 hours, a reduction in hours can be managed in multiple ways. A few of the many options are outlined below.

Option 1: The organization can request that rather than laying off 50 employees, all employees agree to work 75 percent of a FTE. This can be accommodated through closing the plant for one and a quarter days of the week or operating Monday to Friday for six hours. This option involves all employees reducing hours from 40 per week to 30 per week.

Option 2: The organization can request that rather than laying off 50 employees, 168 of the employees agree to work 70 percent of a FTE. This option involves 168 employees reducing hours from 40 per week to 28 per week, while 32 employees continue to work 40 hours per week (full-time).

Option 3: The organization can request that rather than laying off 50 employees, 145 of the employees agree to work 65 percent of a FTE. This option involves 145 employees reducing hours from 40 per week to 26 per week, while 32 employees continue to work 40 hours a week (full-time).

Option 4: The organization can request that rather than laying off 50 employees, 100 of the employees agree to work 50 percent of a FTE. This option involves 100 employees reducing hours from 40 per week to 20 per week, while 100 employees continue to work 40 hours a week (full-time).

Note: Reduction in hours should be voluntary to avoid charges of constructive dismissal.

Wage or Benefit Concessions

In cases where downsizing activities have been triggered by a reduction in profits of the organization, a reduction in wages or benefits can increase profitability of the organization (profit equals revenue minus costs).

Organizations that engage in downsizing as an attempt to reduce costs can reduce labour expenses by asking for wage or benefit concessions from the workforce instead of engaging in headcount reductions. When concessions are requested, organizations must be clear as to how long and under what circumstances the wage or benefit reduction will last. Cuts should also be evenly distributed throughout the organization so that employees perceive the concessions as fair. In unionized organizations, concessions on items outlined in the collective bargaining agreement must be negotiated with the union. Also, at times of profitability, the organization should consider increasing wages or benefits accordingly.

Due to a recall of pet foods in which the company's product was linked to the death of several cats and dogs, Menu Foods Income Fund experienced a shortage of demand for products, rising inventory levels, and a need to contain expenses. As a result, the organization initiated downsizing. When the organization announced a reduction of up to 138 jobs, executives at the firm simultaneously announced they would take wage concessions. The CEO, Paul Henderson, agreed to a 22-percent reduction in base salary, while executives in the organization committed to a 17-percent cut, and Board members agreed to a 20-percent wage concession.[23]

HRP AND STRATEGIC PARTNERS

A Case of a Poorly Managed Labour Surplus

MTD Products Canada is a producer of outdoor power equipment (e.g., lawn mowers, snow blowers, etc.). Due to weather conditions, the company experienced excess snow blower inventory, a product produced at the Kitchener, Ontario plant. As a result, the need for production was significantly reduced. Management approached the union (Canadian Auto Workers Local 1524) and requested the labour surplus be handled using a reduction in hours and wage concessions. The organization wanted wage reductions from workers of approximately $4.00 per hour, and also felt that the demand for the product only warranted that the company be open eight months of the year, rather than year-round. In addition, the organization would still have to reduce 180 of the 500 jobs. The union had a policy forbidding wage concessions, and after many meetings, a consensus between management and the union could not be reached. Shortly after unsuccessful negotiations on wage concessions and work-term changes, MTD Products Canada announced that they had no option but to close the manufacturing operations in the Kitchener plant, resulting in the loss of all manufacturing jobs in the plant, affecting more than 400 workers.[24]

Retraining/Moving Employees

If an organization has a labour surplus in one unit and a labour shortage in another, or a skills mismatch between current and desired skills, retraining or moving employees may be a useful tactic to manage the labour surplus. Employees see these options as an organizational commitment to maintaining the employment of the labour force, and react positively to these options, when they are executed correctly. Another benefit of these options is that they allow the organization to hold on to a targeted group of employees, thus management can maintain some control over the internal workforce composition. However, each method presents some unique challenges, as outlined below.

Retraining employees allows an organization to keep the best and brightest employees. In this scenario the company develops individuals by exposing them to new skills that align with the organization's new strategic direction. Retraining employees is a longer-term option though, and the cost and time of retraining must be accounted for in the HR plan.

Moving employees involves transferring employees from a unit with a labour surplus to a unit with a labour shortage. This can be problematic if the individual skill set is not aligned with the needs of their new jobs, if there is a culture mismatch between the jobs, or if the move feels forced, which could result in the employee not feeling loyal to the new department or not being as productive in the new group. Employees in dual-income families or with non-work related commitments to a location may be reluctant to move; therefore this option might not be realistic for some employees. As well, the cost of relocation (e.g., moving expenses, housing assistance, etc.) may be less than the cost of severance. Thus, a complete cost-benefit analysis is needed to determine if this is a desirable option.

■ MIXED METHODS OF DOWNSIZING

Organizations are not limited to selecting only one strategy to execute a downsizing. In fact, many organizations adopt multiple strategies to achieve the desired reductions. Here are some examples:

- In April 2007, Stelco Inc. announced 300 job cuts to the Hamilton, Ontario plant, as a result of moving hot-strip processing to another location. The 300 cuts involved a combination of retirements, layoffs, and buyouts.[25]
- In July 2007, Canfor Corp. announced layoffs of 130 employees at a mill in Mackenzie, British Columbia. The cuts came from a mix of layoffs, early retirements, and employee relocation activities.[26]
- In November 2007, Casino Windsor laid off 229 employees due to a 30 percent drop in revenue. In total, 23 managers were terminated, 170 employees were laid off, and another 36 employees were given incentives for voluntary separation.[27]

■ THE CHALLENGES OF DOWNSIZING AND METHODS TO OVERCOME THEM

When people factors aren't considered during downsizing, the desired cost reductions and increased efficiencies do not materialize. Empirical evidence suggests that layoffs have a negligible impact on firm profitability. More than half of the companies that executed layoffs indicated that they were soon understaffed, almost 44 percent reported difficulties meeting deadlines, and 26 percent stated that business growth was hindered.[28] Only 46 percent of the companies that underwent mass layoffs reached their expected reduction targets. Barely 32 percent increased their profit to anticipated levels, only 22 percent reached their productivity targets, and 21 percent met their expected return on investment.[29] A study of Fortune 100 companies revealed that financial performance actually declined following the layoff efforts of these firms.[30]

One explanation for the lack of success stems from how the organization decides which employees to layoff.[31] In a four-year study that collected 2,500 questionnaires from companies in the U.S. that downsized, the way in which downsizing occurred was found to be more important in predicting effectiveness of the activity than the size of the workforce reduction or the anticipated cost savings.[32]

Too often companies are focused on reducing headcount with no consideration for the qualifications of the employee mix that remains. Firms found that they laid off the wrong employees, which increased the anticipated costs of the layoffs.[33] Researchers ascertained that the risk of turnover might be the highest among firms' most valuable employees.[34] Organizations trying to downsize poor-performing employees were finding that the employees who worked well were the ones leaving during layoffs.[35] As a result, the company's potential to recover is damaged because the best qualified people may not remain with the organization.[36]

psychological contract theory

Theory suggesting that mutual obligations form during an employee's tenure of employment, and the employer – employee relationship is founded on the expectation that each party will fulfill their obligation

Psychological contract theory suggests a mutual relationship exists between employees and the organization that employs them. There are mutual obligations that form during the tenure of employment and the relationship is founded on the expectation that each party will fulfill their obligations. The employee is expected to perform the functions of the job, work hard, and assist in accomplishing organizational goals. The organization is expected to provide stable employment, safe work environments, and competitive wages and benefits.

During a time of downsizing, employees perceive that the psychological contract has been violated, since the organization is no longer fulfilling its expectation to provide stable employment and a positive work environment.[37] Thus, the employee's commitment to organizational goals, completing work, and working hard are compromised. Almost three out of four senior executives report problems with employee morale and trust post-downsizing.[38] The result is an aversion to risk, innovation, and flexibility.[39]

To compound this issue, the majority of organizations are also finding that survivors of downsizing have high levels of stress, job dissatisfaction, mistrust in management, and lowered productivity. Five years after the layoffs, survivors still suffered the same psychological and work attitude issues that they experienced during the downsizing, including a sense of unfairness, anger towards top management, one-way loyalty, insecurity, and a general lack of motivation.[40] In the literature, this phenomenon is widely known as survivor syndrome.

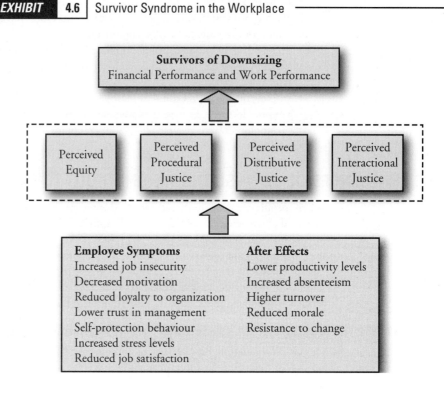

EXHIBIT 4.6 Survivor Syndrome in the Workplace

Survivors of Downsizing
Financial Performance and Work Performance

| Perceived Equity | Perceived Procedural Justice | Perceived Distributive Justice | Perceived Interactional Justice |

Employee Symptoms
Increased job insecurity
Decreased motivation
Reduced loyalty to organization
Lower trust in management
Self-protection behaviour
Increased stress levels
Reduced job satisfaction

After Effects
Lower productivity levels
Increased absenteeism
Higher turnover
Reduced morale
Resistance to change

survivor syndrome

A condition in which survivors of down-sizing struggle with negative psychological states and work atti-tudes towards the organization

Survivor syndrome is a condition in which survivors of downsizing struggle with negative psychological states and work attitudes, such as anger towards the organization, guilt about sur-viving the downsizing, increased job insecurity, lower morale, uncertainty about their future with the organization, uncertainty about organizational expectations, increased anxiety about work, an increased workload, lower job satisfaction, and decreased organizational commitment. Survivor syndrome is summarized in Exhibit 4.6.

Due to loss of morale and the violation of the psychological contract, survivors are more loyal to themselves than to the organization. Thus, organizational recovery post-downsizing may be hindered by survivor syndrome. There are four main constructs used to mitigate survivor syndrome—perceived equity, perceived procedural justice, perceived distributive justice, and per-ceived interactional justice. A high perception of equity and justice minimizes the negative atti-tudes and psychological state of the employee, which increases performance of the survivors.

Other factors play a significant role in determining the reactions of survivors, and ultimately their performance in helping the organization heal post-downsizing. They include: the people involved in the downsizing process, how change is communicated, and what support services are offered to employees affected by the downsizing.

A survey of over 1,200 executives and managers found that 82 to 88 percent of organizations do not consider or implement programs aimed at boosting the performance and confidence of survivors post-downsizing.[41]

Equity Theory

Equity theory postulates that people compare their inputs (e.g., abilities, effort, experience, and education) and their outcomes (e.g., pay, promotion, layoffs, and other effects) with the inputs and outcomes of other people.[42] Suggestions have been made that a decrease in self-esteem may

equity theory

Theory that people compare their inputs (e.g., abilities, effort, experience, and education) and their outcomes (e.g., pay, promotion, layoffs, and other effects) with the inputs and outcomes of other people

increase the work performance of survivors due to feelings of guilt (e.g., positive inequity) about the manner in which downsizing was conducted.[43] If survivors identify closely with leavers, then equity perceptions lead to an increase in negative side effects associated with survivor syndrome. The issue of resentment has been researched as an attribute of equity. Resentment illustrates the equity issues in terms of real and symbolic sacrifices by management and individual employees.[44]

The ratio of exchange is the measure of equity, determined by the amount of a person's input compared with their outcomes. Failure of managers and human resources professionals to maintain consistency with inputs and outcomes of individual employees results in low job performance, lower levels of management trust, as well as higher rates of absenteeism and turnover. Although this is perceptual and grounded in the employee's sense of comparability with co-workers, perceptions of internal equity can affect the survivor's association with the perceived fairness of the firm post-layoff. For example, if employees with high input (e.g., performance, experience, etc.) are laid off, survivors may perceive low levels of equity at work.

Organizational Justice

organizational justice

Employee perception of justice that is driven by perceived fairness in the outcomes and processes of organizational change, including procedural justice, distributive justice, and interactional justice

Similar to equity theory, **organizational justice** is driven by perceived fairness in the outcomes and processes of organizational change. Where equity theory compares the input with the perceptions of the outcomes, organizational justice examines employee's relationships with managers, departments, and the organization as a whole. Employees surviving a downsizing make judgements about balance and correctness of the outcomes. Initially, the topics of distributive justice and procedural justice dominated in academic research, however over the years the topic of interactional justice has also progressed. How survivors and leavers react to a downsizing will be affected by perceived organizational justice at all three levels: procedural, distributive, and interactional.

procedural justice

The perception that the procedures used to make downsizing decisions are fair

Procedural Justice   **Procedural justice,** in this context, is the perception that procedures used to make downsizing decisions are fair. Decision-making processes with high predictability of change and merit-based decisions are perceived by employees as fair and less threatening. If the decision-making process is political or random, the perceptions of procedural unfairness create negative psychological side effects. Violations of procedural justice are focused on the perceived legitimacy or consistency of decision-making factors. For example, an organization that gives notice for the first set of layoffs, but not the following layoffs, is seen as having procedural injustice.

There are six recommended rules for procedural justice:[45]

1. Consistency—Over time, across people
2. Bias suppression—Personal self-interest and blind allegiance to narrow perceptions should be prevented
3. Accuracy—Decision must be based on good information and informed opinions
4. Correctability—Opportunity must exist to modify or reverse a decision based on inaccurate information
5. Representativeness—Allocation process must represent areas of concern for all subgroups or individuals
6. Ethicality—Allocation process must be compatible with prevailing moral ethics

distributive justice

The perception of outcome fairness

Distributive Justice   **Distributive justice** is the perception of outcome fairness. In this context, distributive justice refers to the perceptions of fairness resulting from downsizing outcomes. Distributive justice is difficult to apply to this setting, since entire departments or teams may be eliminated at one time.

Usually, corporations announce workforce reductions first, and then look internally for sources of downsizing. The workforce reduction decision-making procedure usually takes less than two months.[46] Downsizing is also often done indiscriminately, reducing headcount rather than searching broadly for waste. When the focus of downsizing is reducing headcount, employees need to know that the magnitude and outcomes of the layoff (e.g., size, locations, etc.) are legitimate and fair. Perceptions of fairness and justice regarding workforce reduction decisions are important in both the reaction of survivors and of leavers.

interactional justice

Justice related to the perceived fairness level between employee and management relations on an individual scale

Interactional Justice   **Interactional justice** is a relatively new field in academic research that explores the perceived fairness level between employee and management relations on an individual scale. Managers are in a unique position during unstable times since they are in a dual manager–labour position. The executive decision-makers decide what actions must be taken at the firm level, while managers may decide actions at a departmental, group, team, or business-unit level. Work demands increase significantly for line managers during a layoff.[47] As well, managers are dealing with their own emotions of anger, anxiety, cynicism, resentment, resignation, and desire for retribution at the time of a workforce reduction.[48]

In the absence of interactional justice, the lower the level of control an employee feels they have (or the higher the level of control management has) during a layoff time, the more negative psychological side effects they endure, according to survivor studies. Thus, to maintain control of the downsizing, while minimizing survivor syndrome, interactional justice must be considered. Research has shown that management or supervisors have the largest impact in making or breaking employee's reactions to a transition.

Downsizing Agents

downsizing agents

Those with decision-making authority who assist in and carry out decisions about who will stay and who will leave during a time of downsizing

Downsizing agents include those with decision-making authority who assist in and carry out decisions about who will stay and who will leave during a time of downsizing. Generally, these include members from human resources management, department managers, line managers, and supervisors.

Human Resources Management   The HRM team is a critical component of the downsizing decision. HRM usually determines the extent of the labour surplus, plans and executes action to be taken, and establishes the timing of the downsizing based on an HR planning process. Through understanding the existing staffing situation, HR managers can assess the quality (e.g., knowledge, skills, abilities, competencies) and quantity (at each unit) of employees required to support an organization's future workforce needs.

The HRM team can provide guidance on downsizing alternatives, the management of exits and survivors, compensation schemes for employees affected by the reductions, the possibility of retraining or labour movement within the organization, and any transitional issues that need to be addressed.

The HRM team can also assist with determining the best selection criteria for the downsizing. Options include job analysis results, needs assessment, seniority, reverse seniority, skill levels, job performance, and plant or business unit locations, to list just a few.

Department or Line Managers and Supervisors   During employment, direct and indirect communication and interaction between a manager and their employee promotes loyalty and trust and increases job satisfaction. During a layoff, content and consistency in a manager's explanation for a layoff has a positive effect on survivor attitudes. Honest and open communication between the two parties increase an employee's sense of security and belief in the fact that they will be kept informed of future changes in the organization.

As the downsizing agent, managers are feared but also depended on by their employees to guide them through the downsizing. Managers are directly expected to manage negative employee emotions during a downsizing, while at the same time, they are trying to deal with their own negative emotions. Employees may expect managers to provide information about the downsizing that managers may or may not be privy to. When unable to provide guidance during a downsizing, managers may be perceived to be hiding information or unwilling to support employees. As well, managers must play the role of the "grim reaper," to help select and execute the downsizing of employees. At the same time, the employees and management may have formed strong working relationships and friendships, a situation that increases the stress and guilt of the manager during these events.

Often, the first question that an employee will ask is "Why me?" As well, affected employees may demonstrate their grief, communicate their confusion or surprise, or engage in hostile behaviour. The managers are directly exposed to these reactions and are expected to cope with these workplace toxins at the time of a downsizing.

Post-downsizing, managers are held accountable for re-energizing the workforce, maintaining employee morale and productivity, being change agents, brokering communication between the organization and the employee, managing the rumour mill, and at times, having fewer workers do roughly the same amount of work.

As a result, it has been found that managers suffer from the same negative work attitudes and psychological states found in survivor syndrome before, during, and after downsizing events.

HRP AND ETHICS

Ethical Challenges During a Labour Surplus

The decision to reduce the size of the workforce in a labour surplus situation is usually a strategic decision made by top management. The management team has two main stakeholders with competing obligations at a time of a labour surplus.

First is the moral obligation to conduct business with the best interest of the firm in mind, with the ultimate goals of short-term and long-term sustainability. The decision to downsize is largely based on reducing costs, maximizing productivity, and eliminating redundancies in the workplace. In this sense, management teams set aside personal concerns and act in a manner best aligned with their fiduciary duty to shareholders and business owners.

Second is an obligation to maintain employee rights. Based on psychological contract theory (as discussed in this chapter), employees perform the functions of the job in return for workplace security. When management unilaterally makes the decision to change the size, composition, or work terms of its labour force, employees feel that the organization's ethical responsibility to protect the worker is violated.

In a downsizing situation, this violation can occur with the disclosure of information. Management may be caught between the need to disclose only selected information to the employee, to aid in the recovery of the organization, and the employee's sense of entitlement to full disclosure of information regarding the downsizing.

In addition, severance pay is a topic with inherent conflict for management. Management may feel obligated to provide the minimum possible severance package to exiting employees in order to reduce the costs of the labour surplus, and at the same time may feel obligated to provide the maximum severance package to exiting employees since these workers became unemployed through no fault of their own.

The timing of the workforce imbalance correction may also be problematic. Management is again torn between two competing demands. First, there is the obligation to

Continued

HRP AND ETHICS Ethical Challenges During a Labour Surplus

make labour force changes as soon as possible to help the organization refocus and recover. Second, there is the obligation to avoid announcements near holidays, something that is perceived as unethical by employees, and provide advanced notice to employees of any changes.

The topic of advanced notice is also the subject of much debate. If minimum advanced notice is given (e.g., two weeks, as legislated), the risk is that employees may feel unprepared for unemployment and may feel that the organization has not demonstrated a commitment to its employees. In contrast, in the case where minimum notice periods have been exceeded (e.g., 30 days' notice of layoff), employees may no longer be productive, may show higher levels of absenteeism, and may engage in counterproductive behaviours (e.g., gossiping, sabotage, theft).

The challenge for management teams is to conduct the workforce reduction efforts in a manner that is perceived as aligned with the team's ethic responsibility to the organization and shareholders, as well as the moral obligation to the employees. The inherent conflict associated with the decision to change the size, composition, or work-term changes of the internal labour force present a unique challenge for management.

Communication with Employees During a Labour Surplus

During a time of organizational change, communication includes not only the message that is sent to the employee, but also the way that the message is conveyed. The manner in which something is said is just as important as the content of what is said. Yet, at the time of downsizing, horror stories about communication are common. One company videotaped a message and sent it to the employees' homes. Another company announced the names of laid-off personnel one by one over a PA system as their primary method of informing employees of termination. Another company sent out email notifications to the affected employees, insinuating that the employee was responsible for the layoff.[49]

In 2007, when Dell laid off over 50 middle managers, they came to the employees individually and gave them the layoff notice. Affected middle managers were given the choice to either work on the call-centre lines or take seven weeks of severance pay. Immediately following this discussion, employee badges were taken and laid-off employees were escorted to the door. Downsized employees were not allowed to go back to their desk for personal items or to say goodbye to colleagues.[50] A downsizing process that involves employees being immediately escorted off the premises without an opportunity to bid farewell to colleagues causes downsized employees to feel a loss of self-esteem and dignity. This has been found to negatively influence their ability to cope with the job loss and secure re-employment.

Although most jurisdictions in Canada mandate that the layoff notice must be provided to the employee in writing, there are no additional guidelines as to the appropriate timing, method, and execution of downsizing communication. When CanJet decided in 2006 to discontinue regularly scheduled flights and move exclusively to the chartered business, almost 450 jobs were eliminated. The company left layoff notices and severance package information in staff mailboxes around September 6, with a deadline of September 12 to either sign the packages or risk losing severance pay.[51] Generally, emails, letters, and bulletins are considered too impersonal a way to communicate emotion and explanations. Instead, it is better to meet face to face. This allows for two-way communication and gives employees the opportunity to ask questions and get clarification.

In a face-to-face meeting, verbal and non-verbal communication can reinforce the same message. If a manager uses positive and sympathetic body language, employee uncertainty is minimized.[52] When Compaq Computers laid off 15 percent of its workforce in one location (roughly 2,000 employees), it held a mandatory downsizing training session for managers. In this four-hour session, management was explained the rationale for the downsizing, and provided clear instructions on how to conduct the meeting to communicate the change to employees. They were given macro-level information (such as company finances and competitive environment), a list of frequently asked questions, and resources to pass on to the employees during these meetings (e.g., information about outplacement and counselling services). Within a year, the company met the organizational goals that triggered the downsizing, and they attributed a large portion of their success to the employee's willingness to accept the change to the organization and realign themselves with the organization's new strategy.

However, managers are rarely given training on the execution of these meetings; therefore, face-to-face meetings may be missing the desirable elements outlined above. In these meetings, managers should be firm and clear, as well as apologetic. The meeting should provide severance package and benefits information, timelines, information about any outplacement services, and written notice.

For large or geographically dispersed companies, company-wide town hall–style meetings with an explanation by CEO and senior management, followed by an open question-and-answer period are a good idea. The question-and-answer period should encourage employees to address any concerns and ask for clarification as needed. Although it may be difficult to answer all questions, responses should be clear and honest. If the answer is not known, it is best to say so rather than making suggestions on the spot. Any communication during a town hall meeting can be interpreted as a commitment to a solution later by the employees. Communication should be an ongoing process after the initial meeting. The organization can use websites or newsletters to distribute information and updates after the fact.

Employees should be encouraged to deal with the grief (i.e., speaking with supervisors or having counsellors available), rather than made to feel guilty about the layoff as in the previous examples. As well, the message should focus on transition and the ultimate aim of the downsizing, rather than focusing on intended results by a specified date.[53]

Communication should remain open even after the downsizing has occurred so as to better help the organization recover. It has been suggested that a clear and organizational therapeutic process supports survivors post-downsizing, including re-establishment of the psychological contract, as outlined in Exhibit 4.7.[54] By engaging in communication and clarification as outlined in this process, new approaches and expectations of both the employees and the organization can be identified. Rather than being perceived as unilateral one-way communication, this is a mutual process between leaders and followers that can help rebuild relationships and trust in the workplace.

Outplacement Services to Downsized Employees

outplacement services

Services that focus on preparing the terminated employee for post-downsizing activity (e.g., job search, job-loss coping, etc.), with the ultimate aim of minimizing risk to all parties and helping candidates return to work quickly

Outplacement services includes career counselling (including assistance with the job search process, training and development information, and labour market information), legal counselling (including assistance in understanding employee rights), psychological assistance (including job-loss coping mechanisms and counselling), and financial planning assistance (including information about employment insurance and budgeting) to candidates before, during, and after the termination of employment. The process focuses on preparing the terminated employee for post-downsizing activity (e.g., job search, job-loss coping, etc.), with the ultimate aim of minimizing risk to all parties and helping candidates return to work quickly. Studies have confirmed that leavers' access to information about procedures, outplacement, and redeployment are seen as important by the survivors.

These services are generally provided by a specialized outside firm, and the employer pays the fees for terminated employees to gain access to the firm's resources. Examples of services are outlined in Exhibit 4.8. Outplacement services can be offered by an organization to

| EXHIBIT 4.7 | The Organizational Therapy Process |

Communication	Clarification
Frequently and openly talking to employees • explain what is taking place and why • provide ongoing communication • be a visible leader who is willing to engage in personal communication **Facilitating expression behaviours** • give individuals a chance to talk about what they are feeling and why • include Employee Assistance Plans (EAP) as a potential third-party counsellor **Engage in deep listening** • promote and encourage feedback non-defensively	**Clarify strategic direction** • employees want to know where they fit in **Clarify performance expectations** • what results are expected **Clarify key operating values and ground rules** **Clarify new contract expectations** • identify new psychological contract **Clarify new reward** • intrinsic and extrinsic **Clarify employee expectations**

| EXHIBIT 4.8 | Outplacement Services Available to the Recently Unemployed |

Access to private offices and workstations

Administrative support and equipment

Alternative job-search strategies; networking, Internet search, etc.

Alternative lifestyle planning

Career redirection

Coping with job loss and unemployment

Employee rights information

Financial consultation

Financial planning and budgeting training

Guidance using recruitment and placement agencies

Information about government support for unemployed persons

Interest and aptitude assessments

Interview and negotiation preparation

Job placement

Job search assistance

Labour market information

On-site termination support

Personality assessments

Personalized project portfolio

Referral and networking services

Résumé preparation

Retirement counselling

Time-management skill development

Transferable skills analyses

Transition counselling

Self-employment options

Spousal/partner support

Stress reduction workshops

exiting employees; however, employee participation is voluntary. Fees for the service are typically 10–15 percent of the candidate's salary, or group packages (usually a day session of with a maximum of 15 employees) can be organized for $1,000–$3,000 per day per group.

There are many benefits of providing outplacement services during a downsizing. For one, it helps maintain a positive and responsible organizational image, since provision of outplacement services highlights an organization's commitment to the well-being of the employees and the community. It preserves the goodwill of terminated employees who may be advocates of the organization to others (including potential new hires) or may return to the organization in a future time of labour shortage. Outplacement services also reduce stress and guilt of the manager communicating the downsizing, since they are able to offer support to exiting employees. Retention is improved with the use of outplacement services, given that survivors feel that the organization is demonstrating a commitment to its employees and are supportive and fair to those employees affected by the downsizing. Employee morale and productivity is also significantly increased with the use of outplacement services, as these services demonstrate that the company values employees.

In a survey by Murray Axmith and Associates of 693 Canadian firms that conducted downsizing, 63.9 percent of firms provided some form of outplacement services to executives, 53.5 percent offered outplacement services to managers/supervisors, 34.2 percent of professional/technical staff were offered outplacement services, and 20.6 percent of salaried employees were offered outplacement services. It was determined that the higher the position of the downsized employee in the organization, the longer and more comprehensive their outplacement package. Additional factors have a marginal effect on length and comprehensiveness of the outplacement service, including external labour market conditions and an employee's position, age, salary, and health.[55]

■ UNION IMPACT DURING A TIME OF LABOUR SURPLUS

In unionized organizations, management may not have discretion in determining who is affected by the downsizing. Downsizing agents must be sure to review the collective bargaining agreement (CBA) prior to, during, and after downsizing activity. The CBA may have explicit rules in place about layoffs, such as selection criteria, rules for retraining, organizational notice periods, bumping rights, etc. In many cases, when the CBA includes such information, it often exceeds minimum standards legislated. Since the CBA is a legal document outlining terms and conditions of employment between the organization and those covered by the union, the company must follow the terms of the CBA. In manufacturing in Canada, about 55 percent of the jobs lost from 2002 to 2007 were in unionized positions.[56]

Bumping rights are intended to protect employees with seniority in the company by allowing senior employees affected by job termination due to downsizing the right to transfer to jobs held by employees with less seniority. The notion originated from the perception that internal candidates must compete with each other on the basis of capability, performance, and qualifications. In cases where these factors are relatively equal between the two candidates, seniority becomes the determining factor. Thus, an employee who is downsized, but capable of moving to another job (usually a lateral move or downward one), can displace an employee with equal capabilities, but less seniority.

bumping rights

A right that allows senior employees affected by job termination due to downsizing to transfer to jobs held by employees with less seniority

Bumping rights are generally met with some resistance by management, given that they impede efficiency in that arbitrators have ruled that senior employees with no training are able to bump less senior employees with training. In cases where plant-wide layoffs are based on a seniority system, arbitrators also agree that even in cases where bumping rights are not explicit in a CBA, such a right is implied.[57] From an organizational perspective, bumping rights complicate the execution of the downsizing since it may be unclear about the limitations of bumping and the implications on maintaining control of who stays and who leaves.

An example of the complications of bumping can be found in Air Canada's 2007 decision to downsize 100 maintenance mechanics at their Winnipeg location. The Thursday announcement followed an announcement made on Monday of the same week regarding the downsizing of 680 maintenance mechanics in Vancouver. The Vancouver announcement allowed mechanics affected by the downsizing to bump less senior mechanics out of the Winnipeg location. Although 220 of the Vancouver maintenance mechanics wanted to move to Winnipeg for work, there was only space for 100. As a result, 100 of the Winnipeg mechanics were laid off, many with the option of moving to another city (Ottawa, Toronto, or Montreal) to bump less-senior employees.[58] The collective agreement allows employees targeted for a layoff 72 hours to decide if they want to move to another city and bump a less senior employee in the same or similar job, and then the affected employee is given another two weeks to make relocation arrangements. One of the challenges that Lorne Hammerberg, a spokesperson for the International Association of Machinists and Aerospace Workers union, recognized was that the most senior employees would be the most desperate to bump employees in another city, in order to preserve their pensions and maintain employment for the few years they have left until retirement.[59]

In conclusion, the methods outlined above allow an organization to equalize their forecasted HR supply with demand, including immediate workforce reduction strategies, attrition, and changing work terms.

CHAPTER SUMMARY

- A labour surplus exists when the supply of labour exceeds the demand for labour, which can occur with either the quantity of labour or the quality of labour. HR planning includes responding to a labour surplus by taking action to ensure labour equilibrium exists.

- At the general level, downsizing is considered an active organizational activity undertaken with the intent of reducing headcount. Therefore, at a macro level, HR and management respond to a labour surplus with downsizing activity. The methods for managing a labour surplus include immediate headcount reduction strategies (e.g., layoffs, incentives for voluntary separation, leaves without pay); attrition strategies (e.g., hiring freezes, early retirements); or work-term change strategies (job-sharing, reduction in hours, wage or benefit concessions, retraining/mobility).

- An organization considering employee separations as a method to respond to a labour surplus must comply with legislation and regulations. Legislation relating to the notice period and severance of layoffs and employer-initiated (non-disciplinary) separations vary significantly across jurisdictions in Canada.

- The response to a labour shortage does not have to be singular. Instead, a mix of methods can be used to secure the desired number of headcount reductions.

- A significant challenge in responding to a labour surplus is the effect of the downsizing activity on the employees remaining with the organization post-downsizing. Commonly referred to as survivor syndrome, remaining employees experience negative psychological and work attitudes after downsizing. These can be mitigated by demonstrating justice and equity in the downsizing process, but many organizations overlook the impact of the downsizing activity on the survivors. Thus, their ability to recover from the reduction is significantly hindered.

- Downsizing agents have a responsibility to effectively communicate with employees and unions during a labour surplus. As well, union presence may limit an organization's ability to respond to a labour surplus. Contracts that include bumping rights present a unique challenge that HR planners must be prepared for.

KEY TERMS

- attrition   86
- bumping rights   99
- constructive dismissal   88
- distributive justice   93
- downsizing   79
- downsizing agents   94
- early retirements   87
- equity theory   93
- hiring freeze   86
- immediate headcount reduction strategies   81

- incentives for voluntary separations   82
- interactional justice   94
- job-sharing   88
- labour surplus   78
- layoff   81
- leave without pay   86
- organizational justice   93
- outplacement services   97
- permanent layoff   81

- procedural justice   93
- psychological contract theory   91
- reduction in hours   89
- severance pay   84
- survivor syndrome   92
- temporary layoff   81
- work-term change strategies   88

REVIEW QUESTIONS

1. What are the causes for the prevalence of downsizing in the Canadian economy, and what challenges or opportunities does this present for HR planners?
2. Identify and describe eight of the options available for an organization with a labour surplus.
3. What is the role of the downsizing agent and the challenges that a downsizing agent experiences?
4. What communication techniques are recommended for an organization at the time of downsizing?
5. What legislation impacts notice times and severance pay in Canada? Outline how this legislation is consistent and how is it different.
6. What is survivor syndrome and how is it affected by perceived equity and perceived justice?
7. What types of services are typically included during outplacement? How do these benefit the employee?

DISCUSSION QUESTIONS

1. You are a supervisor for a team of six employees in a medium-sized manufacturing firm. This morning, an announcement was made in the local newspaper that your company will be eliminating 20 percent of its positions through layoffs and incentives for voluntary departures. You get to the plant and notice that employees are avoiding you and appear anxious. At the moment you don't have any more information about the layoffs. What would you do? Who would you communicate with, what would the message be, and how would it be delivered? Provide a rationale for your decision.
2. An employee reporting into you recently received a pay raise and is now thinking about buying a larger house. She discloses that she will just be making enough to make all of her

payments. You have information that the organization may conduct a downsizing next quarter. Do you tell her or not? What are the inherent assumptions in your position and the position of your subordinate?

3. Assume your organization has asked you to help facilitate a training session for managers on how to effectively downsize. What would you include in the process and why? What materials might you need for this process? What obstacles or challenges should you address?

4. Review the ethical challenges section of this chapter. Given your newly formed expertise in managing a labour surplus, what would you recommend management do to overcome the inherent conflicts associated with organizational demands and employee perceptions?

WEB EXERCISE

Methods of Downsizing

The Canadian Business and Current Affairs (CBCA) database is one of Canada's largest databases of business and current event news. Most local libraries, colleges, and universities offer access to the searchable full text of the CBCA as a source of information on current issues.

Using some of the common terms highlighted in Exhibit 4.1 for downsizing (e.g., downsizing, layoff, job cuts, reduction in force, rightsizing, and restructuring) conduct a search of the CBCA to find articles within the last six months referring to downsizing activity in Canada. Select 20 different articles on downsizing activity in Canada and review the articles to address the questions below.

Questions

1. What types of downsizing are the companies using? If there is more than one method, are the methods complementary or contradictory?

2. Given your newly formed expertise in communication during a labour surplus, do you find the message provided in the articles demonstrates equity and justice in the downsizing process? Why or why not? What are some of the risks associated with the messaging as it appears in the article? What would you suggest to overcome these risks?

3. What advice would you give public relations representatives about improving the quality of downsizing announcements in Canada? How can your suggestions benefit the company and/or its employees?

CASE INCIDENT

Budgetary Restrictions at Your Educational Institute

University of Canada* recently experienced a 10 percent decline in enrolment. There is no indication of when enrolment will return to previous levels. This has resulted in a labour surplus of professors. Of the 225 professors at the university, 45 percent are tenured (have a strong record of teaching, research and service, as well as inherent job security), 40 percent are tenure-tracked (working towards tenure), and 5 percent have contractually limited appointments (usually three-year contracts). Of the tenured professors, 72 percent are male and 28 percent are female. Of the tenure-tracked professors, 56 percent are male and 44 percent are female. Of the contractual limited appointments, 38 percent are male and 62 percent are female.

The average professor salary at your academic institution is about $75,000 per year, and professors are expected to spend 40 percent of their time teaching students (four to five classes a year), 40 percent of their time conducting research (an important aspect that brings in additional grants and funding, and is important in attracting new students and faculty), and 20 percent of their time doing services (e.g., serving on local, industry, or academic committees). Contractually limited appointments have no expectations of service or research and are paid per course taught.

Given the expertise you developed in this chapter regarding management of a labour surplus, what strategy would you recommend the university adopt to manage the labour surplus, and why? What assumptions did you make in your decision? What risks or disadvantages does this strategy present and what would you recommend the university do to overcome these?
* Fictional university

CASE INCIDENT

Communication During a Labour Surplus

Review a local newspaper, magazine, or public announcement made recently about a company undergoing activity related to a labour surplus. Assume the position of the HR department for this organization heading to work the day after the announcement is made. Based on the information provided in the announcement, as well as your learning about communication and survivor syndrome, prepare a two- to three-minute speech to give workers in your department about how to handle this announcement. What types of challenges can downsizing present to the HR department and how can downsizing agents effectively communicate with employees in this time? Don't forget, a number of your employees may be nervous about being affected by the downsizing themselves. Please address this in your communication.

CASE INCIDENT

Predicting Notice Period and Severance Pay for Permanent Layoffs

You are working in the HR department of a company that has recently announced it will lay off 15 percent of its workforce. There are 300 employees in your organization. You are tasked with determining the total compensation (pay in lieu of notice plus severance pay) for the following two employees. Based on the information provided below, as well as the legislation information in this chapter's Appendix, calculate the total minimum compensation that the following two employees would be eligible for if they fell under: a) the Ontario jurisdiction, b) the federal jurisdiction, and c) the British Columbia jurisdiction.

Louise earns $55.00 an hour. A standard work week is 44 hours, and she has worked for 13 years with this employer.

Martin has worked for the company for 8 years, earns $17.50 an hour, and works 30 hours a week.

◼ APPENDIX: JURISDICTIONAL EFFECTS OF LEGISLATION ON LAYOFFS

Ontario Jurisdiction Employees

In addition to notice of termination or pay in lieu of notice, an employee with five years of employment or more who is dismissed, constructively dismissed, or laid off for 35 weeks or more in a period of 52 weeks due to a permanent discontinuance of the employer's business at an establishment, or whose employer refuses or is unable to continue employing him/her, may be entitled to severance pay. This severance pay is calculated by adding the number of years of employment completed by the employee, including any partial year of employment (number of additional months divided by 12), and multiplying this sum by the employee's regular wages for a regular work week for a total of up to 26 weeks of wages. Severance pay may be paid in installments over a period of up to three years with the agreement of the employee or the approval of the Director of Employment Standards.

This can be written out in the following mathematical equation:

$$S_O = P * H_w * Y$$

Where:

S_O = severance in Ontario
P = rate of hourly pay
H_w = average hours worked/week
Y = years employed (up to a maximum of 26)

Federal Jurisdiction Employees

In addition to termination or pay in lieu of notice, an employee who has completed 12 consecutive months of employment is entitled to either two days wages for each completed year of employment or a total of five days wages, whichever is greater.

This can be summarized in two mathematical equations:

$$S_{F1} = P * H_d * Y * 2$$

and

$$S_{F2} = P * H_d * 5$$

Where:

S_{F1} = severance at the federal level, 1st option (two days wages for each completed year)
S_{F2} = severance at federal level, 2nd option (a total of five days wages)
P = rate of hourly pay
H_d = average hours worked/day
Y = years employed
If $S_{F1} > S_{F2}$, employee is paid S_{F1}.
If $S_{F1} < S_{F2}$ employee is paid S_{F2}.

Using this information, downsizing compensation, using two different cases, can be examined to fully understand the jurisdictional effects on compensation during downsizing in Canada. Ann and John are two of a number of employees who work in a company's administrative department and have been identified as employees to be laid off. These employees are targeted for individual layoffs since the size of the downsizing does not meet mass layoff minimums.

Ann has worked with this employer for 3 years, earning $12.50 an hour with a standard work week of 32 hours. John has worked for the company for 18 years, earns $27.50 an hour, and works 37.50 hours a week.

Within the federal jurisdiction in Canada, Ann would be entitled to $600 severance and 2 weeks' notice (or pay in lieu of notice equalling $800), and John would be entitled to $7,425 severance and 2 weeks' notice (or pay in lieu of notice equalling $2,062.50).

Within the Ontario jurisdiction, Ann is not eligible to receive a severance pay, but would receive 1-week notice (or pay in lieu of notice equalling $400). On the other hand, John would receive a severance pay of $18,562.50 and 8 weeks' notice (or pay in lieu of notice equalling $8,250) in Ontario.

Individuals terminated or laid off in Canada's other provinces would not be entitled to severance pay. For example, in Newfoundland, Ann would be entitled to 1-week notice of termination (or pay in lieu of notice equalling $400), and John would be entitled to 6 weeks' notice (or pay in lieu of notice equalling $6,187.50). Exhibit 4.9 provides a summary comparing Ann and John's compensation across these three different jurisdictions. It is evident based on this analysis that the Canadian landscape lacks consistency in the regulations regarding employment termination.

EXHIBIT | **4.9** | Comparing Downsizing Compensation in Canada ——————

Two Cases of Total Layoff Compensation (Pay in Lieu of Notice Plus Severance Pay)

	Ann	John
Federal	$1,400.00	$ 9,487.50
Ontario	$ 400.00	$26,812.50
Newfoundland	$ 400.00	$ 6,187.50

■ REQUIRED PROFESSIONAL CAPABILITIES REFERENCED IN THIS CHAPTER

86. Develops deployment procedures (e.g., transfers, secondments and reassignments).
87. Implements deployment procedures ensuring necessary compensation and benefit changes, and education plans are addressed.
88. Develops and implements procedures for employee departures.
89. Advises clients on matters of sub-standard performance and discipline.
90. Advises on alternatives to terminations.
93. Participates in the termination process by preparing termination notices, conducting exit interviews, and arranging outplacement services.
96. Provides support and expertise to managers and supervisors with respect to managing people.
99. Provides advice on issues relating to labour and employee relations including hiring, discipline, and termination.
115. Provides advice on the interpretation of the collective agreement.

CAREER DEVELOPMENT

LEARNING OBJECTIVES

- Describe the relationship between human resource planning and career development of employees
- Describe three models of career development
- Describe the balance between organizational and individual needs in the career management process
- Understand career development within the business context (e.g., talent management)

■ PROFILE

Talent Management in the 21st Century

Talent management in the 21st century[1] is a phrase that caught the author's attention. As a human resources leader one is aware of the role human resources as a function plays in helping an organization manage its talent. During the 1950s and 1960s, large organizations created significant internal programs to develop their talent pipeline. The management development programs included executive coaching, job rotation, tuition reimbursement, and time off to take university and graduate programs. During the 1980s, with the large layoffs of white-collar workers, the internal programs all but disappeared in most large organizations. Why develop talent when individuals with the skills you require have just been laid off by your competitor and are looking for work? As an organization, you can pick the best from the pool of talented individuals and help these individuals adapt to your organization's culture.

However, does this really work in the 21st century? Data from various sources has identified significant scarcity of human capital either in numbers or skills.[2-5] McKinsey surveyed fifty-six large and mid-size U.S. companies. Of those surveyed, 89 percent believed it to be more difficult to attract talented people now than three years ago, and 90 percent thought that retention of talent was more difficult now. The original study in 1998 found that if organizations did not manage their talent well, they had one of the key difficulties of recruiting and/or retaining talent.[6]

Today we can see the issue of talent management in the financial centre of Canada, Toronto. The financial sector drives the economic well-being of Toronto. In March 2007, the Toronto Financial Services Alliance's report on Talent Matters reported that "the future growth of the Toronto financial services industry and its ability to remain competitive will rely on its ability to address escalating talent challenges."[7] The research found that the industry was not currently in a talent crisis but that one was pending. If the leaders failed to respond to the pending crisis, they would "limit their ability to conquer new markets, drive growth, embrace new technology, and [would] be constrained by compliance and risk management requirements and hampered by their inability to retain key talent while struggling to attract new talent."[8]

According to a Manpower Inc. study, 66 percent of Canadian employers are having difficulty filling positions due to lack of suitable talent.[9] The research predicts that Canadian labour force growth will drop to less than one percent between 2005 and 2009 and by 2010 immigration will account for 100 percent of the net labour market growth in Canada.[10]

In early 2000 and in 2001, companies in North America were laying off technology employees in large numbers and schools providing education in this field saw enrollments drop significantly. Some programs were even cancelled. However, by 2008 organizations began to identify a need for technology workers. At a conference by the Conference Board of Canada many companies, including Canadian Tire[11], CN[12], and Desjardin[13] made presentations about their issues in managing their technology talent. Canadian Tire's presentation, "Strategies for Securing Our Future, Being on the Offensive,"[14] illustrated their challenges and discussed the need not only to work with colleges and universities to secure talent, but to develop the talent from within. Canadian Tire "brings in internationally educated professionals through college and university internship programs and supports a policy of re-skilling its current workforce based on a resource planning exercise to identify talent and opportunities for movement and development within the company."[15]

The need for specific talent or skilled workers varies with time. Planning by an organization or individual requires that opportunities both in the short term and the longer term be considered.

■ CAREER DEVELOPMENT AND HUMAN RESOURCE PLANNING

In this chapter we will discuss career development with respect to individuals and organizations and its relationship to human resource planning, career models, and talent management. As outlined in Chapter 1 of this text, human resource planning (HRP) is a process used to determine future human resource requirements by anticipating future business demands, analyzing the impacts of these demands on the organization, and making decisions on how to effectively acquire and utilize firms' human resources.

Career development has many different definitions by different researchers. A few examples are outlined below:

- Sears describes career development as the total constellation of psychological, sociological, educational, physical, economic, and chance factors that combine to shape the career of an individual over the life span.[16]
- Brown and Brooks describe career development as "a lifelong process of getting ready to choose, choosing, and typically continuing to make choices from among the many occupations available in our society."[17]
- Ginzberg describes career development as a developmental process that occurs over a number of years, or an occupational choice as a lifelong process of decision making.[18]

career development

An organized, formalized, and planned effort to achieve a balance between the individual's career needs and the organization's work force requirements; helps employees attain their career objectives

All the above definitions focus on individual career development—where most of the research has been done. There is also a need to develop an understanding of career development in organizations, especially with respect to human resource planning. With this in mind, **career development** can be described as "an organized, formalized, and planned effort to achieve a balance between the individual's career needs and the organization's work force requirements."[19] It also helps employees attain their career objectives.

There are a number of ways of looking at career development. Much of the research on career development has focused on career psychology and the needs of the individual. Thus, the outcomes of the research discussed earlier are focused on how the individual makes a career choice and the education and counselling required. Most of the research done on career development is based on how individuals and organizations think about the implementation of career development in the culture of North America. Organizational career research has focused on career development within organizations and until recently there has been little collaboration between researchers in the two areas. Organizations in their planning must take into account the individual and organizational needs if they are going to be successful in developing their human capital. The role of human resources in the planning is to create, with the support of the business team, models and processes to ensure that employees are clear on their responsibilities and the organizational responsibilities with respect to career development. Overall an organizational career development program is a dynamic process that balances the needs of the organization and individual. Individual needs and organizational needs will not always align.

Individuals look to work for organizations that provide them with opportunities to meet their career goals. They are encouraged during their educational years to define their career goals and plan their career path. Today, the selection for roles in organizations begins before the first job. Educational institutions provide co-op and internship opportunities to help students clarify their objectives for work opportunities, and employers use these vehicles to try out students. In the article "The New Fast Track," Gerdes discusses how an accounting major at Pennsylvania State University participated in a pre-internship development program.[20] During the program, Ernst & Young picked her to participate in a development seminar for "high-potential" talent. The student hadn't applied for an internship, let alone a full-time job, but Ernest & Young was hand-picking key talent in a world of talent shortages so that they could meet their organizational needs. This process of hand-picking can lead to a full-time job and then an accelerated career path.

Although most companies still develop their talent the old-fashioned way, some companies, such as Phillips Electronics, identify their top performers who have at least three years of experience at the company and send them off to an evaluation centre for appraisal of their skills and an exploration of career opportunities.[21] A chosen few, identified as individuals who are potential candidates for further organizational development, not only have development plans outlined for them, but as part of the development process they attend frequent lunches with the CEO as part of the networking and mentoring program.

Why Would an Organization Support Career Development?

The presence of a development process in an organization attracts employees to the organization and:

1. Develops promotable employees
2. Lowers turnover
3. Motivates employees
4. Reduces loading on managers
5. Satisfies employee needs
6. Taps employee potential

Who is Responsible for Career Development?

It is a challenge to decide who is ultimately responsible for career development activities. In the traditional bureaucratic organization, career development was something done for individual employees. An organization often had an assessment centre, or used an external organization to assess individuals. During the process, specific employees were identified as having management potential and once their potential was confirmed, the employee was groomed through various activities, including special projects, executive training programs, and international assignments. A development plan was created for the individual based on both the outcomes of the analysis and the organization's needs. However, although the individual was aware of the development plans, they did not participate in the development decisions. For many individuals, their careers were secure in a particular organization so long as they were successful in career development.

In today's organizations there is a move from secure careers within an organization to career ownership and management by the individual.

A key question is how much responsibility an organization has for managing its employees' careers. This is not an easy question to answer but more and more organizations are expecting individuals to maintain their own employability skills.

HRP AND ETHICS

Career Development —Individual versus Organizational Investment

Organizations such as the Federal Government, Canadian Tire, Desjardin, GE, and CN spend considerable time and money investing in their employees. The investment includes reaching into their organization to identify employees with potential in areas where there are gaps. The organization then focuses on developing and retaining these employees who they feel are critical to their survival as an organization.

Many other organizations refuse to make such long-term investments in developing their employees, especially new recruits from colleges and universities who tend to only stay with their first employer a year or two. The investment does not achieve a return that they believe is valuable to the organization. In the past ten years or so, many organizations have invested in their employees, including paying for post-graduate education (e.g., MBA schooling) only to see their highly trained staff hired by other organizations.

Consider employees who have participated in extensive development programs— time off for studies and payments for MBA tuition in the range of $50,000 to $100,000. Do these employees have an obligation to remain with the organization so that the organization realizes a return on their investment?

■ HUMAN CAPITAL

human capital

A reflection of the depth and breadth of employees' talents, education, experience, knowledge, and skills

Employees bring talents, education, experience, knowledge, and skills to their jobs and an organization in general uses some of these. The **human capital** of employees is independent of their current job or employer. Rather, it is a reflection of the depth and breadth of the employee's talents, education, experience, knowledge, and skills.[22] Managers are often surprised to find out what their employees do outside of the workplace. For example, an individual works for a company as a receptionist, but as part of their volunteer work they are the chairperson of a large not-for-profit organization, using skills they don't in the workplace. Often these surprises are discovered when a major change is happening, such as downsizing or expanding the organization. At this time, management is looking at skills to determine who stays in the downsizing or who is promoted in the expansion. If organizations are going to appropriately manage their talent, they need to minimize these surprises and use and acknowledge their employees' capabilities. The long-term success of an organization depends on its ability to attract, retain, enhance, and effectively use its human resources. Human capital is becoming a scarce resource and with the lack of skilled resources it is important that organizations plan so as to ensure that the skilled resources needed are available when required. At one point, many organizations thought that technology could replace people in some roles, but this idea has not worked out well. Most industries in today's knowledge workplace depend on people to ensure their competitive advantage.

Organizations have a number of options and issues to consider as they determine who and when they hire. The planning must consider the following questions:

- Does the organization buy or develop their human capital?
- How does the organization manage their human capital in an era of talent shortages?
- How does the organization determine the potential value of individuals to the organization and ensure that the value is developed?

Buy Versus Develop

During the 1980s many organizations downsized, rightsized, and developed flatter structures to develop and maintain their competitive advantage. Prior to this period, organizations developed and implemented career development processes to ensure that they had the talent in place that they needed in order to grow their business. As a result of downsizing, these career development processes have all but disappeared in many organizations. In many cases the staff development function was the first to be downsized or eliminated. The leadership of many organizations saw no need to invest in the talent of the future, for if they needed specific skills during the period of downsizing, they raided their competition or they found the individual they needed in the ranks of the unemployed. Stewart reported that in general "companies have a hard time distinguishing between the cost of paying people and the value of investing in them."[23] However, in the current work environment, the option of buying is not available to most employers. As the age of the workforce increases, and a large percentage of employees are eligible to retire in the next ten years, the availability of skilled candidates for jobs is dramatically reduced. Gerdes' research shows that 37 percent of North American employers have development programs to accelerate the careers of "high potentials" and employees who will be key to their organization's competitive position.[24]

Talent Crunch

Managing talent is emerging as the most important challenge in a world with a shortage of talent.[25] Krinks and Strack grouped the challenges into three themes:[26]

- Developing and retaining the best employees, using techniques of talent management, including improved leadership development and managing work–life balance

- Anticipating change, through managing demographics, managing change and cultural transformation, and managing globalization
- Enabling the organization to work effectively by becoming a learning organization and transforming HR into a strategic partner

Overall, people with leadership and employability skills and the potential to grow are becoming scarcer, the work environment is becoming more global, the workforce is growing older, and employees are placing more importance on work–life balance. The challenge for organizations is how to attract, develop, and retain their workforce in a changing environment.

Potential Value of an Employee

The potential value of a person to an organization depends on the degree of match between the person's human capital and the needs of the organization.

 153

An organization's investment in the career development of employees needs to be viewed as a long-term investment, not an operating expense or a short-term expedient program. Investing in human capital is a symbiotic relationship; both the employee and the employer must contribute in order for both the gain the benefits.

As part of the organizational planning process, human resources needs to work with the management team to:

- Forecast staffing needs
- Research the marketplace
- Determine talent availability
- Determine talent requirements
- Develop programming to support talent development and retention

Career

career

A course of successive situations that make up a person's work life and usually refers to all the jobs that one has held in their working life

There is a lack of clarity regarding the concept of career, and this ambiguity around its meaning has prevented a common ground of thinking in this area. Traditional definitions of career restrict the definition to one's professional work life.

A **career** is traditionally seen as a course of successive situations that make up a person's work life and usually refers to all the jobs that one has held in their working life. In the past, individuals have looked to the organization to provide a career opportunity. Today, individuals need to continuously develop their employability skills and look for opportunities to fulfill their career needs.

However, researchers have now expanded the term beyond professional work life to include other activities. For example:

- Super, a researcher in the field of career development, defines career as "the sequence of major positions occupied by a person throughout his preoccupation, occupational, and post-occupational life, and includes work-related roles such as those of student, employee and pensioner, together with complementary vocational, familial, and civil roles."[27]
- The Department of Education and Science defines careers as "the variety of occupational roles which individuals will undertake throughout life. Careers include paid and self employment; the different occupations which a person may have over the years; and periods of unemployment and unpaid occupations such as that of student, voluntary worker, or partner."[28]

protean career

A process used by an individual to manage their career, by moving from organization to organization or work setting to work setting to develop skills; the process is shaped by the needs of the individual rather than the organization

Building on these definitions, different types of careers have been defined. For example:

- **Protean career** refers to the notion that in order to adapt and survive in a changing world, the individual needs to be self-generating, or protean.[29] The protean career displaces the notion of a linear and vertical career path and acknowledges flexible and idiosyncratic career construction. It recognizes all aspects of an individual's life as relevant to career and places the individual at the centre of the stage, and organizational and occupational contexts as the stage.

- The concept of the protean career is closely related to the concept of the boundaryless career which emphasizes that career is about an individual not an organization and that the enactment of career reflects an intersection of self organizing and social phenomena.[30–31]

Careers are becoming more varied and more difficult to manage for both individuals and organizations.[32]

Career Path

career path

The sequential pattern of jobs that form one's career

A **career path** is a sequential pattern of jobs that form one's career. For example, a path in HR might be: human resource administration role; human resource recruiting role; human resource compensation role; human resource consultant; human resource manager, director, or recruiter; and finally vice president of human resources. A career path for a public accountant might take the form: staff auditor, senior auditor, audit manager, partner/senior partner.

Due to flatter organizations, employers are faced with the dilemma of how to promote employees when many organizations have eliminated the higher management positions. Additionally, career paths related to moving from employee to supervisor to manager to director to vice president do not exist in many flatter organizations, or the number of opportunities is significantly fewer. Some organizations have created two parallel career paths. One path for managers and another for individual contributors such as engineers, who can move up the non-supervisory path into senior professional positions with many of the rewards that are generally attached to management track positions at the same level.[33] Another option employers use is to move an employee horizontally, or at the same level (e.g., from finance to marketing to human resources) to gain experience in different areas of the company. Many management training programs are designed to include this type of career path.

Career Goals and Career Planning

career goals

Goals that one selects for one's career or future position

career planning

The process of selecting one's career goals and the path to attain these goals

Career goals are goals that one selects for one's career or future position. This process of selecting one's goals usually involves self-reflection, self-assessment, and career orientation.[34] Following the career planning process below will help an individual to facilitate the process of continuously reviewing and setting goals.

Career planning is the process of selecting one's career goals and the path to attain these goals. For example, Andolsen describes a six-step framework for career planning in the field of records and information management that can be applied effectively to other fields of work.[35] The steps include:

- **Self-assessment** to understand your personality, skills, knowledge, values, and interests.
- **Occupational research** to investigate the options available in as comprehensive and exhaustive a way as possible. Techniques include information search, information interviews, job shadowing, and job experience.
- **Making some decisions** that narrow down your career choice, including setting career objectives, personal objectives, and educational objectives.
- **Looking for employment contacts** through job searching, or networking, developing a résumé and cover letter, and hopefully interviews.
- **Accepting work** and evaluating how the role fits your career plan, and continue to work on the plan.
- **Ongoing planning** is required as you change and as the work environment changes.

Career planning is a process. Exhibit 5.1 illustrates the components involved in this process. For example, if an employee is aware of the career paths within an organization, they can set goals, participate in development opportunities (e.g., education, work assignments, etc.),

EXHIBIT **5.1** | Career Planning Process

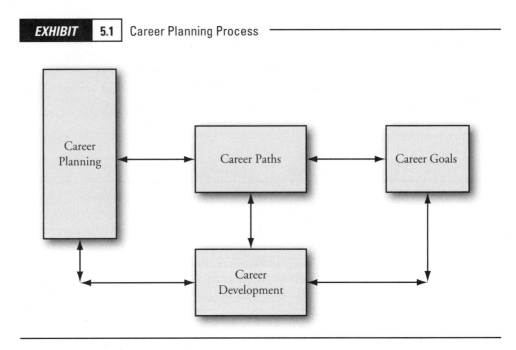

and continuously reevaluate their career plan. Why? While engaged in these development opportunities, the employee may see other career paths that interest them. At this point, the employee could modify or develop new goals and select alternative development opportunities to participate in. Over a work lifetime, employees may choose many different career paths, building on their education and work foundation. For example, a graduate of a technology post-secondary program might start their career in an organization as a technology analyst, work for a few years in this position, receive a promotion to supervisor, participate in further education (such as earning an MBA and participating in a number of different work assignments), then be promoted to manager of operations in a distribution centre. The work assignments would have included not only technology-based ones, but roles in marketing, finance, and the supply chain. In today's work environment, it is expected that knowledge workers will change their work many times during their lifetime and move though many difference career options.

■ CAREER MANAGEMENT AND THE BALANCE BETWEEN ORGANIZATIONAL AND INDIVIDUAL NEED

The challenge in career management is the balance or alignment between organizational and individual needs. Exhibit 5.2 illustrates some issues that need to be considered by both the organization and the individual. For example, at what career stage is the employee just starting out or thinking about retiring? The planning process needs to take into account the needs of both. What type of education and training have they received? Where is the organization in its life cycle? What are the operational issues of the organization? Organizations need to address individual issues when developing a career-planning model for employees, and the employees need to consider the strategic and operational needs of an organization as they plan their career.

As illustrated in Exhibit 5.2, there needs to be some alignment between individual and organizational needs in the career management process. The organization has both strategic and

EXHIBIT | **5.2** | Career Management Balance[36]

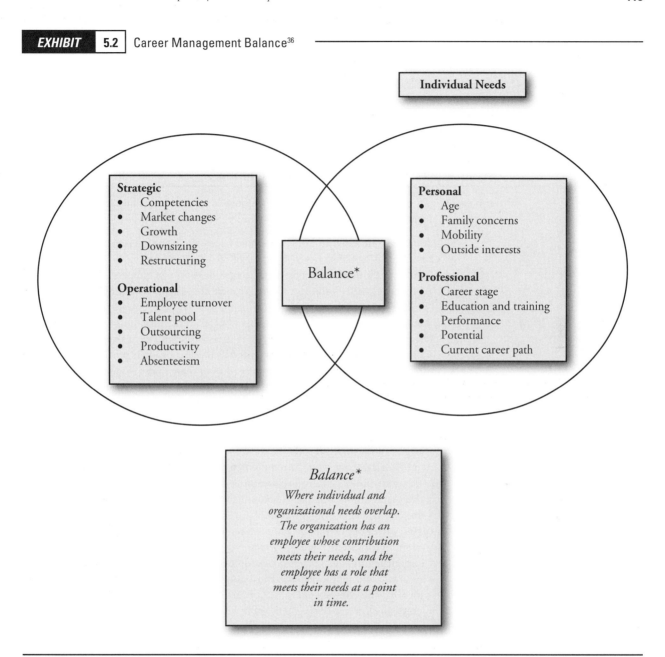

Individual Needs

Strategic
- Competencies
- Market changes
- Growth
- Downsizing
- Restructuring

Operational
- Employee turnover
- Talent pool
- Outsourcing
- Productivity
- Absenteeism

Balance*

Personal
- Age
- Family concerns
- Mobility
- Outside interests

Professional
- Career stage
- Education and training
- Performance
- Potential
- Current career path

*Balance**

Where individual and organizational needs overlap. The organization has an employee whose contribution meets their needs, and the employee has a role that meets their needs at a point in time.

operational needs that must be met, and specific skills are required for each area. Individuals have personal and professional needs and specific skills are required for each area. Organizations plan for employee turnover, growth, product diversification, mergers, and many other options through their forecasting processes. During the organizational planning exercise, discussions should include employee needs, including the skills that are currently available or unavailable in their workforce, and how they will close the gap. Organizational human resource planning should include the identification of employees who have potential to do the identified work, as well as the development of plans that will facilitate individuals achieving the potential through formal training and other activities as needed. The planning should also include the identification of career paths in the organization and opportunities to develop the skills required so that the individual can be considered for the roles on the career paths.

Employees have professional and personal needs. They need to be aware of their own requirements, skills, and aspirations. Additionally, they need to prepare themselves for potential opportunities by continuously developing their employability skills. When organizational needs change, employees need to be able to identify potential opportunities either within or outside of the organization, based on both their personal and professional needs.

Organizational Career Development Planning

As an overall part of human resource planning, the four key areas to consider when developing a career development process in an organization include:

1. Matching the individual and organizational needs while considering the following:
   - Communicating the strategic direction of the company
     - Individuals need to know the strategic direction of the organization and the human resource strategy. Organizations are often competing for individuals with specific skills that are scarce in the marketplace. Employees and potential employees who have these skills have choices. If organizations want to succeed in recruiting and retaining employees with specific skills so as to maintain strategic position in the marketplace, they need to be clear on their processes.
   - Ensuring employees are aware that ownership of their career belongs to them
     - Potential employees in today's market want to have more control over work–life balance. Thus, ownership of their career is important to them.
   - Establishing a process of goal setting and planning, including self-assessment, training, and development opportunities
     - Organizations need to provide the opportunity for individuals to plan and manage their careers within the requirements of the organization. In some cases, organizations provide many opportunities for development that are not specific to the organization, but do so because they believe most development is good for employees and the organization.
2. Identifying career opportunities and requirements
   - Developing competency requirements
     - Organizations need to define the competency requirements for roles in the organization, and employees need to know what is required from them, be able to identify any competency gap they have with respect to specific roles, and how they can close the competency gap.
   - Establishing career paths—professional versus technical
     - Too often the career paths within an organization are unclear. For example, if an individual is a technical expert, what is the career path to move to management or stay in the technical stream? Without this knowledge, individuals find themselves developing competencies for a technical career path when none exists.
3. Identifying employee potential
   - Measure competencies and performance
     - Employees require feedback on an ongoing basis with respect to gaps in their competencies or performance, and what developmental opportunities exist, based on the feedback.
   - Establishing inventories of employee talents
     - As part of the human resource planning process, inventories of employees with specific skills and competencies should be developed and made easily accessible to the management teams who make decisions about staffing opportunities.
   - Establishing succession plans

- For organizations to be competitive, key employee positions that are required for both the strategic and operational business should be identified.
- Employees with potential to fill the key positions should be identified, and to close the gap in competencies, individual development plans need to be created for each identified individual.

4. Identifying career development initiatives
   - Providing developmental feedback
     - Employees need feedback on an ongoing basis. This is the only way they can confirm what is working and what is not working. The feedback needs to be specific to their current role, and opportunities need to be identified for them within the organization.
   - Providing developmental opportunities
     - As part of the feedback process, developmental opportunities of interest to the organization and the employee should be identified. As well, the process for how to participate in the opportunities also needs to be identified.
   - Providing coaching and mentoring
     - Coaching is a great tool to facilitate the development of individuals based on gaps in competencies. Mentoring with a more senior organizational member will provide individuals with ideas for personal development and options to consider for future growth.

■ CAREER MODELS

A number of different career models are used by organizations, but many have common themes—career ladders, competency models, career development, and employee development. We will look at the following three career models:

1. The career ladder, which is based on a series of jobs in which each position is the successor to the next
2. Sonnenfeld's career system typology which facilitates the understanding of organization career systems
3. The Microsoft competency-based model where movement from one job to another is based on the development of competencies

career ladder

A vertical series of jobs starting at entry level and progressively moving to higher-level jobs, based on experience, education, and performance

From the 1950s to the 1970s many large corporations had extensive internal employee development programs. Often the process outlined the career ladder within the organization and the path to reach specific roles. In the 1980s, many organizations cut these development programs because they were costly and skilled workers were available in the marketplace. In general, there was not a shortage of skilled workers. In the 1990s, as the shortage of skilled workers in various areas began to make its way into the marketplace, many organizations began looking at alternative development programs to attract and retain the talent they needed to remain competitive.

Career Ladder

One career model is a **career ladder.** In this model, there is a clear succession of position. The assumption in this progression is that each employee will start at the lowest level and work their way up. Examples of a career ladder are shown in Exhibit 5.3a and 5.3b. During the last 20 years, in most organizations, this model has not had as much relevance due to the development of flatter structures and organizational changes related to globalization, knowledge workforce, and the succession planning models that look for generalists versus specialists.[37]

| EXHIBIT | 5.3a | Career Ladder in Human Resources

Sonnenfeld's Career System Typology Model

Sonnenfeld's career systems typology

A model that facilitates the understanding of organization career systems as a strategic approach

Sonnenfeld's career systems typology, as shown in Exhibit 5.4, is a career model that facilitates the understanding of organizational career systems as a strategic approach.[38] It applies general systems theory to the flow of human resources in and out of the organization in terms of input, throughput, and output. As an open system, an organization's labour supply is subject to external forces in the processes of input (entry) and output (exit).

This model has two dimensions:[39]

1. Supply flow: Supply flow ranges from a completely internal supply to largely external supply of managerial labour. Organizations that focus on an internal supply flow tend to think of people as assets, with long-term developmental value, rather than as cost, which carry an annual expense.

EXHIBIT | **5.3b** | Career Ladder in Accounting ——————————————————

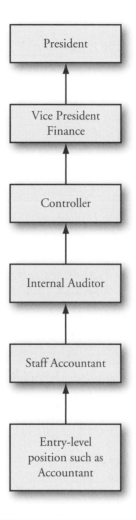

---

2. Assignment flow: Assignment flow refers to the degree to which assignment and promotion decisions are based on individual performance on one side versus overall contribution to the group or organization on the other side. Organizations that focus on individual contribution expect people to be continually producing value, while those that focus on group contribution see people as having intrinsic value.

Within the four-cell typology, four career system types are shown—fortress, club, baseball team, and academy. The characteristics of the four career system types are described in Exhibit 5.5.

Competency-Based Career Model at Microsoft[40]

Microsoft defines career models as "a platform of common standards for identifying, assessing, managing, and developing people to enable the core value propositions to be realized for the company." The Microsoft core value propositions include:

EXHIBIT **5.4**   Sonnenfeld's Career Systems Typology[41]

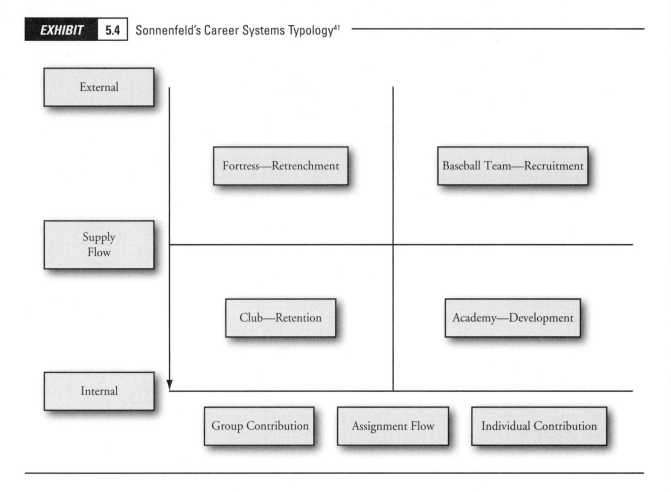

1. **Alignment:** Alignment among the company's business strategy, employee and leader behaviour, and new culture expectations. Two examples of culture change reinforced in the career model are:
   • **Integration:** Career models emphasize the desired collaboration across groups to result in an integrated product or service for users.
   • **Customer and Partner:** Meeting customer and partner expectations are emphasized and rewarded across all career paths.
2. **Employee engagement:** Employee engagement models offer the advantage of clarity. They make transparent the criteria for success.
3. **Discretionary effort:** Employees have clear expectations of current results and information about what is required to achieve personal career aspirations.
4. **Transparency:** Transparency increases trust and reduces the perception of bureaucracy or bias.

The three components of the Microsoft career model include:[42]

1. **Career stage profiles** explain career paths and key stages along a career path, performance expectations for each stage, and what it takes to get to the next stage.
2. **Competencies** that define the behaviours that differentiate outstanding from standard performance and increase the likelihood of success in a career path at Microsoft over time. Competencies are skills, knowledge, and behaviours and include dealing with ambiguity, conflict management, and business acumen.
3. **Experiences** describe key roles and situations that enable growth in important competencies and serve as a tool to guide career planning.

EXHIBIT	5.5	Characteristics of the Four System Types

Career System Type	Entry	Exit	Development Characteristics	Examples of Firms
Academy	Strictly early career. Individuals hired are seen as having the ability to grow.	Low turnover in this type of organization and the reasons for leaving are dismissal for poor performance or retirement.	Elaborate career paths/job ladders Extensive training for specific jobs Primarily a human resource practice Tracking and sponsorship of high-potential employees	Committed to early career hiring and long-term professional growth (e.g., GM, IBM)
Club	Early career with an emphasis on reliability. There is low turnover and it is usually by retirement.	Low turnover and it is usually by retirement.	General, with slow paths Requires many steps and there is an emphasis on commitment	Committed to early career hiring and long-term commitment. Different from Academy as their assignment flow is contribution-based (e.g., government, monopolies such as utilities)
Baseball Team	Credential and expertise. Recruitment at all career stages. Individuals are recruited at all career stages.	High turnover and cross-employer career paths.	On-the-job training Little formal training Little succession planning	Firms for this model include: law firms, advertising, and entertainment
Fortress	Passive recruitment as individuals are drawn to an industry by their own interests/background.	Frequent layoffs, and seniority applies in the layoffs.	Characterized by the organization's effort to retain core talent	Companies include airlines and hotels

Goals of Microsoft's Career Model

According to Tanya Clemens, Corporate Vice President, Capability Microsoft Corporation, the career model process brought "objectivity and consistency to career development, which improved morale and positively affected attrition and overall productivity."[43] The career model provides a dual focus: first on the management career path and second on the individual contributor career path.[44] The career path process sets objective standards for employees and management. It is an important aspect of the employee value proposition and profiles a range of options, particularly for attracting and retaining engineering talent. Prior to the implementation of the current process, there was a lack of a consistent standard transparency. As a result, inconsistent decisions were made by management that affected the organization's ability to retain and reward key people. The outcomes led to frustration among employees and reduced the ability to keep key talent.

The components of the Microsoft career model are integrated into a talent management system that provides for continuous reinforcement and behaviour change required by the organization to achieve culture change objectives. It is important that the two processes are linked because a disconnected talent process would drag on the company's ability to grow and adapt to marketplace challenges, and the disconnects would create or perpetuate barriers to effective change.[45]

■ THE CAREER MODEL OF THE 21ST CENTURY

In the 1970s and 1980s, career success was synonymous with moving up the corporate ladder in the same company over the course of one's career. The company often drove an individual's career, not the individual. However, career management has now moved to the individual. Individuals are being challenged to play a greater role in constructing their own career developments.[46]

Individuals need to focus on their employability skills, rather than on job security, and learn skills to assist them in taking responsibility for the direction and evaluation of their own careers. Career development is now viewed as multi-directional and multi-levelled, rather than linear.

The protean career concept is closely related to the boundaryless career, which emphasizes that career is about an individual organizing, not organizations, and that the enactment of career reflects an intersection of self organizing and social phenomena.[47]

Careers of the 21st century will be driven by the person, not the organization.[48] Hall, a well-known researcher in the field of career development, refers to protean careers, or the notion that in order to adapt and survive in a changing world, the individual needs to be self-generating or protean. The protean career displaces the notion of a linear and vertical career path and acknowledges flexible and idiosyncratic career construction. A protean career includes all aspects of an individual's life that are relevant to their career and places the individual at the centre. The concept of career in this protean model is not a contract with the organization but with one's self and is increasingly a continuous learning model. Thus, individuals need to develop skills related to learning, including how to learn, and how to be adaptable. As individuals develop their career portfolio by proactively moving from employer to employer and working across vocations and countries, they simultaneously develop and utilize their marketable skills. It is this process that is often referred to as a boundaryless career.

Individuals pursing boundaryless careers develop their human capital along dimensions of industry and occupational knowledge.[49, 50] For example, a human resources professional may develop their recruiting knowledge and industry knowledge by moving from one industry to another. Their first role might be as a human resources administrator in retail. After a short period, as they look for more challenges, they take a role as a human resources recruiter in financial services, then move to a role as an executive recruiter for transportation in a recruiting company. Their career is in human resources and their focus is on recruiting. Individuals who pursue careers within an organization develop their knowledge in ways specific to the given organization. Individuals who pursue careers in a professional area may develop knowledge of their profession as well as a number of industries.

Mentoring

mentoring

A developmentally oriented relationship between senior and junior colleagues or peers

Mentoring is a key tool used in the process of career development in the 21st century. Mentoring is a developmentally oriented relationship between senior and junior colleagues or peers. Mentoring relationships, which can occur at all levels and in all areas of an organization, generally take the form of an advising role that involves modeling, sharing contacts, and giving general support to colleagues or peers who have less experience in a particular area.[51] The key goal of mentoring is to support and guide the personal growth of the mentee (the one being mentored). The mentee in the mentoring relationship is in charge of his/her learning.[52] Mentoring provides benefits to both the mentor and mentee. The mentee gains the value, knowledge, and support of the mentor and the mentor receives both increased job and career satisfaction from helping others.

Mentoring is also available through various organizations. For example, NursingNet is an online nursing forum that has mentoring programs for those in health care.[53] Professional associations, such as the Human Resources Professional Association (HRPA), provides mentoring opportunities for their members. Mentoring is an especially critical career development tool for individuals who have boundaryless careers because the support that exists within organizational developmental programs is not available for these individuals as they move from one organization to another as part of their career development.

Another type of mentoring is called "reverse mentoring." Reverse mentoring involves younger employees providing guidance to more senior executives in areas in which they have expertise and the more senior person does not. Examples include using the Web for messaging or using Twitter as a research or marketing tool. Organizations using reverse mentoring include General Motors, Procter & Gamble, and General Electric.[54] The relationship that is developed between the senior executive and the junior employee often benefits the young mentor as the older mentee provides career advice and support.

Networking

networking

Working with your network of contacts to broaden your knowledge of the career areas that you are interested in

Networking is another career development tool. It involves working with your network of contacts to broaden your knowledge of the career areas that you are interested in. Support for networking can include professional associations such as the HRPA and The Institute of Chartered Accountants of Ontario, family or extended family members, professors, or former bosses. Through networking, one can find new jobs, learn about professional trends, or even find support for your ideas as you consider a new job or educational opportunity. The ability to network is critical for professionals. It is particularly important for individuals who are not linked with a specific organization, or for those individuals who are looking for developmental opportunities related to their profession that are not available in their own organization. Career ladders for professionals often require movement between organizations to gain experience, and networking is a tool that can help achieve this.

Coaching

coaching

An ongoing process of providing feedback

Coaching is a tool used for many developmental opportunities. For example, executives hire coaches to help them develop skills related to managing their business, and managers act as coaches for their employees to help them improve their performance. Individuals receive feedback on their performance, usually during performance appraisals, and a discussion of their career goals takes place. Coaching can be defined as an ongoing process of providing feedback. A coachable moment may arise in many situations, including when an employee demonstrates a new skill, asks for feedback, mentions a desire for support for a development program, or expresses an interest

---

EXHIBIT | **5.6** | Career Management at PricewaterhouseCoopers ————————

The career management service at PricewaterhouseCoopers helps "employees to write their own job descriptions and create a more satisfying working life."[55] The service includes an independent career counselling service that helps employees recognize their development needs and work out what they must do to achieve them. Help is given to employees to focus on their career preferences, and the opportunity is given to talk through the options, both within and outside the company. Individuals receive support to set their career objectives. The support provided helps the employee match their needs for development with the needs of the business. Line mangers take on a coaching role to support the development of individual skills, and the organization provides access to a number of self-development tools. Career management and development is a partnership between the organization and individuals, since it is in both parties' interest to collaborate.

in a change in the organization. Coaching under any of these circumstances can have a positive impact on performance.

Coaching can also have a significant impact in creating a positive work environment. According to Block, a UBS Wealth Management Coach, 96 percent of coached financial advisors are retained compared to 84 percent who had not been coached.[56]

■ ROLE OF HUMAN RESOURCES IN FACILITATING CAREER DEVELOPMENT

153

The role of human resources in facilitating career development in the 21st century is moving from the tactile (e.g., developing and delivering training) to being more strategic, with a focus on the long-term needs of an organization, including talent management process and succession planning. Succession planning is a process that organizations use to ensure they have pools of skilled employees trained and available to meet the strategic objectives of the organization. Succession planning involves identifying employees who have potential to assume key positions in the organization and preparing them for these positions. Succession planning will be discussed in greater detail in Chapter 6.

■ TALENT MANAGEMENT

talent

A person's recurring patterns of thought, feeling, or behaviour that can be productively applied

talent management

The ability to attract, develop, and retain engaged talent to meet current and future needs

Talent management is an organizational process in which key senior management define organizational resource needs and put appropriate processes in place to ensure they have the human resource talent they require to meet their strategic objectives. **Talent** refers to a person's recurring patterns of thought, feeling, or behaviour that can be productively applied.[57] **Talent management** can be defined as the ability to attract, develop, and retain engaged talent to meet current and future needs.[58] The talent pool is getting smaller in Canada due to the retirement of baby boomers and the country's slowing birth rate. Due to the lack of skilled older employees, younger people will soon be getting bigger jobs.[59] Thus, it is important that human resources develop talent management processes as part of its planning to ensure the organization has the talent pool it needs to deliver on its business strategy. Labour shortages in specific professional areas in Canada are being reported by many organizations, including at Microsoft, Canadian Tire, CN, and the Toronto Financial Services Alliance.[60] In part, the shortage of labour is the result of a drop in Canada's growth rate, from to 1 percent between 2005 and 2009 to an expected less than 0.5 percent by 2015.

A study by McKinsey et al. of 13,000 senior managers in large and mid-size companies revealed that:[61]

- Only 3 percent strongly agreed that their companies did a good job of developing people effectively
- Only 3 percent strongly agreed that their companies were effective at dealing with poor performers
- Only 16 percent strongly agreed that their companies could even identify the high and low performance leaders

How did this mismanagement of organizational talent, as indicated in this North American study, occur? According to Effron, developing countries such as India and China are more serious about building great talent than North America is.[62] Talent development needs to be the key priority of an organization's leadership if North American organizations are going to meet their strategic plans.

According to Ulrich, talent is equal to competence + commitment + contribution.[63] Individuals who are competent, that is to say they have the knowledge, skills, and values required in the workplace, but are not committed, do not deliver on their competence. Committed and engaged employees deliver. To manage their talent, organizations need to find a way to ensure that competent individuals are engaged and committed.

The Role of Leaders in Talent Management

In his review of organizations, Wexber, CEO of The Limited, recognized that the critical reason for the success of many organizations, such as GE and PepsiCo, is talent management systems.[64] As CEO, he recognized that his role was to manage the talent management system in his organization.

According to Handfeld-Jones et al., the new talent mindset of organizational leaders should include a deep conviction that: [65]

- Better talent leads to better corporate performance
- Managers need to be held accountable for strengthening their talent pool
- Talent management is a central part of how a company is run
- Bold action plans are required to build the talent pool needed

In order for organizations to attract and retain engaged talent and be competitive, they should: [66]

- Develop their direct reports by setting high standards and providing ongoing feedback on performance, as well as giving strong performers new challenges and dealing appropriately with low performers
- Establish a talent standard, including identifying and articulating the characteristics the organization needs in a leader as well as modelling the standards daily
- Influence the hiring, promotion, and firing decisions as much as possible by ensuring all managers use the talent standard set by the organization objectively
- Drive a simple, probing review of talent with the same rigour and intensity as is done with the budget
- Hold managers accountable for the strength of their talent pools
- Instill a talent mindset in managers throughout the organization

Competency-Based Approach to Talent Management

We can examine the competency-based approach to talent management by taking a look at the nuclear industry. The organizational needs of the nuclear industry in Canada are changing. More talent and different talent are needed, according to Dwight Willet.[67] The nuclear industry in Canada is currently a highly skilled workforce close to retirement. The pension and benefits programs of current workers are very attractive and it is expected that many of the workers will retire when eligible, even though they don't have to under current legislation. For a significant period of time, there has been little hiring in the industry and this has created a gap of talent in the marketplace. Thus, the industry needs to look at an integrated long-term vision within a human capital management framework, with a focus what the end state needs to be.

Working with an external partner, Korn/Ferry, Bruce Power has designed and begun the implementation of an integrated talent management system, leadership development programs, and recruitment at all leadership levels in order to fill their shortage. Exhibit 5.7 illustrates their talent management model.

The basis for this talent management model is a competency-based approach around which performance management, recruiting, succession management, and development processes are developed and implemented. Competencies required by Bruce Power include: getting work done through others, dealing with trouble, inspiring others, making tough people calls, and making complex decisions.[68]

The talent management process involves a significant commitment on behalf of the leadership team of Bruce Power, but they have been the leaders in the development of the processes and own the rollout. According to Taylor of Praxis Partners, the steps in the Bruce Nuclear strategy are the steps required to "bullet proof" a talent management strategy and development plan and maximize the effectiveness of the processes.[69]

According to Van Dam, Deloitte's Global Chief Learning Officer, innovative talent management strategies are required in an environment of scarce resources and a develop-deploy-connect

EXHIBIT **5.7** Talent Management Model—Bruce Power[70]

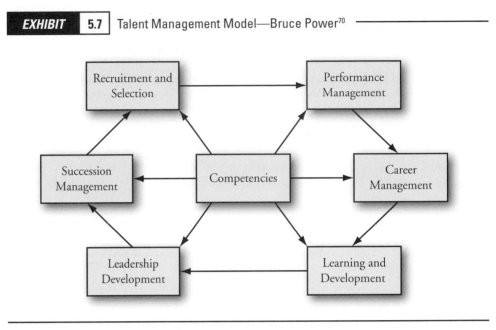

model should be used by organizations as a strategic approach to talent management.[71] This type of model focuses on the "critical components of performance improvement and delivers business results while addressing the career aspirations of individual knowledge workers."[72]

Supply-Chain Model of Talent Development

Most organizations lack formal programs for anticipating and fulfilling talent needs. Since the 1990s, they have tended to rely on the pool of external candidates that had been produced due to the layoffs of white-collar workers in the 1970s and 1980s. As previously discussed, this pool of skilled knowledge workers is decreasing. However, the development and execution of internal development programs is expensive and sometimes ineffective. According to Cappelli, the stable business environment and captive talent pipelines of the 1970s and 1980s that were needed for the success of the old developmental models, no longer exist.[73] So how should organizations approach talent development?

Cappelli believes it is time for a new approach to talent management, using the supply chain model of management. In this approach, he suggests that companies should:[74]

- Balance make-versus-buy decisions by using internal development programs to produce most, but not all, of the needed talent, and fill the gaps by hiring from outside
- Reduce the risks in forecasting the demand for talent by sending smaller batches of candidates through modulized training systems
- Look at improving return on investment in development by adopting novel cost-sharing programs with other organizations and post-secondary education institutions
- Protect investments by generating internal opportunities to encourage newly trained managers to stick with the organization

Talent-Based Approach to Talent Development

Another approach to talent development is based not on competencies, but on talent. As discussed earlier, talent is defined as a person's recurring patterns of thought, feeling, or behaviour that can be productively applied.[75] According to this definition, impatience, charm, strategic thinking,

---

EXHIBIT | **5.8** | CN and Desjardin's Technology (IT) Future

---

CN's Technology (IT) Future

In a Conference Board of Canada presentation, it was stated that the real magic of attracting and retaining IT workers is the way you channel talent in a business direction.[76] This is just the approach that CN is attempting. CN is experiencing a shortage of IT workers with computer skills, including SAO skills, .NET skills, and Java skills, and to address this shortage they are attempting to channel talent in a business direction.

CN hires IT workers who have the "whole package"—the technical skill sets, attitude, and drive required to fit into CN's organizational culture. This of course, tends to narrow the market of eligible candidates in a tight market, but it does make for a better fit and less turnover.

The IT market has many IT consultants who are highly paid and don't want to work for just one company. At one time it was thought that these consultants could be attracted to CN if appropriate medical plans and pensions were added to a good salary. However, for many, medical plans and pensions were not an issue because the consultant's partner worked for a company that provided these, and as a consultant they enjoyed higher wages. To attract top IT talent, CN has started to get its brand known in Canadian universities, and raise awareness of the demand for IT workers at CN. The company is also bringing in more co-op students in order to identify potential future employees before they graduate, and to create career pathways for co-op students who would make a good corporate fit with CN.

How does CN work at retaining the new recruits? CN is aware that new IT recruits often make decisions about whether they will stay or leave the company within the first 6 to 12 months on the job. Investing in the employees during their first two years helps ensure that the company is able to retain them. When hired, CN invests intensively in developing the SAP or JAVA skills of the new recruits, while transforming them into "railroaders." A process called "onboarding" involves taking graduates with a good technical skill base, honing their specialized IT skills to enable them to contribute to the business, and engaging them in the company business of railroading.

Desjardin's Technology (IT) Future[77]

Desjardin, a financial services institution, is also experiencing significant issues finding and retaining IT workers. One of the areas that is particularly challenging is the loss of workers with IT experience in the security area. So what is Desjardin's human resource strategy to address the talent gap? Over the next five years, the organization is taking the following actions:

- Continue to hire IT workers on the open market
- Augment traditional hiring practices by identifying the talents of potential new IT hires who are working summer jobs at Desjardins
- Engage in different initiatives with universities
- Implement a continuous training policy to ensure IT workers are up-to-date in their skill sets
- Work with managers to identify and upgrade the competencies of high-potential candidates within the company

Both CN and Desjardin are creating and implementing a human resource strategy that supports the business strategy.

---

and empathy are all talents. Buckingham et al. states that behavioural competencies cannot be learned and that organizations are wasting their time using them as a basis for talent development.[78] His perspective is that the "competency-based approach chooses to fight against uniqueness and thereby condemns the organization to waste its most precious resource—the talents of its people."[79] Instead, he suggests a "talent-based approach deploying each person's individual talents with discipline, efficiency, and power."[80]

■ TALENT DEVELOPMENT—A BURNING PRIORITY

According to the report by Chambers et al., research shows that executive talent has been the most under-managed corporate asset for the past two decades.[81] Organizations manage their physical and financial assets with sophistication, but have not made people a priority in the same way. In this report, only 23 percent of 6,000 executives surveyed strongly agreed that their companies attract highly talented people, and just 10 percent agreed that they retain almost all their high performers. Superior talent is today's prime source of competitive advance. The updated report found that 89 percent of individuals surveyed found it even more difficult today to attract talent, and 90 percent found that it was more difficult to retain them.[83] The research also illustrates that companies doing the best job managing their talent delivered far better results for the shareholders.

Overall, in the world of a talent crunch, what is the employee value proposition for joining a company, or what attracts individuals to join and stay with an organization? Creating a winning employee value proposition means tailoring a company's brand, products, and the job it has to offer, to appeal to the specific people it wants to find and keep.[84]

So what is the process that ensures attraction and retention of key talent? According to Chambers et al., it is a process that involves: [85]

- Putting people in jobs before they're ready for them, because the key to individual development is "a big job before expected."
- Having a good feedback system in place. Feedback and coaching are important and most companies do not do this well. Seventy-three percent of executives view informal feedback and coaching as essential or very important to development, but only 30 percent rate their company as excellent or very good at providing them. Sixty percent strongly value being mentored, but only 25 percent are content with their own mentoring.
- Understanding the scope of the retention problem. Senior managers tend to focus on the top executives and know little of the situation in the lower and middle ranks of managers—the future talent of the organization. As the number of lower and middle ranks of managers continues to decline, this potential problem could become a significant issue.
- Moving on the poor performers when identified, as the cost of carrying these individuals is high. Their low productivity drags down the organizational performance and the company's employee value proposition is damaged.

There is currently a greater awareness of the shortage of talent in the workplace and the increased competition for it. Even with the economic downturn, many organizations are short of key workers. Research in Motion is hiring thousands of employees with specific skills to ensure that they can continue to hold their position in the marketplace.[86] Company leaders need to make talent development a priority at all levels in the organization by:[87]

- Creating reasons for top talent to choose their organization
- Rebuilding recruiting strategies to reflect the talent need and the opportunities in their organization
- Creating significant opportunities for development and career paths with their organization
- Learning to identify poor performers and deal with them

In conclusion, career development is both an organizational and individual responsibility. The role of human resources in their HR planning is to develop career plans that support the business plan. This will include developing talent from within the organization and recruitment of specific talent from outside the organization.

CHAPTER SUMMARY

- Career development can be described as "an organized, formalized, and planned effort to achieve a balance between the individual's career needs and the organization's work force requirements" and involves helping employees attain their career objectives.
- As part of career planning it is important to align career planning processes and human capital processes with human resources planning if planning is to be successful

- The balance between buying talent and developing talent is a challenge that requires human resource planning to meet the business plan.
- Career planning involves setting goals and the paths to reach these goals.
- Career management involves balancing the organization's and the individual's needs. Organizations are always changing. They do so to meet their customer needs, but they also need to do the same to retain and attract the required talent for the organization. In the 1960s and 1970s, career ladders with international career development paths were common in many large organizations. Individuals joined organizations with the expectation that they would move up the ladder and that the organization would support their development in an effort to do so. That changed in the 1980s when organizations began to downsize and change to flatter structures. Career ladders in most organizations no longer exist.
- Sonnenfeld's career system typology is a model that facilitates the understanding of organizational career systems from a strategic approach. It includes two dimensions—supply flow of employees and assignment flow. The model discusses types of entry into an organization including early career and credential-based. It also discusses exit types, including low employee turnover to high employee turnover. Additionally, the developmental strategies of each type of career system are characterized in the model.
- Career development in organizations is often based on specific competencies, such as dealing with ambiguity and inspiring others. Microsoft uses this competency-based career model.
- The talent management process includes those built on competencies and those built on supply chain concepts.
- Mentoring and networking are key tools for career planning, both for individuals within organizations and those outside organizations, especially in the environment of talent shortages.
- In the environment of talent shortages, talent management has become a significant challenge for many organizations. Organizations are working internally and externally to develop potential talent to meet their future needs.
- The leadership for talent management is a significant part of the senior management's role in organizations. The HR plan needs to support the business plan to ensure the talent required by the organization is available when needed. One of the key roles of leaders in today's organizations should be talent management as it is an organization's strategic advantage.

KEY TERMS

- career   112
- career development   109
- career goals   113
- career ladder   117
- career path   113
- career planning   113
- coaching   123
- human capital   111
- mentoring   122
- networking   123
- protean career   112
- Sonnenfeld's career systems typology   118
- talent   124
- talent management   124

REVIEW QUESTIONS

1. Define the terms "human resource planning," "human capital," and "career path."
2. Why is there a talent shortage in North America? In terms of career development, how should individuals and organizations address this shortage?
3. What are the key components of a talent management system?
4. Describe the difference between a competency-based approach and a talent-based approach to talent management.
5. Identify the components of a talent management system based on competencies.
6. What are the organizational and individual needs that need to be balanced in career management?
7. Describe the role networking can play in career development.

DISCUSSION QUESTIONS

1. Microsoft's career planning model was described in this chapter. What recruitment and retention impact does this type of model have on the organization?
2. If a large international organization asked you to help them develop a career planning model, what would you suggest and why?
3. Developing a talent pool is becoming very important for large Canadian corporations. Capelli suggested developing this pool using supply-chain concepts. If you were asked to participate in this process, what would you consider? Why?
4. Talent management processes usually involve both ongoing assessment and career development opportunities that an organization provides for individuals. What ethical considerations might be discussed in regards to these processes?

WEB EXERCISE

Using the Conference Board of Canada website (www.conferenceboard.ca), access information related to career development. Research how two organizations are managing their career development to meet their business challenges. For example:

1. Do they always buy their talent?
2. Is their talent development model based on a competency model?
3. Do they balance their talent acquisition between buy and build?

EXPERIENTIAL EXERCISE

In groups of four, identify your experience with career development. Select a company you worked for, identify its career development process and how it was applied to you. For example, when you joined the organization, how were the career options described? What role were you to play? What role was your manager to play in the model? What really happened?

CASE INCIDENT

Talent Development

A large North American company has recognized that its management development program is not producing the talent that is required for the new strategic business plan. The new plan calls for expansion into new markets. This will require a number of individuals in new leadership roles to develop the new markets and staff roles in the organization to support the markets.

As the vice president of HR, you have met with both the manager of staffing and the manager of talent development. Together you have identified that the staffing forecast does not include a forecast of this expansion, and will need to be updated to include details of the skills required. Additionally, the talent development process has been under review for some time and you have had difficulty getting leadership participation for roles such as mentoring and coaching.

The good news is as they need talent for this business initiative, the senior management team is now ready to listen to changes that need to be made in the talent development process.

As you sit down with your two managers to discuss the human resource plan to support the strategic business plan, what should be discussed and how are you going to position the processes with the senior management team?

■ REQUIRED PROFESSIONAL CAPABILITIES REFERENCED IN THIS CHAPTER

70. Develops systems and processes that link the career plans and skill sets of employees with the requirements of the organization.
153. Helps supervisors/managers to identify career options for employees that align with business needs.
156. Assists employees in identifying career paths, establishing learning plans and activities required for achieving personal and organizational success.

SUCCESSION MANAGEMENT: PLANNING FOR THE FUTURE

LEARNING OBJECTIVES

- Differentiate between succession management and succession planning
- Explain the reasons why managing succession is an important activity
- Describe the relationship between succession planning, talent management, career development, and workforce (human resource) planning
- Identify the five key elements that characterize an effective succession program
- Describe the succession planning process
- Differentiate between high potentials and high-performing employees
- Discuss the constraints that can impede succession planning

■ PROFILE

The Kellogg's Conundrum—A Leader in the Wings

Kellogg's is an organization known across the nation for producing products such as Frosted Flakes, Special K, Raisin Bran, Rice Krispies, and those delicious Keebler cookies. With sales in 2006 of over $11 billion, Kellogg's corporation has been the world's leading producer of breakfast cereal since 1906, distributing products to over 180 countries. Kellogg's operates in both the U.S. and Canada with a workforce of 25,000 and it is known for its exceptional human resources practices.[1]

Recently, Kellogg's was faced with a major challenge. One of their leaders suddenly resigned, deciding it was *time to go*. The leader who was earmarked as being "next in line" was by all accounts not ready to take the next step. These events had a significant impact on Kellogg's, sending this well-managed company into frenzy!

The beginning of the story dates back to an important call from the White House, when CEO Carlos M. Gutierrez received a call asking him to take the position of Commerce Secretary. Not many people would turn down such an opportunity, and so with only six out of the expected fifteen years' tenure as a CEO completed, Gutierrez decided to step down as CEO and leave the corporation. These events necessitated that the board of directors install his successor. The only problem—their chosen candidate, David Mackay, was not ready!

David was a veteran of Kellogg's, having been with the organization since 1985. He had travelled up the corporate ladder at a swift pace, moving from job to job every two to three years. Early on, it was not very clear what his career projectory was going to be and, in 1992, David MacKay decided to leave Kellogg's for a lucrative position at Sara Lee Corporate. His tenure at Sara Lee was short-lived and in 1998, Kellogg's successfully wooed David back. From that point onwards, his career projectory became much clearer. He moved from head of the U.S. unit of Kellogg's in 2000 to president and COO of the U.S. division in 2003, and he was identified as the major front-runner to take over Carlos Gutierrez's role by the end of 2006.

However, when Gutierrez resigned in 2004, David was not quite ready. He was lacking in boardroom expertise, a critical skill required of a CEO. He did not have any experience per se with boards and no visibility on boards. He did not clearly understand the board members' points of view and needed some significant development is this area. Until David developed these skills, the board felt that he wasn't ready.

The board was convinced that David was the right candidate and so they decided to install an interim CEO—James M. Jenness. His main purpose was to develop David Mackay and to ensure that he was ready to step into the job by December 2006. Over the course of two years, David Mackay received a crash course in what it was like at the top of the house. He was immediately given a seat at Fortune Brands Inc., an $8 billion a year marketer of Jim Beam whiskey, and some golf gear, and he spent the next two years under the wing of James Jenness. Today, the crisis is over at Kellogg's; David has been installed as CEO and all is well in the world of the most famous cereal maker in history.

This chapter will discuss why it is important for organizations to manage succession, the characteristics that determine an effective plan, the process that organizations engage in to determine when employees are ready to move, and which positions should be considered within an organization.

■ WHAT IS SUCCESSION MANAGEMENT?

Effective leadership is the fundamental building block to all successful organizations. Leaders set the vision and goals and provide direction for the organization. Leaders come from many different backgrounds and leadership can be expressed in many different ways. Today, organizations operate in dynamic and fluid environments where changes happen rapidly. An organization's ability to react quickly and with agility while utilizing all its resources optimally is a necessary condition for survival.

Guiding the organization through these challenges requires the right leader with the right skills at the right time and in the right place. Ensuring that an organization has an available supply of talent from its management ranks enables organizations to react and respond accordingly to local and global challenges.[2] Just think about the catastrophe that happened on 9/11. Many companies had to come to terms with the loss of their key executives: Cantor Fitzgerald, Oracle, AON, 3M, and the Fire Department of New York, to name a few. These organizations not only had to deal with the loss of their executive talent, but also suddenly, they were faced with major holes in their management structures. They immediately had to identify what skills they needed, the positions that were critical, and what types of competencies were required.[3]

Succession management is a systematic effort to ensure continuity of leadership across key positions within the organization. It is a deliberate and planned effort that reaches into the organization, identifying critical positions across all levels to ensure that there is an available talent pool of qualified candidates at any given point in time. It is a proactive approach that links to leadership development activities so that the organization will have an available supply of management talent of current and future job successors.[4]

Succession management is active and flexible. It continuously takes into account the dynamic nature of organizations, the numerous constituents that the organizations serve, and the various characteristics of its diverse populations. It is linked to the company's business plan, ensuring that the organization reaches its goals.[5]

Managing succession requires that organizations create a succession plan. The succession plan is a series of steps that enables the organization to review its workforce requirements from the individual and organizational perspective. It guides the organization towards resource decisions. These decisions will help the organization determine if an internal candidate will be ready to take on a leadership role or if the organization must source external talent to fill its leadership roles. The focus is on development of the individual, the identification of key positions within the organization, and the creation of a pool of available talent. This process can be deployed systematically or haphazardly. It can be structured or unstructured or broad or narrow in scope.

Why is managing succession so important? The next section will identify three primary reasons.

succession management

A systematic effort to ensure continuity of leadership across key positions within the organization

WHY IS MANAGING SUCCESSION IMPORTANT?

There are several reasons why managing succession is important for organizations today. The three primary ones, as shown in Exhibit 6.1, focus on organizational sustainability, attraction and retention of key talent, and leveraging the diverse nature of the workforce.

EXHIBIT 6.1 Reasons Why Managing Succession Is Important

Ensures Organizational Sustainability

Research indicates that companies that have effective succession management systems enjoy a higher rate of return and that this higher rate is increased when the systems cover several tiers of management. For example, Scott Paper increased its plant manufacturing output by 35 percent and reduced production defects after implementing a succession management program.[6] Having these systems in place helped to nurture and develop management staff. These systems view development over the long-term and methodically plan the appropriate development opportunities of these individuals over the course of their careers.[7]

Organizations must ensure that they have the right leaders who possess the necessary competencies and skills to sustain the business. This means anticipating the challenges facing the organization from an internal and external perspective.

With the baby boomers set to retire and an increasing demand for leaders, the projection of the number of leaders leaving organizations is disconcerting. A recent study conducted by the Hay Group on succession planning practices indicated that organizations anticipate between 15 to 30 percent or more of their key leaders will be retiring or leaving in the next three to five years. In addition, 52 percent of these organizations indicated that they were not sufficiently prepared for this exodus. They were unclear which roles across their organizations were critical, and they weren't clear on the breadth and depth of the competencies, skills, and knowledge necessary to be able to effectively carry out these roles. Moreover, these organizations felt that they did not have robust development processes in place to ensure that individuals were ready to take on these leadership roles.[8]

Another concern is CEO tenure. Booz Allen Hamilton determined that CEO tenure is shrinking. The global average is 7.6 years compared to 9.5 years in 1995. It is significant to note that two out of every five CEOs fail in the first eighteen months of their position.[9]

High-performing organizations anticipate these changes and ensure that they have a diverse talent pool in which there are candidates readily available to help the organization achieve its business objectives. Consider the events recently taking place at Home Depot. Home Depot decided to expand its market offerings and move into China. In December 2006, Home Depot announced that it was purchasing Home Way, a twelve-store home improvement retailer, in six Chinese cities, including Beijing. Annette Verschuren, an employee for over twelve years with Home Depot, was chosen to lead this venture. Verschuren had a record of accomplishment that included helping Home Depot gain significant market share in Canada and was someone known for exemplary operational skills and an ability to bring teams together under one vision. Annette was *ready* and was Home Depot's chosen candidate to lead this venture.[10] A *Canadian Business* article about Annette observed that "conquering Asia is vital to Home Depot's future."[11] Annette was a known quantity. She was well respected and had the support of Home Depot's employees and board of directors. She built up her creditability through years of demonstrating competence and leadership within a variety of roles and she made a significant contribution to organizational sustainability. She was viewed as a person able to achieve projected revenue targets as well as extend Home Depot's global reach.

This choice will enable Home Depot to continue to grow and compete in a highly competitive marketplace, meeting its financial targets set out by the business plan. The retail industry is waiting to see the outcome!

Attracts and Retains Key Talent

As discussed in Chapter 3, talent shortages are expected over the next several decades. Those organizations that offer talent management programs and care about their employees' development needs are the ones that employees want to work for, and these programs are the ones considered by HR professionals as necessary to ensure retention of top leadership talent.

A recent Critical Issues Survey conducted by the Institute of Management and Administration (IOMA), indicated that talent management, broadly defined to include retention, development, and succession planning, was human resources professionals' number one concern (74.2 percent). This was followed by employee engagement (60.7 percent) and leadership training and development at all levels (59.8 percent).[12] Corporate interest in retention management and succession planning has been growing as many companies worry about long-term workforce requirements and having the leadership to help in today's unstable environments. These numbers are high with about 57 percent concerned with long-term workforce requirements and 61 percent concerned about cost and disruption to the organization due to frequent turnover at the top.[13]

To understand what drives leaders away, we turn to a recent survey conducted by Hewitt Associates of the 50 Best Employers to Work for in Canada. Consistently, employees point to the availability of career development, opportunities for advancement, the ability to make a significant contribution to organizational success, and the willingness on the part of their managers to develop their future replacements as important. These organizations grow their employee capabilities from within, harness employee potential, and focus on getting the right people in the right roles led by the right type of management. Hewitt reported that these companies receive 45 percent more unsolicited applications, and the average turnover rate is 8 percent versus 11 percent at other organizations.[14]

Effective succession management programs highlight the importance of employee contributions to the organization. These programs can be one of a company's best tools for developing and retaining people as it determines who the key individuals are in an organization and determines gaps in work experience and skills, information that is critical for determining training needs.[15] It directs the organization to focus on its *talent* and highlights the importance of the firm's intellectual capital by tapping the abilities and competencies of these individuals. These programs review leadership talent, nurture and develop talent, listen to what the talent needs, and they do so in a systematic fashion. They do this to ensure that they have an optimum supply of manpower so that they can meet business requirements at any given point in time.[16]

The loss of valuable people resources can be catastrophic for an organization, compromising an organization's ability to manage its challenges. For example, SAP, a world leader in business software, recently lost one of its prized stars. Shai Agassi, president of the product and technology group, chose to leave the company because he did not want to wait any longer to progress to a higher level. Agassi was slated to become co-CEO of SAP when the current CEO, Henning Kagermann, was set to retire. However, Kagermann was asked to extend his tenure to continue leading new product launches. This meant that Agassi's appointment to his new role was going to be postponed. He was disappointed that the organization did not deliver on its promise within the timeframe that he expected. He felt thwarted and decided not to wait any longer. Several analysts expressed concern about SAP losing a star performer, one who had significant knowledge and leadership ability.[17]

Leverages Workforce Diversity—A Diverse Talent Tool

Diversity refers to a variety of human difference. Primary characteristics can include race, ethnicity, gender, age, and sexual orientation. Secondary characteristics may include status, educational background, work experience, and leadership capabilities.[18] Managing diversity refers to understanding these differences, valuing these differences, and leveraging these differences to help an organization achieve its business objectives.

Managing diversity is critical today as the demographic landscape changes and organizations are operating in a global environment. According to the Bureau of Labor Statistics, four out of every ten people who will enter into the U.S. workforce will be members of a minority group.[19] Ethnic groups currently represent 30 percent of the U.S. population today; by 2050, it is projected that minority groups will account for 90 percent of the overall population increase in the U.S.[20] In Canada, as per the 2001 census, over 13.4 percent of the total population is a visible minority, over 6 percent of working Canadians have some type of disability, and the projection is that over 85 percent of women in the 18–64 age group will be entering into the labour market in the near term.

A diverse workforce will require managers to develop competencies so that they can better understand the needs of these diverse groups. If managers are going to effectively leverage the talents these individuals possess, they must become aware of cultural differences and they must be aware of cross-cultural practices. This response can be viewed as a firm's *strategic* response to globalization activities and the growing multiculturalism of workforces and marketplaces.[21] It makes business sense, and research indicates that if senior management is not on board, achieving diversity will never happen.

In order to demonstrate commitment to diversity, organizations are expected to "walk the talk," ensuring that the actual demographic of its leadership team reflects diversity. The term **glass ceiling** refers to a systematic, invisible barrier that limits the maximum level to which a member of a demographic minority can rise in an organization. Breaking through this glass ceiling has been a challenge for quite some time.

In the year 2000, women filled 12 percent of corporate office jobs in Canada's 560 largest companies. Only 7.5 percent of directors at Canada's largest companies are women.[22] One company that is working to change this is Scotiabank, a company that has won an international award for advancement of women. At Scotiabank, representation of women at the most senior executive VP/Corporate officer level increased from 26.7 percent in 2003 to 36.8 percent in 2007.[23] If we look at representation at the executive levels with other diverse groups, the statistics are significant. For example, Canadians of Asian and African origins are educated compared to other ethnic groups, yet less than one percent of top executives in the country belong to these groups.[24]

Diversity that is reflected and supported at the executive levels demonstrates commitment—commitment to inclusiveness. This means establishing a succession management program that highlights diversity, and developing a succession plan that monitors diversity within the management ranks by setting goals to ensure a diverse talent pool. These actions will not only enlarge the pool of executive and managerial talent, it will also facilitate recruitment and act as a signal that managing diversity is the right thing to do.[25]

Many companies are visibly active in terms of their diversity initiatives. At Weyerhaeuser, executives are responsible for mentoring diversity and this activity is reflected in their career plans.[26] At RBC, the Diversity Leadership Council (DLC) has established stretch goals for increased representation of women and visible minorities in senior management and pipeline positions. As well, RBC is the founding member of the Canadian Aboriginal and Minority Council whose aim is to boost employment and economic development efforts.[27]

Next, we will discuss the elements that characterize an effective succession program.

glass ceiling

A systematic, invisible barrier that limits the maximum level to which a member of a demographic minority can rise in an organization

■ KEY ELEMENTS THAT CHARACTERIZE EFFECTIVE SUCCESSION MANAGEMENT

Succession management has evolved over the decades. Traditionally, it was viewed solely as a replacement plan, identifying backup for top-level positions. It literally meant *replacement* and focused on person—job fit, determining voids in continuity of leadership, and generating a simple replacement slate.[28] This plan may have identified two or three backups for an executive role or it may have only identified one candidate. It was reactive and focused only on filling the most senior of leadership roles. Candidate choice was based solely on feedback from immediate managers. Its activities could be likened to a form of risk management.[29]

In some organizations, the key leadership candidate was considered the "crown prince." They were "anointed," hand-picked by the CEO. In other firms, candidates literally competed for the top spot. It was a highly charged political process and typically, when the candidate did not win, they left.[30] The process was static, the focus short-range, and it did not consider the external landscape.[31]

Today, researchers view succession management as a way for firms to optimize and leverage their human capital. It is seen as a flexible and robust system that digs deep into the organization

| **EXHIBIT** | **6.2** | Elements That Describe Effective Succession Programs |

These programs:

✓ have stated goals and engage in a structured process to achieve its goals

✓ have established guidelines and a formal operating policy

✓ are aligned to the business environments in which they operate

✓ are linked to other HR– and business-related processes

✓ have developed feedback mechanisms to monitor and evaluate

to access and nurture talent while providing significant leadership and developmental opportunities to a group of individuals.[32] This system takes into account the dynamic nature of the business environments in which a firm operates, and recognizes that organizations are unique in terms of how they decide to manage their succession programs. There is no standardized template and no two succession programs look alike. Factors such as organizational size, industry, commitment of senior management, the dynamic nature of the external environment in which the organization operates, and the degree of importance placed on these activities are all important elements to consider when managing succession.[33]

There are, however, some common elements that can describe effective succession programs, and many researchers have provided examples of high performing organizations that engage in such practices.[34] Listed below are the elements of an effective succession program, also shown in Exhibit 6.2:

1. These programs all have stated goals and engage in a structured process to achieve these goals. This process is called the succession planning process.
2. These programs have established guidelines and have a formal operating policy.
3. These programs are aligned to the business environments in which they operate, and their programs are designed taking into account factors such as size, industry, and product life cycles.
4. These programs are linked to other HR– and business-related processes.
5. These programs have developed feedback mechanisms to monitor, evaluate, and assess their inherent value to organizational sustainability.

Next, we will discuss each of these elements in detail.

The Succession Planning Process

The first common element of an effective succession program is that is has stated goals and engages in a structured process to achieve these goals.

The overall goal of succession management is to ensure that the organization has an ample supply of qualified candidates who possess an array of leadership capabilities and skills at all levels within the organization so that they are able to address current and future business needs.[35] In essence, the organization is creating a leadership pipeline, a matrix of available talent who possess the appropriate skills and competencies, who at any given point in time can be ready to assume a leadership role.[36] To achieve this goal, organizations follow a series of seven key process steps, as outlined in Exhibit 6.3.

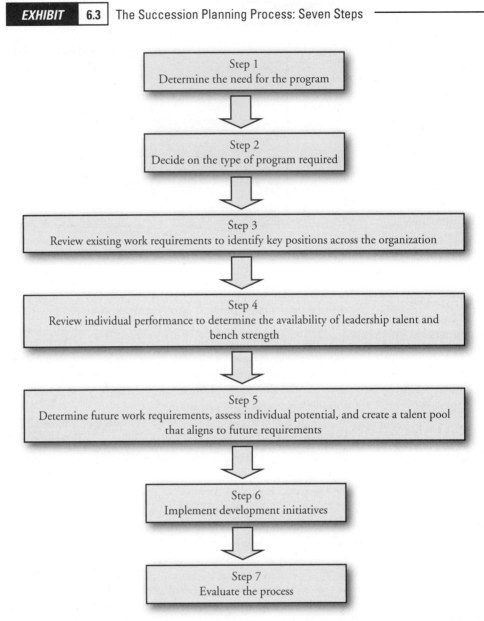

EXHIBIT 6.3 | The Succession Planning Process: Seven Steps

Step 1
Determine the need for the program

Step 2
Decide on the type of program required

Step 3
Review existing work requirements to identify key positions across the organization

Step 4
Review individual performance to determine the availability of leadership talent and bench strength

Step 5
Determine future work requirements, assess individual potential, and create a talent pool that aligns to future requirements

Step 6
Implement development initiatives

Step 7
Evaluate the process

Source: Rothwell, W.J. (2005). Effective Succession Planning: ensuring leadership continuity and building talent from within, 3rd ed., New York: AMACOM.

Step 1: Determine the Need for the Program   Organizations must first determine whether they need a succession program. Some questions that can help ascertain whether such a program is necessary include: Is the organization having difficulty filling key positions? Is the organization having difficulty retaining key employees? Is the organization experiencing some key problems that cannot be resolved without specific leadership skills?

Step 2: Decide on the Type of Program Required   Organizations are all different—in size, the dollars they have to spend on their programs, the challenges they face, the industries in which they operate, and the types of skill sets their employees possess. As such, organizations require varying degrees of sophistication with respect to their succession programs.

There are some important factors that must be considered when choosing a program, including how robust the succession program will be, whether it will operate globally or locally, and the scope of the program in terms of how far down the management levels it will extend. Consideration must be given to organizational size, stage of organizational maturity, and degree of alignment to business plan.

William J. Rothwell, author of *Effective Succession Planning* suggests that organizations that have never engaged in succession planning should start small and develop a basic plan. He describes succession-planning practices, which can range from simple to robust, and suggests that these practices become more sophisticated as organizations evolve. He refers to this evolution as stages that range from 1 to 5.

Initially, organizations typically create a simple replacement plan based solely on replacement for the CEO. As they evolve, organizations will design a plan that takes into account the CEO's direct reports as well (Stages 1 and 2). In the next phase, these plans begin to consider the levels below the senior team and there is evidence of some activities being cascaded to the middle-manager ranks (Stage 3). It is common at this point for organizations to develop a replacement chart that defines backups for top-level positions and some managerial ranks. See Exhibit 6.4 for a sample replacement planning chart.

In Stage 4 there is a movement from a replacement model to a development model where talent pools are created and developed for the future, and everyone is considered a potential successor for the critical positions (Stage 4). Finally, a highly sophisticated plan, referred to as "cutting edge," focuses on developing external sources for future talent, such as suppliers, out-source vendors, the contingent workforce, as well as internal development of the talent pool. The organization uses multi-rater assessments, competency models for the groups targeted, individual development plans, and skills inventories for talent pools outside the organization to help assess its talent. These plans use technology as an aid to facilitate this process (Stage 5).[37] Exhibit 6.5 provides an example of a company that is highly sophisticated in its approach to human resource planning. Chapter 7 will discuss technology in more detail.

Step 3: Review Existing Work Requirements to Determine Critical Positions   The next step in the process focuses on determining the organization's critical positions. Job analysis might be one HR activity used to collect this data. The outcome of this activity is to determine which roles are key positions. A **key position** is one that has considerable impact and influence on an organization's operational and strategic activities. Another term that is used to describe key positions is **"linchpin,"** meaning a position that is essential and of critical importance to the long-term health of an organization.[38]

Step 4: Review Individual Performance to Determine the Availability of Leadership Talent and Bench Strength   The next step is to review the employees' performance. The purpose of this is to create a "talent pool." A **talent pool** is a group of employees who are being developed for advancement. This advancement can be vertical, providing the employees with an in-depth array of skills at their current level. Or the move might involve horizontal opportunities which would mean promotion to a role with greater accountability, decision-making, and responsibility. The objective is to produce a "roster" of available employees. This roster provides the organization with a picture of "strength on the bench," often referred to as bench strength. **Bench strength** is the "organization's ability to fill vacancies from within."[39]

Organizations that are at the initial stage of plan development (Stage 1) would focus on the top levels of the house, whereas organizations that are using sophisticated techniques (Stages 4 and 5) would dig deep into the organization and identify several candidates who could *potentially* fill several different management levels within the organization. For example, at Prudential Financial, the EVP, chairperson, and executives from each business division meet to review the succession plans. This activity is cascaded down to the business units. Prudential has stressed the importance of these reviews, indicating that they can add rigor to the process and provide the organization with a macro view of its potential "talent pool." This view not only targets across

---

key position

A position that has considerable impact and influence on an organization's operational and strategic activities

linchpin

A position that is essential and of critical importance to the long-term health of an organization

talent pool

A group of employees who are being developed for advancement

bench strength

An organization's ability to fill vacancies from within

EXHIBIT **6.4** Illustration of a Replacement Planning Chart: Planning for Succession

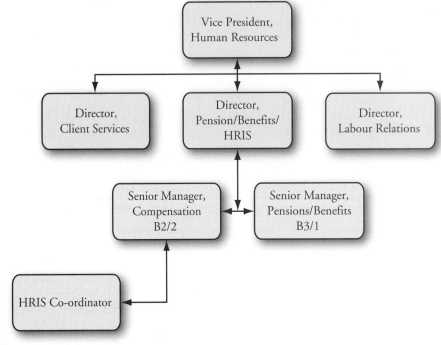

Key

Promotion Availability

A–Ready for promotion
B1–Development required, 6–12 months
B2–Development required, 12–18 months
B3–Development required, 18–24 months

Performance

1–Superior performance, role model
2–Above average
3–Average

---

the functions, but across the organization as well. The reviews help the succession team focus on developing more successors for critical positions and improve diversity across the organization.[40]

Step 5: Determine Future Work Requirements and Assess Individual Performance Potential In this stage, the organization reviews its business strategy and answers the following questions: What types of skills does the organization need? When will they need them? Where will they need them? What are the most critical skills that they must have and what are the most critical linchpin positions?

Once determined, these projections are reconciled to the pool of existing candidates and each individual within the pool is assessed in terms of potential. Assessment is widely regarded as an opportunity to provide an objective view of an individual's strengths and weaknesses. This potential is expressed by further segmenting the group into individuals who are high potentials and strong professionals/performers. Potential refers to future performance. **High potentials** are individuals who typically demonstrate the ability to learn more rapidly than their peers,

high potentials

Individuals who typically demonstrate the ability to learn more rapidly than their peers, show significant emotional maturity and growth in all areas, and are capable of taking on new challenges at work, rapidly mastering the task

---

EXHIBIT **6.5** Weyerhaeuser's Succession Planning Program (Stages 4 and 5) ────────────

An example of a robust succession program can be seen at Weyerhaeuser.[41] Weyerhaeuser is an international forest products company with sales of $21.9 billion annually. It was founded in 1900 and employs approximately 41,000 people, operating in eighteen countries worldwide.[42]

Weyerhaeuser has a robust succession management program. Its process has been in place for over ten years and is described as an "integrated human resources model." It focuses on several key factors: people, leadership diversity, and enhancing work systems. Weyerhaeuser has created a roadmap to help employees understand what they need to do to achieve in these key areas. Employees are rated on these key dimensions and are held accountable for how effectively they deliver. Employees are evaluated in terms of where they are performing within their current jobs and in terms of what they need to do in the future to gain future requisite skills. Weyerhaeuser has a comprehensive assessment system that determines development needs, which includes an assessment by an independent psychologist, 360-degree feedback, and performance reviews of the candidates based on job performance and core competencies.

Weyerhaeuser offers a robust leadership education program. It offers coaching and numerous management development programs with a particular focus on long-term development through experiential learning. What is most unique about this program is the fact that its customers contribute to the curriculum and that its executives and CEO are required to attend these sessions. Individuals are offered many opportunities for cross-functional assignments.

In the past, Weyerhaeuser hired 35 percent of its executives from the outside. That has now changed dramatically. All of its executives are now developed from within. The succession process is centralized for its top 100 "high potentials" across the organization. In addition, the process is deployed within each business unit to ensure that its high performers are assessed, development plans are in place, and that these individuals are visible. The CEO personally "owns" 50 positions. Weyerhaeuser's goal is to ensure continuity of leadership. They aim for "no gaps" when leaders retire or move into other roles.[43]

---

show significant emotional maturity and growth in all areas, and are capable of taking on new challenges at work, rapidly mastering tasks.[44] High potentials are individuals who are recognized as being future leaders.[45] They are capable of advancing two or more levels ahead of their current role in a relatively short time.[46] They manage change with ease, are highly flexible, and seek out significant challenges to help them grow.[47] On the other hand, a high performer is someone whose performance may be above average in only some jobs. They may be considered major contributors within their area of discipline, but when faced with new challenges, they may not always be able to rise to the occasion.[48] We can distinguish between the various levels by examining Exhibit 6.6.

The performance potential grid has two axes—present performance and future potential. The grid used some key terms to describe the various classifications of individuals. *Stars* are considered high potential, high performance individuals. *Workhorses* demonstrate high performance in their current jobs, but have poor potential. *Question marks* currently exhibit poor performance but are thought to have potential. *Deadwoods* are those individuals who demonstrate low performance and have low potential.[49]

Consider the process at Colgate Palmolive. Each subsidiary first determines who its high potentials are and then the general managers review the list and input their views. The list is then revised and the division heads are asked to comment and add or delete candidates. The list is then circulated to the Colgate Palmolive Human Resource Committee (CPHR), which is made up of the CEO, president, COO, and senior vice president of HR, and the senior candidates who are being considered for the top positions in the organization. Human resources then consolidate the list into one master list and cascade the information down where managers once again get an opportunity to challenge the decision. This process at Colgate takes place once a year.[50]

Step 6: Implement Development Programs At this point, those individuals who are in the pool are placed on an individual development plan (IDP). An IDP attempts to narrow the knowledge and experience gap, resulting in a detailed plan of what development is required in order for these individuals to qualify for advancement to the next position.[51]

EXHIBIT 6.6 Performance Potential Grid[52]

Future Potential

		High	Low
Present Performance	**High**	**Stars** Exceptional performers The organization should accelerate the development of these highly valuable employees	**Workhorses** Exceptional performers in their current job, but without significant future potential These individuals need to be motivated and kept productive
	Low	**Question Marks** These individuals have potential, but are not performing well in their current roles These individuals need to be given opportunities to prove that they can be converted to "stars" Development needs to be accelerated	**Deadwood** Poor performers and no potential Manage their performance and either convert them to workhorses or terminate

Adapted from *Effective Succession Planning,* 3rd ed., by William J. Rothwell, 2005.

The organization literally prepares these individuals by providing them with leadership development opportunities. Learning needs are diagnosed and these individuals receive a variety of opportunities, such as coaching, mentoring, formal training, and special assignments. Chapter 5 discusses these various developmental approaches in more detail.

For example, executives will typically receive specific assignments in many different functions across many different units.[53] Those who have been earmarked for CEO roles are given positions with responsibility in increasingly larger and more complex profit-and-loss centres. As well, they are provided with opportunities to manage increasingly more complex organizations. Complexity could refer to products, geographical locations, or size. For example, consider an individual who oversees an organization that operates locally versus one that operates globally.

 70

talent show

A monthly or quarterly meeting to discuss high potentials and determine their level of readiness for the next position

Meetings to discuss high potentials—"The talent show"   To ascertain readiness, it is typical for organizations to have a **"talent show."** This is a monthly or quarterly meeting to discuss high potentials and determine their level of readiness for the next position. Developmental opportunities and promotions are discussed and individuals are earmarked to move ahead. The CEO, senior VPs, senior managers of each division/department, and senior HR professionals attend this meeting.

This meeting is very important because it's as this point that the organization decides if it will be able to fill a role internally or look externally to fill a critical position. Other staffing alternatives may be considered at this point as well.

Step 7: Evaluate the Process   As with any process, continuous improvement and the utilization of measurement tools to ascertain whether the process is adding value is a major tenet of the design. The more sophisticated the organization, the more robust this evaluation process will be. We can expect organizations that are at Stages 4 or 5 to have well-developed feedback mechanisms to monitor and evaluate progress. For a more detailed discussion on the different types of evaluation mechanisms, refer to Chapter 10.

Succession Policies/Guidelines

The second common element that characterizes an effective succession program is the existence of established policies and practices and administrative processes that are well structured. These programs have formalized guiding principles, operating policies, and a formalized succession management policy.

The guiding principles might include the mission and philosophy regarding why the organization has embarked on a program, whether the program will be communicated openly or kept secret, and how much time and attention is required from key decision makers in terms of cultivating talent, appraising performance, and coaching and mentoring others. The policies typically establish the roles and responsibilities of the key stakeholders, the process to be followed, the timing of the process, what groups are included in the succession program, and the administrative details such as forms to be completed, approvals to be obtained, and use of technology.

Several roles are typically described in the policies—an executive, the board of directors, and HR. Often the CEO is the strategic owner and champion of the process. These individuals have accountability for development of their own teams and oversee the process. The board of directors is responsible for ensuring that the CEO has included succession management on their agendas and review the status of the program. For example, at Weyerhaeuser, the CEO owns the top 50 positions and is involved in all other discussions. The executive team is also involved in the top 50 positions.[54] Corporate HR is the process owner, which means they are responsible for ensuring consistency and a seamless deployment of the process. They are responsible for coordinating the programs, administering the system, ensuring that the information is documented, and keeping employees' files updated. In consultation with senior management, they identify how many and what kinds of people will be included, how many people will be involved in the process, and how much individual discretion is allowed. They determine when the talent pools will be updated, when the talent shows will take place, and when promotions will happen.[55] They establish a process regarding how high potentials will be selected and what methods that will be used.[56]

As one might expect, organizations that are beginning their planning efforts may have a low degree of formalization. However, as their process becomes more robust, they will develop more formal guidelines and policies and utilize increasing degrees of technology to help them administer the program. Chapter 7 will discuss how organizations use technology to plan for succession.

HRP AND THE SMALL BUSINESS

Succession Planning in a Family Business

A recent survey conducted by the Deloitte and Touche Centre for Tax Education and Research at the University of Waterloo indicated that three-quarters of leaders who manage family-owned businesses are due to retire within the next fifteen years. Of those businesses, two-thirds had not initiated any type of succession planning process. This lack of a succession plan is the major reason provided why only 30 percent of family businesses survive into the second generation. Over the next fifteen years, $1 trillion worth of assets will change hands, and this could have a major impact on jobs.[57] To ensure success, specialists recommend that businesses develop a succession plan early on and review it on a regular basis. This plan becomes the owner's exit strategy. It is important that family-owned businesses have a plan. If they do not and the owner develops a catastrophic illness, it may mean that the company has no one to take over, and it may have to be sold prematurely, perhaps for a lower value than it is worth.

Continued

HRP AND THE SMALL BUSINESS

Succession Planning in a Family Business

It is a common assumption in many family businesses that the company will be taken over by the owner's children. However, family members may be uninterested and, when asked to take on a position of authority, may not want to do so. In addition, not all family members are capable of running a business and the owner must ascertain competence and commitment and whether they share a common philosophy. Early on, those family members need to receive development to help them acquire the necessary skills. In family-run businesses, there may be issues when one family member is chosen over another and resentments ensue.

One family firm that has been successful at developing its plan is KD Displays. KD Displays is located in Oakville, Ontario. Robert and Joan Shatilla run it. KD provides point of sales displays for merchandisers. Robert and Joan initially developed their succession plan back in 1989. At that point, they thought that they would hand the company over to their children, David and Kim. However, nine years later the plan looks very different. Their son, David was going to become president, but he chose to bring in a non-family partner. The daughter married and she and her husband decided to purchase a division. Later on, the daughter spun off the division and created a separate entity apart from KD Displays.

Family businesses encounter specific challenges when it comes to deciding how best to ensure that the business is sustained through the next generation. To ensure that there is a smooth transition, these firms must start early on, revisit their plans over time, and seek expert counsel on such issues as tax, insurance, and resource matters. One action they can take is creating an advisory board of non-family members. This board can provide advice and counsel and help the family make difficult decisions. They can be impartial and independent and provide the family with an objective view. KD Displays is one such company. They have a seven-person advisory council and they have found this board to be a valuable resource.[58]

Business Environment

The third element of an effective program is one that aligns to the business environment in which it operates, and takes into account factors such as size, industry, and product life cycles.

To illustrate this, let's take a look at the GAP. Many of us know the GAP, a leading specialty retailer with over 150,000 employees across the world. And for those of us who have worked in retail or followed business trends we know just how competitive the retail landscape has become. The competition in retail is mounting exponentially as international competitors enter the marketplace. GAP has been losing market share for quite some time and they are acutely aware that they must embark on a business strategy to regain momentum in a marketplace saturated with players, if they want to return the company to a level of sustained performance. Executives have determined that they need a leader who has demonstrated that they can turn a company around and invigorate it. This individual must possess a certain set of skills and have a proven track record. To that end, GAP recently hired Glenn Murphy to lead this execution strategy. He has a proven track record, having invigorated Loblaws and Shoppers Drug Mart brands. He is considered "a decisive leader with great retail skills" and has an impeccable record of retail success.[59]

Imagine taking the time to find a senior executive to fill this role who does not have these qualities? How effective would the organization's program actually be if it did not understand the business strategy and the key issues facing the organization?

Consider also a start-up company or a small organization that operates in a stable environment where there is an abundance of skills available. These organizations may only develop a plan solely based on a replacement model (Stages 1 or 2). Contrast this to an organization that operates globally, in unstable environments with complex products, where the supply of key talent at all levels is fierce. The greater the business challenges, the more diverse the talent pool.

The steel industry in Canada is an example of an industry that has faced immense challenges. There has been significant consolidation of resources, with Dofasco being purchased by Arcelor, and Stelco, on the verge of merging, restructuring to avoid bankruptcy. Consider what their talent roster should look like.

Links to Other Business and HR–Related Functions[60]

The fourth common characteristic is succession programs that link to and align with other human resources– and business-related processes.

The most significant of these processes are career development, performance management, recruitment, and strategic planning.

A major tenet of managing succession is preparation of the talent pool for the future leadership. This preparation is guided by the identification of leadership competencies and an array of supporting developmental opportunities.[61] While many organizations are unique in terms of how they handle the succession process, they all share one common characteristic—they focus on the development of internal high-potential talent, accelerating learning through rapid assignments.

Business planning is critical as it determines the skills that are necessary for the pool to have at any given point in time. This results in an enhanced talent pool with specific skill sets. As we discussed earlier, a major assumption is that corporate strategy drives succession.[62] Biannually, Eli Lily has an action-training program that brings together potential leaders to focus on a business strategic issue. This is a six-week session where they meet with subject matter experts (SMEs), business leaders, and specialists in the field to analyze what they have learned.[63]

Performance management, via the appraisal process, enables the organization to identify the level of performance and determine the contributions being made by an individual in the talent pool. It is a critical activity used to assess an individual's leadership potential.[64] Once this information is known, managing the performance of high potentials is of the utmost importance. Appraisal feedback will enable the organization to know whether "the right people are moving at the right pace into the right jobs."[65]

In a recent study conducted by Hewitt Associates, it was found that high-performing companies were twice as likely to tie succession to performance management and use 360-degree feedback mechanisms tying these results to succession management. In addition, they found that these corporations were more likely to align and integrate their HR systems.[66]

The recruitment process is linked as well. At some point in the process, decisions are made with respect to sourcing talent internally or externally, the associated costs, and what benefits will result from this decision.

Evaluation, Feedback, and Measurement

The fifth common characteristic of an effective succession program is feedback mechanisms that monitor, evaluate, and assess effectiveness. These mechanisms ensure that the organization has the ability to ascertain if it has the right leaders when they need them, where they need them, and with the right skills.

Using Kirkpatrick's hierarchy of training evaluation as a framework, William Rothwell identified several main evaluation areas that can be utilized to evaluate and monitor the success of the succession program. These areas are customer satisfaction, program progress, effective placements, organizational results, and administration.[67]

Customer Satisfaction   Evaluation of the succession system considers whether the key stakeholders are satisfied. The key stakeholders are the board of directors, the senior management team, the *potential* candidates, and the internal support functions, such as training and development and human resources. Buy-in and commitment are important for any plan to be successful as is whether or not the stakeholders feel that the plan is credible, timely, and meets their stated needs. Prudential, for example, focuses on senior management's view of the process and uses this as one of their key metrics to evaluate effectiveness.[68]

Questions asked reflect how satisfied the chief customers are with each component of the program, such as the appraisal processes and development activities, and if the stakeholders feel that the program is aligned with individual career plans. To gather this information, organizations typically create a survey, which is confidential in nature. They may also have "skip level" meetings. These are meetings an employee has with the individual one level above their own manager. Managers of *high potential* employees regularly meet to discuss their perceptions and are asked for input to determine if the types of growth opportunities are well-received.

Effective Placements   This area looks at the number of vacancies and considers how long they will take to fill and what individual mastery is required. Key indicators include how many vacancies for key positions are filled internally, how quickly these vacancies are filled, and once the individual is in the position, how quickly he or she is able to get up to speed and perform as expected. This information can be gained by reviewing the individual's performance appraisals, individual and multiple raters, data from the HRIS system, and feedback from the candidates themselves.

Process Progress   Process progress relates to whether or not the process achieved what it set out to do. It compares the stated objectives to what actually happened and determines if there was alignment. It also examines if there was a clear understanding of the goal. Some tools that are used to gather data in this area include the design of a pre- and post-test of the level of skill/knowledge, creating SMART (specific, measurable, achievable, relevant, and time-bound) objectives, and gathering data from the stakeholders as to how effectively these goals were achieved.

Organizational Results   This is a macro measure that looks at whether the succession planning program contributed to the success or failure of the strategic plan. Many things must be considered, including if there is a direct line of sight that can be attributed to the succession program, if there is an increase in leadership diversity, if there are now fewer key positions without a ready successor, and if there is an increased percentage of high potential leaders.[69] In addition, the extent to which the organization is able to fill important leadership positions with internal candidates, and just how quickly this takes place, are some of the other areas that are evaluated. Measures such as the number and percentage of vacancies being filled and over what time span, might be considered. For example, at Dow Chemical, 75 to 80 percent is a sign of success.[70]

Administration   Administration of the plan is also an important element that must be evaluated in terms of usability, timeliness, and availability. Some issues to consider are whether the process is timely, well communicated, and clear. In addition, availability of adequate documentation is important to evaluate.

Now that we have discussed the characteristics of an effective program, we will turn our attention to constraints that may impede the success of a program.

■ CONSTRAINTS FACING SUCCESSION PLANNING

Several constraints can impede the succession planning process, as shown in Exhibit 6.7. Lack of senior management commitment; unclear selection criteria, rater error, and questionable data; insufficient attention to leadership development; timing of assignments; and a general lack of respect for the work of the human resources department are some of the more common factors.[71]

Lack of Management Commitment

Have you ever been able to implement a program without senior management's support? As with any programs in an organization, unless the senior team understands the value that can be derived from the program, supports the initiatives surrounding the program, and demonstrates by their actions that they are committed, the program will be bereft of a sponsor. Without a sponsor, the program will be doomed to lip service or another flavour-of-the month initiative. Management engagement in the process is necessary. Numerous researchers have highlighted the importance of senior management commitment and involvement in assessing, selecting, and developing their leadership potentials. Hewitt Consulting conducted a study of over 320 U.S. companies and 600 international firms and found that over 84 percent of the top twenty firms strongly agreed that the CEO must be actively involved, and 37 percent felt that the board of directors must be actively involved in this process.[72]

Unclear Selection Criteria, Rater Errors, and Questionable Data

This succession planning constraint refers to the organization's ability to identify high potentials and differentiate them from high performers. Leadership competencies are often used, but how well these competencies are understood, how clearly they are communicated, the consistency with which appraisals are carried out, and errors that can result from appraising performance, are all concerns that can hinder effectiveness.[73] For example, managers may choose individuals as high potentials because they are similar to them, as opposed to using objective criteria. This is sometimes called the "mini-me syndrome," a situation where executives feel more comfortable filling leadership roles with individuals who are similar to them.[74]

The element of the self-fulfilling prophecy may also play a part with respect to who should be in the elite talent pool. Management may be afraid to change the designation of the anointed individual even when their performance slips. They may also be reluctant to upgrade a regular performer to anointed status.[75] In addition, the evaluation mechanisms used to determine candidate potential might be questionable. For instance, one must consider if the information on performance was current, how many data sources contributed to the appraisal, and whether the data was statistically significant.

EXHIBIT | **6.7** | Constraints Facing Succession Planning —————

✓ Lack of management commitment
✓ Unclear selection criteria, rater errors, and questionable data
✓ Insufficient attention to development
✓ Timing of development assignments
✓ Lack of HR credibility

Insufficient Attention to Development

Managers may not be aware of what type of development is necessary and as such they do not focus on the appropriate type of employee development. Leadership development today focuses on a variety of techniques, encompassing educational with hands-on real-time training. Important things to consider in development include exposure to different bosses, a variety of assignments, and an understanding and utilization of the principles of action learning.[76] A more thorough discussion of this takes place in Chapter 5.

Timing of Developmental Assignments

The timing of assignments can be a constraint. There are several elements to consider. For example, what about the individuals who have the requisite skills and competencies and are ready to move, but are not given applicable assignments in a timely manner? Or perhaps an employee is ready to assume a role and the organization does not have any opportunities at that time. Also, consider a scenario where there may be a role available but more than one candidate ready. In this case, the organization will need to choose between the two candidates. Think about the message the organization should give to the candidate who was not chosen.

Organizations must be cognizant of these issues because lack of attention to timing can lead to unexpected turnover of high potentials.[77] Think about our earlier example about the executive who decided to leave SAP due to his promotion being delayed. Do think that he would have left if the appropriate opportunity had been available?

Lack of HR Credibility

As we discussed earlier, succession planning must be owned and driven by management. HR facilitates the process, but management owns it. Managers assess HR to determine if HR listens to them and whether or not they deliver a level of service that is timely and customer-focused. Managers want to see that HR clearly demonstrates a good understanding of its succession challenges and is truly acting as a strategic partner. If the organization does not feel HR is listening, then the HR department's credibility will be hindered. This can result in a process that is less than optimal.

In the next section, we turn to our attention to trends in succession management and examine a debate that has existed for quite some time—should leadership talent be sourced internally or should the organization look externally to fill a key role? Read the following to get a glimpse of this interesting conundrum.

■ TRENDS IN SUCCESSION MANAGEMENT

Organizations cannot afford to ignore the inevitable necessity of having the right people in the right place at the right time! Escalating worldwide labour shortages will exacerbate this challenge, highlighting just how critical it is for organizations to effectively leverage their talent. Succession management will continue to transform into an activity that will add sustainable value to the organization. It will become more integrated into all aspects of the business and planning and will extend further down the ranks to tap the talent early on, at different managerial levels, and across divisions and subsidiaries. Preparing individuals to manage globally and access their talent globally will become a necessity if organizations are going to manage in a global arena. Issues such as work–life balance will continue to take precedence. Technology will become an integral tool with which to manage information and improve planning. Currently, its use varies widely even within the best proactive organizations, where some human resources systems are aligned and others still operate as a stand-alone function. Chapter 7 will discuss the various technological innovations and challenges facing HR planning.

HRP IN THE NEWS

External Successors Who Did Not Fare Well[78]

Several CEOs have been recently appointed to head up large organizations. All of these CEOs were external to the organization and were well-known prior to joining the organization. Many of them had celebrity status and were widely regarded amongst their peers as major contributors to their past organizations.

Paul Pressler

Paul Pressler was the president of GAP Inc. for four years, leaving in January 2007. Prior to the GAP, he spent fifteen years with the Walt Disney Corporation. Pressler was CEO for only four years because the board felt that he lacked the appropriate retail experience. When Paul Pressler left the board, he appointed Robert Fisher, an insider. Fisher was one of the GAP founders and was chairman of the board. Today Glenn Murphy, an outsider, has been named as the next CEO of GAP. He comes from Loblaws, where he spent his formative years.

Robert Nardelli

Robert Nardelli became CEO of Home Depot in December 2000 and, by 2006, he was asked to leave the company. Robert Nardelli was a recruit from General Electric where, since 1971, he held increasingly senior positions. He was known as "little Jack" and modelled himself after his mentor, Jack Welch. When Jack Welch retired, Robert Nardelli hoped that he would succeed Jack. However, this did not happen, and Nardelli accepted the CEO role at Home Depot. He lasted six years. The board had concerns with his aggressive result-driven style, and when the company's growth declined, he resigned. An insider, Frank Blake, who had been with Home Depot since 2002, took over the helm.

Carleton (Carly) Fiorina

Carly Fiorina started as an AT&T management trainee and rose to become a senior VP by 1995. She then moved to Lucent Technologies from 1995 to 1999. In 1999, she became the CEO of Hewlett Packard. Right from the beginning, she clashed with many long-term executives, and there were concerns about how she would fit with the HP culture. She was dismissed in February 2005 by the board. The reason given was the significant differences regarding how to execute HP strategy. She lasted six years and was replaced by another outsider, Mark Hurd.

One particular issue that will no doubt continue is whether it is best to hire an internal or an external candidate to fill a key executive role.

A Difficult Choice—Hire an External Candidate or Fill the Role Internally

Organizations often are faced with the decision to externally hire leadership talent or develop and grow it from within. In particular, this decision is most pressing when it comes to the CEO position. The data raises a serious question as to which way is the best way to go. In North America, 55 percent of outside CEOs who left their organizations in 2003 were terminated, compared to 34 percent of insiders. The European statistics are even more astonishing, with over 70 percent of outsiders being terminated.[79]

Consulting firm Booz Allen Hamilton concluded that CEOs who were appointed internally outperformed outsiders with respect to shareholder returns.[80] However, outsiders in the first half of their tenure posted significantly greater shareholders gains. But, in the second half of the outsiders' tenure, their performance declined and insiders' contributions markedly increased.[81] Yet, outsiders run more than 37 percent of Fortune 1000 companies.[82]

There are several reasons why organizations choose an external candidate. While there is considerable expense attached to hiring external candidates—fees to retainer firms can be as high as 35 percent of the CEO base pay—firms may not have adequate succession programs in place. This can lead to placement of an external candidate. A recent survey conducted by the Corporate Leadership Council found that only 20 percent of HR executives felt that their succession programs were adequate. Outsiders are chosen for their particular skills, such as significant expertise in management, restructuring, or consolidations. Outsiders may be brought in to shake up the culture and to redesign processes. For example, at Nortel, Mike Zafirovski was hired as an outsider known for his ability to manage costs and restructure organizations. His mandate was to "stop the bleeding" and bring Nortel back to financial health. To do this, Zafirovski focused on cost-cutting research and development, general and administration expenses, and targeting key business initiatives that would once again bring Nortel back to operating margins of 13 percent.[83]

Insiders, however, are chosen because of credibility and knowledge of the business. They are respected, they are a proven quantity and, if they have been developed effectively, have the skills to manage the challenges. However, there are some problems with insiders. Because they are known quantities, they may have a reputation that does not necessarily hold true any longer, or they may have networks in place that hinder change, or they may lack well-developed interpersonal skills. It is interesting to note that about one-third of internally sourced leaders fail, usually because of poor people skills or because they exhibit poor interpersonal competencies such as insufficient self-awareness, poor emotional intelligence, and lack of empathy.[84]

It is difficult to develop leaders, even when the organization has a strong developmental focus. Consider a corporation with 70,000 employees and $25 billion in revenues. There may be 3,000 potential leaders. Of these 3,000, likely 50 to 100 would qualify for one of the ten top jobs, and likely only two or three would be potential candidates for the CEO position.[85]

HRP IN THE NEWS   Rogers Communications Picks a Successor

One such company that considered the internal versus external options was Rogers Communications, a diversified Canadian communications and media company engaged in four primary lines of business: wireless, cable, media, and telecom. When Ted Rogers was president and CEO of the company, he gave considerable thought to finding a successor for his business. It was once thought that his son Edward, who served as president of the cable business, or his daughter Melinda, who at the time was senior VP of strategy and development, would take over the empire. Or at one point, it was thought that John Tory would step into this role. However, Ted Rogers never dismissed the fact that a successor might come from outside the organization. He indicated that when the time came, he expected the board of directors to hire advisors to help them source internal and external candidates.[86] Unfortunately, that time came much sooner than anyone thought when Ted Rogers recently died. Alan Horn, the company's chairman, stepped in at that point to take over the reins as an interim CEO.[87] However, the search continued and on March 30, 2009, Rogers Communication announced that Nadir Mohamed would be the next president and CEO. Highly regarded in the industry, Nadir had 25 years experience in telecom and had since May 2005 served as the president and CEO of the communications division of Rogers.

CHAPTER SUMMARY

- Succession management is a systematic effort to ensure continuity of leadership across the organization. It ensures that there is pool of leadership talent available at the right time with the right leadership skills to lead the organization towards achievement of its business objectives.

- Effective succession management creates a plan of action. This succession plan is future-oriented, systematic, and determines a process to identify critical management positions, and high potential employees, providing these individuals with targeted developmental opportunities.

- Succession management is a critical business activity in that it harnesses the diverse and requisite skills and experience that these individuals possess, leverages these talents, and optimizes the contributions of these individuals.

- Organizations manage succession in different ways. Some organizations engage in limited succession planning while others have robust and highly structured activities. The factors that contribute to how robust the program is largely depend on the environment in which the organization operates—management philosophy, size, and industry characteristics.

- There are several reasons why managing succession is important for organizations today. Some of the key reasons are organizational sustainability, attraction and retention of key talent, and leveraging the diverse nature of the workforce.

- There are five common elements that describe effective succession management programs. These programs all have established goals and engage in some form of a structured process, they have established guidelines and policies, the programs are aligned to business requirements, their activities link to other HR– and business-related functions, and they all engage in some form of evaluation and feedback mechanisms.

- The succession planning process involves seven steps. Step 1: Determine the need for the program; Step 2: Decide on the type of program required; Step 3: Review existing work arrangements to determine critical positions; Step 4: Review individual performance to determine the availability of leadership talent and bench strength; Step 5: Determine future work requirements and assess individual performance potential; Step 6: Implement development programs; and Step 7: Evaluate the process.

- Planning for succession is an important organizational activity that ensures sustainability. It enables an organization to optimally manage its talent. However, management must be aware of the constraints that can impede the implementation of an effective succession program. These constraints include lack of commitment at the senior level; unclear selection criteria, rater error, and questionable data; insufficient attention to detail; the timing of the assignment; and lack of HR credibility.

KEY TERMS

- bench strength   141
- glass ceiling   138
- high potentials   142
- key position   141
- linchpin   141
- succession
  management   135
- talent pool   141
- talent show   144

REVIEW QUESTIONS

1. What is the difference between succession management and succession planning?
2. What are the three main reasons to engage in succession planning?
3. What are the five key elements that can be used to describe some common characteristics of succession plans?
4. What are the steps in the succession planning process?
5. Why would an organization choose an internal versus external candidate?
6. What differentiates a Stage 1 organization from a Stage 5 organization?
7. What are the constraints facing effective succession planning?

DISCUSSION QUESTIONS

1. Do you think leaders should come from within the ranks of an organization? Why or why not?
2. What reasons would you give if you had to convince organizational leaders that succession planning is important?
3. What role do you think the board of directors, the executive team, and human resources should play in helping an organization choose a successor? Do you think that the organization should consult the employees?
4. What are some of the competencies and qualities that leaders should possess? Do you think these qualities should be different for not-for-profit versus profit organizations?
5. How open do you think an organization should be with its succession plans?
6. Do you think that all organizations should have a succession plan in place? Think about the difference between a small and mid-sized organization.

WEB EXERCISE

Over the past eight years, several high profile companies have experienced a change in leadership. Apple, WestJet, and Johnson & Johnson are a few examples. Choose two organizations that have experienced this type of change and compare and contrast these organizations in terms of size, revenues, number of employees, operational sites, and leadership styles. How many leaders has each organization had? Were the leaders sourced internally or externally? Was there a particular business reason for these choices? What competencies did these organizations identify as being most important? Can you differentiate between the firms' succession management practices?

CASE INCIDENT

Nike Inc.—A Doomed Succession Plan?

Nike Inc. is a company that needs no introduction. The swoosh, designed in 1971, is synonymous with Nike. It represents the wing of the Greek goddess *Nike,* meaning victory. Nike was originally called Blue Ribbon Sports. Bill Bowerman, a track-and-field coach at the University of Oregon, and Phil Knight, a University of Oregon business student and middle-distance runner under Bowerman, founded the company in 1964. In 1972, Blue Ribbon Sports introduced a new brand of athletic footwear called Nike. Today, Nike employs approximately 29,000 people worldwide.[88]

Phil Knight has led Nike since the beginning, successfully turning his company into a multi-billion dollar enterprise. Knight has been heralded as a leader with a vision; a vision that focuses on matching pop culture with sports. Celebrities such as Tiger Woods and Michael Jordan all helped this vision come to life. A. Michael Spence, dean of the Stanford Graduate School of Business and a Nike board member has said that, "Phil understands the symbolic power and attractiveness of sports and he helped build that connection in our culture."

Phil Knight is known for being very casual in his dress and he is rarely seen without his Oakley sunglasses. He has been described as eccentric, unpredictable, aloof, and idiosyncratic. He is competitive and he is known for being very hands-on with the day-to-day operations of the business.[89]

He has always acknowledged that succession planning was a top priority, but has had difficulty handing over the reins. In the past, Knight has tried to hand over the reins of power but was unsuccessful. In November 2004, he tried again. This time he hired William Perez, a marketing executive from SC Johnson. It took over one year to find Perez. The company went through 75 résumés and conducted 15 interviews. It then narrowed the search down to three or four candidates and spent a significant amount of time with each candidate. From the onset, Phil Knight decided to hire an outsider. He felt that he needed new blood and was determined to find someone with specific skills and knowledge.

Perez was chosen for his expertise in financial management, his track record of overseeing a consumer products company, and his ability to manage multiple brands globally. Once hired, Perez was asked to review the company strategies, manage the firm's operating costs, ascertain whether Nike had the right growth strategy, and demonstrate an understanding of the company and the industry.

Unfortunately, right from the beginning Phil Knight and fellow executives had issues with Perez. Perez hired the Boston Consulting Group to review the company's strategies and moved very quickly to make changes. He questioned whether Nike had the right growth strategy and appropriate control of operating costs. He made recommendations suggesting that Nike open outlet stores, raising significant concerns about devaluation of the brand. To manage costs, he suggested that Nike outsource security services, daycare, and janitorial services, which was not looked upon favourably. He questioned the impact of Nike's advertising strategy. There were basic differences in their approach to managing the issues. Although Knight wanted Perez to manage costs, he disagreed on the approach. In addition, he felt that Perez did not understand the Nike brand and relied too heavily on spreadsheets and analysis. He did not feel Perez understood Nike's creative mindset.

Just thirteen months from the time Perez was hired, Phil Knight called him into his office on a Monday morning and told him that he was fired. The reason given? That Perez did not fit with the Nike team.[90]

Questions

1. Upon hearing about the Perez situation, Stephanie R. Joseph, president of the Directors Network Inc. said, "It's almost like a death wish coming into that company from the outside."[92] What do you think she means by this statement? Do you agree with this statement?
2. Do you think Nike's succession plan has been well-thought-out? What process would you suggest to follow?
3. Should Knight have chosen someone internally? Do you think it was a mistake to go externally for a candidate?
4. What are some of the constraints that have impeded Nike's succession management process?
5. What recommendations can you make to improve the process?

■ REQUIRED PROFESSIONAL CAPABILITIES REFERENCED IN THIS CHAPTER

1. Contributes to the development of the organization's vision, goals, and strategies with a focus on human capabilities.
2. Translates the organization's business plan into issues, priorities, and human resources strategies and objectives.
5. Keeps current with emerging HR trends.
36. Stays current with professional knowledge.
64. Researches, analyzes, and reports on potential people issues affecting the organization.
66. Identifies the data required to support HR planning.
68. Assess the effectiveness of people and talent management plans.
69. Maintains an inventory of people talent for the use of the organization.
70. Develops systems and processes that link the careers plans and skill sets of employees with the requirements of the organization.

HUMAN RESOURCE PLANNING AND TECHNOLOGY

LEARNING OBJECTIVES

- Describe why a human resource management system (HRMS) is important to human resource planning
- Identify the critical design components required in a HRMS
- Describe how the requirements of a HRMS are established
- Identify issues related to security and confidentiality and the limits to which these can be ensured
- Describe the impact of HRMS on the roles of human resources professionals and line managers

■ PROFILE

Ryerson University

In the fall of 2007, Ryerson University announced to its staff and faculty via email that it was implementing a new human resource management system. Why? The reasons for the change were identified as:[1]

- Facilitation of the university's strategic objective to provide more control of human resources processes to faculties and departments
- Improving both an individual's and a department's access to their human resource information and thus improve the HR services provided
- Reducing the increasing human resources workload in the growth environment of the university by reducing the use of manual- and paper-based human resource processes

As companies grow, changes are necessary in how they collect and manage their human resource data if they are to meet both internal and external reporting requirements. Often, as in the case of Ryerson, organizations outgrow their current system and need to implement more complex systems.

Prior to implementing a new system, Ryerson's used a process that was in part paper-based and required employees to enter data provided on paper by employees, meaning manual processes that took significant time and were prone to error. Also, their system had limited functionality, produced fragmented data, created duplication of data, and required extensive time and resources.[2]

What were Ryerson's objectives for the new human resource system? According to the CampusNews, the objectives included:[3]

- Providing managers and employees with self-service so they can enter data directly or see information about their benefits by personally accessing the system
- Supporting decision making at the department level with respect to human resource management by making data readily available to management
- Providing relevant centralized information to support reporting needs and strategic planning
- Integrating the human resource management system (HRMS) with other critical Ryerson computer systems (e.g., SAS, Financial Services, Research, The Chang School)

In May of 2008, Ryerson sent a campus email to provide the Ryerson Community with a HRMS update, stating that a module that enables faculty and departments to hire and make changes on contracts for temporary and contract employees (called eAppoint) would be operational in 2008.[4] As well, other modules, including self service, time reporting, and recruitment for teaching assistants and graduate assistants would be introduced in early 2009.

To minimize the challenges created by the change, a business process advisory committee, with representatives from faculties and administrative departments, was created as part of the development and rollout of the system. The role of the advisory committee ensured that employee input was heard and that the employees would support the system as it was rolled out.[5]

In this chapter we will discuss:

- Why a human resource management system (HRMS) is important to the human resource planning process in an organization, and why the investment should be made by human resources departments
- The various types of human resource management systems, and the impact of organizational needs on the type of system used
- The factors to be considered in the purchasing, implementation, and security
- Security issues related the collection and storage of human resources data

■ INTRODUCTION—TECHNOLOGY AND HUMAN RESOURCES

It's predicted that from 2005 to 2010 human resource technology in North America will increase seven percent per year on average.[6] This growth is expected to be 11 percent in Europe, 18 percent in the Asia-Pacific market, and 21 percent in Latin America. One of the challenges in implementing a human resource system in a larger organization is that they are often international, and the requirements for the collection and use of data varies by country. Deciding what software to use is difficult because the senior team of an international organization does not want to purchase and implement software that cannot be used in all parts of the organization, especially when it comes to decision making for hiring, talent management, and succession planning.

Many human resource software companies have stated that their systems are international and are flexible enough to be used in international companies. SAP, one of the industry's biggest players, advertises itself as "the world's largest business software company," stating that it has software versions of human resource applications tailored for 46 different countries. To maintain its compatibility in this field, SAP has teams of people monitoring legal developments around the world, and advertises that it delivers legal changes every three weeks.[7] PeopleSoft (Oracle), another large supplier of human resource software, also has software that is applicable internationally. As a company, PeopleSoft also keeps tabs on legal changes around the world and updates its software to make sure PeopleSoft clients are in compliance with local legal requirements.[8]

■ HUMAN RESOURCE PLANNING AND TECHNOLOGY

As a new member in an organization, one of the first things an employee is required to do is complete a number of forms before they are "officially" on the payroll. The type of information usually required includes: name, address, banking information, social insurance number, emergency contacts, benefit plan information, beneficiaries, and martial status. These files used to be paper-based and in some cases still are. In order to keep their records up-to-date, an employee needed to complete an update form, often have the form signed by their manager, and then forward it to human resources where an employee entered the date. The human resources department was and continues to be the custodian of this information in most organizations.

The human resource function in organizations is a rapidly changing area. It needs to continually react to a changing social and organizational environment and rapidly evolving information requirements. The ongoing social and organizational changes exert pressure on human resources to provide expanded services that are higher quality, faster, and seamlessly aligned with other corporate functions.[9] The use of information technology assists human resources professionals in delivering services more efficiently and effectively. However, the use of technology also increases the expectations that employees, managers, customers, suppliers, and regulators have of the human resource function, including providing up-to-date reporting in areas related to turnover, costs of benefit packages, and talent availability for open positions.

Evolution of Data Management in Human Resources

From 1960 to 1980, human resources as a function began to be integrated into the core business of many organizations. During this period the governmental and regulatory reporting requirements for employees increased significantly. Initially, with the use of mainframe computers in North America and the need for increased regulatory reporting, organizations began to use technology to meet record-keeping requirements and to provide some reporting using the analytical capability of the computer.

Over the last two decades, organizations have begun to develop an increasing reliance on human resources for solutions to increase the effectiveness of decision making, including reporting on hiring, turnover, and talent availability.[10] During this period, the use of personal computers with varying types of software has grown exponentially. This growth has resulted in a variety of software being developed so that the needs of all organizations, independent of size, can find the tools needed to meet regulatory reporting requirements as well as help the organization manage its human assets. Human resource management systems have evolved into complex tools designed to manage complex information and provide analytical tools to assist in decision making about human asset management.

The type of technology used by organizations varies depending upon their size, technological capability, and experience. In addition to collecting information such as address, salary, and benefits, organizations are now collecting other data, such as education, training, performance, and roles in the organization or other organizations. The data collected is used by human resources and management to forecast staffing, retirements, staff shortages in specific areas of experience, succession planning, talent management, and learning management.

◼ WHAT IS A HRMS?

human resource management system (HRMS)

A technological system used to acquire, store, manipulate, retrieve, analyze, and distribute pertinent information regarding an organization's human resources

A **human resource management system (HRMS)** is a technological system used to acquire, store, manipulate, retrieve, analyze, and distribute pertinent information regarding an organization's human resources.[11] The technology used for the HRMS can include:

- Word or Access files
- Home-grown technical systems using a variety of programming software
- Open source licensed systems
- Modules in enterprise resource programs, such as PeopleSoft or SAP products[12]

Not all companies require enterprise resource programs to manage their human resource needs, but all companies do have HR–related needs. Research indicates that companies that effectively use technology to manage their human resources function will have a significant advantage in the competitive marketplace in areas such as hiring and retention over companies that do not use technology.[13]

World-class companies now spend 25 percent less than their peers and operate with 16 percent fewer human resources staff. Why? More efficient use of technology is a key factor. Self-service technology appears to play a role in the higher level of efficiency and productivity. Additionally, human resource leaders in these world-class companies have a deep understanding of technology and make a strong effort to derive as much value as possible from the technologies they implement.[14]

As is the case with any complex organizational information system, the HRMS is not limited to computer hardware and software applications (the technical part of the system), but also includes the people, policies, procedures, and data required to manage the human resource function.[15]

The Stakeholders

Contemporary human resource management systems must meet the needs of a number of organizational stakeholders. The typical stakeholders that would interact with the HRMS include human resources professionals, managers in functional areas (e.g., marketing, finance, etc.), and employees.

In many organizations human resources professionals have come to rely on the organizational human resource management systems in their job functions, specifically in areas such as compliance and reporting, compensation analysis, payroll, pension, skill development, and skill inventory. The need for systems with increased computing capability is required if the organization is going to be able to manage and provide the reporting that is required by shareholders, regulators, and governments, let alone the organization.

As organizations recognize the importance of their human capital, functional managers expect to be able to get the data they require to meet their goals and objectives from the HRMS. Managers expect to get data and analysis from the HRMS for performance appraisals and performance management, résumé processes, recruiting and retention, team and project management, assessment and development, and management development.[16]

Individual employees often become end users of many HRMS applications. Previously, human resources collected data on address changes, benefit changes, and any other individual employee changes on paper forms, which were often signed off by a supervisor, and then entered the changes into the human resources system or files. The process was very administrative and took significant human resource administrative time. With the option of web-based access to individual data, and the self-service option in the new HRMS, employees can make the appropriate changes to personal information themselves, monitor benefits or stock option packages, sign up for and even participate in online training. Human resources professionals are then freed up to do more strategic and less transactional work.

Overall Impact of Information Technology on Functional Activities

Changing human resource technology has continually provided the opportunity for organizations to increase the efficiency and effectiveness of managing employee data. The use of computer technology allows for more transactions to occur with fewer resources. For example, calculating the potential cost of a proposed new benefit can be done quickly using HRMS software that has the organizational demographics. It also has the capability of doing what-if scenarios. Rather than spending days calculating, the HRMS system can be programmed to provide the required information within minutes. The accuracy of the data provided using the HRMS system is significantly increased compared to manual calculations in which multiple parameters are involved.

■ WHY IS A HRMS IMPORTANT TO HUMAN RESOURCE PLANNING?

In order to be an effective human resource planner, relevant and current information must be readily available. The management team of an organization looks to human resources to be responsive to the needs of the organizational strategic plan and to provide accurate human resource information in a timely manner.[17] In order to respond and provide data to management in a timely manner, human resources needs to capture data beyond personal information about an employee in a manner that allows human resources or organization management to retrieve the required information in a form/report that can be used for analysis. For example, to do workforce planning, one needs to do a supply analysis that includes "identifying organizational competencies, analyzing staff demographics, and identifying employment trends" and pull this together in such a way that further analysis related to workforce planning can be achieved.[18]

Generally, the data required for each employee within an organization includes the competencies an individual possesses, work experience, age, educational background, evaluation results, career development plans, succession scenarios, training needs. Thus, a HRMS that captures this type of information and can produce the reporting necessary to provide management with the data they require is essential to permit high-quality, informed human resource planning decisions.

Why Invest in an HRMS?

The phrase "war on talent" is used extensively in the news and within the recruiting community as a way of describing a talent shortage.[19] The phrase captures the fact that it is difficult to find certain types of talent or individuals with the key competencies that organizations need to be competitive. A number of research reports have been produced, including the Toronto Financial Services report (TSFE), that illustrate the shortage of skilled talent in many fields including the financial services industry.[20] Organizational leaders recognize that their organization's success relies on the knowledge that employees have and use to do their jobs. These organizational leaders know that their strategic success will depend on the "coordinated, strategic management, and integration of the organization's human resources and information technology."[21] Organizational leaders are addressing the "war on talent" by using talent management solutions, establishing or refining human resource application strategies, aligning employee performance with organizational goals, and measuring results with performance management solutions.[22]

According to Jones and Hoell, to be successful in implementing a strategic plan including the human resource component, it is necessary to develop, implement, operate, and maintain a HRMS that has a broad knowledge of the organization's human resource programs, as well as the relationship between human resource programs and the overall strategic plan.[23]

Thus, organizations must leverage technology to manage human resources activities, especially those related to strategic human resource planning. Data available in the HRMS can be used to report employee participation in training, including types of training, competencies achieved, and competencies identified as needing work, based on performance appraisal information and performance levels, which can then be used by the management team to develop strategic options for the organization. Access to data in the HRMS by not only human resources, but management, will help an organization identify areas of available talent as well as areas where available talent is not sufficient to meet organizational needs.

Specific Applications of a HRMS   Applications including skills inventory, succession planning, replacement charts, and compensation planning are key examples of applications that are useful technology supports for human resource planning.

An inventory of skills for current employees can be maintained on the HRMS system. Data included in a skills inventory include employee name, seniority, job classification, status (full-time versus part-time), job history, education, training, competencies, performance appraisals, future job interests, and recommendations by managers. This data, if easily searchable, can be used to provide reports to management including information on the number of employees who are 60 or over. Or, it can be used in decision making, such as determining whether a particular business strategy can be supported by the current staff or if there is a skills gap in a particular competency area.

Succession planning is another area where technology supports are helpful. Succession planning is a process that prepares employees for future jobs in the organization. The process requires significant information on competencies, development plans, employee pool, performance assessments, and developmental plans. Some human resource management systems have talent management modules that are updated periodically to support management in the decision-making processes related to filling key vacancies.

The use of technology is a benefit in replacement planning. The process of finding replacement employees for key roles in an organization is called replacement planning. Replacement charts can be used to support this process. In this process, individuals who are likely to leave the organization, including potential retirees, can be identified, and a list of potential successors can be named. Data on each of the potential successors, including performance appraisals, competencies, and the needs of the role, is then available to make decisions if one of the identified individuals leaves the organization. Overall, the reporting from the system can provide sufficient information to decisions makers for them to determine if they have enough employees with the talent needed, or if they need to develop or hire individuals with that specific talent. Human capital management systems, a part of the HRMS, provide online navigation of divisional and corporate-wide charts, allowing managers to track candidates and obtain specific information to make decisions.[24]

Another useful application of a HRMS is in compensation planning. Periodically, organizations need to engage in compensation planning, a process to determine the cost of potential compensation packages. To perform this process without software can take significant time (i.e., to get a set of real number salary ranges against jobs based on the size of the organization). A Miami-based company, Town Care Dental Groups, was able to do this with HRMS in 10 minutes instead of 10 to 12 hours of labour intensive work.[25]

Outsourcing

More and more organizations are subcontracting work that is not part of their core business. This is referred to as outsourcing. Nelson Hall, an outsourcing research firm, reported that the outsourcing market will grow 21 percent annually.[26] The growth in human resource outsourcing has been seen in areas related to basic human resource transactions as well as those related to the employee life cycle, such as recruiting.[27] In order to effectively outsource work, one needs to have employee information in an electronic system. Data on employees, such as name, address, age, and benefits can be exchanged accurately and efficiently in a timely manner. For an organization that wants to outsource human resource work, it is important to define the requirements of an HRMS so that they can capture and share data with the outsource company as needed.

Global Needs

Multinational organizations are concerned with establishing human resource systems worldwide to ensure consistent processes for the whole organization. Travelport, a part of the Cendant conglomerate, is trying to install a single source of human resource data worldwide. The belief is that the system will save costs and allow executives to analyze information quickly, helping them to make key business decisions.[28] For certain information, the needs change from country to country. To deal with this, and with challenges such as language differences, patches to the HRMS are used. The development and installation of patches and the ongoing need to upgrade HRMS always take more time than anticipated and cause frustrations. As much as possible, given local laws and customers, many multinationals want to establish a content workforce management system that works internationally. Vendors of human resource software systems promise to help organizations with worldwide rollouts of systems that meet their needs, but the products available leave much to be desired when it comes to meeting the international requirements of an organization. Many applications lack features required to meet country-specific requirements, both legal and cultural.[29]

For example, an applicant-tracking system used by an international organization must configure to various recruiting practices that exist consistently in North America. Most systems have difficulty doing this. Even more challenging is trying to use an application tracking system globally. IBM created their own application system called Professional Marketplace that tracks the skills, availability, and billing rates of Big Blue technical professionals throughout the world. The system captures data for over 90,000 IBM employees.[30] IBM needs software that managers can use in assembling project teams. They also need it to prove to potential clients that IBM has the consulting resources the client's projects need in multiple countries. The challenge for any commercial software trying to meet global needs is immense. IBM, like many global companies, does substantial business worldwide. They operate in 140 countries and employ people in 70 countires.[31] How do you create software to manage the differences that are likely to arise under these circumstances? IBM had to create their own because commercial software was not capable of doing the work.

Some human resource applications may be easier to install and use globally than others. For example, learning management systems don't have as many country-specific laws to consider as recruiting applications. Learning management applications typically track the training and certifications of employees. To do this, the system needs to be able to display and accept multiple languages for global organizations.[32] Thus, as global organizations look at what they need in their HRMS, they need to be clear on their needs, particularly their global needs.

Human Resources Efficiencies

Research by CedarCrestone in the 2006 survey "Workforce Technologies and Service Delivery Approaches" found that use of technology was helping enable human resources departments to become more strategic.[33]

The implementation of self-service using the HRMS technology resulted in operational efficiency so that human resources was not burdened with transaction activity. The efficiency gave the human resources professionals the time and resources to provide strategic value in the following areas:[34]

- Gathering and providing metrics for budgeting and policy making to become more proactive, by sensing trends in metrics
- Providing more business strategy consulting to line managers
- Moving forward with other technology initiatives
- Strategically linking human resources practices and technologies to improve revenue growth

◼ COMPONENTS TO CONSIDER IN THE DESIGN OF A HRMS

In the ever-changing work environment, organizations are faced with many challenges, including globalization, the search for employees who have specific talent, and the need to manage and plan their workforce across international borders—a very competitive business environment. To address these concerns, organizations need tools that will facilitate the management of their human capital. More organizations are beginning to develop or buy information systems that will help them, rather than relying on paper or spreadsheets.

Development of a HRMS

Human resource departments in the past, and even in many cases today, keep data in paper files and move the data to computer systems that simply capture the data electronically. The custodian of this information is the human resources department that produces reports when requested. The reports produced are relatively simple, with little or no analysis being done on the information. Often the data in the human resource files is outdated since updates rely on individuals producing paper forms to be input by human resource staff in a timely manner. Once database technology became more prevalent, human resource data was input and stored in databases that were stored on client servers. The new systems allowed human resources professionals to input data, manipulate the store data, and produce more complex reports that organizations can use to manage their resources. Human resources was, and still is, in many organizations the only group that has access to the data. They are seen by the organization as the owners of the data.

Relational Databases

relational database

A database in which data can be stored to more than one file, each containing different types of data; the different files can be linked so that information from separate files can be used together

With the development of **relational databases,** the world changed. A relational database is a database in which data can be stored to more than one file, each one containing different types of data. The different files can be linked so that information from the separate files can be used together. Relational databases allow information to be added from many sources, and if the database is set up appropriately, the data from many sources can be linked, and complex reports can be generated. Additionally, data from other parts of the organization can be linked with human resource data allowing management to have and use integrated reporting for decision making. The user of the system can customize the human resource data to be investigated and offer a wide variety of possible searches and analyses to be conducted. For example, output of performance reviews could be input by line managers and linked to other employee data that had been input by human resources. Consider a line manager who needs to fill a vacant role requiring:

EXHIBIT   7.1   Relational Database

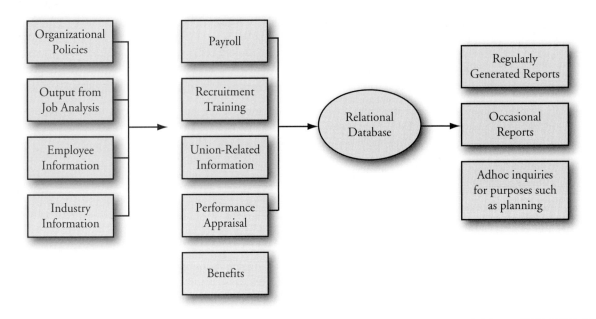

- Specific educational backgrounds (e.g., MBA)
- Minimum of five years of experience in the organization
- Specific work experiences (e.g., training delivery)
- Specific performance review ratings

The line manager could perform a database search of internal staff and produce a report providing the names of the individuals that fit the requirements. Human resources staff, line managers, and others can then look at the report and provide personal input regarding each individual before the list of candidates is finalized.

As illustrated in the Exhibit 7.1, information about the employees and the organization is collected in various databases. Information includes: organizational policies, employee information, benefits, and performance appraisal. Pieces of data can be stored in more than one file and different files can be linked. This linking means that different information from separate files can be used together to generate reports. Thus, a regularly generated report on employee training might link specific employee information such as name and department with training received in the last quarter. Data from the employee information file and training file would be linked through the relational database to create the training report. During the planning period, senior management might ask human resources for a report on current industry trends in compensation and current compensation by employee categories. This report would use data from the industry information file, the employee file, and the benefits file. Using the relational database, human resources would produce the required ad hoc report to be used in the planning.

Web-Based Technology

Web-based applications are applications that use a Web browser as a user interface. Users can access the applications from any computer connected to the Internet via a secure, password-protected login page, and the data from that point forward is encrypted to ensure security. Web-based technology is currently being used by a small number of organizations. One common use of web-based technology is for employees to enter personal data directly, including address change and educational information.

Web-based technology is also currently used to enable employees to see their total rewards on-line at any time. Generally, companies are moving towards a more holistic way of showing how their contributions are rewarded. Last year, the aircraft manufacturer Boeing began giving employees full access to their compensation and benefits information, from pensions to health insurance and childcare referral services. Boeing's director of benefits says, "We want engaged employees and we don't want them to worry about their health or financial future.[35] Having the data online allows employees to see the breadth of the package and helps them to plan for a secure future.

The number of companies using web-based technology is limited but growing. The larger the organization the more likely it uses web-based technology. The most commonly used "e-HR" of web-based human resources technology is recruiting. A significant number of organizations now require potential candidates, both internal and external, to apply for jobs online. The technology system is then set up to screen candidates using key words or phrases related to the job. Thus, the technological systems help reduce the number of applications the human resources recruiter has to screen.

The advancement of technology and its uses have made it possible for human resources professionals to use systems to transform information into knowledge that can be used in decision making.[36] Human resources will likely maintain a key role in the ownership of the data in the system, due to the confidentiality issues that exist around some specific data, but will no longer be the sole owner.

CRITICAL COMPONENTS OF A HRMS

How do organizations determine the tools they require to plan and manage their human resources? Factors such as size of the organization, its complexity, software tools currently in place in the organization, and the talent in the information technology department are important factors in decision making. As organizations think about what software tools they require, they need to take these factors into account. Organizations that don't have the information technology skills on staff might consider using software that is supported by a vendor.

WHAT IS A HRMS USED FOR?

Research of Canadian organizations show that HRMSs are primarily used to capture data related to:[37]

- Basic employee data
- Employee job grades and job history
- Payroll
- Employee compensation
- Benefits information
- Employee absences
- Employee terminations

Why specifically this information? Human resources has legal, tax, and government reporting requirements as well as requirements for reporting to senior managers and shareholders. This type of data is required for legal, tax, and government reporting. As companies grow, especially into international markets, they need tools to manage factors such as the varying legislative requirements, tax requirements on employee salaries and benefits, and different hiring requirements of various countries. In order to manage this type of reporting, technology tools are important if the organization is going to be competitive.

Additional technology capabilities that may be needed for growing organizations, especially those organizations that are global, are available only in larger systems such as enterprise resource planning systems, and include:[38]

- Workforce management: including contractors, consultants, regulatory requirements, and reporting
- Profile management
- Hiring: including data entry by managers as well as managing different hiring practices by region, worker type, and industry
- Training administration
- Career and succession planning

■ IT SOLUTIONS FOR DIFFERENT NEEDS

There are many different software solutions for human resources on the market. Organizations need to define their needs, the financial implications, and the solutions they want in the short term versus the longer term. Some organizations (usually larger ones with enterprise resource planning solutions for other parts of the business) may choose to add the human resource module of their current ERP system. Other organizations may want a specialty product that focuses on a single area such as applicant tracking.

There are numerous speciality products available to address specific HRM needs. For example, many distribution centres have large numbers of employees to manage who do similar jobs. The organizations often use a software system called Kronos to track time, attendance, hours, overtime, and vacation balances of employees. Other specialty packages available include:[39]

- Compensation planning, which provides managers with the means to compare various salary recommendations or scenarios relative to budgets
- Recruiting, which is used by an organization to screen applicants
- Managing training schedules and budgets

Some of the packages in the marketplace can be linked to an ERP system or a more comprehensive HRMS when the organization is ready, but others cannot.

■ ENTERPRISE RESOURCE PLANNING SYSTEMS

enterprise resource planning system (ERP)

A companywide computer software system used to manage and coordinate resources, information, and functions of a business using shared data stores; typically modular in nature so that businesses can add or reconfigure modules as required

Enterprise resource planning system (ERP) solutions are based on software that integrates data from diverse applications into a common database. The system can integrate human resource data with other systems in the organization such as finance, marketing, production, and logistics.

Some organizations have moved to enterprise resource systems (ERP). These systems are comprised of many software models that are linked together. For example, PeopleSoft has modules that include accounts payable, accounts receivable, supply chain, compensation, and training. The complexity of the ERP allows organizations to link various kinds of data so they are able to perform what-if scenarios. What if the organization is looking at the impact of a five percent growth in a specific area of their business on employee hiring? The ERP system contains information on current workforce competencies, costs of payroll, office requirements, etc. The data can be linked based on the various scenarios to produce reporting. The management team can look at the projected impact and make plans on what needs to happen to ensure appropriate business and human resource planning for the five percent growth.

Major suppliers of ERP systems include Oracle (Peoplesoft Enterprise) and SAP. Oracle positions its application as one that allows human resources to manage its employee information, from managing talent to paying employees. SAP is the world's third largest independent software provider with more than 28,000 customers in over 120 countries.[40] Their ERP solution integrates four functional areas, including financials, human capital management, operations, and corporate services.

The following human resource modules are usually included within an ERP solution:

- Global workforce management
- Smart Hire
- Profile management
- Training administration
- Career and succession planning
- Salary planning
- Variable and total compensation
- Global assignment training
- Labour relations management
- Regulatory requirements
- Health and safety base benefits

workforce planning

Tools in an ERP system that use workforce demographic data to help human resources professionals understand current workforce trends, and plan future needs, and link data related to headcount planning, budgeting, and key talent processes to programs such as recruiting and talent development

SAP advertises its SAP ERP Human Capital Management solution as a "complete and integrated human capital management solution that delivers unmatched global capabilities."[41] According to SAP, the "solution equips executives, HR professionals, and line managers to hire the best talent, as well as train and cultivate the skills of their workforce."[42] The Human Capital Management solution provides integrated, enterprise-wide functionality that: [43]

- Allows the organization to assign the right people to the right project at the right time
- Supports both employees and managers throughout the employee life cycle
- Provides real-time information access that accelerates workforce decision making
- Automates HRC processes and seamlessly integrates them across global operations
- Empowers employees to manage processes in a collaborative environment

talent management analytics

Uses data in the ERP system to analyze employee skills and qualifications, evaluate the efficiency of the recruiting processes, and analyze the cost-effectiveness of employee programs

The operation of such capability would give an organization a strategic advantage over their competition.

The following tools[44] help streamline human resources' administrative tasks and provide outputs that staff can use to plan and implement strategic business initiatives: [45]

- **Workforce Planning**—tools to analyze headcount development, turnover rates, and workforce compositions
- **Talent Management Analytics**—tools to identify key attributes of the organization's talent pool, measure the effectiveness of learning programs, and assess the value of succession programs

■ HOW DOES AN ORGANIZATION DETERMINE THEIR HRMS REQUIREMENTS?

HRMS is important to organizations and provides many benefits, but what type of system and what capabilities should a specific organization acquire? Not all organizations can afford millions of dollars for a new system and not all companies have the technological capability to support large systems. Additionally, some organizations have ERP systems for finance and other areas and don't want to add another system to their technology platform. If information is to be exchanged by the various areas, including human resources, then compatibility of systems needs to be addressed.

There are a few things that need to be considered when an organization is thinking of purchasing and implementing a HRMS. First, what do they want in their system and what can they afford? If the organization does not have the technology infrastructure to manage the system, then a system that is housed on-line and maintained outside the organization might be the best option. Some examples are Orange HRM[46] or Halogen Software.[47] Both are software systems that are housed and supported by the vendor with web access by an organization and its employees.

HRP AND STRATEGIC PARTNERS

Oracle at Capital One and Cognos

Capital One and Oracle[48]

Capital One is a financial services corporation with 18,000 employees. The company installed Oracle's Enterprise Portal, Financial Management, and HRMS to provide employees with centralized access to financial and human resources applications. The objective was to "increase organizational productivity and reduce overall operating costs." Employees can maintain their own personal and benefits information online. This ensures information is up-to-date, reduces administrative tasks for human resources, and frees human resources staff to do more strategic work.

Cognos and Oracle[49]

Cognos is a business intelligence software company of 300 employees located in Ottawa. The company installed Oracle's PeopleSoft Enterprise eProfile, eDevelopment, eRecruit, and eRecruit Manager in 2004. Cognos recruits in many countries, including Australia, the United States, the United Kingdom, and Europe. Instead of using tedious manual processes, the eRecruit system works quickly. It attracts more candidates than previously expected, allows online screening, and reduces use of external recruiters, resulting in an increase in the volume of applications. The expectation was that if the system lived up to expectations, there would be less manual work and more recruiting could be done using their own staff, something that would result in significant savings.

Some organizations already have ERP systems for finance or other functional groups and would prefer to add a human resources module from the ERP system. Organizations often have to look at their human resources practices when they are considering buying technology to support them. One decision that organizations have to make is whether to buy a system and use it as is so they can bring best practices into their organizations or purchase a system and customize the software to their existing processes. The first option often has significant change management challenges and the second option will cost the organization not only initially, but in the future when changes need to be made.

When organizations choose to implement an ERP system, or anything that will bring significant change in how employees access or use human resource information, there is a need to follow a project management process, such as the one outlined in Exhibit 7.2.

Investigation of Needs

Just as business needs change, the needs of human resources are constantly changing and evolving. As part of the process of selecting a technology system to support the human resource area, it is important to take time to define organizational needs at a high level, as well as look for flexibility in a system to meet future needs, if possible. A needs analysis would include the factors listed in Exhibit 7.3.

From this needs analysis, a document of requirements is created. This document needs to be reviewed by a cross-functional group of business individuals to ensure business, technology, and human resources needs are addressed, and to provide confirmation that the critical needs have been given the correct priority from all stakeholder perspectives.

EXHIBIT 7.2 Process for Selecting Human Resources Systems

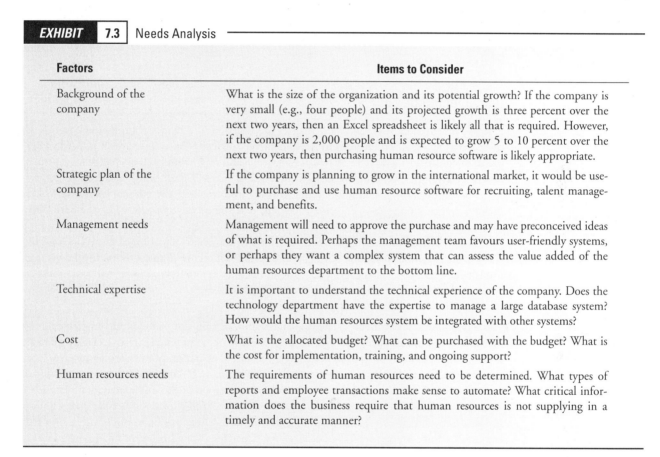

| Investigation of Needs | → | Marketplace Investigation | → | Request for Proposal | → | Evaluation of Products | → | Implementation |

EXHIBIT 7.3 Needs Analysis

Factors	Items to Consider
Background of the company	What is the size of the organization and its potential growth? If the company is very small (e.g., four people) and its projected growth is three percent over the next two years, then an Excel spreadsheet is likely all that is required. However, if the company is 2,000 people and is expected to grow 5 to 10 percent over the next two years, then purchasing human resource software is likely appropriate.
Strategic plan of the company	If the company is planning to grow in the international market, it would be useful to purchase and use human resource software for recruiting, talent management, and benefits.
Management needs	Management will need to approve the purchase and may have preconceived ideas of what is required. Perhaps the management team favours user-friendly systems, or perhaps they want a complex system that can assess the value added of the human resources department to the bottom line.
Technical expertise	It is important to understand the technical experience of the company. Does the technology department have the expertise to manage a large database system? How would the human resources system be integrated with other systems?
Cost	What is the allocated budget? What can be purchased with the budget? What is the cost for implementation, training, and ongoing support?
Human resources needs	The requirements of human resources need to be determined. What types of reports and employee transactions make sense to automate? What critical information does the business require that human resources is not supplying in a timely and accurate manner?

Marketplace Investigation

request for proposal

A written request provided to potential suppliers of a product or service; it usually includes a description of the product or service required, specifications related to the exact structure and format of the supplier's response, references, and timing

As discussed earlier, there are a large number of possible solutions in the marketplace for identified system needs. It is important that the organization familiarize themselves with the vendors, the solutions offered by the vendors, and the flexibility of the product. Additionally, the project team needs to discuss the capabilities and challenges of various systems with representatives of other organizations who have experience with a specific system. Human resources professionals and others on the project team will be able to project a short list of vendor prospects to provide the solution at the end of the investigation. Once the short list is agreed upon, then each vendor is sent a request for proposal.

Request for Proposal   Most organizations have a process for purchasing software systems that requires a **request for proposal (RFP)**. This is a request to potential vendors of the software to provide information about their products, cost of the product, ongoing maintenance costs, and other costs including upgrades. Usually, a select group of vendors are then selected to demonstrate their product to a cross-functional team of management, and based on a defined screening process, a vendor is selected.

Evaluation of Products

Criteria for evaluation of the vendors should be predefined based on the needs outlined in the RFP. The organization provides vendors with an agenda for the demonstration to ensure the issues they are trying to have addressed are covered. References, both technical and functional, from other users of the product should be available at this stage. These references will provide information about the experience of other organizations with the product, including challenges with implementation and servicing.

Implementation

The implementation of the software involves the selection of a vendor team that will work with the purchasing organization team to implement the software. The external team is usually comprised of consultants who have technical knowledge and expertise as well as change management expertise. The internal team is usually comprised of internal users who will be using the system. For example, if the recruiting module is being implemented, the internal team would likely include the recruiting manager, some recruiters, and some line managers who may have direct access to the system.

The process of implementation includes not only the implementation of the technology, but transferring organizational data, testing, piloting, and full rollout of the software to all users. Full implementation means disengaging any systems the human resources function had and providing access to the new system after all users have received training.

The Implementation Process   The implementation of software, especially an implementation involving a significant change in how employees do work, requires an effective change management or organizational development strategy. The implementation process, which involves business, people, and technology changes, requires a project manager and a project team consisting of representatives from technology, business, and human resources. An implementation plan needs to be put together that documents the processes required and provides timelines and resources needed. Generally, for large installations, a steering committee will be in place with senior representatives from human resources, technology departments, and other business areas. During installation, issues will arise that relate to required process changes or software modification. Only senior organizational members will likely be able to make these decisions, as both financial and human resources will be required for such changes. In addition, communication plans, education and/or training plans, and new policies and procedures will have to be developed and delivered.

As in the case of any change, there will be some resistance. It is important that significant effort is taken to help human resources professionals, managers, and employees accept the change and use the new tools to achieve the defined business benefit. A significant part of the implementation effort needs to be focused on this challenge.

■ THE FUTURE OF HUMAN RESOURCES TECHNOLOGY

Over the past 30 years HRMSs have become easier to use and the hardware has transitioned from mainframes to servers and PCs, but the key employee data and human resource functionality has remained essentially unchanged.[50] Vendors have added a lot of nice features to their software, but human resources departments use only 25 to 50 percent of the available features in their current systems.[51]

What will change in the future is how users interface with the software and the degree to which many of the added features of today's human resource software become seamless and standard. In the future, employee and manager self-service modules will not be extra modules requiring separate installation, but will become the standard configuration of all human resource systems. Human resources professionals and employees will have around-the-clock access to software, primarily via the Internet and to a greater extent through wireless technology.[52] Additionally, in the future, fewer companies will license, install, and maintain human resource software on their own computers. The combination of outsourcing and the application service provider model of software delivery will change the way most companies obtain and access human resource software.[53] The future of human resource technology is not about employee recordkeeping or the transactional side of human resources, rather it's "about the strategic acquisition, deployment, and use of technology to minimize costs and enhance human resources' strategic value to the organization."[54]

MEASURING THE PERFORMANCE OF A HR INFORMATION SYSTEM

The expense of buying and implementing a human resource information system is one of the challenges that human resource leadership face. Human resources professionals need to be able to justify the value-added contribution of the HRMS in accomplishing the organization's mission, if they want to convince an organization to spend the money and resources for a HRMS. In 2001, the Central Intelligence Agency[55] (CIA) developed and implemented a balanced scorecard-based performance measurement system for its HRMS so as to justify cost and highlight the effectiveness of the system. Using the scorecard helped the HRMS program director:

- Identify and align the organization's goals, objectives, and measures
- Gather baseline data to measure against established measurement targets
- Measure and demonstrate the value-added contribution of the HRMS

CONFIDENTIALITY VERSUS SECURITY

It is important to differentiate between confidentiality and security in a HRMS environment. The latter involves the protection of proprietary, company-owned information about human resources. Privacy, or confidentiality, however, involves data in the HRMS database that is protected by law and should not be made known universally. Canadian privacy legislation establishes the right for the protection of personal information collected, used, or disclosed in the course of commercial activities. In an "era in which technology increases the circulation and exchange of information, rules to govern the collection, use, and disclosure of personal information in a manner that recognizes the right of privacy of individuals with respect to their personal information and the need of organizations to collect, use, or disclose personal information for purposes that a reasonable person would consider appropriate in the circumstances."[56]

Confidentiality Issues

A key concern in the implementation of human resources systems is who has access to what data, what information gets stored on the systems, and who can change data.[57] For example, should personal medical information be stored on the system? As with any system that houses confidential information, security profiles need to be established. This process must be done before the system is implemented. For example, profiles can be set at screen and field level. These profiles determine who has access to what screen or field and who is authorized to access, view, or change information.

Some of the questions that need to be answered when an employee profile is being created include:

- What should the profile of a human resources administrator who enters employee information look like?
- Should the employee's functional manager have access to information such as SIN and address information or performance appraisal information?

Typically line managers can view but not change information that is relevant to the work situation. They cannot view confidential data that is irrelevant to managing their staff (e.g., the benefits that the employee selects). Exhibit 7.4 illustrates a chart that considers function, role, and data access.

It needs be made clear to all individuals working with a HRMS system, that they must adhere to the company's confidentiality and code of ethics policies.

Security Issues

ERP systems have varying levels of security built into them that enable the systems to be set up so access to information is restricted to an individual or a role in the organization. Although the human resources department is likely the custodian of the modules related to human resource information, others can access data and reporting depending on their level of authority. The security features ensure that line managers, executives, and human resources professionals are able to access data and reports to manage their workforce, determine how the talent of their employees lines up with the needs of the strategic direction of the organization, and help them plan a human capital strategy that supports the business strategy.

Some systems are not hosted on site; instead employees access data through the Internet. As with other business systems, the appropriate level of security needs to be in place to prevent theft of knowledge. In North America more employees are working outside the office using portable electronic devices. However, there are risks in this type of work as they access company data through the Internet. Incidents of employee data breaches are often in the headlines and for companies that are involved, reducing the damage and rebuilding trust with employees is a long, expensive process.

For example, when the Royal Canadian Mounted Police (RCMP)[58] needed to upgrade their HRMS, one of the key points to be considered in the upgrade was enhanced security. The HRMS had two components. One component allowed human resources professionals to access the system through client/server technology to administer human resources functions. The second component was an HR–online one that allowed access via intranet/Internet technology.

EXHIBIT 7.4 Users of Human Resources Data

Data	Employee	Line Manager	Human Resources Staff
Input data	X	X	X
Forecasting and Planning		X	X
Benefits	X		X
Talent Management/ Succession Planning		X	X
Strategic		X	X
Decision Making	X	X	X

The HRMS system was defined as a protected application with the maximum security afforded to it.

In the case of human resources, it is wise to take a proactive approach to protect against breaches of employee data.[59]

■ THE IMPACT OF A HRMS ON HUMAN RESOURCES PROFESSIONALS AND LINE MANAGERS

Generally, in organizations the human resources data is the responsibility of the human resources department. When line staff need to hire, they generally work with human resources staff. The human resources staff posts the job on the human resources system, if the organization uses recruiting software. Once the résumés are received, the line staff expects the human resources staff to access the information on the system and provide them with the résumés or summary of candidates. The line staff does not expect to access the recruiting software. However, the implementation of manager self-service software will change this. Line managers will be expected to access human resources data online and use the data to make decisions.

management self service (MSS)

The use of software and the corporate network to automate paper-based personnel-related processes that require a manager's approval, recordkeeping, or input

Broadly defined, human resource **management self service (MSS)** is the use of software and the corporate network to automate paper-based personnel-related processes that require a manager's approval, recordkeeping, or input.[60] These are processes that support the manager's job. Simple examples include approving employee requests for travel, supplies, expenses, or vacation. We can see an example of management self service at Mapic Inc., an Atlanta-based developer of enterprise resource planning software. Mapic Inc.[61] had a million-dollar problem. Managers did not know how much vacation time their several hundred widely dispersed workers took each year. The paper-based tracking system was often inaccurate. Likely many Mapic employees did not even use all the vacation they had. Mapic Inc. wiped out accrued vacation within several months after it adopted MSS software and implemented a new vacation policy. Advanced processes in MSS include performance reviews, compensation planning, and recruitment.

Challenges of MSS Rollout and Implementation

employee self service (ESS)

The use of software by employees to manage their own personal information such as address changes online without having to fill in paperwork that is then entered manually, usually by a human resources administrator

The rollout of MSS has the same challenges as rolling out **employee self service (ESS),** including getting cooperation from the technology and human resources departments, understanding the processes that are impacted, and getting people to accept and do things differently. Convincing people to do things differently is a significant challenge with MSS. Many managers still like human resources to handle the people transactions that MSS requires managers to do. Employee self-service is seen as empowering the user, while management self-service is often seen as an imposition. Effective implementation of MSS in an organization will require initiatives to help managers make the required changes in attitude about the benefits of the system.

At Florida Power & Light Co., the rollout of SAP's MSS applications required considerable change management work.[62] The biggest challenge they encountered, according to their general manager of human resources shared services, was helping users understand all the features available and why they were using them. Managers continued to call human resources for reports that were available to them through the MSS. However, overall, the ROI was significant. The MSS application let the company automate a weekly payroll review process to prevent mistakes. In the past, the organization was not even sure which managers were reviewing payroll.

■ THE IMPACT OF A HRMS IN ORGANIZATIONS

Overall, the roles of the human resources professionals and line managers are changing as the result of the use of human resource technology. Human resources professionals are doing less transactional work as employees can update their own data and managers can update data themselves from activities such as performance appraisals. Human resources professionals are freed up to do more strategic work. Line managers have immediate access to data without going through human resources and can manage payroll, vacation, and other employee information directly.

There is growing evidence that HRMSs are being used to support strategic tasks and more organizations are becoming reliant on technology. Human resource planning requires organizations to have accurate data on their employees, including number of employees, labor turnover, skills audits, demographic profiles, productivity levels, performance levels, absenteeism, and personal, technical, and management competencies. As a tool, the HRMS allows the organization to go beyond the automation of data and enables human resources professionals and management to analyze data and make informed decisions within the context of human resource planning.

For example, an organization needs to identify and retain talented leaders and managers in a very competitive marketplace. If the organization defines the requirements of their talent pool, collects data within their HRMS, and reports and manages this pool as part of human resource planning, then reporting from the HRMS will provide management with information on what training is required, what developmental opportunities have been undertaken, and will identify the individuals that have the skills the organization requires to meet business needs. Additionally, if the HRMS is continually updated as individuals develop new skills or participate in assignments to develop management capabilities, then managers can use the reporting capability to identify potential candidates with the required skills for roles that come open when individuals leave the organization.

Human resource planning encompasses all employees in an organization. The goal of an effective human resource planning program is to have the best available employees working in the appropriate job at the appropriate time. This will ensure that the organization is maximizing its productive capacity. To fulfill this goal means that future employee needs are forecasted accurately, based on annual employee turnover and expected strategic direction. For example, if the strategic goals of an organization are to increase market share by five percent over the next three years, the number of new employees needed in multiple job categories will change. With accurate estimates of employee turnover in specific categories added to the forecasted employee needs based on the strategic goal, the organization can begin planning to recruit new employees and as well as train current employees. To make the forecasts, accurate data related to job descriptions are required. The HRMS is a tool to ensure data of job descriptions are accurate and readily available for planning purposes.

In conclusion, the use of technology in human resources is freeing up time from transactional work for the human resources professional to spend on strategic work. Additionally, employees can manage and access their own personal data such as benefit plans to ensure they are up-to-date. Also, managers have immediate access to the data of direct reports and can manage vacation leave and professional development plans.

CHAPTER SUMMARY

- Human resources needs relevant and current information in order to be effective in planning and they need to link the human resource plan to the strategic plan of the organization. This data needs to be accessed and linked to organizational data.
- Smaller organizations may be able to manage their human capital using Excel spreadsheets. Larger organizations, however, especially those operating across international

borders, need to be able to meet compliance requirements in various countries or provinces, provide up-to-date reporting on costing (such as benefits), provide what-if scenarios on various topics such as salary or benefit increases in preparation for labour negotiations, and provide reporting on talent available for roles in the international arena. Due to the size and complexity of such organizations, a HRMS is likely needed.

- In the past, management of human resource data was very much a paper-based manual system, but with the development of technology, and especially the Web, organizations are now able to use relational databases to link information. This not only helps them to meet informational compliance needs but also to manage informational needs for strategic decision making.

- Due to the global nature of many businesses, there is a need to bring consistency to talent management practices (e.g., recruiting, management, development, etc.) However, many HR technology systems do not provide this opportunity. It is difficult to incorporate language, legal, and cultural needs into one system. Thus, some companies, such as IBM, have developed their own tools that support the development of international proposals for work, identifying staffing needed through their IT systems.

- Organizations generally use a HRMS in Canada for basic employee data, employee job grades, job history, payroll, employee compensation, benefits information, employee absences, and employee terminations.

- Options available in ERP systems include: global workforce management, recruiting, training administration, career and succession planning, salary planning, labour relations management, regulatory requirements, health and safety base benefits, and variable and total compensation management.

- HR technologies for many companies now provide employee self-serve where employees can access their personal information, such as address, benefits, etc., through the online services.

- The purchase and implementation of an ERP HRMS system is a major decision for a company and is only appropriate for larger companies. The process for determining the modules needed depends on many variables, including the current systems in place, IT capability, human resources capability, price, and needs for future developments.

- Security of data is a major issue for most companies. Who can view what data and who can change data needs to be defined and communicated. Human resources professionals need to be proactive in their approach to confidentiality and security. They need to define who has access to what data and why. There is considerable sensitivity around this issue and loss of personal data or access to personal data without appropriate business need can lead to mistrust by employees and resistance to use of systems.

KEY TERMS

- employee self service (ESS)   175
- enterprise resource planning system (ERP)   168
- human resource management system (HRMS)   161
- management self service (MSS)   175
- relational database   165
- request for proposal (RFP)   171
- talent management analytics   169
- workforce planning   169

REVIEW QUESTIONS

1. Define the term "human resource management system."
2. Explain why HRMS is important to human resource planning.
3. Explain why an organization may need to invest in a HRMS.
4. Define the term "relational database."
5. List three areas in which Canadian organizations commonly use a HRMS.
6. Describe three other capabilities that are available in most ERP human resource management systems.
7. What factors should an organization consider when planning to purchase a HRMS?
8. What factors should an organization consider with respect to confidentiality when implementing a HRMS system?
9. Describe how the forecasting of employee needs by an organization could be supported by a HRMS.

DISCUSSION QUESTIONS

1. As a human resources professional, what reasons would you give management for the purchase and implementation of a HRMS system.
2. What role would an information technology group play in the selection and implementation of a HRMS?
3. What feedback would you provide to a manager who expressed concern about confidentiality when, as a human resources professional, you suggested that your organization implement a HRMS?
4. Describe the circumstances under which an organization might choose an ERP HRMS versus an online supported system.

WEB EXERCISE

Search the web, specifically news sites, as organizational sites will not likely have this information, for two companies that have implemented a HRMS system in the past five years. What did they hope to achieve with the implementation? Why? What were the outcomes of the implementation? Did they choose an ERP HRMS? Why?

CASE INCIDENT

Developing a Request for Proposal

As a director in the HR department of ABB Company, you have been asked to develop a request for proposal (RFP) for the purchase and implementation of a human resource management system. ABB Company is a Canadian retailer with stores in all provinces that has now expanded to the United States and the United Kingdom as a result of a purchase of a company called Jones Retail.

ABB Company has HR data that is managed in a homegrown Access system. Up until now it has been used for reporting benefits, salaries, etc. as required.

Jones Retail is an international company that has run separate companies in the United States and the United Kingdom with their own HR system for each country. There has not been very much exchange of data between the United States division and the United Kingdom division. They have pretty much run as separate companies.

ABB Company has developed a strategic plan for the organization and part of that plan includes developing and sharing talent across international borders.

You need to develop the RFP in the next month.

Questions

1. What information from the strategic plan of ABB Company do you need?
2. What additional information do you need?
3. How do you propose to get the information?
4. What concerns or issues do you have?

■ REQUIRED PROFESSIONAL CAPABILITIES REFERENCED IN THIS CHAPTER

15. Ensures the HR information management function is fully capable of supporting the organization's strategic and operational needs.
16. Provides the organization with timely and accurate HR information.
17. Ensures compliance with legislated and contractual requirements for information management (e.g., records of hours worked, records of exposure to hazardous substances).
18. Contributes to development of specifications for the acquisition and/or development of HR information management systems and for their implementation.
19. Evaluates alternatives for meeting current and future information management needs.
21. Ensures the availability of information needed to support the management decision making processes.
22. Ensures HR administrative requirements conform to organizational policies as well as best practices, balancing confidentiality and operational requirements.
24. Develops requests for proposals (RFP) and reviews submissions by third parties.

International Human Resources: Planning for Resources in a Global Economy

LEARNING OBJECTIVES

- Define the term "global human resource planning" and explain the difference between resource planning in a firm that operates domestically versus a firm that operates globally
- Identify the external and internal contextual factors that influence global human resource planning
- Explain why cross-cultural awareness is integral to managing talent globally
- Discuss the importance of corporate social responsibility and its impact on global resource planning
- Describe the advantages and disadvantages of staffing a firm with a host country national, a parent country national, or a third country national
- Differentiate between the various types of global staffing assignments and their impact on international HR planning
- Outline the elements that constitute a successful expatriate experience

■ PROFILE

HONDA—A Global Company with Significant Resource Opportunities

The Civic, the Accord, the Odyssey, the Shadow 750, the Honda Goldwing —all models of cars and motorcycles, and all highly profitable lines for Honda! Honda Motor Company Ltd., established in 1948, has grown to be one of the world's leading manufacturers of automobiles and motorcycles, and is the third largest manufacturer in Japan after Toyota and Nissan. Honda is truly a global company with a network of 454 subsidiaries and affiliates, 144,785 employees, and global operations in Japan, South America, Asia, North and Central America, Europe, Middle East, Africa, and China.[1]

Honda operates under basic principles of respect for the individual and believes that everyone who comes in contact with Honda, whether it be selling, buying, or creating, should share a sense of joy through that experience.[2] Honda is a company that provides the highest quality products at reasonable prices for worldwide customer satisfaction. In addition, the company takes corporate social responsibility seriously. A key phrase, "together for tomorrow," illustrates Honda's concern and commitment to the communities in which it operates and its concern for the next generations—creating a safe and healthy environment for the future.[3]

Honda's strategic objectives are to establish advanced manufacturing systems and capabilities, enabling its growth in its overseas markets. The company recently opened an advanced production facility and research and development centre in Japan and plans to extend these initiatives across the globe.

Honda anticipates increased demand for its products and is expanding its facilities. This growth is evidenced by a number of plants opening across the globe. In Argentina, Honda just opened a motorcycle plant with an annual production capacity of 15,000 units, with a potential to increase to 45,000 units.[4] In Brazil, a plant that currently produces 80,000 units is slated to increase to 100,000. In Rajasthan, India, Honda has just unveiled a forecast for a new plant with an initial capacity of 60,000 units and projections to accommodate 200,000 units. This plant is expected to generate employment for over 1,000 people in the first phase.[5] In Greensburg, Indiana, Honda just announced plans to build a plant that will employee 2,000 employees with an annual production of 200,000 units/vehicles.[6]

However, Honda is cautious with respect to its growth strategy, as there are real bona fide concerns that could potentially limit this growth. Factors such as an economic slowdown; loss of customers due to increasing fuel prices; threats from non-compliance of environmental regulations; and increasing costs of raw materials, oil, and energy may impact demand and adversely affect production.

What does this mean from an HR planning perspective? What types of skills will Honda need? When will they need them and where? How will they source these skills? Will Honda decide to hire local talent or will they transfer its existing management to head up a plant? How will Honda tap the skills and experience of its existing talent? To what extent will Honda decide to utilize its knowledge base worldwide? What is the context that they will be operating in?

multinational enterprise (MNE)

An organizations that has operations and subsidiaries across the globe

This chapter will discuss the human resource planning challenges facing a **multinational enterprise (MNE),** those organizations that have operations and subsidiaries across the globe. We will discuss how these firms effectively engage in leveraging their global workforce to ensure that they have the right people with the right skills at the right time and in right place. We will describe the internal and external contextual factors that influence resource planning, consider the various staffing options available to these organizations, and explore the HR policies and practices that an MNE adopts to achieve their strategic goals.

■ INTRODUCTION—HUMAN RESOURCE PLANNING IN A MULTINATIONAL ENTERPRISE

The globalization of business has increased significantly over the past decade. National borders are no longer barriers to trade and more and more organizations are exploring ways to enhance their markets, manage cost, and better control efficiencies across the globe. New buzzwords about

business ecosystem

A series of tightly knit intercompany relationships that allows the business to attain a competitive advantage

global human resource planning

Planning that estimates employment needs and develops plans for meeting those needs from the available global labour force

international human resource management (IHRM)

The worldwide management of talent from a staffing perspective; provides HR support across many different countries and the employment of many different national categories of employees

global human resource management (GHRM)

A more robust IHRM that views HRM in a global context and, in a less traditional sense, as one that contributes and delivers on organizational capabilities

strategic planning have emerged. Terms such as "co-evolution," "business ecosystem," and "white space opportunities" are being used to describe how global firms effectively capitalize on these opportunities. A **business ecosystem** is a series of tightly knit intercompany relationships that allow the business to attain a competitive advantage. These terms describe organizations as a system, one that interacts with many stakeholders, such as customers, suppliers, and even competitors. It acknowledges that each stakeholder is driven by its own goals and that these goals can be achieved more effectively if they work together and collaborate to gain greater competitive advantage. Successful companies will be those that get others in their *universe* to buy into their vision, and finding the opportunity, which will be of mutual benefit, creating a win-win opportunity for all. Leading organizations do this by pursuing mergers and acquisitions, joint ventures, and strategic alliances. These opportunities can be anywhere, any time, and with anyone, and require organizations to be very flexible, adaptable, and ready to seize the opportunity.[7] We might think about these activities like "My Space" for corporations, creating a network, a community of interested parties who are in the corporation's universe and can add value to the community in some way. Currently, the Bank of Nova Scotia plans to buy a minority stake in China's Bank of Dalian Co. Ltd. and expand its operations into China, establishing a strategic alliance benefiting both parties.[8]

However, in order to seize these opportunities, organizations must clearly understand their human resource capabilities and the talent that resides within its global organization. From a resource perspective, a major advantage for these firms is that they potentially have a significant supply of talent across the globe to choose from. However, the challenges are how to transfer and exchange knowledge so that learning is deployed across its global units and how to effectively utilize these skills on a real-time basis.[9]

For these global firms, the goal of human resource planning does not change; it is still the right time, right place, and right skills. What is different is the size of its talent pool, the geographic, economic, and legal differences of each country, and the major cultural and ethical issues that arise as firms participate and plan in a global economy. **Global human resource planning** "estimates employment needs and develops plans for meeting those needs from the available global labour force" and determines the viability of MNEs in their ability to align their workforce forecasts with the supply for global talent.[10]

International human resource management (IHRM) is about the worldwide management of talent from a staffing perspective. It is about providing HR support across many different countries and the employment of many different national categories of employees.[11] Traditionally, the IHRM focus has been on staffing across borders. Recently, the term **global human resource management (GHRM)** has been used to describe a more robust IHRM process. It views HRM in a global context and in a less traditional sense as one that contributes and delivers on organizational capabilities. GHRM focuses not just on staffing, but on those activities that contribute to organizational efficiency, information exchange, knowledge transfer, and also contributes to the convergence of core business processes. GHRM takes into account the distinctive local and national issues that firms encounter when operating in a global space, and is sensitive to the balance between global integration and local management. From a resource planning perspective, it is about leveraging a firm's talent pools, creating robust career development and succession programs, and optimizing a firm's resource supply while balancing the need to attract local talent to meet demand.[12]

Depending on the size of an organization and the markets that it operates within, the scope of resource planning and the type of human resources management activities can be very different. Next, we will describe four different stages of operations as firms grow, and highlight the differences.

Four Stages of Corporate Evolution: Resource Planning Implications

There are four basic stages of corporate evolution: domestic, international, multinational, and global. Researchers have determined that each stage brings with it different and increasingly more complex HR–related practices and challenges that impact resource planning in different ways.[13] See Exhibit 8.1.

EXHIBIT 8.1	Resource Planning Implications: Four Stages of Corporate Evolution

Type of Firm	Characteristics	HR Planning Implications
Domestic	• Focuses on domestic market • Operates locally • Importance of international business is minimal	• Staffing is primarily local/regional
International Firms	• Firms choose to operate internationally when foreign sales reach 10–20% of total revenue	• Resource planning becomes more complex as the firms available talent pool expands • Beginning of employees being sent abroad on short-term assignments • Some relocation from home country • Emergence of national staffing categories—PCN/HCN/TCN
Multinational Firms	• Branches and subsidiaries in many countries • Each subsidiary operates independently	• Global HRP begins • Employees sent with increasing frequency on international assignments • HR provides relocation services and deals with international compensation and benefit issues
Global Firms	• No borders • Headquarters can be anywhere • These firms are comprised of employees from many different cultures who work together and who are used to operating in the international arena	• Maximum leverage of talent pool

Domestic Firms and HRP Implications   This firm focuses on its domestic markets. It operates locally and some larger domestic firms may export their products or services as they expand their reach. The importance of international business is minimal for these firms.

Resource planning in these firms is local. The firm's practices are dictated by local (provincial or federal) legislation and the focus is typically on ensuring legislative requirements such as employment equity are met. Cross-cultural issues are minimal. Staffing is primarily local or regional depending on the firm's demand and supply requirements. As firms grow, they may need to fill some key positions nationally. Staffing involves employees within one national boundary.[14]

International Firms and HRP Implications   In this stage, exports become a part of the organizational plans. A firm may choose to form international divisions when its foreign sales reach over 10–20 percent of total revenues.[15] Initially, the choice will involve only export to foreign customers in one country or import of one or a few products. The international activity has little impact on the business as foreign operations are viewed as sites that copy and duplicate what is carried out at home. These firms typically expand to the nearest border and their focus becomes marketing. As the firm expands beyond national boundaries, the focus is on three national categories—the parent company, which refers to where the firm is headquartered; the host country, which refers to a subsidiary; and the other countries where the firms operate.[16]

Resource planning becomes more complex as the firm's available pool of talent expands significantly. We begin to see employees sent abroad on short-term assignments and some individuals temporarily relocated from their home country. The firm typically relies on a few key managers and technical experts to deal with overseas linkages and the transfer of technology, if necessary. These firms may subcontract some work out as well and might have to deal with foreign suppliers. Cultural sensitivity becomes more important and managers require some training in understanding cultural differences. Human resources practices are dictated from home office, and divisions abroad tend to align with parent company practices. A major HRP challenge is ensuring that those internal management resources are *ready* to go abroad when needed, that they receive cultural sensitivity training, and that the distractive elements (e.g., work permits) are taken care of. The managers sent on these assignments are not necessarily senior personnel. They are chosen for their technical expertise or to help manage and maintain a secure link between the home office and the division.

In this stage, various national staffing categories emerge, and three distinct types of employees become available to IHRM professionals.[17] These three categories are **parent country nationals (PCNs), host country nationals (HCNs),** and **third country nationals (TCNs).** PCNs are citizens of the country where headquarters are located. HCNs are citizens of a county of a foreign subsidiary, hired to work at a subsidiary located in their home country. TCNs are citizens of a country other than the parent country.[18]

We will discuss these categories in more detail later in the chapter.

parent country nationals (PCN)

■ Citizens of the country where headquarters is located

host country nationals (HCN)

■ Citizens of a country of a foreign subsidiary, hired to work at subsidiary located in their home country

third country nationals (TCN)

■ Citizens of a country other than the parent country

Multinational Firms and HRP Implications   A multinational company can have branches and operations in many countries. A firm may establish a subsidiary in multiple countries. Each subsidiary typically operates independent of its operations in other countries and often independent of its parent company headquarters. This type of firm focuses on price and sourcing labour and resources with a focus on the cost and quality. The staff works together from all parts of the organization and across many boundaries, necessitating the need to develop cross-cultural skills. The cultures in these types of organizations are less unified, rigid, and less dominated by one national culture. These types of firms develop strategic capabilities that allow them to be very sensitive and responsive to differences in national environments around the world.[19]

It is at this point that we begin to see firms engage in global HR planning. As the firm increases its global presence, the organization sends its employees on international assignments with increased frequency. These assignments are viewed as significant developmental opportunities for high-potential employees. Managers who are sent to these subsidiaries are typically senior and hold high positions in the organization. These managers are seen as an important link to the home office. The HR role at this stage becomes more involved, providing services such as relocation and dealing with international compensation and benefits issues for individuals who have been assigned to foreign locations. Human resources may coordinate the human resource management activities and practices of many subsidiaries. Typically, at this point in their evolution, companies conform to local HR practices and the practices are largely decentralized, corporate HR tries to seek some consistency with the culture and policies of the parent company. They establish a global set of rules and processes to facilitate coordination of their efforts, such as establishing a recruitment process and key selection criteria for candidates who will be considered. The planning considerations focus on greater integration of key personnel into the local culture, choosing from a variety of staffing options, weighing the costs of the options and benefits, ensuring that the key personnel are ready when an opportunity arises with the applicable capabilities, and dealing with the administrative elements like work-permit applications.

Global Firms and HRP Implications   Global firms do not have any borders. They operate on the basis that products or services can be created anywhere, and the world is seen as one big market to be tapped for resources. These firms are focused on cost and quality. They organize and manage subsidiaries in many countries and seek to achieve economies of scale and spread development costs over a large area. Efficiency is the primary concern. Headquarters can be located anywhere in the world and people working in these subsidiaries can be from anywhere. These firms are comprised of employees from many different cultures who work together and who are used to operating in the international arena. Managers are sent abroad as the glue to ensure strategic synergy. These managers are chosen from a robust talent management system, have been identified as high potentials, and are ready for the next step in their careers. These firms build efficiency and are competitive on a global scale. They are responsive nationally and leverage learning on a worldwide basis.[20]

Many companies have emerged as major contenders in the multinational area. For example, Embraer, located in Brazil, builds aircraft and is the only aerospace company who has been successful at entering into the commercial jet market. They have delivered $446 million in profits and $3.83 billion in revenues in 2005, and 93 percent of sales were outside of Brazil. Techtronic Industries of Hong Kong is another such firm. This firm manufactures cordless power tools and distributes them across the world. Utilizing manufacturing and engineering expertise in China, this firm manages costs and is on the cutting edge of innovation. Since 2000, their sales have increased fivefold to $3 billion.[21] Walmart is yet another example. Walmart recently established an alliance with Bharti enterprises in India. They plan to enter into the Indian market and set up a joint venture.[22]

As discussed earlier, for a global firm, the most significant planning challenge is helping the global organization optimize its human resource capability. That may mean sourcing from the robust and multiple talent pools across the organization; individuals and their families can be relocated abroad for extended periods; and individuals may be sent on short-term assignments. The firm engages in whatever resource options makes the most sense from a cost/benefit perspective. Here we see sophisticated HR practices with HR creating policies based on best practices from companies who operate worldwide. There is a significant emphasis on valuing cross-cultural diversity. Global HR planning is in full swing, "managing the balance between overall coordinated systems and sensitivity to local needs."[23]

We can see that as an organization evolves, the scope of its resource planning broadens significantly, the availability of talent increases exponentially, and the role of HR expands within a global context. However, there are many factors that can impact resource planning when operating in the international arena.

Next, we will explore these internal and external factors.

HRP IN THE NEWS   Faskens Goes Global—Farsighted Journey into Africa

One such company going global is Faskens. Over the past several years, the law firm of Fasken Martineau DuMoulin LLP has seen its historic clients devoured by takeovers. Born out of necessity, Fasken decided to embark on a global strategy to focus on upstart mining companies. They opened an office in Johannesburg to provide services to these emerging mining players, providing legal advice to these organizations seeking to raise capital. At the time, this move was not considered that strategic, but over time, with markets shrinking, competitors now have a very different view.

Recently Fasken expanded its reach yet again, announcing a merger with Stringer Saul LLP, a U.K. firm with significant expertise in mining and high technology. This expansion further positions Fasken from an international perspective. The merger adds thirty additional mining specialists to the firm's 620 lawyers, offering advisors for clients in Africa, the U.K., and Canada.

Fasken's strategy is to continue this global expansion. Mr. David Corbett, managing partner of Faskens, said, "I believe the key for us is to look for a strategy on a global stage, and you have to be aggressive."[24]

| **EXHIBIT** | **8.2** | Internal and External Contextual Factors that Influence ———— Planning Decisions |

External Factors	**Internal Factors**
• Country culture	• Firm's commitment to corporate social responsibility
• Labour economy	• Managerial staffing preference
• Labour leglislation	
• Immigration policies	

HUMAN RESOURCE PLANNING—EXTERNAL AND INTERNAL FACTORS THAT INFLUENCE PLANNING DECISIONS

The challenges of an MNE are great as they grow their enterprise through the establishments of subsidiaries and divisions in other countries across the globe. Some key factors are critical to consider when developing an HR plan for an MNE firm. These factors relate to the external context in which the MNE will be operating and the internal preferences of the parent corporation.

As shown in Exhibit 8.2, the external contextual factors are culture, labour economy, labour legislation, and immigration policies. The internal factors refer to a firm's predilection to local responsiveness versus global integration—managerial staffing preferences and commitment to global corporate social responsibility (CSR).[25]

EXTERNAL CONTEXTUAL FACTORS

Country Culture

Countries across the globe are very different in terms of their history, beliefs, laws, and behaviour patterns. Understanding these values is important so that we can avoid conflict and work in harmony. Culture is one of the most important issues affecting MNEs and can impact their success.[26] For example, in France it is very common for work to stop for a few hours during the lunch break. The French enjoy their food and they value downtime and rest. However, in Canada, we eat on the run and we rush through lunch so we can get back to work. Adapting to a different culture can be a challenge for employees who are sent abroad. Different cultures have many different views on issues related to gifts, child labour, and bribery. A particularly interesting example involves an employee who was employed by an MNE. This employee was caught stealing and was fired by the manager. To the manager's horrific surprise, this employee was executed.[27]

Managing successfully with an increasingly diverse workforce can be a major challenge for HR and executives of MNEs and is a key priority today.[28] In a recent study conducted by Korn/Ferry, China was one of the easiest countries in which to attract executives, but one of the most difficult in which to succeed. The most common reason was lack of cultural fit. Some countries are easier to adapt to than others. For example, this study determined that Western Europe, North America, and South were locations where executives were more successful in terms of adapting to cultural differences, whereas countries where it was harder to integrate were North Asia, Japan, and South Korea.[29]

Numerous researchers have studied cross-cultural values and analyzed differences among cultures. From Geert Hofstede, in his seminal work on culture that surveyed over 100,000 employees from IBM in forty countries, to a more recent study called the GLOBE (the globe leadership and organizational behaviour effectiveness study), and an ongoing research project into

assertiveness

The degree to which people are assertive in society and the extent to which they are confrontational

gender differentiation

How society views differences in gender roles and affords higher status to certain roles

uncertainty avoidance

The degree to which people are consistent and seek structure in their lives

power distance

The degree to which people are separated by power and authority

in-group collectivism

The degree to which a society feels loyal toward either their family or other collective groups

performance orientation

The extent to which society recognizes and rewards positive performances

leadership and natural culture from 825 organizations in sixty-two countries, these researchers have identified key dimensions that can be used to determine differences in cultures.

Hofstede identified five dimensions of culture—individualism versus collectivism, power distance, masculinity versus femininity, uncertainty avoidance, and long-term versus short-term orientation. Individualism versus collectivism relates to the importance of being tied to a group versus when a society tolerates and accepts more individualism. The U.S. scored high on individualism, whereas Columbia scored high on collectivism. Power distance refers to the extent to which individuals in a society accept that power is not distributed equally. For example, Spain and Russia are high in power distance.[30] Masculinity and femininity depend on the degree to which traditional gender roles are assigned in a society. Masculine countries value behaviours that are more assertive, whereas feminine countries value more modest and caring attitudes. Japan scored high on masculinity and Denmark scored high on femininity. Uncertainty avoidance refers to the extent to which people feel discomfort with the unknown or unstructured circumstances. South Korea scored high on uncertainty avoidance but Jamaica scored low on this dimension. Long-term versus short-term orientation deals with how important the future is as opposed to the past or present. China scored the highest on this dimension and Pakistan scored the lowest.[31]

The GLOBE study determined that nine dimensions can be used to describe cultural differences. These dimensions are assertiveness, gender differentiation, uncertainty avoidance, power distance, in-group collectivism, performance orientation, humane orientation, institutional collectivism, and future orientation.[32] **Assertiveness** focuses on how assertive people are in society and the degree to which they are confrontational. **Gender differentiation** focuses on how society views differences in gender roles and affords higher status to certain roles. Turkey and Egypt scored high on gender differentiation, whereas Canada scored lower. **Uncertainty avoidance** refers to the degree to which people are consistent and seek structure in their lives. **Power distance** focuses on the degree to which people are separated by power and authority. **In-group collectivism** focuses on the degree to which a society feels loyal toward either their family or other collective groups. **Performance orientation** focuses on the extent to which society recognizes and rewards positive performances. **Humane orientation** focuses on the degree to which societies focus on altruistic behaviour and generosity. The Philippines scored high in human orientation, whereas France scored low. **Institutional collectivism** refers to the degree to which institutions want individuals to integrate into the large structure even if this is at the cost of individual freedom. **Future orientation** refers to the degree to which people delay current rewards in order to reap these rewards at a later date.[33]

From a resource planning perspective, these cultural beliefs, which highlight countries' different approaches, can have an effect on a firm's actions as it relates to resource planning and staffing. It is important to consider the parent company's value system and its overall belief structures. If a firm is altruistic and benevolent, strongly believes in equality of the genders, and believes that decision making should be pushed down to the lowest possible levels, which countries do you think that this firm would be most comfortable operating within? Where do you think they may choose to set up a subsidiary, enter markets, or source individuals? What type of person would be attracted to one company versus another? For example, if you were offered a job at a company that did not value altruistic behaviour, would you want to work there?

Labour Economy

As we discussed in Chapter 3, understanding labour economic conditions is critical for planners. For MNEs, the added complexity of operating in countries where the economy is different or unfamiliar is an added challenge for the human resource planner. Firms that are able to understand the economic challenges facing the regions in which they will be operating will be able to more effectively determine the demand and supply of their resources and create a more comprehensive human resource plan from a global perspective.

The points below illustrate some examples of how global labour information can potentially add very valuable input into a firm's global HRP and help a firm effectively balance its demand and supply across its subsidiaries.

humane orientation

The degree to which societies focus on altruistic behaviour and generosity

institutional collectivism

The degree to which institutions want individuals to integrate into the large structure even at the cost of individual freedom

future orientation

The degree to which people delay current rewards in order to reap these rewards at a later date

- Skills Shortages in India's Call Centre Industry—According to Gartner Consulting, there is a skill shortage in the call centre industry in India. This shortage is going to get worse and the Indian government has determined that there is a need for one million trained and qualified employees in call centres in 2009, and a likely shortfall of over 260,000 workers. This shortage can potentially impact MNEs who are located in India and anticipating a stream of workers.[34]

- Software and IT Services Industry Growth in China (IT/Telecom)—The Chinese IT and telecom markets are growing exponentially. Research conducted by The China Electronic and Information Development Academy estimates that the software industry grew by 20 percent in 2004 and the IT service grew by 26 percent. The group forecasts continued growth for the combined industries in the range of 16 percent over the next five years. What does this mean for firms who operate in this market? Where do you think is a logical place for them to expand? Is it any surprise that IT companies such as Oracle, SAP, and Bearing Point all have implemented aggressive hiring plans and are setting up shop in China?[35]

- Labour Costs in Emerging Economies—Labour demand is strong and rising in Asia and in Central and Southern Europe, and labour costs have been reported as 20 to 80 percent below U.S. labour costs. Firms that are focused on cost control might consider expanding their operations in these regions, and HR professionals should proactively explore the labour situations within these emerging countries.[36]

- Labour Force Participation—In 2003, China had the highest labour force participation rates for both men and women. Brazil and India's rates for women were below 50 percent. Mexico and Korea had the lowest rates of unemployment.[37] The highest gap in female and male labour force participation rate was in the Middle East and North Africa where the male labour force rates exceeded the female rates by 48 percent in 2004. Developing countries are experiencing a significant increase in the working age population, and a significant number of young people are entering the workforce. The reverse is true in developed countries where economists have reported slowing rates of population growth. These countries are experiencing static or declining numbers of young people entering the workplace. This fact, combined with increased health in midlife, has increased the mature group portion of the working-age population.[38] Labour force participation rates are a valuable indicator of the size of the supply of labour available, indicating what portion of an economy's working age population is economically active.

Labour Legislation—Employment

Another factor that impacts global planning is labour legislation because it differs around the world. Each country has its own rules regarding employment standards, including hours of work, rest periods, overtime, termination provisions, severance costs, and vacations, and the variations between countries can be significant. It is imperative for human resource planners to be cognizant of these laws and how they can affect their global resource plan. The following examples illustrate some of these differences and the resource implications.

Leave Entitlements/Vacation   In Ontario, employees receive two weeks' vacation and eight statutory holidays after one year of service. In France, employees receive twenty-five days of leave and eleven public holidays. The Netherlands gives 31.5 days of leave and eight public holidays and Ireland employees get twenty days' leave with nine public holidays. For the resource planner, the implications relate to increased vacation, coverage when employees are not working, and lost productivity.[39]

Termination Provisions/Severance Cost

What if it was so administratively onerous and expensive for your firm to terminate someone in a particular country that adherence to this legislation was going to have a significant impact on your firm's sustainability? This is exactly what happened at Jody Dharmawan's jeans factory operating in Indonesia. This firm, after several years of poor revenues, decided to lay off some of its workforce in Indonesia. However, due to Indonesia's inflexible labour laws, the owner found that this was going to be a significant problem because the legislation required that dismissed workers receive up to several years in severance pay; even employees who quit were entitled to payouts. These costs were excessive and posed a significant problem for Jody Dharmawan's factory.[40] Severance provisions in each country differ. For example, Finland requires one to three months of notice and a minimum of one-month salary for lower-level employees and ten months of salary for senior employees. In France, an inspector must approve all terminations, and payment to seniors can exceed up to three months in salary.[41] Germany allows for three to six months' salary, and an executive board and the unions must review all dismissals.

Organizations must consider the implications from a resource planning perspective. Before a firm decides to hire employees from a particular country, it is imperative that they understand employment legislation and the labour costs as well as the administrative burden. When firms take the time to explore the impact of terminating employees they may decide to establish their operations in countries where the costs can be more effectively managed.

Human Rights and Anti-Discrimination   This legislation differs in each country and among countries these differences vary considerably. Countries such as Canada, the U.S., and the U.K. have highly developed laws, but there is a lack of uniformity across the globe. Most countries ban discriminatory practices based on gender, ethnic orientation and race, but countries vary in terms of discrimination based on sexual orientation, age, social class, and disability. For example, Canada is the only country that forbids discrimination with respect to "aboriginal status." A common form of gender discrimination is sexual harassment, but the definitions of harassment and the protections afforded to those who bring a claim vary broadly. In fact, Malaysia does not have a separate legislation for sexual harassment and their scope of protection is limited. In South Korea and Hong Kong, sexual harassment is considered a criminal offence whereas, in Sri Lanka, it is not.[42] From a global planning perspective, MNEs who choose to hire individuals from these countries will need to reconcile their home countries' policies and philosophies with local traditions. If the burden is too onerous, planners may consider an alternative staffing option, such as sending someone on a short-term assignment, using virtual teams, or outsourcing.

Labour Legislation—Labour Relations

There are wide variations from country to country with regards to labour practices, union representation, and the ways in which union relations are managed. In some countries, union activity is primarily economic with a focus on collective bargaining regarding hours of work, benefits, etc., while in others, union activity is focused on achieving its goals through political action. In some countries, union relations are decentralized or may be based on industry-wide practices or national bargaining. For example, the level of union representation varies. Denmark and Sweden have over 75 percent union membership, but Japan has considerably lower numbers, with only 25 percent belong to unions.[43] Currently, Belgium, Finland, and Ireland bargain at the intersectoral level, whereas bargaining is carried out at the sectoral level for countries such as Austria, Germany, Greece, Italy, and Spain.[44]

Global firms need to understand the level of union involvement, the types of employees who are unionized, and the proportion of the workforce who are unionized in each country they plan to operate within. This information will provide the planner with valuable input and will help them make decisions regarding the best way to ensure that the skills needed are obtained in the most cost-effective fashion. That may mean deciding to send someone from the home office on an assignment rather than filling the role locally.

Immigration Policies

If you have ever worked in another country you know just how difficult it can be to get a working visa and the advanced planning required to ensure you have your papers when you need them. HR planners must be cognizant of countries' immigration policies when planning for resources in a global context. Virtually every country exercises control over their immigration practices, requiring a visa for business travel and residency. It is imperative for companies to understand the various types of visas required, the procedures that must be followed, the details that must be obtained from the applicant, the length of time that it takes to seek approval, the renewal requirements, and the potential roadblocks that may impede this process.

The visa process can be very onerous, time-consuming, and costly. For example, largely as a result of the aftermath of September 11, 2001, the U.S. authorities decided to implement a stringent series of visa regulations. These regulations were reported as so onerous that in a survey by The Santangelo Group over 73 percent of the individuals sampled experienced significant problems in processing business travel visas, and 60 percent reported suffering some form of material impact.[45] The result was that the number of business travellers to the U.S. decreased by 10 percent in 2005 from the previous year.[46]

The HR planner must factor into the resource plan the relevant immigration information regarding each country in which they operate so that they are cognizant of the timing issues and are able to develop a contingency plan with alternative staffing options, just in case the employee's visa approval is delayed.

Below are some examples to illustrate the difference in immigration policies.

Canada   It has been reported that more than 90,000 foreign workers enter Canada on a temporary basis every year. These individuals may provide specialized services and help ameliorate the skills shortage situation. Business permits can only be obtained after an individual receives an offer of employment and the company can demonstrate that the employment of this worker will have a "neutral" or "positive" effect on the labour market in Canada. "Such applications must be initiated in advance as there are several steps in the process and significant information required from the applicant. The procedure may involve many ministries and government agencies and can last up to three to four months depending on the circumstances.[47]

Japan   Similar to Canada, Japan will issue a work visa when it is demonstrated that the person is bringing a skill that is not readily available. The term for these permits is one to three years. There are fourteen major classes of occupation work. Visas are easy to obtain, but landed status is not. There are many conditions and significant documents. There are different methods to obtain a work visa. One method, the quickest, is to obtain a "company obtained certificate of eligibility." This certificate confirms the qualifications, the position description, and job parameters. The process can take four to six weeks.[48]

The U.K.   The U.K. visa application has two tiers. Tier one deals with company transfers, investments, and senior managers, and provides for individuals who want to work due to a labour shortage. Tier two is for individuals who are not nationals who want to come and work in the U.K. The permit can be issued for up to five years. The work permit application must be made by a U.K. employer. The U.K. also has some special visas status considerations for certain occupational groups and categories. For example, specific consideration is given for someone who is termed an innovator, investor, lawyer or solicitor.[49]

Now that we have explored four external factors that influence global HRP, we will turn our attention to the internal factors that can influence global HRP.

■ INTERNAL CONTEXTUAL FACTORS

There are two main internal factors that can influence HRP. The first is a firm's demonstration of its commitment to social responsibility. The second is management's preference with respect to staffing the MNE. This preference relates to management's view about how much control headquarters should exert over its subsidiaries and its preference for staffing subsidiaries with HCNs versus TCNs or PCNs. See Exhibit 8.3.

How Corporate Social Responsibility Influences the Global HR Plan

Corporate social responsibility is a concept that identifies a company's obligation to its constituents. It is a way for organizations to demonstrate, through proactive programs, their commitment to economic, social, and environmental issues, which impacts their operations and its ethical approach to labour.

Over the past decade there has been a significant increase in how public perceptions are influenced by a firm's corporate social citizenship, and public pressure is expected to increase even further over the next twenty years. This has placed a significant demand on firms to exhibit appropriate forms of CSR. This expectation is not just about what organizations say they are doing, it's about them *walking the talk*.[50]

How a firm demonstrates its commitment is an important factor that can influence a firm's resource plan. It is not uncommon for the parent firm (headquarters) of a large MNE to set the overarching CSR principles. However, it is often the responsibility of each subsidiary to align its programs accordingly. Having said this, local conditions must factor into how a subsidiary conforms, as there is "no single, comprehensive, and universally applicable definition."[51] CSR can have a wide range of meanings and the tools, which are employed to enhance a firm's performance in this regard, vary considerably.[52]

EXHIBIT | **8.3** | Internal Contextual Factors That Influence HRP ────────────

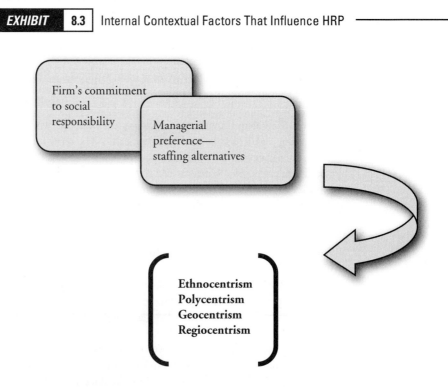

HRP AND ETHICS

Nike Inc. and Corporate Responsibility

Consider Nike, founded by Bill Bowerman, the legendary University of Oregon track and field coach, and Phil Knight, a University of Oregon business student and middle-distance runner. These two have built the world's leading designer, marketer, and distributor of authentic athletic footwear, apparel, and equipment. In 1972, they introduced a new brand of athletic footwear called Nike, named for the Greek winged goddess of victory, and the company has grown exponentially since then. Nike employs approximately 29,000 people worldwide and, in addition, approximately 650,000 workers are employed in Nike-contracted factories around the globe. Although Nike is known for producing its products in less developed countries with cheap labour, its beliefs and values with respect to its corporate social responsibility are articulated, acted up, and well documented to uphold this standard.

However, in 1996, Nike experienced a major backlash when an article about child labour in Pakistan appeared in *Life* magazine showing a picture of a twelve-year-old boy sewing a Nike soccer ball. Although the factory was not run by Nike, but by a subcontractor, Nike's ethical views were questioned. A movement to boycott Nike products gained speed, and Nike's labour practices were scrutinized. In fact, in their show *48 Hours*, CBS reported on working conditions in Vietnam, featuring Nike and the abuse of its workers.[53]

What level of responsibility do you think an MNE should have with respect to its suppliers, customers, and the countries in which they operate?

It is no surprise that countries across the globe can have very different views about social responsibility, and global firms make decisions with respect to what country they will operate in, and how they will conduct themselves with respect to employment practices. Choices are made regarding where work will be done and by whom—which subsidiary locally will carry out the work. In addition, the firm may decide to outsource the work to another company in another country and must decide its level of comfort with the firm that it outsources to with respect to CSR. Some global firms establish "hyper norms," broad-based universal principles and are very demanding regarding conformity. For example, Ernst and Young, a professional services accounting firm, has a global code of conduct that it requires all of its subsidiaries to adhere to. Another example is Honda, a company that adheres to global standards with respect to safety and environmental issues. Read about Nike's challenges, above, when it engaged a third party back in 1996 to help produce its products.

Managerial Preference—Staffing Alternatives

The second internal factor that influences resource planning within an MNE is managerial preference. This refers to the orientation of senior executives with respect to staffing and is based on a firm's business strategy. It relates to the degree of domination an organization feels it should have over its subsidiary. Executives are always concerned about how to optimally balance and coordinate a firm's global standards, set by the home country, with local practices.[54] It brings to light the issue as to how much local presence is important, and researchers have debated for quite some time about the degree to which headquarters should be present in a local market and just how important local responsiveness is when an MNE operates in a foreign country. Researchers Bartlett and Ghoshal proposed that MNEs are comprised of a number of units that must be coordinated and integrated in some way.[55]

These managerial preferences, shown in Exhibit 8.3, are referred to as ethnocentrism, polycentrism, geocentrism, and regiocentrism.[56] Next, we will highlight the reasons why managers may prefer to choose one approach as opposed to another.

 64

ethnocentrism

A view in which managers use a home-country standard as reference for managing activities

polycentrism

Characterized by firms that are staffed by host country managers and are characterized by decentralized and autonomous operations

Ethnocentrism   **Ethnocentrism** refers to the view in which managers use a home-country standard as reference for managing activities. Individuals from headquarters fill key positions. Decision-making is centralized and is driven from the home country where control over operations is exercised. Subsidiaries are controlled by the PCN and there are very few opportunities for HCNs to hold key positions or be promoted outside their operation.[57] Their strategy is based on transferring and adapting the parent company's knowledge or expertise to foreign markets while maintaining considerable influence.[58]

Polycentrism   In **polycentrism,** firms are staffed by host country managers and are characterized by decentralized and autonomous operations. These firms are managed via tight financial and operational controls from their headquarters. The opportunity for promotion within the subsidiaries is available, but outside of the subsidiaries it is limited.

Geocentrism   With **geocentrism,** the managerial outlook focuses on creating a global network and follows a strategy that integrates and is dependant on the global firm's strengths. It is of the view that the best person for the job can be found from anywhere.[59]

Regiocentrism   **Regiocentrism** focuses on the regions in which organizations operate. This view chooses the best manager in the region, and transfers within the region are common.

The Staffing Mix—Advantages and Disadvantages of PCNs, TCNs, and HCNs

geocentrism

A managerial outlook that focuses on creating a global network and follows a strategy that integrates and is dependant on the global firm's strengths

regiocentrism

A focus on the regions in which organizations operate

What is the optimum mix? Should an organization respect local traditions? Should it manage from the head office? It has often been said that high performing organizations "think globally, but act locally." Next, we will explore the advantages and disadvantages of employing a PCN, a TCN, or an HCN. See Exhibit 8.4 for a summary of these advantages and disadvantages.

Host Country National—Local Presence   There are many benefits to using host country nationals—employees of the MNE who are citizens of the subsidiary. These employees know the culture, the local politics, and economic situations. They share a common language and can communicate effectively. They are less expensive than bringing someone from the home country. When firms are staffed with local talent, these individuals tend to fit well with the culture and they understand local practices. They may lack familiarity with the parent country's culture. However, this may not be a major issue, depending on to what degree the MNE's headquarters takes the time to socialize the HCN and where this takes place. For example, deciding if the HCN is to be socialized at the parent headquarters or at the host country subsidiary. For the parent company, a disadvantage of using HCNs is the time and energy it takes to understand the local market, and managing without an expatriate means less coordination between headquarters. Typically, we would see local hires and international transferees.[60]

Parent Country National—Integrating Global Standards   PCNs, employees of the MNE who are citizens of the country where the MNE has its corporate headquarters, can also be beneficial. PCNs are familiar with the MNE corporate culture, can communicate effectively with headquarters, are able to exert control over the subsidiary's operations, and will ensure that the MNE's strategic objectives, policies, and goals will be understood and complied with.[61] MNEs continue to send PCNs as technical troubleshooters, structure reproducers, and general management operatives. Other important reasons PCNs are used: position fillers when HCNs are not available, to

| **EXHIBIT 8.4** | Advantages and Disadvantages of Staffing Choices | |

Staffing Choice/Nationality	Advantages	Disadvantages
Host Country National (HCN) • Employees of the MNE who are citizens of the subsidiary	• Knows local culture, politics, and economic situation • Shares common language and can communicate effectively • Less expensive than bringing an employee from the home country	• Lacks familiarity with parent country's culture
Parent Country National (PCN) • Employees of the MNE who are citizens of the country where the MNE corporate headquarters reside	• Familiar with MNE corporate culture • Can communicate well with headquarters • Ensures that the MNE strategic objectives are understood and complied with	• Can be expensive to send • Resentment due to possible inequities as it relates to reward/compensation packages between PCN and HCN • Limited awareness of local culture • Work permit issues
Third Country National (TCN) • Citizens neither of the country where the MNE is headquartered, or where the foreign subsidiary is located	• Identifies with the global firm • Mobile • Culturally sensitive • Highly developed language and cultural skills	• May not be perceived as legitimate representatives of headquarters • May be cultural biases if TCN is from a country where there is a long history of conflict

develop and mentor others, to support organizational development and change efforts, and to provide lead time for HCNs to reach acceptable performance standards. Some possible disadvantages of using PCNs are that they can be expensive, and there may be perceived reward inequities between how the HCNs and the PCNs are compensated. In addition, PCNs may have limited awareness of local culture.[62]

Third Country National—Integrating Global Standards   TCNs are not citizens of countries where the MNE is headquartered, nor are they citizens of the country where the foreign subsidiary is located. TCNs identify with a global firm and do not overly identify with either the parent or the host country. They may not be as expensive as a PCN. They are mobile and culturally sensitive. They typically have better language and cross-cultural skills than headquarter expatriates and they can make an important contribution in the cultural socialization of management. They may be chosen for their language ability rather than for their managerial or technical abilities. While TCNs may have greater linguistic and cross-cultural skills, many TCNs are not perceived as legitimate representatives of their headquarters, and there may be cultural biases if the TCN comes from countries where there is a history of conflict. Another possible disadvantage of using this group relates to the fact that they may experience work-permit problems.[63]

Recently, a fourth pool of expatriate candidates have been identified, referred to as TCKs—*third culture kids*. Third culture kids (TCK) are comfortable with many different cultures. Having spent their formative adolescent years in several different cultures, these individuals do not fully subscribe to any particular culture.[64]

No matter which option organizations decide to choose, ultimately the goal is to *optimize their talent pool* and do so in the most cost-efficient and effective manner. Next, we will discuss some current trends in organizations today.

CURRENT TRENDS IN STAFFING THE INTERNATIONAL ORGANIZATION—"THE ASSIGNMENT"

Have you ever worked on a project where you had to travel to deliver the service? Over the past decade, there has been a considerable trend toward staffing internationally through the use of the assignment. A recent survey conducted by PWC indicated that over 50 percent of the surveyed firms expected short-term assignments to increase in the future.[65]

Assignments have become a popular staffing option as technology enables communication across wide boundaries, firms enter into collaborative business relationships, employees become more concerned about work–life balance, and firms have greater access to a global workforce. There are many different types of assignments that organizations consider, depending on the business needs, whether there be a short- or long-term requirement for a particular skill set, whether individuals can be interchanged or if the same person must deliver the service, and whether the service can be delivered continually or intermittently. There are many different variables that determine the type of assignment. These ways have been categorized by researchers in four ways: short-term, commuter, frequent flyer, and expatriate.

The term **international commuter** refers to an employee who frequently commutes from their home country to a place of work in another country, typically on a weekly or biweekly basis. A frequent flyer is an employee who travels with increasing frequency on international business trips to accomplish a specific task. The term **flexpatriate** has also been used to describe a person who is on a short-term assignment and engages in frequent travel without relocation. Typically, short-term assignments are for less than one year and refer to the commuter and frequent flyer as well.

The term **expatriate** describes an individual who is sent on an assignment outside of their home country for a period of time. This period is usually over one year. Expatriates are of special concern for organizations. Questions such as whether the expatriate will need to relocate, if they can travel back home or must bring their family with them, and the length of the assignment must be considered.[66]

Next, we will discuss the costs and benefits associated with sending someone on a long-term assignment outside their home country (as an expatriate), and explore what organizations must do to ensure that these assignments are successful.

---

international commuter

An employee who frequently commutes from their home country to a place of work in another country, typically on a weekly or biweekly basis

 36

flexpatriate

A person who is on a short-term assignment and engages in frequent travel without relocation

expatriate

An individual who is sent on an assignment outside of their home country for a period of time

---

The Expatriate—Costs and Benefits

You are an employee of an MNE and you are born and bred in Canada, a parent country national. You joined this firm right out of university and one of the reasons you chose to work with this firm was that someday you envisioned there would be an opportunity to work in one of their global subsidiaries. You have always wanted to travel and so after being in your current job for over three years, you decided to apply for an internal job posting for a two-year assignment at one of the firm's subsidiaries in Germany. To your surprise, you got the job and the subsidiary is expecting you to start in sixty to ninety days. You think the time frame is reasonable, but you are not sure. Your mind races with all kinds of questions about what it is like to live and work in Germany. Some of your queries are very practical, relating to Germany's visa requirements, how long it takes to get a business/work visa, who will do the paperwork, the cost of living in Germany, if your company will help relocate you to a home that is similar to yours, if your spouse will be able to work, and how important it is to learn the German language. Also, you want to know if the company will pay for trips back home. After all, if you do not come home for the holidays, your parents will be very upset! There are many unanswered questions and many hurdles to cross before you actually feel comfortable accepting the assignment.

International assignments are important for several reasons. They are viewed as an opportunity to develop employees and they demonstrate a firm's commitment to the development of its human capital. Employees are provided with exposure to other cultures and management styles and the opportunity to work with different nationalities. From an employer perspective, sending an employee on an international assignment enables the firm to transfer its knowledge and skills. It can fulfill skills in which there is scarcity or a shortage, it enables headquarters to establish its policies at its subsidiaries, and it can facilitate the exertion of control and coordination.[67]

However, international assignments can be expensive. The average costs associated with sending U.S. expatriates overseas has been recorded as anywhere between $150,000 U.S. and $250,000 U.S. per year.[68] Other reports have indicated the average of a one-year assignment to be about 500,000 euro. For example, a recent survey by Agence France-Pressee reported on the cost of living in Shanghai. They found that rent in Shanghai for a furnished Western-style apartment is higher than an equivalent space in New York or Tokyo, starting at $2,000 a month for a two-bedroom apartment. The average tuition fees to educate children in private school are approximately $20,000 a year. This is 20 percent higher than in New York.[69]

To ensure success of such an assignment, a number of elements must be considered. Formal HRM, travel, and relocation policies must be developed and supported by a robust administrative infrastructure. Special attention must be given to setting objective selection criteria to ensure that the person chosen will be the best fit for the assignment. In addition, upon completion of the assignment, consideration must be given to bringing the employee back to their home country. We will discuss these key elements next.

Key Elements of a Successful Expatriate Experience

There are four elements that must be considered when using an expatriate, as shown in Exhibit 8.5. They are the creation of formal HRM, travel, and relocation policies; well-structured and consistent administrative processes; clearly defined candidate staffing criteria; and a well-thought-out plan for the candidate's reentry to their home country. A recent survey conducted by PWC indicated that less than 50 percent of surveyed companies had formalized policies in place regarding tax, social security, and visa requirements. Of those that did, 50 percent indicated that they followed one policy and did not differentiate between the different types of assignments. Over 80 percent of those surveyed felt that changes to their existing policies needed to be made.[70]

Policies—HRM, Travel, and Relocation   Policies must be standardized, well structured, consistently applied to all employees who are on assignment, and easy to comprehend so that the

---

EXHIBIT 8.5   Key Elements of a Successful Expatriate Experience ———————

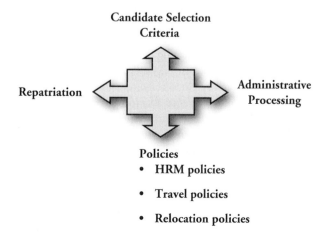

expatriate can clearly understand what the organization commitment is. There are several policies that pertain to the expatriate. These range from HRM policies created by the HR department responsible for international employees to travel policies, which typically are created by the accounting department, and relocation policies which are jointly developed by both HR and accounting.

HRM Policies Some of the HR policies that are relevant to the expatriate include training and development, compensation, and performance management. In terms of training and development policies, firms must consider the type of language training and cultural sensitivity experiences needed to desensitize the individual and whether there are any special country conditions that must be understood. This would include a country where there may be safety and security issues. The degree and level of training will differ based on the type of assignment. Performance management is another area that must be considered. How will the firm manage an individual's performance to ensure that the individual's performance is aligned with the overall goals and objectives of the organization? Consideration must be given to individuals who will manage the person's performance, how often it will be managed, and the mechanisms that will be put in place to document this performance. Again, depending on the type of assignment, it is a lot easier for someone who is going on a short-term assignment versus someone who will be relocated for a longer term. Compensation programs must be developed to ensure that they are locally relevant and globally equitable. Compensation for a short-term assignment will be a lot easier to determine than in the case of an individual relocating to a particular country, where factors such as cost of living need to be taken into account.[71]

Travel In terms of travel, it must be determined how many trips the expatriate can take back to their home country and at what cost per trip. Will the company allow individuals to fly first class or economy? If someone were on a short-term assignment, consideration must be given to their daily allowance for meals, entertainment, etc., and whether this allowance will fluctuate based on the country, or should be unlimited or capped.

Relocation Policies Relocation has been cited as one of the most stressful situations an employee can encounter. The focus of a formal relocation policy is the transport of an employee, the family, and their household goods to the new site with minimal disruption. The policy typically includes housing, cost of living adjustments, temporary living expenses, spousal assistance, cross-cultural training, destination and setting up services.[72] Relocation can be very costly. According to a recent study by Atlas Van Lines, the average cost of relocation is about $45,000 for a domestic move and twice that for an international move.[73] Firms such as Runzheimer International and Prudential Relocation are specialists in helping employees relocate.

Administrative Processing Another important element to consider is administration. Lack of attention to details and potential errors in administrative processes can hinder an individual's positive experience and has been cited as one of the most frustrating issues that expatriates can experience. Managing the *basics* is an expectation of anyone who works for an organization. Some examples are ensuring that the assignment terms and conditions are documented and that the individual agrees to these terms and conditions, ensuring that payroll processing and tax administration is managed according to this agreement, offering assistance with the visa application to ensure that the documentation compiled is complete according to the immigration regulations, as well as handling any issues and concerns related to a spouse or dependant(s). In addition, providing administrative support with respect to relocation is very important. Considerations such as engaging a relocation firm to help the assignee find suitable accommodation, managing the vendors who will be providing services to the assignee, and building in supports to help with family concerns, such as schools to attend or community groups to join are important.[74]

Candidate Selection Criteria Arguably, one of the most critical considerations is *fit* and whether the individual chosen is the best fit for the assignment. Large multinational firms who do this well have established specific criteria for candidate selection, giving thought to the importance of nationality and whether sending a PCN, a TCN, or an HCN will enhance the fit for the role and the achievement of a firm's objectives.[75] These firms document and communicate the criteria to potential candidates. Some of the elements are race, gender, adaptability, flexibility, cultural awareness, previous work experience, and level of interest. A recent survey of EMBA students in China and South Korea examined whether race and gender were important factors in selecting executives to head foreign operations of a U.S. multinational in China and South Korea and a newly acquired U.S. operations of a Korean multinational. In both examples, competencies were considered more important than race and gender in a senior executive appointment; however, in the Korean example, race and gender were more important than competencies in assignments to Korea.[76]

Repatriation   The final consideration is how effective an organization is at reintegrating an individual back to their home country firm after they have been on a long-term assignment. These individuals can be a major resource within a company as they have significant knowledge that they have built up over time. If their knowledge is fully employed, these individuals can play a significant role in helping firms sustain their competitive advantage. However, there is ample evidence to suggest that when expatriates return home from an extended assignment, it is often difficult for some of them to adjust back to the parent country. This phenomenon has been called "reverse culture shock." This experience refers to how an individual adjusts to his or her environment upon return. They may miss the special benefits they received while working internationally. For example, in some countries having a chauffer is common and even necessary if there are safety issues. Another common problem is that the individual often expects a promotion upon return and this does not always happen in a timely fashion. In addition, the returning individual may also feel disconnected as the company may have hired new personnel that the returning individual does not know who have become integral parts of the team.[77] All of this may contribute to an individual's decision to leave the firm.[78] One survey suggested that as many as 25 percent of expatriates leave their companies within two years of returning home.[79]

HR Planning Implications   The human resource planning repercussions of not addressing these issues can significantly affect the individual's experience on an assignment. Policies and practices that are inconsistent, inequitable, and not managed properly can have a profound effect on an individual's perception regarding how effective an organization is at managing its employees abroad. Individuals may choose not to go on assignments and the word *assignment* can take on a negative tone. If employees do not see the assignments as valuable, the firm will have difficulty managing its shortages. In addition, individuals who are on an assignment may feel frustrated and decide to leave the firm. This loss of personnel will ultimately hurt a firm as valuable knowledge "walks out the door." The firm will lose its prized intellectual capital and its knowledge base will be depleted. In addition, labour costs will rise due to turnover, as the firm will most likely have to hire new employees.[80]

CHAPTER SUMMARY

- As corporations have evolved, they have become increasingly more complex with respect to the markets they serve and the human resource planning challenges they face. As firms grow, they move through four stages of evolution: domestic, international, multinational, and global. A firm that operates in a domestic market operates locally whereas a firm that is global operates across the world and its products or services can be created anywhere in the world. As organizations expand their global reach, their available pool of talent expands and the complexities with respect to managing employees with diverse cultures and in different countries increase exponentially.

- HRM has responded to these challenges and, as a discipline, it has evolved from providing solely domestic support to providing services on a global basis. International human resource management (IHRM) is about the worldwide management of talent. It is about providing HR support across many different countries and the employment of many different national categories of employees. Primarily, the focus for IHRM has been on staffing across borders.

- Recently, the term global human resource management (GHRM) has been used to describe a more robust IHRM process. It views HRM in a global context and in a less traditional sense as one that contributes and delivers on organizational capabilities. GHRM focuses not just on staffing, but on those activities that contribute to organizational efficiency, information exchange, knowledge transfer, and the convergence of core business processes. Global HR planning determines employment needs and develops plans for meeting these needs from the available global labour force.

- There are external and internal factors that can influence global HR planning. The external contextual factors are country culture, labour economy, labour legislation, and immigration policies.

- The internal contextual factors that influence global human resource planning are a firm's commitment to corporate social responsibility (CSR) and managerial preferences with respect to international staffing. These staffing preferences relate to ethnocentrism, polycentrism, geocentrism, and regiocentrism

- Managers have several options when deciding how to effectively staff an MNE. There are three types of international employees: host country nationals (HCNs), parent country nationals (PCNs), and third country nationals (TCNs). Deciding which category is most appropriate will depend on managerial preference and staffing needs. HCNs know the culture and language of the host country and are less expensive. PCNs are familiar with the MNE's culture and are able to cross-communicate effectively, which will ensure the goals are understood. TCNs do not identify with the host country or the MNE. They are mobile and although they are able to more effectively communicate cross-culturally, they do not have any direct ties to either company.

- There are various types of global staffing assignments that managers of MNEs consider. They include short-term, commuter, frequent flyer, and expatriate.

- To ensure a successful expatriate experience, there are several policies that need to be well documented and consistently applied to each employee involved in the assignment. Expatriates must be given cultural sensitivity and language training and compensated accordingly. The firm's travel and relocation policies must be clear. In addition, companies need to effectively manage the basics, such as documenting the arrangement, helping the expatriate and their families find appropriate accommodation, aiding with visa requirements, and helping with moving costs to ensure a smooth transition.

KEY TERMS

- assertiveness   188
- business ecosystem   183
- ethnocentrism   194
- expatriate   196
- flexpatriate   196
- future orientation   189

- gender differentiation   188
- geocentrism   194
- global human resource management (GHRM)   183

- global human resource planning   183
- host country nationals (HCN)   185
- humane orientation   189
- in-group collectivism   188

- institutional collectivism   189
- international commuter   196
- international human resource management (IHRM)   183

- multinational enterprise (MNE)   182
- parent company nationals (PCN)   185
- performance orientation   188
- polycentrism   194
- power distance   188

- regiocentrism   194
- third country nationals (TCN)   185
- uncertainty avoidance   188

REVIEW QUESTIONS

1. What are the four categories used to describe the evolution of an MNE firm?
2. What are the four external contextual factors that HR professionals must consider when planning internationally?
3. What are the two internal contextual factors that HR professionals must consider when planning internationally?
4. Managers have a specific orientation with respect to staffing its subsidiaries. What are these preferences?
5. There are advantages and disadvantages to consider when employing a PCN, a TCN, and/ or an HCN. What are the reasons why a manager would choose one option versus another?
6. A successful expatriate experience requires that the organization consider several elements. What are these elements?

DISCUSSION QUESTIONS

1. What are the advantages and disadvantages of being an international commuter?
2. How effective are expatriates in transferring knowledge and skills to their home countries?
3. What are some the ethical issues that would arise when working in countries such as Russia, China, and the U.S.?
4. What do you think are the key competencies of an international manager?
5. Cross-cultural knowledge is considered a very important aspect of working in the international environment. What aspects of cross-cultural knowledge do you consider the most important: language, media, non-verbal communication, or written?
6. What sets the CSR initiatives of multinationals apart from domestic organizations?

WEB EXERCISE

Many global companies are developing programs to help expatriates prepare for the experience and to help them become acclimated once in a new country. For example, KPMG International has invested in a "buddy system" to help expatriates manage the stress of moving to a foreign country.[81]

1. Find three articles online that describe what some global companies are doing to help make the expatriate experience a positive one. Consider the types of programs these companies offer, the type of training and/or support they provide, and what they should consider providing to their expatriates. Some companies to consider are: DuPont Chemical, KPMG, and Schindler Group. Here are some sites to visit:

   http://www.fm200.org/Career_Center/en_US/career_paths/career_paths.html
   http://findarticles.com/p/articles/mi_m3495/is_6_50/ai_n14700370/
   http://www.reuters.com/article/pressRelease/idUS174580+16-Feb-2009+BW20090216
   www.schindler.com (career, human resource policies)

2. Go to www.youtube.com and view a podcast called "Mobility Matters at Ernst and Young." Discuss the impact that the international assignment had on the employee. What benefits do you think the employee received from the assignment? What did the employee learned from this assignment?

CASE INCIDENT

Coal Company Wants to Hire Chinese Workers for B.C. Mine—Is Importing Workers from China the Answer to Mining's Labour Shortage?

Canadian Dehau International Mines Group Inc. is embarking on a coal-mining project in Northern B.C. and plans to have a mine up and running in 2009. They have proposed bringing in 400 workers from China to staff the mine.

It is no surprise that the mining industry has faced a severe labour shortage and has had to find creative ways to staff their facilities. However, the idea of bringing workers from China with specific skills in underground mining has been challenged as perhaps not an optimum way to manage this shortage.

Labour groups and the Mining Association of British Columbia have raised concerns about bringing foreign workers into northern B.C. towns, specifically regarding the cultural and social ramifications a major influx of Chinese people would have on a small community. The projected site is northwest of Chetwynd, which has a population of 2,500 people, and has Indian reserves nearby that have significant traditional ties to the areas. Concerns have also been raised about bringing in workers from foreign countries versus developing talent locally. Currently, Aboriginals underrepresented in mining, could be a source of labour. Wages are also an issue with regard to whether the workers would accept less than the going rate of $20.00 to $30.00 an hour and what impacts this would have on the industry.[82]

Do you think that importing workers is the answer to Dehau's labour problem?

Questions

1. Discuss the cultural impacts on the northern communities if 400 Chinese workers were hired.
2. Discuss the current immigration policies, how long it will take to bring these individuals to B.C., and how long can they stay.
3. Discuss the ethical and CSR issues that the company is facing. Discuss the health and safety concerns as well.
4. Discuss how employment legislation is affected (employment equity, BFOR, etc.).
5. What other staffing options might Dehau consider? Where could they source labour?

■ REQUIRED PROFESSIONAL CAPABILITIES REFERENCED IN THIS CHAPTER

2. Translates the organization's business plan into issues, priorities, and human resources strategies and objectives.

5. Keeps current with emerging HR trends.

36. Stays current with professional knowledge.

64. Researches, analyzes, and reports on potential people issues affecting the organization.

69. Maintains an inventory of people talent for the use of the organization.

70. Develops systems and processes that link the career plans and skill sets of employees with the requirements of the organization.

MERGERS AND ACQUISITIONS

LEARNING OBJECTIVES

- Explain the terms "merger" and "acquisition" and identify the types of mergers and acquisitions
- Explain why organizations merge and the methods used to achieve a merger or acquisition
- Describe the impact of mergers and acquisitions on employees
- Describe the relationship between mergers and human resource planning
- Evaluate the organizational skills required to maximize the success of a merger or acquisition

■ PROFILE

The Urge to Merge

CBC News reported that mergers continue to be significant in the Canadian marketplace and that the main debate today revolves around acquisitions of well-known Canadian companies by foreign-owned companies.[1] The following is a list of companies that have fallen under foreign control or are due to become foreign-owned:[2]

- Hamilton steelmaker Dofasco was bought by Luxembourg-based Arcelor SA.
- Graphics chip-maker ATI Technologies of Markham, Ontario was sold to California-based Advanced Devices Inc.
- The Fairmont Hotel chain, including the Chateau Frontenac, Banff Springs Hotel and others, was bought by an investors group led by a Saudi Arabian prince
- Sleeman Breweries of Guelph, Ontario was bought by Japan's Sapporo Breweries

Additionally, Canadian cross-border takeovers include Manulife Financial's $15 billion takeover of Boston-based John Hancock Financial in 2003, and TD Bank's $5 billion acquisition of New England's Banknorth.[3]

Depending on the literature you read, 50 to 85 percent of these mergers, takeovers, or acquisitions are unsuccessful, and only 30 to 50 percent of international mergers and acquisitions create shareholder value.[4, 5] Research indicates that merger and acquisition failures stem from poor communication, differences in management style, and cultural differences.[6]

During the late 1990s, school boards and hospitals in the province of Ontario were required by law to merge. After much study, commissions of the government decided that by merging hospitals and school boards, significant financial benefits could be obtained. This merger has not been very positive and there has been major resistance from stakeholders (e.g., staff, students, parents on behalf of school boards, and staff and patients on behalf of hospitals). The University of Toronto opposed the merger of Sunnybrook Medical Centre and Women's College Hospital and noted that the merger could harm many programs.[7] Subsequently, Women's College Hospital has de-amalgamated from Sunnybrook Health Sciences Centre as the merger never delivered the planned outcomes.

The Toronto District School Board, which is the result of the 1998 merger of the school boards for the former municipalities of York, East York, North York, Scarborough, Etobicoke, and the Metropolitan Toronto Public School Board has had significant issues from the start.[8] The proposed outcomes of the merger were reduced costs, streamlined operations, and a consistent educational experiences for all students in the Toronto area.[9] Since the merger, significant issues related to budget overruns, service needs not being met, and program challenges in the schools have been reported in the media. According to reports, the Board Governance Committee is currently discussing options such as de-amalgamation, including a proposal that would be similar to the model that existed in Toronto prior to school-board amalgamation.[10, 11]

Mergers and acquisitions are major change initiatives that organizations undertake. The success of these initiatives is directly linked to the people strategies and operations of an organization. In this chapter we will discuss the role of human resources in supporting a merger or acquisition and how business planning and human resource planning of the merger can maximize the success of the initiative.

■ MERGERS AND ACQUISITIONS

merger

A combination of two organizations to create a third organization

A **merger** is the combination of two organizations to create a third organization.[12] For example, Daimler-Benz and Chrysler merged and a new company, DaimlerChrysler, was created. There are three major categories of mergers. They include:

1. **Horizontal merger:** A merger of two competitors. An example of this type of merger would be a merger between TELUS and Bell Canada.

horizontal merger

◾ A merger of two competitors

vertical merger

◾ A merger of a buyer with a supplier or buyer

conglomerate

◾ Merger of one company with another where the two companies have no competitive or buyer-seller relationship

acquisition

◾ The purchase of a company or a controlling interest in a company by another company

2. **Vertical merger:** A merger of a buyer and supplier to achieve synergies of controlling factors. An example would be a cone company buying an ice cream company or a clothing company buying its material supplier.
3. **Conglomerate:** Merger of one company with another where the two companies have no competitive or buyer-seller relationship. An example would be a financial institution buying an airline.

An **acquisition** is the purchase of a company or a controlling interest in a company by another company.[13] The result is that the company taken over no longer exists.

In the case of either a merger or an acquisition, the end result is the creation of a new company. For the purpose of this chapter we will discuss mergers and acquisitions as one category.

Typically, organizations only use the term "merger" when one company completely takes over another company. However, the term also includes the following: one company acquiring another company and running it as a separate holding (e.g., Canadian Tire acquired Marks Work Warehouse and continues to run it as Marks Work Warehouse), or acquiring another company and managing it as a subsidiary.

◾ A CANADIAN OVERVIEW OF MERGERS

In 2007, there were 1,941 mergers and acquisitions in Canada totalling $370 billion. More than 60 of the transactions were over $1 billion in value. According to McKinsey and Company, the historical value of merger and acquisition activity is a significant percentage of the GDP in Canada. Overall, Canada has provided a more robust merger and acquisition market than the United States.[14] See Exhibit 9.1 for a summary of deals from 2003 to 2007 in Canada. As the economic downturn that started in 2008 continues, many companies that have a good financial bottom line are looking for growth opportunities, and it is predicted that the number of mergers will increase.

Recent megadeals involving foreign purchases of large Canadian companies have raised concerns that Canada is being "hollowed out."[15] However, over the past 15 years, Canadian companies have been more active in acquiring foreign companies than foreigners have been in purchasing Canadian entities. This is true even in the large-deal category when the purchase price is over one billion dollars. In the last two years foreign companies have bought out companies such as Hudson's Bay Company, Fairmont Hotels & Resorts, Inco, and Falconbridge. See Exhibit 9.2 for examples of some of the takeovers that transpired in 2007. In the fall of 2007, the biggest foreign takeover in Canadian corporate history took place when Rio Tinto acquired Alcan Inc. for approximately $40 million.

Between 1994 and 2007[16] the total number of merger and acquisition deals involving foreign companies acquiring Canadian companies, where the value is great than $1 billion, is virtually equal to the number of Canadian companies taking over foreign companies. Since 1994, the number of transactions valued at less that $1 billion where Canadians have purchased foreign assets has been higher than the number of deals involving foreign acquisition of Canadian companies. "Thus, the idea that foreign-controlled companies operating in Canada will turn us into a 'branch-plant' economy is out of touch with the current global realities."[17] See examples in Exhibit 9.3.

EXHIBIT | 9.1 | Mergers and Acquisitions in Canada[18]

Year	Number of Deals	Canadian Dollars (billions)
2003	833	83
2004	859	115
2005	1,613	165
2006	1,968	257
2007	1,941	370

EXHIBIT **9.2** Examples of Foreign Takeovers of Canadian Companies in 2007[19]

Announcement Date	Deal Value (C$)	Target	Acquiror
January 4, 2007	19,873,000,000	Inco Limited	Companhia Vale do Rio Doce
March 30, 2007	8,7000,000,000	Shell Canada Limited	Shell Investments Limited
July 5, 2007	8,619,500,000	Thomson Learning	Apax Partner
October 25, 2007	39,833,550,000	Alcan Inc.	Rio Tinto

Source: Theriault, L. and Beckman, K. (February, 2008). Trends in Foreign Direct Investments and Mergers and Acquisitions, International and Canadian Performance and Implications, The Conference Board of Canada, Ottawa.

EXHIBIT **9.3** Examples of Canadian Takeovers of Foreign Companies in 2007[20]

Announcement	Deal Value (C$)	Acquiror	Target
June 11, 2007	6,534,230,000	Brookfield Asset Management Inc	Multiplex Group
August 3, 2007	4,597,320,000	Great-West Lifeco	TH Lee, Putnam Capital, Limited Partnership
October 2, 2007	8,479,600,000	TD Bank	Commerce Bancorp, Inc.
October 8, 2007	18,976,440,000	Thomson Corporation	Reuters Group PIC

Source: Theriault, L. and Beckman, K. (February, 2008). Trends in Foreign Direct Investments and Mergers and Acquisitions, International and Canadian Performance and Implications, The Conference Board of Canada, Ottawa.

The research of Theriault et al.[21] has shown that the lower interest rates and booming corporate profitability in Canada has had a significant impact on merger and acquisition activity. Additionally, the analysis shows that for each percentage point decline in the long-term interest rate, Canadian mergers and acquisitions abroad increase by 1.3 percent, and foreigners' mergers and acquisitions in Canada increase by 0.8 percent. The current sub-prime mortgage crisis and the negative effect on borrowing will affect merger and acquisition activity.[22]

WHY MERGE?

Senior management in organizations and the boards of directors, especially in public companies, see it as their role to add shareholder value. One option to add shareholder value is to grow the organization. This includes growing their companies. It is difficult to create a world-class organization through growth only, since most companies grow at a relatively slow pace. Thus, companies turn to mergers and acquisitions to achieve business opportunities that include:[23]

1. Market share growth
2. Becoming a leader in a specific industry
3. Enhancing company brand
4. Reducing operating/overhead costs due to acquisition of capability

5. Entering new industry and/or expanding their product market portfolio
6. Accessing talent and/or management capabilities
7. Accessing new technologies or know-how
8. Accessing manufacturing capabilities and/or expertise

Exhibit 9.4 illustrates some Canadian takeovers of companies in 2007.

Overall, organizations generally see strategic and financial benefits to mergers and thus take action to find opportunities to merge and increase shareholder value. In some cases, CEOs feel a personal need to expand their organization and they try convincing their leadership team to look for possible acquisitions. Expansion of a company because of an individual's need may not have the support of the full leadership team and may set the company off on a high-risk path.

STRATEGIC BENEFITS OF MERGING

If an organization develops a strategic direction and sets goals to achieve strategic benefits, then the merger or acquisition can lead to success. Some of the strategic benefits could include:[24]

- **Growth and expansion** into new markets, especially internationally. For example, Compaq's market was focused on the individual market and HP was focused on the business market. When HP acquired Compaq the new HP that was formed included both the home and business market.
- **Strengthening competitive positions.** For example, pharmaceutical Pfizer took over Warner-Lambert to obtain a specific cholesterol drug, Lipitor, which was the market leader.
- **Operating synergy.** An example is the cost reductions achieved by economies of scale produced by a merger or acquisition. This was the case in the former cities of North York,

---

| *EXHIBIT* | **9.4** | Examples of Growth by Acquisition |

Both Scotia Bank and Pitney Bowes developed a strategy to grow by acquisition. They prepared a strategic direction and set criteria to evaluate the various options in the marketplace, selecting only those options that fit their plan. The process was part of their strategic plan. The planning process reduced their risk and maximized the opportunity to achieve their goals.

Scotiabank

Scotiabank is Canada's most international bank. It has over 55,000 employees serving 10 million customers in over 50 countries, and has grown significantly by using acquisition. Scotiabank added over 9,000 employees from 2005 to 2007 through acquisitions, and as of 2006, 50 percent of all Scotiabank employees were located outside Canada. In 2005, Scotiabank acquired Banco de Comercio in El Salvador. This was their first acquisition in eight years. After the acquisition, the number of branches increased from 20 to 67, the number of employees increased from 430 to 2,000, and the market share and customer base increased correspondingly.[25]

As a result of the acquisition, Scotiabank grew its market share, enhanced its brand, and developed new markets internationally.

Pitney Bowes

Pitney Bowes, originally known for its postage meters, spent $1.7 billion on acquisitions from 2001 to 2005 in an effort to expand its market share and become a world leader in production mail and business services, including mailroom and document outsourcing. The growth strategy included acquiring organizations that were related to the stand-alone meters that Pitney Bowes was famous for, including shipping and sorting meters. It also included growth through businesses that were not directly related to meters, such as bar-coding and voice processing. The overall strategy included mainstream expansion, document management, global penetration, and cross-selling.[26]

The criteria for acquisitions included: business fit, near-term strategies, earnings accretion, compatible operations, and attractive price. Danka and PostLinx are examples of Canadian companies that Pitney Bowes acquired.

For Pitney Bowes, the result of these acquisitions was increased market share, new markets, enhanced brand, and new technology and talent.

East York, etc. forming Toronto. Another example is the merger of HP with Compaq. This merger created a very large company who by virtue of their size were able to negotiate contracts at reduced rates with their supplier for items such as memory chips and hard drives.

- **Accessing new markets.** When Air Canada and SAS joined the Star Alliance network, they were able to access markets such as Asia, where access had been previously denied.
- **Diversification.** Examples include a ski resort acquiring a golf course, or GE Electronics acquiring a credit card company.
- **Vertical integration.** An example is KFC, Taco Bell, and Pizza Hut being acquired by PepsiCo—products that are distributed in these establishments.
- **Horizontal integration.** An example is TELUS merging with BC Telecom to become a stronger regional telephone company better able to compete with Bell Canada.
- **Acquisition of complementary skills or resources.** An example is acquiring specific talent for developing game software.

■ FINANCIAL ADVANTAGES

All business strategies that include mergers or acquisitions are positioned as a way of increasing shareholder value for the company. Some of the financial advantages of a successful merger or acquisition include:[27]

- A reduction in variability of cash flow, as not all resources will be from one company
- A growing business that will fund a mature business
- Expectation of tax advantages as the tax loss of the acquired business will offset the income of a parent company
- Financial gain as the company that is acquired is undervalued

Many organizations claim their mergers have succeeded from a financial perspective. Analysis by Hall et al. has found that the financial benefits of many mergers, including the return to shareholders, is small or negative.[28] Generally, in the planning process, the expectation regarding increased earnings per share are high, but the risks are also high. The leadership in the planning and acquisition phase tends to focus on business risks including financial, marketing, customer, and shareholder, and ignores the people (employee) risks. The costs of the employee risks can outweigh the business risks, however they are not generally seen or addressed by the organizational leadership until the merger has been completed.

Managerial Needs

One of the goals for the leadership of most organizations is growth. In many organizations, the objectives of the strategic plan and the benefits package for the leaders include rewards for growth, specifically in size and shareholder value.[29] A new CEO hired by a board of directors will have a set of commitments that must be met as part of their performance contact. One of the commitments often includes growth of the business at a specific rate, or diversification of the business within a specific period of time. As outlined earlier, diversification or growth of any significance is unlikely without the development of a merger and/or acquisition strategy.

Some CEOs have a personal need to expand their business control and see a merger or acquisition as a means to increase their business control. These individuals will build a case with their senior team to ensure that the organizational business strategy includes mergers and/or acquisitions as one of their strategic platforms.

In either case, the concern that arises is that the need of the leadership might drive the strategy, rather than strategy driving the need. The result may be a merger and/or acquisition without a business need, which could have a negative impact on the outcome of the merger.

■ HOW DO MERGERS OCCUR?

Friendly Mergers

friendly merger

A merger in which two companies want to join together; both organizations see the merger as beneficial to each other and they work together to create the new organization

In an environment that is friendly, a merger is a relatively simple process. For example, in a **friendly merger** the management of one company contacts the management of another company to initiate talks. The initial contact could be CEO to CEO or it could entail using an intermediary, such as an investment banker or a colleague. These are considered friendly takeovers, where both companies see an advantage in coming together. Often, the leadership of both companies engages in open communication about business options, so employees are prepared in part for the change.

Hostile Mergers

hostile merger

A merger in which one of the two companies in the merger does not want to merge; the organizational environment of the company being taken over is hostile

When one company tries to buy out another company that does not want to be bought out, the environment becomes hostile. In a **hostile merger,** the process can be long and drawn out and can include potential issues with shareholders and employees when the information leaks to the press, despite efforts to keep the merger confidential. Situations may vary, but often the media highlights the negative aspects of the situation, which causes employees and shareholders to react in an undesirable manner. Some examples of hostile takeovers include: Air Canada's takeover of Canadian Airlines, US Airways and Delta Airlines, and Yahoo and AOL versus Microsoft. See Exhibit 9.5.

| **EXHIBIT** | **9.5** | Examples of Hostile Takeovers |

Air Canada

In 1999, business magnate Gerald Schwartz obtained a favourable court ruling to obtain a merger vote between Air Canada's shareholders and Canadian Airlines.[30] In general, Air Canada's top brass was not in favour of the merger, which they viewed as a hostile merger attempt by shareholders of Schwartz's company Onex Corp.

Delta Airlines

In December of 2006 the headlines read "Delta Airlines Rejects US Airways Hostile Merger Bid."[31] Why? Delta was in bankruptcy and one means of exiting bankruptcy was merging with another airline. However, the bid from the US Airways Group Inc. of $8.38 billion was rejected as Delta's plan was to exit bankruptcy as an independent company with a value of as much as $12 billion. US Airways saw Delta's situation as a means to grow, but put a limit on how much they were prepared to spend to acquire the company. The bid was rejected by Delta's leadership because they believed they were in a good position to come out of bankruptcy with a value of as much as $12 billion and return to financial stability. This was based on the estimated recovery value to the unsecured creditors as well as a detailed analysis that showed why the US Airways proposal was a poor strategy.

Yahoo

In February 2008, Yahoo restarted merger talks with AOL as a means of defending itself against the $45-billion hostile bid approach from Microsoft.[32] Yahoo rejected the Microsoft offer in part because their board believed that Microsoft had undervalued Yahoo. In a statement to the media, Yahoo announced that the board of Yahoo would not even consider starting talks with Microsoft unless the suitor group offered at least an additional $12 billion.

Microsoft wanted to take over Yahoo because Google's dominance in the online search advertising market posed a threat to Microsoft's future. In this example, the changes in the marketplace were forcing Microsoft to look for merger solutions to the threat posed by Google, and for Yahoo to look for merger solutions to the potential buyout by Microsoft at a value less than they believe was appropriate. The discussions about the potential merger that took place in the media were not favourable to either Microsoft or Yahoo. These discussions created a very hostile environment both in the business community and within Yahoo and Microsoft. In the end, the merger did not go through.

Waves of Change

In all cases, hostile or not, mergers and/or acquisitions have a ripple effect that impacts both business processes and people. Unless these changes are managed, business performance can decrease as the leadership concentrates their time on the needs of the merger while ignoring the existing business and their employees who are becoming more uncertain about their future. One of the results of the change is increased employee resistance, which can result in loss of productivity and loss of highly skilled employees who are looking for a more stable work environment.

Research shows that between 40 and 80 percent of mergers fail to provide any benefit for the shareholders and up to half can destroy shareholder value.[33] Research suggests that up to 85 percent of failed mergers are attributable to mismanagement of cultural issues.[34,35]

■ MERGER AND ACQUISITION PROCESS

The merger and acquisition process, as illustrated in Exhibit 9.6, can be divided into four steps: pre-deal, due diligence, integration planning, and implementation. We will now explore these steps in greater detail.

Pre-Deal Stage

pre-deal stage

The stage of the merger and acquisition process that occurs when organizations decide they would like to grow by merger and begin to look for opportunities, including partners or business ventures that they would like to consider as an acquisition

In the **pre-deal stage,** business leaders are looking for compatible business ventures that will provide an opportunity to expand their business. Some companies have business units devoted to this process, or they may use external resources. If a company's strategic plan includes the use of mergers and acquisitions as a growth strategy, the process taken is likely documented in the same way as a strategic business plan and discussed with employees. In many cases, the organization does not communicate the process or the business strategy beyond the senior team. Thus, any announcement of a merger comes as a surprise to the employees. The surprise often creates uncertainty for employees, shareholders, and the public, and may affect factors such as share price, public support of the company, and employee performance.

One Canadian retailer, Canadian Tire, developed a strategy in the 1990s to grow by mergers or acquisitions. They hired a vice president of business development whose responsibility was to implement their strategy. The company's past experience with acquisitions in the international

EXHIBIT | **9.6** | Merger and Acquisition Life Cycle Process[36]

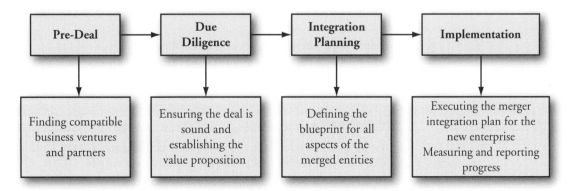

Source: Adapted from Laviolette, K. and McDowell, T. (2005). Assembling a Post-Merger Integration Team, Conference Board of Canada. Reproduced with the permission of the authors Katya Laviolette, CBC Radio-Canada, and Tom McDowell, Partner, Oliver Wyman Delta.

marketplace had not been successful and resulted in a negative financial impact that affected share price. The job of the vice president was to develop:

- A strategy and plan for opportunities the organization might pursue
- Criteria for evaluating the opportunities
- Processes to ensure that potential opportunities are consistently evaluated prior to consideration for pursing them

Due Diligence Stage

due diligence stage

The stage of the merger and acquisition process when an organization has found a potential acquisition and begins the process of determining if it a sound decision from a financial, human resource, and shareholder perspective

In the **due diligence stage,** the business leaders work to ensure that the deal is sound. Questions to be discussed include:

- Will the Board buy into it?
- What will the impact be on business, financials, and hopefully employees?
- How will the value proposition be positioned, especially to the market and the shareholders?
- Will the outcome be a merger or an acquisition?

In the Canadian retailer situation described earlier, there was a real concern for how the team worked on the merger and how the marketplace would see the acquisition given the organization's prior history with acquisitions.

Integration Planning Stage

In the integration planning stage, a blueprint for all aspects of the merger must be defined. Usually a team of senior leaders work on the various pieces of work that need to be accomplished, the financial and human resources required, as well as the timelines that must be considered. The plan often includes creating task teams that will define the work in detail (e.g., communications team, human resources team, etc.).

Transcontinental, a company of over 13,000 employees in Canada, the U.S., and Mexico, developed a post-merger integration plan to help in the merger process.[37] The plan was defined as a 100-day process. The timelines were important to the leaders in the organization as they believed the focus must be on maintaining both the integration of the two companies and the benefits while completing the work in the shortest time possible. The 100-day integration plan was set up as a project plan that included:

- A detailed integration/project management approach for integration
- Task forces for the implement plan
- Outcomes that ensure synergy objectives are met (e.g., increased revenue and decreased costs)
- Processes that exceed employee expectations in communications
- A plan that will complete the process in 100 days (e.g., all decisions made and communicated), although some projects could take longer

Implementation Stage

In this stage, the integration team must execute the merger integration plan. Critical success factors that would be in most merger integration plans at this stage include:[38]

- Clarification regarding project accountabilities
- Effective project management
- Tight timelines to ensure management focus
- Decision-making processes and forums that are clear and efficient
- Consistent communications vehicles to ensure common visions for activities

- Organizational aspects of the integration efforts (i.e., the new organizational design and the placement of people in jobs for the new organization need to be addressed early in the process)
- People issues, including culture, must be considered, acted upon early, and integrated into business decisions

◼ HOW CAN HUMAN RESOURCES PROFESSIONALS ADD VALUE TO A MERGER?

In 2000, a survey by the Towers Perrin and the SHRM Foundation provided insights into how human resources professionals currently added value to a merger or acquisition so as to determine ways they could play a more pivotal role in the future. Of the 440 senior human resources professionals involved in three or more mergers over the past five years, primarily in North America, two-thirds indicated that human resources professionals had significantly less involvement in the earliest strategic stages (i.e., pre-deal and due diligence versus the integration planning and implementation). Research indicated that human resources professionals can positively influence decisions that will ultimately determine the success of a merger. This is based on their involvement in the earlier stages, including the fit of the two organizations and whether the two companies' managements and cultures will be compatible.[39]

Human resources professionals are rarely involved in the pre-deal and due diligence stages, and at times they are not even involved in the integration planning stage. Why? Although, there is increasing awareness that human factors have an influence over the success of a merger, senior executives often struggle with how to address the issues or how to use their human resources professionals to support the merger. First, they are so absorbed with the business deal and in securing their own interests that the organizational implications of the deal are only considered once the deal has been set. Second, they don't see their human resources staff as having the skills required to add value to the discussions in the initial stages. Often business leaders see the role of the human resources professional as one that provides transaction services (e.g., reviewing benefits packages, restructuring plans, and downsizing strategies) as needed once the business issues are addressed. However, research illustrates that the companies that succeed in mergers and acquisitions likely have human resources professionals with strategic competencies that lead to higher levels of meaningful involvement across the full range of merger and acquisition activities.[40]

If an organization mishandles a merger from the employee prospective, they run the risk of losing key people—the key people who constitute the significant market value that was key in attracting the acquiring organization in the first place.[41] If managers do not anticipate and prepare for the emotional response of employees at the beginning of the merger, the benefit of the knowledge and skills of these employees may be destroyed, and they may leave the company. In order to achieve the benefits from merging the organizations and to achieve shared business goals, employees and the organization must work together to:[42]

- Talk with one another
- Work with one another
- Learn from one another

For an organization to be successful in merger or acquisition activity, employees need to be involved in the process. To facilitate this process of involving employees, human resources professionals need to be involved in the merger process, especially at the due diligence stage.

◼ MAJOR OBSTACLES TO SUCCESSFUL MERGERS AND ACQUISITIONS

The major obstacles in achieving success in mergers and acquisitions stem from the following key issues:[43–46]

1. Lack of financial performance
2. Loss of productivity
3. Incompatible cultures

9.7   Components of Culture[48, 49]

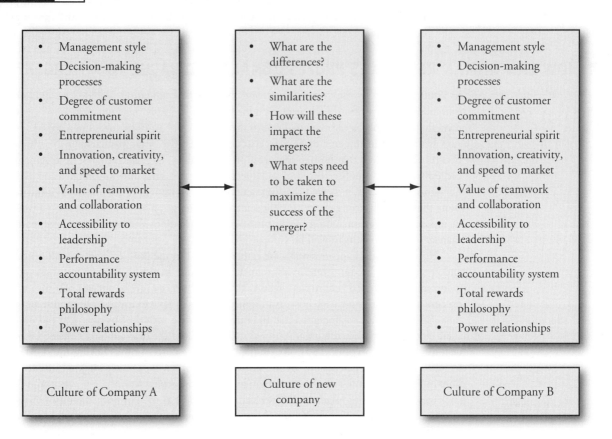

4. Loss of key talent (talent necessary to keep the organization performing at the expected level)
5. Clash of management styles and/or egos
6. Inability to manage and/or implement change
7. Objectives or synergies not well understood

All of the issues described above are directly or indirectly related to the strategic management of people, with the single highest barrier to success being the management of cultural differences.

Corporate culture is a company's culture and includes the values, norms, and behaviours that characterize the organization and its work environment (e.g., employee behaviours, how they are held accountable, and the way they're rewarded). The "purpose of culture is to supply shared meaning—a sane, systematic way of giving the organization and the people within it a sense of identity, a knowable place of belonging, a way of working together and a way of relating to the outer environment."[47] Overall, how are people suppose to work together when they hold different values and expectations about how work is to be done?

Research has confirmed that one of the keys to a successful merger is the ability for the integration team from both companies to understand each other's culture, including identifying and addressing potential issues early in the process.[50]

Exhibit 9.7 illustrates how the culture of two companies can be different, and the questions that need to be addressed to begin the process of developing a culture for the new organization as a result of the merger.

Schein's research, which focused on the executives involved in mergers, determined that 87 percent of executives agreed or strongly agreed that cultural issues were at least equivalent to the importance of financial issues in the successful outcome of the transaction.[51] Corporate culture can be both managed and changed. Culture manifests itself through numerous organizational events and thus, it can be managed by changing concrete aspects of an organization's functioning. [52]

Human Resources Due Diligence

Companies spend a significant amount of time carrying out due diligence to ensure the proposed deal is sound from financial, legal, environmental, operational, people/cultural, and intellectual capital perspectives. Findings of research reported by Schein show that cultural issues are equal to financial factors in making a merger deal successful.[53] However, many merger teams often fail to involve human resources professionals in the due diligence process and skip the people/cultural and intellectual capital perspectives of the due diligence process. Human resources professionals are often brought in by the purchasing organization after the deal is signed and then asked to help with the people issues that arise. What is HR's due diligence and what is to be gained by bringing human resources professionals into the process sooner?

human resources due diligence

The analysis of the cultural risks of a merger, including similarities and differences of culture affecting the merger and an assessment of whether or not the risks are manageable through the cultural integration of the merger

Human resources due diligence includes analysis of cultural risks, including the differences and similarities affecting the integration of the two companies and an assessment of whether or not the risks are manageable through cultural integration.[54] Additionally, an analysis of human resource risks include determining:

- How or if alignment and motivation of employees is possible
- The potential key talent (i.e., employees essential to the performance of the business) that you want to keep

An approach to cultural due diligence would include:

- Gaining an understanding of cultural compatibility and incompatibility of the two organizations by using cultural diagnostics to identify differences and to surface cultural dilemmas
- Identifying the cultural objectives for the merged organization and identifing key components for the integration plan.

 11, 42

The overall question out of this exercise is: Are the differences too challenging to overcome in order to achieve the business objectives? If so, is the organization prepared to walk away from the deal? If not, what are the potential consequences?

HRP IN THE NEWS   AT&T

In early 1990, AT&T acquired NCR. AT&T was late in discovering significant cultural differences between the companies. For example, AT&T's union staff objected to working in the same building as NCR's non-union staff.[55] Staff and managers spent time discussing who worked where, and managers insisted that teams consisting of staff from both organizations work together on projects. The overall environment became quite toxic. The clash of the conservative management style of NCR, where managers directed work, with the coaching model at AT&T, where managers coached employees rather than directing them, also created a toxic work environment. This work environment led to a high turnover of NCR executives. Of the 30 executives, 26 left the organization. This turnover had a negative impact on the merger because they lost the knowledge of the NCR senior management who left the company, and also because of the inability of employees to work together. AT&T eventually sold NCR. The cost to AT&T was $3 billion, and NCR lost approximately half of its market share.[56]

It is to be expected that in any merger significant differences will exist in:

- Virtually every element of how HR functions are positioned
- The key strategic objectives of HR
- Human capital–related programs and processes

The question is not if there are differences, but if the differences can be overcome so that the combined organization can achieve the business objectives that the merger was expected to achieve.

IMPACT OF MERGERS AND ACQUISITIONS ON EMPLOYEES

Most frequently, employees in an organization don't know about a merger or acquisition until the deal is complete. When the senior team makes the announcement, they create immense change–management issues. The outcomes of the changes include:[57]

- Potential loss of key talent
- Turnover, especially key managers
- Context of work during mergers
- Communication challenges
- Clash of corporate cultures

We will discuss these potential outcomes in detail below.

Loss of Key Talent

Once the announcement is made, a strong message is sent to the acquirer's competitors and to recruiting firms. Individuals with the key skills required in the marketplace are available, but these individuals don't know if they have a job, where they will be located, the new company's structure, or how much pay they will receive.[58] Once the merger announcement is made, individuals will begin to receive many calls about their interest in changing employment. Recruiting firms know the key talent in the company and they begin the raid. Key talent knows they have marketable skills and they are in a good position to negotiate for new or more stable positions. How can this situation be avoided or reduced? As part of the planning for the implementation of the merger, key talent needs to be identified. Then, a plan to communicate with them prior to, or shortly after, the announcement can be developed. If key talent in either organization needs to be retained, they need to feel comfortable that they have a role in the organization during and after the transition.

Turnover—Especially of Key Managers

There is a need to ensure that as the merger moves forward there is staff available to continue the business. The transition to the new organization takes time, and during this transition process customers need to be serviced so they do not move to a new source for their product or service. For those employees who remain, there will be confusion as a result of the differences in decision-making styles, something that could lead to non-productive behaviour.[59] For example, managers can postpone decisions or block the making of decisions. The result of this behaviour can be stalling of the integration, and productivity then declines. In the struggle for power, the impact of personal and organizational stress, the voice of the customer may be lost. The shift of focus inward and away from the customer will make the partners in the merger vulnerable to aggressive competitors. According to Harding and Rouse, nearly two-thirds of companies lose market share in the first quarter after a merger, and by the third quarter the figure increases to 90 percent.[60] It is important that turnover is kept to a minimum during the transition.

Context of Work During Mergers

During a merger, the context in which an individual does work will change. Additionally, the workload and the number of conflicting agendas that an individual encounters will increase. This change in the context of work, increased workload, and conflicting agendas will all have to be managed by the individual within very tight timelines dictated by the senior team. Many key activities and deliverables must be achieved in the transition. This transition is often set as a 100-day plan.

Overall, managers have to deal with a large number of people regarding issues that tend to be more complex under the circumstances. As part of the transition planning, manager competencies in this area need to be analyzed and addressed so they are prepared to deal with the workload and people-related issues. Thus, it is important that key managers are identified and their roles during the transition clearly identified and managed. For example, which managers/teams are to focus on ensuring current customers transition to the new organization? The managers and their teams need to know what is expected of them and they need to be held accountable for delivery of their goals. If their accountabilities are not clear, deliverable, identified, and measured, there will be a tendency to sit and wait for new direction and/or begin to look for alternative positions.

Communication Challenges

Lack of communication creates a void and in that void employees grow concerned about what is going to happen. To minimize the void, a high-level communications plan should be developed and implemented that includes details of short-term activities that are to be undertaken and a high-level set of longer term activities. In the absence of direction from the senior team, employees begin to wonder how they benefit from a merger. If they can't provide an answer, they begin to create answers based on their perceptions. As individuals tend to be frightened by this type of change, rumours about the impact of the changes tend to be significant (e.g., the whole marketing team of the acquired company will be let go). Based on the rumours, individuals become very concerned and start looking for alternative employment. At the same time, their productivity reduces and resistance increases.

The general communications process will not work in this situation. There is a need for a strategic communication plan that starts with the senior management's announcement. Following the announcement, key managers need to be prepared to discuss the change with their employees. They need a communication's tool key that provides the information employees need to know and lets them know where to get the answers. Some organizations have provided vehicles such as a merger hotline, ongoing newsletter, or a company website where questions and answers are posted. Overall, the communication plan needs to include the timing, frequency, and repetition of updates. Some senior managers have learned that it is better to communicate, even when no update is available. The communication keeps employees from creating their own updates. The ongoing communication provides an opportunity to ask questions and for senior managers to get a feel for employees' feelings in the process.

Clash of Corporate Cultures

Corporate teams working on the merger frequently ignore the tensions that cultural discrepancies can create, including:[61]

- Task versus relationship orientations
- Communication styles
- Decision-making approaches
- Performance management
- Office space management
- Benefits packages

Initially, after a merger, the employees of the two companies will likely be asked to work together on various initiatives. The task will be clear, but the employees of one company may be more task-oriented than the employees of the other company. Trying to get work done can be challenging under these circumstances. Clashes can result and are caused mainly due to the differences in approaches, communication styles, or decision-making approaches.

Each organization will have a different approach to performance management. In one organization, when goals are not achieved, the management may rely on discussions with employees to determine the cause and to help with the solution. In another organization, the management may be more dictatorial and they may set goals very difficult to reach with no discussion. If individuals from both organizations are working on a project and something goes wrong, the feedback from management will depend on which organization the manager is from. Either way, a disconnect will occur for some members of the team. This disconnect will cause confusion as well as suspicion that there is a problem, which will result in productivity disruption.

Office set-up will vary, but is an important factor in positioning for most organizations. The size, furniture, and location of an office usually reflect one's position in the organization. For example, a larger office usually denotes higher rank. As the merger moves forward and individuals get moved around to work on transition projects, the assigned office areas can be perceived as an indication of promotion or demotion. If for example, two people, one from each organization, are assigned to share a space, the perception may be that one of them will not be in the organization after the merger.

Benefits packages can be as important to employees as their salaries. It can be expected that the benefits packages of the two companies will be different. A change to benefits will be a difficult change to implement and will take significant communication and selling, especially to the employees that end up having significant changes in their packages. Employees need to know that this is being considered early in the transition, and the processes for changes need to be clear to reduce issues.

The manageability of culture by the corporate leadership cannot be overemphasized. Corporate culture is manageable and can be changed. Leadership that understands the importance of culture, and understands how to change when necessary, will have a powerful handle on guiding the merger to a successful conclusion from a people perspective. As a General Electric executive said, "We spend most of our time on culture change."[62]

■ MERGERS AND HUMAN RESOURCE PLANNING

As part of human resource planning, the human resource function needs to have the requisite skills to work with an organization's senior team during times of mergers. Individuals with key human resource skills need to have a seat at the planning table to provide management with critical insights into how the merger will affect the newly formed company's people. The human resources team needs to be considered a strategic business partner. During the planning process, the human resources members of the team will develop a clearer understanding of where the management is going. Based on this knowledge, the human resources team needs to develop strategies that will recommit and engage the employees who will make the new company a success, and help managers to implement these strategies. Early identification of sensitive issues, such as pay, benefits, and severance packages for those who will not have a job, can become significant issues if not addressed early in the process. If human resources professionals are not part of the strategic team, they will likely be overtaken with operational and mechanical issues, such as providing severance packages, rather than participating in a more strategic role that ensures the transition plan for human resources has the same priority as other business areas, such as finance.

Senior management will often say that employees are their firm's most precious asset. However, evidence illustrates the contrary. In the planning and execution of a merger, employees in both companies are often not given high priority when it comes to implementation of the new organization. In the merger, the human resources staff needs to ensure the company's people plans include identifying and addressing the needs of employees from both companies. This type of planning ensures that the key people assets required are in place to move the human resources through the transition, to operate the new organization, and to continuing meeting the needs of the customer.

Human Resources as Part of the Merger Team

It is important that human resources members be a part of the merger team. As part of the planning process, it is important that the people factors are reviewed during the due diligence stage. When Company A buys out Company B, it does not mean that all of the human resource practices that Company A uses will be those used by the new Company. Perhaps Company B has better benefits or talent development processes that the new Company would like to incorporate. The following questions need to be addressed early in the process:[63]

- Which key people need to be kept? What is the new company prepared to do to hold on to their key talent?
- Which core areas of competence should be retained? What is the new company prepared to do to ensure core areas of competence are retained?
- Are there major cultural discrepancies with the target? Will these discrepancies cause major defection or other losses in productivity? Is the organization willing to resolve them?
- What executive compensation contracts, including golden parachutes (lump sum payments) would be made to executives who lose their jobs as a result of the merger or acquisition? What collective agreements are in place and how do they affect jobs?

All the above questions need to be addressed prior to the implementation stage.

Other Areas to Consider as Part of Human Resource Planning

Once the merger is agreed to and the announcement is made, human resources needs to be part of the transition and integration teams that address redundancies, organizational structure, staffing decisions, talent retention, communication, compensation, labour relations, performance appraisals, and training and development.

Redundancies   There are likely to be redundancies in a merge situation. Human resources, with management, needs to define fair principles with respect to the handling of redundancies, including ensuring that key talent continues in place during the transition, even though some will no longer be with the merged company in the end. For example, a key financial person from the acquired company may be required to ensure that the financial information is integrated into the merged company. However, at the end of the transition, this individual is no longer required. He/she has very employable skills, but the merged company leadership does not want him/her to leave until the transition is complete. If the need is identified early in the transition process, there are means by which the organization can attract the individual to stay, including a bonus package payable in installments or at the end of the required/negotiated work. The package might include a bonus and support to transition to a new role in another company at the end of the transition.

Organizational Structure   As a result of the merger, changes will occur in the structure of both the acquired organization and the organization that is doing the acquiring. One of the roles of the transition team will be to define a structure for the new organization, starting with the executives and moving down the organization by divisions. Based on this structure, the following questions must be addressed:

- What are the implications on staffing, including who gets appointed/hired into the roles?
- What processes will be used to make these decisions?
- How quickly will most of the decisions be made?

As a member of the transition team, one of the roles of the human resources professional is to define the new structure and the process to be used to fill the roles.

Staffing Decisions   Staffing decisions are critical in the transition to the new organization. Some staff will be terminated, hired, or moved as a result of the change, and human resources staff need to use the new processes to make staffing decisions. Data gathered in the due diligence stage will have determined if one or both companies have succession planning and/or talent management and what the differences and similarities are. Job analysis will need to be performed quickly to determine where there will be gaps or duplication in the new organization. For example, there will likely be two CFOs. Which one will be retained? Some employees within both companies will be very marketable based on their skills and knowledge. During the uncertainty after the merger is announced, the talented individuals will move on if they are not aware of opportunities for them. As part of the transition plan, there needs to be a human resource plan to address these issues. This plan should identify key individuals whose skills are required and the options that can be used to help retain them.

Key talent is critical to the success of the new organization. Processes need to be put in place to ensure the retention of talent, select individuals for the new organization, and integrate human resources programs.

Communication   Communication of what is known, what plans are in place, and how continued communication will occur is very important. Without a clear picture of what to expect, key talent will begin to look for new roles in other places, and productivity will come to a standstill. Additionally, stress will increase as employees know that there are likely two persons for each job and are concerned about who will be kept and who will not. Good merger management with respect to communication includes:

- A formal announcement that includes the rational for the merger and what benefits the senior team expects to gain from the change
- General information about the structure and the key senior staff that will be retained
- How the change will be managed, including any changes in the reduction of staff and how the team will work with any union
- How ongoing communication will be managed

Compensation   Reviewing the compensation systems and developing the principles of the new organization's compensation system is something that needs to be carried out near the beginning of the transition to the new organization. If the two companies that merge have different compensation systems, then the options are to merge the systems, adopt one of the systems, or develop a new one. Retention of employees will be dependent on comfort with the compensation plan. The major challenge for the human resources department is dealing with two benefits plans. The major concern in a merger is managing costs, and benefits packages can add significantly to employment costs. If the buying company's plan is less expensive, they will want to use it. However, the employees from the acquired company will be resistant to the change in their benefits plans. Cost-benefit analysis is one of the ways to look at the costs. However, the buyer may want to extend some of the more costly benefits of the company they bought so as to maintain the employees required to maintain productivity.

Labour Relations   Union employees are covered by a collective agreement, which is a legally binding document. If the employee in both or one of the companies is covered by a union agreement, the buyer will have to abide by the conditions of the agreement with respect to issues such as job changes. Some agreements have successorship clauses that require both the employer and the successor to adopt the agreement.[64] As the process moves forward, the issue will become whether the union employees continue to work on the current collective agreement or whether it will be renegotiated. In the short term, the conditions of the agreement with respect to layoffs, job security, etc. will have to be adhered to.

In some situations, union representation is involved from the beginning of the process. Generally, union representatives are seen by employees as independent of management and can help obtain the trust and confidence of employees. As such, if the union believes a change program is in the best interest of the employees, this will help persuade employees to participate.

Performance Appraisal   During a merger, productivity in the organizations tends to decrease. Employees are unsure of what is expected of them. Managers and job descriptions change. The long-term goals are no longer clear and it is hard to focus on short-term goals. Human resources needs to work with management to help them determine the reasons for the performance issues and to help facilitate a resolution to the issues. Perhaps the employees don't have the skills to do the assigned work now, and training might be required. Perhaps employees don't know what to do, and additional or alternate types of communication may be required. In some cases, employees might not be willing to do the work assigned because of the change. Human resources can help management develop or improve the performance management process.

Training and Development   Managers and peers may need additional training to support their staff during the transition. Coaching skills would be helpful for managers as they work through the transition and help their employees to do the same. Training related to managing stress, through programs such as relaxation, would also be helpful.

■ ORGANIZATIONAL SKILLS REQUIRED TO SUPPORT A SUCCESSFUL MERGER

Management Capabilities

The management capabilities of an organization vary. Most executives are by nature very action-oriented and keen to get through the difficult business of reorganization and job loss and onto the new organization as quickly as possible. The integration project of the transition is often set with specific timelines, such as a 100-day plan. This short timeframe is implemented to ensure management focus is on the integration and that the benefits are realized in the shortest time.[65] Line managers also play a key role in the various project teams during the transition. Management teams consisting of members of both organizations need to quickly come together with a common approach, especially regarding human resources issues. Human resources will likely need to be prepared to provide development of team-building skills. Additionally, human resources needs to be prepared to identify where specific skills are required and identify processes to quickly develop the skills during the transition. Skills needed include:[66]

- Strategic management skills, especially with regard to understanding how to add value in the new business
- Integration skills, such as being able to make decisions about structure, roles, and dealing with sensitive issues
- Change management skills to help in the process of productively bringing employees with them through the change
- Cultural skills, including being able to understand the dynamics of organization culture, and dealing with culture classes and the emergence of a new culture
- People skills, including being able to recognize and understand the reactions and concerns of the employees, and supporting them through the change
- Communication skills, since one of the key roles during the merger transition is sustaining communications at a level that helps address the emotional issues, and convinces the employees of the benefits at an emotional level not simply a rational level

The Skill of Communication   This skill of communication is critical to the success of the merger implementation. After the merger announcement, there is often a period of time where information is not available or no change is seen. Managers need to be prepared to sit down with their teams and discuss what is happening, what is not happening, and communicate even if they have nothing to communicate. The need for two-way communication is critical. Listening to the employees' questions and concerns will help managers adjust their style so that they are able to minimize the negativity of the change.

Consider as an example, the merger of two professional services organizations. Line managers were given the chance to reflect on how they were going to help implement the organizational changes. For some, the main challenge was "getting staff into confidence mode." Additionally, managers felt the need to ask questions of their management, rather than assuming they were being kept in the dark. A wide range of management styles applied appropriately to different circumstances is required to move through the transition.[67]

◼ HUMAN RESOURCE CAPABILITIES

In addition to good leadership, human resource, and management skills, human resources professionals require good business skills if they are to be considered by the leadership team as value-added resources to the merger team. To be considered for a role in the due diligence stage of the merger process, human resources professionals need to make a case for themselves. The following are capabilities that the human resources professional needs:[68]

- Ability to evaluate another company
- Ability to advice regarding employee sensitivities/attitudes
- Mergers and acquisition literacy and integration know-how
- Ability to plan and lead complex integration projects
- Knowledge of best people practices/systems
- Ability to motivate and retain critical talent
- Expertise with people/organization/culture integration
- Expertise in putting together or helping put together a communications plan that will be flexible

Without this knowledge, it is difficult to see the human resources professional as adding value during the due diligence stage.

◼ GAPS IN HUMAN RESOURCES SKILLS

Research illustrates that the gaps in human resource competence among human resources professionals as related to mergers are as follows:[69]

- Lack of merger and acquisition literacy and integration know-how
- Lack of experience in planning and leading complex integration projects
- Lack of ability and experience in evaluating another company's people processes

Thus, human resources professionals are often left out of the planning phase and only asked to participate in the implementation. During the implementation there is a need to effectively integrate the following:[70]

- Remuneration plans, including a possible redesign to meet the new performance requirements
- Benefits packages including those for individuals who are leaving the organization
- Terms and conditions of the new roles
- Culture and management style of both organizations into the new organization
- Career and other development issues, including helping managers and employees understand changes in roles, outlining possible new career paths, and implementing different training and development processes
- Employee relations, as organizations may have different processes in place, including different unions and union agreements for similar levels of work, and also working with management on the differences, especially in organizations where there may be employees of different unions working together under very different agreements

Overall, the human resources professional, in addition to developing and implementing the human resources programs, provides support and feedback to managers as the new organization roles out. Over time, people issues related to new roles, new skills, and concerns about benefits and compensation packages will arise. The human resources professional needs to constantly watch for disconnects and support managers in the ongoing implementation of the change.

In conclusion, the need for human resource planning in a merger or acquisition is vital to the success of the initiative. Many mergers fail due to culture incompatibilities and other people issues. Human resources professionals bring knowledge and skills to the initiative that are vital to its success. They need to be involved in the initial stages of the process and illustrate not only their human resources skills but the application of these skills to the business challenges.

CHAPTER SUMMARY

- A merger is the combination of two organizations to create a third organization. An acquisition is the purchase of a company, or the controlling interest of a company, by another company. Both are usually carried out to facilitate the growth of market share, to enhance the brand, to acquire new technology talent or capability, or to enter into new markets.
- Canadian companies are actively involved in the purchase of foreign companies, and for deals under $1 billion they are more actively involved in the marketplace than foreign companies are in buying Canadian companies.
- Strategic benefits of mergers include: growth and expansion into new markets, strengthening of competitive position, cost reduction due to operating synergy, diversification, vertical and horizontal integration, and acquisition of complementary skills or resources.
- Financial advantages include: reduction in variability of cash flow, a growing business acquisition that can help fund a mature business, tax reductions due to tax loss, and financial gain as the acquired company is undervalued.
- The merger or acquisition cycle includes the pre-deal, due diligence, integration planning, and implementation stages.
- Human resources professionals can add value to the mergers prior to the rollout if they are involved in either the pre-deal and/or due diligence stages. Cultural issues are key factors that impact the success of the deal and they are often not dealt with until the deal is finalized.
- Major obstacles that impact the success of mergers and acquisitions include: lack of financial performance, loss of productivity, incompatible cultures, loss of key talent, clash of management style/egos, and objectives not being well understood.
- Human resources due diligence initially needs to focus on culture, including gaining an understanding of cultural compatibility and incompatibility, and helping identify issues so plans can be developed to address them.
- The impact of mergers on employees includes: potential loss of key talent, turnover, stress and anxiety, disengagement, clash of cultures, and communication concerns.
- Changes in performance management, decision-making processes, and benefits packages can have negative effects on employee morale and must be managed effectively.
- Redundancies, organizational structure, staffing decisions, talent retention, communication planning and implementation, compensation, labour relations, performance appraisals, and training and development all need to be reviewed and changed as appropriate to support the merger.
- Management capabilities to deal with change, including strategic management skills, integration skills, cultural skills, people skills, and communication skills need to be supported during the transition.

KEY TERMS

- acquisition   206
- conglomerate   206
- due diligence stage   212
- friendly merger   210
- horizontal merger   206
- hostile merger   210
- human resources due diligence   215
- merger   205
- pre-deal stage   211
- vertical merger   206

REVIEW QUESTIONS

1. Define the term "merger."
2. Illustrate a horizontal merger.
3. Define the term "due diligence" with respect to a merger. What activities should human resources participate in during the due diligence stage of the merger?
4. What are the reasons why companies engage in a merger?
5. What are the key factors that have been identified as contributing to the failure of a merger?
6. What skills do human resources professionals need to be successful in helping a transition team during a merger?
7. What skills do managers require to be successful in the implementation of a merger?

DISCUSSION QUESTIONS

1. Describe the effects that a merger can have on employees. What can management do to reduce the effects of a merger on employees? What can employees do to protect themselves when they hear rumours of a merger?
2. One of the concerns executives have when they announce a merger is the loss of key talent. How would you define key talent? What programs can be used to minimize the loss of key talent during and after a merger?
3. Human resources professionals should be involved early in the merger process. What skills do they need if they want to be of value to the organization at the early stage of the merger process? What key people issues can they address in the planning process of a merger?

WEB EXERCISE

Identify a company that has been involved in a merger in the past five years. Visit the website of the company and a couple of newspaper sites, such as The Globe and Mail (www.theglobe-andmail.com), and identify the following:

1. The processes used for transition to a new organization
2. The processes used to deal with redundancies, benefits, and talent retention
3. The role human resources played in the transition to the new organization
4. The issues that have been identified as outstanding

CASE INCIDENT

The Role of Human Resources in an Acquisition

You work for a large retail organization that has decided, as part of its business strategy, to grow by acquisition. They have hired a business development executive who has developed processes and procedures that will be used to determine potential opportunities for acquisition. Last week, the senior team told the human resources team that ABC Company was under consideration for acquisition. Next week you need to meet with the business development executive to discuss the role that the human resources department should play in the decision-making processes prior to finalizing the acquisition.

Questions

1. What suggestions would you make with respect to the role of human resources in the pre-deal stage of the acquisition?
2. If the business development executive agrees that human resources should be involved in the pre-deal stage, what are the required skills of the human resources person working with the executive?
3. If the acquisition moves to the due diligence stage, what is required of human resources?

■ REQUIRED PROFESSIONAL CAPABILITIES REFERENCED IN THIS CHAPTER

10. Applies business fundamentals of production, operations management, accounting and finance, information technology, marketing, and strategic planning to people management issues.

11. Gathers, analyzes, and reports relevant business and industry information (including global trends) to influence the development of strategic business HR plans.

42. Guides and facilitates change in organizational culture and/or values consistent with business strategies.

43. Serves as a change agent to support OD interventions.

50. Plans for and manages the HR aspects of organizational change.

69. Maintains an inventory of people talent for the use of the organization.

SPECIFIC APPLICATIONS IN HUMAN RESOURCE MEASUREMENT SYSTEMS

LEARNING OBJECTIVES

- Describe the balanced scorecard approach and the HR scorecard approach to the strategic management and evaluation of human resources

- Discuss the importance of aligning HR measures with organizational goals and selecting the right types of HR measures to use

- Identify the four stages of the HR life cycle and the impact of return on investment, economic value added, and productivity throughout the life cycle

- Explain at least five major metrics for each stage of the HR life cycle

■ PROFILE

Sysco Corporation

Sysco Corporation is a leading foodservice operator in North America. In 2007, Sysco (an acronym for Systems and Services Company) secured over $35 billion in revenue. The organization had over 170 locations and a diverse group of more than 50,000 employees. Roughly 75 percent of Sysco's operating costs were human resource costs.

To better understand the human resources side of the organization, Sysco started tracking three key metrics. First, the company evaluated and measured work climate or satisfaction level, on the theory that committed employees should be more productive. Second, the organization determined the number of employees needed for each 100,000 cases sold. This metric was considered a productivity metric, as it examined the impact of employees on the production of core business products or services. Third, the organization tracked employee retention levels for each function group, as well as along the warehouse, sales, and finance administration divide.

Not only did Sysco determine and collect the important HR metrics, but they demonstrated a true understanding of business strategy by interpreting the results effectively. For Sysco, a strong relationship existed between work climate scores, productivity, retention, and operating pre-tax earnings. By identifying what HR metrics affect financial metrics over time, the organization was able focus their effort and resources on value-added tasks that aligned with organizational success.

Using this information, Sysco was able increase the retention rate of its delivery associates from about 65 percent to 85 percent. Including all costs associated with turnover, this move resulted in almost $50 million in annual savings. This translated into a value of 10 cents per share.[1]

In an era of hyper-competition, dynamic organizations, and globalization, the need to justify organizational decisions and measure their impact on organizational or strategic success is vital. This chapter introduces multiple human resource measurement systems, identifying the strengths, weaknesses, uses, and potential target audiences of this information.

■ THE BALANCED SCORECARD APPROACH

Co-created by Robert Kaplan and David Norton,[2] the Balanced Scorecard (BSC) aims to help an organization implement strategy, and provides a way to measure business performance using a strategic map (evaluating how the strategy is implemented, rather than just measuring what the strategy is). The notion behind the balanced scorecard is relatively simple. Financial measures are important in evaluating an organization's performance and alignment with strategy, but they must be supplemented with other indicators of an organization's success to provide a realistic and comprehensive view of an organization's future.

balanced scorecard

An approach that provides a balanced view of organizational performance by measuring financials, internal processes, customers, and an organization's human capital

The **balanced scorecard** approach provides a balanced view of organizational performance by measuring financials, internal processes, customers, and an organization's human capital (see Exhibit 10.1). Unlike historical measures of performance (such as traditional financial measures that are inherently past oriented), the BSC attempts to actively engage employees with the strategic implementation process of the organization by providing specific vital measures, assessing them, regularly communicating the measures within the organization, and having management ensure that the entire organization is actively engaged in the strategy implementation.[3]

The balanced scorecard includes four main perspectives: financial, customer, internal business processes, and learning and growth (as a measure of an organization's human capital).

Financial Perspective: Financial measures (e.g., revenue, profit, operating expenses) provide ways to determine if an organization is achieving its desired results in an efficient manner, including cost minimization.

Customer Perspective: This perspective answers the questions "Who are our target customers?" and "What value proposition are we presenting or serving them with?" This helps to create a focus that will differentiate an organization from its competitors, as well as identifies where an organization should focus its efforts.

EXHIBIT	10.1	Sample Balanced Scorecard

Strategy: High Value and Diversification

	Objectives	Measures	Targets	Initiatives
Financial	Increase margins	Number of fixed bid projects Billing rates	25% of revenue 15% increase	Refine bidding Target new regions
Customer	More service	New specialized offerings	2 per account	Brownbag seminar
Internal Business Processes	Forecast accuracy	Forecast vs. actual hours	Margin of error +/− 10%	Estimation standards and guidelines
Learning & Growth	Implement knowledge management	# of shared assets	250 per year	Knowledge harvesting

Sourced from: www.processdriven.org/balanced_scorecard.html

Internal Business Processes Perspective: This perspective recognizes the key processes that an organization must excel in to ensure that they are continuously aligning with long-term strategy and serving their customers. This perspective centres on efficient operations, service development/delivery, partnerships, and reporting of these internal processes.

Learning and Growth Perspective: This perspective is also referred to as the organization's human capital perspective. This is the foundation on which the entire scorecard is built. Sustainable performance can only be achieved by identifying gaps in current versus desired employee skills, information systems, and organizational climate, and by focusing learning and growth activities on efforts that will close these gaps.

Although the BSC helps to keep a manager's attention on strategic issues and management of the implementation of strategy, it is important to remember that the BSC itself has no role in the formation of strategy. In fact, BSCs can comfortably co-exist with strategic planning systems and other tools.

The BSC is currently adopted by almost 50 percent of the world's Fortune 1000 companies, and was hailed as one of the 75 most influential business ideas of the 20th century by Harvard Business Review.[4] The success of a BSC is based on the fact that it takes the strategy of an organization, and transforms it into "simple objectives and measures that drive real people to real behaviours, leading to real results."[5]

The HR Scorecard Approach

HR deliverables

Measures of HR activity that add value to the organization and increase its ability to help an organization achieve its strategic goals

It is widely believed that a primary source of an organization's competitive advantage is their human resources. Many organizations claim that "people are our strongest assets," yet organizations fail to measure the impact that the human resources have on value creation and success of the business. With continuous investment in human resources, the ability to effectively manage employees is becoming increasingly critical.

HR deliverables help integrate HR into a business performance measurement system.[6] The HR deliverables are measures of HR activity that add value to the organization and increase its ability to help an organization achieve its strategic goals. There is no core set of HR deliverables that can be applied to every organization. Instead, each organization's HR deliverables will be determined by the employees' desired core competencies and how these competencies can help deliver organizational success. This provides a clear validation of the strategic value of HR activity.

| **EXHIBIT** **10.2** | The HR Scorecard Approach |

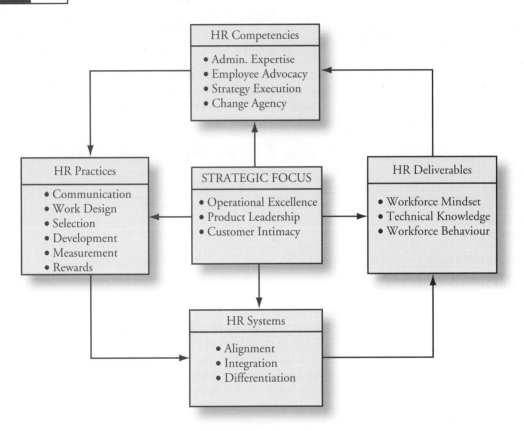

Sourced from: http://www.watsonwyatt.com/services/integrated/workforce/Oct03_HRScorecard.pdf

The HR scorecard focuses on HR deliverables and their influence on implementing the business strategy. Complementing the balanced scorecard approach, the HR scorecard uses the same standard four measurement dimensions: financial, customer, processes (operations), people/human capital management (learning and growth). However, rather than attempting to measure the value added throughout the organization from all perspectives, the HR scorecard maintains a focus on human resources value-add and measurements.

Thus, the **HR scorecard,** shown in Exhibit 10.2, is a measurement and evaluation system to help define the role of HR as a strategic partner. The existence of a unified framework to guide HR managers' priorities and key deliverables provides a consistent approach to HRM within an organization and clarifies the expectations of the HR team. This framework forces managers to evaluate the consequences of their investments in intangible human assets in a well-defined measurable manner.

The HR Scorecard has five key elements:[7]

- Workforce Success: Has the workforce accomplished the key strategic objectives for the business?
- Right HR Costs: Is total investment in the workforce (not just the HR function) appropriate (not just minimized)?
- Right Types of HR Alignment: Are HR practices aligned with the business strategy and differentiated across positions, where appropriate?

HR scorecard

A measurement and evaluation system to help define the role of HR as a strategic partner

- Right HR Practices: Has the organization designed and implemented world-class HR management policies and practices throughout the business?
- Right HR Professionals: Does the organization's HR professionals have the skills needed to design and implement a world-class HR management system?

We can see that the HR scorecard is a slight modification of the balanced scorecard approach. It highlights the strategic role of intangible assets within an organization and clarifies the alignment of human resources with the organizational goals through HR deliverables. This aids in securing HR as a strategic, value-added partner in the organization through development of measurable, strategically aligned results.

One major design challenge of the HR scorecard is justifying the choice of measures. Of all the metrics available to measure HR success, why were these selected? The metrics selected should generate value-related information, linking HR functions, activity, and investment with the overall business strategy.

ALIGNMENT OF HR MEASURES WITH ORGANIZATIONAL STRATEGY

Most researchers use publicly available metrics in their human resources calculations, such as revenue, profit, operating expenses, and productivity. While these measures are easily accessible and have some level of standardization (e.g., profit = revenue − costs), there is minimal justification as to selection of measures. "Researchers rarely justify their choice of measures and . . . the primary goal is to demonstrate plausible potential effects from investing in HR activities and/or strategies."[8]

The selection of HR measures used should align with the corporate strategy. The choice of metrics should convey the values, priorities, and organizational structure of the company, and also operate at the individual employee level to drive performance in specific key areas that are measured.

A hypothetical example of a sales employee in a telecommunications company can illustrate this point. If this employee is measured on annual sales revenue, then he or she will be rewarded for maximizing the volume of networking equipment sold to customers in a given year. That might mean the employee gives volume discounts to ensure that the revenue is high (regardless of profit margins), sells the predicted expansions for next year this year (negatively impacting future revenue), and uses very aggressive pressure tactics in the customer relationship to close the sale (while potentially losing a long-term customer). If this employee is measured on profits for the year, he or she may be hesitant to give out discounts. Comparatively, if this employee is measured on a three- or four-year track record with the same customer, he or she would not sell the entire inventory upfront. Instead, the employee would benefit by creating a long-term sustainable relationship with the customer. Also, customer satisfaction would be brought to the forefront and the salesperson might discover that the use of aggressive measures is not beneficial.

Clearly, careful selection of HR metrics is imperative to organizational success and the actions of individual employees. When selecting HR metrics, the organizational values conveyed to all stakeholders must be considered.

Again, the point can be illustrated using a hypothetical example. This example assumes a small burger restaurant has the choice in determining the number of burgers they make—10, 20, 30, or 40 (see Exhibit 10.3). Cost per burger decreases as the number of burgers made increases, due to economies of scale (e.g., buying materials in bulk, overhead cost is spread out over more burgers). We can also expect the price per burger to decrease as we increase the number of burgers made, due to basic supply and demand economics.

Maximizing revenue can be accomplished by increasing sales price, sales volume, or both. Maximizing profit margins can be accomplished by maximizing the difference between the sale price and the costs. A company may choose to focus on one or both of these targets. As demonstrated in this example, if the company goal is to maximize revenue, it would hire and train enough human resources to make 40 burgers a day. In turn, it would be operating at the lowest

EXHIBIT 10.3 ABC Burger Restaurant

Number of burgers made a day	Cost per burger ($)	Price per burger ($)	Total revenue ($)	Profit per burger ($)
10	2.00	3.50	35.00	1.50
20	1.80	3.20	64.00	1.40
30	1.60	2.90	87.00	1.30
40	1.40	2.50	100.00	1.10

profit margin. However, if the company goal is to maximize marginal profit, it would only hire and train enough employees to make 10 burgers a day. In turn, it would be operating at the lowest revenue point. When determining which metrics to use, it is imperative to know the company strategy in order to correctly analyze the information and develop an action plan accordingly.

According to Jack Phillips, CEO of Performance Resource Organization, less than one percent of human resources budgets are spent on managing and tracking HR metrics, with almost no funding available in small- to medium-sized businesses.[9] Generally, human resources personnel do not have training in financial metrics, nor is it a job requirement. There is an intrinsic hesitancy for those without strong financial backgrounds to use quantitative analysis.

HRP AND THE SMALL BUSINESS

Challenges in Implementing a HRMS

Small businesses face a number of challenges when it comes to the successful adoption and implementations of a human resource measurement system (HRMS). With a limited number of employees, each employee may be responsible for more than one role or position at a time. Thus, it may be difficult to evaluate individual employee contribution to organizational success. It is also slightly more difficult to establish benchmarks in small businesses due to the dynamic nature of the small business. Without the appropriate support (HR expertise or software to track information), small businesses may be focused on revenue-generating activity without truly understanding and capitalizing on human resource alignment with organizational strategy.

Additionally, when a small business does collect metrics, they tend to focus on cost- and time-related metrics. This is due to the fact that a single employee's activities can largely impact an organization's success. For example, in a larger organization with 50 salespeople, a single employee's exit from the sales department can be absorbed temporarily within the organization (e.g., accounts can be transferred, overtime can be used to accommodate the loss). Thus, pressures to ensure that a vacant position is filled as soon as possible can be balanced with the need to ensure that the right candidate is selected for the right position, and that the replacement is provided with adequate training and development opportunities to maximize future contributions to the organization. By comparison, in a small business, there may only be two salespeople. A small business might have to focus on filling the position as soon as possible while overlooking the quality, development, and utilization metrics associated with long-term organizational success.

The Saratoga Institute specializes in measuring performance and cost metrics. They suggest five key measures need to be included in HR metrics: cost, time to do something, quantity involved, quality involved, and human reaction. The Saratoga Institute also suggests three key success factors for adoption of metrics by the human resources department:

1. Collecting data regularly—create a routine and analyze problems before cutting expenses
2. Having metrics that match company strategy
3. Having metrics that match human resources goals

The problem is that most managers do not know *what* should be measured, let alone how. Since historical information does not exist, the human resources department may not be sure where to start. Systems are expensive and time-consuming to set up. As well, the value derived from creating such a system may not be tangible until multiple years of data collection are complete. Combined, this creates multiple entry barriers for companies to start using HR metrics systems efficiently.

What Defines Meaningful HR Metrics?

Success of human resource measurement systems (HRMS) depend on four key elements.[10] First, the kind of data available must align with the kind of data required to make projections and calculations. It is easier to merge data after the fact than to segment data based on variables. For example, data separated by business unit can easily be merged for aggregate-level analysis, whereas it may be more difficult to separate aggregate-level data based on business unit. Second, the data must be accurate. This will be explored more in the upcoming validity section. Third, the cost of collecting data limits what types of data an organization can access. For example, it would not make strong financial sense to spend $15,000 to evaluate the effectiveness of a program that cost $5,000. Lastly, the difficulty in securing data to analyze in a HRMS limits the use of data.

Exhibit 10.4 identifies an approach to the development of HR metrics, as outlined in the book *Ultimate Performance: Measuring Human Resources at Work.* Throughout the HRMS process, users should continuously return to their underlying motivation for data collection and the potential uses of this data to ensure well-founded decisions about data collection are made. As well, the HR decisions should focus on understanding the value of employees and how specific measures enhance or reduce this value.

Within the four steps in the development of a metrics approach, it is critical to determine what HR metrics are meaningful to an organization before embarking on HRMS activity. Some core issues to consider when evaluating the significance of HR metrics include:[11]

- Does the metric reflect the corporate culture's definition of what is important?
- Does the metric measure something that is truly significant in terms of the employer's strategic goals?

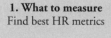 **10.4** Development of Metrics Approach

1. What to measure
Find best HR metrics

2. How to measure
Decide which measure and analysis technique to use

3. What does this mean?
Determine the method Interpret the metric

4. What to do about it
Make a recommendation for appropriate action

- Is the metric limited to three to five specific measures for any outcome or result?
- Does the metric drive continuous improvement?
- Are the metrics easy to calculate and compare?
- Are the metrics periodically reviewed and refined?

■ PREPARING FOR HR MEASUREMENT

When implementing human resource measurement systems, the first major issue is determining what to measure. This will depend on the purpose of the information and its intended use. As well, the target audience for the HR measures should be considered, including their potential use of the measure. There are also limitations based on cost, time, resources, and availability of data that need to be considered. Ultimately, the organization's mission is not to measure every possible variable, but to select key variables that will provide the information required for the organization to be successful in finding, recruiting, training, developing, and retaining employees who can help the organization succeed.

No one measure has to be used in isolation. A combination of measures or a hybrid between two measures may be most useful. Additionally, an alteration on a specific measure may make more sense for an organization. Thus, the examples covered in this chapter are intended to provide an awareness of the range and use of HR measures as an introduction to a wide range of possible measures. The measures selected by an organization, their reporting, and the interpretation of that information for decision-making purposes, should fit the culture, strategy, and goals of the

HRP AND ETHICS   Staying Objective and Managing Privacy

Using HR metrics, human resources managers are expected to compile and analyze data in order to inform decision making, problem solving, and future activities of the organization. This assumes objectivity and limited disclosure in the collection, analysis, and distribution of HR metrics, and is a requirement for the analysis to be considered ethical.

Objectivity

Employee-related metrics must be reported in an objective, rather than subjective way. When presenting information, HR should be careful to keep the interpretation of data free from intentional or unintentional subjectivity. For example, consider two ways that HR could present productivity information. One, the HR employee says "the marketing department's productivity increased *only* five percent." Two, the HR employee says "the marketing department's productivity increased *by a whopping* five percent." Adding subjectivity to the results clearly influences the way that results are interpreted, so metrics should be reported clearly and objectively.

Disclosure/Employee Privacy

When requests for HR metrics are made, the HR team must be careful to report only the results requested, rather than providing access to additional information or complete files. For example, if a manager requests performance information for each employee in their team, with the intent that they may discipline or dismiss employees based on poor performance, any additional information provided inadvertently has the potential to bias management action. In this example, if HR provided access to the complete employee file, include the employee's gender, age, marital status, etc., this information could be unintentionally used in the decision-making process. Therefore, the disclosure of information at the individual level must be controlled.

organization. Measures should also be periodically reviewed to ensure that they continue to meet organizational needs.

ALTERNATIVE APPROACHES TO SEGMENTING HR METRICS

Given the vast number of HR measurements available, there are many possible approaches to segmenting these metrics. While this chapter focuses on the life-cycle approach to categorizing and understanding these metrics, an awareness of alternative approaches is provided in this chapter, since these metrics are highly flexible and adaptable based on organizational need and strategy.

MEASURES USING THE LIFE-CYCLE APPROACH

attraction and acquisition of talent

Encompasses efforts to staff an organization with the right types of people, in the right positions, at the right time

development of talent

Providing personnel with the knowledge and skills required for current and future job-related success

utilization of talent

The production-related activities of the workforce

separation

The exit of talent from the organization, including all forms of exits

The life-cycle approach to HR assumes that HR activity can be divided into a number of unique clusters or stages, based on the nature and scope of activity. Rather than occurring in a linear function, these clusters are considered cyclical, in that each segment in the cycle has a direct impact on the subsequent stage (see Exhibit 10.5).

There are four main stages in the HR life cycle. First is the stage focused on the **attraction and acquisition of talent.** This includes recruitment and selection activity, and encompasses efforts to staff an organization with the right types of people, in the right positions, at the right time. Measures of the effectiveness and efficiency of these functions include cost, quality, quantity, and time metrics.

Once human resources have been added to an organization, the next cluster of metrics in the HR life cycle focus on the **development of talent.** This development involves providing employees with the knowledge and skills required for current and future job-related success. There are multiple HR measures within this stage of the life cycle, which can be divided into subsections such as cost, time, efficiency, internal mobility, and succession.

The next stage of the life cycle is the **utilization of talent.** In the context of HR management systems, utilization is associated with the production-related activities of the workforce. This includes performance, lost productivity, span of control, and overtime measures.

The last stage of the life cycle is the **separation** stage. This stage focuses on the exit of talent from the organization, including all forms of exits (e.g., voluntary or involuntary, permanent or temporary, functional or dysfunctional). These are generally viewed as either turnover-related metrics or vacancy-related metrics. This stage usually initiates a need for attraction and acquisition of new talent, thus completing the HR life cycle.

As highlighted in Exhibit 10.5, the life cycle does not operate in isolation from the rest of the organization. The cycle is highly dependant on the strategic focus of the organization, as highlighted throughout this book. In addition to the four main clusters within the life-cycle approach, there are three metrics that impact every stage of the life cycle. These are return on investment, economic value added, and productivity. These three core metrics are ubiquitous HR metrics. We will begin with a discussion of these three metrics that are associated with all stages of the life cycle before exploring metrics within each stage of the life cycle.

Return on Investment

return on investment (ROI)

Ratio of value creation for the organization based on HR activity and the associated expenses for HR activity in a given period of time

Return on investment (ROI) is typically considered a financial measure, but is being increasingly applied in HR to demonstrate the financial viability of HR initiatives. ROI is the ratio of value creation for the organization based on HR activity and the associated expenses for HR activity in a given period of time.

ROI can be used in multiple aspects of HR measurements. A total-rewards perspective measures how effective a work-life, compensation, and benefits program might be in reducing costs or generating revenue. It can also be used to evaluate the success of a training or recruitment program. Although there are multiple measures of ROI, and each organization should

EXHIBIT   **10.5**   HR Life-Cycle Model

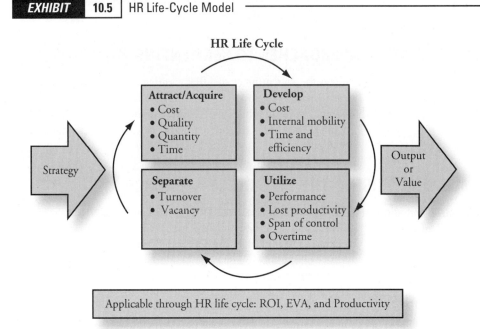

develop their own ROI metrics, there are four common guidelines to use when developing these measures:[12]

1. Include all direct and indirect costs associated with the activity, program, or process
2. Base the analysis on quantifiable results
3. Base the analysis on observable results
4. Be consistent with methods to quantify changes and the assumptions that are required for the data

Economic Value Added

economic value added (EVA)

The calculation of all revenue eliminating the cost of all capital (e.g., human, production, and other)

Considered one of the most dynamic measurements to properly account for all ways in which value can be added or lost, **economic value added (EVA)** determines the economic profit of business activity.[13] Originating in the accounting realm, the basic measure of economic value added is the calculation of all revenue eliminating the cost of all capital (e.g., human, production, and other).

In the context of HR metrics, the economic value added is also referred to as **human capital value added,** which can be calculated as all organizational revenue minus the cost of operating expenses and total compensation per FTE. This answers the question about what people are worth to the organization, and can be used at multiple stages in the life cycle. Organizations add value to their shareholders if the revenue value exceeds the value of all capital costs. Some organizations use this metric to judge the feasibility of HR activities.

human capital value added

All organizational revenue minus the cost of operating expenses and total compensation per FTE

$$\text{EVA (in HR context)} = \text{revenue} - \text{operating expenses} + [(\text{compensation cost} + \text{benefit cost}) / \text{total FTE}]$$

*Note: FTE = Full-time equivalent—a way to standardize measurement of workforce size, as discussed in Chapter 4.

EVA is considered a method that can clearly connect capital budgeting and strategic investment decisions with a methodology for subsequent evaluation of actual performance. By forecasting economic profit, this measurement produces a series of targets for management to achieve to justify the valuation, which can also be readily communicated to and understood by operational management. EVA is a powerful metric because it can be collected at the business-unit level, allowing for comparison and benchmarking within an organization.

Productivity

productivity

Ratio of outputs to inputs in a given production situation

Most organizations define productivity as time spent accomplishing the mission of the department or the organization. Generally speaking, organizations view **productivity** as a ratio of outputs to inputs in a given production situation. Regardless of how it is measured, rising productivity means that the same inputs result in higher outputs, and falling productivity means the same inputs result in lower outputs. Productivity also spans levels and can be defined at the individual, process, job, department, firm, industry, or economy level.

There are four common types of productivity indexes:[14]

1. Single factor productivity is defined as the ratio of a measure of output quantity to the quantity of a single input used.
2. Labour productivity is defined as the ratio of a measure of output quantity to some measure of the quantity of labour used, such as total hours worked.
3. Multifactor productivity is defined as the ratio of a measure of output quantity to a measure of the quantity of a bundle of inputs often intended to approximate total input.
4. Total factor productivity is defined as the ratio of a measure of total output quantity to a measure of the quantity of total input.

Input can be labour, capital, or time. When labour is measured as input, it is highly recommended that FTE count be used instead of headcount, since it provides a more standardized value that can be translated into a meaningful, non-skewed result. FTE was described in detail in Chapter 4. Labour as an input can be split based on various factors (e.g., job, skill, organization, separate inputs, etc.). When capital, rather than labour, is measured as input, the metric is more complex. Capital measures evaluate the value of investment of assets as input over a certain period of time, to determine the relevant price of these capital goods or services. When non-tangible, depreciating, or difficult-to-measure capital is used in the HR metric, it becomes less precise and more complicated. When time is measured as input, a predetermined period of time dictates when the outputs are measured. Output can be either gross output or value-added output.

The reason why this metric spans the HR life cycle is that value is something the organization defines based on its organizational objectives, goals, and strategy. For example, value can be derived from a competitive talent acquisition practice, the development of a learning organization, stability in the internal workforce, or high performance in the workplace. Each of these metrics would be found in a different part of the life cycle, thus this metric is applicable throughout the entire HR life cycle.

Stage 1 of the HR Life Cycle: Attract and Acquire

The first stage of the HR life cycle is the attraction and acquisition of talent. In order for an organization to be successful, it must first populate itself with the right quantity and quality of human resources at the right time. See Exhibit 10.6 for a summary of the metrics associated with the attract-and-acquire stage.

A valuable HRMS that most organizations can easily access is an applicant tracking system (ATS), also sometimes referred to as a talent management system (TMS). The ATS is a tool used for data collection and analysis during the recruitment and selection process. Applicant data is uploaded into the system by the candidates themselves (through web-based job applications) automatically using software (that reads and codes résumés and CVs) or by the HR department.

EXHIBIT 10.6 Summary of Metrics in the Attract-and-Acquire Stage

Stage 1 of the HR Life Cycle: Attract and Acquire

Cost Metrics	Quality Metrics	Quantity Metrics	Time Metrics
• Cost per hire • Recruiting cost ratio • Recruiter efficiency	• Quality of new hire • Quality of candidate • Ratio of offers accepted to number of applicants • New employee separation rate	• Total number of applicants received • Selection ratio • Hires per recruiter	• Actual to contracted time to start • Time to break even on employee contribution

This provides a comprehensive database of candidates that can be searched using multiple search functions, as well as for gaining information about job postings (e.g., number of candidates who applied, quality of candidates, time-related issues with the job posting), which can be used for evaluation and comparison purposes.

The selection of the software depends on a number of organizational factors, including projected use of the software, size of the company, time and resources required to maintain the software, and organizational strategy. An ATS can be procured through a software service provider, purchased off the shelf, or created as proprietary software for the company.

Attract and Acquire: Cost Metrics   For all elements of HR, there are associated cost-related metrics. Accurately identifying direct and indirect costs can be highly beneficial when conducting a cost-benefit analysis of HR decisions or programs. Specifically, the attraction and acquisition process is expensive and time-consuming, directly affecting a firm's ability to achieve its overall strategy.

Cost Per Hire   The cost-per-hire measure is a form of measuring ROI based on the recruitment function that most senior managers readily understand. It provides an awareness of the expenses related to each new hire and can be used to gauge the effectiveness of the recruiting function. This metric is often used because it can be readily calculated and benchmarked against department, organization, and industry averages.

HRP AND STRATEGIC PARTNERS

Capital One

Capital One, a provider of Visa and MasterCard credit cards, has over 44 million customers and 15,000 call-centre employees. Given turnover levels and growth projections, Capital One hires more than 3,000 call-centre employees each year.[15] Recognizing the need for much recruitment and selection activity, Capital One initiated an online recruitment and screening process. The average time between initial contact and employment offer in the company before the online recruitment and screening process was in place was 22 days. Once the HRMS was implemented, the time from initial contact to offer was reduced to just less than 14 days on average. Thus, the organization increased efficiency in the recruitment and selection of human resources and they were better able to meet increasing demand for labour.

Cost per hire is calculated by adding direct costs of recruitment activity (e.g., recruiters' salary, advertisements, etc.) with the indirect costs of this activity (e.g., travels costs, overhead, etc.) for each new hire. Some companies add an extra 10 percent of the time it takes to conduct all recruiting activity to account for the recruiters' additional overhead costs (e.g., printing, supplies, administration, etc). This information may not be available for each and every position so the option of aggregating all costs and dividing that by the total number of positions available provides an average cost per hire for an organization.

Although widely used, there are three significant challenges to using this metric. One, since the focus is managing recruitment expenses, there is no mention of quality in this metric. Two, the cost per hire is not compared to the cost or value of a position within an organization. For example, it should cost more to hire a CEO than a delivery person, but without an awareness of the position being filled, the cost-per-hire metric might not be interpreted correctly. Lastly, indirect costs are often underestimated in the cost-per-hire metric, and therefore this metric may be deflated.

Recruiting Cost Ratio   Addressing the weaknesses of the cost-per-hire metric, the recruiting cost ratio metric or benchmarks the overall efficiency of the recruiting department. It determines the total cost of recruiting activity as a percent of total compensation for the vacant position (assumed to be reflective of value of the position to the organization). This provides a standard number that can be used to measure the effectiveness of one recruiter versus another, something that can be interpreted as recruiter efficiency.

For example, two recruiters attempt to fill two similar positions in an organization. The first recruiter's job posting has a total compensation cost to the organization of $100,000, and the second recruiter's job posting has a total compensation cost to the organization of $75,000. The direct and indirect expenses that the first recruiter required to fill the position were $23,000, while the second recruiter spent $18,000. Although in absolute cost of recruiting, the second recruiter's activity cost less than the first recruiter's, the first recruiter's cost ratio was 23 percent, and the second recruiter's cost ratio was 24 percent. Therefore, when using recruiting cost ratios, the first recruiter was more efficient in their recruitment activity than the second recruiter.

Recruiter Efficiency   An extension of recruiter cost ratio, recruiter efficiency is measured as a value between 0 and 1, as defined by $1 -$ recruiter cost ratio. Therefore, in the example above, the recruiter efficiency was 77 percent for the first recruiter and 76 percent for the second recruiter. The closer the value of the recruiter's efficiency is to one, the more cost-effective the recruiter's activity.

Attract and Acquire: Quality Metrics   Hiring the right quality of talent is critical to long-term organizational success. It is also a critical component in controlling costs—through management of training, lost productivity, and turnover costs. According to a 2008 survey of HR professionals by *Canadian HR Reporter,* 2 percent of HR staff admit that they are often pressured into hiring someone not as qualified as another candidate, while 5.7 percent of respondents felt that this occurred fairly regularly for them (see Exhibit 10.7).[16] An effective attraction-and-acquisition stage should ensure that high-quality resources are being added to the firm.

Quality of New Hires   In a hrmetrics.org survey of C-level executives, new-hire quality was rated the top metric that executives cared about.[17] The two goals of this measure are to determine alignment with business strategy and to determine the ability to staff the organization with employees who will make a business impact. This metric attempts to determine the quality of a new hire through developing performance standards for success in the position prior to selection of a new hire, then evaluating the performance of the new hire against those standards at a later date (usually 3 or 6 months of employment).

The purpose of this measure is to determine whether the new hire is meeting the expectations that were set before they began, and can be used as an evaluation tool for both the

EXHIBIT   **10.7**   Pressure to Hire Candidates Not as Qualified as Others[18]

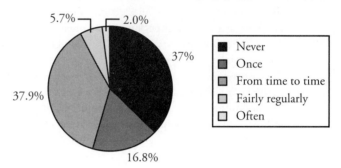

Have you ever been asked or pressured into hiring someone not as qualified as another candidate?

- ■ Never
- ■ Once
- ■ From time to time
- □ Fairly regularly
- □ Often

5.7%   2.0%   37%   37.9%   16.8%

*percentages do not add up to 100 due to rounding

new employee and the hiring manager. For example, if a specific hiring manager is consistently selecting candidates who are not qualified for a given role, the performance measure after the hiring will indicate this disconnect. The organization can take appropriate actions to remedy the situation as needed (e.g., retrain the employee, assess the hiring manager, potentially discharge the employee if they are still on probation, etc.). This metric is easy to use because it can be sufficiently determined by looking at the job performance ratings, and it is useful in assessing if the new hire was a good fit.

Quality of Candidate   Similar to the quality of a new hire, an organization may be interested in the quality of candidates that originally applied for a position (pre-selection). This can be determined by evaluating the number of qualified applicants per requisition (job posting). For example, if there were 40 applicants for an open posting, but only 8 of those were qualified for the position as per the details provided in the job posting, then the quality of candidate metric would equal 20 percent (total number of qualified applicants divided by total number of applicants). This would suggest that the recruitment effort yielded a low quality of candidates. On the other hand, if there were 24 qualified candidates, the quality of candidate metric would be 60 percent, suggesting a more effective recruitment effort.

This measure is more valuable than counting the number of applicants, as it provides a gauge of the effectiveness of the HR recruiting process. It can also be used to evaluate different forms or sources of applicants (e.g., web-based, referrals, walk-ins, etc.) to help guide future searches.

Ratio of Offers Accepted to Number of Applicants   To help with the HR planning process, it is valuable to know how many of the job offers were accepted. Applicants may apply for more than one job at a time, may determine that the organization is not a good fit, or they may have additional non-work related demands that result in the job offer being turned down.

Using a simple example, let's assume a local Wendy's restaurant needs to hire 3 front counter staff. They know from previous experience that their ratio of offers accepted to number of applicants is 2 percent. Thus, HR or management can estimate that they will need to secure at least 150 applications to fill the 3 positions (total number of positions available divided by the ratio of offers accepted to number of applicants). In comparison, a local used car dealership that needs to hire 3 sales people and has a ratio of offers accepted to number of candidates of 75 percent would only need to attract 4 potential applicants.

The ratio of offers accepted to the number of applicants can help benchmark the minimum number of applicants needed to fill a vacancy, which can be very useful in the HR planning process, and can help evaluate the effectiveness of the HR recruiting process. This information can be useful in determining the means, target, budget, and scope of recruitment activity.

New Employee Separation Rate   As another measure of attraction and acquisition success, the new employee separation rate determines the percentage of new hires that remain with the company for a pre-determined period of time as a percentage of all exits. Some organizations use a one-year mark, while others are interested in determining the number of employees that stay employed past a pre-determined probationary period. This measure is intended to be an indicator of performance as a quality measure of HR and new employee activity. Ideally, this measure should also take into account if the exits were voluntary (employee initiated) or involuntary (employer initiated) to help understand the reason for any potential misfits.

For example, an organization hires 40 new employees in January 2010. By January 2011, 10 of these new hires have left the organization (6 quit = voluntary departures, 4 were dismissed = involuntary departures). In total, in the organization, there were 100 employee separations from January 2010 to January 2011. Therefore the new employee separation rate is 10 percent (total number of new hire separation divided by total number of separations in the organization); the new employee voluntary separation rate is 6 percent (total number of new hire voluntary separations divided by total number of separations in the organization); and the new employee involuntary separation rate is 4 percent (total number of new hire involuntary separations divided by total number of separations into the organization).

This information can help guide future HR efforts as well as determine the desired number of new hires according to projected future demands and commitments of these new hires. In the example above, new employees are more likely to quit than to be dismissed. This might indicate that some of the new employee needs are not being met, and HR can explore this.

Attract and Acquire: Quantity Metrics   Although quality is an important metric to evaluate the success of attraction and acquisition activity, quantity metrics (which require an objective measure and easily accessible data manipulation) are more readily available and easier to calculate using HRMS than quality-related metrics (which require some objective measure or manipulation of data). Therefore, often quantity measures are presented to help evaluate HR efficiency and effectiveness.

Total Number of Applicants Received   This simple metric provides a count of the number of applicants received within a set period of time (e.g., per month), regardless of the means used to collect the applications. This provides a quick review of the potential number of interested applicants, or of the breadth of interest in joining a firm. For example, Google receives more than one million applicants a year.[19] The sheer volume of the applications warrants automated pre-screening and a scientific, rather than intuitive approach, to recruitment. Given the high number of total applicants received, Google adopted an approach to recruitment in which predictors of high performance are scientifically determined—an online survey collects predictive information from applicants and then rates them on a scale to indicate the alignment with predictors of high performance.

Selection Ratio   The selection ratio is the number of applicants hired divided by the total number of applicants. A low ratio (e.g., 1:4) suggests that the organization might not have attracted enough applicants, and should therefore look more closely at the quality of the candidates and whether the recruitment program was cast wide enough. In jobs with a labour shortage, skills shortage, or high specialization, it can be expected that the selection ratio will be lower. A selection ratio can be increased by increasing the pool of potential candidates through more aggressive or more diverse recruitment strategies.

In the case of a high selection ratio (e.g., 1:100), the organization has more leverage in assessing fit and quality of the candidate. A selection ratio can also be too high (e.g., Google), indicating a need to find ways to automate the screening-out process, to avoid applicant overload while maintaining good quality candidates. This will reduce the labour hours required by HR to screen résumés and assist in the selection of the right candidate.

Hires per Recruiter   As a measure of HR activity, some organizations calculate the number of hires per recruiter within a predetermined time frame. For example, an HR department has five recruiters, and all recruiters successfully hired seven new employees this month, with the exception of one recruiter who hired only three. This metric would then highlight a need to explore the reasons why the one recruiter had lower than expected results. Were the jobs they were attempting to fill more complex and the applicants more difficult to find? Was the recruiter using effective recruitment methods? Is the offer-to-acceptance ratio lower for this recruiter, and does that indicate some problems with the recruiter? There may be multiple reasons for a lower than expected or lower than average hires per recruiter, but this metric identifies recruiter performance that may warrant further investigation.

Attract and Acquire: Time Metrics   Several HR analysts express frustration with their inability to change time-related metrics.[20] This can be due to resource constraints, the lack of control they have in dictating the time line of new hires, and the pressure that HR feels to balance quality and time. Regardless, time-related metrics are commonly used as a measuring stick for the service level agreement between the hiring managers (e.g., department representative, supervisor, etc.) and HR. If these two teams work together in partnership, then the time-related metrics can be used to increase efficiency in the attraction and acquisition process.

Actual to Contracted Time to Start   Traditionally, HR measures included a focus on the time to fill a position (the time between the determination of an opening and the selection of a suitable candidate for that position) and the time to start (the time between the determination of an opening and the actual start date of a candidate) as measures of recruitment effectiveness. However, these measures are subject to demands beyond organizational control (e.g., a candidate can present time constraints with both of these measures, the hiring department can dictate a desired start date, the HR department can struggle with finding a qualified pool of candidates, etc.).

A recommended alternative to use is the actual to contracted time to start. Prior to recruitment efforts, the hiring manager and HR collectively determine a desirable start date (contracted time to start). The actual time to start is measured as the number of days between the start of the recruitment process and the date that the employee first starts employment. This assesses whether the organization's expectations are realistic and allows for a focus on quality and timeliness. In addition, this method is preferred as it promotes shared ownership of the recruitment process.

Time to Break Even on Employee Contribution   Originally used as a learning and development measure, this metric identifies the time required for new hires to achieve targeted performance levels. This measure is essential in organizations that rely heavily on freelance or temporary workers or that have high turnover levels, as it provides information about how long it takes an employee to understand the position needs and organizational culture. It addresses the question of how long it takes before the costs of acquisition, training, compensation, and benefits of an employee are aligned with employee contribution to an organization. Another way to understand this is to ask "How long does it take before the organization gains profitability from an employee?"

Stage 2 of the Life Cycle: Develop

Employee development is a future-oriented activity grounded in the identification and growth of essential job skills aligned with organizational strategy. Development-related metrics focus on measurements pertaining to the training, learning, and education of an existing workforce. These

| EXHIBIT 10.8 | Summary of Metrics in the Develop Stage |

Stage 2 of the HR Life Cycle: Develop

Cost Metrics	Internal Mobility Metrics	Time and Efficiency Metrics
• Percentage of budget allocated to training • Training costs per employee • Learning and development metrics	• Internal mobility rate • Internal promotion rate • Candidate succession planning depth	• Average time to promotion • Training penetration rate • Cycle time from transfer request to transfer completion

include many direct and indirect measures, but for clarity these are presented as cost, internal mobility, or succession metrics, and time and efficiency metrics. The most effective approach to measuring development is the pretest-posttest design. In this measure, an organization assesses an employee's performance or abilities prior to the training, development, or learning experience. This is compared to measures after the experiences. The differences between the pre- and posttests identify the effect of the activity on the development of an employee. Since there may be other variables affecting the results, these tests may not pass the criteria to be considered "scientific," however they should be sufficient as practical measures of HR development. See Exhibit 10.8 for a summary of the metrics associated with the develop stage.

Develop: Cost Metrics   The average Canadian company spends 1.6 percent of their payroll spending on training.[21] Within the shift to a knowledge-based economy, and a focus on learning organizations, the costs associated with the development of human resources in an organization will have to be increasingly justified. Executives will be interested in the ROI on development initiatives, while HR and managers will be more interested in the impact of the development on the employee, department, or organization.

Percentage of Budget Allocated to Training   The percentage of budget allocated to training is calculated as the total training expenses divided by total HR, labour, or operating budget. Total training expense includes costs of labour (when training occurs during business hours as part of paid employment), direct training costs (e.g., seminar fees, registration), and indirect costs (e.g., lunches, parking, travel to sites, etc.). This metric allows for interpretation of the organization's learning focus and may indicate an organization's ability to respond to changing demands on the workforce, through a commitment to preparing the existing workforce for anticipated future needs.

In a Mercer study of over 400 Canadian and U.S. companies, both Canadian and U.S. companies were increasing their investment in training and development as an HR strategy to respond to uncertain economic climates. In 2008, 24 percent of Canadian companies surveyed instituted additional training and development programs, while 22 percent considered this action. In the U.S., the numbers were 14 percent and 20 percent respectively.[22] In a report by the Canadian Public Service Agency on federal and departmental government agencies' learning, training, and development activities, an average of 4.5 days were allocated to each employee for learning, with an average cost of $1,000 per employee. The average organization's salary operating budget dedicated to learning was 3 percent.[23]

Training Costs per Employee   The training cost per employee metric determines how much money is spent on training for each employee as a measure of training program evaluation. By standardizing the costs of a training program (e.g., training session on work premises), HR and managers can evaluate multiple alternatives available for training delivery. For example, if a two-day training session on people management skills costs $15,000 and has a 20-person capacity, but individual training sessions on people management skills cost $1,000 per person, then the training cost per employee for the two-day session is $750, compared with $1,000 for the individual session (total cost of training divided by the number of employees attending training). Thus, the group session has a lower individual employee costs. While this provides a clear and easy-to-use metric to calculate training costs per employee, HR must be careful to evaluate the quality of the training session, additional indirect costs (e.g., loss of employee productivity for two days), and be cognizant that development of different skills can require different teaching pedagogies. Therefore, a simple cost ratio may not be ideal to use in all situations.

Learning and Development Metrics   There are hundreds of learning and development metrics to measure the effectiveness of training and development programs, and the impact of these programs on individual, group, and organizational performance. Common questions include: Has safety training helped reduce workplace accidents? What processes have been streamlined or standardized through training? Have managers improved since getting their last set of feedback from employees, or since their last management training session? Each question warrants the use of a unique metric to measure the effectiveness of the learning or development experience. When a new venture is launched with a desired effect on learning or development, HR must decide prior to participation in the activity what the desired outcome is, how it will be measured, and how results will be interpreted. As highlighted above, the pretest-posttest design is useful in assessing the impact of such activities.

Develop: Internal-Mobility Metrics   Internal mobility measures focus on the ability of the organization to utilize its internal labour force to achieve the workforce requirements of today and tomorrow. Rather than selecting an individual from outside of the organization to fill the needs of the organization, through effective recruitment, selection, training, and development of internal staff, an organization may be able to achieve its strategic goals.

Internal Mobility Rate   Internal mobility measures are also referred to as transfer rate. This determines the percentage of employees that were transferred during a specific reporting period, which is critical in predicting future staffing needs. For example, Truckers Assist has 50 employees. From January 1st to June 30th (half a year), 5 employees transferred or changed positions in the organization. As the most basic measure of internal mobility, the transfer rate or internal mobility rate for the organization can be measured at 10 percent (total number of employees transferred divided by total number of employees). Therefore, 10 percent of staff changed positions within the specified period of time, and the remaining 90 percent of the employees (1 − internal mobility rate) maintained their positions during the same period.

In an organization with a relatively high internal mobility rate, it may be important to develop core skills, generic business acumen, or organization-specific training. In an organization with a relatively low internal mobility rate, job-specific training or development would be useful since it is more likely that employees will be staying in their existing jobs for a longer period of time. As well, the internal mobility rate can determine the qualities, generic or job-specific, to assess during the attraction-and-acquisition phase of the HR life cycle.

Internal Promotion Rate   The internal rate of promotion is more specific than the internal mobility rate in that it determines the rate at which current employees are promoted. This exposes the general need for internal advancement opportunities, which can be useful information within and outside of the organization (e.g., for planning reasons, information to share with new recruits, as a measure of retaining key employees, etc.).

Candidate Succession Planning Depth   Candidate succession planning depth determines the percentage of key roles that have a succession pool of unique candidates. According to the Conference Board of Canada,[24] one in every ten senior executive positions has no identified potential

| **EXHIBIT** **10.9** | How Robust Is the Leadership Pipeline?[25] |

Position	**Ratio of High-Potential Successors to Positions**
Senior executive	0.50
Other executive	0.44
Key leverage roles*	0.40

*Pivotal roles not considered executive

successor, indicating a very poor HR plan to deal with the departure of key personnel. In addition, a succession study conducted by the Conference Board of Canada indicates that less than half of executive positions in Canada (e.g., senior executive, executive, or key leverage roles) have a high-potential successor identified (See Exhibit 10.9). Therefore, training, development, and preparedness of potential successors become critical to the success plan. This measure is used to indicate the level of preparedness for succession planning, and can indicate if more planning is required.

Develop: Time and Efficiency Metrics   Measuring development in terms of time and efficiency of initiatives provides easily understandable metrics that can be used at multiple levels within the organization. HR can use these metrics to determine if the development activities are well-organized and securing the return on time invested in them. Management can use these metrics to evaluate their performance on development relative to other groups within the organization, or as a measure of departmental success. Executives value this information because it provides an awareness of the level of preparedness of the internal labour force in a meaningful way that is comprehendible to them.

Average Time to Promotion   The average time to promotion determines the average number of months required for an employee to be promoted within an organization. Not only does this metric help with succession planning initiatives, it also helps determine the average amount of time it takes an employee to gain enough knowledge about the organization and their position in order to be promoted. From an HR planning perspective, this information is extremely valuable in planning internal mobility issues, timelines, succession planning, and replacement planning.

Training Penetration Rate   The training penetration rate assesses the percentage of employees who have completed a specific course or content training, and assesses specific skill or knowledge dissemination within an organization. This information aids in the evaluation and development of the workforce skills and can be used by HR planning for budgeting of future training expenses.

For example, a cultural sensitivity training program is launched at a local police dispatch centre. Of the 75 dispatchers, 20 have completed the training program by a certain time (e.g., December 1st). For HR, this information can be interpreted to measure a cultural sensitivity training penetration rate of 26.7 percent (number of employees who have completed the training divided by the total number of employees), suggesting that at the existing point of time, roughly one in every four dispatchers have the skills required to deal with culturally sensitive calls. As well, if this training is important to job success, the cost of achieving 100 percent penetration in the future can be calculated using the costs of the previous program. For example, if the cost of training for the 20 dispatchers was $25,000, then the budgeting for training the remaining 55 employees would be $68,750 ($25,000 divided by 20 employees equals $1,250 per employee). Likewise, if the training penetration rate was only four percent (i.e., three employees are trained on cultural sensitivity) and a requirement for a position with that training comes up, HR and management would have a much smaller pool of potential candidates to select from.

Cycle Time from Transfer Request to Transfer Completion   Another important measure for internal mobility—all forms of changes within the internal labour force including replacement planning, succession planning, and horizontal and vertical movements—is the cycle time required to complete a transfer request. Specifically, this measures the total days required from the time of a transfer request to transfer completion. For example, an employee working in department A requests a transfer to department B on June 1st, 2010. The transfer is completed by October 1st, 2010. Thus, the cycle time from transfer request to transfer completion is 153 days (the number of days between June 1st and October 1st). HR must utilize this information to determine if the transfer time is perceived as adequate. They can also apply this information in other ways, including to help manage replacements for vacant positions, to motivate and reward an employee who is in a department or position that they would like to leave temporarily, to determine project assignments, and other such operational issues.

Stage 3 of the Life Cycle: Utilize

Once the right human resources are acquired and developed, the organization focuses on optimizing the utilization of these resources. The metrics associated with this stage include performance, productivity (including lost productivity), span of control, and overtime. Since productivity was presented as a core HR metric spanning multiple stages of the HR life cycle, this section will introduce the unique notion of lost productivity as a utilization-specific measure of productivity. See Exhibit 10.10 for a summary of the metrics associated with the utilize stage.

Utilize: Performance Metrics   Performance-related metrics are "formal, structured systems for measuring, evaluating, and improving an employee's job-related behaviour and output."[26] An organization can focus on increasing productivity and improving its competitive advantage by measuring each employee's contribution towards achieving the organization's goals.

Revenue per Employee   As a traditional metric, revenue per employee is relatively easy to collect and well understood by almost all users. Many managers consider this to be a measure of employee productivity, since it is an overall measure of revenue secured per employee. This metric is also valuable in benchmarking, but due to a high degree of variability based on organizational characteristics (e.g., industry, organizational size, etc.), users must be careful to clearly outline the parameters of the organization used as benchmarks.

The revenue generated per employee can also be used by HR to defend compensation levels of employees. For example, in Canada, the average revenue for an employee in the service sector is $154,973, while the average revenue per employee in the primary industries is $1,597,675.[27] Therefore, there may be more flexibility in negotiating wage rates in the primary services industry (which has low labour intensity), than in the services industry (which is highly labour intensive).

| **EXHIBIT** | **10.10** | Summary of Metrics in the Utilize Stage |

Stage 3 of the HR Life Cycle: Utilize			
Performance Metrics	**Lost-Productivity Metrics**	**Span of Control Metrics**	**Overtime Metrics**
• Revenue per employee • Work performance	• Absenteeism • Employee illness absence rate • Injury rate • Absence cost factor	• HR-to-employee ratio • Management ratio	• Overtime expense per FTE

As well, if total compensation cost is known, then the revenue per employee can easily be translated into an economic value-added metric per employee.

Work Performance   This measure determines if an employee is operating above, at, or below the expectations set. This is useful in determining what performance incentives to give an employee, identifying employees for promotion, and managing retention efforts. There are several factors to consider when determining work performance, including, but not limited to: external factors, organizational capability, employee capacity, compensation, motivation, limitations, and factors beyond the employees' control.

A commonly used work performance measure is that of the employee's actual performance divided by performance expectations. Any value over 1 would indicate an employee surpassing performance expectations, and would indentify a high performer. A value under 1 would indicate an employee not meeting expectations. In the rare case of a work performance value of 1, the employee is meeting expectations. For example, if the expectation of a typesetter at a publishing house is to complete an average of 8 pages of typesetting an hour, and the employee completes an average of 9 pages an hour, then the work performance metric would be 1.125 (actual performance divided by performance expectations). Thus, this employee would be exceeding work performance expectations. Exhibit 10.11 identifies executive positions and the ratio of employees with exceptional performance ratings in that position. These values can be used for benchmarking purposes and to identify areas of potential growth, training, or improvement in the organization.

Utilize: Lost-Productivity Metrics   While productivity is discussed as a core HR life-cycle metric, lost-productivity measures provide an understanding of behaviours or performance that detract from an organization's ability to translate expected inputs into expected outputs. These events (e.g., absence, injury, illness) prevent employees from participating at a desired level of productivity.

absenteeism

Time that an employee is absent or away from work, including sick days, excessively long breaks, lateness, etc.

Absenteeism   **Absenteeism** refers to the time that an employee is absent or away from work, including sick days, excessively long breaks, lateness, etc. According to the Human Resources Professional Association (HRPA) Ultimate HR Manual, the average employee is absent from work six to seven days per year. Exhibit 10.12 provides a summary of average days of absenteeism per employee based on major industry grouping. Industry averages can be used as benchmarks to assess if absenteeism is problematic in a specific organization. If there are significant or costly absenteeism issues, the organization should establish attendance management programs. Is there a certain group that is more likely to be absent than others? What alternative explanations could there be for absenteeism?

There are generally four main causes of excessive absenteeism: lifestyle factors (e.g., chronic illness, poor general health, smoking, substance abuse), workplace factors (e.g., workload, low morale, health and safety concerns, shift work), general stress factors (e.g., job dissatisfaction, low supervisory support, peer conflict), and domestic factors (e.g., lack of work–life balance, child or elderly care, finances).

EXHIBIT 10.11	Is Talent Performing to Its Potential?[28]

Position	Ratio of Incumbents with Exceptional Performance Ratings to Positions
Senior executive	0.46
Other executive	0.24
Key leverage roles*	0.38

*Pivotal roles not considered executive

Source: Strategic Value of People: Human Resource Trends and Metrics. (2006, July). The Conference Board of Canada, p. 9.

| **EXHIBIT** | **10.12** | Average Absenteeism days per Employee, by Industry[29] |

Industry	Average Days per Employee
Overall	6.4
Education and health	9.6
Chemical, pharmaceutical, and allied products	8.1
Natural resources	7.9
Government	7.8
Wholesale trade	7.2
Food, beverage, and tobacco products	6.3
Transportation and utilities	6.3
Manufacturing	6.1
Finance, insurance, and real estate	5.9
Not-for-profit	5.8
Retail trade	5.8
Communications and telecommunications	5.7
Oil and gas	5.7
High tech	4.3
Services	3.8

To evaluate the effect of absenteeism on the labour costs of an organization, the average salary is multiplied by average absenteeism, and then divided by the number of working days per year. There are also indirect costs of lost productivity—including the costs associated with replacement workers or overtime and employees' diminished morale—that are difficult to correctly determine, but can be estimated with some accuracy if needed.

Employee Illness Absence Rate   The employee illness absence rate is an individual employee's measure of the days lost (as a percent of total working days available), within a specific time period (usually a year). For example, within a department there are three employees who used sick days within the last year. The first employee was absent 5 days, the second 10 days, and the third 22 days. Assuming that there are 210 working days in a year, the employee illness absence rate for the first employee is 2.4 percent, the second employee is 4.8 percent, and the third employee is 10.5 percent (number of days lost to sickness divided by total number of working days). This information can assist in determining if there is a larger issue to explore for an employee with a high absence rate.

Injury Rate   The injury rate evaluates the number of injured employees at a given period of time within the organization as a whole. This information is rarely presented at the departmental level. This metric allows for the evaluation of workplace safety, as well as assisting with the determination of budgeting for safety-related training and efforts.

Absence Cost Factor   The most common measure of absence cost factor is the determination of the revenue lost when an employee is not at work. The calculation uses average revenue per employee per year to compute average daily revenue generated by each employee. If an employee is absent, the number of days absent multiplied by the average daily revenue generated by each employee is multiplied to give an absence cost factor. While this measure may be useful in estimating the value lost when an employee is not at work, it only captures averages, not actual revenue. The metric is popular nonetheless, since it is fairly easy to calculate, usually readily available, and relatively easy to understand within and outside of the organization.

Utilize: Span-of-Control Metrics   Span-of-control metrics provide useful information regarding the number of administrative or management staff as a ratio of the number of employees (including

| **EXHIBIT** | **10.13** | HR Staff Ratios by Organization Size, Sector, and Industry[30] |

	HR–Employee Ratio	**HR Cost per Employee**
Size		
100 to 499 employees	2.21	$2,865
500 to 900 employees	1.00	2,817
1,000 to 3,999 employees	1.64	2,329
4,000 to 9,999 employees	1.6	1,799
10,000 or more employees	1.43	1,185
Sector		
Private	1.57	2,239
Public	2.08	2,383
Industry		
Primary industry	1.62	3,241
Manufacturing	1.69	2,624
High tech, communications, and telecommunications	1.48	2,091
Transportation	1.75	2,089
Finance, insurance, and real estate	2.08	3,102
Wholesale and retail	1.18	1,492
Education and health	1.15	1,554
Government	2.49	2,082
Services	1.45	1,872
All Organizations	1.76	2,301

Source: The Strategic Value of People: Human Resource Trends and Metrics. (2006, July 7). The Conference Board of Canada.

permanent employees and contractors on payroll). This provides an evaluation of organization structure—how tall or flat an organization is. This information is used to help assess the value created by the management or administrators and evaluate the appropriateness of the organization structure.

HR-Employee Ratio　　This metric provides information about the number of employees each HR person serves as a measure of HR cost-effectiveness and capabilities. The ratio of HR staff to number of employees in an organization varies by organizational size, sector, and industry. In Exhibit 10.13, it is expressed as the number of HR staff for each 100 employees. The HR cost per employee is also a measure commonly used to assess the use and activities of the HR department. Similar to the HR-to-employee ratio, the HR cost per employee varies by organizational size, sector, and industry.

Generally, the HR-employee ratio decreases as the size of the company increases, and the HR cost per employee decreases accordingly, suggesting that large organizations are benefiting from economies of scale, standardizing or automating processes, or potentially from outsourcing HR functions.

Management Ratio　　The management ratio establishes the number of non-management employees relative to the number of managers, providing a measure of the span of control in an organization. For example, an organization has 100 employees in total, of which 20 are at management level. This suggests that the organization has a management ratio of 4 to 1. Thus, each manager has an average of four subordinates (non-management employees). In comparison, if an organization has a management ratio of 2.5 to 1, this suggests that for every 3.5 employees actively involved in organizational production, there is one manager. This benchmark is useful in revealing possible structural obstacles to productivity and efficiency.

Utilize: Overtime Metrics   When an organization is not adequately staffed, overtime can be used to meet organizational demands for labour. In Canada, overtime pay rates are regulated by provincial and federal governments. After the first 40–48 hours (dependant on jurisdiction), an employer is mandated to compensate an employee at a predetermined multiplier of their regular rate of pay. There are exemptions in the legislation, and in certain cases managers and supervisors are exempt from securing overtime pay. However, recent lawsuits (e.g., CIBC and KPMG) are challenging the exemption clause.

Overtime Expense per FTE   Overtime expense per FTE determines the average compensation associated with overtime per full-time equivalent employee. For example, an organization needs 12 full-time employees, but is currently understaffed and only has 10 full-time employees. Each employee is paid $20 per hour and works an eight-hour shift. If the organization was staffed at the right level, then daily direct compensation would be $1,920 ($20/hr × 8 hours × 12 employees). However, due to the labour shortage, an additional 16 hours of work must be paid at an overtime rate. Assuming a 1.5 times multiplier is the overtime rate, then daily direct compensation would be $2,080 ($20/hr × 8 hours × 10 employees + 30/hour OT × 16 hours OT). In fact, it costs the organization an extra $160 to use overtime. Thus, overtime expenses might reduce short-term organizational efficiency.

Stage 4 of the Life Cycle: Separate

A key HR planning responsibility is to predict and manage employee exits, determine labour needs, and figure out ways to bridge the gap between the two. While some separations will not demand replacements, others do. As well, separations can be initiated by the employee or the employer, and they can be planned or unplanned. Therefore, workforce planners must act both proactively and reactively when assessing and responding to separations. See Exhibit 10.14 for a summary of the metrics associated with the separate stage.

Separate: Turnover Metrics   Turnover is costly to organizations. Although the calculation of basic turnover is a simple mathematical equation, the analysis of turnover metrics can be powerful in helping HR interpret, predict, and respond to movement of labour inside and outside of the organization. Using historical data to assess trends in turnover is useful in identifying systemic problems within the organization, labour market, or other societal factors outside of the organization. This trend analysis can aid in guiding HR practices. For example, if an identifiable demographic group has an unusually high turnover level, this may warrant investigation of potential causes of the exodus, as well as identifying a need for a retention strategy aimed specifically at

---

EXHIBIT   10.14   Summary of Metrics in the Separate Stage

Stage 4 of the HR Life Cycle: Separate

Turnover Metrics	Vacancy Metrics
• Turnover levels	• Vacant period
• Turnover cost	• Cost of vacancy
• Attrition rate	
• Rate of retirement	
• Involuntary separation rate	
• Dismissal percentage	
• Permanent resignation percentage	

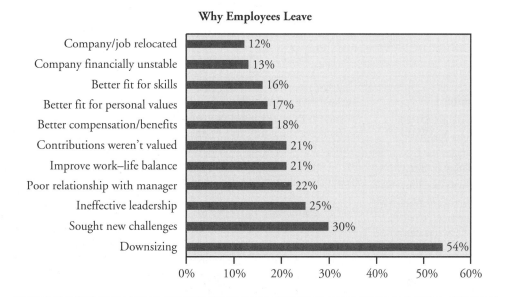

EXHIBIT 10.15 Causes of Turnover in Canada[31]

Why Employees Leave

Cause	Percentage
Company/job relocated	12%
Company financially unstable	13%
Better fit for skills	16%
Better fit for personal values	17%
Better compensation/benefits	18%
Contributions weren't valued	21%
Improve work–life balance	21%
Poor relationship with manager	22%
Ineffective leadership	25%
Sought new challenges	30%
Downsizing	54%

this group. There are multiple causes of turnover, as shown in Exhibit 10.15. A valuable HRMS program can help identify reasons for employee exits, which in turn can help develop programs focused on retention of key performers.

Turnover Levels   Turnover levels are usually expressed as the number of people whose employment relationship with an organization has been severed as a percent of the total employee population of the organization. This presents the simplest form of a turnover calculation and does not take into account the nature or cause of the employee exit. However, the basic turnover rate should be used a number of ways, including possible analysis by department, branch, manager, etc. A higher rate of turnover in one department may indicate a need to investigate potential training issues, management styles, or subcultures within that group. Similarly, a lower than average rate of turnover within a business unit might result in exploration of common best practices of the group that can be used throughout the organization.

Turnover levels are often used for benchmarking purposes by executives to gauge the performance of the HR department (keeping in mind that turnover levels vary significant by industry, company size, location, etc.). They are also used internally by the HR department to help with HR planning efforts. HR can also complement turnover level information with a review of work performance of exiting employees to help distinguish functional from dysfunctional turnover. Functional turnover is desirable since it results in the exit of substandard performers, which would have a positive effect on organizational performance and outcomes.[32] Dysfunctional turnover is the separation of high performers from the organization. Organizations are interested in managing turnover since it has an impact on recruitment, training, and corporate memory-loss costs.

Turnover Cost   Cost of turnover includes the cost of separation and the cost of replacement. Separation costs include severance pay, outplacement fees, exit interview costs, and possible litigation costs. Replacement costs include costs of new hires as outlined in the attraction-and-acquisition phase. In addition to these expenses, there are indirect costs that can be estimated, such as lost productivity, lost sales, and learning curve costs.

It is estimated that the average cost of turnover ranges from 35 percent to 150 percent of an employee's salary, so managing these costs is an important component of HR budgeting and organizational financial success.[33] For example, in a company with 3,000 employees, with an average compensation per employee of $50,000, and a turnover rate of 15 percent, the organization would experience an annual cost of turnover of $16.875 million, using a conservative estimate of 75 percent of salary as the cost of turnover. A small reduction of the cost of turnover, from 75 percent of salary to 70 percent of salary, would result in a savings of $1.125 million.

attrition

The natural and continuous departure of employees in an organization through methods that affect the population at large, such as quits, retirements, disability, and deaths

Attrition Rate **Attrition** is defined in Chapter 4 as the natural and continuous departure of employees in an organization through methods that affect the population at large, such as quits, retirements, disability, and deaths. Therefore, the attrition rate can be calculated by adding the number of retirements, resignations, deaths, and disabilities and dividing that by the total number of employees in an organization. This information can be historical, using past records of exits, or future-oriented, by predicting these values based on trends or expert forecasts.

Rate of Retirement For HR, retirement poses a significant challenge on workforce planning. The average age of retirement in Canada has been declining in recent years. With mandatory retirement, organizations were able to predict the number of employee exits based on either an employee's age or a combination of age and tenure.

The rate of retirement is measured by identifying all persons predicted to retire within a set period divided by the total number of employees. As outlined in Exhibit 10.16, the rate of retirement is highly dependant on industry, with ranges in Canada of 1.7 percent to 3.7 percent. Therefore, in a university with 15,000 employees, it can be predicted that 555 positions will need to be filled due to retirement activity (3.7 percent of 15,000). In contrast, in a customer-service centre with the same number of employees, it can be predicted that 345 positions will be vacated due to retirement (2.3 percent of 15,000). These metrics provide guidance for HR planning professionals in terms of recruitment initiatives, succession planning, and replacement planning.

Involuntary Separation Rate Employees may involuntarily separate from an organization in the form of layoffs and dismissals/terminations. This information is useful to understand the nature

EXHIBIT   10.16 Expected Retirement by Occupational Group in Canada (2007–2012)[34]

Occupational Group	Number of Retirees	Rate of Retirement (%)
Sales and service	438,100	2.3
Business, finance, and administration	445,900	2.9
Trades, transportation, and equipment operations	315,500	2.5
Social science, education, government service, and religion	224,200	3.7
Health	153,500	3.1
Processing, manufacturing, and utilities	130,700	2.2
Natural and applied sciences	91,500	1.7
Primary industry	60,500	2.3
Arts, culture, recreation, and sport	49,500	2.4
Total	**1,909,400**	**2.6**

of employee separations. The involuntary separation rate is calculated by dividing the number of involuntary exits by the number of total exits within a specific time period. For example, in the month of May an organization had 300 employee separations. One hundred of these separations were due to involuntary reasons, suggesting that 33.33 percent of the separations were initiated by the organization for business or performance reasons (number of involuntary separations divided by total number of separations).

This information is valuable to the HR department to help compare levels of voluntary versus involuntary departures. In the example above, two of every three exits were based on the employees initiating separation from the workforce. In the HR planning, the involuntary separation rate can be benchmarked against industry standards.

Dismissal Percentage Unlike the involuntary separation rate, the dismissal percent and permanent resignation rate (discussed below) do not use the number of separated personnel as the base. Instead, these values divide the exits by the total number of employees in the organization.

Dismissal percentage identifies the percentage of headcount that was dismissed during a specific period. This is a useful metric in assessing and comparing dismissal rates within the organization (e.g., between departments), but it does not specifically outline reasons for the dismissal (e.g., poor performance, insubordination, violence in the workplace, tampering, etc.).

Permanent Resignation Percentage Similar to dismissal percentages, resignation percentage identifies the percentage of headcount that resigned during a specific period. This metric can assist with future succession planning by identifying potential employee-initiated exits from an organization. To calculate the resignation percentage, calculate the number of resignations within a specified period and divide that value by total number of employees in the organization.

Separate: Vacancy Metrics There are a number of vacancy-related metrics that focus on the period of time between when an employee leaves an organization and when a replacement is secured. During this period, an organization is running a deficit of labour, since there are not enough human resources available for operations. HR planners must attempt to fill vacancies in a timely and cost-effective manner. According to the Conference Board of Canada, the range of time required to fill a vacancy and the cost of the vacancy differs by employee group (see Exhibit 10.17).[35] Executive and senior executive positions remain vacant for roughly three months after the incumbent has left the job, which can pose significant challenges for organizational operations and long-term success. Thus, the importance of identifying potential losses and using succession management (as highlighted in Chapter 6) is solidified.

Vacant Period The vacant period measures how many days, weeks, or months it takes to fill a position once it is determined that the position is vacated. For example, if an employee gave notice on

---

EXHIBIT 10.17 Vacancy Metrics in Canada

Employee Group	How Long Does it Take to Fill a Vacancy?	What Will the Vacancy Cost?
Clerical, service, and production	43 days	$5,000
Technical	48 days	$7,000
Professional	54 days	$12,000
Management	62 days	$16,000
Other executive	89 days	$36,000
Senior executive	91 days	$48,000

January 1st that they would be vacating a position on January 15th and a replacement was hired who began on January 30th, then the position was vacant for 15 days. This metric can be benchmarked against industry averages to identify any inefficiencies. The metric is relatively easy to collect and compare. However, there is no review of replacement quality, so depending too heavily on this metric can lead to a trade-off of quality for timeliness. Additionally, it is assumed that the recruiter has control over the length of the recruitment process, but as highlighted earlier in this chapter, there are multiple extraneous factors that can limit a recruiter's ability to control the vacant period.

Cost of Vacancy   The cost of a vacancy is a calculation similar to the cost of turnover. Both direct and indirect costs associated with the vacant position are included in this metric. Direct costs include the required overtime from other human resources to cover off any work requirements of the vacated position, while indirect costs include opportunity cost, loss of potential business, increased stress among workers who are left to complete work with a labour shortage, etc.

As time passes, HR managers and planners may begin to weigh the cost of the vacancy with the cost of recruitment to justify actions. For example, if the cost of keeping a position vacant for a week is $5,000, then incurring a $3,000 expense in order to fill the position one week earlier than expected can be justified. The net savings to the organization from the recruitment activity would be $2,000.

STRATEGIC VERSUS OPERATIONAL METRICS

The role of the HR group in an organization involves both strategic and operational contributions. HR managers are expected to deliver services effectively and efficiently, aligned with organizational strategy and objectives.

Operational contributions are focused on keeping the organization functioning. These metrics tend to be more reactive in nature, concentrated on administering programs, reporting on results of past activity, staffing jobs that have been vacated, complying with labour laws and policies, and overseeing training and compensation.

In contrast, strategic contributions, which were highlighted in Chapter 1, can be identified as activities that have a contributing effect on the strategic direction and success of the organization. Strategic HR metrics include those that are proactive, help develop and revise policies and procedures, evaluate strategic strengths and weaknesses, identify organizational gaps (e.g., training needs), are involved with HR planning, or can be used to develop plans focused on employee performance or talent retention.

Given that operational contributions are focused on keeping the organization running (or at least maintaining a status quo), while strategic contributions impact long-term success and direction of the organization, some users of HR metrics prefer to segment the metrics according to the two categories above—strategic and operational.

TARGET AUDIENCE

Another approach to segmenting HR metrics is to think of them in terms of the intended target audience. The four main audiences for the metrics can be grouped as *up, down, in,* and *out. Up* refers to the executives and C-level members of the organization (e.g., CEO, CFO, COO). This audience is usually interested in metrics that meet executive-level goals, focus on larger business impact, and align with strategy. *Down* refers to members, units, or departments within the organization that are not in executive or C-level roles. *In* refers to the HR department of the organization, since they are often the source for collecting and analyzing HR metrics. Both *down* and *in* are focused on impact to the organization. These groups are interested in metrics that they can take action on or ones that focus on performance optimization. *Out* refers to any intended target outside of the organization. There are limitations regarding the level of information an organization is either mandated to share or is comfortable sharing with audiences outside of the organization. As well, when providing data, consideration must be given to privacy concerns.

As outlined above, each target audience has different potential uses of the HR metrics, different demands, and different expectations of the information. According to a 2006 survey of C-level executives by HRmetrics.org, chief human resources officers (CHROs, considered the *in* group) identified the most important HR metrics as HR employee-to-total-employee ratio, cost per hire, time to fill, vacancy rate, and turnover ratio, while other C-level executives (considered the *up* group) selected new hire quality, line manager satisfaction, recruiting staff efficiency, time to start, and vacancy rate as the most important metrics. Therefore, another potential way to segment the metrics includes the separation of metrics based on target audiences.

The need to measure and evaluate human resource activity is ever present. Although significant HRMSs were introduced in this chapter, an organization should ensure that the HR metrics selected by the organization represent the values, strategies, resources, and long-term goals of the organization.

CHAPTER SUMMARY

- Human resource measurement systems (HRMS) depend on a method of collecting, analyzing, and integrating HR measures to aid in decision-making (through providing internal and external benchmarks). The use of HRMS is increasing as organizations want to ensure a link exists between the organizational strategy and human resources, allowing human resources departments to be strategic partners.

- The balanced scorecard approach develops a framework or map to help an organization implement strategy and measure business performance by measuring financials, internal processes, customers, and human capital. Building on this, the HR scorecard maps and measures the impact of human capital on value creation and business success using the same four perspectives of the balanced scorecard.

- There are many HR measures. An organization should only use measures that reflect business strategy and success within the organization's time, money, and resource constraints. Ultimately, the selection of HR metrics should convey the values, priorities, and organizational structure of the company, while providing information that can be used to drive individual performance in these areas.

- Metrics must address the questions of what to measure, how to measure, what the results mean, and what the organization should do about the results.

- Ethical and other issues in using HR metrics include the challenges associated with the objectivity of data analysis and issues of information disclosure. These must be addressed to ensure accuracy and appropriateness in the interpretation of the metrics.

- Metrics can be categorized according to the four stages of the HR life cycle—attract and acquire, develop, utilize, and the separate stage. Applicable throughout the HR life cycle are measures of return on investment, economic value added, and productivity.

- Attract-and-acquire metrics include those that focus on the cost, quality, quantity, and time metrics related to the successful recruitment and selection of human resources in an organization.

- Development-related metrics focus on employee orientation and performance-enhancing activities to reach desired productivity levels. These are generally focused on cost, internal mobility, time, and efficiency.

- Utilization of employees examines the impact of fully functional employees on the achievement of organizational strategies, HR goals, and desired performance. These focus on performance, lost productivity, span of control, and overtime-related metrics.

- Separation of employees from an organization include multiple measures of turnover and vacancy.

KEY TERMS

- absenteeism   247
- attraction and acquisition of talent   235
- attrition   252
- balance scorecard approach   228
- development of talent   235
- economic value added (EVA)   236
- human capital value added   236
- HR deliverables   229
- HR scorecard   230
- productivity   237
- return on investment (ROI)   235
- separation   235
- utilization of talent   235

REVIEW QUESTIONS

1. Why is HRMS important and who is the target audience for the use of such information?
2. What different strategies does a HRMS complement? Identify two to three metrics that align with each organizational strategy.
3. In addition to the HR life cycle, what other approaches can be used to segment HR metrics, and when is each approach useful?
4. What are the four stages of the HR life cycle, and which metrics are core to all stages of the HR life cycle?
5. What is the purpose of the balanced scorecard approach and how has this developed into an HR scorecard?
6. Why is turnover such a big issue for organizations? How can you use HR metrics to defend the implementation of a retention program?

DISCUSSION QUESTIONS

1. You are working in the HR department of a large Canadian firm in the telecommunications industry. The firm is currently conducting cost-cutting measures and has asked each department to defend their value-add. What metrics would you choose to defend the value that the HR department adds and why?
2. In your role as student, how is the professor currently measuring your productivity (e.g., attendance, retention of knowledge, ability to write reports)? Do you think these measures are appropriate? Why or why not? Suggest additional measures that can be used to measure student productivity in the classroom.
3. Your organization has recently identified a high need for internal training. Would you recommend use of "percentage of budget allocated to training" or "training costs per employee" to analyze the value of the training to your organization? Why did you select this metric?

WEB EXERCISE

Developing HR Deliverables

1. Using a web search and published reports (e.g., magazine articles, annual reports, press releases), select a company in your local area. Based on information you have gathered, try to understand and summarize the business strategy of the organization. Using this business

strategy, try to develop HR deliverables linked with organizational strategy. Present this information using the five main segments in the HR scorecard.

a) Workforce Success: Has the workforce accomplished the key strategic objectives for the business?

b) Right HR Costs: Is the total investment in the workforce, not just the HR function, appropriate and not just minimized?

c) Right Types of HR Alignment: Are HR practices aligned with the business strategy and differentiated across positions where appropriate?

d) Right HR Practices: Has the company designed and implemented world-class HR management policies and practices throughout the business?

e) Right HR Professionals: Do HR professionals have the skills they need to design and implement a world-class HR management system?

CASE INCIDENT

Calculate and Interpret Turnover Metrics

ABC Company has 1,200 employees at the start of the year. Over the course of the year 150 employees were laid off, 42 quit, 58 retired, 78 were fired (dismissed), and 3 passed away. Using this information, calculate the attrition rate, rate of retirement, involuntary separation rate, dismissal percentage, and permanent resignation rate. Do you think any of these are problematic, threatening the long-term sustainability of the organization? Defend your opinion.

■ REQUIRED PROFESSIONAL CAPABILITIES REFERENCED IN THIS CHAPTER

2. Translates the organization's business plan into issues, priorities, and human resources strategies and objectives.
6. Develops and implements a human resources plan that supports the organization's strategic objectives.
9. Evaluates the effectiveness of HR strategies, applying various measurement and assessment programs.
10. Applies business fundamentals of production, operations management, accounting and finance, information technology, marketing, and strategic planning to people management issues.
16. Provides the organization with timely and accurate HR information.
18. Contributes to development of specifications for the acquisition and/or development of HR information management systems and for their implementation.
52. Provides performance feedback, coaching, and career development to teams and individuals to maximize their probability of success.
68. Assesses the effectiveness of people and talent management plans.
76. Evaluates effectiveness of the recruitment process.
81. Evaluates the effectiveness of selection processes, tools, and outcomes.
99. Provides advice on issues relating to labour and employee relations including hiring, discipline, and termination.
147. Monitors and reports on the impact of development activities on organizational performance.
152. Develops and implements measurement tools and processes to evaluate program effectiveness.
158. Monitors, documents, and reports on career development activities.
164. Develops training budgets and monitors expenditures.

FUTURE DEVELOPMENTS IN THE FIELD OF HUMAN RESOURCE PLANNING

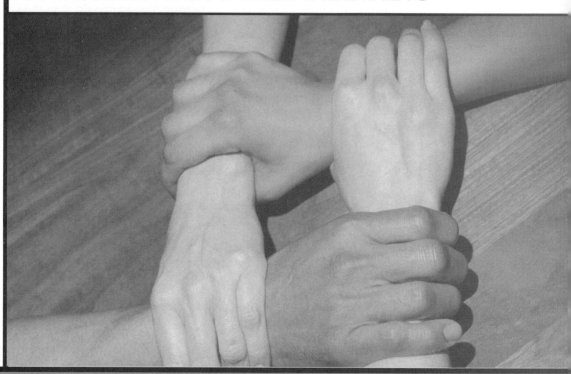

LEARNING OBJECTIVES

- Understand the changing nature of the labour force in Canada, including trends associated with the aging of the workforce, diversity management, and projected labour shortages

- Evaluate how alternative work arrangements can assist in overcoming future HR planning challenges, and understand the strengths and weaknesses of each arrangement

- Examine the causes and consequences of outsourcing departments to an organization, including organizational, social, ethical, financial, and HR implications

- Evaluate the feasibility of outsourcing operational versus strategic HR functions

■ PROFILE

Recommendations for Canada's Future Economic and Labour Prosperity

A report released in August 2008 by the Public Policy Forum, sponsored by the Certified General Accountants Association of Canada (CGA-Canada), gathered material on the Canadian labour economy from a cross-section of participants—government, business, labour, post-secondary education, aboriginal and immigrant communities, and youth. The report suggests that Canada's future prosperity is highly dependant on education, specifically skills training and learning.[1]

Twelve key recommendations were made to address the skills shortage and to maintain an active labour force in Canada:

1. Encourage apprenticeship programs and training among small- and medium-sized enterprises.
2. Develop and track strategies and best practices to aid immigrants' and their families' integration into the workforce and across Canadian society.
3. Refine the recruitment process so that Canada's medium- to long-term employment needs and skills of immigrants are better aligned.
4. Offer additional incentives to employers who offer jobs to skilled immigrants.
5. Facilitate agreement on mutually recognized credentials to improve inter-provincial labour mobility.
6. Improve information sharing about the workforce among various levels of government.
7. Simplify the process for international students to obtain permanent residency in Canada.
8. Eliminate barriers associated with childcare programs, and encourage Aboriginal and immigrant women to acquire skills training and jobs.
9. Directly confront issues in the education system and workplace that directly or indirectly contribute to latent racism and cultural obstacles.
10. Encourage academic mobility and life-long adult learning through a national credit transfer system.
11. Encourage retirement-aged workers to remain in the workforce longer (on a full-time, flextime, or part-time basis) through incentives and adapted pension eligibility rules.
12. Encourage intergenerational transitions in the workplace through the establishment of Generation Y networks.

Human resource planners must be aware of developments in the HR field in order to optimize an organization's ability to predict and respond to these trends. The changing nature of the workforce, employment–work arrangements, and hyper-competitive business environment create an ever-changing organizational dynamic, as discussed in this chapter. This chapter highlights future developments in the field of HR planning by creating an awareness of employment and organizational trends aligned with labour force changes, alternative work arrangements, and outsourcing.

An awareness of present day employment and organizational trends allows organizations to take the steps necessary to be prepared and respond appropriately. This chapter reviews a number of existing trends in the HR field that are expected to continue in the future. The purpose of these discussions is to provide an awareness of the changes in the Canadian landscape so as to prepare future HR managers to address and respond to these changes. Specifically, this chapter is segmented into three core areas, each aligned with specific trends:

1. Labour Force Changes
   a) Labour shortage and talent mismatch
   b) The aging workforce
   c) Diversity management

2. Alternative Work Arrangements
   a) Flextime
   b) The compressed workweek
   c) Annualized or banked hours
   d) Reduced hours or part-time work
   e) Telecommuting
3. Outsourcing
   a) General outsourcing trends
   b) Outsourcing of HR

■ LABOUR FORCE CHANGES

Labour Shortage and Talent Mismatch

The Canadian labour market experienced healthy growth from 1996 to 2006, at 2.0 percent annually, but this is predicted to decrease at an annual average rate of 1.1% from 2006 to 2015.[3] Although this represents a slowdown in employment growth over previous years, in the next ten years it is expected that 1.9 million jobs will be added to the Canadian market. At the same time, it is predicted that labour force growth will decelerate, based on challenges to population growth and the aging Canadian population. Over the next ten years, it is predicted that 70 percent of all job openings will be associated with the replacement of retiring workers. Thus, a labour shortage in Canada is imminent. Exhibit 11.1 shows that the expected labour force growth (supply) will be outpaced by the expected employment growth (demand) on labour required for the next few years in Canada.

While there is substantial debate in the media suggesting that Canada is experiencing a serious labour shortage, there is also evidence suggesting that Canada is misusing the labour available and that the skill supply available does not match what's in demand. Supply and demand across occupations keeps changing for a number of reasons, including the adoption of new production technologies, shifts in consumer preferences, demographic developments, and changes in the relative prices of goods and services.[4] Thus, some organizations are experiencing difficulty predicting the

EXHIBIT 11.1 Labour Market Outlook in Canada, 2002–2015[2]

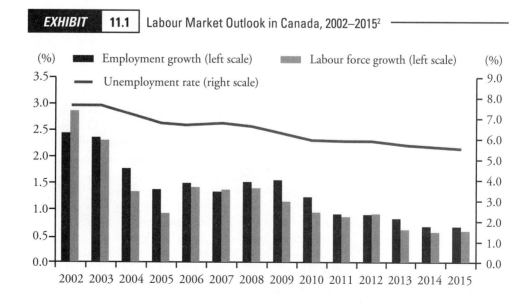

desired supply and demand of resources and skills in their organization. The methods highlighted in Chapter 2 can help alleviate potential problems in forecasting supply and demand.

At the national level, the health care sector has the largest number of occupations showing signs of shortage. The labour force growth in the health care sector has been outpaced by demand due to the increased needs of an aging population, increases in government funding for health care, and a relatively high number of retirements within the existing workforce. Supply for labour in health care has not been able to keep pace due to accelerated retirement of health care workers, limited or controlled enrolment in training programs, a lack of recognition of foreign credentials, and strong world demand for health care workers. As well, in the technology sector it is expected that from 2008 to 2011, Canada requires an additional 89,000 IT workers. If those positions go unfilled, the Canadian economy is expected to lose $10 billion per year, and Canada's ability to compete globally will be negatively affected. Furthermore, this will lead to serious productivity gaps.[5]

Additionally, management occupations (e.g., senior management, human resources managers, and accommodation service managers) are expected to experience a labour supply shortage as a result of high levels of retirement. Employers' emphasis on recruiting and retaining quality employees to handle the increasingly complex jobs in our economy results in a high demand for human resources professionals.[6]

Yet, there exists an oversupply of labour in certain industries. Office equipment operators and machine operators are experiencing a reduction in labour demand due to automation, advances in technology, international competition, and organizational restructuring activity in Canada. This suggests a skills mismatch in the demand and supply for labour in Canada.

Additionally, from 2006–2015, the employment growth rate in Canada's service sector will be 50 percent higher than the predicted growth rate in the goods producing (manufacturing) sector. In addition, two of every three jobs created will require a post-secondary education. Yet, only 20 percent of Canadian-born persons have university education.[7] This suggests a mismatch between labour demand and supply that HR must be aware of and accommodate for.

When it comes to labour shortages in Canada, Alberta took the lead from 2005 to 2008. Due to a combination of poor natural growth rates (birth rates minus death rates), the aging of the workforce, Calgary's strong economic growth, and the boom in the oil industry, Alberta's employers took a heavy hit when it came to finding and retaining labour. In a 2006 study of organizations in Alberta, one in four manufacturing organizations identified a labour shortage as a primary business concern. The study results suggested the labour shortage was partially attributable to the mining and construction industries whisking away potential employees.[8] In a survey completed by Alberta Employment, Immigration and Industry in 2008, four out of five companies experienced problems hiring employees, and of those, 71 percent said this was due to the problem of high turnover.[9]

The Aging Workforce

The baby-boom generation refers to individuals born between 1944 and 1964. Since 1964, fertility and birth rates have been consistently declining in Canada. The baby-boom generation is the result of a period of significantly increased fertility and birth rates, which led to a disproportionately large increase in the Canadian population. The outcome is a population bulge that moves through society as one large cohort. The first effect was a straining of the hospitals that had to manage the significant increase in birth rates, followed by the growth of educational institutions as this cohort completed their academic training. And now, this large portion of the labour force is nearing retirement, and HR planners must be able to adjust and plan accordingly.

In addition to the effect of the baby boom, individuals are healthier and living longer than before, due to more active lifestyles and an overall improvement in health care. This is reflected in an increased average life expectancy—75.8 years for men and 81.4 years for women.[10] As a result, the average age of a member of the Canadian labour force increased from 37.1 years old in 1991 to 41.2 years old in 2006.

At the same time the population ages, mandatory retirement laws in Canada have been deemed a discriminatory practice under human rights legislation, and have largely been abolished. With the exception of cases justified as "bona fide occupational requirements," organizations are no longer allowed to force employees to retire at the age of 65.

The elimination of mandatory retirement enables those employees without sufficient savings to sustain long-term retirement the opportunity to continue a stable income. Approximately 61 percent of baby boomers are concerned that they will outlive their retirement funds.[11] Moreover, these individuals may also be part of the sandwich generation, facing increased expenses as they financially support their elderly parents and children at the same time.[12] In addition, employees who enjoy working can continue to do so past the age of 65. Therefore, many mature employees continue working, some as a matter of choice and some due to financial circumstances.

With the combination of this large sector of the population nearing retirement, increased life expectancies, and decreased fertility and birth rates, Canada's labour force will experience a dramatic decline. Studies conducted by the Investors Group have demonstrated that 67 percent of individuals aged 45 to 64 plan to continue working past the age of 65.[13] Several baby boomers are postponing retirement due to the elimination of mandatory retirement legislation, increased life expectancies, high productivity levels among older workers, and the need for continued income.

Therefore, HR planning activities become increasingly complex as retirement predictions become increasingly complex. Given the challenges associated with accurate predictions and the variation of retirement preferences, issues of succession planning, planning replacements, forecasting, and talent retention become increasingly difficult for organizations.

Employers need to retain the institutional knowledge and organizational commitment that many older workers possess. Studies demonstrate that mature workers are more loyal and less likely to leave an organization than their younger counterparts.[14] Also, older employees often possess highly specialized skills and tacit knowledge about the organization that can have a direct impact on organizational profitability.

Concurrently, older workers are often confronted with age stereotypes in the workplace. Some of the most prevalent prejudices held against older workers pertain to the state of their health, their assumed lack of physical or cognitive abilities, their willingness or capacity to learn new technology or skills, and the ability to adapt to new situations.[15] These stereotypes have created barriers in training and development policies, as well as in the recruitment and selection practices associated with older workers.[16] Nevertheless, research studies indicate that most, if not all, of these biases are unjustified.[17]

As the baby boomers begin to retire in large numbers, a labour shortage is imminent. Human resources will have to plan for the shortage to ensure that there are enough qualified candidates available to fill vacant positions. Human resources teams will also have to adjust future labour projections so that they incorporate the departure of retirees from the organization. In addition, the decline in fertility rates since 1964 means that the size of the labour force after the baby boom is not as big. Thus, the competition for labour may be fiercer, and HR planners need to recognize the impact of these changes on their internal and external labour force supply.

Diversity Management

diversity management

A strategy to promote the perception, acknowledgement, and implementation of diversity in organizations and institutions

Diversity management is a strategy to promote the perception, acknowledgement, and implementation of diversity in organizations and institutions. The practice of diversity management is used to ensure all employees are treated equally, regardless of gender, ethnicity, physical/mental ability, sexual orientation, religious beliefs, or any other protected grounds in Canada. Although the intentions of such a program may be clear, the successful implementation of these programs requires a great deal of time, effort, and resources. In Canada, immigrants, visible minorities, women, and people with disability have experienced long-standing patterns of unemployment, lower than average pay rates, and a concentration in low-status jobs.

glass ceiling

A systematic, invisible barrier that limits the maximum level to which a member of a demographic minority can rise in an organization

A term often used to discuss the diversity challenges in Canada is **glass ceiling.** The glass ceiling refers to a systematic, invisible barrier that limits the maximum level to which a member of a demographic minority can rise in an organization. Those who have difficulty breaking through the glass ceiling are fully qualified with ample amounts of experience, but stereotypes that do not support the traditional view of strong leadership ability are keeping minorities from reaching top decision making roles in organizations.[18]

For many organizations, there has been a shift from viewing workforce diversity as a human rights and employment equity issue to viewing it as an asset and competitive advantage.[19] While this shift is occurring, the levels of diversity in the workforce and in executive positions are far too low. Diversity management programs can be successful in remedying this imbalance as well as in enhancing an organization's performance. Yet, only one-third of companies have an actual diversity definition, and few Canadian companies actively track their workforce diversity or set specific goals to increase diversity.[20] Despite the fact that 46 percent of companies claim to have a commitment to workforce diversity within their mission statement, only 14 percent have a diversity hiring action plan, and only 18 percent set measurable goals for workforce diversity.[21] Without measurable goals in place or tracking of workforce diversity, there can be only limited success.

immigrant population

Individuals born outside of Canada who are granted the right to live in Canada by immigration authorities

Immigrants   This era of globalization promotes not only movement of goods and services between countries, but also movement of labour, via immigration, across the world. This has led to growing diversity in the labour market, which has a direct and significant impact on organized labour.[22] In Canada, the 1990s brought on a serge of immigration. The **immigrant population** refers to individuals born outside of Canada who are granted the right to live in Canada by immigration authorities.[23] In Canada, the majority of immigrants remain in the country and secure Canadian citizenship.

According to the 2006 census completed by the Canadian federal government, one in every five individuals residing in Canada was born outside of the country. This is the highest proportion of immigrants in the population in Canada in the last 75 years.[24]

Between 2001 and 2006, Canada's foreign-born population increased by 13.6 percent, but the growth rate of the Canadian-born population during the same period was only 3.3 percent. Almost half of all new immigrants are between the ages 25–44 (labour-force ready), as compared to less than one-third of the Canadian population. Additionally, immigrants accounted for 70 percent of the labour force growth between 1991 and 2001.

In the long run, higher educational attainment levels among immigrants will result in a greater ability to adjust to the demands of the Canadian labour market.[25] According to a survey published in the *HR Reporter,* 20 percent of Canadian-born persons have university-level education, compared with much higher percentages among foreign-born persons living in Canada (see Exhibit 11.2). This suggests that Canada will be increasingly dependant on immigrants and people of different ethnicities to fulfill job demands that require post-secondary education.

Yet, immigrants experience a much higher unemployment rate than Canadian-born persons. Specifically, the unemployment rate among core working-age immigrants is almost 50 percent higher than the unemployment rate of Canadian-born persons.[26] As well, recent immigrants are the most susceptible to underemployment in Canada.[27] Recent immigrant cohorts have higher levels of earnings inequality than those who came to Canada in the early 1980s. Although foreign education, the inability to speak one of the official languages, and birthplace, explain a large part of immigrants' unequal earnings (roughly 40 percent of the income variance), much of this wage disparity remains unexplained.

By 2011, immigration is expected to account for all net labour market growth in Canada. Immigrants face difficulty in securing employment for several reasons, including: non-recognition of credentials, education level or experience abroad, lack of clarity on foreign education quality and standards, language barriers, weaker social networks, and a general lack of information regarding the Canadian job market or recruitment strategies in Canada.

In order to plan for, attract, and retain human resources, HR planning activities must be cognizant of the changing nature of the Canadian labour force. The growth of immigrants in

EXHIBIT **11.2** University Education by Ethnicity among Canadian Population

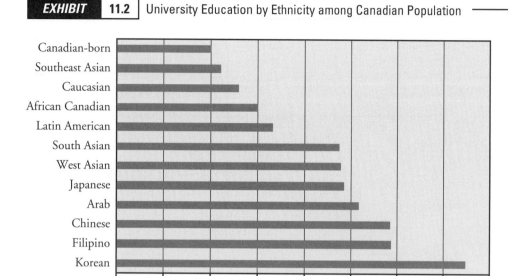

the labour force will compel organizations to be more aware of the direct and indirect obstacles that immigrants face. The methods for evaluating foreign credentials, training, and experience become increasingly important. If the internal HR department doesn't have the expertise to manage the diversity in the labour pool, they can develop partnerships with external sources to build, evaluate, and manage a larger candidate pool. The Canadian Information Centre for International Credentials (www.cicic.ca) assists employers in the assessment of foreign credentials. Also, Services Canada offers basic English and French language training for newcomers to Canada, including language assessment centres in local communities.

visible minorities

Persons, other than Aboriginal peoples, who are non-Caucasian in race or non-white in colour

Visible Minorities   **Visible minorities** are defined by the Employment Equity Act as persons, other than Aboriginal peoples, who are non-Caucasian in race or non-white in colour.[28] Thirty percent of the visible minority population was born in Canada.[29] This translates to 1.19 million members of the Canadian population (4 percent of the population) who are visible minorities, but not immigrants. Comparatively, from 1996 to 2001, 75 percent of the immigrant population was a visible minority. This translates to 1.36 million members of the Canadian population (4.6 percent of the population) who are immigrants, but not visible minorities. There exists a generation of visible minorities born and raised in Canada who cannot be classified as immigrants. Similarly, a number of new immigrants are not visible minorities. Therefore, immigrants and visible minorities are in fact two separate categorizations. The two categorizations cannot be interchanged.

A 2004–2005 annual report on employment equity submitted to Parliament revealed that in comparison to other designated groups, visible minorities remain underrepresented to a higher degree in executive level positions. The gap between visible minority representation in the workforce and representation in executive positions is 10.4 percent. Additionally, a study conducted by the HRPA found that half of the companies studied had no visible minority among senior management, and 30 percent of these companies had no visible minority among their top paid or executive level employees.[30]

Although visible minorities comprise only 11 percent of the labour force, they produce over one-third of Canada's GDP. Some argue that there exists a glass ceiling keeping visible minorities from attaining positions in core decision-making roles (as discussed earlier in this chapter).

EXHIBIT **11.3** Average Total Income in Canada by Gender and Age

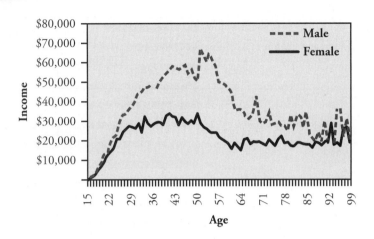

Women   In July 2008, the participation rate of men over the age of 25 in the Canadian labour force was 73.7 percent, while participation of women in the same age bracket was 62 percent.[31] Although there has been an increase in labour force participation among women, employment of females is largely concentrated in lower-level positions. The gap in employment levels decrease as educational attainment levels increase, suggesting that education attainment dramatically increases the likelihood of women being employed.

By their mid-20s, women secure significantly lower incomes than men of the same age. As women gain work experience and knowledge, the discrepancy grows. During what are generally considered to be peak earning years (e.g., age 50), women's average incomes remain below 70 percent of average male incomes in the same age bracket.[32] As highlighted in Exhibit 11.3, the average woman's income is consistently lower than the average man's income in Canada, regardless of age.[33]

Additionally, in management occupations in Canada, men occupy 65 percent of positions, while women occupy 35 percent.[34] Of Canada's top 500 corporations, men make up 86 percent of corporate officer positions, while women make up 14 percent of these positions.[35]

No one factor influences the wage and opportunity disparity women experience in Canada, rather it is a combination of factors. Issues such as labour market discrimination, government policies, and social attitudes integrate together to influence the role of women in the labour market.[36] Social attitudes contribute to the fact that women still bear the brunt of the family and home responsibilities outside of the workplace. In Canada, almost one in every five women who work part-time said that they did so because of family or personal responsibilities. In sharp contrast, only three percent of men claim to work part-time because of family or personal responsibilities. There is also systemic labour market discrimination resulting in the underemployment of women. In 2006, almost one in every four women who worked part-time wanted to work full-time but could not secure full-time employment. As well, there is a concentration of females in nursing in health-related occupations, where 87 percent of all employees are female; clerical and administrative occupations, where 75 percent of all employees are female; and education, where 64 percent of all teachers are female. These occupations traditionally pay less than occupations that are male dominated (e.g., doctors, pharmacists, engineers, lawyers, judges, university professors).

From an HR planning perspective, the underutilization of women in the workforce presents two significant challenges. First, the pool of candidates for a vacant position might be incomplete if direct or indirect discriminatory labour market factors influence the participation of women. As the labour market continues to shrink, the participation of all available talent will be critical to ensure organizational continuity.

Second, evidence suggests that the participation of women in the workforce is beneficial for an organization. Fortune 500 companies with women in executive positions (e.g., CEO, CFO, COO) reported higher profits overall than companies with no women in executive positions. On average, companies with a higher proportion of female corporate officers earned 34 percent higher returns than companies with a lower proportion of women in these positions. One rationale for the benefits of women in executive positions is that the organization promotes the best qualified employee for the position regardless of gender. The selection of the best qualified candidate, free from direct and indirect discrimination, increases organizational success.

disability

The result of complex interactions between a health problem or functional limitations and a person's social, political, cultural, economic, and physical environment

Persons with Disability   In Canada, a **disability** is defined as the result of complex interactions between a health problem or functional limitation and a person's social, political, cultural, economic, and physical environment. These factors, in combination with personal factors such as age, gender, and level of education may result in a disability—often referred to as a disadvantage. Courts try to determine the link between a functional limitation and disadvantage when investigating disability-based human rights complaints. In 2005, 50 percent of the cases lodged with the Canadian Human Rights Tribunal (CHRT) were complaints citing disability as the grounds of discrimination.[37]

Almost one out of every two persons with a disability who participate in the labour force full-time, full-year is under-utilized in the workforce (65.3 percent participation rate full-time, full-year in 2004). Overall, workers with disabilities in Canada are more likely than those without disabilities to earn wages in the lowest wage quartile—31 percent compared with 24.6 percent respectively. However, persons with and without disability who have similar levels of work experience—25 or more years of experience—have similar wage profiles.[38] This suggests that disability does not lead to an income disadvantage if the employee has reached an advanced career stage. Unfortunately, disabled workers in early-career stages still experience significant wage disadvantages.

As well, parents of children with disabilities are changing the nature of the working relationship to adapt to home and personal priorities. Almost 50 percent of parents of disabled children aged 5 to 9 years identify their children's disability as a factor that severely influenced their decision to decline a job, or work fewer hours. Of this group, one in three parents has quit a job, while slightly fewer have refused a promotion so that they can manage their child's disability.[39]

Workers with disabilities are slightly less likely to participate in training programs than the non-disabled population.[40] Here, one area of concern is that 7.3 percent of persons with severe or very severe disabilities report that they have been denied training over the last five years because of their disability.

Collectively, this data suggests that Canada is significantly underutilizing the disabled worker population. Additionally, the lack of opportunities for the disabled population indicates that either there are systemic limitations or barriers within an organization for the advancement and inclusion of the disabled populations, or that HR policies may be lacking clarity or focus on disabled persons. The challenges faced by disabled employees and parents of disabled children may result in a need to participate in flextime, reduced workweeks, or part-time work. In order to attract and retain these persons, HR planners should demonstrate an understanding of these challenges and offer flexibility in work terms.

Impact of Labour Force Trends on Human Resource Planning

In 2006, the high school dropout rate in rural Alberta was the highest in the country, at 25 percent.[41] The labour shortage and accompanying wage premium means a number of younger people deciding to forgo training and investment in future skills to take advantage of a tight labour market today. A lack of educational attainment and future skills development in the labour force suggests that organizations, the local communities, and Canada may not be able to respond to current and long-term expansion of a skilled labour market.

For HR planners, the issues of training and development as part of a job requirement become more critical. As well, replacement and succession planning (which usually requires more than a job-specific skill set development) become challenging. This has an impact on many levels.

First, competition among employers for a shrinking pool of qualified and skilled employees has resulted in a dramatic increase in turnover rates in Canada.[42] Wages are rapidly increasing in booming sectors due to increased HR demand. This further encourages turnover.[43] As discussed in Chapter 10, turnover is not only costly to an organization, but also very disruptive to long-term organizational success. To reduce turnover levels, HR must focus on enhancing retention strategies by understanding the challenges that the changing Canadian labour force presents and the unique responses or needs that an organization should formulate to respond to these changes. Rather than managing these changes reactively, by staying abreast of trends in the Canadian labour force, an organization can proactively manage change.

Second, replacement and succession management may be hindered due to a lack of available human resources. Rather than developing core skill sets before entry into the labour force, many employees have only job-specific training in a tight labour market. Therefore, the organization and planners will require longer lead time to develop personnel, as this development may have to happen at work or in parallel to full-time work for many employees. For example, if a position requires an MBA, and the organization expects to fill the position internally, but none of the existing talent has an MBA, then a number of high-performing employees can be given incentives (e.g., sabbaticals, funding, etc.) for completing executive education to help develop their abilities. If the employee works full-time, then they may only be able to complete additional training part-time, which lengthens the time to fill a vacancy with in-house talent.

Third, budgeting must take into account the possibility that an organization may be forced to carry the expenses of skills development, or that in a time of a labour shortage, a premium on wages or compensation may be demanded. An increased focus on training and development in areas of diversity and language skills will allow an employer to maximize employee contribution given Canada's diverse workforce. As well, an increasing number of retirees re-entering the workforce creates an increased focus on job redesign and workplace accommodations.

Using a hypothetical example, an organization has a $300,000 budget for additional positions in a growing department. In the past year, the industry average compensation for that position was $50,000 per year, but due to a labour shortage, the organization might have to budget $60,000 to fill the position. Additional training expenses of $10,000 per year may have to be included in the budget to accommodate for population trends. As well, signing bonuses or retention expenses could add up to $5,000 per employee in this example. Thus, without the impact of population trends, the organization may have been able to afford six additional employees to join the department to help meet forecasted demand ($300,000 budget divided by $50,000 per employee). However, with the supply-demand imbalance, based on recent Canadian trends, the organization can either afford only four employees ($300,000 budget divided by $75,000 per employee), or will be forced to request and justify an increase in human resources or labour budget by 50 percent.

Fourth, recruitment and selection strategies need to be more specific, given the trends identified above. While organizations facing recruitment challenges may already be utilizing aggressive strategies to attract applicants, it is important to also consider non-traditional recruitment and selection techniques. Southland Transportation, a bus company in Calgary, Alberta effectively escaped a labour shortage by advertising to stay-at-home mothers and retirees.[44] Creating strategic alliances or partnerships with post-secondary educational institutes is recommended to minimize skills mismatch and ensure that the talent pipeline outside of the organization is sustainable. Furthermore, by creating such partnerships, opportunities for co-operative education programs, on-campus recruitments, and branding as an employer of choice will help meet the needs of the organization.

Fifth, employers must be aware of the impact of the aging workforce on HR and the organization. The aging of the workforce will impact mentoring programs within the organization. Once older workers begin to retire, the company will lose a great deal of corporate knowledge unless it is transferred to replacement workers. Thus, mentoring programs should be strategically devised to ensure the flow of information from older employees to newer employees.

Training costs will also likely increase as a result of the baby-boom generation. First, older workers need to be continuously involved in training programs to ensure that their skill set is

HRP AND THE SMALL BUSINESS

Helping to Hire Immigrants

Given the impact of immigrants on the labour force, the importance of aiding small and medium enterprises (SMEs) in attracting, acclimatizing, and integrating a diverse workforce is becoming increasingly critical for organizational sustainability.

While SMEs account for the majority of Canadian jobs, most don't have the HR support or know-how to comfortably hire skilled immigrants. Hireimmigrants.ca's mandate is to help SMEs overcome real and perceived barriers to hiring skilled immigrants, including links to agencies that serve local immigrant communities and organizations that assess international credentials. In 2008, hireimmigrants.ca launched a year-long campaign to raise awareness among small businesses about the advantages of hiring skilled immigrants. The campaign and website aimed to provide SMEs with interactive tools and resources to help them find, interview, hire, promote, and retain skilled immigrants.

current and integrated with the organizational goals. Second, as these employees leave, the firms will have to dedicate a significant amount of time and resources into preparing and training workers to fulfill vacant positions.

Organizations looking to keep senior workers on board should look at shorter workweeks and flexible hours. According to a survey of 2,052 Canadians, workers 65 and older said they would prefer to work reduced hours over a shorter workweek (e.g., Tuesday to Thursday from 9 a.m. to noon). Canadians 55 years and older also said they would like to have an average of 6.4 weeks of vacation per year, while 60 percent value extended health-care benefits, 47 percent prefer flexible work hours, 34 percent value a guaranteed wage/salary, and 24 percent want phased retirement.[45]

Sixth, organizations must develop accommodations for a diverse workforce. Whether it is language training for immigrants; flexible benefits and hours for female, disabled, or older employees; or elimination of the glass ceiling, these limitations must be addressed to encourage continued participation of employees in an organizational internal labour force. Diversity management will continue to become increasingly critical to an organization's ability to retain talent in a time of labour shortages and skills mismatch.

■ ALTERNATIVE WORK ARRANGEMENTS

alternative work arrangements

Flexible arrangements or alternate schedules from the traditional Monday to Friday, 9 to 5, working day and week

The use of alternative work arrangements in the employment relationship is increasing. **Alternative work arrangements** are defined as flexible arrangements or alternate schedules from the traditional Monday to Friday, 9 to 5, working day and week. These can be initiated by the employer or employee. An employee may request a different work schedule to maintain a work–life balance, to manage nonwork priorities, or as a personal preference. Alternatively, as discussed in chapters 3 and 4, employers may initiate various schedules to meet organizational, management, or customer needs.

In a survey of 1,311 executives from around the world, conducted by the Association of Executive Search Consultants, 53 percent of executives feel they have not achieved a satisfactory work–life balance, with 46 percent suggesting that work–life balance has deteriorated over the last five years. For HR, work–life balance as a priority among employees becomes even more evident as 87 percent of executives state that the level of work–life balance is critical in their decision to join or remain with an employer. In fact, 56 percent would strongly consider refusing a promotion if it negatively affected work–life balance, and 24 percent would definitely refuse a promotion that negatively affected work–life balance.[46]

According to the Canadian Centre for Occupational Health and Safety, alternative work arrangements have many organizational benefits, such as an increased ability to attract, retain, and motivate high-performing and experienced employees. Management benefits from a reduction in absenteeism and an increased energy level and creativity among employees. Employees also benefit from an increased job satisfaction and ability to handle to stress.[47] Common alternative workplace arrangements include flextime, a compressed workweek, annualized/banked hours, reduced hours/part-time work, and telecommuting.

Flextime

flextime

A work arrangement that gives employees flexible start and end dates to a given workday, usually with the condition that all employees are present during core business hours

Flextime provides employees with flexible start and end dates to a given workday, usually with the condition that all employees are present during core business hours. While this does not affect total hours worked by each employees, it permits some personalization of start and end times, allowing the employee and employer to predetermine the expectations of work attendance. For example, in one department, core hours can be 10:00 a.m. to 3:00 p.m., with an expectation that all employees work 8 hours per day. Given this situation, a mother with young children may decide to work 8:30 a.m. to 4:30 p.m. to give her the flexibility to work around childcare requirements. An employee who commutes a long distance may elect to work from 7:00 a.m. to 3:30 p.m. to avoid rush hour. An employee enrolled in a continuing education class in the evenings may want to start at 10:00 a.m. and end work at 6:30 p.m. These hours should become routine for each employee so everyone knows the schedules in a team that works on flextime.

Compressed Workweek

compressed workweek

A reduction in the number of days per week in which full-time work is performed, but not in the number of weekly hours

A **compressed workweek** is an arrangement where employees work for longer periods of time each day or shift in exchange for a day or more off in a given working period. Although compressed workweeks are usually initiated by the employee, an employer may initiate this in order to improve operational efficiency, maximize production (through reduced daily startup time and costs), or manage customer service (through establishing longer business hours).

The most common compressed workweek arrangement is four days of the week at ten hours per day, although some organizations offer flexibility such as working an extra hour a day in exchange for one day off every two weeks or working an extra half hour a day in exchange for an extra day off every four weeks.

An employee may prefer a compressed workweek to help secure additional days off in a given workweek without reducing total hours worked, minimize commuting and preparation time, or reduce overtime expectations each day. In addition, this option may help an employee improve work–life balance.

Annualized or Banked Hours

annualized or banked hours

A situation in which employees choose their days and hours of work, within set boundaries, as long as the weekly, monthly, or annual hours (as agreed to) are completed within the predetermined time frame

Another alternative work arrangement includes the use of **annualized or banked hours.** In this arrangement, employees choose their days and hours of work, within set boundaries, as long as the weekly, monthly, or annual hours (as agreed to) are completed within the predetermined time frame. Employees and employers negotiate in advance the arrangements, as well as the boundaries under which annualized hours can be used. The ultimate aim is that employers can benefit from having employees work at their peak productive times, while minimizing overtime expenses.

As an example of annualized hours, an organization can determine the total number of hours an employee would work in a year, month, or week, depending on the period of time that the employee and employer want to focus on. Assuming that a full-time employee would work 2,000 hours per year (five days a week, eight hours a day, fifty weeks per year), the employer and employee can negotiate new ways to work the 2,000 hours. For example, perhaps working five days of the week at ten hours a day would be desirable. In this case, the employee would work for forty weeks of the year. An alternative could be working six days of the week for nine hours a day. In this case, the employee would work slightly more than 37 weeks a year. This benefits the organization because they can accommodate peak seasons or high-demand times without having to pay overtime to the employee. As well, an employee would benefit because they are able to manage their working hours and increase the number of weeks off in a year. This arrangement is ideal in fields with seasonal variations or peak-hour demands. Challenges include the difficulties in managing, monitoring, and coordinating the work of annualized employees.

Banking hours is a slight variation on annualized hours, which simplifies the process for the employee. Rather than pre-negotiating terms of annualized hours, any overtime that an employee completes is put in a virtual time bank with the organization. Rather than getting paid overtime for the hours, the hours are available for the employee to use for future days off. The notion of managing the number of hours an employee works and reducing costs is the same in banking hours as it is in annualized hours, but this option is slightly easier to explain to employees and can be used on an as-needed basis.

Reduced Hours or Part-Time Work

There is a growing concentration of part-time workers compared to full-time workers in Canada. For clarification, the definition of "part-time" and "full-time" employment differs across Canada, as these definitions are based on labour regulations in each province or labour sector. However, there are some commonalities within all definitions. In general, part-time work is considered fewer than 32 hours per week and may not have employment-related benefits, while full-time employees work a minimum of 32 hours per week and usually have some form of job security and benefits associated with employment.

In 2008, part-time employment increased at nearly twice the rate of growth of full-time jobs.[48] There are suggestions that the number of "involuntary" part-time workers increased recently due to the Canadian labour market's inability to provide full-time jobs. In July 2008, over 241,000 Canadians worked part-time because they were unable to find a full-time job, up 10 percent from a year ago. This trend does not appear to be reversing, as year-over-year growth in part-time jobs (2.3 percent) is still significantly outpacing year-over-year growth in full-time jobs (0.4 percent).[49]

HR specialists must be able to understand what created this trend and what can be done to accommodate the changing workforces, as this employment trend will affect a large number of organizations and employees. Employers are embracing the use of part-time employees as a way to potentially save on benefits, allow flexibility to employees, and tap into an employee base that may not be interested in full-time work.

Employees may choose to work fewer than the standard 37.5 or 40 hours per workweek. These arrangements may be on a temporary or permanent basis depending on individual circumstances. This may also be considered in cases for employees with health problems or disabilities. Work hours may be negotiated, or they may be chosen to coincide with peak workload hours depending on the type of business. However, employee benefits and qualification for government programs, such as employment insurance or pension plans, may be affected, and should be examined thoroughly before commencing part-time options.

Telecommuting

telecommuting (telework)

A situation where an employee conducts at least some of his/her regular work from home instead of going into the office setting

Telecommuting (also known as telework) occurs when an employee conducts at least some of his/her regular work from home instead of going into the office setting. Telecommuting has increased in popularity due to advances in technology, the increased acceptance of a virtual work-force, boundaryless organizations, and the existing labour shortage. Currently, about 1.5 million Canadian employees telecommute for at least some of the workweek.[50]

There are three main ways to organize telecommuting. Home-based teleworking involves employees working from home, sometimes with periodic or alternating requirements to work at the employer site for some of the week. Telecentre-based telecommuting relies on specialized telecentres equipped with all the necessary technological and office fittings. Employees can work

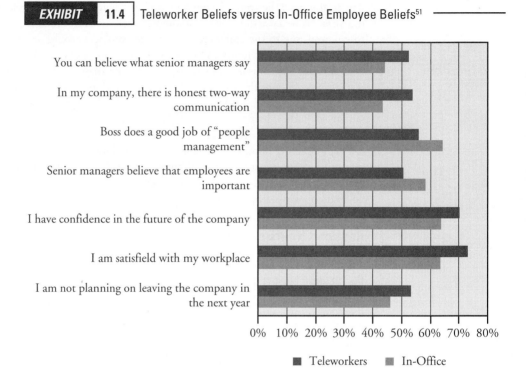

EXHIBIT 11.4 Teleworker Beliefs versus In-Office Employee Beliefs[51]

from a remote telecentre instead of the traditional office for some or all of the workweek. Mobile telecommuting is best suited for sales or services people, as these employees can work from remote or mobile offices—often cars or vans equipped with required office equipment—and maintain the ability to conduct work from multiple locations in a given day or week.

A Kenexa Research Institute survey of 10,000 American employees found that teleworkers generally feel better about their employment relationships and organization than in-office work-ers.[52] See Exhibit 11.4. However, more in-office workers agreed that senior managers believe that their employees are important. This may be due to an "out of sight, out of mind" perspective, where employees who work from home may not have the same visibility, on the part of the senior managers, that in-house employees do.

Impact of Alternative Work Arrangements on Human Resource Planning

Alternative work arrangements present some complications for HR planners. They must assist the department in determining core hours, help manage the requirements for work, communicate with the compensation group regarding expectations of each worker, and manage more adminis-trative tasks around individualized working times. Of course, HR planning should also be clear if there is no option of alternative work arrangements. For example, in a manufacturing firm all employees may be required to work the same hours on the plant floor to maintain production. Also, if there are options, selection into an arrangement needs to be perceived as fair, free from bias, and non-discriminatory.

Additionally, HR planners must be aware that flextime adds additional management require-ments. In the examples above, the department manager may work 9:00 a.m. to 5:30 p.m., which would mean that employees who work outside of those hours would not have management pres-ent for part of their shift. Alternatively, HR can determine that there is a need for one manager to work 6:30 a.m. to 3:00 p.m. and another manager to work from 10:00 a.m. to 6:30 p.m. to ensure that there is always a manager present. Thus, HR planners must be aware of, help manage, and respond accordingly to alternative work arrangements.

There are many implications for HR managers who work for companies that employ tele-workers. The ability to recruit employees from a global labour market has increased because potential employees do not have to relocate if hired. This also reduces some recruitment expenses. Forty-three percent of employees would switch companies in order to telework, and 33 percent would choose teleworking instead of a raise. Telecommuting has become a way for HR managers to reduce costs—office rental space, overhead, etc. The annual savings generated by an average teleworker is approximately $2,000 per employee. As well, organizations benefit from increased productivity. In 2008, a study by the Canadian Telework Association estimated that productivity and job performance increased an average of 20 percent per teleworker.

■ OUTSOURCING

outsourcing

The subcontracting of activities (production processes or services) that are not regarded as part of a company's core business in an effort to reduce costs by transferring portions of work to outside suppliers rather than completing it internally

Outsourcing is defined as the subcontracting of activities (production processes or services) that are not regarded as part of a company's core business in an effort to reduce costs by transferring portions of work to outside suppliers rather than completing it internally. Initially started by manufacturing companies, outsourcing has grown at a rapid pace to become one of the most widely used cost-cutting procedures within organizations today. Research in outsourcing shows that the top services that management currently outsource are:

1. Information Technology: Computer hardware, software, or networking, as well as other technology products. In 2007, almost 50 percent of Canadian companies reported outsourcing some aspect of information technology.[53]
2. Human Resources Services: Recruitment, selection, training, development, occupational health and safety, and human resource planning are all experiencing a growth in outsourcing.
3. Manufacturing Services: Production and development of products. By outsourcing manufacturing services, companies attain 5 to 20 percent savings on material and labour costs and a 10 percent reduction in overhead costs.[54]
4. Call Centres: Internal and external clients often require phone or web-based assistance. With the continued growth and outsourcing of business services, call centers in Canada experienced a 5 percent annual average increase in revenue every year from 1998 to 2006.[55]
5. Finance and Accounting Services: Accounts payable and receivable, collections, billing, and income tax services are being outsourced.
6. Legal Services: Contracts, advice, lawsuit assistance, etc.

Outsourcing will remain a core organizational procedure in the future as organizations focus on their core competencies (thus outsourcing non-core functions). For many companies, this means drastic managerial and operational changes to their labour force.

Labour Market Trends Impacting Outsourcing

Labour market trends which push an organization to outsource their services can vary greatly depending on organizational needs, goals, strategies, objectives, and business operations. In recent years, the following labour market trends that have had the greatest impact on an employer's decision to outsource:

- Business process outsourcing (BPO) refers to an entire business process that is supported by an outside vendor. Currently, BPO outsourcing is the fastest growing sector of outsourcing, indicating an increased acceptance of outsourcing at an organizational and business process level.

- Increased wage rates in Canada are pushing companies to eliminate departments or processes that are not part of their core competencies, in an effort to save costs and reduce expenses. A large number of Canadian companies are offshoring—having some or all components of a process performed in a foreign country to take advantage of labour cost arbitrage—in an attempt to maintain costs.[56]
- The aging workforce in Canada creates challenges in replacing existing employees who may have knowledge, skills, and abilities that are hard to imitate. This was discussed in greater detail earlier in the chapter.
- An increased demand for skilled and educated workers means that organizations must work harder to acquire and retain employees aligned with an organization's core competencies. Outsourcing provides access to specific skills that may be high in demand.
- Shared service centres can reduce costs through integrating support functions across organizations and utilizing common structures, technology, and processes, such as human resources, accounting, and legal processes.[57]
- Developments in information, communication, and technology (ICT) have increased the demand for and facilitation of outsourcing. This has enabled companies to have more collaborative work environments with around-the-clock work cycles, which are especially significant for call centers and information technology services.

With the reduction of trade barriers and increasing integration of world markets, firms may switch from low-skill intensive producers in Canada to foreign producers in low-wage countries. Therefore, foreign outsourcing may lead to a decline in the demand for unskilled labour and increase the demand for skilled labour in Canada.

The Outsourcing of HR

Outsourcing HR functions can be a part of the overall HR business strategy. As mentioned above, the outsourcing of HR is a common activity within organizations. Non-strategic and routine HR functions can be outsourced as part of a company's strategy to reduce its administrative burden and allow for more value-added human resource management. Strategically, outsourced functions should be routine, easy to define, simple to manage, and completed by easily accessible providers.[58] The willingness to outsource HR functions has increased over the years and will continue as a future development that HR must adapt to. According to the Conference Board of Canada, there has been a 14 percent increase in willingness to outsource HR functions in Canada.[59] Common functions outsourced include pre-employment background screening, recruitment, performance management, compensation, benefits, and training.

Pre-Employment Background Screening   One vital service that more and more organizations are utilizing is pre-employment background screening for new employees. There are four primary reasons why an employer would consider outsourcing this function. First, tasks such as verifying professional designations and contacting past employers are time-consuming and may require specialized knowledge, something that can take time away from vital strategic HR functions. Second, the time and money required to train HR professionals to successfully screen in-house and abide by all appropriate laws may be more that the cost of outsourcing this function to a third-party vendor. Third, both employers and employees can enjoy legal protection, as most pre-employment screening organizations take extra steps to ensure compliance with both federal and provincial legislation. Lastly, many organizations believe that as a matter of their corporate culture, outsourcing pre-employment background screening to a third party reduces a new hire's feeling of being investigated, which promotes a greater sense of employee privacy.[60]

Recruitment   Effective recruitment can mean the difference between the success or failure of a firm. The never-ending need to fill job openings, in addition to its costly and administrative-heavy

Ethical Challenges with Outsourcing

When making financially driven decisions, organizations often fail to look through an ethical lens and consider the human cost of the decision. This is especially true in the case of outsourcing, since the corporation becomes removed from much of its operations through the use of vendors. Organizations must consider whether or not they will hold the vendor accountable to same ethical standards as the organization, since often the vendors standards are significantly lower.

Some of the earliest foreign outsourcing partners were described as sweatshop operators. Concerns about poor work environments and exploitative work policies were indicative of other nations' lower standards regarding the treatment of employees. For instance, American-owned Gap was recently accused of exploiting workers in India. They were exposed as using a vendor in India that relied on child labour for production, and maintained employee relationships at a level compared to slavery. Children were purchased from human traffickers and then forced to pay off their cost of purchase by working for the vendor. Often, these children were gagged, beaten, and not given the small amounts of money that they had earned.[61]

When work is contracted offshore, cultural differences become problematic in regions where bribery is considered culturally acceptable. In North America, bribery is seen as a conflict of interest, a means to influence decision making, and an unethical business practice. Use of bribes for outsourced vendors may be deemed an unethical practice by the organization.

If an organization makes the decision to outsource, it must also determine the level of accountability of the vendor–employee relationships, including compliance with rules and regulations governing an industry or workplace. This can be done in the original outsourcing contract, clearly outlining penalties associated with unethical behavior. Companies engaged in outsourcing activity should be clear as to the ethical expectations of vendors, since vendor actions reflect upon the company as a whole.

---

nature, can make recruitment a burden in some firms. The future of recruiting does not appear to be any less demanding. The battle for talent will likely intensify as the talent pool becomes smaller and skills shortages become more prevalent, causing the recruitment function to weigh more heavily on time and resource constraints.[62] As such, many organizations have turned to outsourcing of the recruitment function. In fact, recruitment and selection continues to be one of the most highly outsourced HR functions.[63]

Performance Management   While performance management is not usually considered a function that is conducive to outsourcing, doing so can offer many of the same benefits of outsourcing traditional HR functions. Outsourcing performance management refers to outsourcing the transactional processes, not employee performance itself. The performance management outsourcer will give advice and information about how to manage and improve the workforce performance process, and can help develop systems for evaluating employee performance, but they do not actually conduct the evaluation for the organization. Performance management outsourcers are experts in workforce alignment methods.[64] As such, they are able to align technology with workforce performance and an organization's overall business strategy. This results in a system that can support the organization's goals and expectations. It is critical to note that outsourcing performance management requires a connection with the workforce so that the performance management system is accurately measuring what management is looking to have measured (i.e., it is valid).

Compensation   Compensation continues to be outsourced for a number of reasons. Over the past decades, a number of firms have moved towards incentive-based compensation programs to complement or replace base pay. This increases the workload demands for the compensation department, including timely tracking of employee status and monitoring the incentive plan to ensure accuracy and consistency of compensation. With the use of technology, ways to measure, observe, input, report, and analyze data can be automated, reducing the need for in-house HR personnel. As well, with globalization, the need for outsourced compensation specialists will continue to increase as expertise will be needed on international legislation, pay rates, compensation strategies, pay equity issues, etc.

Outsourced compensation should be strategically aligned with the organization. Typically, it is less expensive to outsource the collection of salary data or administration of merit increases than it is for the company to do it themselves. If a company's strategy involves reducing costs, compensation outsourcing would align with this strategy. Outsourcing non-strategic, routine, or administrative compensation duties (e.g., payroll) allows an organization to focus on strategic activities such as retention.

Benefits   There are various ways that benefits can be outsourced. The administration and delivery of benefit and pension plans are commonly outsourced. As well, the actuary responsible for the plan may also be handled externally. Record-keeping and benefit accounting services are services that are also offered by many benefit vendors.[65]

Outsourcing of benefits has been a common HR practice since the 1980s and will continue to be an element in future developments of HR. The initial interest in outsourcing benefits was driven by the introduction of the 401(K) plan in the U.S., where the complicated administration of the plan led to its inevitable outsourcing.[66] In addition, the rapid pace of technological change has quickly outdated legacy systems that organizations used, resulting in a consistent need to create new and up-to-date universal benefit systems. The constant need to update technology and software has been a driving reason why organizations outsource this function.[67]

Training   A new era of outsourcing training debuted in 2000, when Nortel Networks signed a large contract with PriceWaterhouseCoopers to perform a variety of activities, including the management of its enterprise-wide training programs. As of 2003, an estimated 28 percent of all training expenditures go to outside vendors.[68] By outsourcing training, an organization is no longer limited to the areas of subject matter expertise that can be found within the organization. Instead it can access a wide range of professional experts on a broad range of topics. Outsourcing of training can be more cost-effective because procedures, training programs, and manuals may already be developed, reducing the initial overhead costs of curriculum and training program development for an organization.

Impact of Outsourcing on Human Resource Planning

Human resource planning is greatly affected by outsourcing. Outsourcing changes the overall landscape of planning and it challenges internal departments to operate efficiently and effectively to protect themselves from potentially cheaper outsourced alternatives.

Outsourcing can help focus HR efforts away from daily operations to more strategic functions. It reduces the need for an organization to hire and train employees and managers to oversee a particular department, process, or function. Outsourcing enables a company to dip into a

HRP AND STRATEGIC PARTNERS	**Professional Designations**

Strategic partnerships in HR planning include the recognition of specialized skills and the standardization of desired skills through certification procedures. In the world of HR there are multiple professional certifications, such as certified human resources professional (CHRP), registered professional recruiter (RPR), and certified employee benefits specialist (CEBS). Due to recent increased focus on outsourcing, the International Association of Outsourcing Professionals (IAOP) introduced a new designation in Canada called the certified outsourcing professional (COP). The program, launched in 2006, uses a point system to demonstrate a candidate's professional capabilities through work experience, education, and core-knowledge development.

The COP designation covers a breadth of expertise, including defining, effectively communicating, and leading outsourcing projects; integrating outsourcing as an organization's strategy; selecting the appropriate outsourcing service providers; developing the pricing and financial analysis of outsourcing opportunities; negotiating outsourcing contracts; and managing the transition of outsourcing activities.[69] More information on this designation and the IAOP can be found at www.outsourcingprofessional.org.

larger talent pool, through access to specialized skills, experts, low-skill workers, and independent subcontractors. This provides HR with the flexibility to secure human resources on an as-needed basis. Outsourcing can improve talent quality, as the resource provider may be a specialist in a specific area. Moreover, small companies can gain access to a specialized skill set that they want without having the responsibility for securing permanent employment for the individual. Additionally, the organization can avoid costly benefits provided to regular employees, which reduces the demand on HR for benefit management. Lastly, outsourcing allows the company to utilize technology that they might not be able to otherwise afford. These advantages help reduce time and money spent in the human resources department, while ensuring that HR efforts are aligned with strategic, value-added functions.

Outsourcing Challenges

Although there are many advantages to outsourcing certain organizational functions, significant issues can arise. Companies often move hastily toward downsizing and eliminating in-house departments, attempting to find cheaper, but higher-quality alternative solutions without considering all the associated monetary and non-monetary costs.

Organizations often engage in outsourcing for cost-savings purposes. However, the perceived savings may not be aligned with expectations. Organizations have to be careful in their decision-making process to determine if outsourcing is a worthwhile effort. For example, when JP Morgan decided to outsource its IT department to IBM (a $5-million deal), it seemed like a viable cost-savings solution. However, for several years following the outsourcing decision, the CIO at JP Morgan became aware of the impact of the outsourcing decision on employees' diminished morale, decreased productivity, and general loss of trust with management.[70] Eventually, JP Morgan decided that outsourcing the IT department was not working and they brought the IT department back in-house. The entire process was costly, difficult, and took years to recover from. Other companies have experienced similar problems. A study of IT outsourcing revealed that 60 percent of managers were dissatisfied with the impact that IT outsourcing had on the organization, and 40 percent of managers were actively trying to bring IT functions back in-house.[71]

There are advantages to keeping a department or process in-house. One of these advantages includes improved control of operations and resource management. On-site employees are better able to address unexpected changes in the business if they do not have to manage remote workers. Beyond contract administration, the organization has little control over the performance and management of outsourced services.[72]

Another advantage to keeping services and processes in-house is that it reduces the likelihood of cultural or linguistic barriers often faced in international outsourcing or offshoring.[73] It is also politically correct to keep employees in-house, and this can be used as a valuable public relations tool.[74] Both employees and the public feel cheated and may lose faith in a company when it is forced to downsize due to outsourcing or offshoring initiatives.

In conclusion, HR planners must ensure they respond to the existing and upcoming HR needs of an organization. Through monitoring HR trends within and outside of the organization, planners will be better prepared to address current and future organizational human resources requirements.

CHAPTER SUMMARY

- Labour force changes include the aging of the workforce in Canada, the increasing importance of diversity management (including immigrants, visible minorities, women, and persons with disability), and Canada's current and future labour shortage/talent mismatch. HR planning must prepare for these changes, realizing their impact on training and development, turnover, replacement planning, succession planning, budgeting, internal mobility, mentoring, and the need to accommodate employees.

- Alternative work arrangements allow an organization to respond to labour demands and preferences by offering flexible arrangements of schedules that deviate from the traditional workweek. Through the use of flextime, compressed workweeks, annualized or banked hours, reduced hours or part-time employment, and telecommuting HR can balance the needs of the organization with the needs of the employees. Often, these changes increase the potential talent pool available for an organization, but they do add additional management and forecasting variances that affect HR planners.

- Outsourcing refers to the increasing trend to outsource other teams or departments within an organization, as well as the increasing trend to outsource the HR of an organization. Outsourcing is an organizational response to increased wage rates; the aging workforce; increased demand for skilled labour; a desire to reduce costs; developments in information, communication, and technology; and a general acceptance of the outsourcing of business processes.

- The outsourcing of HR includes the outsourcing of operational, rather than strategic, HR functions such as pre-employment background screening, recruitment, performance management, compensation, benefits, and training.

KEY TERMS

- alternative work arrangements   269
- annualized or banked hours   270
- compressed workweek   270
- disability   267
- diversity management   263
- flextime   270
- glass ceiling   264
- immigrant population   264
- outsourcing   273
- telecommuting (telework)   271
- visible minorities   265

REVIEW QUESTIONS

1. Outline how alternative work arrangements can help an organization respond to changing demands in Canada. Which of these alternative work arrangements do you think will continue in the near future and why?
2. Select one alternative work arrangement. Develop an HR policy regarding that arrangement for professors at your academic institution. What are the strengths and weaknesses of the arrangement? What effect would these arrangements have on HR planning or forecasting?
3. What are the top services that an organization outsources and why?
4. What are the labour market trends leading to an increase in outsourcing in Canada?
5. What are the implications of outsourcing HR for a company? Which elements of HR are outsourced most often and why?

DISCUSSION QUESTIONS

1. Review the groups of people discussed in the diversity management section. What factors do you think contribute to the disadvantages that these groups experience in Canada?
2. Outline the barriers that exist in securing a skills match within the Canadian workforce. How can HR managers be better prepared to manage these barriers?
3. As full-time jobs are replaced with part-time jobs in Canada, more and more employees are forced to work part-time jobs, although they would prefer full-time employment. What challenges does this present for an organization's ability to attract, retain, and motivate employees?
4. Assume you are an HR manager in an organization that is currently experiencing difficulty attracting and retaining talent. Review the report highlighted in the opening profile (Getting on the Same Page: Report on the CGA-Canada Summit on Skills and Learning, organized by the Public Policy Forum). Using the information presented in the report, and the twelve key recommendations highlighted in the chapter opening profiles, develop concrete, deliverable, and measurable policies that you can recommend to your organization to overcome labour resource obstacles.
5. Briefly identify the factors that led to a labour shortage or labour skills mismatch in Canada. Consider the perspective of multiple stakeholders (e.g., employees, managers, HR, government). What can be done to minimize the effect of either the labour shortage or the labour skills mismatch?

WEB EXERCISE

Statistics Canada (www.statcan.gc.ca) is Canada's central statistics agency, providing regularly updated statistics to help better understand Canada's population, resources, economy, society, and culture. In addition to the Canadian census, Statistics Canada completes and compiles over 350 additional surveys on a regular basis. For example, the Labour Force Survey (LFS) is completed on a monthly basis, highlighting recent developments in the Canadian labour market. It also includes information on a variety of current labour force characteristics, such as employment and unemployment for Canada, the provinces, metropolitan areas, and economic regions.

Review the latest labour force survey release and compare this to the labour force release for the same month one year earlier.

1. What has changed in the Canadian labour market over the year (e.g., unemployment levels, types of employment, industry employment growth, regional employment changes, etc.)?
2. What are some of the causes for these changes?
3. How do you think HR planning will be affected by these changes?
4. Given your newly developed expertise in HR planning, what recommendations would you make to the HR managers, department managers, or executive managers regarding how the organization can adapt to these changes and manage the potential impact of these changes on the organization?

CASE INCIDENT

Diversity in the Workplace

You have been hired as a consultant for a large bank in Canada. The bank just completed a basic HR inventory to determine the diversity of their internal labour force. They currently have a labour shortage and will need to hire at least 1,500 employees to fill expected vacancies and an expected increase in demand throughout the organization.

The external labour force includes 48 percent women, 4 percent persons with disability, and 18 percent recent immigrants. Using the information below, which positions have an underrepresentation of each category—women, persons with disability, and immigrants? Which positions have an overrepresentation of each category?

	Total Current Number of Employees	Total Current Number of Women	Total Current Number of Persons with Disabilities	Total Current Number of Recent Immigrants	Additional Employees Needed
Executives	35	1	0	0	7
Branch managers	220	12	3	0	43
Department managers	780	210	5	18	152
Account manager	2,120	815	20	940	413
Teller	4,535	3,125	85	1,550	885
Total	7,690	4,163	113	2,508	1,500

What is the impact of this over- or underrepresentation on the organization's ability to operate? What actions would you recommend to align the internal labour force with the external labour force? How would the organization benefit by following these recommendations?

CASE INCIDENT

Alternative Work Arrangements

Company ABC recently experienced an unusually high level of turnover. Historically, voluntary turnover levels in the organization have been 12 percent, but over the last three years this number has risen to 16 percent, 18 percent, and 22 percent respectively. The company decided to engage in exit interviews and they hired a third-party company to conduct the interviews. Here are some of the comments they received:

Susan, aged 33, worked for the company for six months: I just couldn't handle the long commute to work. I live in Guelph and the drive in to Toronto was taking me over an hour and a half one way. I have two young children at home and my husband works long hours. I don't want to spend three hours a day on the road.

Gary, aged 62, worked for the company for 27 years: I am tired. I just finished paying off my house mortgage and my wife was eligible for retirement. We want to rent a yacht and sail around the world.

Tina, aged 57, worked for the company for 22 years: I like the company, I really do, but I have been stuck in my job for the last 11 years. I haven't had a promotion in just as long and I sit at my desk watching others get promoted, even though my performance appraisals are great year after year. I just feel undervalued and unappreciated. I'd rather be paid less in a place that appreciates me.

Mandeesh, aged 42, worked for the company for two years: I am very appreciative of the opportunity that the company gave me when I started working for them a couple of years ago. They hired me just when I needed a job the most. My wife was arriving from India and I had been in Canada for almost six months with no attractive job prospects. When I was hired, the company looked at my six months of experience working in a restaurant and at pizza shops and brought me in at the lowest customer service level they had. No one cared that I had completed my training as an engineer at IIT (Indian Institute of Technology, a world leader in Engineering education) and I worked for a large multinational company for nine years as an engineer. Although I applied numerous times to engineering positions within the company, they said I didn't have Canadian experience or education. I am not happy here anymore.

Sandy, aged 28, worked for the company for one month: I was so excited to get the administrative assistant position at the company! I just love interacting with people and think I am really organized, but since I was a kid I have been afraid of confined spaces. My doctor says that I am claustrophobic. When I got to work the first day I was horrified to see that my office was this small cubicle with tall walls all around. The desk was U-shaped so I barely had room to move my chair. The walls were so tall that I couldn't see over them when I was standing. I hated going to work in that cubicle.

Looking at the results of some of the exit surveys, which employee exits could have been prevented? What alternative work arrangements would you have considered offering these employees? How would these options have benefited both the employee and the employer?

■ REQUIRED PROFESSIONAL CAPABILITIES REFERENCED IN THIS CHAPTER

5. Keeps current with emerging HR trends

31. Ensures the organization's HR policies and practices align with human rights legislation.

53. Develops processes to engage and involve employees in achieving the objectives of the organization.

64. Researches, analyzes, and reports on potential people issues affecting the organization.

67. Develops people plans that support the organization's strategic directions.

99. Provides advice on issues relating to labour and employee relations including hiring, discipline, and termination.

153. Helps supervisors/managers to identify career options for employees that align with business needs.

BUILDING STRATEGIC PARTNERSHIPS

■ STRATEGY DEVELOPMENT

In setting business strategies, line managers need to be fully in tune with their stakeholders and where the business is going. One key stakeholder for any business is the customer. Business leaders need to understand their customers and what they want from the organization. In the same way, human resource managers need to be in tune with their customers, who are the business leaders, and what they need to support the organizational plan. Human resource strategies need to be in tune with each organizational unit as well as the organization as a whole. For example, acting together, human resources professionals and line managers need to think through the type of culture that is needed in each unit if the people in the unit are to be able to deliver the business strategy.

Strategic Human Resources

Strategic human resources is a set of policies and procedures created by the organization to facilitate the achievement of organizational strategy. An example of such would be a talent management process with an outcome of attracting, retaining, and developing talent to achieve business strategy. From the traditional perspective, HR planning includes forecasting surpluses and shortages with a focus on the tactical needs of managing employees. Currently, many organizations are asking HR functions to demonstrate their real value rather than articulating their perceived value. Thus, HR functions are working with line functions to develop HR strategies that support business strategies.

■ STAKEHOLDERS

Many business leaders express the concern that while human resources professionals have skills and knowledge with respect to human resources, they do not know the business they support. Based on this belief, human resources staff are not involved in the process of business planning. If human resources professionals are to be successfully involved in the business planning process, they need to be strategic partners with the business and they need to be seen as understanding the business needs. Once accepted as a business partner, the human resources professional can work with their business colleagues to ensure the human resources plan is linked to and supports the business plan. As well, human resources professionals need to be able to translate the business strategies into human resource implications. They can demonstrate their understanding of the businesses they serve by communicating with business leaders and line managers in terms of business needs, not just human resource needs. If the human resources professional can link human resource activities, such as hiring practices and leadership development, to the business needs, they can illustrate how human resource activities will support business initiatives. To do this, human resources professionals must involve line managers in the development of the human resource initiatives that make a difference in how people are managed, developed, and rewarded.

HRP IN THE NEWS   **GBCS**

In July 1992, Global Business Communications Systems (GBCS) was formed by the merger of two business units of AT&T—Business Communications Systems, which sold telecommunications systems and services to large clients, and General Business Systems, which served smaller customers. The GBCS business environment was highly competitive with thin profit margins. The integration of two distinct cultures and business processes was very challenging.[1] The three major changes made to transform the organization into a global leader included: infusion of new leadership talent with the subsequent reformulation of mission, objectives, and strategies; a human resources effort to recast policies and programs into tools for linking the new business principles to daily life; and the reorganization of the human resource function to support the strategic business linkage.

To operationalize the human resource planning process, human resources professionals need to be linked to the business they support. HR needs to transform itself from its role as "provider of basic personnel services" to one with a strategic function, and one that adds value to the entire organization. At GBCS, human resources was repositioned as a key member of the senior management team with responsibility for providing leadership on strategic human resource issues and in areas such as diversity, labour, and human resource strategic planning.[2] This ensured that key human resources professionals had input into the business strategy as it was being formulated, ensuring any people issues were discussed and addressed as part of the business strategy, not as an add-on after the strategy had been agreed to. Exhibit A.1 illustrates the linking of the business strategy to the human resource mission and plan at GBCS.

Strategic Partnerships

Jack Welch, former head of General Electric, has stated: "I am the ultimate believer in people first, strategies second."[3] What are the implications of this sentiment for human resources and line managers? For those who worked for Jack Welch, their first priority was hiring the right people, developing them, and evaluating them. Their second priority was the business strategy. In many organizations, the senior management team looks at strategy first, and only once the strategy is accomplished do they work at getting people in place to implement the strategy.

strategic partnership

A formal alliance between the business and human resources to maximize the value added of human resources to the business; human resources is seen as a partner with business, not a supplier of services

Researchers such as Ulrich[4] and Brockbank[5] argue that human resources professionals need to be strategic partners with the business. In effect, the human resources department needs to create a **strategic partnership** with organizational line managers. Research shows that competitive advantage may be derived from the integration of the business strategy and human resource planning because:[6]

- When there is a strategic partnership between human resources and line managers, the ability to implement strategic initiatives increases as strategic business and human resource plans merge.
- Merging strategy and human resource planning increases the organizational capacity to change. People resist change when they fail to understand the change, when the change

may lead to negative outcomes, or when the perceived risks associated with change are greater than the perceived benefits. Most strategic initiatives imply change. To reduce the potential for resistance, human resource practices need to be engaged. For example, if competitive pressures and financial restructuring fundamentally change business strategy, a number of human resource practices can be used to overcome individual resistance to change. For example:

- Staffing decisions are made that require employees to have different skills. Now, development and training programs can be developed and offered to help employees acquire new competencies consistent with the new strategies.
- Incentive systems are changed to focus more on customer service, and profit and communication activities can be aligned to help employees understand the new business requirements.

Strategic initiatives often require change; human resources practices help overcome resistance to change, which results in a competitive advantage.

As a result of a strategic partnership between the business and human resources, the efforts of human resources become significantly more meaningful and congruent with the needs of the organization's strategic objectives. Additionally, the human resources professional will achieve a stature within the organization that truly reflects the strategic contribution they should be providing.[7]

Emergent Approach to Planning

emergent approach

A planning approach that involves human resources waiting for the business to determine their strategy and then attempting to provide human resource services, such as recruitment, to meet the strategy

Some human resource teams do not take a planned approach to planning but instead prefer to take an **emergent approach.** That is to say they prefer to wait until there is a clear business strategy on which to model their human resource strategy. This approach often results in missed opportunities due to the time required for business strategies to become clear. Human resource teams that react to business needs, rather than plan with the business, often do so because they are concerned about being seen either as creating their own policy in the absence of business strategy, or as driving business strategy. In many organizations, the links between human resources and the business are complex. One issue is the ownership of human resource strategy. Does the human resource strategy and plan belong to the human resources group or the business? In the example of GBCS, if human resources is repositioned as a key member of the senior management team, with responsibility for providing leadership on strategic human issues, then the human resource strategy is owned by the business and human resources works with the business to implement the strategy in support of the business strategy.[8]

For many organizations, merging strategic and human resource planning activities has become a critical source of competitiveness.[9] When strategy initiatives (e.g., growth, diversification, mergers, privatization, customer service) merge with human resource plans (e.g., staffing, developing, appraising, rewarding, organizing, communicating with employees), businesses may perform in a unique way, such as the ability to transfer strategy to employee action, to align systems and strategies, and to make strategies happen.[10]

Human resource planning is a systematic process of merging or linking human resource practices and systems with business demands to build an organization's capability and competitive advantage, as shown in Exhibit A.2.

■ LINKING HUMAN RESOURCE PLANNING WITH BUSINESS PLANNING

Human resource planning that is linked and aligned with business planning can have a significant impact on the design, development, and implementation of an organization's strategic objectives, including human resources policies and programs. In many organizations, human resources

EXHIBIT A.1 GBCS's Example of Linking the Business Strategy with HR Mission and Plan

GBCS Business Principles	GBCS HR Strategic Imperatives	HR Mission	Focus Areas	HR Plan Initiatives
Make people a key priority	Associates actively take ownership for the business success at all levels, individually and as teams, by improving associate value	To create an environment where the achievement of business goals is realized through an acceptance of individual accountably by each associate and by his/her commitment to performance excellence	• Cultural change • Rewards and recognition • Ownership	• Learning forums • Communication platform • Diversity platform • Progress sharing plan • Recognition platform • Performance excellence partnership, including associate surveys and organization effectiveness

EXHIBIT A.2 Human Resource Planning[11]

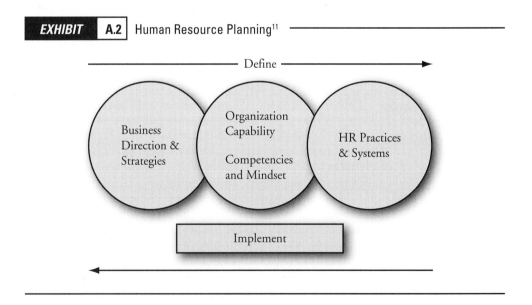

programs and policies are reactive to the business needs and not well received by the management team. However, if they are planned as part of the business processes then they will be viewed as critical to the success of the organization and supported.

Reactive vs. Proactive Human Resource Response

As part of the business planning process, business units define their human resource needs. For example, during the process the following needs are identified:

reactive human resource response

A planning approach that involves human resources professionals waiting until the business plan is complete and then reacting to the business leaders' needs

proactive human resource response

A planning approach that involves human resources professionals being involved in the business plan and inputting human resource needs into the business plan during the planning exercise

- A business unit in the marketing department confirms the need for 10 people with skills in marketing design
- Another unit in the finance department documents the need for five people at the entry level with an accounting credential, preferably a CA

If HR was not involved in the planning process, then it must now reactively respond to the approved needs. In this **reactive human resource response,** the HR professional assigned to each unit working with the business owner would post the jobs as defined and use the policies and procedures of the organization to complete the hiring. During this process, the HR professional might have concerns about bringing in so many new staff at once or concerns about the skills that are being considered, based on their knowledge of current skills in the organization. They may also have concerns about the ability to provide support to the new staff as they participate in the orientation programs of the organization, or about how many new staff will report to one manager. But often their concerns are met with significant resistance because approval through the business planning process has been received. In the end, the human resources professional often ends up doing the job for the business unit and dealing with people issues, such as hiring too many junior staff in Finance, when they arise.

If human resource planning is linked and aligned with business planning, then human resources will no longer be reacting to business needs, but proactively involved in the design, development, and implementation of organizational strategic initiatives. This is considered a **proactive human resource approach.**

Strategic Staffing

strategic staffing

Process where HR assesses the cumulative vacancies an organization may have over a period of time, for instance five years in selected critical job families, and creates a plan to address the vacancies, including creating career paths or new retention strategies

Peters et al. suggest that human resources professionals should be focused on **strategic staffing** as a means to link business and human resource planning, and that this approach will facilitate the development of a strategic partnership with the business.[12]

Using the model illustrated in Exhibit A.3, human resources' primary function under input is staffing. Their objective is to get the right people in the right jobs at the time. Under throughput, human resources designs and implements development, appraisal, and reward systems to transform the input as required by the needs of the organization. The output would be the performance of the staff. The performance of the staff is measured by feedback mechanisms, which are referred to as **human resource accounting.**

The implications of this model are that development, rewards, and appraisal systems are built on the needs of the organization once the right staff has been hired. That is to say, the development, rewards, and appraisal systems are based on business need. For example, IBM as a business demands superior talent. The focus of IBM's HR staff is on acquiring the right staff so as to ensure the organization has superior talent, or the right people at the right time.

Focus on Throughput Rather than Input

human resource accounting

A process that involves using accounting principles to identify, measure, and communicate information about human resources to facilitate effective management

An example outlined by Peters et al. illustrates the importance of focusing on throughput.[14] A Fortune 100 company set in motion the downsizing of a strategic business unit (SBU). The organization directed human resources to downsize the unit by 13,000. However, at the same time, the same SBU hired 3,000 new people. Why? Even though the SBU had the best internal development programs, sound reward systems, and institutionalized appraisal system, they did not have the right people at the right time to meet the strategic direction of the company. Human resource planning was not linked with business planning. In fact, human resource planning was focused on throughput (see Exhibit A.3), emphasizing development, appraisal, and rewards, and not on input (e.g., staffing).

EXHIBIT   **A.3**   Strategic Approach to Human Resource Planning[13]

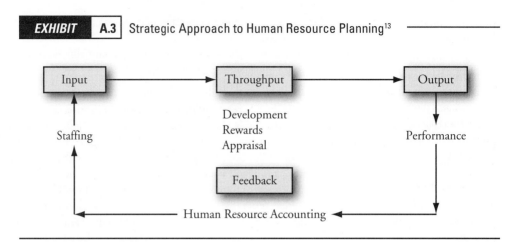

MODELS FOR LINKING BUSINESS AND HR PLANNING[15]

Described below are three models that illustrate how business can be linked to human resource planning:

1. The first model involves executives identifying a business strategy, and once the strategy is defined, human resource planning is conducted and various human resource practices are derived (e.g., staffing, training, appraisal, rewards, etc.) in order to accomplish the strategy.

2. The second model involves executives linking business strategy and human resource strategy through the core values of the company. For example, one of the core values could be service. The business strategy would include the service strategy, and the human resource planning would involve creating human resource plans to support the defined service strategy.

3. The third model involves both HR and the business working together as a team to plan and integrate the business and human resource plan.

All three models are used in varying degrees in companies depending on the role human resources has been assigned by the senior team. If the line managers leave the people plans to the human resource function with little or no leadership, then human resource activities are likely to be seen as belonging to human resources and only implemented if there is a significant push by the senior business team.

Human Resource Planning Follows Completion of Business Planning

In the first model, human resources is not at the table during business planning, and the people issues of the plan are likely not considered with the same importance as the business and financial issues. As such, human resources must take time following the completion of the business plan to develop supporting human resource processes. This reactive response often leads to human resources attempting to sell various people strategies to a business team that has moved to implementation of the business plan without the human resource input needed to support the business plan. Additionally, the budget created based on the business plan likely does not include human resource initiatives. Thus, the human resource function must fight for dollars to support initiatives that they believe will support the business plan. However, the business team may not see the need in the same way that human resources does.

Linking the Business Strategy and Human Resource Strategy through Core Values

In the second approach, the senior team builds plans for both business and human resources based on the core values of the organization. If a core value of the organization is customer service, then human resource strategies that support this core value will be supported by the business and the budget will be allocated accordingly. The challenge in this scenario is that human resource strategies or activities that are not seen as supporting a core value will be a hard sell to the business leaders and will often go unsupported.

Business and Human Resource Planning Together

In the third approach, there is a strategic partnership between human resources and the business. The discussions of people strategies to support business strategies occur as part of the planning process, which includes both business and human resources. Thus, the buy-in and budget for the identified work is committed.

In this model, illustrated in Exhibit A.4, the boundaries between the human resource and line management teams are often blurred—some of the human resource management tasks are transferred to the line managers, human resource staff are often deployed to the business units, and business unit staff are often rotated through human resources.

At the corporate level in organizations, the development of business strategy and operational objectives is done on a yearly basis. Most organizations have a three- or five-year plan in place that is updated yearly. As in the example of GBCS, the organizational leadership develops

EXHIBIT | A.4 | Factors Associated with HR as a Strategic Partner[17]

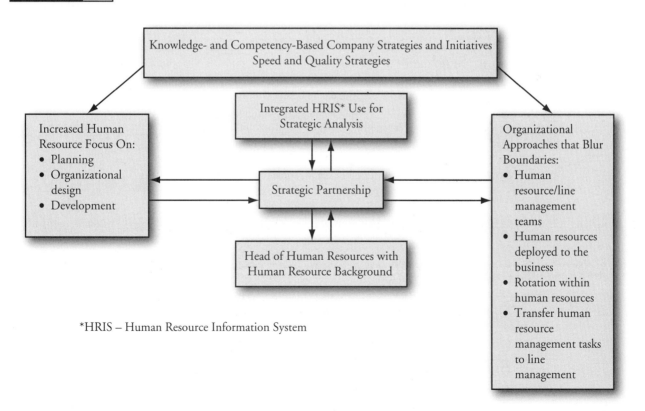

*HRIS – Human Resource Information System

and/or updates the vision, mission, values, and objectives during this planning cycle. At GBCS, management's belief that its people were its only "sustainable competitive advantage" was key to how they developed their strategy, business plan, and the role of human resources in the planning process. As part of the planning process, human resources was asked to examine "all aspects of the people dimension of the organization with the focus of engaging the workforce and creating an environment that supports our people as our only sustainable, competitive advantage."[16]

STRATEGIC PARTNERING PROFESSIONAL SKILLS

In order to produce the human resource plan and link it with the business plan, what skills does the HR professional require? Research has shown that in addition to professional skills related to human resources, the following **strategic partnering professional skills** are crucial if human resources professionals are to be successful as strategic business partners:[18]

strategic partnering professional skills

Business skills needed by human resources professionals to be successful strategic business partners

- Knowledge of the business
  - Where is the business going in three to five years?
  - What talent is needed to accomplish the strategic plan?
  - What is the gap? How can it be filled?
- Professional competence within the HR department
  - What skills sets do human resources professionals have in the organization?
  - What are the gaps?
  - How can the gaps be closed?
- Ability to anticipate pressures for organizational change and be responsive
  - Most strategic plans require organizational change. How prepared is human resources to provide that support?
  - What line manager skills exist to support change?
- Ability to distinguish line/staff roles and responsibilities
  - What roles do each group have?
  - Do the various areas have the trust and support needed to do the work required?
- Customer-driven focus
  - What are the organization's customer needs?
  - How are they linked to the business strategy?
  - How can the human resource strategy support these needs?
- Ability to capitalize on simple successes and sell them
  - What successes have occurred as a result of various human resource initiatives in the past?
  - How can the successes be used to sell a more strategic approach to business needs?
- Ability to link human resource tools to long-term success
  - What talent management tools are in place?
  - How do they link to business strategy?
  - How can the business use these?

COMPETENCY MODEL FOR HUMAN RESOURCE PROFESSIONALS

The International Personnel Management Association (IPMA) has developed a model to illustrate the competencies that human resources professionals require to be successful as a strategic partner with the business. At the centre of this model is the role of change agent. Surrounding the change agent are four key competency areas that support this role. The areas are leader, advocate, human resources expert, and business partner. Exhibit A.5 illustrates how the model fits together.[19]

This model illustrates that human resource expertise competencies are only part of the competency set that human resources professionals require. Of the twenty competencies that IPMA Canada has identified as required by human resource professionals, only one relates to human resource expertise.[21]

EXHIBIT   **A.5**   Competency Model for Human Resources Professionals[20]

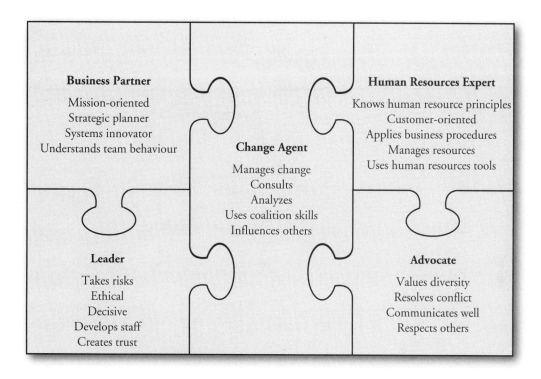

Business Partner

Mission-oriented
Strategic planner
Systems innovator
Understands team behaviour

Change Agent

Manages change
Consults
Analyzes
Uses coalition skills
Influences others

Human Resources Expert

Knows human resource principles
Customer-oriented
Applies business procedures
Manages resources
Uses human resources tools

Leader

Takes risks
Ethical
Decisive
Develops staff
Creates trust

Advocate

Values diversity
Resolves conflict
Communicates well
Respects others

Thus, to successfully integrate human resource planning with business planning, as a partner with the business, human resources professionals need to build relationships with business leaders, illustrating first their business skills and then their human resource expertise.

In the late 1980s, Eastman Kodak faced a very competitive environment that resulted in many changes in their core business.[22] The human resource function had to reshape to focus on the strategic dimension of human resources, as illustrated in Exhibit A.6. The vocabulary of the human resources staff changed from equity, fairness, and respect; employee advocacy; and compliance to competitive advantage, customer focus, value creation, and business partnership. Working together in what they call "an integrative ensemble," business and human resources have been able to do the necessary planning and integration to implement the outcomes successfully.

■ LINKING HUMAN RESOURCES PROFESSIONALS WITH LINE MANAGERS

What should human resources professionals and line managers do in the planning process? In the Kodak example, instead of human resources dictating the needs of staff, they involved the top management in the planning process, setting the direction for human resource planning. Together, line managers and HR staff discussed the challenges and opportunities and set a corporate human resources agenda together. The HR competencies needed to develop and deliver on the needs of the business were also defined. Together the human resource and business team drove the planning process. In order to implement a business strategy, the HR professionals create or develop human resources systems and tools that give the employees the capability to execute business strategy. Working together, the business managers and human resource staff build a shared conceptual framework and initiate the contracting process for human resource planning.

Many HR professionals see the work they do through the eyes of a functional specialist and they fail to see it through the eyes of their business partners. If they are to be viewed as critical

EXHIBIT   A.6 | Kodak's Model of Planning[23] ————————————

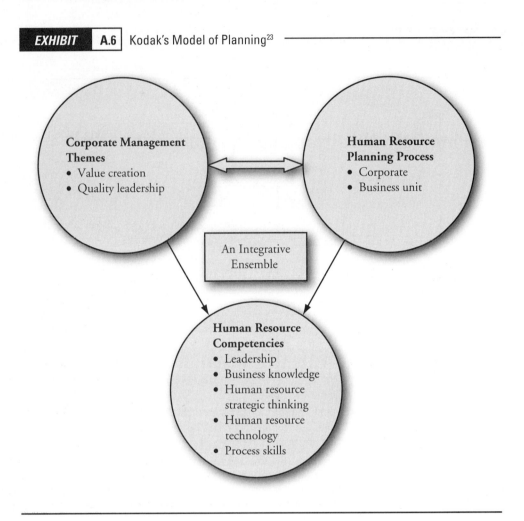

to the delivery of the business strategy, they need to develop skills that their business partners consider useful. These skills include:[24]

- Thinking strategically
- Being a personal and professional sounding board
- Being transparent and candid
- Avoiding politics
- Developing credibility

All of these skills are crucial for a human resources professional. Developing these skills and linking them with human resources professional skills are critical if the HR professional wants to be proactively involved in the business.

Challenges

Many of the challenges that arise between business and human resources are related to understanding the value that strategic people processes can bring to the shareholder value of a company. For example, many executives believe that leadership development is a job for the human resources department. However, this may be the "single biggest misconception they can have."[25] Executives who are good at growing leaders, and set this as a priority over developing a world-class business strategy, create leading-edge organizations such as General Electric. Leadership teams that recognize growing great leaders is a key aspect of organizational success have included accountability for developing direct reports in the line manager's performance. In many cases, the operating manager's own evaluation, development plans, and promotions depend on how successfully they develop their subordinates.[26] Human resource staff have the knowledge and skills to create the tools to help line managers achieve this accountability, through their leadership development and performance management activities. Thus, building a business/people strategy together by linking areas such as talent management can have a significant positive impact on shareholder value.

■ THE IMPACT OF LINKING HUMAN RESOURCE AND BUSINESS PLANNING[27]

centres of excellence (COE)

Physical or virtual centres focused on specific issues; they concentrate on existing capacity and resources to facilitate collaboration across disciplines and organizations on programs or projects with direct relevance to human needs

Corning Inc. provides us with an example of the impact of linking HR and business planning. Corning went through major business challenges in the late 1990s and early 2000s with the telecommunications boom and then the collapse of the telecom bubble. Human resources had been set up around **centres of excellence (COE),** including compensation and benefits, learning and development, employee relations, and recruiting. The COE approach resulted in deployment of initiatives that were not aligned with the priorities of business units. The outcome was that some of the human resources initiatives were unsuccessful because they did not gain the support of the business. The corporate structure of COEs resulted in field HR organizations of Corning taking on COE–like roles so their structure lined up with the corporate structure. Overall, the result was that human resources was not aligned with the needs of the business and the cost to deliver human resource services was high, which raised concern.

The human resources leadership decided to change how it did business. The key focus of human resources became understanding Corning's business strategies and the human capital requirements necessary to achieve its business results at both the divisional and enterprise level. To facilitate focus, the leadership worked with human resource staff to help them draw a direct connection between the strategies of the corporation's businesses and the human capital implications of the strategies. Being able to draw this connection helped the staff to understand the future talent requirements of the corporation in terms of numbers, type, and quality of people needed to execute the business strategy. Once the connection was drawn, the HR staff needed to understand the actions required to realize the maximum return from the investment in the talent.

The planning of the human capital needs became central to HR's approach for linking their plan to Corning's five-year business plan. Other human resource activities supported this process, keeping them aligned with the business strategy and operational objectives.

Exhibit A.7 illustrates the link needed between business and human resources to create a successful ongoing pool of employees. The global and scalable goals of the business address the need to build capability where and when the client businesses need, and the top quartile cost goal ensures that HR remains within the boundaries of appropriate total cost to deliver required services.

EXHIBIT A.7 Human Resource Transformation Goals[28]

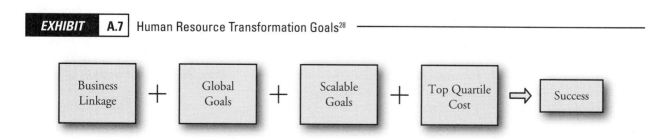

■ ALIGNING HUMAN RESOURCES AND BUSINESS STRATEGY

Many articles, books, and studies argue that human resources needs to become a strategic partner with the business to align strategy. What does this mean in terms of operationalizing the human resource plan? If the HR strategy contributes to the business strategy, and the business strategy contributes to the human resources strategy, there should be minimal or no disconnect. HR senior management would be part of the process to develop and implement business plans, and business management would do the same with HR plans. In this context, HR is facilitating the development of an organizational strategy that is owned and developed by line managers. All human resources programs would be created to solve real business problems and add to value to the delivery of the business strategy. The HR programs should be indistinguishable from business programs. The objectives of people development should be set so as to support the business objectives.

Implications

Human resources staff need to understand the language of business, the numbers of business, and the analyses presented by marketing, supply chain, finance, and other operational areas. They need to be prepared to do cost-benefit analysis of human programs with their colleagues from the business. Business staff need to be able to identify the human resource capabilities of their staff and work with human resources staff to develop people strategies. In doing so, they will support the development of the people resources needed to meet business needs. Additionally, business staff need to develop skills to deal effectively with some human resource responsibilities, or more correctly called, people strategies.

As a result, employees will be more engaged in the people programs as these programs will be seen as part of the delivery of the business objectives. The business objectives will be part of the business plan. The evaluation of programs will be based on the objectives that are set as part of the business plan instead of being evaluated against some human resources objectives.

CHAPTER SUMMARY

- Human resource planning linked with business planning can create a strategic partnership that may result in a competitive advantage for an organization.
- A strategic partnership between human resources and business will result in human resources efforts being significantly more meaningful and congruent with the needs of the organization.
- Human resources professionals need to be fully in tune with their line managers to develop an HR plan that supports the organizational plan.
- Linking of human resource and business planning can be executed in three ways: Defining the business strategy, followed by human resource planning; linking the human resource and business strategy through the core values of the company; or integrating the business and the human resource plan.
- Strategic professional skills required by human resources professionals include: knowledge of the business, ability to distinguish line/staff roles and responsibilities, complexity management, being customer-driven, the ability to capitalize on simple successes and sell them, and the ability to link HR tools to long-term success.
- An integrative ensemble links corporate management themes, human resource planning processes, and human resource competencies to ensure that human resource planning supports business strategy.

- Line managers should have more accountability for people strategies and be more involved in the development of these strategies as part of the business planning process.
- Linking the development of the people strategy with the business strategy creates: a better understanding of the needs of the business and the capability of the employees to deliver the business strategy; a clear link between the budget and the people strategy; and opportunities to ensure measures are in place to measure the people strategy against the business deliverables.

KEY TERMS

- centres of excellence (COE)   293
- emergent approach   285
- human resource accounting   287
- proactive human resource response   287
- reactive human resource response   287
- strategic partnership   284
- strategic partnering professional skills   290
- strategic staffing   287

REVIEW QUESTIONS

1. List four business skills that HR professionals need in order to work strategically with the business to link the HR planning process with the business planning process.
2. Define the emergent approach to planning and why HR staff often use this approach.
3. Outline three models that can be used to link business and HR planning.
4. List four HR competencies documented in Kodak's model of planning.

DISCUSSION QUESTIONS

1. HR planning linked to business planning is critical if HR is to be seen as a strategic partner within an organization. How do centres of excellence negatively impact this concept?
2. A reactive response by HR to business needs may result in frustration for HR staff if they hire staff based on business-unit needs only to lay them off the following year. What would be the result of a reactive response to hiring in such a scenario? How would linking business and HR planning reduce this risk?
3. A number of organizations use strategic staffing or human capital planning as a means of integrating HR and business planning. Why? Provide two examples of how HR activities result from this approach.

WEB EXERCISE

Use a web search to find two organizations that link business and HR planning and illustrate how they do this. How is the performance of the people strategy measured? Do the roles of line managers change? Do line managers have more responsibility for people strategies?

GLOSSARY

absenteeism Time that an employee is absent or away from work, including sick days, excessively long breaks, lateness, etc.

acquisition The purchase of a company or a controlling interest in a company by another company

actuarial losses Life events that affect all populations (i.e., death, disability, and retirement)

alternative work arrangements Flexible arrangements or alternate schedules from the traditional Monday to Friday, 9 to 5, working day and week

analyzers Firms that can operate in both a stable and unstable environment; they combine the strengths of the defender and prospector into one system and can operate in product areas that are low-cost or innovative

annualized or banked hours A situation in which employees choose their days and hours of work, within set boundaries, as long as the weekly, monthly, or annual hours (as agreed to) are completed within the predetermined time frame

appropriate planning horizon A judgement about how far into the future predictions can be made, taking into consideration acceptable levels of operational, organizational, and environmental uncertainties

assertiveness The degree which people are assertive in society and the extent to which they are confrontational

attraction and acquisition of talent Encompasses efforts to staff an organization with the right types of people, in the right positions, at the right time

attrition The natural and continuous departure of employees in an organization through methods that affect the population at large, such as quits, retirements, disabilities, and deaths

balanced scorecard An approach that provides a balanced view of organizational performance by measuring financials, internal processes, customers, and an organization's human capital

bench strength An organization's ability to fill vacancies from within

bumping rights A right that allows senior employees affected by job termination due to downsizing to transfer to jobs held by employees with less seniority

business ecosystem A series of tightly knit intercompany relationships that allows the business to attain a competitive advantage

business strategy A strategy that identifies how businesses compete in the areas they have selected

career A course of successive situations that make up a person's work life and usually refers to all the jobs that one has held in their working life

career development An organized, formalized, and planned effort to achieve a balance between the individual's career needs and the organization's work force requirements; helps employees attain their career objectives

career goals Goals that one selects for one's career or future position

career ladder A vertical series of jobs starting at entry level and progressively moving to higher-level jobs, based on experience, education, and performance

career path The sequential pattern of jobs that form one's career

career planning The process of selecting one's career goals and the path to attain these goals

centres of excellence (COE) Physical or virtual centres focused on specific issues; they concentrate on existing capacity and resources to facilitate collaboration across disciplines and organizations on programs or projects with direct relevance to human needs

coaching An ongoing process of providing feedback

competency A set of behaviours that encompass skills, knowledge, abilities, and personal attributes, that taken together, are critical to successful work accomplishment

competency model A future-oriented model that first reviews competencies that are aligned with an organization's mission, vision, and strategy, and then aims to identify an ideal workforce in terms of these competencies

compressed workweek A reduction in the number of days per week in which full-time work is performed, but not in the number of weekly hours

conglomerate Merger of one company with another where the two companies have no competitive or buyer-seller relationship

constructive dismissal Occurs when the employer unilaterally makes changes to the employment terms and conditions (reduction in salary, work locations, hours of work, authority or position) thereby altering work terms and the employee resigns within a reasonable time after these changes occur

consultants Professionals who provide expert advice and counsel in a particular area

contingent workforce The class of individual workers who are not regular, full-time employees of a company

contractor Someone who provides goods or services to another entity under the terms of a specific contract

corporate strategy The selection of business areas in which organizations will compete

cost leadership A strategy that focuses the organization on becoming the lowest cost provider of goods or services

crowdsourcing Act of taking on a function once performed by employees and outsourcing it to an undefined (and generally large) network of people in the form of an open call

defenders Organizations that operate in stable markets and simple markets; they compete on cost and their strategy is to protect their market share by cost controls and operational efficiencies

Delphi method A method of forecasting HR demand that involves a panel of experts using their judgements to make estimates of short-term future demands

demand analysis Analysis that identifies the future workforce requirements needed to maintain the organization's mission and goals

development of talent Providing personnel with the knowledge and skills required for current and future job-related success

differentiation An emphasis on the creation of value through being unique

disability The result of complex interactions between a health problem or functional limitations and a person's social, political, cultural, economic, and physical environment

distributive justice The perception of outcome fairness

diversity management A strategy to promote the perception, acknowledgement, and implementation of diversity in organizations and institutions

downsizing An intentional organizational action that affects work process, which involves workforce reduction in an effort to improve efficiency and effectiveness of the organization

downsizing agents Those with decision-making authority who assist in and carry out decisions about who will stay and who will leave during a time of downsizing

due diligence stage The stage of the merger and acquisition process when an organization has found a potential acquisition and begins the process of determining if it a sound decision from a financial, human resource, and shareholder perspective

early retirements A situation that allows employees with either long service or older age, or a combination of the two, to retire before their eligible retirement date

economic value added (EVA) Economic profit of business activity

emergent approach A planning approach that involves human resources waiting for the business to determine their strategy and then attempts to provide human resource services, such as recruitment, to meet the strategy

employee self service (ESS) The use of software by employees to manage their own personal information such as address changes online without having to fill in paperwork that is then entered manually, usually by a human resources administrator

enterprise resource planning system (ERP) A companywide computer software system used to manage and coordinate resources, information, and functions of a business using shared data stores; typically modular in nature so that businesses can add or reconfigure modules as required

environmental scanning A process of systematic surveillance and interpretation designed to identify events, elements, and conditions of the environment that have potential relevance and impact for an organization

equity theory Theory that people compare their inputs (e.g., abilities, effort, experience, and education) and their outcomes (e.g., pay, promotion, layoffs, and other effects) with the inputs and outcomes of other people

ethnocentrism A view in which managers use a home-country standard as reference for managing activities

expatriate An individual who is sent on an assignment outside of their home country for a period of time

external labour force Potential sources of human resources outside of an organization that can affect the future supply of employees

flex hours Variable start and stop times

flex schedules Any type of variation in traditional work schedules

flexible retirement Optimizing the talent of recent retirees by extending their contributions and continuing their engagement in organizational activities

flexpatriate A person who is on a short-term assignment and engages in frequent travel without relocation

flextime A work arrangement that gives employees flexible start and end dates to a given workday, usually with the condition that all employees are present during core business hours

focused differentiation A strategy that is a combination of cost leadership and differentiation; it focuses on a segment of the market, providing a product or service to this segment

forecasting The interaction between the decision maker's perceptual and cognitive processes and the objective characteristics of their environment

friendly merger A merger in which two companies want to join together; both organizations see the merger as beneficial to each other and they work together to create the new organization

full-time employee An employee who works 37.5 to 40 hours in a workweek

functional strategy Strategies implemented by making decisions and taking actions that support this process

future orientation The degree to which people delay current rewards in order to reap these rewards at a later date

gap analysis Analysis that identifies the differences between the forecasted HR supply and the forecasted HR demand, focusing on balancing the number and characteristics of employees needed and available to ensure that supply equals demand

gender differentiation How society views differences in gender roles and affords higher status to certain roles

geocentrism A managerial outlook that focuses on creating a global network and follows a strategy that integrates and is dependant on the global firm's strengths

glass ceiling A systematic, invisible barrier that limits the maximum level to which a member of a demographic minority can rise in an organization

global human resource management (GHRM) A more robust IHRM that views HRM in a global context and, in a less traditional sense, as one that contributes and delivers on organizational capabilities

global human resource planning Planning that estimates employment needs and develops plans for meeting those needs from the available global labour force

groupthink The tendency for group members to avoid introducing novel ideas that are outside of the group's normal mode of thinking for fear that they will disrupt the group consensus process

high potentials Individuals who typically demonstrate the ability to learn more rapidly than their peers, show significant emotional maturity and growth in all areas, and are capable of taking on new challenges at work, rapidly mastering the task

hiring freeze A form of attrition where openings created from natural attrition (e.g., quits, resignations, retirements, etc.) are not filled with new employees

horizontal merger A merger of two competitors

host country nationals (HCN) Citizens of a country of a foreign subsidiary, hired to work at subsidiary located in their home country

hostile merger A merger in which one of the two companies in the merger does not want to merge; the organizational environment of the company being taken over is hostile

HR deliverables Measures of HR activity that add value to the organization and increase its ability to help an organization achieve its strategic goals

HR scorecard A measurement and evaluation system to help define the role of HR as a strategic partner

human capital A reflection of the depth and breadth of employees' talents, education, experience, knowledge, and skills

human capital value added All organizational revenue minus the cost of operating expenses and total compensation per FTE

humane orientation The degree to which societies focus on altruistic behaviour and generosity

human resource accounting A process that involves using accounting principles to identify, measure, and communicate information about human resources to facilitate effective management

human resource audit A systematic examination and analysis of an organizational workforce in an effort to create an understanding of the current staffing situation

human resources due diligence The analysis of the cultural risks of a merger, including similarities and differences of culture affecting the merger and an assessment of whether or not the risks are manageable through the cultural integration of the merger

human resource management system (HRMS) A technological system used to acquire, store, manipulate, retrieve, analyze, and distribute pertinent information regarding an organization's human resources

human resource planning (HRP) A process used to determine future human resource requirements by anticipating future business demands, analyzing the impacts of these demands on the organization, and making decisions on how to effectively acquire and utilize firms' human resources

immediate headcount reduction strategies Strategies for addressing labour surpluses that focus on severing the employment relationship for non-natural reasons

immigrant population Individuals born outside of Canada who are granted the right to live in Canada by immigration authorities

incentives for voluntary separations An organization's attempt to entice employees to self-select employment termination during a time downsizing in exchange for a monetary benefit (e.g., cash bonuses, retraining expenses, outplacement service); also called buyouts

in-group collectivism The degree to which a society feels loyal toward either their family or other collective groups

institutional collectivism The degree to which institutions want individuals to integrate into the large structure even at the cost of individual freedom

interactional justice Justice related to the perceived fairness level between employee and management relations on an individual scale

internal labour force Those who perform the work or provide services within the company under the control or supervision of the organization's management team

international commuter An employee who frequently commutes from their home country to a place of work in another country, typically on a weekly or biweekly basis

international human resource management (IHRM) The worldwide management of talent from a staffing perspective; provides HR support across many different countries and the employment of many different national categories of employees

involuntary turnover Employer-initiated turnover, mainly in the form of dismissals or layoffs

job-sharing A work-term change strategy where the duties, compensation, and/or benefits of one position are split among two or more employees

key position A position that has considerable impact and influence on an organization's operational and strategic activities

labour shortage A shortage that occurs when there is not enough qualified talent to fill the demand for labour

labour surplus A condition when labour supply exceeds demand of labour in an organization or business unit

layoff A permanent or temporary separation of employees from employment for business or economic reasons

leave without pay A situation where an employee agrees to a temporary leave of absence without compensation while retaining seniority and, in some cases, benefits

linchpin A position that is essential and of critical importance to the long-term health of an organization

management self service (MSS) The use of software and the corporate network to automate paper-based personnel-related processes that require a manager's approval, recordkeeping, or input

manpower planning A process by which management determines how the organization should move from its current to its desired human resources position

Markov analysis Analysis that helps predict internal employee movement from one year to another by identifying percentages of employees who remain in their jobs, get promoted or demoted, transfer, and exit out of the organization

mentoring A developmentally oriented relationship between senior and junior colleagues or peers

merger A combination of two organizations to create a third organization

multinational enterprise (MNE) An organization that has operations and subsidiaries across the globe

networking Working with your network of contacts to broaden your knowledge of the career areas that you are interested in

nominal group technique (NGT) A method of forecasting HR demand that involves multiple experts (usually line and department managers) meeting face to face to discuss independently formulated positions of an organizational issue, with the ultimate aim of securing an accurate assessment of a given situation

organizational justice Employee perception of justice that is driven by perceived fairness in the outcomes and processes of organizational change, including procedural justice, distributive justice, and interactional justice

outplacement services Services that focus on preparing the terminated employee for post-downsizing activity (e.g., job search, job-loss coping, etc.), with the ultimate aim of minimizing risk to all parties and helping candidates return to work quickly

outsourcing The subcontracting of activities (production processes or services) that are not regarded as part of a company's core business in an effort to reduce costs by transferring portions of work to outside suppliers, rather than completing the work internally

parent country nationals (PCN) Citizens of the country where headquarters is located

part-time worker Employed persons whose normal hours of work are less than those of a comparable full-time worker; they typically work approximately 20 to 25 hours per week

people equity An approach used by an organization to measure and manage human capital using three elements—alignment, capabilities, and engagement

performance orientation The extent to which society recognizes and rewards positive performances

permanent layoff Layoffs where the organization has no intent to re-establish a working relationship with the employee and there are no recall rights; also called terminations

polycentrism Characterized by firms that are staffed by host country managers and are characterized by decentralized and autonomous operations

power distance The degree to which people are separated by power and authority

pre-deal stage The stage of the merger and acquisition process that occurs when organizations decide they would like to grow by merger and begin to look for opportunities, including partners or business ventures that they would like to consider as an acquisition

proactive human resource response A planning approach that involves human resources professionals being involved in the business plan and inputting human resource needs into the business plan during the planning exercise

procedural justice The perception that the procedures used to make downsizing decisions are fair

productivity Ratio of outputs to inputs in a given production situation

prospectors Organizations that operate in unstable, dynamic, and complex environments; they compete on innovation and creativity

protean career A process used by an individual to manage their career, by moving from organization to organization or work setting to work setting to develop skills; the process is shaped by the needs of the individual rather than the organization

psychological contract theory Theory suggesting that mutual obligations form during an employee's tenure of employment, and the employer–employee relationship is founded on the expectation that each party will fulfill their obligation

ratio analysis Analysis that determines future HR demand based on ratios between assumed casual factors and the number of employees needed

reactive human resource response A planning approach that involves human resources professionals waiting until the business plan is complete and then reacting to the business leaders' needs

reduction in hours A situation where work hours for full-time employees are reduced to less than full-time

regiocentrism A focus on the regions in which organizations operate

regression analysis A method of estimating HR demand that provides statistical projections using mathematical formulas to determine the correlation between multiple measureable output factors (independent variables) and an organization's employment level (dependent variable)

relational database A database in which data can be stored to more than one file, each containing different types of data; the different files can be linked so that information from separate files can be used together

replacement chart A chart used to estimate vacancies in higher level jobs and identify how potential HR supply can fill these vacancies via internal movements from lower levels jobs

request for proposal A written request provided to potential suppliers of a product or service; it usually includes a description of the product or service required, specifications related to the exact structure and format of the supplier's response, references, and timing

resource-based view (RBV) An organization's resources, such as financial and physical; it highlights the importance of the skills and competencies possessed by a firm's human resources

return on investment (ROI) Ratio of value creation for the organization based on HR activity and the associated expenses for HR activity in a given period of time

scenario analysis A method that provides multiple estimates of future HR demand, contingent on a unique set of assumptions and circumstances for each scenario

separation The exit of talent from the organization, including all forms of exits (e.g., voluntary or involuntary, permanent or temporary, functional or dysfunctional)

severance pay Additional compensation provided to employees whose employment relationship with an organization is severed due to an organizational decision to reduce workforce size

strategic human resource management (SHRM) The linking of HRM with the strategic goals and objectives of the organization to improve organizational performance

strategic partnering professional skills Business skills needed by human resources professionals to be successful strategic business partners

strategic partnership A formal alliance between the business and human resources to maximize the value added of human resources to the business; human resources is seen as a partner with business, not a supplier of services

strategic staffing Process where HR assesses the cumulative vacancies an organization may have over a period of time, for instance five years in selected critical job families, and creates a plan to address the vacancies, including creating career paths or new retention strategies

skills inventory A computerized or manual system designed to take stock of information about current employees' experience, education, compensation history, and/or unique abilities

solutions analysis Analysis that creates a strategic plan to address labour surpluses or shortages, including creating an awareness of changes that continually occur in the workforce (e.g., retirements, turnover, etc.)

Sonnenfeld's career systems typology A model that facilitates the understanding of organization career systems as a strategic approach

staffing table A clear graphical view of all organizational jobs and the current number of employees at each job

strategic partnership A formal alliance between the business and human resources to maximize the value added of human resources to the business; human resources is seen as a partner with business, not a supplier of services

strategic partnering professional skills Business skills needed to be successful strategic business partners

strategic plan A macro-level set of directives that identify how the organization will achieve its mission and move toward its vision

strategic staffing Process where HR assesses the cumulative vacancies an organization may have over a period of time, for instance five years in selected critical job families, and creating a plan to address the vacancies, including creating career paths or new retention strategies

strategy An organization's plan of action, a pattern of decisions that determines objectives and purposes, and produces principles, policies, and plans for achieving these goals

succession management A systematic effort to ensure continuity of leadership across key positions within the organization

survivor syndrome A condition in which survivors of downsizing struggle with negative psychological states and work attitudes towards the organization

talent A person's recurring patterns of thought, feeling, or behaviour that can be productively applied

talent management The ability to attract, develop, and retain engaged talent to meet current and future needs

talent pool A group of employees who are being developed for advancement

talent show A monthly or quarterly meeting to discuss high potentials and determine their level of readiness for the next position

telecommuting (telework) A situation where an employee conducts at least some of his/her regular work from home instead of going into the office setting

temporary layoff Layoff where employees experience a temporary interruption of the employment relationship due to a lack of work and have the potential for recall

third country nationals (TCN) Citizens of a country other than the parent country

total turnover Total number of employees leaving an organization divided by the total number of employees in an organization, regardless of whether the turnover was voluntary or involuntary

trend analysis A method of forecasting that assumes past trends and ratios in employee movement are stable and indicative of future trends and ratios in employee movement

turnover Termination of an individual's employment with an organization

uncertainty avoidance The degree to which people are consistent and seek structure in their lives

utilization of talent The production-related activities of the workforce

vertical merger A merger of a buyer with a supplier or buyer

visible minorities Persons, other than Aboriginal peoples, who are non-Caucasian in race or non-white in colour

voluntary turnover Employee-initiated turnover, mainly in the form of quits or resignations

workforce planning Tools in an ERP system that use workforce demographic data to help human resources professionals understand current workforce trends, plan future needs, and link data related to headcount planning, budgeting, and key talent processes to programs such as recruiting and talent development

work-term change strategies Strategies aimed at minimizing or removing the need for mass headcount reductions in a time of labour surplus through changing the terms of employment for multiple employees

ENDNOTES

Chapter 1

1. VANOC Communications. (2003, July). "Vancouver Named Host City of the 2010 Olympic and Paralympic Winter Games!" Retrieved January 11, 2007, from http://www.vancouver2010.com/en/OrganizingCommittee/MediaCentre/NewsReleases/2006/01/12/74_0601121245-767.

2. VANOC Communications. (2005, November). Transcript of John Furlong's speech to the Vancouver Board of Trade. Retrieved January 11, 2007 from http://www.vancouver2010.com/en/OrganizingCommittee/PublicCommunications/Speeches/November2005VBOT.

3. VANOC Communications. (2006, October). Transcript of John Furlong's speech to the Vancouver Board of Trade. Retrieved January 11, 2007 from http://www.vancouver2010.com/en/OrganizingCommittee/PublicCommunications/Speeches/October2006VBOT.

4. "Job Opportunities." Retrieved March 23, 2009 from http://careers.peopleclick.com/careerscp/client_vanoc/external/en-ca/search.do.

5. Jackson, S.E. & Schuler, R. (1990). Human Resource Planning. Challenges for Industrial/Organizational Psychologists [Electronic version]. *American Psychologist,* 223–239; Walker, J.W. (1992). *Human Resource Strategy.* The United States: McGraw-Hill, Inc.; Boroski, J. W. (1990). Putting It Together: HR Planning in "3D" at Eastman Kodak [Electronic version]. *HR. Human Resource Planning,* 13(1), 45–56.

6. Rothwell, W.J. (2005). *Effective Succession Planning* (3rd ed.). New York: Amacom.

7. Jackson, S.E. & Schuler, R. S. (1990). Human resource planning. Challenges for Industrial/Organizational Psychologists [Electronic version]. *American Psychologist,* 223–239.

8. Ibid; Boroski, J. W. (1990). Putting it together: HR planning in "3D" at Eastman Kodak [Electronic version]. *HR. Human Resource Planning,* 13(1), 45–56; Walker, J.W. (1992). *Human Resource Strategy.* The United States: McGraw-Hill, Inc.

9. Smith, B.J., Boroski, J.W., & Davis, G.E. (1992). Human resource planning [Electronic version]. *Human Resource Management,* 31(1/2), 81–93.

10. Johnson, G.L. & Brown, J. (2004). Workforce planning not a common practice, IPMA-HR Study finds [Electronic version]. *Public Personnel Management,* 33(4), 379–388.

11. Smith, B.J., Boroski, J.W., & Davis, G.E. (1992). Human resource planning [Electronic version]. *Human Resource Management,* 31(1/2), 81–93; Walker, J.W. (1992). *Human Resource Strategy.* The United States: McGraw-Hill, Inc.

12. Bechet, T.P. & Walker, J.W. (1993). Aligning staff with business strategy [Electronic version]. *HR. Human Resource Planning,* 16(2), 1–16; Mills, D.Q. (2001). Planning with people in mind. *Harvard Business Review,* 97–105; Gubman, E. (2004). HR strategy and planning: From birth to business results [Electronic version]. *HR. Human Resource Planning,* 27(1), 13–23.

13. Walker, J.W. (1992). *Human Resource Strategy.* The United States: McGraw-Hill, Inc.

14. Gubman, E. (2004). HR strategy and planning: From birth to business results [Electronic version]. *HR. Human Resource Planning,* 27(1), 13–23.

15. Walker, J.W. (1992). *Human Resource Strategy.* The United States: McGraw-Hill, Inc.

16. Walker, J.W. (1992). *Human Resource Strategy.* The United States: McGraw-Hill, Inc; Schuler, R. S. (1989). Scanning the environment: Planning for human resource management and organizational change

[Electronic version]. *Human Resource Planning,* 12(4), 257–276; Mills, D.Q. (2001). Planning with people in mind. *Harvard Business Review,* 97–105; Walker, J. W. (1974). Evaluating the practical effectiveness of Human Resource Planning applications [Electronic version]. *Human Resource Management,* 13(1), 19–27.

17. Walker, J.W. (1992). *Human Resource Strategy.* The United States: McGraw-Hill, Inc.

18. Walker, J. W. (1974). Evaluating the practical effectiveness of Human Resource Planning applications [Electronic version]. *Human Resource Management,* 13(1), 19–27.

19. Wright, P. M., Dunford, B. B., & Snell, S. A. (2001). Human resources and the resource based view of the firm [Electronic version]. *Journal of Management, 27,* 701–721.

20. Boroski, J. W. (1990). Putting it together: HR planning in "3D" at Eastman Kodak [Electronic version]. *HR. Human Resource Planning,* 13(1), 45–56.

21. Smith, B.J., Boroski, J.W., & Davis, G.E. (1992). Human resource planning [Electronic version]. *Human Resource Management,* 31(1/2), 81–93; Bechet, T.P. & Walker, J.W. (1993). Aligning staff with business strategy [Electronic version]. *HR. Human Resource Planning,* 16(2), 1–16.

22. Buhler, P.M. (2006). Managing in the new millennium: Are you addressing the talent shortage? [Electronic version]. *SuperVision,* 67(11), 19–22.

23. Ulrich, D. & Smallwood, N. (2004). Capitalizing on capabilities [Electronic version]. *Harvard Business Review,* 82(6), 119–127; Wright, P. M., Dunford, B. B., & Snell, S. A. (2001). Human resources and the resource based view of the firm [Electronic version]. *Journal of Management, 27,* 701–721.

24. Ibid.

25. Grundy, T. (1997). Human resource management—a strategic approach [Electronic version]. *Long Range Planning,* 30(4), 507–517.

26. Walker, J.W. (1992). *Human Resource Strategy.* The United States: McGraw-Hill, Inc; Grundy, T. (1997). Human resource management—a strategic approach [Electronic version]. *Long Range Planning,* 30(4), 507–517.

27. Boroski, J. W. (1990). Putting it together: HR planning in "3D" at Eastman Kodak [Electronic version]. *HR. Human Resource Planning,* 13(1), 45–56.

28. Ibid.

29. Walker, J.W. (1998). Are we global yet? [Electronic version]. *HR Human Resource Planning,* 21(4), 8–10.

30. Walker, J. W. (1990). Human resource planning, 1990's style [Electronic version]. *HR. Human Resource Planning,* 13(4), 229–240.

31. Grundy, T. (1997). Human resource management—a strategic approach [Electronic version]. *Long Range Planning,* 30(4), 507–517.

32. Schuler, R. S. (1989). Scanning the environment: Planning for human resource management and organizational change [Electronic version]. *Human Resource Planning,* 12(4), 257–276.

33. Grundy, T. (1997). Human resource management—a strategic approach [Electronic version]. *Long Range Planning,* 30(4), 507–517.

34. Johnson, G.L. & Brown, J. (2004). Workforce planning not a common practice, IPMA-HR Study finds [Electronic version]. *Public Personnel Management,* 33(4), 379–388.

35. Biesada, A. (n.d.). Zara International, Inc. Retrieved April 26, 2007, from http://www.hoovers.com/zara/--ID—109755--/free-co-factsheet.xhtml.

36. Capell, K. (2006, September 4). Fashion conquistador. *BusinessWeek,* 38–39.

37. "Inditex and Trent of the Tata Group agree to open stores in India beginning 2010." Retrieved March 23, 2009, from http://www.inditex.com/en/press/press_releases/extend/00000689.

38. Gubman, E. (2004). HR strategy and planning: From birth to business results [Electronic version]. *HR. Human Resource Planning,* 27(1), 13–23.

39. Thomas, D. (2006). World-class HR focuses on planning [Electronic version]. *Personnel Today,* 6.

40. Wright, P. M., Dunford, B. B., & Snell, S. A. (2001). Human resources and the resource based view of the firm [Electronic version]. *Journal of Management, 27,* 701–721; Ulrich, D. & Smallwood, N. (2004). Capitalizing on capabilities [Electronic version]. *Harvard Business Review,* 82(6), 119–127.

41. Restivo, K. (2005, March 30). Cognos to add 1,600 to workforce by 2008. [National Edition]. *National Post,* p. FP.3.

42. Walker, J.W. (1992). *Human Resource Strategy.* The United States: McGraw-Hill, Inc.

43. Likierman, Sir A. & Ready, D.A. (March 2008). How Effective Are Your Company's Strategic Talent Management Initiatives? Retrieved March 23, 2009 from http://www.talentmgt.com/assessment_evaluation/2008/March/576/index.php.

44. Gubman, E. (2004). HR strategy and planning: From birth to business results [Electronic version]. *HR. Human Resource Planning,* 27(1), 13–23.

45. Voelker, M.P. (2006). Optimizing the human supply chain [Electronic version]. *Intelligent Enterprise,* 9(1), 35–37.

46. Dofasco, Solutions in Steel. (n.d.). Talented, dedicated and energized people. Retrieved February 4, 2007, from http://www.dofasco.ca/bins/content_page.asp?cid=339-9516-9557-9864.

47. Mills, D.Q. (2001). Planning with people in mind. *Harvard Business Review,* 97–105.

48. Pitts, G. (2005, November 5). GM economic aftershocks set to hit southern Ontario. *The Globe and Mail,* p. B22.

49. Van Alphen, T. (2009, February 18). CAW set for crunch time talks. *Toronto Star,* pp B1, B7.

50. Lam, S. S. K. & Schaubroeck, J. (1998). Integrating HR planning and organizational strategy [Electronic version]. *Human Resource Management Journal,* 8(3), 5–19; Schuler, R. S. (1989). Scanning the environment: Planning for human resource management and organizational change [Electronic version]. *Human Resource Planning,* 12(4), 257–276.

51. Schuler, R. S. (1987). Personnel and human resource management choices and organizational strategy. *HR. Human Resource Planning,* 10(1), 1–17; Jackson, S.E. & Schuler, R. S. (1990). Human resource planning. Challenges for Industrial/Organizational Psychologists [Electronic version]. *American Psychologist,* 223–239; Bechet, T.P. & Walker, J.W. (1993). Aligning staff with business strategy [Electronic version]. *HR. Human Resource Planning,* 16(2), 1–16.

52. Smith, B.J., Boroski, J.W., & Davis, G.E. (1992). Human resource planning [Electronic version]. *Human Resource Management,* 31(1/2), 81–93.

53. Edwards, C. (2006, January 9). Inside intel. *Business Week,* p. 46.

54. Smith, B.J., Boroski, J.W., & Davis, G.E. (1992). Human resource planning [Electronic version]. *Human Resource Management,* 31(1/2), 81–93.

55. Mintzberg, H. & Quinn, J. B. (1992). *The Strategy Process—Concepts and Contexts.* Englewood Cliffs, NJ: Prentice Hall.

56. Harrison, J. S. & St. John, C. H. (2002). *Foundations in Strategic Management.* Ohio: South Western.

57. Ibid.

58. Duane, M. J. (1996). *Customized Human Resource Planning.* Wesport, CT: Quorum Books.

59. Harrison, J. S. & St. John, C. H. (2002). *Foundations in strategic management.* Ohio: South Western; Miles, R. E. & Snow, C. C. (1984). Designing strategic human resources systems. *Organization Dynamics,* 13(1), 36–52.

60. Harrison, J. S. & St. John, C. H. (2002). *Foundations in Strategic Management.* Ohio: South Western.

61. Walker, J.W. (1992). *Human Resource Strategy.* The United States: McGraw-Hill, Inc.

62. Duane, M. J. (1996). *Customized Human Resource Planning.* Wesport, CT: Quorum Books.

63. Ibid.

64. Miles, R.E. & Snow, C.C. (1984). Designing strategic human resources systems [Electronic version.] *Organization Dynamics,* 13(1), 36–52.

65. Jackson, S.E. & Schuler, R. (1990). Human resource planning. Challenges for industrial/organizational psychologists [Electronic version]. *American Psychologist,* 223–239.

66. Schuler, R. S. (1987). Personnel and human resource management choices and organizational strategy. *HR. Human Resource Planning,* 10(1), 1–17.

67. BioWare Corp. (n.d.) About BioWare. Retrieved May 2, 2007, from http://www.bioware.com/bioware_info/about/.

68. CTV.ca News Staff. (2005, March 21). Canada the new hotspot for video game creators. Retrieved May 2, 2007, from http://www.ctv.ca/servlet/ArticleNews/story/CTVNews/20050321/canimators050316/20050321/.

69. Mills, D.Q. (2001). Planning with people in mind. *Harvard Business Review,* 97–105.

70. Brush, M. C. & Ruse, D. H. (2005). Driving strategic success through human capital planning: How Corning links business and HR strategy to improve the value and impact of its HR function [Electronic version]. *HR. Human Resource Planning, 28*(1), 49–60.

71. Davenport, T. H. (1993). *Process innovation.* Boston, Mass: Harvard Business School Press.

72. Walker, J.W. (1992). *Human Resource Strategy.* The United States: McGraw-Hill, Inc; Boudreau, J.W. & Ramstead, P.M. (2005). Talentship and the new paradigm for human resource management: From professional practices to strategic talent decision science. *HR. Human Resource Planning, 28*(2), 17–26.

73. Duane, M. J. (1996). *Customized human resource planning.* Wesport, CT: Quorum Books; Jackson, S.E. & Schuler, R. (1990). Human resource planning. Challenges for industrial/organizational psychologists [Electronic version]. *American Psychologist,* 223–239.

74. Effron, M., Gandossy, R., & Goldsmith, M. (Ed.). *Human Resources in the* 21st *Century.* (2003). Hoboeken, New Jersey: John Wiley and Sons.

75. Boudreau, J.W. & Ramstead, P.M. (2005). Talentship and the new paradigm for human resource management: From professional practices to strategic talent decision science [Electronic version]. *HR. Human Resource Planning, 28*(2), 17–26.

76. Schiemann, W. A. (2006). People equity: A new paradigm for measuring and managing human capital [Electronic version]. *HR. Human Resource Planning, 29*(1), 34–44.

77. Gubman, E. (2004). HR strategy and planning: From birth to business results [Electronic version]. *HR. Human Resource Planning, 27*(1), 13–23.

78. Davenport, T. H. (1993). *Process Innovation.* Boston, Mass: Harvard Business School Press.

79. Zabarenko, D. (2007, May 2). Arctic thawing faster than forecast. *Toronto* Star, p. A3.

80. Mittelstaedt, M. (2007, January 31). The fallout of global warming: 1000 years. *The Globe and Mail,* p. A1.

Chapter 2

1. Pirruccello. J. E. (Nov. 2005). Contingent worker protection from client company discrimination: Statutory coverage, gaps, and the role of the common law. *Texas Law Review.* Austin: Nov 2005. Vol. 84, Iss. 1; pg. 191, 33 pgs.

2. Vosko, L. F., Zukewich, N. & Cranford C (2003.) "Precarious jobs: A new typology of employment." *Perspectives on Labour and Income,* vol. 4, no. 10.

3. http://www.statcan.ca/Daily/English/030211/d030211a.htm

4. Source: http://www.jobfutures.ca/en/brochure/JobFuture.pdf, page 3.

5. Gulli, C. & Lunau, K. "Adding Fuel to the Doctor Crisis," *Maclean's.* Toronto: Jan 14, 2008. Vol. 121, Iss. 1; pg. 62, 6 pgs.; CBC News, Canada's doctor shortage to worsen without changes: Fraser report, Monday, August 28, 2006; Bains, C. "Severe doctors' shortage predicted in Canada." The Canadian Press, Canada Health Profile; Kingston, A. "Doctors for Hire" *Maclean's.* Toronto: May 19, 2008. Vol. 121, Iss. 19; pg. 46, 1 pgs; Anonymous. "Fixing a Doctor Crisis". *Maclean's.* Toronto: Mar 17, 2008. Vol. 121, Iss. 10; pg. 2, 1 pgs.

6. Mobley, W. (1982) "Employee Turnover: Causes, Consequences and Control." Reading: Addison-Wesley.

7. Mobley, W., Griffeth, R., Hand, H & Meglino, B (1979). A review and conceptual analysis of the employee turnover process. *Psychological Bulletin,* 86, 493–522; Steers, R. & Mowday, R. (1981) Employee Turnover and Post Decision Accommodation Process: in L. Cummings and B. Staw "Research in Organizational Behaviour." JAI Press, Connecticut.

8. http://www.jobfutures.ca/en/brochure/JobFuture.pdf, page 4.

9. Slavenski, L. & Buckner, M. (November 15, 1993). "Succession Planning." American Society for Training & Development.

10. Helmer-Hirschberg, O. (1966). *The Use of the Delphi Technique in Problems of Educational Innovations.* RAND Corporation, Santa Monica, CA.

11. Milkovich et. al. 1972 ; Dyer and Blancero 1992.

12. A. L. Delbecq and A. H VandeVen. "A Group Process Model for Problem Identification and Program Planning." *Journal Of Applied Behavioral Science* VII (July/August, 1971), 466–91 and A. L. Delbecq, A. H. VandeVen, and D. H. Gustafson, *Group Techniques for Program Planners* (Glenview, Illinois: Scott Foresman and Company, 1975).

13. Martin, L. (2001) "More Jobs for the Boys?: Succession Planning in SMEs," *Women in Management Review* 16(5): 222–31; Bachkaniwala, D., Wright, M. and Ram, M. (2001) "Succession in South Asian Family Businesses in the UK." *International Small Business Journal* 19(4), 15–27.

14. Bjuggren, P. and Sund, L. (2001) "Strategic Decision Making in Intergenerational Succession of Small- and Medium-Size Family-owned Businesses." *Family Business Review* 14(1), 11–23.

15. Davis, P. S. and Harveston, P. D. (1998) "The Influence of Family on the Family Business Succession Process: A Multi-Generational Perspective." *Entrepreneurship Theory and Perspective* 22(3): 31–49; Kets de Vries, M. F. R. (1993). "The Dynamics of Family Controlled Firms: The Good News and the Bad News." *Organizational Dynamics* 21(3), 59–71.

Chapter 3

1. Statistics Canada. (2006). Canada's population. *The Daily.* Retrieved June 18, 2007, from http://www.statcan.ca/Daily/English/060927/d060927a.htm.

2. Cross, P. & Bowlby, G. (2006). The Alberta economic juggernaut: The boom on the rose. [Electronic version]. *Canadian Economic Observer,* 19(9), 3.1–3.12. Retrieved September 23, 2007, from http://www.statcan.ca/english/freepub/11-010-XIB/11-010-XIB2006009.pdf.

3. Alberta Human Resources and Employment. (2005). Alberta's Aging Labour Force and Skills Shortages. Retrieved September 23, 2007, from http://employment.alberta.ca/documents/LMI/LMI-LMF_Ageing_Skill_Shortages.pdf.

4. Government of Alberta. (2009). Labour Force Developments January 2009. Retrieved from http://www.finance.alberta.ca/aboutalberta/labour_force/2009/2009_01_developments.pdf.

5. Terrett, J. (2006). Addressing Alberta's skills shortage [Electronic version]. *Plant,* 1(1), 3.

6. Payne, S. (2008). Survey Find Talent Shortage is Largest Concern for E&PS. *Oil & Gas Investor-This Week* 16(11), 3. Retrieved April 21, 2009, from Business Source Complete.

7. Government of Alberta (2008). Workforce Partnerships. Retrieved from http://employment.alberta.ca/cps/rde/xchg/hre/hs.xsl/3105.html.

8. Potter, M. (2006, June/July). Stemming the loss of knowledge. *HR Professional,* 21–26.

9. Thorpe, J. (2007, January 22). Workers may be real shortage. *Financial Post,* p. FP1.

10. Building and Educating Tomorrow's Workforce. (2006). Inventory government of Alberta initiatives.

11. Dychtwald, K., Erickson, T.J., & Morison, R. (2006). *Workforce Crisis.* Boston: Harvard Business School Press.

12. Meisinger, S. (2005). Looming talent, skills gap challenge HR. [Electronic version]. *HR Magazine,* 50 (10), 12.

13. World Health Organization (2008). Monitoring education and training for health workers. *Spotlight on Statistics: A fact file on health workforce statistics.* Retrieved from http://www.who.int/hrh/statistics/spotlight3/en/.

14. World Health Organization (2008). "World Health Report calls for return to primary health care approach." Kazakhstan.

15. Borsellino, M. (2006). It's not just about money anymore [Electronic version]. *Medical Post,* 42(29), 37–38.

16. Leger, L. (2006). Canada must train more MDs: Fraser Institute [Electronic version]. *Medical Post,* 42(28), 6.

17. Love, M. (2006). Manitoba town finds job sharing one solution to rural MD shortages [Electronic version]. *Medical Post,* 42(20), 56.

18. McKenna, V. (2006). A nurse's story: How not enough nurses is harming quality care [Electronic version]. *Our Times,* 25(1), 14.

19. (2008, January 8). Shipping Industry faces severe labour shortage over next decade. *Daily Commercial News and Construction Record.* Retrieved February 24, 2009 from http://www.dailycommercialnews.ca/ article/id25940.

20. Sorensen, J. (2006, November 27). ASTTBC forecasting critical shortfall by 2010. *Journal of Commerce,* AT3.

21. Kennedy, P. (2006, August 9). B.C. aviation firms face skills shortage. *The Globe and Mail,* p. B3.

22. George-Cosh, D. (2008, January 21). Labour Shortage could cripple Canada's tech industry: report [Electronic Version]. *Financial Post.* Retrieved April 21, 2009 from http://www.financialpost.com/story.html?id=253575.

23. Bolan, S. (2001). Numbers prove skills gap real. *Computing Canada,* 27(15), 24.

24. Sankey, D. (2006, March 14). Another inconvenient truth. *The National Post:* WK5.

25. Sallot, J. (2007, January 1). The hottest postsecondary field? Intelligence. *The Globe and Mail,* p. A2.

26. Coy, P. & Ewing, J. (2007, April 9). Where are all the workers? *Business Week,* 28–31.

27. Lane, K., Pollner, F. (2008). How to address China's talent shortage. *McKinsey Quarterly,* 2008 (3). Retrieved April 21, 2009 from Business Source Complete.

28. Ford, A. (2007, May 1). Disabled form untapped talent pool; Pan Pacific Hotel manager challenges industry to review hiring practices; [Final Edition]. [Electronic version]. *The Province Vancouver B.C.,* p. A29.

29. Bowes, B (2007, January 27). Co-op option. *Winnipeg Free Press,* p. G.1.

30. Taylor, P. S. (2005, March 14–27). Help wanted. *Canadian Business,* 29–34.

31. Waisberg, D. (2006, November 8). Top gun for hire, *National Post,* p. WK1.

32. Khanna, S. (2005). An HR planning model for outsourcing. [Electronic version]. *HR. Human Resource Planning,* 28 (4), 37–43.

33. Ibid.

34. Ibid.

35. Hamm, S. & Ante, S. E. (2005, April 18). Beyond blue. [Electronic version]. *Business Week,* 3929, 68.

36. BMO Financial Group to outsource human resources processing services to Exult, Inc. (2003, April 23). *HRO Today.* Retrieved June 20, 2004, from http://www.hrotoday.com/News.asp?id=224

37. Walsh, B. (2006). HR needs to keep evolving to tackle future challenges [Electronic version]. *Business Day,* 10.

38. Howe, J. (2006). The rise of crowdsourcing. *Wired.* Retrieved March 13, 2007 from http://www.wired.com/wired/archive/14.06/crowds.html.

39. Schick, S. (2006, August 10). 'Crowdsourcing'—idea power from the people. *The Globe and Mail,* p. B6.

40. Polivka, A. E. (1996). Contingent and alternative work arrangements, defined. [Electronic version]. *Monthly Labour Review,* 3–9.

41. Ibid.

42. Cardon, M. S. (2003). Contingent labor as an enabler of entrepreneurial growth. [Electronic version]. *Human Resources Management,* 43(4), 357.

43. More contingent workers are a blessing and sometimes a challenge for H.R. (2006). *HR Focus* 83(1), S1–S4.

44. Greble, T.C. (1997, February). A leading role for HR in alternative staffing. *HR Magazine,* 42(2), 99–104.

45. More contingent workers are a blessing and sometimes a challenge for H.R. (2006). *HR Focus* 83(1), S1–S4.

46. Bowlby, G. (2001). The labour market: Year-end review. *Statistics Canada,* 2(1). Retrieved September 23, 2007 from http://www.statcan.gc.ca/english/studies/75-001/00101/hi-fs_200101_01_a.html

47. Ibid.

48. Labour Statistics Division (2003). The Canadian labour market at a glance. Retrieved August 29, 2007 from http://www.statcan.ca/english/freepub/71-222-XIE/71-222-XIE2004000.pdf.

49. Ibid.

50. Ibid.

51. Contingent workforce brings more questions than answers. (2005). *HR Focus,* 82(7). 26–7.

52. Daly, R. (2006, December 8). MPPs target 'temp' boom. *Toronto Star,* p. A1. Talaga, T. (2008, December 10). Ontario unveils new rights for temp workers [Electronic version]. *Toronto Star,* 1-3. Retrieved February 25, 2009 from http://www.thestar.com/print Article/551312.

53. MacDougall, S. L. (2005). Identifying tangible costs, benefits and risks of an investment in intellectual capital: Contracting contingent knowledge workers. [Electronic version]. *Journal of Intellectual Capital,* 6(1), 53–71.

54. More contingent workers are a blessing and sometimes a challenge for H.R. (2006). *HR Focus* 83(1), S1–S4.

55. McCallum, C. (2006). Unstable work hours a fact of life for many employees [Electronic version]. *OH & S Canada,* 22(6): 25.

56. Manage overtime: Pros and cons of overtime. *Department of Trade and Industry.* Retrieved March 1, 2007, from http://www.businesslink.gov.uk/bdotg/action/detail?r.l1=1073858787&r.l3=1074414310&type=RESOURCES&itemId=1074415479&r.l2=1073858926&r.s=sc.

57. Cohen, T. (2007, June 5). CIBC faces lawsuit. *Canadian Press.* Retrieved June 22, 2007, from http://www.thestar.com/printArticle/221663.

58. CIBC News. (2007). Suit seeks overtime pay for CIBC tellers. Retrieved June 22, 2007, from http://www.cbc.ca/money/story/2007/06/05/cibctellersuit.html.

59. Olive, D. (2007, June 8). Overtime lawsuit is hardly surprising. Retrieved June 24, 2007 from http://www.thestar.com/printArticle/223032.

60. Deveau, S. (2007, June 11). Companies divided on overtime pay issues. [National Edition]. *National Post,* p. FP2.

61. Treatment of overtime wages for employees. (2005). *Human Resources Advisor Newsletter,* 3.

62. British Columbia Ministry of Labour and Citizen's Services (2002). Employment Standards Act Factsheet. Employee or independent contractor? Retrieved November 27, 2006 from http://www.labour.gov.bc.ca/esb/facshts/pdfs/employee-or-contractor.pdf.

63. Hargrove, B. (2005). In praise of less work-time: Canadians work too much, need more time for rest and families. *CCPA Monitor,* 12(5), 7.

64. Campione, M. & Williams, L. (2006). Diverse labour force demands diverse options. [Electronic version]. *Canadian HR Reporter,* 19(18), 14.

65. Dychtwald, K., Erickson, T.J., & Morison, R. (2006). *Workforce Crisis.* Boston: Harvard Business School Press.

66. Hammer, L. B. & Barbara, K. M. (1997). Toward an integration of alternative work. *HR Human Resource Planning,* 20(2), 28–36.

67. Dychtwald, K., Erickson, T.J., & Morison, R. (2006). *Workforce crisis.* Boston: Harvard Business School Press.

68. Dychtwald, K., Erickson, T.J., & Morison, R. (2006). *Workforce crisis.* Boston: Harvard Business School Press.

69. Ibid.

70. Conlin, M. (2006, December 11). Smashing the clock. *Business Week,* 60.

71. Campione, M. & Williams, L. (2006). Diverse labour force demands diverse options. [Electronic version]. *Canadian HR Reporter,* 19(18), 14.

72. Ministerial Statement (2006, December 12). Statement to the Legislature by the Honourable Steve Peters Minister of Labour regarding: The end of mandatory retirement.

73. Khanna, S. (2005). An HR planning model for outsourcing. [Electronic version]. *HR. Human Resource Planning,* 28 (4), 37–43.

74. Meisinger, S. (2005). Looming talent, skills gap challenge HR. [Electronic version]. *HR Magazine,* 50 (10), 12.

75. Duane, M. J. (1996). *Customized Human Resource Planning.* Westport, Connecticut: Quorum Books.

76. Ministry of Labour. (2006). Termination of employment and severance pay. Retrieved September 23, 2007 from http://www.labour.gov.on.ca/english/es/factsheets/fstermination.html.

77. Ying, J, Ash, A. D. & Sly, T. (2007). Preparing for a pandemic [Electronic version]. *The Internal Auditor,* 64(3), 64–68.

78. Cooper, J. (2007). Global warnings [Electronic version]. *CMA Management,* 81(2), 52–54.

79. Ibid.

80. Ying, J, Ash, A. D. & Sly, T. (2007). Preparing for a pandemic [Electronic version]. *The Internal Auditor,* 64(3), 64–68.

81. Cooper, J. (2007). Global warnings [Electronic version]. *CMA Management,* 81(2), 52–54.

Chapter 4

1. Associated Press. (April 7, 2009). *Canada Offers to Help Auto Sector.* Retrieved June 1, 2009 from http://blog.cleveland.com/business/2009/04/canada_offers_help_to_auto_sec.html; Bronski, C. (April 30, 2008) *CAW Agrees to Massive Concessions with Ford Canada.* Retrieved June 1, 2009 from http://www.wsws.org/articles/2008/apr2008/caw-a30.shtml; Krollicki, K. (May 25, 2009). *Canada Union Ratifies GM Concessions.* Retrieved June 1, 2009 from http://www.bclocalnews.com/news/national/46016352.html?c=y&curSection=/bc_thompson_nicola/kamloopsthisweek&curTitle= National%20News; Owram, K. (April 16, 2009). *Canada Says Chrysler Must Slash Labour Costs,* manufacturing.net. Retrieved on June 1, 2009 from http://www.manufacturing.net/News-Canada-Says-Chrysler-Must-Slash-Labor-Costs-041609.aspx?menuid=276; Ramsay, J. (March 12, 2009). *GM Canada Workers Approve Contract Concessions.* Retrieved June 1, 2009 from http://www.autoblog.com/2009/03/12/gm-canada-workers-approve-contract-concessions/.

2. Marshall, R., & Briggs, V. (1989). *Labor Economics, Theory, Institutions and Public Policy* (6th ed.). Homewood: Irwin.

3. Wagar, T. H. (1997). Factors affecting permanent workforce reduction: Evidence from large Canadian organizations. *Canadian Journal of Administrative Sciences,* 14(3), 303–314.

4. Barrick, M. R., Mount, M. K., & Strauss, J. P. (1994). Antecedents of involuntary turnover due to a reduction in force. *Personnel Psychology,* 47(3), 515.

5. Cameron, K. S. (1994). Strategies for successful organizational downsizing. *Human Resource Management,* 33(2), 183.

6. Cameron, K., Freeman, S., & Mishra, S. (1991). Best practices in white-collar downsizing: Managing contradictions. *Academy of Management Executive,* 5, 57–73.

7. Cravotta, R. & Kleiner, B. H. 2001. New developments concerning reductions in force. *Management Research News,* 24(3/4), 4; Dugan, R. D. (1996). Corporate executions: The ugly truth about layoffs—How corporate greed is shattering lives, companies, and communities. *Personnel Psychology,* 49(4), 998; White, S. (2003). Reduction in force—Benefit or detriment? A look at some tangible and intangible results of federal sector reductions in force (RIF). *International Journal of Public Administration,* 26(10/11), 1145.

8. Belcourt, M. & McBey, K., (2006). *Strategic Human Resources Planning,* (3rd ed.). Toronto: Thomson Nelson.

9. Woolhouse, M. (2005, April 28). Tax hike is aimed mostly for schools, average bill would jump $232 if measure passes. *The Boston Globe,* p.1.

10. Mulrane, M., (March 5, 2008), TD Economics Special Report: What's Behind the Canadian Manufacturing Sector Recession? Retrieved June 5, 2009 from http://www.td.com/economics/special/mm0308_canmfg.pdf; Weir, E. (2007, May). Canada's manufacturing crisis, *CCPA Monitor,* 14 (1), 17.

11. Zatzick, C. D., Iverson, R. D., (2006). High-involvement management and workforce reduction: Competitive advantage or disadvantage? *Academy of Management Journal,* 49(5), 999–1015.

12. Statistics Canada, March, (2004), *Have permanent layoffs increased in Canada?* Catalogue No. 11F0019MIE-No. 218, Ottawa, ON: Business and Labour Market Studies Analysis Division.

13. Statistics Canada, September, (1997). *Permanent layoffs in Canada: Overview and longitudinal analysis,* Catalogue No. 11F0019MPE-No. 103, Ottawa, ON: Business and Labour Market Studies.

14. Smith, P. C. & Walker, J. W. (2000). Layoff policies as a competitive edge. *Competitiveness Review,* 10(2), 132.

15. McCune, J. T., Beatty, R. W., & Montagno, R. V., (1988). Downsizing: Practices in Manufacturing Firms. *Human Resource Management,* 27(2), 145.

16. Rardin, K. (2006, November 27). *Merge Healthcare announces "rightsizing" and reorganization initiative.* Retrieved February 1, 2007 from http://www.nema.org/media/ind/20061127a.cfm.

17. Dichter, M. & Trank, M. (1991). Learning to Manage Reductions-in-Force. *Management Review,* 80(3), 40.

18. Lau, J. (2002). Auditing human capital. *Malaysian Business,* (July 16), 60.

19. Friesen, J. (1997). Mandatory notice and jobless duration of displaced workers. *Industrial and Labor Relations Review,* 50 (4), 652–666.

20. People First Solutions Inc. (2008). *The hidden cost of attrition: Why retaining top talent remains mission critical.* Retrieved on June 14, 2008 from http://www.peoplefirstsolutions.com/resources/reports/pfs cost_of_attrition.pdf.

21. MacGregor, D. (2005). Yes: Right to work is fundamental, even for people over 65. *CCPA Monitor,* 12 (7), 24.

22. Human Resources and Social Development Canada. (2008, February 15). *Mandatory Retirement in Canada Legislation of General Application.* Retrieved April 13, 2008 from http://www.hrsdc.gc.ca/en/lp/spila/clli/eslc/19Mandatory_Retirement.shtml.

23. Flavelle, Dana. (2007, October 11). Menu raises recall costs, to slash jobs. *The Toronto Star,* 417.

24. Hammond, M. (2007, May 12). MTD plant closes, 400 jobs lost. *Guelph Mercury,* 573.

25. Keenan, G. (2007, April 5). Stelco cuts 300 jobs, shuts hot strip mill. *The Globe and Mail,* CTVglobemedia Publishing Inc.

26. Canfor says Mackenzie, B.C. mill to open but 130 jobs will be lost. (2007, July 27). *Canadian Press,* 600.

27. Smith, J. J. (2007, November 15). Casino Windsor cuts workers as sales fall. *The Detroit News,* 343.

28. Lehrer, S. (1997). Effectively coping with downsizing: A four-phase model. *The Government Accountants Journal,* 45(4), 12.

29. Cameron, K., Sutton, R., & Whetton, D. (1988). *Readings in organizational decline: Frameworks, research and implications.* Boston, MA: Ballinger.

30. De Meuse, K., Bergmann, T., Vanderheiden, P., & Roraff, C. (2004). New evidence regarding organizational downsizing and a firm's financial performance: A long-term analysis. *Journal of Managerial Issues,* 16 (2), 155.

31. Iverson, R. & Pullman, J. (2000). Determinant of voluntary turnover and layoffs in an environment of repeated downsizing following a merger: An event history analysis. *Journal of Management,* 26, 977.

32. Cameron, K., Freeman, S., & Mishra, S. (1991). Best practices in white-collar downsizing: Managing contradictions. *Academy of Management Executive,* 5, 57–73.

33. Mirvis, P. (1997). Human resource management: Leaders, laggards, and followers. The *Academy of Management Executive, 11(2),* 43.

34. Sutton, R. I. (1983). Managing organizational death, *Human Resource Management,* 22(4), 391.

35. Knapp, T. J. (2001). How to set up a reduction-in-force program. *Journal of Organizational Excellence,* 20(4), 75; Mone, M. (1994). Relationship between self-concepts, aspirations, emotions and intent to leave a downsized organization. *Human Resource Management,* 33, 381–398; Simone, A. & Kleiner, B., H. (2004a). Workforce reduction guidelines. *Southern Business Review,* 29(2), 16.

36. Robert, M. & Lyle, Y. (1994). Planning for a restructured, revitalized organization. *Sloan Management Review,* 35, 81–92.

37. Rousseau, D. (1993). Psychological and implied contracts in organizations. *Employee Responsibilities and Rights Journal, 2,* 121–139.

38. De Meuse, Kenneth P., & Tornow, W. W., (1993). The tie that binds has become very, very frayed! *HR Human Resource Planning.* 3(3), 203; Robinson, S., Kraatz, M., & Rousseau, D., (1994). Changing the obligations and the psychological contract, *Academy of Management Journal,* 37, 437–452.

39. Henkoff, R. (1990). Cost cutting: How to do it right. *Fortune,* 121(8), 40–47.

40. Bagshaw, M. (1998). Coaching, mentoring and the sibling organization. *Industrial & Commercial Training,* 30(3), 87–89.

41. Noer, D. (1993). Healing the Wound: Overcoming the trauma of layoffs and revitalizing downsized organizations. In G. Huber & Glick (Eds.), *Organizational change and redesign: Ideas and insights for improving performance* (pp. 19–65). New York: Oxford University Press.

42. Boroson, W. & Burgess, L. (1992). Survivors' Syndrome, *Across the Board,* 41–47.

43. Falkenberg, L., Stone, T., & Meltz, N. (1999). *Human Resource Management in Canada* (4th ed.). Toronto: Dryde.

44. Brockner, J., Davy, J., & Carter, C. (1985). Layoffs, self-esteem, and survivor guilt: motivational, attitudinal and affective consequences. *Organizational Behaviour and Human Decision Process,* 36, 229–244.

45. O'Neill, & H., Lenn, J. (1995). Voices of survivors: Words that CEO's should hear. *Academy of Management Executives,* 9, 23–34.

46. Rousseau, D. (1995). *Psychological contracts in organizations.* Thousand Oaks, CA: Sage Publications.

47. Smith, P. C. & Walker, J. W. (2000). Layoff policies as a competitive edge. *Competitiveness Review,* 10(2), 132.

48. Newell, H., Dopson S. (1996). Muddle in the middle: Organizational restructuring and middle management careers. *Personnel Review,* 25(5), 4–20.

49. O'Neill, H., Lenn, J. (1995). Voices of survivors: Words that CEO's should hear. *Academy of Management Executives,* 9, 23–34.

50. Pfeil, M, Setterberg, A, ORouke, J. (2003). The art of downsizing: communicating lay-offs to key stakeholders. *Journal of Communication Management,* 8(2), 130–141.

51. Over 50 Dell staff laid off in Edmonton; company cuts workforce 10%. (2007, October 12). *The Edmonton Journal,* 315.

52. Auld, A. (2006, September 7). More than 450 CanJet employees to lose jobs with end of scheduled flights, *Canadian Press,* 557.

53. Noer, D. (1995). After the Pink Slip, *Executive Female,* 18(4), 42.

54. Guiniven, J. (1999). Communicating downsizing: Companies should address grief not guilt. *Public Relations Tactics,* 6 (6).

55. Stoner, C., & Hartman, R. (1997). Organizational therapy: Building survivor health and competitiveness. *S.A.M. Advanced Management Journal,* 62(3), 25–41.

56. Murray Axmith & Associates. (1990). Canadian Termination Practices Survey, Toronto, Ontario.

57. Beltrame, J. (2008, April 16). Canada is losing high quality jobs, bank report warns. *The Spectator,* p. A13.

58. BNA Editorial staff. (2003). *Grievance Guide,* 11th edition, Washington, DC: Bureau of National Affairs Inc. Retrieved July 01, 2005, from http://findarticles.com/p/articles/mi_m3495/is_7_49/ai_n6127820.

59. Giroday, G. (2007, June 21). Vancouver layoffs cost city AirCan jobs up to 100 workers here may get bumped. *Winnipeg Free Press,* 393.

60. Santin, A. (2007, April 25). 200 face job loss at air Canada. *Winnipeg Free Press,* 423.

Chapter 5

1. Cappelli, Peter, (2008). Talent Management for the Twenty-First Century, *Harvard Business Review,* Vol. 86, Issue 3, p. 74–81, retrieved June 23, 2008.

2. Chambers, E.G., Foulton, M., Handfield-Jones, H., Hankin, S.M., & Edward G., (1998). The War for Talent, *McKinsey Quarterly,* Issue 3.

3. Effron, M., Rowan, L. and Sobczak, E. (2007). The talent crisis is real, *Workforce Management,* Vol. 86, Issue 15, p. 57.

4. Schiemann, W.A. (May 2008). From Crunching Numbers to Counting Human Capital, *Financial Executive,* p. 53–55, retrieved electronically June 30, 2008.

5. Axelrod, E.L., Handfield-Jones, H. & Welsh, T.A. (2001). War for Talent, Part Two, *McKinsey Quarterly,* Issue 2, p. 9–12.

6. Chambers, E.G., Foulton, M., Handfield-Jones, H., Hankin, S.M., & Edward G. (1998). The War For Talent, *McKinsey Quarterly,* Issue 3.

7. Talent Matters, Shaping Talent Strategies in a Changing World (March 2007). *Toronto Financial Services Alliance and Deloitte,* p. 4.

8. Ibid., p. 4.

9. http://22848.vws.magma.ca/EPRO_2527/presentations/plen6/player.html, retrieved June 30, 2008.

10. Ibid.

11. Eubanks, M. (June, 2008). Being on the Offensive, Canadian Tire's IT Future, Case Study from *The Conference Board of Canada, Education and Learning,* p. 3.

12. Grigsby, Fred R. (June 2008). Lining Up Individual and Organizational Value Propositions, CN's IT Future. Case Study from *The Conference Board of Canada, Education and Learning.*

13. Halley, R. (June, 2008). Replacing Retiring IT Workers. Case Study from *The Conference Board of Canada, Education and Learning.*

14. Eubanks, M. (June, 2008). Being on the Offensive, Canadian Tire's IT Future, Case Study from *The Conference Board of Canada, Education and Learning,* p. 3.

15. Ibid.

16. Sears, S. (1982). A definition of career guidance terms: A National Vacation Guidance Association Perspective, *Vocational Guidance Quarterly, 31:* p. 139

17. Brown, D., and Brooks, L., (1996b), Introduction to career development, in D. Brown and L Brooks (Eds.) *Career choice and development: Applying contemporary theories to* practice (2nd ed., p. 1–12), San Francisco: Jossey-Bass.

18. Ginzberg, E. (1984). Career development, in D. Brown & L. Brooks (Eds), *Career Choice and Development; Applying contemporary theories to practice* (p. 172–190). San Francisco: Jossey-Bass.

19. Leibowitz, Z. B., Farren, C., and Kaye, B. L. (1986). *Designing Career Development Systems.* San Francisco: Jossey-Bass, p. 4.

20. Gerdes, L. (2008). The New Fast Track. *Business Week,* September 15, 2008, Issue 4099, p. 44.

21. Ibid., p. 44.

22. Schiemann, W.A. (May 2008). *From Crunching Numbers to Counting Human Capital, Financial Executive,* p. 53–55, retrieved electronically June 30, 2008.

23. Stewart, T, A. (2001). The wealth of knowledge: intellectual capital and the twenty-first century organization, Toronto, *Currency.*

24. Gerdes, L., (2008). The New Fast Track, *Business Week*, September 15, 2008, Issue 4099, p. 44.

25. Krinks, P. & Strack, R. (2008). The talent crunch, *People Management,* Vol. 14, Issue 13, p. 30–31.

26. Ibid., p. 30–31.

27. Department of Education and Science. (1989). *Careers education and guidance from 5-16.* London: HMSO.

28. Super, D. E. (1976). Career Education and the Meaning of Work, *Monographs on Education, Washington,* DC; Department of Education.

29. Hall, D.T. & Mirvis, P.H. (1996). The new protean career: Psychological success and the path with a heart. In D.T Hall & Associations, *The career is dead: Long life the career. A relational approach to careers.* San Francisco: Jossey-Bass, p. 13–45.

30. Arthur, M.B., and Rousseau, D.M (1996). *The boundaryless career: Individual action and economic change,* London: Sage.

31. Littleton, S.M., Arthur, M.B., & Rousseau, D.M., (2000). The future of boundaryless careers, in A. Collin & R.A. Young (Eds). *The future of career.* Cambridge, UK; Cambridge University Press, p. 101–114.

32. Arnold, J. (1997). Managing careers into the 21st century. London: Paul Chapman.

33. Tucker, R, Moravee, M., and Ideus, K. (1992). Designing a Dual Career-Track System, Training and Development 6, p. 55–58.

34. Cole, N.D., & Dessler, G. (2005). *Human Resources Management in Canada.* Pearson, Prince Hall, p. 224–244.

35. Andolsen, A.A. (2008). Six Steps to Your Successful Career Path, *The Information Management Journal,* July/August, p 56–60.

36. Belcourt, M. (2002). *Managing Human Resources.* Thomson Nelson, p. 195–198.

37. http://ilearn.senecasc.on.ca/careers/goals/establishing_goals.html, retrieved July 16, 2008.

38. Baruch, Y. and Peiperl, Y. (2003). An empirical Assessment of Sonnenfeld's career systems typology, *International Journal of Human Resource Management* 14:7 p. 1267–1283.

39. Sonnenfeld , J.A. and Peiperl, M. A. (1988). Staffing Policy as a Strategic Response: A Typology of Career Systems, *Academy of Management Review,* 13(4): p. 568–600.

40. Olesen, C., White, D. and Lemmer, I. (2007 spring). Career Models and Culture Change at Microsoft, *Organization Development Journal,* Vol. 25, No. 1, p. 31–35.

41. Ibid.

42. Ibid., p. 32

43. Ibid., p. 33

44. Ibid., p. 33

45. http://www.microsoft.com/business/peopleready/business/operations/casestudy/careercomp. Retrieved July 9, 2008.

46. Watts, A.G. (1996a). Toward a policy for lifelong career development: A transatlantic perspective, *The Career Development Quarterly,* 45, p. 46.

47. Hall, D.T. & Mirvis, P.H. (1996). The new protean career: Psychological success and the path with a heart. In D.T Hall & Associations, *The career is dead: Long life the career. A relational approach to careers,* San Francisco: Jossey-Bass, p. 13–45.

48. Hall, D. T. (1996). Protean Careers of the 21st Century, *Academy of Management Executive* Vol. 10 No. 4 p. 8.

49. Littleton, S.M., Arthur, M.B., & Rousseau, D.M., (2000). The future of boundaryless careers, in A. Collin & R.A. Young (Eds), *The future of career.* Cambridge, UK; Cambridge University Press, p. 101–114.

50. Gasteiger, R., and Briscoe, J.P. (December 2005). What Kind of Organizations do Protean People Prefer? The Case of Germany and the United States, *Human Resource Management Review;* Vol. 15, Issue 4, p. 281–304.

51. Coaching and Mentoring, How to Develop Top Talent and Achieve Stronger Performance. (2004). *Harvard Business Press.*

52. Ibid.

53. www.NursingNet.com

54. Lewis, D. (2001). "That's Right, Double Click There, Sir." *Globe & Mail*, May 31, p. B14.

55. Holbeche, L. (1999). Aligning Human Resources and Business Strategy, Elsevier, Butterworth, Heinemann, p. 223–224.

56. Block, B. (2008). Streettalk, *ONWALLSTREET,* www.onwallstreet.com, retrieved September 24, 2008.

57. Karamanos, M. (June 2008). Engagement, Performance, Leadership and the Talent Challenge, *Conference Board of Canada,* http://22848.vws.magma.ca/EPRO_2634/Presentations/keynote1/player.html, retrieved June 30, 2008.

58. Ibid.

59. Woods, K. (June, 2008). Leadership, *Conference Board of Canada,* http://22848.vws.magma.ca/EPRO_2634/Presentations/plen1/player.html, retrieved June 30, 2008.

60. Khan, S. (June 2008). How HR Can Make Strategic Contribution Through Innovative Strategies That Address Talent Shortages, *Conference Board of Canada,* http://22848.vws.magma.ca/EPRO_2527/presentations/plen6/player.html, retrieved June 30, 2008.

61. Gupta, A. (2001). Talent management crisis, *Mid-American Journal of Business,* Fall 2001, Vol. 16, issue 2, p. 2.

62. Effron, M., Rowan, L, Sobczak, E. (2007). The talent crisis is real, *Workforce Management,* Vol. 86, Issue 15, p. 57.

63. Ulrich, D. (2008). Not-So-Standard Deviation, www.peoplemangment.co.uk/features, retrieved September 24, 2008.

64. Handfield-Jones, H., Michaels, E. and Axelrod, B. (2001). Talent Management: A critical part of every leader's job, *Ivey Business Journal,* Dec/Nov 2001.

65. Ibid.

66. Ibid.

67. Willet, D. (2008). Talent Management at Bruce Power, *Conference Board of Canada,* http://22848/vwa.magma.ca/EPRO_2634/presentations/plen6/player.html.

68. Ibid.

69. Taylor, I. (2008). Raising Your Organization's Game: Moving Average Performers Up the Talent Curve, *Conference Board of Canada,* http://2848.vws.magma.ca/EPRO_2634/presentations/plen4/player.html. Retrieved June 30, 2008.

70. Ibid.

71. Van Dam, N. (June 2005). Innovative Talent Management Strategies, www.clomedia.com, retrieved June 2008, p. 13.

72. Ibid.

73. Cappelli, P. (2008). Talent Management for the Twenty-First Century, *Harvard Business Review,* Vol. 86, Issue 3, p. 74–81, retrieved June 23, 2008.

74. Buckingham, M, and Vosburgh, R. M. (Dec. 2001). "The 21st century human resources function: It's the talent, stupid! One person at a time, becomes our defining challenge." *Human Resource Planning,* 24, 4, 17. Retrieved electronically September 25, 2007.

75. Buckingham, M., and Vosburgh, R. M. (Dec 2001). "The 21st century human resources function: It's the talent, stupid!, one person at a time, becomes our defining challenge." *Human Resource Planning,* 24, 4, 17. Retrieved electronically September 25, 2007.

76. Grigsby, Fred R. (June 2008). Lining Up Individual and Organizational Value Propositions, CN's IT Future, Case Study from *The Conference Board of Canada, Education and Learning.*

77. Halley, R. (June, 2008). Replacing Retiring IT Workers, Case Study from *The Conference Board of Canada, Education and Learning.*

78. Ibid., p. 5.

79. Ibid., p. 5.

80. Ibid., p. 8.

81. Chambers, E. G., Foulton, M., Handfield-Jones, H., Hankin, S.M. and Michaels, E.G. (1998). The War for Talent, *McKinsey Quarterly,* Issue 3, p. 44–57.

82. Axelrod, E. L, Handfield-Jones, H, and Welsh, T.A. (2001). War for talent, part two, *McKinsey Quarterly,* Issue 2, p. 9–12.

83. Chambers, E. G., Foulton, M., Handfield-Jones, H., Hankin, S.M. and Michaels, E.G. (1998). The War for Talent, *McKinsey Quarterly,* Issue 3, p. 44–57.

84. Ibid.

85. http://www.rim.com/careers. Retrieved Aug. 29, 2009.

86. Chambers, E. G., Foulton, M., Handfield-Jones, H., Hankin, S.M. and Michaels, E.G. (1998). The War for Talent, *McKinsey Quarterly*, Issue 3, p. 44–57.

Chapter 6

1. Weber, J. (2007, April 23). The accidental CEO. *Business Week,* 64–72.

2. Greengard, S. (2001). Why succession planning can't wait [Electronic version]. *Workforce,* 34–36.

3. Ibid.

4. Walker, J. W. (1998). Perspectives [Electronic version]. *HR. Human Resource Planning,* 21(3), 9–11; Rothwell, W. J. (2002). Succession planning for future success [Electronic version]. *Strategic HR Review,* 1(3), 30–33.

5. Rothwell, W. J. (2002). Succession planning for future success [Electronic version]. *Strategic Review,* 1(3), 30–33.

6. Huang, T. (2001). Succession management systems and human resource outcomes [Electronic version]. *International Journal of Manpower,* 22(8), 736–747.

7. Fulmer, R. (2005). Keys to best practice succession management. Retrieved April 8, 2007 from http://www.humanresourcesmagazine.com.au/articles/DD/0C02A0DD.asp?Type=60&Category=919.

8. HayGroup. (2006). Succession planning: A crisis is brewing. Retrieved November 4, 2007, from http://www.haygroup.com/downloads/ca/Succession_Planning-_A_Crisis_is_Brewing_March_2006.pdf.

9. Charan, R. (2005). Ending the CEO succession crisis. [Electronic version]. *Harvard Business Review,* 83(2), 72–81.

10. Nutall-Smith, C. & York, G. (2007, March). Orange China. *Report on Business,* 24–38.

11. Olijnyk, Z. (2007, January 29). World-Beater. *Canadian Business,* 38–41.

12. Critical issues in HR drive 2006 priorities: #1 is talent management [Electronic version]. (2006). *HR Focus,* 83(1), 1–4.

13. The ROI of succession planning [Electronic version]. (2006). *HRMagazine,* 51(4), 16.

14. Hewitt Associates. (2005). From attraction/retention to financial results, 50 best employers outshine the competition, says Hewitt Associates [Electronic version]. *Canada NewsWire,* 1.

15. Joinson, C. (1998). Developing a strong bench—succession planning. *HR Magazine.* Retrieved March 2, 2007 from http://findarticles.com/p/articles/mi_m3495/is_n1_v43/ai_20389988.

16. Frauenheim, E. (2006). Succession progression [Electronic version]. *Workforce Management,* 85(1), 31–34.

17. Gohring, N. (2007). SAP executive changes may leave leadership gap. *Computer World.* Retrieved April 8, 2007 from http://www.computerworld.com.au/index.php?id=1098106170.

18. Konopaske, R. & Ivancevich, J. (2004). *Global management and organizational behavior.* New York: McGraw-Hill Ryerson.

19. Campbell, T. (2003). Diversity in depth [Electronic version]. *HRMagazine,* 48(3), 152.

20. White, M. (2002). Paying more than lip service to diversity [Electronic version]. *Chief Executive,* 20–21.

21. Boyden World Corp. (n.d.). Reaching consensus on diversity. Retrieved May 3, 2007 from http://www.boyden.com/news_articles/conf_perspectives_diversity.htm.

22. Schwind, H., Das, H. & Wagar, T. (2005). *Canadian Human Resource Management. A Strategic Approach.* Toronto: McGraw-Hill Ryerson.

23. Chromminska, S. "Sylvia Chrominska Speech —April 4, 2007." Presentation to Catalyst Canada. Toronto. 4, Apr. 2007.

24. Schwind, H., Das, H. & Wagar, T. (2005). *Canadian Human Resource Management. A Strategic Approach.* Toronto: McGraw-Hill Ryerson.

25. Schreiber, C. T., Price, K. F. & Morrison, A. (1993). Workforce diversity and the glass ceiling: Practices, barriers, possibilities [Electronic version]. *HR. Human Resource Planning,* 16(2), 51–64; Campbell, T. (2003). Diversity in depth [Electronic version]. *HRMagazine,* 48(3), 152.

26. Risher, H. (2002). Current practices [Electronic version]. *HR. Human Resource Planning,* 25(1), 5–12.

27. Diversity at RBC: 2005 Highlights. *Diversity Progress Report 2005.* Retrieved July 17, 2007 from http://www.rbc.com/uniquecareers/diversity/diversity_progress_report2005.pdf.

28. Metz, E. J. (1998). Designing succession systems for new competitive realities [Electronic version]. *HR. Human Resource Planning, 21*(3), 31–37.

29. Rothwell, W. J. (2005). Effective succession planning (3rd ed.). New York: Amacom.

30. Tichy, N. (1996). Simultaneous transformation and CEO succession: Key to global competitiveness [Electronic version]. *Organizational Dynamics, 25*(1), 45–58.

31. Leibman, M., Bruer, R. A. & Maki, B. R. (1996). Succession management: The next generation of succession planning [Electronic version]. *HR. Human Resource Planning, 19*(3), 16–29.

32. Frauenheim, E. (2006). Succession progression [Electronic version]. *Workforce Management, 85*(1), 31–34.

33. Leibman, M., Bruer, R A. & Maki, B. R. (1996). Succession management: The next generation of succession planning [Electronic version]. *HR. Human Resource Planning, 19*(3), 16–29; Rothwell, W. J. (2002). Succession planning for future success [Electronic version]. *Strategic Review, 1*(3), 30–33; Huang, T. (2001). Succession management systems and human resource outcomes [Electronic version]. *International Journal of Manpower, 22*(8), 736–747; Greengard, S. (2001). Why succession planning can't wait [Electronic version]. *Workforce,* 34–36.

34. Huang, T. (2001). Succession management systems and human resource outcomes [Electronic version]. *International Journal of Manpower, 22*(8), 736–747; Metz, E. J. (1998). Designing succession systems for new competitive realities [Electronic version]. *HR. Human Resource Planning, 21*(3), 31–37; Rothwell, W. J. (2002). Succession planning for future success [Electronic version]. *Strategic Review, 1*(3), 30–33; Walker, J. W. (1998). Perspectives [Electronic version]. *HR. Human Resource Planning, 21*(3), 9–11; Tichy, N. (1996). Simultaneous transformation and CEO succession: Key to global competitiveness [Electronic version]. *Organizational Dynamics, 25*(1), 45–58.

35. Rothwell, W. J. (2002). Succession planning for future success [Electronic version]. *Strategic Review, 1*(3), 30–33.

36. Charan, R. (2005). Ending the CEO succession crisis. [Electronic version]. *Harvard Business Review*, 82 (2), 72–81.

37. Rothwell, W. J. (2002). Succession planning for future success [Electronic version]. *Strategic Review, 1*(3), 30–33.

38. Conger, J. A. & Fulmer, R. M. (2003). Developing your leadership pipeline [Electronic version]. *Harvard Business Review, 81*(12), 76–84.

39. Rothwell, W. J. (2002). Succession planning for future success [Electronic version]. *Strategic Review, 1*(3), 30–33.

40. Risher, H. & Stopper, W. G. (2002). Current practices [Electronic version]. *HR. Human Resource Planning, 25*(1), 5–11.

41. ibid.

42. Weyerhaeuser. (n.d.). Retrieved July 17, 2007 from, http://www.weyerhaeuser.com/aboutus.

43. Risher, H. & Stopper, W. G. (2002). Current practices [Electronic version]. *HR. Human Resource Planning, 25*(1), 5–11.

44. Walker, J. W. & LaRocco, J. M. (2002). Perspectives: Talent pools: The best and the rest [Electronic version]. *HR. Human Resource Planning, 25*(3), 12–14.

45. Cope, F. (1998). Current issues in selecting high potentials. *HR. Human Resource Planning, 21*(3), 15–17.

46. Rothwell, W. J. (2002). Succession planning for future success [Electronic version]. *Strategic Review, 1*(3), 30–33.

47. Walker, J. W. & LaRocco, J. M. (2002). Perspectives: Talent pools: The best and the rest [Electronic version]. *HR. Human Resource Planning, 25*(3), 12–14.

48. Cope, F. (1998). Current issues in selecting high potentials. *HR. Human Resource Planning, 21*(3), 15–17.

49. Rothwell, W. J. (2005). Effective succession planning (3rd ed.). New York: Amacom.

50. Charan, R. (2005). Ending the CEO succession crisis. [Electronic version]. *Harvard Business Review, 83*(2), 72–81.

51. Rothwell, W. J. (2002). Succession planning for future success [Electronic version]. *Strategic Review, 1*(3), 30–33.

52. Rothwell, W. J. (2005). *Effective Succession Planning* (3rd ed.). New York: Amacom.

53. Walker, J. W. & LaRocco, J. M. (2002). Perspectives: Talent pools: The best and the rest [Electronic version]. *HR. Human Resource Planning,* 25(3), 12–14.

54. Ibid.

55. Rothwell, W. J. (2002). Succession planning for future success [Electronic version]. *Strategic Review,* 1(3), 30–33.

56. Cope, F. (1998). Current issues in selecting high potentials. *HR. Human Resource Planning,* 21(3), 15–17; Metz, E. J. (1998). Designing succession systems for new competitive realities [Electronic version]. *HR. Human Resource Planning,* 21(3), 31–37.

57. Buckstein, J. (2003, May 22). Never too early to put succession plans in place. *The Globe and Mail.* Retrieved June 27, 2007 from www.globeandmail.com/partners/adp/sbr/globe/52222003.html.

58. Ibid.

59. Strauss, M. (2007, July 27). Former Shoppers CEO has tough task waiting at GAP. *The Globe and Mail,* p. B1.

60. Conger, J. A. & Fulmer, R. M. (2003). Developing your leadership pipeline [Electronic version]. *Harvard Business Review,* 81(12), 76–84.

61. Leibman, M., Bruer, R A. & Maki, B. R. (1996). Succession management: The next generation of succession planning [Electronic version]. *HR. Human Resource Planning,* 19(3), 16–29.

62. Risher, H. & Stopper, W. G. (2002). Current practices [Electronic version]. *HR. Human Resource Planning,* 25(1), 5–11; Frauenheim, E. (2006). Succession progression [Electronic version]. *Workforce Management,* 85(1), 31–34; Bernthal, P. & Wellins, R. (2006). Trends in leader development and succession [Electronic version]. *HR. Human Resource Planning,* 29(2), 31–40; Leibman, M., Bruer, R A. & Maki, B. R. (1996). Succession management: The next generation of succession planning [Electronic version]. *HR. Human Resource Planning,* 19(3), 16–29.

63. Conger, J. A. & Fulmer, R. M. (2003). Developing your leadership pipeline [Electronic version]. *Harvard Business Review,* 81(12), 76–84.

64. Bernthal, P. & Wellins, R. (2006). Trends in leader development and succession [Electronic version]. *HR. Human Resource Planning,* 29(2), 31–40; Conger, J. A. & Fulmer, R. M. (2003). Developing your leadership pipeline [Electronic version]. *Harvard Business Review,* 81(12), 76–84.

65. Conger, J. A. & Fulmer, R. M. (2003). Developing your leadership pipeline [Electronic version]. *Harvard Business Review,* 81(12), 76–84.

66. How to succeed at succession plans. (2004). *HR Focus,* 81(11), 1–4.

67. Rothwell, W. J. (2002). Succession planning for future success [Electronic version]. *Strategic Review,* 1(3), 30–33.

68. Risher, H. & Stopper, W. G. (2002). Current practices [Electronic version]. *HR. Human Resource Planning,* 25(1), 5–11.

69. Bernthal, P. & Wellins, R. (2006). Trends in leader development and succession. *HR. Human Resource Planning,* 29(2), 31–40.

70. Conger, J. A. & Fulmer, R. M. (2003). Developing your leadership pipeline [Electronic version]. *Harvard Business Review,* 81(12), 76–84.

71. Leibman, M., Bruer, R A. & Maki, B. R. (1996). Succession management: The next generation of succession planning [Electronic version]. *HR. Human Resource Planning,* 19(3), 16–29; Cope, F. (1998). Current issues in selecting high potentials. *HR. Human Resource Planning,* 21(3), 15–17; Frase-Blunt, M. (2003). Moving past 'Mini-Me' [Electronic version]. *HRMagazine,* 48(11), 95; Risher, H. & Stopper, W. G. (2002). Current practices [Electronic version]. *HR. Human Resource Planning,* 25(1), 5–11.

72. How to succeed at succession plans. (2004). *HR Focus,* 81(11), 1–4; Bernthal, P. & Wellins, R. (2006). Trends in leader development and succession. *HR. Human Resource Planning,* 29(2), 31–40.

73. Walker, J. W. & LaRocco, J. M. (2002). Perspectives: Talent pools: The best and the rest [Electronic version]. *HR. Human Resource Planning,* 25(3), 12–14.

74. Frase-Blunt, M. (2003). Moving past 'Mini-Me' [Electronic version]. *HRMagazine,* 48(11), 95.

75. Walker, J. W. & LaRocco, J. M. (2002). Perspectives: Talent pools: The best and the rest [Electronic version]. *HR. Human Resource Planning,* 25(3), 12–14.

76. Conger, J. A. & Fulmer, R. M. (2003). Developing your leadership pipeline [Electronic version]. *Harvard Business Review,* 81(12), 76–84.

77. Risher, H. & Stopper, W. G. (2002). Current practices [Electronic version]. *HR. Human Resource Planning,* 25(1), 5–11.

78. Weber, J. (2007, April 23). The accidental CEO. *Business Week,* 64–72.

79. Charan, R. (2005). Ending the CEO succession crisis. [Electronic version]. *Harvard Business Review,* 83(2), 72–81.

80. Frauenheim, E. (2006). Succession progression [Electronic version]. *Workforce Management,* 85(1), 31–34.

81. Weber, J. (2007, April 23). The accidental CEO. *Business Week,* 64–72.

82. Charan, R. (2005). Ending the CEO succession crisis. [Electronic version]. *Harvard Business Review,* 83(2), 72–81.

83. DeCloet, D. (2007, February 8). Can Nortel shrink its way down to fat margins? Slim chance. *The Globe and Mail,* p. B18.

84. Bernthal, P. & Wellins, R. (2006). Trends in leader development and succession. *HR. Human Resource Planning,* 29(2), 31–40.

85. Charan, R. (2005). Ending the CEO succession crisis. [Electronic version]. *Harvard Business Review,* 83(2), 72–81.

86. McLean, C. (2006, December 6). Rogers eyes successor beyond family. *The Globe and Mail,* p. B7.

87. Austen, I. (2008, December 3). 2 Canadian phone giants in different struggles. *International Herald Tribune.* Retrieved from http://www.iht.com.

88. Roth, D. (2005, April 4). Can Nike still do it without Phil Knight? *Fortune,* p. 58–68.

89. Krentzman, J. (n.d.). The force behind the Nike Empire. *Stanford Magazine.* Retrieved June 26, 2006 from http://www.stanfordalumni.org/news/magazine/1997/janfeb/articles/knight.html.

90. Holmes, S. (2006). Inside the coup at Nike. *Business Week,* 34.

91. Ibid.

Chapter 7

1. CampusNews@ryerson.ca (October 5, 2007), Ryerson Implements a New Human Resources Management System.

2. Ibid.

3. Ibid.

4. CampusNews@ryerson.ca (May 12, 2008), Ryerson Implements a New Human Resources Management System.

5. Ibid.

6. Frauenhelm, E. (2006). Bumps in the road to going global. *Workforce Management,* Vol. 85, Issue 19, p. 20–31.

7. Ibid., p. 20–31.

8. Ibid., p 20–31.

9. Pfeffer, J. (1997). "Does Human Resources Have a Future," in Ulrich, D., Losey, M.R., and Lake, G., eds. Tomorrow's HR Management: 48 Thought Leaders call for Change. New York: John Wiley, p. 190–196.

10. Hendrickson, A.R. (2003). Human resource information systems: Backbone technology of contemporary human resources. *Journal of Labor Research,* Vol. 24, Issue 3, p. 381–394.

11. Samir Shrivastava, and James B. Shaw (Fall 2003). Liberating HR Through Technology, *Human Resource Management,* Vol. 42. No. 3, 201.

12. http://www.orangehrm.com/product-features.shtml, retrieved May 14, 2008.

13. A.S. Targowski and S.P. Deshpande (Autumn, 2001). The Utility and Selection of an HRMS. Advances in Competitiveness Research, p. 42.

14. Frauenhelm, E. (2006). Bumps in the road to going global. *Workforce Management,* Vol. 85, Issue 19, p. 20–31.

15. Hendrickson, A.R. (2003). Human Resource Information Systems: Backbone Technology of Contemporary Human Resources. *Journal of Labor Research,* Summer 2003, Vol. 24, Issue 3, p. 381–394.

16. Fein, S. (2001). Preface, in Walker, A.J. ed., *Web-Based Human Resources.* New York: McGraw-Hill, p. vii–x.

17. Shrivastava, S. and James B. Shaw, (Fall 2003). Liberating HR through technology. *Human Resource Management*, Vol. 42. No. 3, p. 201.

18. Anderson, M. (Retrieved September 29, 2007). The metrics of workforce planning. *Public Personnel Management* 33.4 (Winter 2004) p. 1.

19. Benest, F. (June 2008). The role of benefits in winning the war on talent. *Benefits and Compensation Digest*, Vol. 45 Issue 6, 42–45.

20. "Talent Matters, Shaping Talent Strategies in a Changing World." (March 2007). Toronto Financial Services Alliance and Deloitte, p. 4.

21. William J. Jones and Robert C. Hoell. (Fall 2005). Human Resource Information System Courses: An Examination of Instructional Methods. *Journal of Information Systems Education*, Vol. 16(3), p. 321.

22. HR Technology Trends to Watch in 2007. (January 2007). *HRFOCUS*, p. 10–15.

23. Bulmash, J. (2008). "Human Resources Management and Technology, in Human Resources Management in Canada," Dessler, G. and Cole, N.D., Pearson, Prentice Hall, Toronto, p. 52.

24. http//www.oracle.com/applications/peoplesoft/hcm/ent/module/stock_admin.html, retrieved January 22, 2008.

25. McCormack, J. (2004). Compliance tools. *HRMagazine*, Vol. 49, Issue 3, p. 95–98.

26. Bulmash, J. (2008). "Human Resources Management and Technology, in Human Resources Management in Canada," Dessler, G. and Cole, N.D., Pearson, Prentice Hall, Toronto, p. 52.

27. Ibid., p. 53.

28. Frauenhelm, E. (2006). Bumps in the road to going global. *Workforce Management*, Vol. 85, Issue 19, p. 20–31.

29. Ibid.

30. Ibid.

31. Ibid.

32. Ibid.

33. HR Technology Trends to Watch in 2007. (January 2007). *HRFOCUS*, p. 10–15.

34. Bulmash, J. (2008). "Human Resources Management and Technology, in Human Resources Management in Canada," Dessler, G. and Cole, N.D., Pearson, Prentice Hall, Toronto, p. 54

35. Robb, D. (2007 Aug). A total view of employee rewards. *HRMagazine*, Vol. 52, Issue 8, p. 93–93.

36. Bulmash, J. (2008). "Human Resources Management and Technology, in Human Resources Management in Canada," Dessler, G. and Cole, N.D., Pearson, Prentice Hall, Toronto, p. 54.

37. http://www.bestpricecomputers.co.uk/glossary/human-resource-management-system.htm.

38. Pearson, G. (2001). HRMS does make a difference. Canadian HR Reporter, Guide to HR Technology Supplement, Oct 22, G1.

39. http//www.oracle.com/applications/peoplesoft/hcm/ent/module/stock_admin.html, retrieved January 22, 2008.

40. http://www.sap.com/Canada/about/index.epx, retrieved September 3, 2009.

41. http://www.dap.com/solutions/busines-suite/erp/hom/indix.exp, retrieved Jan 22, 2008.

42. Ibid.

43. Ibid.

44. Schramn, J. (2006). HR technology competencies: New roles for HR professionals. *HRMagazine*, Vol. 51, Issue 4, p. 1–18.

45. http//www.oracle.com/applications/peoplesoft/hcm/ent/module/stock_admin.html, retrieved January 22, 2008.

46. http://www.orangehrm.com/projct-features.shtml, retrieved May 14, 2008.

47. http://www.capterra.com/human-resrouce-softwar/spotlight/76778/Employee%20 Performance, retrieved June 13, 2008.

48. http://www.dap.com/solutions/busines-suite/erp/hom/indix.exp, retrieved Jan. 22, 2008.

49. Oracle Customer Summary, Capital One, http://www.oracle.com/Retrieved Jan. 22, 2008.

50. HR technology trends to watch in 2007. (January 2007). *HRFOCUS*, p. 10–15.

51. Ryder, J.A. (2005). Future of HR technology. *HRMagazine*, Anniversary Issue 13, Vol 50, p. 67–69.

52. Ibid., p. 68

53. Ibid., p. 69.

54. Hagood, W.O and Friedman, L. (Winter 2002). Using the balanced scorecard to measure the performance of your HR information system. *Public Personnel Management*, Vol. 31, Issue 4, p. 543–553.

55. Hubbard, J.C. Forcht, K.A. and Thomas, D.S. (1998). Human resources information systems, an overview of current ethical and legal issues, *Journal of Business Ethics*, 17, 1319–1323.

56. Isenhour, L.C. (2009). HR Administration and HRIS, in Human Resource Information Systems, Kavanagh, M.J. and Thite, M. (eds), Sage, London , p. 239.

57. Ibid., p. 239–240.

58. Privacy Impact Assessment –Human Resources Management Information System (HRMIS. (2008). HTTP:www.rcmp-grc.gc.ca/pia/hrmis-e.htm, retrieved September 22, 2008.

59. Moss, D. (Oct 2006). Three key HR technology issues. *HRMagazine*, Vol. 51, Issue 10, p. 12.

60. Isenhour, L.C. HR Administration and HRIS, in Human Resource Information systems, Kavanagh, M.J. and Thite, M. (eds), Sage, London, p. 239–240.

61. Roberts, B. (Jun 2004). Empowerment or impositions? *HRMagazine*, Vol. 49, Issue 6, p. 157–166.

62. Ibid., p. 157–166.

Chapter 8

1. Anonymous. (2007). Honda Motor: 2007 company profile edition 1: SWOT analysis, 15–16.

2. Company overview. (n.d.). Details of Honda's head office. Retrieved May 18, 2007, from http://world.honda.com/profile/overview/.

3. Community. (n.d.). The key phrase: Together for tomorrow. Retrieved May 18, 2007, from http://world.honda.com/community/.

4. Honda Worldwide. (2006). Honda holds opening ceremony of new motorcycle plant in Argentina. Retrieved May 18, 2007, from http://world.honda.com/news/2006/c060802PlantinArgentina/printerfriendly/index/html.

5. Honda Worldwide. (2007). Honda unveils plans for new plant in Rajasthan. Retrieved May 18, 2007, from http://world.honda.com/news/2007/c070503NewPlantinRajasthan/printerfriendly/index.html.

6. Honda Worldwide. (2006). Honda officially breaks ground for new auto plant. Retrieved May 18, 2007, from http://world.honda.com/news/2007/c070319ManufacturingIndiana/printerfriendly/index.html.

7. Byrne, J. (1996, August 26). Strategic planning. Retrieved May 2, 2007 from, http://www.businessweek.com/1996/35/b34901.htm.

8. Friend, D. (2007, March 20). Scotiabank explores China buy. *Toronto Star,* p. D3.

9. Brewster, C., Sparrow, P. & Harris, H. (2005). Towards a new model of globalizing HRM [Electronic version]. *International Journal of Human Resource Management,* 16(6), 949–970; Ling, Y. & Jaw, B. (2006). The influence of international human capital on global initiatives and financial performance [Electronic version]. *International Journal of Human Resource Management,* 17(3), 379–398; Schuler, R. S., Budhwar, P. S. & Florkowski, G. W. (2002). International human resource management: Review and critique [Electronic version]. *International Journal of Management Reviews,* 4(1), 41–70.

10. Briscoe, D. R. & Schuler, R. S. (2004). International human resource management (2nd ed.). New York: Routledge.

11. Collings, D. G., Scullion, H. & Morley, M. J. (2007). Changing patterns of global staffing in the multinational enterprise: Challenges to the conventional expatriate assignment and emerging alternatives [Electronic version]. *Journal of World Business,* 42, 198–213.

12. Brewster, C., Sparrow, P. & Harris, H. (2005). Towards a new model of globalizing HRM [Electronic version]. *International Journal of Human Resource Management,* 16(6), 949–970.

13. Adler, Dr. N. J. (1990). Globalization and human resource management: Strategic international human resource development [Electronic version]. *Pacific Region Forum;* Tarique, I., Schuler, R. & Gong, Y. (2006). A model of multinational enterprise subsidiary staffing composition [Electronic version]. *International Journal of Human Resource Management,* 17(2), 207–224.

14. Collings, D. G., Scullion, H. & Morley, M. J. (2007). Changing patterns of global staffing in the multinational enterprise: Challenges to the conventional expatriate assignment and emerging alternatives [Electronic version]. *Journal of World Business,* 42, 198–213.

15. Ibid.

16. Ibid.

17. Ibid.

18. Tarique, I., Schuler, R. & Gong, Y. (2006). A model of multinational enterprise subsidiary staffing composition [Electronic version]. *International Journal of Human Resource Management,* 17(2), 207–224.

19. Mor Borak, M. E. (2005). Managing Diversity. Thousand Oaks, California: Sage Publications Inc.

20. Bartlett, C. A. & Ghoshal, S. (1992). What is a global manager? [Electronic version]. *Harvard Business Review,* 70(5), 124–132.

21. Engardio, P., Arndt, M. & Smith, G. (2006, July 31). Emerging giants. *BusinessWeek,* 40–49.

22. Mahapatra, R. (2006, November 28). Wal-Mart juggernaut gets set to roll into India. *Toronto Star,* p. D3.

23. Brewster, C., Sparrow, P. & Harris, H. (2005). Towards a new model of globalizing HRM [Electronic version]. *International Journal of Human Resource Management,* 16(6), 949–970.

24. McNish, J. (2006, December 6). Faskens' farsighted journey into Africa. *The Globe and Mail,* p. B9.

25. Tarique, I., Schuler, R. & Gong, Y. (2006). A model of multinational enterprise subsidiary staffing composition [Electronic version]. *International Journal of Human Resource Management,* 17(2), 207–224; Wiechmann, D., Ryan, A. & Hemingway, M. (2003). Designing and implementing global staffing systems: Part I – leaders in global staffing [Electronic version]. *Human Resource Management,* 42(1), 79; Brewster, C., Sparrow, P. & Harris, H. (2005). Towards a new model of globalizing HRM [Electronic version]. *International Journal of Human Resource Management*m 16(6), 949–970; Briscoe, D. R. & Schuler, R. S. (2004). *International Human Resource Management* (2nd ed.). New York: Routledge.

26. Briscoe, D. R. & Schuler, R. S. (2004). *International Human Resource Management* (2nd ed.). New York: Routledge.

27. Briscoe, D. R. & Schuler, R. S. (2004). *International Human Resource Management* (2nd ed.). New York: Routledge.

28. Mor Borak, M. E. (2005). *Managing Diversity Toward a Globally Inclusive Workplace.* Thousand Oaks, California: Sage Publications Inc.

29. Marshall, J. & Heffes, E. M. (2006). China: Recruiting easy, but success difficult [Electronic version]. *Financial Executive,* 22(10), 12.

30. Mor Borak, M. E. (2005). *Managing Diversity Toward a Globally Inclusive Workplace.* Thousand Oaks, California: Sage Publications Inc.

31. The Open Learn University. (n.d.). An introduction to business cultures. Retrieved November 4, 2007 from, http://openlearn.open.ac.uk/mod/resource/view.php?id=210375.

32. Javidan, M. & House, R. J. (2001). Cultural acumen for the global manager: Lessons from Project GLOBE [Electronic version]. *Organizational Dynamics,* 29(4), 289.

33. Javidan, M., Stahl, G. K., Brodbeck, F. & Wilderom, C.P.M. (2005). Cross-border transfer of knowledge: Cultural lessons from Project GLOBE [Electronic version]. *Academy of Management Executive,* 19(2), 59–75.

34. Out-Law News. (2005). Indian labour shortage may affect offshoring, says Gartner. Retrieved May 13, 2007 from, http://www.out-law.com/page-6116-theme=print.

35. Anonymous. (2006). Employment trends and opportunities [Electronic version]. *Going Global Career Guides,* 18–33.

36. Hansen, K. (2006). Balancing the global workforce [Electronic version]. *Workforce Management,* 85(23), 44.

37. Guillard, M. (2006). A visual essay: International labor market comparisons [Electronic version]. *Monthly Labor Review,* 33-40.

38. Mor Borak, M. E. (2005). *Managing Diversity.* Thousand Oaks, California: Sage Publications Inc.

39. Carley, M. (2003). Industrial relations in the EU, Japan and USA, 2001. *Eurofound.* Retrieved March 14, 2007 from, http://www.eurofound.europa.eu/eiro/2002/12/feature/tn0212101f.html.

40. Wright, T. (2006, December 7). Indonesia chained by labour law. *The Globe and Mail,* p. B19.

41. Briscoe, D. R. & Schuler, R. S. (2004). *International Human Resource Management* (2nd ed.). New York: Routledge.

42. Mor Borak, M. E. (2005). *Managing Diversity Toward a Globally Inclusive Workplace.* Thousand Oaks, California: Sage Publications Inc.

43. Briscoe, D. R. & Schuler, R. S. (2004). *International Human Resource Management* (2nd ed.). New York: Routledge.

44. Industrial relations in the EU, Japan and USA, 2001. (2002). Eurofound. Retrieved March 14, 2007 from, http://eurofound.europa.eu/eiro/eiro/2002/12/feature/TN0212101F.html.

45. Yamamoto. (2004). US visa backlog costing exporters billions. Retrieved June 6, 2007 from, http://groups.google.ca/group/soc.culture.thai/browse_thread/thread/45a00e0e552e6f0c/7f4f71a65f379a3c?lnk=st&q=OT%3A+Thai+Visa+rules&rnum=1&hl=en#7f4f71a65f379a3c.

46. Bliss, J. & Hughes, J. (2007). World's worst visa system scares business away from the U.S. Retrieved June 6, 2007 from, http://www.bloomberg.com/apps/news?pid=20601087&sid=a1F10udeixLM&refer=home

47. Dongier, I. (2005). H1B blues: Canada's HR options [Electronic version]. *Area Development Site and Facility Planning,* 42–44.

48. Work permits and visas. (2005). Going Global Inc. presents career information and resources for Japan. Retrieved November 4, 2007 from, http://www.goinglobal.com/CareerGuide.asp.

49. Helping people migrate. (n.d.) Retrieved September 6, 2007 from, www.migrationexpert.com/uk.

50. Arthaud-Day, M. L. (2005). Transnational corporate social responsibility: A tri-dimensional approach to international CSR research [Electronic version]. *Business Ethics Quarterly,* 15(1), 1–22.

51. Industry Canada. (2005). Corporate social responsibility. Retrieved June 8, 2007 from, http://strategis. ic.gc.ca/epic/site/csr-rse.nsf/en/Home.

52. Ibid.

53. Soccer gets on the ball (prevention of the US soccer ball industry's use of child labor in Pakistan) [Electronic version]. (1998). *Bobbin,* 39(11), 46; Colljnsa, E., Zochb, L. & Mcdonalda, C. (2004). When [professional] worlds collide: implications of Kasky v. Nike for corporate reputation management [Electronic version]. *Public Relations Review,* 30(4), 411–417.

54. Kamouche, K. (1996). The integration-differentiation puzzle: A resource-capability perspective in international human resource management [Electronic version]. *The International Journal of Human Resource Management,* 7(1), 230–243

55. Schuler, R. S., Budhwar, P. S. & Florkowski, G. W. (2002). International human resource management: Review and critique [Electronic version]. *International Journal of Management Reviews,* 4(1), 41–70.

56. Collings, D. G., Scullion, H. & Morley, M. J. (2007). Changing patterns of global staffing in the multinational enterprise: Challenges to the conventional expatriate assignment and emerging alternatives [Electronic version]. *Journal of World Business,* 42, 198–213.

57. Ibid.

58. Mor Borak, M. E. (2005). *Managing Diversity Toward a Globally Inclusive Workplace.* Thousand Oaks, California: Sage Publications Inc.

59. Briscoe, D. R. & Schuler, R. S. (2004). *International Human Resource Management* (2nd ed.). New York: Routledge.

60. Tarique, I., Schuler, R. & Gong, Y. (2006). A model of multinational enterprise subsidiary staffing composition [Electronic version]. *International Journal of Human Resource Management,* 17(2), 207-224; Collings, D. G., Scullion, H. & Morley, M. J. (2007). Changing patterns of global staffing in the multinational enterprise: Challenges to the conventional expatriate assignment and emerging alternatives [Electronic version]. *Journal of World Business,* 42, 198–213.

61. Briscoe, D. R. & Schuler, R. S. (2004). *International Human Resource Management* (2nd ed.). New York: Routledge; Tarique, I., Schuler, R. & Gong, Y. (2006). A model of multinational enterprise subsidiary staffing composition [Electronic version]. *International Journal of Human Resource Management,* 17(2), 207–224

62. Scullion, H. & Collings, D. G. (2006). *Global Staffing.* New York: Routledge.

63. Reynolds, C. (1997). Strategic employment of third country nationals [Electronic version]. *HR. Human Resource Planning,* 20(1), 33–39. Scullion, H. & Collings, D. G. (2006). *Global Staffing.* New York: Routledge.

64. Scullion, H. & Collings, D. G. (2006). *Global Staffing.* New York: Routledge.

65. Collings, D. G., Scullion, H. & Morley, M. J. (2007). Changing patterns of global staffing in the multinational enterprise: Challenges to the conventional expatriate assignment and emerging alternatives [Electronic version]. *Journal of World Business,* 42, 198–213.

66. Mayerhofer, H., Hartmann, L. C., Michelitsch-Riedl, G. & Kollinger, I. (2004). Flexpatriate assignments: A neglected issue in global staffing [Electronic version]. *International Journal of Human Resource Management,* 15(8), 1371–1389.

67. Schiuma, G., Bourne, M. & Harris, H. (2006). Assessing the value of international workers [Electronic version]. *Measuring Business Excellence,* 10(1), 60–71.

68. Collings, D. G., Scullion, H. & Morley, M. J. (2007). Changing patterns of global staffing in the multinational enterprise: Challenges to the conventional expatriate assignment and emerging alternatives [Electronic version]. *Journal of World Business,* 42, 198–213.

69. Immen, W. (2006, July 5). Working in China comes with a price. *The Globe and Mail,* p. C1.

70. Collings, D. G., Scullion, H. & Morley, M. J. (2007). Changing patterns of global staffing in the multinational enterprise: Challenges to the conventional expatriate assignment and emerging alternatives [Electronic version]. *Journal of World Business,* 42, 198–213.

71. Collings, D. G., Scullion, H. & Morley, M. J. (2007). Changing patterns of global staffing in the multinational enterprise: Challenges to the conventional expatriate assignment and emerging alternatives [Electronic version]. *Journal of World Business,* 42, 198–213.

72. Moakler, C. & Reinhart, G. (2003). Apply international lessons to domestic moves [Electronic version]. *Canadian HR Reporter,* 16(21), 21.

73. Mumma, J. S. (1993). How to control relocation costs [Electronic version]. *HRMagazine,* 38(8), 67–69.

74. Schuler, R. S., Budhwar, P. S. & Florkowski, G. W. (2002). International human resource management: Review and critique [Electronic version]. *International Journal of Management Reviews,* 4(1), 41–70.

75. Ibid; Collings, D. G., Scullion, H. & Morley, M. J. (2007). Changing patterns of global staffing in the multinational enterprise: Challenges to the conventional expatriate assignment and emerging alternatives [Electronic version]. *Journal of World Business,* 42, 198–213.

76. Tung, R.L. (2008). Do race and gender matter in international assignments to/from Asia Pacfic? An exploratory study of attitudes among Chinese. *Human Resource Management,* 47(1), 91. Retrieved March 11, 2009 from ProQuest database.

77. Contreras, C.D., Bravo, F. (2003). Should you accept an international assignment? *Chemical Engineering Process,* 99(8), 67. Retrieved March 14, 2009 from ProQuest database.

78. Fink, G., Meierewert S., Rohr, U. (2005). The use of repatriate knowledge in organizations [Electronic version]. *HR. Human Resource Planning,* 28(4), 30–36.

79. Contreras, C.D., Bravo,F. (2003). Should you accept an international assignment? *Chemical Engineering Process,* 99(8), 67. Retrieved March 14, 2009 from ProQuest database.

80. Collings, D. G., Scullion, H. & Morley, M. J. (2007). Changing patterns of global staffing in the multinational enterprise: Challenges to the conventional expatriate assignment and emerging alternatives [Electronic version]. *Journal of World Business,* 42, 198–213.

81. Krell, E. (2005). Budding relationships: formal global buddy programs can help ease the transition for expatriates and improve retention and productivity. *HR Magazine.* Retrieved November 2, 2007 from, http://findarticles.com/p/articles/mi_m3495/is_6_50/ai_n14700370/print.

82. Stueck, W. (2007, May 28). Coal company wants to hire Chinese workers for B.C. mine. *The Globe and Mail,* p. B1.

Chapter 9

1. CBC News in Depth. (February 26, 2007). The urge to merge. Retrieved December 28, 2007, from http:www.cbc.ca/news/background/mergers/.

2. Ibid.

3. Ibid.

4. Brahy, S.(Autumn, 2005). Six Solution Pillars for Successful Cultural Integration of International M &As. *Journal of Organizational Excellence,* p. 53.

5. Miller, R. (September–October 2000). How Culture Affects Mergers and Acquisitions, *Industrial Management,* p. 22.

6. Brahy, S. (Autumn, 2005). Six Solution Pillars for Successful Cultural Integration of International M &As, *Journal of Organizational Excellence,* p. 53.

7. The Bulletin, University of Toronto. (November 20, 1995). Retrieved Dec 28, 2007, http:/www. newsandevents.utoronto.ca/bin/bulletin/nov20_95/art6htm.

8. Wikipedia, the free encyclopedia, (2006), Toronto District School Board, retrieved December 28, 2007, http://en.wikipedia.org/wiki/Toronto_District_School_Board.

9. Ibid.

10. thestar.com editorial. (Dec 21, 2007). Proceed carefully on school board, retrieved December 28, 2007, http://www.thestar.com/article/287576.

11. Trustees look at changing the TDSB, *North York Mirror,* Wednesday, December 26, 2007, p. 3.

12. Investopedia, Mergers and Acquisitions: Definition, Retrieved December 28, 2007. http:/www.investopedia.com/university/mergers/mergers1.asp.

13. Ibid.

14. "Mergers and Acquisitions." (2008). http://www.investinontario.com/siteselector/befs_604.asp, retrieved April 24, 2009.

15. Theriault, L. and Beckman, K. (February, 2008). *Trends in Foreign Direct Investment and Mergers and Acquisitions, International and Canadian Performance and Implications.* The Conference Board of Canada, Ottawa.

16. Ibid., p. 16.

17. Ibid., p. 17.

18. "Mergers and Acquisitions." (2008). http://www.investinontario.com/siteselector/befs_604.asp, retrieved April 24, 2009.

19. Ibid., p. 16.

20. Ibid., p. 18.

21. Ibid., chapter 5.

22. Ibid., chapter 5.

23. Lafaix, F. (2002). The Pre-Deal Stage in *Making Mergers Work, The Strategic Importance of People,* ed. by Jeffrey A. Schmidt. A Towers Perrin/SHRM Foundation Publication, p. 70.

24. Lafaix, F. (2002). The Pre-Deal Stage in *Making Mergers Work, The Strategic Importance of People,* ed. by Jeffrey A. Schmidt. A Towers Perrin/SHRM Foundation Publication, p. 71.

25. Hawkrigg, J., and Drover, B. (April 16, 2007). Successful Transformation through Acquisition, Conference Board of Canada, http:// 22848.vws.magma.ca/EPRO_1549/max/e/s06/pdf/Hawkrigg.pdf, retrieved September 21, 2008.

26. Martin, M. (November 2005). *Growing Through Acquisition,* Conference Board of Canada, http://22848.vws.magma.ca/EPRO_1549/max/e/s06/pdf/Martin.pdf, retrieved September 21, 2008.

27. Ibid., p. 72

28. Hall, P. and Norburn, D. (1987). The Management Factor in Acquisition Performance, *Leadership & Organization Development Journal,* No.8.

29. Lafaix, F. (2002). The Pre-Deal Stage in *Making Mergers Work, The Strategic Importance of People,* ed. by Jeffrey A. Schmidt. A Towers Perrin/SHRM Foundation Publication, p. 73.

30. http://archives.cbc.ca/economy_business/transport/clips/6191/, retrieved September 22, 2008.

31. http://www.us.all-biz.info/news/index.php?newsid=315, retrieved September 22, 2008.

32. http://business.timesonline.co.uk/tol/business/industry_sectors/technology/article3346356.ece, retrieved September 22, 2008.

33. Harding, D., & Rouse, T. (April, 2007). Human Due Diligence, *Harvard Business Review,* 85(4), 124.

34. Miller, R. (2000). How Culture Affects Mergers and Acquisitions, *Industrial Management,* September–October 2000, p. 22.

35. Gitelson, Gene, Bing, John W., Ed.D. and Laroche, Lionel. The Impact of Culture on Mergers & Acquisitions, http://www.itapintl.com/mergersandacquisitions.htm. Retrieved December 28, 2007; Schmidt, Jeffrey A. (2002). The Strategic Importance of People, p. 5. in *Marking Mergers Work, The Strategic Importance of People,* A Towers Perrin/SHRM Foundation Publication, Towers Perrin, p. 5.

36. Laviolette, K. and McDowell,T. (2005). Assembling the Post-Merger Integration Team, Conference Board of Canada, http://22848.vws.magma.ca/EPRO_1549/max/e/s06/pdf/laviolette/pdf, retrieved September 19, 2008. Reproducd with the permission of the authors Katya Laviolette, CBC Radio-Canada, and Tom McDowell, Partner, Oliver Wyman Delta.

37. Schmidt, Jeffrey A. (2002). The Strategic Importance of People, in *Marking Mergers Work: The Strategic Importance of People,* A Towers Perrin/SHRM Foundation Publication, Towers Perrin, p. 3–21.

38. Ibid., p. 3–21.

39. Ibid, p. 3– 21

40. Holbeche, L. (1999). *Aligning Human Resources and Business Strategy,* Elsevier, Butterworth Heinemann, London. p. 395.

41. Ibid., p. 395.

42. Gitelson, G., Bing, J. W., and Laroche, L. The Impact of Culture on Mergers & Acquisitions, http://www.itapintl.com/mergersandacquisitions.htm. Retrieved December 28, 2007.

43. Schmidt, Jeffrey A. (2002). The Strategic Importance of People in *Marking Mergers Work: The Strategic Importance of People,* A Towers Perrin/SHRM Foundation Publication, Towers Perrin, p. 5.

44. Pekala, N. (May/June 2001). Merger They Wrote: Avoiding a Corporate Culture Collision, *Journal of Property Management,* Vol. 66, Issue 3.

45. DeMattos, Claudio and Salciuviene, L. (2007). Cultural Compatibility in the Implementation of Mergers and Acquisitions: The Banking Sector, *Economics & Management,* p. 338–345.

46. Schmidt, Jeffrey A. (2002). The Strategic Importance of People, in *Marking Mergers Work: The Strategic Importance of People.* A Towers Perrin/SHRM Foundation Publication, Towers Perrin, p. 9.

47. Harihanan, R. (Nov 2005). HR due diligence in mergers and acquisitions, http://22848.vws.magma.ca/EPRO_1549/max/e/s07/pdf/Harihanan.pdf. Retrieved September 19, 2008.

48. Maines, D.R. (2002). Charting Futures of Sociology: Culture and Meaning, *Contemporary Sociology,* Vol. 29, No. 4, p. 588.

49. Galpin, T. J. and Herndon, M. (2000). The Complete Guide to Mergers and Acquisitions: Process Tools to Support Mergers and Acquisitions Integration at Every Level, *Jossey-Bass Publishers,* p. 9.

50. Schein, L. (November 2001). Managing Culture in Mergers and Acquisitions, The Conference Board of Canada, Research Report, R-1302-01-RR.

51. Ibid., p. 11.

52. Schein, L. (2001). Managing Culture in Mergers and Acquisitions, The Conference Board Research Report R1302-01-RR. p. 1–87.

53. Ibid., p. 6.

54. Cong, D & Ogden, D. (Nov 30, 1998). A Match Made in Heaven? Find Out Before You Merge, *Wall Street Journal,* p. A22.

55. Mirvis, P.H. and Marks, M. L. (1992). The Human Side of Merger Planning: Assessing and Analyzing "Fit," *Human Resource Planning,* Vol. 15, No. 1, p. 77.

56. Cong, D & Ogden, D. (Nov 30, 1998). A Match Made in Heaven? Find Out Before You Merge, *Wall Street Journal,* p. A22.

57. Kay, Ira T. and Shelton, M. (2000). The people problem in mergers, *McKinsey & Company Quarterly.*

58. Harding, D. & Rouse T. (2007, April). Human Due Diligence, retrieved October 15, 2007, from Business Source Complete database, *Harvard Business Review,* 85(4), 124–131.

59. Ibid., p. 124–131.

60. Ibid., p. 124–131.

61. Brahy, S. (Autumn, 2005). Six Solution Pillars for Successful Cultural Integration of International M &As, *Journal of Organizational Excellence,* p. 53 –63, retrieved October 15, 2007, from Business Source Complete database.

62. Harding, D. & Rouse T. (2007, April) Human Due Diligence, retrieved October 15, 2007, from Business Source Complete database, *Harvard Business Review*, 85(4), 124–131.

63. Wheeler, H.N. (1989). Trade Unions and Takeovers: Labor's Response to Mergers and Acquisitions, *Human Resource Planning,* Vol. 12, No. 2, p. 167–177.

64. Harding, D. & Rouse T. (2007, April). Human Due Diligence, retrieved October 15, 1007, from Business Souce Complete database, Harvard Business Review, 85 (4), p. 124–131.

65. Schein, L. (November 2001). Managing Culture in Mergers and Acquisitions, The Conference Board of Canada, Research Report, R-1302-01-RR, p. 11.

66. Holbeche, L. (1999). *Aligning Human Resources and Business Strategy,* Elsevier, Butterworth Heinemann, London. p. 395.

67. Ibid., p. 416.

68. Ibid., p. 417.

69. Galpin, T. J., and Herndon, M. (2000). The Complete Guide to Mergers and Acquisitions, Process Tools to Support Mergers and Acquisitions Integration at Every Level, *Jossey-Bass Publishers,* p. 14.

70. Schmidt, Jeffrey A. (2002). The Strategic Importance of People, in *Marking Mergers Work, The Strategic Importance of People.* A Towers Perrin/SHRM Foundation Publication, Towers Perrin, 2002, p. 20.

Chapter 10

1. Cascio, W. (2005). From Business partner to driving business success: The next steps in the evolution of HR management. *Human Resource Management, 44*(2), 159–163.

2. Kaplan, R.S., & Norton, D.P. (1996). *The Balanced Scorecard: Translating Strategy Into Action.* Boston: Harvard Business School Press.

3. Ultimate performance: Measuring human resources at work. (2008). *Canadian HR Focus.*

4. Niven, R. P. (2005). *Balanced Scorecard Diagnostic: Maintaining Maximum Performance,* New York: Harvard Business School Press.

5. Niven, R. P., (2005). *Balanced Scorecard Diagnostic: Maintaining Maximum Performance,* New York: Harvard Business School Press, p. 17.

6. Haridas, M. The HR Scorecard. Retrieved July 13, 2008 from rad1986.pbwiki.com/f/human%2520 resources%2520scorecard.pdf

7. Huselid, M. (2007). The HR Scorecard. Retrieved February 4, 2008 from http://www.markhuselid.com/hr.html

8. Dyer, L., & Shafer, R. (1998). From human resource strategy to organizational effectiveness: Lesson from research on organizational agility, CAHRS Working Paper 98(12), 10.

9. Grossman, R. J. (2000, January). Measuring up: Appropriate metrics help HR prove its worth. *HR Magazine.*

10. Ultimate performance: Measuring human resources at work (2008). *Canadian HR Focus.*

11. Ibid.

12. Davison, B. (2003). Reviewing corporate financials shows how HR measures up. *Employment Relations Today;* 30(1), 7.

13. Cash Focus. Strategic Focus-concepts. Retrieved August 4, 2008 from http://www.cashfocus.com/sf_overview.htm

14. Diewert, E., Nakamura, A. (2005). *Concepts and Measures of Productivity: An Introduction, Service Industry and Knowledge Based Economy,* The University of Calgary Press.

15. Romeo, J. (2003 October). Answering the Call. *HR Magazine,* 48 (10).

16. Pulse survey. (2008, 16 June). *Canadian HR Reporter,* 7.

17. Pulse survey. (2008, 16 June). *Canadian HR Reporter,* 7

18. Pulse survey. (2008, 16 June). *Canadian HR Reporter,* 7.

19. Sullivan, J. (2007 February, 7). Growing the Google Talent Machine. *Human Resources Magazine.*

20. Burkholder, N. (2007). *Ultimate Performance: Measuring Resources at Work,* John Wiley & Sons, p. 66.

21. Sougue, J.P. (1996). Focusing on Competencies, Training and Development, Practices, Expenditures, and Trends. *Conference Board of Canada,* 177–196.

22. Mercer. (2008). Compensation and Staffing Implications of a Changing Economic Climate—Snapshot Survey.

23. Canada Public Service Agency. (2004). Annual Report on Learning, Training, and Developmental Activities.

24. The Strategic Value of People: Human Resource Trends and Metrics. (2006, July). The Conference Board of Canada, 21.

25. Ibid.

26. Fleming, M. J. (2001). Effective HR measurement techniques. *Society for Human Resources Management,* 7.

27. The Strategic Value of People: Human Resource Trends and Metrics. (2006, July). The Conference Board of Canada, 21.

28. Ibid., p. 9.

29. HR by the number (2006, September 11). *Canadian HR Reporter,* 4.

30. The Strategic Value of People: Human Resource Trends and Metrics. (2006, July 7). The Conference Board of Canada, 21.

31. What Canadian are happy and unhappy about at work (2007, September 24). *Canadian HR Reporter,* p. 7.

32. Koys, D. J. (2001). The effects of employee satisfaction, organizational citizenship behaviour, and turnover on organizational effectiveness: A unit-level, longitudinal study. *Personnel Psychology;* Tsui, A., Pearce, J., Porter, L., & Thpoli, A. (1997). Alternative approaches to the employee organization relationship: Does investment in employees pay off? *Academy of Management Journal,* 4(40), 1089–1121; Dalton, D., Krackhardt, D., & Porter, L. (1981). Dysfunctional turnover reflects loss of effective performers or highly skilled and/or trained personnel that are not easily replaceable, Functional turnover: An empirical assessment. *Journal of Applied Psychology,* 66.

33. Carroll, T. (2007, December 19). Calculating the High Cost of Employee Turnover, tamm Communications.

34. Service Canada. Job Futures World of Work. National Edition, 4. Retrieved February 12, 2007, from http://www.jobfutures.ca/en/brochure/JobFuture.pdf.

35. The strategic value of people: Human resources trends and metrics as cited in How long does it take to fill a vacancy? What will it cost? (2008, September 16). *Canadian HR Reporter,* 4.

Chapter 11

1. Public Policy Forum. (2008 March). Report on the CGA-Canada Summit on Skills and Organizational Learning. Ottawa: Certified General Accountants.

2. Lapointe, M., Dunn, K., Tremblay-Cote, N., Bergeron, L., & Ignaczak, L. (2006). Looking Ahead: A 10-year Outlook for the Canadian Labour Market (2006-2015), Labour Market and Skills Forecasting and Analysis Unit, Human Resources and Social Development Canada.

3. Human Resources and Social Development of Canada. (2006). Advancing the Inclusion of People with Disabilities. Retrieved March 3, 2008 from http://www.hrsdc.gc.ca/en/disability_issues/reports/fdr/2006/page00.shtml.

4. Human Resources and Social Development of Canada. (2006). Advancing the Inclusion of People with Disabilities. Retrieved March 3, 2008 from http://www.hrsdc.gc.ca/en/disability_issues/reports/fdr/2006/page00.shtml.

5. Klie, S. (2008 February, 11). Price tag of IT shortage: $10 billion per year. *Canadian HR Reporter,* 21(3)

6. Human Resources and Social Development of Canada. (2006). Advancing the Inclusion of People with Disabilities. Retrieved March 3, 2008 from http://www.hrsdc.gc.ca/en/disability_issues/reports/fdr/2006/page00.shtml.

7. HR by the numbers. (2008, June 16). *Canadian HR Reporter,* 4.

8. Bowlby, G. & Cross, P. (2006). The Alberta economic juggernaut: The boon on the rose. *Canadian Economic Observer,* Statistics Canada. Retrieved March 14, 2008 from www.statcan.ca/english/freepub/11-010-XIB/00906/feature.htm.

9. Alberta Employment, Immigration and Industry. (2008). *Employer Labour Market News*, 3, 1. Retrieved March 12, 2008 from, http://employment.alberta.ca/documents/RRM/RRM-CG08janE.pdf.

10. Malatest & Associates Ltd. (2003). The Aging Workforce and Human Resources Development Implications for Sector Councils. Retrieved February 28, 2008 from http://cpsc-ccsp.ca/PDSF/Aging%20Workforce%20Final%20Report.pdf.

11. HRM Guide, 2007, from www.hrmguide.net.

12. McCraken, R. (2007, February 5). Booming Numbers. *The Ottawa Citizen*, 1.

13. Powers, G. (2008, March 18). Phased Retiremenet Slowly Catching On. *Sympatico MSN Finance.* Retrieved March 18, 2008, from http://finance.sympatico.msn.ca/retirement/gordonpowers/articles.aspx?cp-documentid=6526884.

14. HRM guide, 2007, from www.hrmguide.net.

15. Streb, C.K., Veolpel, S.C, & Leibold, M. (2008). Managing The Aging Workforce: Status Quo and Implications for the Advancement of Theory and Practice. *European Management Journal*, 26, 1–10.

16. Malatest & Associates Ltd. (2003). The Aging Workforce and Human Resources Development Implications for Sector Councils. Retrieved February 28, 2008 from http://cpsc-ccsp.ca/PDSF/Aging%20Workforce%20 Final%20Report.pdf.

17. McMahan, S. & Sturz, D. (2006). Implications for an Aging Workforce. *Journal of Education for Business,* 82(1), 50–55.

18. Brannae, M. (2008). Glass ceiling becoming slightly thicker in Canada. *The Montreal Gazette.*

19. Talbot-Allen, N. (2005 June). Diversity in the Workforce. *CMA Management,* 69(3).

20. HR Benchmarking. (2008). March Madness at Work; Defining Diversity; Syncing the CEOs up with executives. *PR NEWS,* 64.

21. HRPAO (2007). Corporate Diversity Assessment Report.

22. Chhinzer, N. (2007). "Immigrant versus Non-immigrant Differences in Demand for Unions: A test of the Self-Protection Model." Gender and Diversity Division, in Proceedings of Administrative Sciences Academy of Canada Annual Conference, Ottawa, ON, Canada.

23. Statistics Canada, (2003). Ministry of Industry, 92(378), 21.

24. Statistics Canada, (2007, December 4). 2006 Census: Immigration, citizenship, language, mobility and migration. Retrieved May 18, 2008 from http://www.statcan.ca/Daily/English/071204/d071204a.htm.

25. Ostovsky, Y. (2008, April 9). Earnings Inequality and Earnings Instability of Immigrants in Canada. Retrieved May 13, 2008 from http://www.statcan.ca/english/research/11F0019MIE/11F0019MIE2008309.htm.

26. Statistics Canada. (2008 May, 13). Canada's Immigrant Labour Market. Retrieved July 28, 2008 from http://www.statcan.ca/Daily/English/080513/d080513a.htm.

27. Galarneau, D. & Morissette, R. (2004). "Immigrants: Settling for less?" *Perspectives on Labour and Income,* Vol.16, No. 3, Autumn 2004, Statistics Canada, Catalogue no. 75-001-XPE.

28. Statistics Canada, 2003. Catalogue No. 92-378-XIE, *Ministry of Industry,* revised April 2003.

29. Study: Demand for Skills in Canada: The Role of Foreign Outsourcing and Information Communication Technology. (2005 October, 28). Statistics Canada.

30. HRPAO. (Oct 2007). Corporate Diversity Assessment Report (www.hrpa.ca)

31. Statistics Canada. (2001). Experienced labour force 15 years and over by occupation and sex, by province and territory (2001 Census). Retrieved March 1, 2008 from http://www.statcan.ca/english/Subjects/Labour/ LFS/lfs-en.htm.

32. Lahey, K. (2001). The Impact of Relationship Recognition on Lesbian Women in Canada: Still Separate and Only Somewhat 'Equivalent.' *Status of Women in Canada:* Ottawa.

33. Lahey, K. (2005). Women and Employment: Removing Fiscal Barriers to Women's Labour Force Participation: Ottawa, 17.

34. Statistics Canada. (2001). Experienced labour force 15 years and over by occupation and sex, by province and territory (2001 Census). Retrieved March 1, 2008 from http://www.statcan.ca/english/Subjects/Labour/ LFS/lfs-en.htm.

35. Steele, S.W. (2004). The best and the brightest. *Canadian Business,* 77, 4-1.

36. Lahey, K. (2005). Women and Employment: Removing Fiscal Barriers to Women's Labour Force Participation: Ottawa, 17.

37. Human Resources and Social Development of Canada. (2006). Advancing the Inclusion of People with Disabilities. Retrieved March 3, 2008 from http://www.hrsdc.gc.ca/en/disability_issues/reports/fdr/2006/ page00.shtml.

38. CCDS. (2004) Disability Information Sheet. Retrieved March 11, 2008 from http://www.ccsd.ca/drip/ research/drip16/drip16.pdf.

39. Statistics Canada. (2002) A Profile of Disability in Canada, Participation Activity Limitation Survey (PALS), Catalogue no. 89-577-XIE.

40. CCDS. (2004) Disability Information Sheet. Retrieved March 11, 2008 from http://www.ccsd.ca/drip/ research/drip16/drip16.pdf.

41. Bowlby, G. & Cross, P. (2006) The Alberta economic juggernaut: The boon on the rose, *Canadian Economic Observer,* Statistics Canada. Retrieved March 14, 2008 from www.statcan.ca/english/freepub/ 11-010-XIB/00906/feature.htm.

42. Alberta Employment, Immigration and Industry. (2008). Employer Labour Market News 3, 1. Retrieved March 12, 2008 from, http://employment.alberta.ca/documents/RRM/RRM-CG08janE.pdf.

43. Alberta Human Resources and Employment. (2005). Understanding Alberta's Labour Force: Looking to the Future, 1–25.

44. "The Year in HR." (December 15, 2008). www.personneltoday.com.

45. The ideal work week for seniors. (2008, May 5). *Canadian HR Reporter,* 4.

46. HR by the numbers. (2006, September 11). *Canadian HR Reporter,* 4.

47. Canadian Center for Occupational Health and Safety. (2002, February 12). Retrieved February 19, 2008 from http://www.ccohs.ca/oshanswers/psychosocial/flexible.html.

48. Beauchesne, E. (2008, June 06). Part-time work props up Canada's job growth. *Canwest News Service.* Retrieved March 18, 2008 from http://72.14.205.104/search?q=cache:BMrGrOVPgIEJ:www.nationalpost.com/news/story.html%3Fid%3D569378+Growth+in+Part-time+workers+in+Canada&hl=en&ct=clnk&cd=3&gl=ca.

49. Laurentian Bank Securities. (2008 August, 8). No matter how we slice it the labour market's conditions are deteriorating. Retrieved August 1, 2008 from http://cebl.vmbl.ca/Economics/1/CEQ%2008082008_e.pdf.

50. Akyeampong, E.B. (2007 June). Working at home: an update. *Perspectives on Labour and Income,* 8.

51. Absence makes the heart grow fonder? (2007, September 24). *Canadian HR Reporter,* 4.

52. Absence makes the heart grow fonder? (2007, September 24). *Canadian HR Reporter,* 4.

53. Canada News Wire. (2007). The Race is On! Research Revels IT Outsourcing and Offshoring are Taking Competition to a New High.

54. Mossison, T. (2007). Outsourcing heat treating by manufacturers brings profit to the bottom line. *Industrial Heating,* 74(2).

55. Vincent, R. & McKeown, L. (2008 February 15). Trends in the telephone call centre industry, *Statistics Canada.*

56. The Canadian Chamber of Commerce. (2005). Offshoring Outsourcing: Opportunities and Challenges for the Canadian. Retrieved March 5, 2008 from www.chanber.ca/cmslib/general/OutSourcing050113.pdf.

57. Parsons, S. (2004). You're thinking about outsourcing. . .now what? *Mercer.*

58. Embleton, P.R, & Wright, P.C. (1998). A practical guide to successful outsourcing. *Empowerment in Organizations,* 6(3), 94–106.

59. Adkins, D. (2005, June). Outsourcing Performance Management. *Working Performance Solutions.*

60. Garvey, C. (2001, March 25). Outsourcing Background Checks. *HR Magazine.*

61. McDougall, D. (2007). Child Sweatshop Shame Threatens Gap's Ethical Image, *The Observer.*

62. Berry, M. (2006). Creativity should be a weapon of choice in war for talent. *Personnel Today.* Retrieved March 18, 2008 from http://personneltoday.com/articiles/2006/02/24/34072/creativity.

63. Ordanini, A. & Silvestri, G. (2008). Recruitment and selection services: Efficiency and competitive reasons in the outsourcing of HR practices. *The International Journal of Human Resource Management,* 19(2), 372–391.

64. Adkins, Sam S. (2005). Outsourcing Performance Management. *Workforce Performance Solutions.* June 2005.

65. Hewitt Associates. (2008). Our Services: HR outsourcing. Retrieved March 11, 2008 from http://www.hewittassociates.com/Intl/NA/en-US/OurServiceLine.aspx?sln=HR=Outsourcing.

66. DeFerhen, R. (2003). Outsourcing benefit administration services: A methodical approach of organization success. *Employee Benefit Review,* 58(2), 43–47.

67. Sharratt, A. (2005). Benefit Canada Magazine: what lies below. Retrieved March 11, 2008 from http://www.benefitscanada.com/news/article.jsp?content=20060721_131046_5420.

68. Harris, P. (2005 January). Training and Development: Training Outsourcing Finds its Identity. *HRO Today.*

69. Powers, C. (2007 September 24). Outsourcing gets its own designation. *HR Reporter,* 15.

70. Overby, S. (2005, September 1). Backsourcing Pain. *CIO magazine,* www.cio.com.

71. Lacity, M.C. and Hirscheim, R. (1993) The information systems outsourcing bandwagon. *Sloan Management Review* 35, 73–86.

72. Hall, R. (2008 March). Outsourcing, contracting-out and labour. *Asia Pacific Journal of Human Resources.*

73. Margulius, L, D. (2007). Staying Stateside. Retrieved March 19, 2008, from www.inforworld.com.

74. Ibid.

Appendix A

1. Plevel, M.J., Lane, F., Nellis, S., and Schuler, R.S. (Winter 1994). AT&T global business communications systems: Linking HR with business strategy. *Organizational Dynamics,* Vol 22 Issue 3, p. 59–72.

2. Ibid.

3. Slater, R. (1990). *Jack Welch and the GE Way,* McGraw Hill.

4. Ulrich, D. (1997). Human Resources Champions, Harvard Business School Press, Boston.

5. Brockbank, W. (1999). If HR were really strategically proactive: Present and future directions in HR's contribution to competitive advantage, *Human Resource Management,* 38, 337–352.

6. Ibid.

7. Holbeche, L. (2001). *Aligning Human Resources and Business Strategy,* Elsevier, Butterworth, Heinemann, London.

8. Peter, J.W. and Wargo and Company. (1988). Strategic staffing: A key link in business and human resource planning. *Human Resource Planning,* Vol. 11, No. 2, p. 151–158.

9. Plevel, M.J., Lane, F., Nellis, S., and Schuler, R.S. (Winter 1994). AT&T global business communications systems: Linking HR with business strategy. *Organizational Dynamics,* Vol 22 Issue 3, p. 59–72.

10. Ulrich, D. (1992). Strategic and human resource planning: Linking customers and employees. *Human Resource Planning,* Vol. 15, No. 2. pg. 47–62.

11. Cohn, J.M, Khurana, R, and Reeves, L. (October 2005). Growing talent as if your business depended on it. *Harvard Business Review,* p. 67.

12. Peter, J.W. and Wargo and Company. (1988). Strategic staffing: A key link in business and human resource planning. *Human Resource Planning,* Vol. 11, No. 2, p. 155.

13. Ibid., p. 157.

14. Ibid., p. 158.

15. Boroski, J.W. (1990) Putting it together: HR planning in "3D" at Eastman Kodak. *Human Resource Planning,* Vol. 13, No. 1, p. 45.

16. Beniaminovich, M. and Fortier, G. (March 2007). Building Effective HR Strategies Aligned with Changing Business Plans.

17. Lawler III, E.E. & Mohrman, S.A. (2003). HR as a strategic partner: What does it take to make it happen? *Human Resource Planning,* Vol. 26, No. 3, 15–28.

18. Ulrich, D. (1992). Strategic and human resource planning: Linking customers and employees. *Human Resource Planning,* Vol. 15, No. 2, p. 47–62.

19. http://www.opm.gov/studies/teamsapp.pdf., retrieved Oct, 2009.

20. Ibid

21. http://www.ipma-aigp.ca/certification/competencyTable-new.htm

22. Boroski, J.W. (1990). Putting it together: HR planning in "3D" at Eastman Kodak. *Human Resource Planning,* Vol. 13, p. 1.

23. Ibid., p. 48.

24. Peters, J.W. and Wargo and Company. (1988). Strategic staffing: A key link in business and human resource planning. *Human Resource Planning,* Vol. 11, No. 2, p. 154.

25. Ulrich, D. (1992). Strategic and human resource planning: Linking customers and employees. *Human Resource Planning,* Vol. 15, No. 2. pg. 47–62.

26. Cohn, J.M, Khurana, R., and Reeves, L. (October 2005). Growing talent as if your business depended on it. *Harvard Business Review,* p. 62–70.

27. Brush, M.C, Ruse, D.H. (2005). Driving strategic success through human capital planning. *Human Resource Planning* Vol. 28, No. 1. p 49–60.

28. Ibid., p. 51.

NAME INDEX

ABB Company, 178–179
ABC Company, 225, 257, 281
ADP, 59
Advanced Devices Inc., 205
Agassi, Shai, 137
Agence France-Pressee, 197
Air Canada, 82, 100, 209, 210
Alberta Employment, Immigration
    and Industry, 262
Alcan Inc., 72, 206, 207
Al-Qaeda, 55
Andolsen, A. A., 113
AOL, 210
AON, 135
Apax Partner, 207
Apple Computer, 13, 154
Applied Science Technologists &
    Technicians of British Columbia
    (ASTTBC), 54–55
Arcelor SA, 147, 205
Associated Press, 82
Association of Executive Search
    Consultants, 269
AT&T, 151, 215, 284
ATI Technologies, 205
Atlas Van Lines, 198

Banco de Comercio, 208
Banff Springs Hotel, 205
Bank of Dalian Co. Ltd, 183
Bank of Montreal (BMO), 60
Bank of Nova Scotia, 138, 183
Banknorth, 205
Bartlett, C. A., 193
BC Telecom, 209
Bearing Point, 189
Bell Canada, 205, 209
Bell South, 82
Berkeley University, 82
Best Buy Company Inc., 68
Bharti Enterprises, 186
BioWare Corp., 15
Blake, Frank, 151

Block, B., 124
Blue Ribbon Sports, 155
BMO (Bank of Montreal), 60
Boeing, 167
Booz Allen Hamilton, 136, 152
Boston Consulting Group, 155
Bowerman, Bill, 155, 193
British Columbia Ambulance Service, 2
British Petroleum, 6
Brockbank, W., 284
Brookfield Asset Management Inc., 207
Brooks, L., 109
Brown, D., 109
Bruce Nuclear, 125
Bruce Power, 125–126
Buckingham, M., 127
Bureau of Labor Statistics, 137
BusinessWeek, 55

Cambridge House, 61
Cameron, Kim, 79
Canadian Aboriginal and Minority
    Council, 138
Canadian Airlines, 210
Canadian Auto Workers (CAW), 78, 90
Canadian Centre for Occupational Health
    and Safety, 270
Canadian HR Reporter, 239
Canadian Human Rights Tribunal
    (CHRT), 267
Canadian Information Centre for
    International Credentials, 265
Canadian Manufacturers and Exporters, 72
Canadian Medical Association (CMA),
    33, 34
Canadian Occupational Projection System
    (COPS), 32
Canadian Public Service Agency, 243
Canadian Telework Association, 273
Canadian Tire Corp., 108, 110, 124,
    206, 211
Canadian Tourism Human Resource
    Council, 32

Canfor Corp., 91
CanJet, 96
Cantor Fitzgerald, 135
Capability Microsoft Corporation, 121
Capellie, P., 126
Capital One, 69, 170, 238
Casino Windsor, 91
CBC, 82, 205
CBS, 193
CedarCrestone, 165
Cendant, 164
Central Intelligence Agency (CIA), 173
Ceridian, 59
Certified General Accountants Association
    of Canada (CGA-Canada), 260
Chambers, E. G., 127, 128
The Chang School, 159
Chateau Frontenac, 205
The China Electronic and Information
    Development Academy, 189
Chrysler Corporation, 10, 78, 205
CIBC, 66, 250
Clemens, Tanya, 121
CN Rail, 108, 110, 124, 127
Cognos Inc., 8, 170
Colgate Palmolive, 143
Commerce Bancorp, Inc., 207
Companhia Vale do Rio Doce, 207
Compaq Computers, 97, 208, 209
COMPAS Inc., 66
Conference Board of Canada, 108, 127,
    130, 244, 245, 253, 274
Construction Sector Council, 32
Corbett, David, 186
Corning Inc., 17, 293
Corporate Leadership Council, 152

Daimler-Benz, 205
DaimlerChrysler, 205
Danka, 208
Day, Brian, 34
Dehau International Mines
    Group Inc., 202

Delbecq, A. L., 43
Dell, 13, 60, 96
Deloitte and Touche, 145
Deloitte Consulting, 125
Delta Airlines, 210
Department of Education
     and Science, 112
Desjardin, 108, 110, 127
Dharmawan, Jody, 190
Directors Network Inc., 156
Dofasco Inc., 9, 147, 205
Dow Chemical, 148
DuPont Chemical, 82, 202

Eastman Kodak, 5, 6, 291
Effron, M., 124
Eli Lily, 147
Embraer, 186
Emergency Preparedness Canada, 72
Environment Canada, 22
Environmental Careers Organization
     (ECO Canada), 55
Ernst and Young LLP, 109, 193, 202
Exult, 60

Fairmont Hotels and Resorts, 205, 206
Falconbridge, 206
Fasken Martineau DuMoulin LLP, 186
The Financial Post, 55
Fiorina, Carleton (Carly), 151
Fire Department of New York, 135
Fisher, Robert, 151
Florida Power & Light Co., 175
Ford Motor Company, 10, 78, 82
Fortune Brands Inc., 134
48 Hours, 193
Freedman, Audrey, 61
Friesens Corp., 57
Furlong, John, 2

the Gap Inc., 146, 151, 275
Gartner Consulting, 189
GE Electronics, 209
General Electric (GE), 110, 123, 151,
     218, 284, 292
General Motors Corporation (GM),
     10, 78, 82, 123
Gerdes, L., 109, 111
Ghoshal, S., 193
Ginzberg, E., 109
Global Business Communications
     Systems (GBCS), 284, 285, 286,
     289, 290
Globe and Mail, 224
Google Inc., 9, 14, 210, 241, 242
Great-West Lifeco, 207
Grundy, Tony, 7
Gutierrez, Carlos M., 134

Hall, D. T., 122
Hall, P., 209
Hammerberg, Lorne, 100
Handfeld-Jones, H., 125
Harding, D., 216
Hay Group, 136
Henderson, Paul, 89
Hewitt Associates, Inc., 67, 137, 147
Hewitt Consulting, 149
Hewlett-Packard (HP), 60, 82, 151,
     208, 209
Hoell, Robert C., 163
Hofstede, Geert, 187, 188
Home Depot, 136, 151
Home Way, 136
Honda Motor Company Ltd., 78, 182, 193
Horn, Alan, 152
Howe, Jeff, 61
HP. *See* Hewlett-Packard (HP)
HR Reporter, 264
hrmetrics.org, 239
Hudson's Bay Company, 206
Human Resource Planning Society, 5
Human Resources and Skills Development
     Canada, 22
Human Resources and Social Development
     Canada (HRSDC), 30, 32, 74
Human Resources Professional Association
     (HRPA), 123
Hurd, Mark, 151

IBM, 9, 60, 82, 164, 187, 277, 288
Inco Limited, 206, 207
Indian Institute of Technology (IIT), 281
Inditex (Industria de Diseno Textil), 7
Industria de Diseno Textil (Inditex), 7
Information Technology Association
     of America (ITTA), 55
Institute of Chartered Accountants
     of Ontario, 123
Institute of Management and
     Administration (IOMA), 137
Intel, 11
International Association of Machinists
     and Aerospace Workers (IAM), 100
International Association of Outsourcing
     Professionals (IAOP), 277
International Personnel Management
     Association (IPMA), 290, 291
IPMA-HR (International Public
     Management Association for Human
     Resources), 3, 7
Ipsos-Reid, 86
iStockphoto, 59, 61

Jackson, S. E., 15
Jenness, James M., 134
Job Futures, 22, 32, 36

John Hancock Financial, 205
Johnson & Johnson, 154
Jones, William J., 163
Jones Retail, 178–179
Jordan, Michael, 155
Joseph, Stephanie R., 156
JP Morgan, 277

Kagermann, Henning, 137
Kaplan, Robert, 228
KD Displays, 146
Kellogg's, 134
Kenexa Research Institute, 272
KFC, 209
Kirkpatrick, 148
Knight, Phil, 155, 156, 193
Kodak. *See* Eastman Kodak
Korn/Ferry, 125, 187
KPMG International, 201, 202, 250
Krinks, P., 111

Laval University, 34
Life magazine, 193
The Limited, 125
Loblaws, 146, 151
Lucas, George, 15
Lucent Technologies, 151

McDonald's, 14
Mackay, David, 134
McKinsey and Company, 108, 124, 206
Manpower Inc., 108
Manulife Financial, 205
Mapic Inc., 175
Marine Institute, 54
Marks Work Wearhouse, 206
MasterCard, 238
Menu Foods Income Fund, 89
Mercer, 243
Merge Technologies Inc., 82
Metropolitan Toronto Public School
     Board, 205
Microsoft, 9, 117, 119–122, 124, 129, 210
Miles, Raymond, 13, 14
Mills, Daniel Quinn, 16, 21
Mining Association of British
     Columbia, 202
Ministry of Labour, 10, 32, 86
Mohamed, Nadir, 152
MTD Products Canada, 90
MTV, 5
Multiplex Group, 207
Murphy, Glenn, 146, 151
Murray Axmith and Associates, 99

Nardelli, Robert, 151
The National Post, 55
NCR, 215

Nelson Hall, 164
Nike Inc., 155, 193
Nissan, 182
Nortel Networks, 82, 152, 276
Norton, David, 228
NursingNet, 122

Onex Corp., 210
Ontario Chamber of Commerce
    and Public Safety CHECK, 72
Ontario Nurses' Association, 54
Oracle Corporation, 135, 160, 168,
    170, 189
Organization for Economic
    Co-operation and Development
    (OECD), 33
Otellini, Paul, 11

Pan Pacific Hotel, 57
Pandemic Studios, 15
Pennsylvania State University, 109
PeopleSoft Enterprises, 160, 161, 168
PepsiCo, 209
Perez, William, 155, 156
Performance Resource Organization, 232
Peters, J.W., 287, 288
Peters, Stephen, 57
Pfizer, 208
Phillips, Jack, 232
Phillips Electronics, 109
Pitney Bowes, 208
Pizza Hut, 209
Porter, Michael, 13
PostLinx, 208
Praxis Partners, 125
Pressler, Paul, 151
PricewaterhouseCoopers (PWC),
    123, 197, 276
Procter & Gamble, 61, 123
Prudential Financial, 141
Prudential Relocation, 198
Public Policy Forum, 260

RAND corporation, 43
RBC (Royal Bank of Canada), 138
Research in Motion Ltd. (RIM), 128
Reuters Group PIC, 207
Revenue Canada, 57, 58, 64, 74
Rhino Foods, 60
Rio Tinto, 206, 207
Robinson, Mark, 61
Rogers, Edward, 152
Rogers, Melinda, 152
Rogers, Ted, 152
Rogers Communications, Inc., 152
Rothwell, William J., 141, 148
Rouse, T., 216
Royal Bank of Canada (RBC), 138

Royal Canadian Mounted Police
    (RCMP), 174
Runzheimer International, 198
Ryerson University, 159

The Santangelo Group, 191
SAP, 137, 150, 160, 161, 168–169,
    175, 189
Sapporo Breweries, 205
Sara Lee Corporate, 134
Saratoga Institute, 233
SAS, 159, 209
SC Johnson, 155
Schein, L., 215
Schiemann, W., 19
Schindler Group, 202
Schuler, R., 15
Schwartz, Gerald, 210
Scotiabank, 138, 183, 208
Scott Paper, 136
Sears, 109
Semco, 60
Services Canada, 265
Shatilla, David, 146
Shatilla, Kim, 146
Shatilla, Robert and Joan, 146
Shell Canada Limited, 207
Shell Investments Limited, 207
Shoppers Drug Mart, 146
SHRM Foundation, 213
Sleeman Breweries, 205
Snow, Charles, 13, 14
Software Human Resource Council, 55
Sonnenfeld, J.A., 117, 118, 120, 129
Southern Alberta Institute
    of Technology, 55
Southland Transportation, 268
Spence, A. Michael, 155
Stanford Graduate School of Business, 155
Star Alliance, 209
Statistics Canada, 22, 32, 55, 65, 66,
    74, 279
Stelco Inc., 91, 147
Stewart, T. A., 111
Strack, R., 111
Stringer Saul LLP, 186
Sunnybrook Health Sciences Centre, 205
Sunnybrook Medical Centre, 205
Super, D. E., 112
Supreme Court of Canada, 87
Sysco Corporation, 228
Systems and Services Company, 228

Taco Bell, 209
Talver, Brent, 75
Tata Group, 7
Taylor, I., 125
TD Bank, 205, 207

Techtronic Industries, 186
TELUS, 205, 209
TH Lee, Putnam Capital, Limited
    Partnership, 207
Theriault, L., 207
Thomson Corporation, 207
Thomson Learning, 207
3M, 135
Toronto District School Board, 205
Toronto Financial Services Alliance,
    108, 124, 162–163
Tory, John, 152
Towers Perrin, 213
Town Care Dental Groups, 164
Toyota, 78, 182
Transcontinental, 212
Travelport, 164
Truckers Assist, 244
Trump, Grant, 55

Ulrich, D., 124, 284
United Airlines, 82
University of Canada, 102–103
University of Montreal, 34
University of Toronto, 205
University of Waterloo, 145
US Airways Group Inc., 210

Van Dam, N., 125
Vancouver Board of Trade, 2
Vancouver Olympic Committee, 2
VandeVen, A. H., 43
Verschuren, Annette, 136
Viking Air Ltd., 55
Visa, 238

Walker, James W., 5
Walmart, 186
Walt Disney Corporation, 151
Warner-Lambert, 208
Watson Wyatt Worldwide, 67
Welch, Jack, 151, 284
WestJet, 154
Wexber, 125
Weyerhaeuser, 138, 143, 145
Willet, Dwight, 125
William Mercer, 68
Wired, 61
Women's College Hospital, 205
Woods, Tiger, 155
World Health Organization
    (WHO), 54

Yahoo, 210

Zafirovski, Mike, 152
Zara, 7–8
Zebra Ltd., 75

SUBJECT INDEX

Aboriginal peoples
　Employment Equity Act, 265
　skills training, 260
aboriginal status discrimination, 190
absence cost factor, 248
absenteeism, 247–248
　and downsizing, 96
academic mobility, 260
accounting budget analysts
　role in HR planning, 28
acquisitions. *See* mergers and acquisitions
actuarial losses, 35
administration
　in evaluating succession management, 148
aerospace industry, labour shortage, 55
age discrimination, 87, 190
Alberta, workforce planning strategies,
　53, 262
alternative staffing strategies, 56–61
　see also staffing strategies
　alternative staffing sources, 7
　contingent workforce, 61–69
　contract workers, types of, 58–61
　contracting out, 58–61
　factors in determining best options,
　　69–71
　financial constraints, 70
　hiring of employees, 56–57
　internal employee development, 64
　managerial preferences, 70–71, 193–194
　revocability, 71
alternative work arrangements
　annualized (or banked) hours, 270–271
　case incident, 281
　compressed workweek, 67, 270
　flextime, 270, 272
　impact on HR planning, 272–273
　part-time work, 271
　reduced hours, 271
　telecommuting, 67, 271–272, 273
　trends in, 261, 269–270
　work arrangements, leveraging, 65–69

analyzers, 14
annualized hours, 270–271
anti-discrimination legislation,
　globally, 190
applicant tracking system (ATS),
　237–238
appropriate planning horizon, 27–28
assertiveness, 188
attraction and acquisition of talent, 235
　cost metrics, 238–239
　quality metrics, 239–241
　quantity metrics, 238, 241–242
　time metrics, 238, 242
attrition, 252
attrition rate, 252
attrition strategies
　early retirement, 87–88
　forms of, 79–80
　hiring freezes, 86–87

baby-boom generation
　retirement of, 53, 262–263
balanced scorecard approach,
　228–231
balanced scorecard-based performance
　measurement system, 173
banked hours, 270–271
behavioural competencies, 127
bench strength, 141
benefits
　harmonization of in mergers, 218
　outsourcing of, 276
　wage or benefit concessions, 89, 90
boundaryless career, 113
　mentoring programs in, 122–123
bumping rights, 99–100
business ecosystem, 183
business planning
　impact of linking human resource
　　planning with, 293
　linking with human resource planning
　　(HRP), 285–288

models for linking with human resource
　planning (HRP), 288–290
reactive vs. proactive human resource
　response, 286–287
business strategic plan
　link with human resource planning, 5
business strategy, 12
　aligning with human resource planning
　　(HRP), 294
　alignment of HRP to, 11–12
　competitive strategies, 13
　functional strategies, 14
　growth strategies, 13–14
　link with human resource management, 14
buyouts, 82

Canada
　automotive sector, 78
　average annual layoff rate, 81
　average retirement age, 87
　average total income by gender
　　and age, 266
　cause of turnover in, 251
　cross-border takeovers, 205, 206–207
　downsizing compensation
　　comparison, 105
　foreign workers in, 191
　future labour force growth, 108
　labour market outlook, 261, 263
　mandatory retirement, 68, 87, 263
　manufacturing sector decline, 80
　mergers and acquisitions in, 206–207
　projected job growth by occupational
　　grouping, 32
　Public Policy Forum
　　recommendations, 260
　retirement by occupational group,
　　expected, 252
　university education by ethnicity, 265
　vacancy metrics, 253
　visible minorities in workforce, 137–138
Canada Labour Code, 57

Canadian Occupational Projection System (COPS), 32
career, concept of, 112–113
career development, 108–132
  career management balance, 115
  career models, 117–122
  co-operative student programs, 57, 109
  defined, 109
  feedback mechanisms, 117, 128
  as HRP objective, 6
  human capital, 111–114
  and human resource planning, 108–110
  individual vs. organizational investment, 110
  internal-mobility metrics, 244–245
  internships, 57, 109
  mentoring programs, 109, 122–123
  networking programs, 109, 123–124
  organizational support of, 110
  planning process, 116–117
  reasons for employee exits, 137
  responsibility for, 110
  role of human resources in, 124
  role of individual in 21st century, 122
  and succession management, 147
  talent management, 124–127
  and training, 15
career goals, 113
career ladder, 117, 118, 119
career management
  organizational vs. individual need, 114–117
  PricewaterhouseCoopers, 123
career management balance, 115
career models
  career ladder, 117, 118, 119
  competency-based model (Microsoft), 117, 119–122
  protean career of 21st century, 122
  Sonnenfeld's career system typology, 117, 118–119, 120, 121
career path, 113
career planning, 113–114, 116–117
case incidents
  alternative work arrangements, 281
  budgetary restrictions at educational institute, 102–103
  call centre supply and demand prediction, 49–50
  communication during labour surplus, 103
  diversity in the workplace, 280
  importing workers, 202
  Nike Inc., succession plan, 155
  notice period and severance pay, predicting, 103
  ratio analysis, use of in forecasting, 50

request for proposal (RFP), developing, 178–179
  role of human resources in acquisitions, 225
  talent development, 131
  turnover metrics, 257
  weather and human resource planning, 22
  Zebra Ltd., 75
centres of excellence (COE), 293
childcare programs, 260
coaching
  in career development planning, 117, 123–124, 128
co-evolution, 183
collective bargaining agreements
  impact of in labour surplus, 89, 90, 99–100
compensation
  benefit eligibility, 57
  compensation systems of mergers, 220
  contingent workforce considerations, 64
  outsourcing of, 276
  overtime wages, 65–67
  tax deductions remittances, 57
  wage or benefit concessions, 89, 90
compensation planning
  as HRMS application, 163–164
competency, and competency models, 36
competency-based model (Microsoft)
  career development, 117, 119–122
  and talent management, 125–126
Competitive Strategy (Porter), 13
compressed workweek, 67, 270
concentration, as corporate strategy, 12
confidentiality vs. security, 173–175
conglomerate, 206
constructive dismissal, 88
consultants, 58
contingent workforce, 29, 61–69
  administrative considerations, 63–64
  compensation considerations, 64
  defined, 61, 62
  legal considerations, 64
  as management technique, 61–62
  operational considerations, 64
  trends in, 62–63
continuity planning, 71–72
contractors and contract workers, 58
  as contingent workforce, 62
  vs. employees, employment relationship of, 63–64
  outsourcing, 59–61
  Revenue Canada contractor status, 58, 64, 74
  as temporary workers, 57
  types of, 58–61

co-operative student programs, 57, 109
corporate culture
  clash of, in mergers and acquisitions, 217–218
  components of, 214
  management of, in mergers and acquisitions, 213, 214–215
corporate evolution
  stages of, and resource planning implications, 183–186
corporate social responsibility, 192–193
corporate strategy, 12–13
cost leadership, 13
cost metrics
  attraction and acquisition of talent, 238–239
  development-related, 243–244
  turnover costs, 251–252
country culture, 187–188
cross-cultural issues
  handling of in domestic firms, 184
  in international human resource planning, 185, 187–188
cross-cultural skills
  development of in multinational firms, 185
  of Third Country Nationals, 195
  value of in global firms, 186
crowdsourcing, 59, 61
cultural sensitivity, 185
culture, dimensions of, 188
customer perspective, of balanced scorecard, 228
customer satisfaction
  in evaluating succession management, 148

data management, evolution of, 160–161
defenders, and defender strategy, 13
  organizational growth, 13, 14
Delphi method, 41, 43, 44, 45
demand analysis, 39
  factors in, 39–40
  quantitative techniques in forecasting, 40–43
demographic factors
  effect on external labour force, 30
  in forecasting internal HR supply, 35
  in labour shortages, 54
department managers
  as downsizing agent, 94–95
  nominal group technique (NGT) involvement, 43–44
  role of in HR planning, 28
develop-deploy-connect model approach to talent management, 125–126
development of talent, 235

development programs
  individual development plans (IDP),
    143–144
development-related metrics
  cost metrics, 243–244
  internal-mobility metrics, 244–245
  time and efficiency metrics, 245
differentiation, 13
disability, 267
  see also persons with disabilities
discrimination
  age discrimination, 87, 190
  anti-discrimination legislation,
    globally, 190
  disability-based, 267
  and diversity management, 263–267
  racism, 260
  reverse discrimination, 4
dismissal percentage, 253
distributive justice, 93–94
diversification
  as corporate strategy, 12–13
  through mergers and acquisitions, 209
diversity management, 263–267
  diversity in the workplace, 280
  glass ceiling, 138, 264
domestic firms
  resource planning implications, 184
downsizing
  challenges of, 91–99
  compensation comparison, 105
  and employee participation in decision-
    making, 82, 85
  labour shortages post-downsizing, 83
  mixed methods of, 90–91
  organizational downsizing, facets of, 79
  organizational recovery post-downsizing, 92
  outplacement services, 97–99
  synonyms for, 79
downsizing agents, 94–96
due diligence stage, of mergers and
    acquisitions, 211, 212
  role of HR professionals in, 222

early retirement, 80, 87–88
  see also retirement
economic factors
  effect on external labour force, 30
economic value added (EVA)
  as HR metric, 235, 236–237
effective placements
  in evaluating succession
    management, 148
Effective Succession Planning
    (Rothwell), 141
emergent approach to planning, 285
employability skills, 116

employee data
  collection of, 160, 161
  confidentiality issues, 173–174
  privacy of, 234
  security issues, 174–175
employee engagement
  in competency-based career model, 120
  as concern of HR professionals, 137
  and flexible work arrangements, 67
  and organizational performance, 228
  and talent management, 124
employee illness absence rate, 248
employee recruitment
  internal vs. external recruiting, 57
employee selection
  in defender strategy, 14
employee self service (ESS), 175
employee swapping, 60
employee value proposition
  talent attraction, 128
employees
  absence cost factor, 248
  absenteeism and, 247–248
  applicant tracking system (ATS),
    237–238
  communication with during labour
    surplus, 96–97
  contingent workforce, 29
  vs. contractors, employment relationship
    of, 63–64
  effect of layoffs on morale, 81–82
  employability skills, development of, 116
  equity theory, 92–93
  high potentials, 142–143, 144
  hiring, full-time or part-time decisions,
    56–57
  Host Country Nationals (HCNs), 185,
    194, 195
  impact of mergers and acquisitions on,
    216–218
  injury rate, 248
  as intellectual capital, 4
  internal labour force, 28
  organizational justice as perception of
    fairness, 93–94
  outplacement services, 97–99
  Parent Company Nationals (PCNs), 185
  Parent Country National (PCNs),
    194–195
  payment of, 57
  performance potential grid, 143, 144
  psychological contract theory, 91–92
  stress of overtime work arrangements, 65
  survivor syndrome, 82, 91–92
  Third Country Nationals (TCNs),
    185, 195
  turnover metrics, 250–253

employment equity
  and diversity management, 264
Employment Equity Act, 265
employment relationships
  types of, 56–57
enterprise resource planning systems
    (ERP), 161, 168–169
  needs analysis, 170–171
  product evaluation, 172
  software implementation process, 172
  software solutions, 168–169, 170
environmental occupations, labour
    shortage, 55
environmental scanning, 7
equity partnerships, 60
equity theory, 92–93
ethics and HRP
  career development, 110
  corporate responsibility, Nike, 193
  ethical challenges with outsourcing, 275
  forecasting techniques, 41
  labour surplus, ethical challenges during,
    95–96
  managing privacy, 234
  overtime lawsuit, 66
ethnicity, discrimination against, 263
ethnocentrism, 194
executive talent
  as under-managed corporate asset,
    127–128
executives
  role of in HR planning, 28
expatriates
  costs and benefits, 196–197
  elements of successful experience,
    197–199
external contextual factors in international
    human resource planning
  country culture, 187–188
  immigration policies, 191
  labour economy, 188–189
  labour legislation, employment, 189
  labour legislation, labour relations,
    190–191
  termination provisions/severance
    costs, 190
external co-sourcing, 60
external labour force
  forecasting supply of, 31–35
  and HR planning, 30
external recruitment, 57

feedback mechanisms
  in evaluating succession management,
    147–148
finance analysts
  role of in HR planning, 28

financial perspective, of balanced
    scorecard, 228
flex hours, 67
flex schedules, 67
flexible retirements, 67–68
flexpatriate, 196
flextime, 270, 272
float and transfer work arrangements,
    68–69
focused differentiation, 13
forecasting
    Canadian Occupational Projection
        System (COPS), 32
    defined, 27
    doctor shortage in Canada, 33–35
    ethical issues in, 41
    external HR supply, 31–35
    HR demand, 39–46
    HR supply, 31–39
    importance of, 26–27
    internal HR supply, 35–39
    labour demand and supply, 18–19, 26–51
    projected job growth by occupational
        grouping, 32
    successful forecasting, information
        required for, 27–30
    workforce needs, 14
full-time employees, 56
    reduction in hours, 89
functional strategy, 12, 14
future orientation, 189

gap analysis, 46
gender differentiation, 188
gender discrimination, 190, 263
Generation Y networks, 260
geocentrism, 194
glass ceiling, 138, 264, 265
global firms
    resource planning implications, 184,
        185–186
global human resource management
    (GHRM), 183
global human resource planning, 183
globalization
    and environmental scanning, 7
    and increased flexibility of HRP, 6–7
    labour shortages, 53–56
GLOBE study, 188
groupthink, 27

high potentials
    developmental opportunities, 185
    identifying, 149
    individual performance potential,
        142–143, 144
    turnover, 150

hiring freezes, 86–87
horizontal mergers, 205, 206, 209
Host Country Nationals (HCNs), 185,
    194, 195
hostile takeovers, 210
HR deliverables, 229
HR metrics
    attraction and acquisition of talent, 235,
        237–242
    development of, 233–234
    economic value added (EVA), 235,
        236–237
    life-cycle approach, 235–254
    productivity, 235, 237
    return on investment (ROI), 235–236
    separation, 235, 250–254
    strategic vs. operational metrics, 254
    target audience, 254–255
    utilization of talent, 235, 246–250
HR scorecard, 230
HR scorecard approach, 229–231
HRP and strategic partners
    Best Buy, 68
    labour surplus, poorly managed, 90
    online recruiting/screening process
        (Capital One), 238
    Oracle Corporation, 170
    professional designations, 277
HRP and the small business
    Bioware, and the gaming industry, 15
    challenges in implementing an
        HRMS, 232
    downsizing, 85
    hiring immigrants, 269
    planning challenges, 45
    succession planning, 145–146
HRP in the news
    alignment to business strategy
        (Intel), 11
    AT&T, 215
    doctor shortage in Canada, 33–35
    external successors, 151
    Faskens global strategy, 186
    GBCS (Global Business Communications
        Systems), 284
    IBM transformation, 60
    manufacturing sector decline, 80
    Rogers Communications, Inc., 152
    sophisticated human resource planning
        (SHRP, Corning Inc.), 17
HR-to-employee ratio, 249
human capital
    buy vs. develop, 111
    career planning, 112–114
    employees, potential value, 112
    HR systems as enablers of, 6
    and people equity, 19

sophisticated human resource planning
    (SHRP, Corning Inc.), 17
talent crunch, managing, 111–112
human capital value added, 236
human resource accounting, 287–288
human resource audits
    and competency models, 36
    and HR inventory, 29–30
human resource inventory, 29–30
human resource management systems
    (HRMS)
    balanced scorecard-based performance
        measurement system, 173
    defined, 161
    design components, 165–167
    enterprise resource planning systems
        (ERP), 161, 168–169
    impact of HRMS in organizations,
        175–176
    impact of on HR professionals and
        managers, 175
    importance of to planning, 162–165
    needs analysis, 170–171
    reporting requirements, 167
    requirements, determining, 169–172
    role in planning process, 159
    specific applications, 163–164
    stakeholders, 161–162
    uses for, 167–168
    "War on Talent", 162
human resource measurement systems,
    228–258
    alignment of HR measures with
        organizational strategy, 231–234
    attraction and acquisition of talent, 235,
        237–242
    balanced scorecard approach, 228–231
    cost metrics, 238–239
    development-related metrics, 242–246
    employee retention levels, 228
    HR metrics, development of, 233–234
    HR scorecard approach, 229–231
    life-cycle approach, 235–254
    new employee separation rate, 238, 241
    preparing for measurement, 234
    productivity metric, 228
    quality metrics, 239–241
    Saratoga Institute metrics, 233
    satisfaction level metric, 228
    separation metrics, 235, 250–254
    strategic vs. operational metrics, 254
    target audience, 254–255
    time metrics, 238, 242
    *Ultimate Performance: Measuring Human
        Resources at Work,* 233
    utilization of talent metrics, 235, 246–250
    work climate metric, 228

human resource planning (HRP)
  about, 2–21
  aligning with business strategy, 294
  alignment to business strategy, 11–12
  alternative work arrangements, 261
  appropriate planning horizon, 27–28
  defined, 3
  emergent approach to planning, 285
  evolution of, 3–7
  expatriate management, 197–199
  external labour force analysis, 30
  flexibility in, 6–7, 10–11
  fundamental elements of, 5
  future developments, 260–282
  groupthink, and team diversity, 27
  impact of alternative work arrangements
    on, 272–273
  impact of labour force changes on,
    267–269
  impact of linking business planning
    with, 293
  impact of outsourcing on, 276–277
  importance of, 7–9
  integration across processes, 14–15
  key characteristics, 9–15, 20–21
  labour force changes, 260
  linking with business planning, 285–288
  models for linking with business
    planning, 288–290
  outsourcing, 261
  planning sophistication, stages of, 16–18
  process, 18–19, 21
  professional designations, 277
  the Readi paradigm, 8–9
  redundancies, handling of, 219
  resource-based view (RBV), 4, 5–6
  role of in mergers and acquisitions,
    218–221
  staffing patterns, determination of, 4
  strategic approach to, 287
  strategic partnering professional skills,
    290
  strategic partners in, 28
  strategic partnerships, 284–285
  work arrangements, 71
human resource transformation goals, 293
human resources due diligence, 215–216
human resources (HR)
  efficiencies, 165
  outsourcing, 164, 274–276
human resources information systems
  (HRIS), 30
human resources management (HRM)
  as downsizing agent, 94
  expatriate management, 197–199
  integration with planning processes,
    14–15

human resources professionals
  competency model for, 290–291
  impact of HRMS on managers and, 175
  role of in HR planning, 28
human rights legislation
  global standards, 190
humane orientation, 189

Iacocca: An Autobiography, 6
immediate headcount reduction strategies,
    80–86
  layoffs, 81–82
  layoffs and terminations, statutory notice
    periods, 83–84, 85
  leaves without pay, 86
  notice periods, and timing of
    terminations, 83–84
  severance pay, 84, 86
  voluntary separations, 82–84
immigrant population
  educational attainment levels, 264–265
  employment patterns, 263
  hiring, 269
  integration into workforce, 260
  labour force changes, 264–265
  in staffing strategies, 57
immigration policies
  as external contextual factor in
    international human resources, 191
immigration programs
  in workforce planning strategies, 53, 57
implementation stage, of mergers and
    acquisitions, 211, 212–213
  role of HR professionals in, 222–223
In Search of Excellence, 6
information technology
  see also technology
  confidentiality issues, 173–174
  employee data, collection of, 160, 161
  global needs, 164
  impact on functional activities, 162
  knowledge theft, 174
  relational databases, 165–166
  security issues, 174–175
  web-based technology, 166–167
in-group collectivism, 188
injury rate, 248
institutional collectivism, 189
integration planning stage, of mergers
    and acquisitions, 211, 212
  role of HR professionals in, 221–222
intellectual capital, 4
intelligence and security industry, labour
    shortage, 55
interactional justice, 94
internal business processes perspective, of
    balanced scorecard, 229

internal contextual factors in international
    human resource planning, 192–195
  corporate social responsibility, 192–193
  managerial preference: staffing
    alternatives, 193–194
  staffing mix, 194–195
internal human resources
  forecasting methods for, 35–39
  resource-based view (RBV) of, 5–6
internal labour force
  defined, 28
  development of, 64
  evaluating current HR situation, 28–29
internal recruitment, 57
internal mobility metrics, 244–245
international assignments
  staffing trends, 196–199
international commuter, 196
international firms
  resource planning implications, 184–185
international human resource management
    (IHRM), 183
  staffing categories, 185
international human resource planning,
    182–203
  external contextual factors, 187–191
  internal contextual factors, 192–195
  planning decisions, internal and external
    contextual factors, 187
Internet
  confidentiality vs. security, 173–175
  "InnoCentive" website, 61
  use of in open call outsourcing, 61
internships, 57, 109
involuntary turnover, 35, 252–253
IT professionals
  industry skills shortage, 55
  role of in HR planning, 28
IT technology future, 127, 172–173
  ERP software solutions, 168–169, 170
  impact of HRMS in organizations,
    175–176
  impact of HRMS on HR professionals
    and managers, 175
  industry growth, 189
  product evaluation, 172
  software implementation process, 172

Japan, work visas, 191
job postings
  applicant tracking system (ATS), 237–238
  ratio of offers to applicants, 238,
    240–241
job sharing
  as alternative to layoffs, 88
  as labour shortage solution, 54
joint ventures, 60

key position, 141
knowledge, skills, abilities, and other characteristics (KSAOs), 31
knowledge management, 6
knowledge theft, 174

labour costs in emerging economies, 189
labour demand and supply
   Canadian Occupational Projection System (COPS), 32
   doctor shortage in Canada, 33–35
   forecasting, 18–19, 26–51
   forecasting external HR supply, 31–35
   forecasting labour demand, 39–46
   forecasting labour supply, 31–39
   projected job growth by occupational grouping, 32
labour economy
   as external contextual factor in international human resources, 188–189
labour force changes
   aging workforce, 262–263
   alternative work arrangements, 269–273
   diversity management, 263–267
   immigrant population, growth of, 264–265
   impact on human resource planning, 267–269
   labour shortage, and talent mismatch, 261–262
   outsourcing, 273–278
   persons with disabilities, 267
   visible minorities, 265
   women, 266–267
labour force participation rates
   global labour information, 189
labour legislation: employment and global planning, 189
labour legislation: labour relations globally, 190–191
labour mobility, inter-provincial, 260
labour relations
   labour legislation, globally, 190–191
   organizational justice as perception of fairness, 93–94
   union employees, mergers and, 220–221
labour shortages, 7
   Alberta workforce planning strategies, 53, 262
   alternative staffing strategies, 56–61
   contingent workforce, 61–69
   defined, 53
   factors in determining best options, 69–71
   global examples, 54–56
   global labour information, 189

job sharing as solution, 54
pandemics, and continuity planning, 71–72
post-downsizing, 83
and talent mismatch, 261–262
variables affecting, 54
labour surplus
   attrition strategies, 80, 86–88
   Canadian automotive sector, 78
   constructive dismissal, 88
   defined, 78
   downsizing, 82, 83, 85, 90–91, 91–99
   early retirement, 87–88
   employee communication during, 96–97
   employee relocation, 90
   ethical challenges, 95–96
   immediate headcount reduction strategies, 80–86
   job-sharing, 88
   managing, 79–80
   work-term change strategies, 80, 88–90
layoffs
   impact on firm profitability, 91
   notice periods, and timing of terminations, 83–84, 85
   phased approach to, 82
   types of, 81–82
leadership development
   attention to, 150
   as concern of HR professionals, 137
   determining availability of, 141–142
   developmental assignments, timing of, 150
   manager's "mini-me" syndrome, 149
   performance potential grid, 143, 144
   and succession management, 134–135, 147
leadership styles
   planning sophistication and, 16–18
learning and growth perspective, of balanced scorecard, 229
learning organizations, 6
leave entitlements, 189
leaves without pay, 79, 86
legislation
   Canada Labour Code, 57
   compliance, 160
   contract law, 58
   Employment Equity Act, 265
   Employment Standards Act (Ontario), 66
   Federal jurisdiction employees, 104–105
   global employment standards, 189
   human rights legislation, globally, 190
   layoffs and terminations, statutory notice periods, 83–84, 85
   mandatory retirement, 68, 87, 263
   Ontario jurisdiction employees, 104–105

overtime provisions, 65–66
severance packages, 86
temporary agencies practices, 64
legislation requirements
   HR inventory, 30
   labour shortages, 54
linchpin, 141
line managers
   as downsizing agent, 94–95
   impact of HRMS on HR professionals and, 175
   linking human resources professionals with, 291–293
   nominal group technique (NGT) involvement, 43–44
   role in HR planning, 28
   role in staffing patterns, 4

management development programs, 108
management ratio, 249
management self service (MSS)
   impact of HRMS on HR professionals and managers, 175
managerial preferences
   staffing alternatives, 193–194
   workforce planning, 70–71
manpower planning, 4–5
Markov analysis
   in forecasting HR demand, 41
   and internal HR supply, 37–39
measurement systems. *See* human resource measurement systems
mentoring programs, 109
   and aging workforce, 268–269
   in career development planning process, 117, 122–123
mergers and acquisitions, 205–226
   acquisitions defined, 206
   as business ecosystem, 183
   Canadian overview, 205, 206–207
   change, management of, 211
   communication challenges, 217
   communication during transition, 220
   compensation systems, 220
   context of work during, 217
   corporate culture clash, 213, 214–215, 217–218
   employee impact, 216–218
   financial advantages, 209
   friendly mergers, 210
   growth by acquisition, examples, 208
   hostile mergers, 210–211
   and human resource planning, 218–221
   human resources skills, gaps in, 222–223
   labour relations, 220–221
   life cycle process, 211–213
   managerial needs, 209

mergers and acquisitions–*Cont.*
  mergers defined, 205–206
  obstacles to, 213–216
  organizational diversification, 13
  organizational skills for successful
    mergers, 221–222
  organizational structure in transition, 219
  performance appraisals, 221
  reasons for, 207–208
  role of HR professionals in, 213,
    221–222, 225
  staffing decisions, 220
  strategic benefits of, 208–209
  toxic work environment (AT&T), 215
  training and development, 221
  transition and integration teams,
    219–221
multinational enterprises (MNE)
  human resource planning (HRP),
    182–186
  resource planning implications, 184, 185

networking programs, 109
  as career development tool, 123
nominal group technique (NGT),
  43–44, 45
notice periods, and timing of terminations
  ethical challenges during labour
    surplus, 96
  for voluntary departures, 86
nurse shortage, Canada
  "Not Enough Nurses" campaign, 54

offshoring, 60
open call outsourcing, 59, 61
organizational career development programs
  employee potential, as long-term
    investment, 112
  organizational vs. individual need, 109,
    110, 114–117
  planning process, 116–117
organizational downsizing, 79
organizational goals
  in establishing HR objectives, 46
  and layoff policies, 81–82
  role of leadership in establishing, 3
organizational justice, 93–94
organizational performance
  balanced scorecard approach, 228–231
  employee contribution to, 137
  and employee engagement, 228
  low productivity, effect on, 128
organizational results
  in evaluating succession management, 148
organizational strategy
  alignment with HR measures, 231–234
  and strategic human resources, 283

organizational structures, 13–15
  planning sophistication and, 16–18
organizational sustainability
  through succession management, 136
organizational therapy process, 98
outplacement services, 97–99
outside vendors as staffing source, 59
outsourcing
  challenges in, 277–278
  ethical challenges with, 275
  of human resources, 164
  and labour market trends, 273–278
  offshoring, 60
  open call outsourcing, 59, 61
  request for proposal (RFP), 61
  trends in, 261
  types of, 59–61
overtime metrics, 246, 250

Parent Company Nationals (PCNs), 185
Parent Country National (PCNs), 194–195
part-time work, 271
part-time workers, 57
people equity, 19
people resources, 3
"People Soft", 17
performance appraisals during mergers, 221
performance management
  competency-based approach to, 125
  in corporate culture, 218
  outsourcing of, 275–276
  and succession management, 147
performance orientation, 188
performance potential grid, 143, 144
permanent layoffs, 81
persons with disabilities
  employment patterns, 263
  hiring practices, 57
  labour force changes, 267
  parents of, 267
phased-in retirement, 87–88
physician shortage, Canada, 33–35, 54
planning procedures
  formality of, 10
planning process, 31–47
  Canadian Occupational Projection
    System (COPS), 32
  design and implementation of HR
    programs, 46–47
  evaluation of HR programs, 47
  forecasting labour demand and supply,
    31–46
  objectives, establishment of, 46
polycentrism, 194
power distance, 188
pre-deal stage, of mergers and acquisitions,
  211–212

pre-employment background screening
  outsourcing of, 274
privacy
  confidentiality vs. security, 173–175
  HRP and ethics, 234
proactive human resource response,
  286–287
procedural justice, 93
process progress
  in evaluating succession management, 148
productivity
  absenteeism and, 247–248
  as HR metric, 235, 237
  lost productivity metrics, 247–248
  performance metrics, 246–247
productivity indexes, types of, 237
professional associations
  mentoring programs, 122–123
prospectors, and prospector strategy, 14
  decentralized organizational structure of,
    14–15
protean career, 112–113, 122
psychological contract theory, 95
  and survivor syndrome, 91–92

qualitative techniques in forecasting, 43–44
  ethical issues in, 41
quality metrics
  of new hires, 238, 239–241
  separation rate, new employees, 238, 241
quantitative techniques in forecasting,
  40–43
  ethical issues in, 41
quantity metrics
  HR efficiency, evaluation of, 238,
    241–242

ratio analysis, 40–42
reactive human resource response, 286–287
Readi paradigm, 8–9
recruitment
  alignnment with skills of immigrant
    population, 260
  competency-based approach to, 125
  cost metrics, 238–239
  in defender strategy, 14
  hires per recruiter, 242
  internal vs. external recruiting, 57
  and labour force changes, 268–269,
    272–273
  from outside vendor, 59
  outsourcing of, 274–275
  quality metrics, 238, 239–241
  quantity metrics, 238, 241–242
  and rate of retirement, 252
  recruiting cost ratio, 239
  selection process, 15

selection ratios, 238, 241–242
 and succession management, 147
 web-based technology, 167
reduction in hours, 89, 271
redundancies, handling of, 219
regiocentrism, 194
regression analysis, 42–43
relational databases, 165–166
relocation packages, 53
 expatriates, 198
repatriation
 reverse culture shock, 199
replacement charts, 36, 37, 142
 CEO replacement, 141
replacement planning
 and the aging workforce, 262–263
 as HRMS application, 163
 and rate of retirement, 252
request for proposal (RFP), 61, 171–172,
 178–179
resource-based view (RBV), 16
 of human resource planning, 4
 internal human resources, 5–6
retirement
 and the aging workforce, 262–263
 bona fide occupational requirement
  (BFOR), 87, 263
 early retirement, 87–88
 flexible retirements, 67–68
 as labour shortage factor, 53, 262
 mandatory retirement, 68, 87, 263
 phased-in retirement, 87–88
 rate of, 252
return on investment (ROI), 235–236
 talent development, 126
Revenue Canada
 contractor status, determining, 58, 64, 74
 tax deductions remittances, 57
revenue per employee
 as measure of productivity, 246–247
reverse culture shock, 199
reverse discrimination, 4
reverse mentoring, 123
revocability, 71
reward packages, 53
ROWE program, 68

sandwich generation, 263
Saratoga Institute metrics, 233
scenario analysis
 in forecasting HR demand, 44, 45
selection process
 recruitment and, 15
senior leaders
 role of in HR planning, 28
separation
 exit of talent, 235

separation metrics
 attrition rate, 252
 dismissal percentage, 253
 involuntary separation rate, 252–253
 new employee separation rate, 238, 241
 permanent resignation percentage, 253
 and rate of retirement, 252
 turnover metrics, 250–253
 vacancy metrics, 253–254
severance pay, 84, 86, 95
sexual harassment, 190
sexual orientation discrimination, 190, 263
signing bonuses, 53
skills development
 and labour force changes, 267–269
skills inventory
 and competency models, 36
 and HR inventory, 29–30
 as HRMS application, 163
skills shortage, 53, 189
 global examples, 54–56
 Public Policy Forum recommendations, 260
SMART objectives, 148
solutions analysis, 46
Sonnenfeld's career system typology, 117,
 118–119, 120, 121
sophisticated human resource planning
 (SHRP), 17–18, 21
staffing categories
 of international human resource
  management (IHRM), 185, 194–195
staffing strategies
 see also alternative staffing strategies
 contingent workforce, 61–69
 contract workers, 58–61
 determination of, 4
 employee recruitment, 56–57
 factors in determining best options,
  69–71
 internal employee development, 64
 international human resource planning,
  194–195
 staff ratios, 248–249
 work arrangements, leveraging, 65–69
staffing tables, 37
strategic human resource management
 (SHRM), 5
strategic human resource planning, 163
strategic human resources
 and organizational strategy, 283
strategic management process, 12–14
strategic partnering professional skills, 290
strategic partners
 factors associated with HR, 289
 role of in HR planning, 28
strategic partnerships, 284–285
 emergent approach to planning, 285

stakeholders, 283–285
 strategy development, 283
strategic plan, 31
strategic planning systems, co-existence
 with balanced scorecard, 229
strategic staffing, 287–288
strategy, 12
succession management, 134–157
 in attraction and retention of talent,
  136–137
 business environment as factor, 146–147
 CEO tenure, 136
 competency-based approach to, 125
 defined, 135
 Effective Succession Planning (Rothwell), 141
 elements of effective management,
  138–148
 evolution of, 138–139
 external successors vs. internal, 151–152
 feedback mechanisms, 147–148
 glass ceiling, 138
 HR credibility, 150
 HR-related functions, 147
 importance of, 135–138
 individual performance potential,
  142–143
 internal-mobility metrics, 244–245
 labour force changes, 268
 leadership development, 134–135
 leadership talent, determining availability
  of, 141–142
 management commitment, 149
 Nike Inc., 155
 and organizational sustainability, 136
 performance potential grid, 143, 144
 planning process, 139–144
 policies and guidelines, 145
 rater errors, 149
 selection criteria, 149
 trends in, 150–152
 types of programs, 140–141
 work requirements, review of, 141
 workforce diversity, 137–138
succession planning, 36
 and the aging workforce, 262–263
 constraints facing, 149–150
 as HRMS application, 163
 as HRP objective, 6
 and rate of retirement, 252
 in small businesses, 45
 at Weyerhaeuser, 143
supply-chain model of talent
 management, 126
survivor syndrome, 82
 and equity theory, 92–93
 in managers, 95
 psychological contract theory and, 91–92

talent, defined, 124, 126–127
talent management
  and the aging workforce, 262–263
  attraction and acquisition of talent, 235, 237–242
  attraction and retention of talent, 128, 136–137
  Bruce Power model, 125–126
  competency-based approach to, 125–126
  development of talent, 235
  employee engagement, 120, 124
  executive talent, 127–128
  as HRMS application, 163
  labour shortage, and talent mismatch, 261–262
  leaders role in, 125
  loss of through mergers, 216
  in North American organizations, 124
  as primary concern of HR professionals, 137
  separation, 235
  succession management process, 139–144
  supply-chain model, 126
  talent retention, 108
  talent-based approach, 126–127
  utilization of talent, 235, 246–250
talent management analytics, 169
talent management system (TMS), 237–238
talent pool, 141
talent show, 144
technology
  see also information technology
  data management, evolution of, 160–161
  design components of HRMS, 165–167
  eAppoint, 159
  employee data, collection of, 160, 161
  enterprise resource planning systems, 161
  enterprise resource planning systems (ERP), 168–169
  ERP software solutions, 168–169, 170
  future of, 172–173
  global needs, 164
  growth expectations, 160
  impact of HRMS in organizations, 175–176
  impact of HRMS on HR professionals and managers, 175
  IT future, 127
  Professional Marketplace (IBM), 164
  relational databases, 165–166
  Ryerson University, 159
  and succession management, 150
  use of in management systems, 159
  web-based technology, 166–167
telecommuting, 67, 271–272, 273
telework, 271–272

temporary layoffs, 81
temporary workers, 57
termination provisions/severance costs
  as external contextual factor in international human resources, 190
Third Country Nationals (TCNs), 185, 195
third culture kids (TCK), 195
throughput, focus on, 288
time and efficiency metrics, 245
time horizons, 10
time metrics, 238, 242
total quality management (TQM) practices, 5–6
total turnover, 35
training and development
  and aging workforce, 268–269
  apprenticeships, 260
  budget percentage allocated, 243
  career development, 15
  costs per employee, 243–244
  in defender strategy, 14
  float and transfer work arrangements, 68–69
  as HRP objective, 6
  learning and development metrics, 244
  during merger transition, 221
  outsourcing of, 276
  persons with disabilities, 267
  retraining, 90
  training penetration rate, 245
training evaluation, hierarchy of evaluation areas, 148
trend analysis
  in forecasting HR demand, 40
  in forecasting HR internal supply, 35–36
turnover, 35
  causes of in Canada, 251, 267–268
  cost metrics, 251–252
  dismissal percentage, 253
  involuntary separation rate, 252–253
  levels, 251
  permanent resignation percentage, 253
  through mergers and acquisitions, 216
  turnover metrics, 250–253

Ultimate Performance: Measuring Human Resources at Work, 233
uncertainty avoidance, 188
unemployment rates
  immigrant population, 263, 264
unions and union relations
  impact of in labour surplus, 99–100
  variation in international representation, 190–191
  wage or benefit concessions, 89, 90
United Kingdom, work visas, 191

utilization of talent, 235
utilization of talent metrics, 235, 246–250
  lost productivity metrics, 246, 247–248
  overtime metrics, 246, 250
  performance metrics, 246–247
  span of control metrics, 246, 248–249

vacancy metrics, 253–254
vacations, 189
Vancouver 2010 Olympics, 2
vendor co-sourcing, 60
vertical integration
  as corporate strategy, 12
  through mergers and acquisitions, 209
vertical mergers, 206
visa process
  and permanent residency, 260
  work visas, 191
visible minorities
  employment patterns, 263
  labour force changes, 265
voluntary departures, 86
  reasons for employee exits, 137
voluntary separations, 79
  incentives for, 82–84
voluntary turnover, 35

web-based technology, 166–167
white space opportunities, 183
women
  employment patterns, 263
  labour force changes, 266–267
  labour force participation, 138, 189, 260
  underemployment of, 266
work arrangements
  compressed workweek, 67
  factors in determining best options, 69–71
  flex hours, 67
  flex schedules, 67
  flexible retirements, 67–68
  float and transfer, 68–69
  HR role in managing, 71
  overtime, 65–67
  telecommuting, 67
  types of, 65–69
workforce concerns
  employee morale, and workforce reduction, 81–82, 91–92
  equity theory, 92–93
  and planning horizons, 27–28
workforce diversity
  and diversity management, 263–264
  managing, 137–138
workforce planning
  and the aging workforce, 262–263
  Alberta's strategies, 53, 262

alternative staffing strategies, 56–61

attrition strategies, 80

as concern of HR professionals, 137

contingent workforce, 61–69

continuity planning, 71–72

contract workers, 58–61

defined, 169

employee recruitment, 56–57

factors in determining best options, 69–71

Host Country Nationals (HCNs), 185

immediate headcount reduction strategies, 80–86

importance of, 7–9

internal employee development, 64

labour force reduction methods, 79–80

labour shortages post-downsizing, 83

layoffs and terminations, statutory notice periods, 83–84

managerial preferences, 70–71

Parent Company Nationals (PCNs), 185

public agency use of, 7

retirement, rate of, 252

Third Country Nationals (TCNs), 185

work arrangements, leveraging, 65–69

workforce imbalances, 46–47, 262

work-term change strategies, 80

workforce reduction methods

immediate headcount reduction strategies, 80–86

managing, 79–80

workforce trends

identification of through HR inventory, 29–30

and labour force changes, 267–269

Public Policy Forum recommendations, 260

work-life balance

and doctor burnout, 33–34

and flexible work arrangements, 67

as labour shortage factor, 53

overtime lawsuit, 66

and succession management, 150

work-term change strategies, 80, 88–90

constructive dismissal, 88

employee relocation, 90

reduction in hours, 89

retraining, 90

wage or benefit concessions, 89, 90

wrongful dismissal

and employee involvement in decision-making, 81, 82

PHOTO CREDITS